The New
Horizon
Ladder
Dictionary
of the English Language

The New Horizon Ladder Dictionary

of the English Language

By JOHN ROBERT SHAW
with JANET SHAW

A SIGNET BOOK

NEW AMERICAN LIBRARY

Published by arrangement with John Robert Shaw and Janet Shaw

 SIGNET TRADEMARK REG. U.S. PAT. OFF. AND FOREIGN COUNTRIES
REGISTERED TRADEMARK—MARCA REGISTRADA
HECHO EN DRESDEN, TN. U.S.A.

SIGNET, SIGNET CLASSIC, MENTOR, ONYX, PLUME, MERIDIAN AND NAL BOOKS *are published by NAL PENGUIN INC.,* *1633 Broadway, New York, New York 10019*

FIRST SIGNET PRINTING, SEPTEMBER, 1970

16   17   18   19   20   21   22   23   24

PRINTED IN THE UNITED STATES OF AMERICA

CONTENTS

Acknowledgments

The research and preparation of the manuscript of this dictionary was supported by the United States Information Agency, which wanted a dictionary in simple English for use in its overseas program among foreign readers of English as a second language.

We want to express our deep gratitude to Donald E. McNeil for encouraging us to undertake this project and for giving us invaluable advice and help. We also want to thank Ann Newton for the phonetic system she provided for the dictionary.

Introduction

The New Horizon Ladder Dictionary is based on 5,000 of the most frequently used words in written English—words a person will most often see and need to know in reading general English literature. The 5,000 words constitute a vocabulary developed by the United States Information Agency as a result of reviewing frequency word counts and English-teaching word lists and consulting a number of English teachers. The vocabulary has been used, tested, and revised over a period of twelve years in the preparation of books in English at differing levels of reading difficulty for readers of varied ages and interests.

For English-teaching purposes, the 5,000 words are divided into five levels or ladder rungs of approximately one thousand words each, according to the frequency of their use. After each appears a number in parentheses ( ) which shows the level at which the word is located. Words on the first level, shown by *(1)*, are among the thousand most frequently used words in written English. Those on the second level, shown by *(2)*, are among the second thousand most frequently used words. Those on the third *(3)*, fourth *(4)*, and fifth *(5)* levels follow the same pattern of frequency.

The most frequently used prefixes and suffixes, though not counted as words, are included in the body of the dictionary and have a word level. There are also in the dictionary a number of additional entries—combined words—which do not have a word-level designation. Most of these are words or phrases which are constructed from two or more of the 5,000 basic words, prefixes, and/or suffixes which are frequently used in English. They are listed separately because in combined form they have a new meaning. The meaning of the word *afternoon* is clear from the two words that combine to make it, *after* and *noon*. The usual meaning of *high school*, however, is not clear from the two words *high* and *school*. *High school*, therefore, is included as an entry word. Other examples are *firecracker* and *runner-up*.

The words in this dictionary are arranged in order according to the letters of the alphabet: A, B, C, D, E, F, G, H, I, J, K, L, M, N, O, P, Q, R, S, T, U, V, W, X, Y, Z. For example, the word **clear** comes after the word **clean** because "r" comes after "n" in the alphabet; both come before the word **clench** because "a" comes before "n."

When you look at the word **clear** in this dictionary, this is what you will find:

clear (1) [kli:r'], *adj.* 1. easily understood; plain. **Ex.** *His explanation was clear.* 2. bright; uncloudy. **Ex.** *The sky is clear today.* 3. free from doubt; certain. **Ex.** *It was a clear case of murder.* 4. free of anything that might block. **Ex.** *The road is clear.* —*v.* 1. remove persons or things; empty. **Ex.** *She clears the table after meals.* 2. prove or declare innocent. **Ex.** *The lawyer's defense cleared the accused man.* 3. become clear. **Ex.** *The weather will clear in the afternoon.* —**clear'ance, clear'ness,** *n.* —**clear'ly,** *adv.* —**clear'ing,** *n.* land where there are no trees. —**clear out,** make a cleared place. **Ex.** *He cleared out the room.* —**clear up,** 1. make clear or plain. **Ex.** *He cleared up the mystery.* 2. make neat. **Ex.** *He cleared up the room.*

The word **clear** is printed in dark type so that it is easy to find. It is the entry word. The word **clear** and all the information about it that follows is called an entry. Following the entry word is the number *(1)*. This shows that **clear** is on the 1,000-word vocabulary level.

Next the pronunciation of the word in the United States is shown in this way [kli:r']. The pronunciation key is located elsewhere in the book and, in an abbreviated form for quick reference, at the bottom of every fourth page. This pronunciation key, an adaptation of the Trager-Smith transcription system, is used widely by experts in teaching spoken English.

Following the pronunciation, the part of speech is shown by the letters *adj.*, which is an abbreviation for the word *adjective.* The abbreviations for parts of speech used in the dictionary are:

noun—*n.*	verb—*v.*	conjunction—*conj.*
pronoun—*pron.*	adverb—*adv.*	interjection—*interj.*
adjective—*adj.*	preposition—*prep.*	

See definitions of each of these parts of speech in the dictionary, and see also "A Brief Explanation of English Grammar."

Four meanings are given for the word **clear** used as an adjective. The meaning numbered 1. is the most frequently occurring meaning. The meanings numbered 2., 3., etc., occur in that order of frequency. This rule should not be regarded too strictly, however, since the frequency of meanings may be extremely close in some cases.

In order to help make each meaning of a word easily understood, an example is usually given showing how the word is used in a sentence conveying that meaning. These examples, which are preceded by the letters **Ex.,** also assist the reader to incorporate that meaning into the vocabulary he is readily able to use.

Following the meanings and examples of **clear** as an adjective is the letter *v.* As we have seen above, this is the abbreviation for *verb* and means that the word **clear** is also used as a verb. Three meanings are then given for the word **clear** as a verb with an example for each.

Next are the words **clear'ance** and **clear'ness,** divided into syllables and followed by the letter *n.* for *noun,* and the word **clear'ly** followed by the letters *adv.* for *adverb.* Since the most common meaning of *clear* as a noun or adverb when combined with the suffixes *-ance, -ness,* and *-ly* can be understood from the meanings for the adjective and adverb and from the meaning for the suffixes, no separate meanings or examples are given. **Clear'ing** as a noun has a different meaning, and this is explained.

Two expressions are included. The first, **clear out,** is formed by adding the word *out* to **clear** used as a verb, and the second, **clear up,** is formed by adding the word *up* to **clear** used as a verb. Expressions like these are common uses of the entry word in a phrase or combined form. Meanings and examples of use are given for many of the phrases. The reader will find, too, that often the extra word does not change the meaning but is added to give emphasis or liveliness to the language. **Clear out** means substantially the same thing as **clear.**

As we noted in discussing combined forms, not every possible combination of an entry word with all the prefixes, suffixes, and other entries is listed in the dictionary. Similarly, the various tenses of regular verbs, plurals formed by regular means, the extent or degree of adjectives and adverbs usually formed by adding *-er* or *-est,* are also seldom included. If a form of one of the basic 5,000 words of the vocabulary cannot be located in the dictionary, the reader can usually determine its meaning by studying the meanings given for the basic word and the prefixes or suffixes involved, together with "A Brief Explanation of English Grammar" that follows.

Ladder Dictionary Pronunciation Key

symbol	example	symbol	example
a	far	b	boat
æ	am	d	dark
e	get	f	far
ey	late	g	go
i	in	h	home
iy	see	k	cold
ɔ	all	l	let
ow	go	m	man
u	put	n	net
uw	too	p	part
ə	but, ago	r	red
ər	fur	s	sit
aw	out	t	ten
ay	life	v	very
oy	boy	w	went
		y	yes
		z	zoo
ŋ	ring		
θ	think	:	preceding vowel lengthened
ð	that	'	primary stress on syllable preceding
ž	measure		
š	ship	`	secondary stress on syllable preceding
ǰ	edge		
č	child	( )	sounds enclosed by parentheses are frequently not pronounced

A Brief Explanation of English Grammar

Parts of Speech

The names given to words according to the work which each does in a sentence are called the parts of speech. The eight common parts of speech in English are:

noun	*adverb*
pronoun	*preposition*
adjective	*conjunction*
verb	*interjection*

The definition of each of these eight parts of speech is contained in the main part of this dictionary under the word entry. The abbreviations for these parts of speech used in this dictionary are indicated in the "Introduction" and "Appendix II."

Special forms of these eight parts of speech are also sometimes given special names. For example, a verb form used as a noun is called a *gerund*. A verb form usually preceded by the word *to* and used as a noun, adjective, or adverb is called an *infinitive*. A verb form used as an adjective or used as a verb when combined with forms of the verb *be* or *have* is called a *participle*.

Pronouns

Pronouns are given various names according to the kind of person or thing which the pronoun replaces or according to the special work which the pronoun does in the sentence.

Personal pronouns take the place of particular persons or things.

	Singular	Plural
1st person	I, me	we, us
2nd person	you	you
3rd person	he, him she, her, it	they, them

Indefinite pronouns take the place of any person or thing; some of the most common are:

each, either, neither, one, everybody, everyone, nobody, no one, anybody, anyone, somebody, someone, several, few, both, many, some, any, none, all, most

Relative pronouns introduce a clause and relate to another word or idea in the main clause. The most common relative pronouns are:

who, whom, whose, which, that

Interrogative pronouns ask a question. The interrogative pronouns are:

who, whom, whose, which, what

Construction of a sentence

The essential parts of a sentence are the subject and the verb. The subject is that which does something or that about which something is said. The verb is the word which shows the action or state of being.

Ex. *She laughed.*
She is the subject which does something; *laughed* is the verb which shows the action.

Ex. *Mother was very old.*
Mother is the subject about which something is said; *was* is the verb that shows the state of being of the subject.

The word which receives the action of a verb is called the direct object.

Ex. *The birds ate the seed.*
Seed is the direct object which receives the action of the verb *ate*.

Sometimes a word following a verb is not an object but refers to or modifies the subject. The verb joins the two.

Ex. *The house looks new.*
New describes the subject *house* and is joined to it by the verb *looks*.

Ex. *That boy is my friend.*
Friend refers to and describes the subject *boy* and is joined to it by the verb *is*.

Modifiers

Modifiers are words or groups of words which describe other words. The most common modifiers are adjectives, which describe nouns or pronouns, and adverbs, which describe verbs, adjectives, or other adverbs.

Ex. *The old man walked slowly to the door.*
Old is an adjective which describes the noun *man,* and *slowly* is an adverb which describes the verb *walked*.

ositional phrases are groups of words used as modifiers
sist of a preposition, a noun or pronoun, and often one or
ives which describe the noun or pronoun. These phrases

are used in the same ways that adjectives or adverbs are used. The noun or pronoun in the phrase is called the object of the preposition.

Ex. *The girl in the red hat is my sister.*
In the red hat is a prepositional phrase used like an adjective to describe *girl*. *Hat* is the object of the preposition.

Participial and infinitive phrases are groups of words used as modifiers which consist of a participle or an infinitive and one or more other words. Participial phrases are always used as adjectival modifiers. Infinitive phrases may be used as either adjectival or adverbial modifiers.

Ex. *He went to buy bread.*
To buy bread is an infinitive phrase used as an adverb.

Ex. *I waved to the boy riding the bicycle.*
Riding the bicycle is a participial phrase used as an adjective.

Clauses

Clauses are groups of words which contain a subject and a verb and usually other words such as objects and modifiers but which are written as a part of a sentence. If the clause could have been written as a separate sentence, it is called a main clause.

Ex. *We saw a flash of lightning, and then we heard thunder.*
In this sentence there are two main clauses: one, *we saw a flash of lightning,* and two, *then we heard thunder.*

A clause which is not the main clause is called a subordinate clause and may be used as an adjective or adverb. Such a clause is usually introduced by a relative pronoun or by a conjunction.

Ex. *When he came, I was ready.*
When he came is a subordinate clause used as an adverb; *I was ready* is the main clause.

Clauses are also used as nouns.

Ex. *That he liked to spend money was well known.*
That he liked to spend money is a noun clause used as the subject of the sentence.

Changes of form—nouns

A change in the form of a noun is usually used to show whether it is singular or plural, one or more than one. The plural of most nouns is formed by adding -*s*.

Exs. *School, schools; book, books; car, cars.*

The plural of some nouns is formed by adding *es*.

Exs. *Box, boxes; dress, dresses.*

The plural of some nouns ending in *y* is formed by changing *y* to *i* and adding *-es*.

Exs. *Fly, flies; lady ladies.*

The plural of a few nouns is formed by considerable change in spelling. When the plural of a noun is formed in this manner, the singular and plural forms are usually listed in the dictionary as separate entries.

Exs. *Child, children; tooth, teeth.*

The singular and the plural of a few nouns are the same.

Exs. *Sheep, sheep; deer, deer.*

The possessive of nouns is used to show that something is owned by or is related to someone or something. The possessive is formed by adding an apostrophe (') and the letter *-s* to a singular noun and by adding an apostrophe to a plural noun ending in the letter "*s*" and by adding an apostrophe and the letter "*s*" to a plural noun not ending in the letter "*s*."

Exs. *John's book; the box's cover; the boys' hats; the children's toys.*

Changes of form—adjectives, adverbs

A change in the form of an adjective or an adverb, used to show differing extent or degree, is called comparison. For most adjectives and adverbs this comparison change is made by adding *-er* or *-est*.

Exs. *Old, older, oldest; fast, faster, fastest.*

More or *most* and *less* or *least* are used before some adverbs and adjectives for the same purpose.

Exs. *Beautiful, more beautiful, most beautiful; rapidly, less rapidly, least rapidly.*

Some adjectives and adverbs use a different word for each difference of extent or degree.

Exs.		
good	better	best
well	better	best
many	more	most
bad	worse	worst

Changes of form—verbs

A change in the form of a verb is used to show differing times a particular action or state of being occurs, occurred, or will occur. The different time forms are called tenses. Some of the more frequently used tenses are:

Present tense—shows action or being now.

Past—	"	"	"	"	before now.
Future—	"	"	"	"	not yet begun.
Present Perfect—	"	"	"	"	in the past and continuing into the present.
Past Perfect—	"	"	"	"	completed in the past before some other past action.
Future Perfect—	"	"	"	"	which will be completed before some other future action.

The tenses of most verbs are formed in the same way. For example, -ed is added to the present tense of the verb to form the past tense. Use of the word *will* forms the future tense. Such verbs are called regular verbs. The tenses of regular verbs are all formed in the same way as the verb *walk* which is given as an example.

Present   **Present Perfect**

Singular	Plural	Singular	Plural
I walk	*we walk*	*I have walked*	*we have walked*
you walk	*you walk*	*you have walked*	*you have walked*
he walks	*they walk*	*he has walked*	*they have walked*

Past   **Past Perfect**

I walked	*we walked*	*I had walked*	*we had walked*
you walked	*you walked*	*you had walked*	*you had walked*
he walked	*they walked*	*he had walked*	*they had walked*

Future   **Future Perfect**

I will walk	*we will walk*	*I will have walked*	*we will have walked*
you will walk	*you will walk*	*you will have walked*	*you will have walked*
he will walk	*they will walk*	*he will have walked*	*they will have walked*

Certain verbs are called irregular because the various tenses are not formed in the same way. These verbs, of which examples are *be* and *go,* usually have separate dictionary entries for each of the differing forms. The following are the tenses of the most frequently used verb, *be.*

Present

Singular	Plural
I am	*we are*
you are	*you are*
he is	*they are*

Present Perfect

Singular	Plural
I have been	*we have been*
you have been	*you have been*
he has been	*they have been*

Past

I was	*we were*
you were	*you were*
he was	*they were*

Past Perfect

I had been	*we had been*
you had been	*you had been*
he had been	*they had been*

Future

I will be	*we will be*
you will be	*you will be*
he will be	*they will be*

Future Perfect

I will have been	*we will have been*
you will have been	*you will have been*
he will have been	*they will have been*

A

A, a (1) [ey¹], *n.* the first letter of the English alphabet.

a (1) [ey¹, ə], *adj.* 1. one, one kind of; each; any. **Ex.** *I planted a tree.* 2. used with groups or numbers. **Exs.** *A few; a certain number; a thousand. A* is also called an indefinite article and is used before words beginning with most letters except a, e, i, o, and u.

a- (1) [ɔ], *prefix.* on, to, toward, in, into. **Exs.** *Sleep, asleep; live, alive; side, aside.*

abandon (3) [əbæn'dən], *v.* leave completely and finally. **Ex.** *The fisherman abandoned his sinking boat.* —*n.* careless or wild freedom. **Ex.** *He spent money with abandon.*

abbreviate (5) [əbriy'viyeyt'], *v.* shorten by cutting out part. **Ex.** *His book was abbreviated and appeared in a magazine.*

abbreviation (5) [əbriy'viyey'šən], *n.* a shortened form of a word or group of words. **Exs.** *Mr. for mister; Sun. for Sunday; St. for street.*

abdomen (5) [æb'dəmən, æbdow'mən], *n.* the middle part of the body which contains the stomach and other important inner parts. —**ab·dom'i·nal,** *adj.*

abide by (4) [əbayd' bay¹], act in accordance with; obey. **Ex.** *We will abide by your decision.*

ability (2) [əbil'ətiy], *n.* power or skill in mental or physical action. **Ex.** *He has the ability to carry heavy loads.*

able (1) [ey'bəl], *adj.* 1. having the power or ability to do something. **Ex.** *He was not able to return home.* 2. showing unusual skill or knowledge; clever. **Ex.** *An able teacher helped him in school.* —**a'bly,** *adv.*

-able (1) [əbəl], *suffix.* 1. that can or may be done. **Exs.** *Drink, drinkable; read; readable.* 2. that exists as a condition. **Exs.** *Fashion, fashionable; peace, peaceable.*

abnormal (5) [æbnor'məl], *adj.* not usual; odd. **Ex.** *His abnormal behavior shows that something is wrong.* —**ab·nor'mal·ly,** *adv.* **Ex.** *The dry season was abnormally long.* —**ab'nor·mal'i·ty,** *n.*

---

a, far; æ, am; e, get; ey, late; i, in; iy, see; ɔ, all; ow, go; u, put; uw, too; ə, but, ago; ər, fur; aw, out; ay, life; oy, boy; ŋ, ring; θ, think; ð, that; ž, measure; š, ship; ǰ, edge; č, child.

aboard (4) [əbɔrd'], *adv., prep.* on, in, or into a ship, bus, train, etc. **Exs.** *The captain of the ship welcomed the visitors aboard. The passengers aboard the plane were served dinner.*

abode (4) [əbowd'], *n.* home; a place where one lives. **Ex.** *The woodcutter's abode was a house in the forest.*

abolish (3) [əbal'iš], *v.* end completely; destroy. **Ex.** *We are trying to abolish disease.* —**ab·o·li'tion,** *n.* total ending of. **Ex.** *He hoped for the abolition of all wars.*

abominable (5) [əbam'ənəbəl], *adj.* hateful; bad and unpleasant. **Ex.** *Murder is an abominable crime.*

about (1) [əbawt'], *prep.* concerning; of. **Ex.** *A dictionary is a book about words.* —*adv.* 1. almost; nearly. **Ex.** *It is about five o'clock.* 2. in all directions; around. **Ex.** *The man looked about before crossing the street.*

above (1) [əbəv'], *prep.* 1. in or at a higher place than. **Ex.** *His room is above mine.* 2. higher in rank than. **Ex.** *A general is above a captain.* —*adv.* in or at a higher place; overhead. **Ex.** *The clouds above were moving fast.*

abreast [əbrest'] *adv., adj.* beside; not in front or behind. **Ex.** *The runners finished the race abreast of each other and were co-winners.*

abridge [əbrij'], *v.* shorten in length, usually a book. **Ex.** *The 150 pages of the book were abridged to 100.* —**a·bridged',** *adj.* —**a·bridg'ment,** *n.* act of abridging.

abroad (2) [əbrɔ:d'], *adv.* in a foreign country. **Ex.** *They are traveling abroad.*

abrupt (4) [əbrəpt'], *adj.* 1. unexpected; sudden. **Ex.** *The car came to an abrupt stop.* 2. unpleasantly short. **Ex.** *His abrupt words made me unhappy.*

absent (2) [æb'sənt], *adj.* 1. not present; away. **Ex.** *The student was absent from school.* 2. not existing; lacking. **Ex.** *The adventures he read about were absent from his own life.* —**ab'sence,** *n.* the condition of being not present. **Ex.** *His absence was noticed.* —**ab'sen·tee',** *n.* someone not present.

absent-minded [æb'sənt mayn'dəd], *adj.* absent mentally; forgetful.

absolute (2) [æb'səluwt'], *adj.* 1. perfect; complete. **Ex.** *I have absolute faith in his honesty.* 2. without limit. **Ex.** *The king had absolute authority.* —**ab'so·lute'ly,** *adv.*

absolve (5) [əbsalv'], *v.* free from guilt, responsibility, or punishment for a sin or crime. **Ex.** *The judge absolved the man of the crime.* **—ab'so·lu'tion,** *n.*

absorb (4) [əbsɔrb'], *v.* 1. hold the full attention. **Ex.** *He was so absorbed in his work he did not hear the teacher speak.* 2. take in; suck up. **Ex.** *Most paper absorbs water.* **—ab·sorb'ent,** *adj.* **—ab·sorp'tion,** *n.*

abstract (5) [æb'strækt], *adj.* 1. considered apart from matter and from specific cases. **Ex.** *The judge was criticized for having only an abstract idea of justice.* 2. expressing a quality apart from any object. **Ex.** *Beauty is an abstract idea.* 3. difficult to understand. **Ex.** *Some authors are not popular because their writings are too abstract.*

absurd (4) [əbsərd'], *adj.* so unreasonable as to be laughable; foolish. **Ex.** *Your story is too absurd to believe.* **—ab·surd'ly,** *adv.* **—ab·surd'i·ty,** *n.* state or quality of being foolish. **Ex.** *The absurdity of the situation made everyone laugh.*

abundance (4) [əbən'dəns], *n.* a large amount. **Ex.** *There is an abundance of food this year.* **—a·bun'dant,** *adj.*

abuse (4) [əbyuwz'], *v.* 1. use incorrectly or wrongly. **Ex.** *The judge abused his authority.* 2. treat badly, either physically or in speech. **Ex.** *He abused the man by beating and cursing him.* **—n.** 1. wrong or bad use. **Ex.** *His abuse of power has turned his friends against him.* 2. cruel treatment. **Ex.** *The man's abuse of the horse made people angry.* **—a·bu'sive,** *adj.*

academic (3) [æk'ədem'ik], *adj.* 1. concerning a school, college, or university, or teaching. **Ex.** *He left the business world to return to academic life.* 2. concerning theory; not expected to produce a practical result. **Ex.** *Philosophy is an academic subject.* **—ac'a·dem'i·cal·ly,** *adv.*

academy (5) [əkæd'əmiy], *n.* 1. a school of advanced learning. **Ex.** *After graduating from the academy, he went to college.* 2. a place of training in a special subject. **Ex.** *His daughter attends an academy of music.*

accent (3) [æk'sent'], *n.* 1. stronger force given to a word or part of a word in speaking. **Ex.** *The accent in the word "about" is on "bout."* 2. a special national or regional way of speaking. **Ex.** *She speaks English with a foreign accent.* **—v.** say a word or part of a word with increased force. **Ex.** *Do not accent the "a" in "about."* **—accent mark:** '.

accept (1) [əksept'], *v.* take a thing that is offered. **Ex.** *He was happy to accept the gift.* 2. receive with favor. **Ex.** *We accept* *your offer.* 3. believe, agree to. Ex. *Do you accept what he is saying?* —ac·cept'a·ble, *adj.* —ac·cept'a·bly, *adv.* —ac·cept'ance, *n.*

access (5) [æk'ses'], *n.* 1. the right to enter, approach, or use. Ex. *You have access to a good library.* 2. a way or place of approach. Ex. *Access to the park is by this street.* —ac·ces'si·bil'i·ty, *n.* —ac·ces'si·ble, *adj.*

accessory (5) [əkses'əriy], *n.* something which adds to comfort, appearance, or usefulness but is not needed. Exs. *A radio is an accessory in a car. A woman's hat and gloves are accessories.*

accident (2) [æk'sədənt], *n.* 1. a happening that causes damage or hurt. Ex. *He broke his leg in an automobile accident.* 2. an unexpected and unplanned happening. Ex. *It was an accident that we arrived at the party at the same time.* —ac'ci·den'tal, *adj.* —ac'ci·den'tal·ly, *adv.*

accommodate (5) [əkam'ədeyt'], *v.* 1. do a favor for; help; aid. Ex. *He accommodated his friend with a loan.* 2. provide with room and sometimes with food. Ex. *The hotel can accommodate ten guests.* —ac·com'mo·dat'ing, *adj.* —ac·com'mo·da'tion, *n.*

accompany (2) [əkəm'pəniy], *v.* 1. join; go with. Ex. *I will accompany him on the trip.* 2. put with; cause to go with. Ex. *He accompanied his talk with pictures.* 3. play music with a singer or another performer or performers. Ex. *The pianist accompanied the singer.* —ac·com'pa·ni·ment, *n.* that which goes with. —ac·com'pa·nist, *n.* one who accompanies.

accomplice [əkam'plis], *n.* one who assists in a criminal act. Ex. *The robber's accomplice was also caught.*

accomplish (2) [əkam'pliš], *v.* do; perform; finish successfully. Ex. *We accomplished our task.* —ac·com'plish·ment, *n.* a completed task; a skill. Ex. *We admire her accomplishments.*

accord (4) [əkord'], *v.* 1. be in agreement. Ex. *Their story did not accord with the facts.* 2. grant; reward. Ex. *He was accorded the honors he deserved.* —*n.* agreement. Ex. *They were in accord.* —ac·cor'dance, *n.* —ac·cord'ing·ly, *adv.* in the proper manner. Ex. *Be patient and you will be treated accordingly.*

according to (1) [əkɔr'diŋ tuw], 1. in agreement with. Ex. *The building of the road was completed according to plan.* 2. said or declared by. Ex. *According to the newspaper, it will* *rain tomorrow.* 3. in a certain order. Ex. *They stood in line according to height.*

account (2) [əkawnt'], *v.* give a reason for; explain. Ex. *How do you account for your accident?* —*n.* 1. story; explanation. Ex. *Give an account of your trip.* 2. record of money received and paid. Ex. *The bank sent me a monthly report of my account.* —**ac·coun'tant,** *n.* one whose work is keeping or examining accounts or business records. —**on account,** as partial payment. Ex. *He paid him some money on account.* —**on account of,** because. Ex. *We stayed home on account of the rain.*

accumulate (4) [əkyuwm'yəleyt'], *v.* collect or bring together; increase in amount or number. Ex. *He wants to accumulate more paintings.* —**ac·cu'mu·la'tion,** *n.*

accurate (4) [æk'yurət], *adj.* exact; correct; right. Ex. *A good clock keeps accurate time.* —**ac'cu·ra·cy,** *n.* —**ac'cu·rate·ly,** *adv.*

accuse (2) [əkyuwz'], *v.* charge with a wrongdoing or crime; blame; find fault with. Ex. *They accused him of stealing.* —**ac·cus'er,** *n.* one who accuses. —**ac'cu·sa'tion,** *n.* —**ac·cus'ing·ly,** *adv.*

accustom (2) [əkəs'təm], *v.* become familiar with by use or habit. Ex. *She could not accustom herself to a hot climate.* —**accustomed to,** in the habit of. Ex. *He is accustomed to sleeping late.*

ache (3) [eyk'], *v.* suffer continued pain. Ex. *My tooth aches.* —*n.* pain. Ex. *I have an ache in my foot.*

achieve (3) [əčiyv'], *v.* 1. accomplish; complete successfully; do. Ex. *They were able to achieve their purpose quickly.* 2. get through effort. Ex. *The men fought bravely and finally achieved victory.* —**a·chieve'ment,** *n.*

acid (3) [æ'səd], *n.* 1. a chemical substance containing hydrogen that can be replaced by a metal. 2. a sour substance. Ex. *Vinegar is an acid.* —*adj.* sharp or biting to the taste. Ex. *The lemon is an acid fruit.* —**ac'id·ly,** *adv.* —**a·cid'i·ty,** *n.*

acknowledge (4) [əknal'ij], *v.* 1. admit as true. Ex. *She acknowledged her mistake.* 2. answer or express thanks for something. Ex. *They acknowledged the gift.* —**ac·knowl'edg·ment,** *n.*

a, far; æ, am; e, get; ey, late; i, in; iy, see; ɔ, all; ow, go; u, put; uw, too; ə, but, ago; ər, fur; aw, out; ay, life; oy, boy; ŋ, ring; θ, think; ð, that; ž, measure; š, ship; ǰ, edge; č, child.

acorn (5) [ey'kɔrn], *n.* nut, or fruit, of the oak tree.

acquaint (5) [əkweynt'], *v.* 1. make known to; make familiar. Ex. *Please acquaint me with the facts.* 2. know personally. Ex. *These two women are acquainted with each other.* —ac·quaint'ance, *n.*

ACORN

acquire (3) [əkwayr'], *v.* get as one's own; become the owner of; gain by some means. Exs. *He acquired a fortune. She acquired a Ph.D. after many years of study.*

acre (2) [ey'kər], *n.* piece of land that measures 43,560 square feet; 2.471 acres = 1 hectare. See **Weights and Measures.**

across (1) [əkrɔ:s'], *prep.* 1. from one side of to the other. Ex. *He walked across the bridge.* 2. on the other side of. Ex. *He lives across the street.* —*adv.* from one side to another. Ex. *A big ship brought her across.*

act (1) [ækt'], *n.* 1. thing which is done. Ex. *Feeding the child was a kind act.* 2. law; judgment. Ex. *The lawmakers passed an act to increase taxes.* —*v.* 1. do something. Ex. *Think before you act.* 2. produce an effect. Ex. *The medicine acted immediately.* 3. behave. Ex. *His dog acts in a strange manner.* 4. perform on the stage. Ex. *He acted the part of the king in the play.*

action (1) [æk'šn], *n.* 1. something done; act. Ex. *His action was wise and helpful.* 2. process of doing something. Ex. *We need less talk and more action.* —**in action**, moving; doing. —**take action**, do something about. Ex. *He will take action on our problem.*

active (2) [æk'tiv], *adj.* 1. busy; moving all the time. Ex. *She is a very active person.* 2. working; in progress or motion. Ex. *He was active in community affairs.* —ac'tive·ly, *adv.* —ac·tiv'i·ty, *n.*

actor (3) [æk'tər], *n.* one who performs in a play or motion picture. Ex. *The actor spoke his lines clearly.*

actual (2) [æk'čuwəl], *adj.* really existing; real; true. Ex. *He is the one who has the actual power.* —ac'tu·al'i·ty, *n.* —ac'tu·al·ly, *adv.*

acute (4) [əkyuwt'], *adj.* 1. very severe. Ex. *The pain was acute.* 2. keen and quick in seeing, hearing, smelling, thinking. Ex. *A dog has an acute sense of smell.* —a·cute'ly, *adv.*

adapt (5) [ədæpt'], *v.* change to fit needs or new conditions. **Ex.** *Old people find it difficult to adapt themselves to modern life.* —a·dapt'a·ble, *adj.* —ad'ap·ta'tion, *n.*

add (1) [æd'], *v.* 1. join to increase the number, size, or importance. **Ex.** *The new baby adds to the size of the family.* 2. find the sum of two or more numbers. **Ex.** *When you add 5 and 2, the total is 7.* 3. say or write further. **Ex.** *She said that she would be late and added that she was sorry.* —ad·di'tion, *n.* —ad·di'tion·al, *adj.*

address (2) [ədres'], *n.* 1. number, street, and place where one lives. **Ex.** *To what address shall I deliver this package?* 2. speech or writing directed to a person or group. **Ex.** *He gave an address to the graduates.* —*v.* speak to; talk to. **Ex.** *He always addressed us kindly.*

adequate (4) [æd'əkwət], *adj.* as much as required; enough; sufficient. **Ex.** *They had an adequate amount of money for the trip.* —ad'e·qua·cy, *n.* —ad'e·quate·ly, *adv.*

adhere (5) [ədhi:r'], *v.* 1. hold tightly to. **Ex.** *His wet clothing adhered to his body.* 2. be devoted to. **Ex.** *He no longer adheres to those beliefs.* —ad·her'ence, *n.* the act of adhering. **Ex.** *He was well known for his adherence to the rules.* —ad·her'ent, *n.* a person who adheres. **Ex.** *The candidate was surrounded by his adherents.*

adjacent (5) [əjey'sənt], *adj.* near or next to; neighboring. **Ex.** *There is a school adjacent to my house.*

adjective (5) [æj'əktiv], *n.* one of the parts of speech which describes or tells something about the noun or pronoun with which it is used. **Ex.** *In the sentence, "The new teacher is very young," the words "new" and "young" are adjectives.*

adjoin (4) [əjoyn'], *v.* be joined with or to; be next to and touching. **Ex.** *His land and mine adjoin.*

adjourn (4) [əjərn'], *v.* end a meeting until a future time. **Ex.** *The meeting was adjourned until next week.* —ad·journ'ment, *n.*

adjust (4) [əjəst'], *v.* 1. change or move into position for use. **Ex.** *You can adjust your chair to make it more comfortable.* 2. fix; arrange the parts to make work correctly. **Ex.** *Please adjust my watch.* 3. settle; put in order. **Ex.** *Adjust the accounts to make them correct.* —ad·just'ment, *n.* —ad·just'er, *n.*

administer (5) [ədmin'əstər], *v.* 1. manage; be in charge of. **Ex.** *The principal administers the school.* 2. give out. **Ex.**

The courts administer justice. 3. give medicine or treatment. **Ex.** *The nurse administered the medicine.*

administration (3) [ədmin'əstrey'šən], *n.* 1. management of work or of an office. **Ex.** *Who is responsible for the administration of this office?* 2. the operation or functioning of a government. **Ex.** *The mayor is responsible for the administration of the city.* 3. group of men who have the powers to operate a government. **Ex.** *The present Administration is very capable.* —ad·min'is·tra'tor, *n.* —ad·min'is·trate, *v.*

admiral (4) [æd'mərəl], *n.* an officer of the highest rank in the navy; commanding officer of a fleet of ships or a navy.

admire (2) [ædmayr'], *v.* regard with wonder, pleasure, and approval. **Ex.** *He admired her beauty very much.* —ad'mi·ra'tion, *n.* —ad'mi·ra·ble, *adj.* deserving high praise; worth great respect. **Ex.** *Her patience is admirable.* —ad'mi·ra·bly, *adv.*

admission (3) [ədmiš'ən], *n.* 1. permission to enter. **Ex.** *Admission to the school is open to everyone.* 2. price paid for entering. **Ex.** *Admission to that theater is expensive.* 3. confession of a belief, error, or crime; admitting that something is true or false. **Ex.** *His quick admission of his mistake was in his favor.* —ad·mis'si·ble, *adj.* allowed; permitted. —ad·mis'si·bil'i·ty, *n.*

admit (2) [ədmit'], *v.* 1. tell the truth about; confess. **Ex.** *The criminal admitted his guilt.* 2. allow to enter. **Ex.** *Please admit me to the room.* —ad·mit'tance, *n.* —ad·mit'ted·ly, *adv.*

admonish (5) [ədman'iš], *v.* warn of a fault; advise against doing something. **Ex.** *He admonished his friend not to be late for work.* —ad'mo·ni'tion, *n.* —ad·mon'ish·ment, *n.*

ado (5) [əduw'], *n.* trouble; fuss. **Ex.** *There was much ado about the President's visit.*

adolescence (5) [ædəles'əns], *n.* period between being a child and an adult; youth. —ad'o·les'cent, *n.* a boy or a girl between the ages of 13 and 19. **Ex.** *As an adolescent, he had many problems.* —ad'o·les'cent, *adj.*

adopt (3) [ədapt'], *v.* 1. take and use as one's own. **Ex.** *He adopted their customs without difficulty.* 2. choose and take as a member of one's family by law. **Ex.** *The family adopted the child.* 3. choose or follow. **Ex.** *They decided to adopt the suggestion.* —a·dop'tion, *n.*

adore (5) [əd·ːr¹], *v.* regard with the greatest love and respect. Ex. *He adores his wife.* —ad'o·ra'tion, *n.*

adorn (4) [ədɔrn¹], *v.* add beauty; decorate; making pleasing to the eye. Ex. *Jewels adorned her neck and arms.* —a·dorn¹ment, *n.*

adult (2) [ədəlt¹], *n.* a person who is fully grown or of responsible age according to law. Ex. *An adult went with the children.* —*adj.* 1. fully developed in body and mind. Ex. *He is an adult person.* 2. designed for grown people. Ex. *The school offers adult courses.*

advance (1) [ədvæns¹], *v.* 1. move or go forward. Ex. *The army advanced up the hill.* 2. help to move forward; help to succeed. Ex. *They advanced the cause of peace.* —*n.* 1. forward movement. Ex. *The army has made an advance.* 2. raise in rank. Ex. *His new job is an advance for him.* —*adj.* 1. in front. Ex. *Ten soldiers formed the advance guard.* 2. ahead of time. Ex. *Please give me two weeks' advance notice.*

advantage (2) [ədvæn¹tij], *n.* 1. superior or favored position. Ex. *His excellent education gives him an advantage in his new job.* —ad'van·ta'geous, *adj.* —ad'van·ta'geous·ly, *adv.* —take advantage of. 1. make use of. Ex. *Take advantage of the low prices to save money.* 2. make unfair use of. Ex. *He takes advantage of his employer's absence and does no work.*

adventure (2) [ədven¹čər], *n.* 1. an exciting and often dangerous thing to do. Ex. *Hunting lions is an adventure.* 2. an unusual and stirring experience. Ex. *It was an adventure to ride in an airplane for the first time.* —ad·ven'tur·ous, *adj.* —ad·ven¹tur·ous·ly, *adv.*

adverb (5) [æd¹vərb], a part of speech which describes or tells something about a verb, adjective, or another adverb. Ex. *In the sentence "The boy laughed happily," "happily" is an adverb.*

adverse (5) [æd¹vərsˋ, ədvərs¹], *adj.* 1. acting against. Ex. *Adverse winds prevented the boat from entering the harbor.* 2. opposed; opposed to one's interests. Ex. *Adverse circumstances caused him to lose all his money.* —ad·verse'ly, *adv.* —ad·ver'si·ty, *n.* trouble. —ad'ver·sar·y, *n.* a person against whom one fights; an opponent.

advertise (3) [æd¹vərtayzˋ], *v.* praise some product publicly,

---

as in a newspaper, on radio or television, or by a similar means, to cause people to want to buy it. Ex. *Most manufacturers advertise their products.* —ad'ver·tis`er, *n.*

advertisement (3) [ædvərtayz'mənt, ədvər'tizmənt], *n.* a public announcement, usually in a newspaper or on radio or television, advertising some product. Ex. *He learned that the house was for sale through an advertisement.*

advice (2) [ədvays'], *n.* opinion about what to do or how to do something. Ex. *He gave me some good advice about building a house.*

advise (3) [ədvayz'], *v.* 1. suggest an action; warn. Exs. *The doctor advised him to rest. They were advised of the danger.* 2. inform. Ex. *He advised us of an increase in taxes.* —ad·vis'er, *n.*

advocate (4) [æd'vəkeyt`], *v.* speak or write in favor of. Ex. *We advocate peace.* —*n.* one who speaks and writes in support of a cause. Ex. *He is an advocate of reforms in the tax laws.*

affair (2) [əfe:r'], *n.* happening; event; business matter. Exs. *The wedding was a big affair. The sale of the house will be a difficult affair.*

affect (2) [əfekt'], *v.* 1. act on or produce an effect on; change. Ex. *Any change in the weather affects the crops.* 2. make an impression on the mind or feelings. Ex. *The sad news affected him deeply.*

affection (2) [əfek'šən], *n.* warm liking; friendly feeling or emotion. Ex. *The girl had great affection for her little sister.* —af·fec'tion·ate, *adj.* —af·fec'tion·ate·ly, *adv.*

affirm (4) [əfərm'], *v.* say something with certainty. Ex. *He affirmed his innocence.* —af·firm'a·tive, *adj.* —af·firm'a·tive·ly, *adv.*

afflict (5) [əflikt'], *v.* cause pain or suffering; trouble greatly. Ex. *There are many illnesses which afflict old people.* —af·flic'ted, *adj.* —af·flic'tion, *n.*

afford (2) [əfɔrd'], *v.* 1. have the money for. Ex. *They can afford to buy a house.* 2. be able to spare or give up for some purpose. Ex. *He could not afford the time for a vacation.* 3. do something without damage to health, good name, etc. Ex. *A public official cannot afford to have his honesty doubted.*

afraid (1) [əfreyd'], *adj.* feeling fear; frightened. Ex. *I am afraid of big dogs.*

after (1) [æf'tər], *prep.* 1. following behind. Ex. *The soldiers* *walked in line, one after another.* 2. later in time than. **Ex.** *I will see you after lunch.* 3. as a result of; because of. **Ex.** *After what he said, I do not want to see him again.* —*adv.* later; behind. **Ex.** *He left an hour later.* —*conj.* following the time that something else happened. **Ex.** *They arrived after the others had left.*

aftermath (3) [æf'tərmæθ'], *n.* result of; aftereffect, usually bad. **Ex.** *He had to wear eyeglasses as an aftermath of the accident.*

afterward (2) [æf'tərwərd], *adv.* later. **Ex.** *First we will go to the theater, then afterward to dinner.*

again (1) [əgen', əgeyn'], *adv.* 1. once more; another time. **Ex.** *I do not understand; tell me again.* 2. repeatedly. **Ex.** *I have explained it again and again.* 3. as before. **Ex.** *He left home for a while but is back again.*

against (1) [əgenst'], *prep.* 1. not in agreement with; opposed to. **Ex.** *The soldiers fight against the enemy.* 2. in contact with. **Ex.** *The boy leaned against the wall.* 3. in the other direction. **Ex.** *He swam up the river against the current.*

age (1) [eyj], *n.* 1. length of life; number of years old. **Ex.** *What is your age?* 2. period of life. **Ex.** *He studied painting in his old age.* 3. a time or period. **Ex.** *This is the space age.* —*v.* grow old. **Ex.** *He is aging quickly.*

-age (1) [ij], *suffix.* 1. act of; state of. **Exs.** *Marry, marriage; parent, parentage.* 2. cost of; amount of. **Exs.** *Post, postage; foot, footage.* 3. place for. **Ex.** *orphan, orphanage.*

agency (3) [ey'jənsiy], *n.* office or business of a person or company. **Ex.** *An employment agency helps people find jobs.*

agent (3) [ey'jənt], *n.* 1. a person who represents another. **Ex.** *He is the agent for a steel company.* 2. a substance that causes an effect. **Ex.** *A chemical agent is used to make paper white.*

aggregate (5) [æg'rəgit], *adj.* considered as a group or total. **Ex.** *His aggregate debts amounted to 300 dollars.* —*n.* the total; the complete amount. **Ex.** *The aggregate of his debts was 300 dollars.*

aggressive (5) [əgres'iv], *adj.* 1. ready to attack or fight others. **Ex.** *He is so aggressive that others avoid him.* 2. active; energetic. **Ex.** *We need an aggressive leader.* —**ag·gres'sive·ly,** *adv.* —**ag·gres'sion,** *n.* the starting of an attack, a fight, or a war. **Ex.** *Arresting our citizens was an act of aggression by that country.* —**ag·gres'sive·ness,** *n.* quality of being aggressive. **Ex.** *His aggressiveness made us dislike him.* —**ag·gres'sor,** *n.* one who starts a fight or war.

agile (5) [æǰ'əl], *adj.* moving quickly and easily; active. **Ex.** *A good dancer must be agile.* —**a·gil'i·ty,** *n.* quality of being able to move quickly.

agitate (4) [æǰ'əteyt`], *v.* 1. excite; move violently; shake. **Ex.** *The wind agitated the trees.* 2. attempt to excite into action. **Ex.** *The newspapers were agitating for a change in the tax laws.* —**ag'i·tat`ed,** *adj.* —**ag'i·ta`tor,** *n.* one who agitates. **Ex.** *Agitators made the crowd angry.* —**ag`i·ta'tion,** *n.* the state of being agitated or of agitating.

ago (1) [əgow'], *adj.* past; gone; before now. **Ex.** *It happened two days ago.* —*adv.* in the past. **Ex.** *I knew him long ago.*

agony (4) [æg'əniy], *n.* great pain; suffering. **Ex.** *He was in agony from his illness.* —**ag'o·nize,** *v.* —**ag'o·niz`ing,** *adj.* causing suffering. **Ex.** *It was an agonizing illness.* —**ag'o·niz`ing·ly,** *adv.*

agree (1) [əgriy'], *v.* 1. think the same. **Ex.** *We both agree that it is a good book.* 2. consent to. **Ex.** *They agreed to the plan.* —**a·gree'a·ble,** *adj.* cooperative; friendly. **Ex.** *He is an agreeable person.* —**a·gree'a·ble·ness,** *n.* —**a·gree'a·bly,** *adv.*

agriculture (3) [æg'rik:l`čər], *n.* art or science of farming; raising crops, cattle, and other farm animals. —**ag`ri·cul'tur·al,** *adj.*

ahead (2) [əhed'], *adv.* in front; in advance. **Ex.** *He walked ahead of me in the line.*

aid (2) [eyd'], *n.* help. **Ex.** *A nurse gave the wounded man aid.* —*v.* help; assist. **Ex.** *Will you aid me with this problem?*

ail (5) [eyl'], *v.* feel sick. **Ex.** *The old man is ailing and needs a doctor's care.* —**ail'ment,** *n.* sickness; illness. **Ex.** *His ailment is not serious.*

aim (2) [eym'], *n.* 1. purpose. **Ex.** *His aim was to prevent trouble.* 2. act of pointing a gun. **Ex.** *His aim was bad and he did not kill the animal.* —*v.* 1. try; direct one's efforts toward a purpose. **Ex.** *She aimed at perfection.* 2. point or direct something at a person or object. **Ex.** *He aimed his questions at the speaker.*

air (1) [e:r'], *n.* 1. the mixture of gases which are on and above the earth and which we breathe. **Ex.** *Birds fly in the air.* 2. general feeling or influence. **Ex.** *He spoke with an air of secrecy.* —*v.* 1. allow air to enter. **Ex.** *We opened the* *windows to air the warm room.* 2. give public expression to thoughts. **Ex.** *He aired his opinions to all of his friends.* —**air'i·ly,** *adv.* in a light manner. **Ex.** *He spoke airily about his bad luck.* —**air'y,** *adj.*

airplane (1) [e:r'pleyn'], *n.* a flying machine used for carrying people and materials through the air.

AIRPLANE

airport (2) [e:r'port'], *n.* a specially prepared place where airplanes are loaded and fueled, leave the ground, and come down to the ground.

aisle (4) [ayl'], *n.* a path for walking between or along the rows of seats, such as in a theater. **Ex.** *The aisle was wide enough for only one person.*

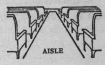

AISLE

-al (3) [əl], *suffix.* 1. the act or process of. **Exs.** *Refuse, refusal; arrive, arrival.* 2. of, like, or suitable for. **Exs.** *Accident, accidental; music, musical.*

alarm (3) [əlarm'], *n.* 1. sudden fear caused by possible danger. **Ex.** *They were filled with alarm when they saw the fire.* 2. any sound or signal warning of danger. **Ex.** *They rang the bell to sound the alarm.* 3. a device for making a warning noise. **Ex.** *They rang the fire alarm.* —**a·larm'ing,** *adj.* —**a·larm'ing·ly,** *adv.* —**a·larm'ist,** *n.* a person who is easily frightened. **Ex.** *Only the alarmists thought there was danger of war.*

album (5) [æl'bəm], *n.* book with blank pages in which to place pictures, stamps, etc. **Ex.** *He had placed all his stamps in an album.*

alcohol (3) [æl'kəhɔl'], *n.* a strong colorless liquid usually made from grains. **Ex.** *Drinks such as beer, whiskey, and wine contain alcohol.* —**al'co·hol'ic,** *adj.* of or containing alcohol. **Ex.** *Beer is an alcoholic drink.* —*n.* a person suffering from drinking too much alcohol. —**al'co·hol·ism,** *n.* the condition of being an alcoholic. **Ex.** *Alcoholism is a serious illness.*

ale (5) [eyl'], *n.* an alcoholic drink similar to beer. **Ex.** *He liked the bitter taste of the ale.*

alert (4) [ələrt], *adj.* 1. watchful and ready. **Ex.** *The policeman on the corner was alert.* 2. quick in thought or action. **Ex.**

The old man was still alert. —*n.* an alarm; a warning. Ex. *During the war, people ran for shelter when the alert was sounded.* —*v.* warn. Ex. *They alerted everyone to the danger.* **a·lert'ly,** *adv.* —**a·lert'ness,** *n.*

alien (4) [ey'liyən], *n.* a foreign-born person who is not a citizen of the country in which he lives. Ex. *The government keeps a record of all aliens.* —*adj.* belonging to a different country or people; strange; foreign. Ex. *After ten years his alien speech was still noticeable.* —**al'ien·ate,** *v.* make unfriendly. Ex. *His bad manners alienated his former friends.* —**al'ien·a'tion,** *n.*

all (1) [ɔ:l'], *adj.* 1. the whole of. Ex. *All the money has been spent.* 2. each one of. Ex. *I invited all my friends.* 3. any whatever. Ex. *He is guilty beyond all doubt.* —*pron.* the whole quantity. Ex. *Eat all of your dinner.* —*n.* everything, everyone. Ex. *All was lost in the fire.* —**after all,** despite everything. Ex. *After all, he tried to be good.* —**all but,** except for. —**all over,** 1. ended. Ex. *The party is all over.* 2. everywhere. Ex. *You see him all over town.* —**all right,** 1. satisfactory; good; correct. Ex. *Is it all right for me to leave?* 2. unhurt; well. Ex. *Is she all right?* 3. yes. Ex. *All right, I will go with you.* —**at all,** under any condition. Ex. *He did not see her at all.*

allay (5) [əley'], *v.* quiet; put at rest. Ex. *The doctor's friendly manner helped allay the patient's fears.*

allege (4) [əlej'], *v.* 1. declare positively but without proof. Ex. *The shopkeeper alleged the boy stole some fruit.* 2. declare as a reason; give as an excuse for an act. Ex. *He alleged poor vision as a cause of the accident.* —**al·leg'ed·ly,** *adv.* —**al·le·ga'tion,** *n.*

allegiance (4) [əliy'jəns], *n.* 1. loyalty or faithfulness to a government or ruler. Ex. *A country needs the allegiance of its citizens.* 2. loyalty or devotion to friends or causes.

alley (4) [æl'iy], *n.* a narrow street between or behind buildings. Ex. *The truck was too large to pass through the alley.*

alliance (4) [əlay'əns], *n.* 1. the act of uniting; a union of interests, especially between states, by agreement or treaty, or between families, by marriage. 2. the agreement itself. Ex. *The alliance between the two nations strengthened each of them greatly.*

allot (5) [əlat'], *v.* give each his share; distribute. Ex. *Prizes were allotted to the winners.* —**al·lot'ment,** *n.*

allow (1) [əlaw'], v. 1. permit. Ex. *Smoking is allowed here.* 2. provide for. Ex. *Allow enough time for breakfast before you leave.* —al·low'ance, n. an amount of food, money, etc. given for a special purpose. Ex. *He gave his wife a weekly allowance to buy food.* —al·low'a·ble, adj. that can be allowed; that can be permitted. Ex. *Certain mistakes are allowable.* —make allowance for, consider the circumstances. Ex. *He is young, so you must make allowance for his mistakes.*

alloy (5) [æl'oy], n. substance consisting of two or more metals melted and mixed together. Ex. *An alloy of gold and copper is harder and less costly than gold alone.* —v. 1. mix metals by melting together. 2. reduce in worth by adding something of less value. Ex. *Their pleasure was alloyed by misfortunes.*

allude (5) [əluwd'], v. refer to or mention in a slight or indirect way (always followed by to). Ex. *Your letter alludes to a matter which I had forgotten.* —al·lu'sion, n. a reference to. Ex. *In his talk, he made several allusions to the Bible.*

allure (5) [əlu:r'], n. charm. Ex. *For me, the country has more allure than the city.* —al·lur'ing, adj.

ally (4) [æ`lay', əlay'], n. a country or person joined with another for some special purpose. Ex. *Canada is an ally of the United States.* —v. 1. join by agreement, treaty, or marriage. 2. bind together; connect; associate. Ex. *They are allied by their common interest in music.*

almost (1) [ɔl'mowst], adv. nearly; a little less than; not quite. Ex. *It is almost ten o'clock.*

alone (1) [əlown'], adj. 1. away from others; by oneself. Ex. *He lives alone.* 2. not including anyone or anything else. Ex. *Man cannot live by bread alone.* —adv. by oneself. Ex. *Don't bring anyone with you; come alone.*

along (1) [əlɔ:ŋ'], prep. on or beside the length of. Ex. *They walked along the road.* —adv. 1. forward; onward. Ex. *They were late and had to hurry along.* 2. together. Ex. *I will go along with you.* —get along, manage. Ex. *How can you get along on such a small salary?*

aloof (5) [əluwf'], adj. distant; disinterested. Ex. *He has few friends because of his aloof manner.* —adv. at a distance but within view; apart. Ex. *He stood aloof from the others.* —a·loof'ness, n.

alphabet (3) [æl'fəbet`], n. the letters used in a language, arranged in a certain order. Ex. *The first three letters of the*

English alphabet are A, B, C. —al`pha·bet'i·cal, *adj.* —al'
pha·bet·ize, *v.* arrange in the order of the alphabet.

already (1) [ɔlred'iy], *adv.* before a certain time. Ex. *When
I reached the house, he had already gone.*

also (1) [ɔ:l`sow'], *adv.* as well; besides; too. Ex. *He is tall
and also strong.*

altar (4) [ɔl'tər], *n.* a raised structure or table used in religious services. Ex. *The marriage ceremony was performed
at the altar.*

alter (3) [ɔl'tər], *v.* make different in some way; change. Ex.
The tailor will alter the suit to fit you. —al`ter·a'tion, *n.* a
change.

alternate (4) [ɔl'tərneyt`], *v.* 1. say or do by turns, one after
the other in regular order. Ex. *The teacher alternated written and spoken work.* 2. vary at regular intervals. Ex. *Day
alternates with night.* —al'ter·nate·ly, *adv.*

alternative (5) [ɔltər'nətiv], *n.* choice between two or more
things, only one of which can be chosen. Ex. *He had the
alternative of coming with us or staying at home.* —*adj.*
offering a choice between two or more things. Ex. *We had
alternative plans if it rained on the day of the picnic.* al·ter'
na·tive·ly, *adv.*

although (1) [ɔlðow'], *conj.* even if; in spite of the fact. Ex.
I will go, although I would rather stay home.

altitude (4) [æl'tətuwd`, æl'tətyuwd`], *n.* 1. height above a
certain level, especially above sea level. Ex. *At what altitude
is the plane flying?* 2. a position that is high. Ex. *The altitude made it difficult to breathe.*

altogether (3) [ɔltəgeð'ər], *adv.* completely; entirely. Ex.
This noise is altogether unnecessary. 2. considering everything. Ex. *Altogether, I decided to move to another place.*

aluminum [əluw'mənəm], *n.* a silvery gray metal, which is
light in weight, does not rust, and is widely used in manufacturing. Ex. *These pots and pans are made of aluminum.*

always (1) [ɔl'weyz], *adv.* 1. at all times. Ex. *He is always
happy.* 2. forever. Ex. *His bravery will always be remembered.*

am (1) [æm'], *v.* present tense of the verb *be,* used with *I.*
Ex. *I am a student now.*

amateur (4) [æm'əčər], *n.* 1. one who does something for enjoyment rather than professionally for money. Ex. *The*

actors in the play were very good amateurs. 2. an unskilled person. Ex. *This artist paints like an amateur.* —*adj.* in the manner of a beginner or amateur. Ex. *He is an amateur gardener, but his flowers are beautiful.* —**am·a·teur'ish,** *adj.* —**am·a·teur'ish·ly,** *adv.*

amaze' (4) [əmeyz'], *v.* surprise; astonish greatly. Ex. *I was amazed by his skill at the piano.* —**a·maze'ment,** *n.* —**a·maz'ing,** *adj.* —**a·maz'ing·ly,** *adv.*

ambassador (4) [æmbæs'ədər], *n.* an official of the highest rank sent by one government as its representative to another. Ex. *Ambassadors usually live in the capital of a country.* —**am·bas'sa·dor'i·al,** *adj.*

ambition (3) [æmbi'šən], *n.* 1. eagerness or great desire for success, wealth, honor, or power. Ex. *His ambition caused him to work hard.* 2. the object of such desire. Ex. *To become a scientist was his ambition.* —**am·bi'tious,** *adj.* determined to succeed. Ex. *Because he is ambitious, he may develop into a great scientist.* —**am·bi'tious·ly,** *adv.*

amend (3) [əmend'], *v.* 1. make correct; change for the better; improve. Ex. *I would like to amend the statement I made yesterday.* 2. alter. Ex. *The Constitution of the United States has been amended many times.* —**a·mend'a·ble,** *adj.* —**a·mend'ment,** *n.*

amiable (5) [ey'miyəbəl], *adj.* friendly; good-natured. Ex. *He spoke in an amiable manner.* —**a'mi·a·bil'i·ty,** *n.* —**a'mi·a·bly,** *adv.*

amid (5) [əmid'], *prep.* surrounded by; in the middle of. Ex. *The teacher stood amid the crowd of students.*

amiss (5) [əmis'], *adv.* improperly; in the wrong way. Ex. *From his angry looks, we knew something had gone amiss.* —*adj.* improper; faulty; wrong. Ex. *If anything is amiss in the house, it will be repaired.*

ammunition (5) [æm'yəniš'ən], *n.* 1. anything that is hurled or shot from a weapon or exploded, such as bullets, bombs, etc. Ex. *The soldiers still had their guns but were out of ammunition.* 2. any material useful in defense or attack. Ex. *The truth was his ammunition against liars.*

among (1) [əmən'], *prep.* 1. in company with; in the midst of. Ex. *There are strangers among us.* 2. in the class or group

---

a, far; æ, am; e, get; ey, late; i, in; iy, see; ɔ, all; ow, go; u, put; uw, too; ə, but, ago; ər, fur; aw, out; ay, life; oy, boy; ŋ, ring; θ, think; ð, that; ž, measure; š, ship; ǰ, edge; č, child.

of. Ex. *There were disagreements among the members of
the family.* 3. with shares to each. Ex. *Divide this money
equally among you.*

amount (1) [əmawnt'], *n.* 1. quantity. Ex. *Only a small amount
of sugar was used.* 2. total of. Ex. *The amount of money
needed to pay the whole bill was very little.* —*v.* reach a
total of. Ex. *The bill amounts to more than I can pay.*

ample (4) [æm'pəl], *adj.* 1. large in size; having enough space.
Ex. *Two people could sit on the ample chair.* 2. sufficient for
the purpose or the needs; more than enough. Ex. *Their supply of food was ample for the winter.* —**am'ply,** *adv.*

amuse (3) [əmyuwz'], *v.* 1. entertain; cause to laugh. Ex. *The
actors amused us all.* 2. cause time to pass agreeably. Ex.
The guests amused themselves by playing a game. —**a·mus'-
ing·ly,** *adv.* —**a·muse'ment,** *n.*

an (1) [æn', ən], *adj.* or *art.* 1. one; one kind of; any. Ex. *He
told an interesting story.* 2. in or for each. Ex. *The car's
speed was 25 miles an hour. An* is also called an *indefinite
article* and is used instead of *a* before words beginning with
a vowel sound.

-an (3) [ən], *suffix.* 1. belonging to; relating to. Exs. *America,
American; Mexico, Mexican.* 2. one who works in or in the
field of. Exs. *Library, librarian; history, historian.*

analysis (4) [ənæl'əsəs], *n.* separation of a whole into parts;
also an examination of each of the parts. Ex. *A blood analysis was made at the hospital.*

analyze (5) [æn'əlayz'], *v.* examine something by separating
it into parts. Ex. *Farmers learn to analyze soil.* —**an'a·lyst,**
n. —**an'a·lyt'ic,** *adj.* —**an'a·lyt'i·cal·ly,** *adv.*

-ance (1) [əns], *suffix.* act of, condition of, or quality of. Exs.
Assist, assistance; grieve, grievance; avoid, avoidance.

ancestor (4) [æn'sestər], *n.* a person in one's family who lived
many years before. Ex. *His ancestors came to this country
200 years ago.* —**an·ces'tral,** *adj.* —**an'ces·try,** *n.* ancestors
as a group. Ex. *His ancestry is European.*

anchor (3) [æŋ'kər], *n.* something, usually made of metal,
lowered by a chain to the bottom of the sea to hold a ship
in a particular place. —*v.* 1. fasten with an anchor. Ex. *The
fisherman anchored his boat near the shore.* 2. fasten firmly.
Ex. *The pupils' desks were anchored to the floor.* —**an'chor·
age,** *n.* a place where ships anchor; harbor.

ancient (2) [eyn'šənt], *adj.* 1. in the early years of history; belonging to the distant past. **Ex.** *We are reading the history of ancient Rome.* 2. very old. **Ex.** *That ancient ruin was once a temple.*

and (1) [ænd'], *conj.* 1. with. **Ex.** *His brother and his sister are going.* 2. also. **Ex.** *The soup is good and hot.* 3. added to. **Ex.** *Four and five are nine.*

anecdote (5) [æn'ikdowt'], *n.* a brief account of an interesting event. **Ex.** *He told many anecdotes about his experiences as a teacher.* —a'nec·do'tal, *adj.*

angel (3) [eyn'jəl], *n.* 1. a spiritual, heavenly being; a messenger of God, usually pictured with a human body and wings. 2. a person with the good qualities of such a being. **Ex.** *The children were angels while you were gone.* —an·gel'ic, *adj.* —an·gel'i·cal·ly, *adv.*

anger (1) [æŋ'gər], *n.* strong, unfriendly feeling usually caused by thoughts that one has been wronged. **Ex.** *The king's unjust laws caused great anger.* —v. cause this feeling. **Ex.** *The man angered her when he hit the child.*

angle (3) [æŋ'gəl], *n.* 1. figure made by two straight lines going out from a point, or the space inside two such lines. 2. a particular way of thinking. **Ex.** *We must consider this problem from all angles.*

ANGLE 1

angry (1) [æŋ'griy], *adj.* feeling or showing anger. **Ex.** *An angry crowd gathered in the street and shouted loudly.* —an'gri·ly, *adv.*

anguish (4) [æŋ'gwiš], *n.* great pain, either of body or mind. **Ex.** *In his anguish, the wounded man screamed.* —an'guished, *adj.*

animal (1) [æn'əməl], *n.* any living being, not a plant, that can feel and move by itself. **Ex.** *Dogs, birds, fish, and people are animals.* —adj. relating to animals. **Ex.** *Meat contains animal fats.*

ankle (3) [æŋ'kəl], *n.* the joint between the foot and the leg. **Ex.** *She broke her ankle.*

annex (5) [əneks'], *v.* attach, join, or add, especially to something larger or more important. **Ex.** *The city annexed neighboring villages.*

annex (5) [æ'neks], *n.* an addition to a building. **Ex.** *He built* *an annex to his house to use as an office.* —**an'nex·a'tion,** *n.* the adding or joining of something to something else.

anniversary (5) [æn'əvər'səriy], *n.* 1. yearly date on which some special event occurred in the past. Ex. *August 24th is our wedding anniversary.* 2. the celebration of such a date.

announce (2) [ənawns'], *v.* 1. cause to be known; give first public notice. Ex. *They will announce the names of the winners tonight.* 2. state the approach or the presence of. Ex. *A man stood at the door to announce the arrival of the guests.* —**an'nounc'er,** *n.* one who announces. —**an'nounce'ment,** *n.* that which is announced.

annoy (3) [ənoy'], *v.* anger slightly; worry; disturb; bother. Ex. *Loud noises annoy many people.* —**an·noy'ance,** *n.* —**an·noy'ing,** *adj.*

annual (3) [æn'yuwəl], *adj.* once in each year. Ex. *New Year's Day is an annual holiday.* —**an'nu·al·ly,** *adv.*

another (1) [ənəð'ər], *adj.* and *pron.* 1. a second; a further. Ex. *When you finish your cake, have another piece.* 2. a different; of a different kind. Ex. *We know that story; tell us another.* —**one another,** each other. Ex. *They love one another very much.*

answer (1) [æn'sər], *n.* 1. a reply to a question or argument. Ex. *What is your answer to this question?* 2. the solution to a problem. Ex. *The teacher said his answer was correct.* —*v.* give a reply in words, action, or writing. Ex. *He answered my letter quickly.* —**an'swer·able,** *adj.* required to give an accounting; responsible. Ex. *He is answerable to the manager of the company for this money.*

ant (3) [ænt'], *n.* a small insect. Ex. *Ants live in large, organized groups.*

-ant (1) [ənt], *suffix.* a person or thing that does something, is acted upon, or is used for. Exs. *Serve, servant; command, commandant.* 2. doing; showing; having. Exs. *Extravagance, extravagant; reliance, reliant.*

ANT

antagonist (5) [æntæg'ənəst], *n.* one who is opposed to another, especially in battle or in a contest; opponent; rival. Ex. *The enemy was a powerful antagonist.* —**an·tag'o·nism,** *n.* —**an·tag·o·nis'tic,** *adj.*

antelope (5) [ænt'təlowpˋ], *n.* small animal similar to a deer.

anticipate (4) [æntis'əpəytˋ], *v.* 1. expect. **Ex.** *Everyone anticipated the party with pleasure.* 2. think of and deal with something in advance. **Ex.** *A good secretary anticipates her employer's needs and is always prepared for them.* —**an·tic'i·pa'tion,** *n.*

ANTELOPE

antique (5) [æntiykˋ], *adj.* of a time long past. **Ex.** *They have some beautiful antique furniture.* —*n.* an object of ancient art. **Ex.** *The antiques of Greece and Rome may be seen in museums.* —**an·tiq'ui·ty,** *n.* ancient times. —**an'ti·quat'ed,** *adj.* old in fashion; no longer useful.

anxiety (2) [æŋzay'ətiy], *n.* worry caused by uncertainty about the future. **Ex.** *She felt great anxiety when told of her daughter's accident.*

anxious (2) [æŋk'šəs], *adj.* 1. greatly troubled; worried. **Ex.** *He is anxious about his health.* 2. desiring greatly. **Ex.** *These merchants are anxious to please.* —**anx'ious·ly,** *adv.*

any (1) [en'iy], *adj.* 1. of an undetermined amount. **Ex.** *Do you have any money?* 2. of no particular one. **Ex.** *Take any book you like.* 3. some. **Ex.** *Do you want any cream in your coffee?* 4. every. **Ex.** *He can answer any question.* —*adv.* to any degree; to any extent. **Ex.** *Is the patient any better?*

anybody [en'iybəˋdiy, en'iybaˋdiy], *pron.* any person. **Ex.** *Can anybody tell me the time?*

anyhow (3) [en'iyhawˋ], *adv.* in any case; regardless of difficulty or argument. **Ex.** *Though her father did not like the young man, she married him anyhow.*

anyone [en'iywənˋ], *pron.* any person. **Ex.** *I did not meet anyone I knew on the street.*

anything [en'iyθiŋˋ], *pron.* any thing, act, condition, event, or fact. **Ex.** *Did you do anything interesting during your vacation?* —*adv.* in any degree. **Ex.** *Their house is not anything like ours.* —*n.* a thing of any kind. **Ex.** *Did you buy anything to eat?*

anyway [en'iywayˋ], *adv.* in any case; nevertheless. **Ex.** *He was told not to go, but he went anyway.*

---

a, far; æ, am; e, get; ey, late; i, in; iy, see; ɔ, all; ow, go; u, put; uw, too; ə, but, ago; ər, fur; aw, out; ay, life; oy, boy; ŋ, ring; θ, think; ð, that; ž, measure; š, ship; ǰ, edge; č, child.

anywhere [en'iyhwe:r`], *adv.* at, in, or to any place. **Exs.** *I cannot find the book anywhere. Are you going anywhere this evening?*

apart (2) [əpart'], *adv.* 1. separately, in place or time. **Ex.** *He lived apart from his parents while he attended school.* 2. in two or more parts. **Ex.** *The children took the clock apart to see how it worked.* —*adj.* separated. **Ex.** *Artists consider themselves a group apart from the rest of society.*

apartment (2) [əpart'mənt], *n.* a room or group of connected rooms for a single household. **Ex.** *There are several apartments for rent in that building.*

ape (5) [eyp`], *n.* a large monkey with no tail.

apologize (3) [əpal'əjayz`], *v.* express regrets for a mistake made or injury done. **Ex.** *He apologized for his error.* —**a·pol`o·get'ic**, *adj.* —**a·pol`o·get'i·cal·ly**, *adv.* —**a·pol`o·gist**, *n.* one who defends an idea; one who apologizes.

APE

apology (3) [əpal'əjiy], *n.* expression of regret for; statement that one is sorry. **Ex.** *I owe you an apology for being late.*

appall (5) [əpɔ:l'], *v.* fill with horror, shock, or fear. **Ex.** *They were appalled by the sight of the bloody shirt.* —**ap·pall'ing**, *adj.*

apparatus (4) [æp`ərey'təs, æp`əræt'əs], *n.* tools or equipment for a special kind of work. **Ex.** *The town has recently purchased some new fire-fighting apparatus.*

apparel (5) [æpær'əl, əper'əl], *n.* a person's outer clothing; suit; dress. **Ex.** *A shop selling women's apparel is at the corner.*

apparent (3) [əpær'ənt, əper'ənt], *adj.* 1. evident; capable of being clearly seen or understood. **Ex.** *His fear was apparent to all.* 2. seeming rather than actual. **Ex.** *The apparent spot on the wall was only a shadow.* —**ap·par'ent·ly**, *adv.*

appeal (2) [əpiyl'], *v.* 1. ask for aid. **Ex.** *After their house burned, they appealed for clothing.* 2. offer attraction, interest, or enjoyment. **Ex.** *The large house appealed to him.* 3. ask a higher court to review a law case. —*n.* 1. a call for aid, support, or mercy; a request. **Ex.** *Their appeal for money was soon answered.* 2. power to attract. **Ex.** *His ideas had great appeal for young people.* 3. a request for a review of a law case by a higher court. —**ap·peal'ing**, *adj.* —**ap·peal'ing·ly**, *adv.*

appear (1) [əpi:r'], *v.* 1. seem; look as if. Ex. *He appears to be happy.* 2. come into sight. Ex. *The ship appeared far away.* 3. come, or be placed, before the public. Ex. *She appeared in a new movie.* —ap·pear'ance, *n.* 1. act of appearing. Ex. *She made a late appearance at the party.* 2. outward look. Ex. *From his appearance, we knew he was ill.*

appease (5) [əpiyz'], *v.* 1. satisfy; make quiet; calm. Ex. *The food appeased his hunger.* 2. make peace, often by sacrificing a moral principle. Ex. *Only complete surrender would appease the enemy.* —ap·peas'er, *n.* —ap·pease'ment, *n.*

append (5) [əpend'], *v.* add or attach as something extra. Ex. *The author appended a list at the end of his book.* —ap·pend'age, *n.*

appendix (5) [əpen'diks], *n.* 1. material added to a complete book, usually in the back. Ex. *The appendix contains some useful information.* 2. a small tube in the body which has no known use.

appetite (4) [æp'ətayt˅], *n.* 1. a desire to eat or drink. Ex. *A sick person often has a small appetite.* 2. any desire. Ex. *Most children have an appetite for learning.* —ap'pe·tiz'ing, *adj.* —ap'pe·tiz'er, *n.* small pieces of food or drink taken before a meal to improve appetites. Ex. *Fruit juice was served as an appetizer.*

applaud (4) [əplɔ:d'], *v.* 1. express approval by hitting the hands together. Ex. *The audience applauded the actors.* 2. praise; express approval. Ex. *We applaud your decision.*

applause (4) [əplɔ:z'], *n.* hand-clapping, shouting, or other outward expressions of approval. Ex. *The applause was loud and long.*

apple (1) [æp'əl], *n.* a red, yellow, or green round, firm fruit with small seeds.

appliance (5) [əplay'əns], *n.* a device for a particular use, usually electrically operated. Ex. *The modern house has many useful electrical appliances.*

APPLE

apply (2) [əplay'], *v.* 1. use. Ex. *You must apply what you know in your work.* 2. place in contact with; put on. Ex. *Apply this medicine to the wound.* 3. ask for. Ex. *She applied for the job.* —ap'pli·ca·ble, *adj.* —ap'pli·ca·bil'i·ty, *n.* suitability. —ap'pli·cant, *n.* one who applies for a job. —ap'pli·ca'tion, *n.* a request.

appoint (2) [əpoynt'], *v.* 1. select for a position; place in office. Ex. *They appointed him president of the company.* 2. decide upon. Ex. *We must appoint a time and place for the meeting.* —**ap·poin'tive,** *adj.*

appointment (2) [əpoynt'mənt], *n.* 1. selection for position or office. Ex. *The committee favored the appointment of the new secretary.* 2. established time; engagement. Ex. *I have an appointment with my doctor at four o'clock.*

appreciate (3) [əpriy'šiyeyt'], *v.* 1. recognize or feel the worth of. Ex. *He does not appreciate art.* 2. be grateful for. Ex. *The boy appreciated the gift.* 3. recognize; understand; sympathize. Ex. *We should appreciate the problems of other people.* —**ap·pre'ci·a·tive,** *adj.* —**ap·pre'ci·a·tive·ly,** *adv.* —**ap·pre·ci·a'tion,** *n.*

apprehend (5) [æp'rihend'], *v.* 1. arrest. Ex. *The police apprehended the criminal.* 2. understand. Ex. *He fully apprehended what he read.*

apprehension (4) [æp'rihen'šən], *n.* 1. dread or fear of coming evil. Ex. *He had some apprehension about going into the forest alone.* 2. the power of understanding ideas. Ex. *She could neither see nor hear, but her apprehension was very great.* 3. act of catching or arresting. Ex. *The apprehension of the thief was done quickly.* —**ap'pre·hen'sive,** *adj.* —**ap'pre·hen'sive·ly,** *adv.*

apprentice (5) [əpren'təs], *n.* a person helping a skilled worker in a trade in order to learn; a learner; a beginner. Ex. *He is an apprentice in the building trade.* —*v.* put under the care of an employer for instruction in an art or trade. Ex. *The young man was apprenticed to a shoemaker.* —**ap·pren'tice·ship,** *n.*

approach (2) [əprowč'], *v.* 1. move near to in space, time, quality, etc. Ex. *The car approached the city.* 2. go to with a request. Ex. *The boy approached his father for permission to go on the trip.* —*n.* 1. act of coming closer. Ex. *They were frightened by the man's approach.* 2. means of entrance; road or path. Ex. *The approach to the house was lined with trees.* —**ap·proach'able,** *adj.* friendly; willing to talk and listen.

appropriate (4) [əprow'priyət], *adj.* proper or fitting for a particular person, purpose, or occasion. Ex. *He made a*

speech appropriate to the holiday. —ap·pro'pri·ate·ly, *adv.*
—ap·pro'pri·ate·ness, *n.*

appropriate (4) [əprow'priyeyt'], *v.* 1. set apart for a special
purpose. Ex. *The city appropriated money for a new bridge.*
2. take possession of; take for one's self. Ex. *After the boy's
parents died, an uncle appropriated their property.* —ap·
pro·pri·a'tion, *n.* 1. act of appropriating. 2. that which is
appropriated.

approve (3) [əpruwv'], *v.* 1. speak or think favorably of; consider to be good. Ex. *Do you approve of my choice?* 2. give
one's consent to. Ex. *The president did not approve the
plan.* —ap·prov'al, *n.* —ap·prov'ing, *adj.* —ap·prov'ing·ly,
adv.

approximate (3) [əprak'səmət], *adj.* very similar; not exact,
but nearly so. Ex. *What is the approximate amount you
need?* —v. be or make very similar. Ex. *This copy ap-
proximates the original.* —ap·prox'i·mate·ly, *adv.* —ap·prox'-
i·ma'tion, *n.*

April (1) [əy'prəl], *n.* fourth month of the
year.

apron (4) [ey'prən], *n.* article of clothing
worn over the front part of one's clothes
to cover and protect them while working.

apt (4) [æpt'], *adj.* 1. suitable; proper. Ex.
*Although not prepared to talk, he made
some apt remarks.* 2. likely. Ex. *Please
remind me, for I am apt to forget.* 3.
quick to learn. Ex. *The girl is an apt pupil.* —apt'ly, *adv.*
—apt'ness, *n.*

APRON

-ar (3) [ər], *suffix.* 1. belonging to; referring to; like; of the
nature of. Exs. *Pole, polar; line, linear.* 2. one who. Exs.
Beg, beggar; lie, liar.

arbor (5) [ar'bər], *n.* a place shaded by trees or vines. Ex.
They sat under the grape arbor.

arc (5) [ark'], *n.* a curved line; a line that is part of a circle.

a, far; æ, am; e, get; ey, late; i, in; iy, see; ɔ, all; ow, go; u, put; uw, too;
ə, but, ago; ər, fur; aw, out; ay, life; oy, boy; ŋ, ring; θ, think; ð, that;
ž, measure; š, ship; ǰ, edge; č, child.

arch (2) [arč¹], *n.* 1. a curved part of a building used to hold up the material above it. 2. any curve in the form of an arch. —*v.* 1. cover or provide with an arch. **Ex.** *The bridge arches the river.* 2. form or bend into the shape of an arch. **Ex.** *She arched her eyebrows in surprise.*

ARCH

architect (4) [ar¹kətekt¹], *n.* a person who designs buildings. **Ex.** *We employed an architect to design our house.*

architecture (4) [ar¹kətek¹čər], *n.* 1. the art or science of designing buildings. 2. a method or style of building. **Ex.** *Greek architecture and modern architecture are quite different.* —ar¹chi·tec¹tur·al, *adj.* —ar¹chi·tec¹tur·al·ly, *adv.*

are (1) [a:r¹], *v.* present tense of the verb *be* used with *you, we, they,* and plural nouns. **Ex.** *We are friends now.*

area (2) [er¹iyə], *n.* 1. a region on the earth's surface. **Ex.** *They traveled to a mountain area.* 2. an amount of space within boundaries. **Ex.** *The area of their land is two acres.* 3. extent of a subject. **Ex.** *The study of the deep oceans is a new area of research.*

argue (2) [ar¹gyuw], *v.* 1. offer reasons for or against something. **Ex.** *They argued against going home.* 2. disagree. **Ex.** *The drunken man argued loudly.* —ar¹gu·ment, *n.* —ar¹gu·able, *adj.* —ar·gu·men¹ta·tive, *adj.* always ready to quarrel.

arise (3) [ərayz¹], *v.* 1. move upward; stand up; get out of bed. **Ex.** *I always arise at seven o'clock in the morning.* 2. appear; come into being. **Ex.** *New problems arise every day.*

aristocrat (5) [əris¹təkræt¹], *n.* 1. a person of high rank, birth, or title. **Ex.** *For many years only aristocrats were members of the government.* 2. one who has the characteristics of a ruling or upper class of society. **Ex.** *The governor came from a poor family but was an aristocrat at heart.* —a·ris¹to·crat¹ic, *adj.* —a·ris¹to·crat¹i·cal·ly, *adv.*

arithmetic (5) [əriθ¹mətik¹], *n.* the science or study of using numbers. **Ex.** *Reading, writing, and arithmetic are the basis* *of an education.* —ar'ith·met'i·cal, *adj.* —ar' ith·met'i·cal·ly, *adv.*

arm (1) [arm'], *n.* 1. part of the human body from the shoulder to the hand. 2. anything like a human arm. **Ex.** *The coat was hanging on the arm of a chair.* —*v.* 1. give guns or other things with which to fight. **Ex.** *The soldiers were armed with guns.* 2. strengthen, furnish with protection. **Ex.** *He was armed against the cold with warm clothing.* — armed, *adj.*

ARM 1

armament (5) [ar'məmənt], *n.* the weapons and military force for fighting a war. **Ex.** *A large percentage of the budget is for armaments.*

armistice (5) [ar'məstəs], *n.* the ceasing of fighting for a brief time, by agreement. **Ex.** *During the armistice, they developed a plan for ending the war.*

armor (3) [ar'mər], *n.* 1. protective covering on a ship, plane, truck, etc. **Ex.** *Nothing could break through the armor of the truck.* 2. protective covering for the body, usually made of metal.

arms (1) [armz'], *n.* guns and other things soldiers use to fight in battle; weapons. **Ex.** *The soldiers laid down their arms and surrendered.*

army (1) [ar'miy], *n.* 1. a large group of soldiers organized for land war. **Ex.** *The army fought to save the country from the enemy.* 2. a great number. **Ex.** *An army of children marched down the street.*

arose (3) [ərowz'], *v.* past tense of *arise.* **Ex.** *He arose early today.*

around (1) [ərawnd'], *adv.* 1. in a circle; on every side. **Ex.** *People were standing around us.* 2. in the opposite direction. **Ex.** *They turned around and ran.* —*prep.* 1. about; encircling. **Ex.** *She wore some beads around her neck.* 2. here and there. **Ex.** *Let us drive around the city for a while.* 3. somewhere in or near. **Ex.** *Stay around the school until I come for you.* 4. near in time or amount. **Ex.** *I will see you around five o'clock.*

arouse (5) [ərawz'], *v.* 1. awaken. **Ex.** *They aroused the boy from a deep sleep.* 2. excite to action or a high degree of emotion. **Ex.** *The speaker aroused the crowd.* —a·roused', *adj.*

arrange (2) [əreynĵ'], v. 1. put in order. Ex. *Arrange the papers on the table.* 2. prepare; plan. Ex. *We will arrange a meeting for next week.* —ar·range'ment, n. —ar·rang'er, n. person who arranges, especially music for different instruments.

array (4) [ərey'], v. 1. clothe in fine garments. Ex. *The dancers were arrayed in colorful costumes.* 2. place in order; line up, or arrange, especially soldiers. Ex. *The soldiers were arrayed in front of the general.* —n. 1. order; battle order. Ex. *The troops were in battle array.* 2. an impressive group of things on exhibition. Ex. *There was an array of jewels in the shop window.*

arrest (3) [ərest'], v. 1. seize a person by legal authority. Ex. *The policeman arrested him.* 2. stop. Ex. *We must arrest the flow of blood or he will die.* 3. attract. Ex. *The story arrested my attention.* —n. seizure by force, physical or moral. Ex. *They placed the man under arrest.*

arrive (1) [ərayv'], v. 1. come to a planned place. Ex. *I will arrive on the two o'clock bus.* 2. reach a point or a state by effort. Ex. *After much discussion, they arrived at a decision.* —ar·riv'al, n.

arrow (3) [ær'ow, er'ow], n. 1. a long, thin piece of wood with a sharply pointed tip used as a weapon and shot from a bow. 2. a mark in the form of an arrow which shows direction. Ex. *Follow the arrows on the wall.*

art (1) [art'], n. 1. the expression or doing of something that is beautiful. Ex. *Painting, music, the dance, etc. are arts.* 2. certain fields of study outside science, such as history, music, languages, etc. 3. skilled workmanship. Ex. *This ring is a fine example of the jeweler's art.* 4. the general principles of an area of learning. Ex. *She is skilled in the art of cooking.* —art'ist, n. —ar·tis'tic, adj. —ar·tis'ti·cal·ly, adv. —art'ful, adj. cunning; clever.

artery (5) [ar'təriy], n. 1. a blood vessel which carries blood from the heart to other parts of the body. 2. a channel of transportation or communication. Ex. *The river was once a main artery of transportation in America.* —ar·te'ri·al, adj.

article (1) [ar'təkəl], n. 1. a piece of writing on a special subject. Ex. *Have you read this newspaper article?* 2. an individual piece or thing. Ex. *A coat is an article of clothing.* 3. the indefinite articles *a* and *an* and the definite article *the*.

artificial (4) [ar'təfiš'əl], *adj.* 1. made by humans; not natural. **Ex.** *The artificial flowers were made of paper.* 2. not true; not honest. **Ex.** *Her smile is artificial.* —ar'ti·fi'cial·ly, *adv.* —ar'ti·fi·ci·al'i·ty, *n.*

artillery (4) [artil'əriy], *n.* 1. large, heavy guns moved on wheeled carriers. **Ex.** *The artillery was the deciding factor in the battle.* 2. the part of the army that uses such guns.

-ary (1) [əriy] *suffix.* relating to; connected with; like. **Exs.** *Honor, honorary; custom, customary; bound, boundary.*

as (1) [æz'], *adv.* 1. equally; in the same amount or degree. **Ex.** *She is as pretty as her mother.* 2. for example. **Ex.** *Some occupations, as engineering or medicine, require many years of study.* —*conj.* 1. to the same degree or amount that; in the same manner. **Ex.** *He grew straight as a tree.* 2. while. **Ex.** *As I sat there, I thought of many things.* 3. because. **Ex.** *As you are not dressed yet, I will leave without you.* —*pron.* 1. who; which; that. **Ex.** *The store is in the same building as my office.* 2. a fact that. **Ex.** *It is red, as anyone can see.* —*prep.* in the idea, character, or condition of. **Ex.** *He was treated as a child.*

ascend (4) [əsend'], *v.* climb or move upward; rise. **Ex.** *He ascended the stairs to the second floor.* —as·cen'sion, *n.* act of rising.

ascent (5) [əsent'], *n.* 1. act of rising; upward movement; rise. **Ex.** *His ascent in the business world was quick.* 2. way or means of going up; upward slope. **Ex.** *The ascent to the top of the hill was steep.*

ash (3) [æš'], *n.* the powdery material that remains after burning. **Ex.** *The paper burned to ashes.* —ashen, *adj.* pale; the color of ashes.

ashamed (3) [əšeymd'], *v.* feeling shame because one has done wrong. **Ex.** *I feel ashamed of the way I acted at your party.*

ask (1) [æsk'], *v.* 1. put a question to; seek information. **Ex.** *Ask her when the train leaves.* 2. demand as a price. **Ex.** *You are asking too much for this furniture.* 3. invite. **Ex.** *We asked guests for dinner.*

asleep [əsliyp'], *adj.* sleeping. **Ex.** *I was asleep and did not hear him knock.*

---

a, far; æ, am; e, get; ey, late; i, in; iy, see; ɔ, all; ow, go; u, put; uw, too; ə, but, ago; ər, fur; aw, out; ay, life; oy, boy; ŋ, ring; θ, think; ð, that; ž, measure; š, ship; j, edge; č, child.

aspect (3) [æs'pekt`], *n.* 1. appearance, look. **Ex.** *To the men in the boat the rocky shore had a frightening aspect.* 2. a way in which a thing may be viewed or considered. **Ex.** *All aspects of the question must be examined.*

aspire (5) [əspayr'], *v.* desire eagerly, especially something high or great. **Ex.** *He aspired to be a leader.* —as·pir'ant, *n.* —as·pi·ra'tion, *n.*

assail (4) [əseyl'], *v.* attack violently, either by words or by repeated blows. **Ex.** *He assailed them with bad language.* —as·sail'ant, *n.* attacker. **Ex.** *The assailant has been caught by the police.* —as·sail'able, *adj.*

assault (4) [əsɔlt'], *n.* violent attack with weapons or blows, or by words and arguments. **Ex.** *We were not prepared for the assault.* —*v.* make an attack.

assemble (3) [əsem'bəl], *v.* 1. collect; gather into one place or group. **Ex.** *The students assembled in the classroom.* 2. put or fit parts together. **Ex.** *The workmen assembled the new machine.* —as·sem'blage, as·sem'bly, *n.* —As·sem'bly, *n.* parliament; legislature.

assent (5) [əsent'], *v.* agree; admit the truth of; consent. **Ex.** *He assented to the plan.* —*n.* agreement; act of assenting.

assert (5) [əsərt'], *v.* 1. state as true; declare; state with certainty. **Ex.** *He asserted that he was innocent.* 2. insist on having. **Ex.** *Every citizen must assert his rights.* —as·ser'tion, *n.*

asset (5) [æ'set`], *n.* something of value that is owned; a quality of value. **Ex.** *Honesty is an asset.*

assign (3) [əsayn'], *v.* 1. give as a job or work. **Ex.** *The teacher assigned a lesson.* 2. appoint. **Ex.** *Two new teachers were assigned to the science department.* 3. select; fix exactly. **Ex.** *We must assign a day for the meeting.* —as·sign'ment, *n.*

assist (3) [əsist'], *v.* aid. **Ex.** *Please assist me with my work.* —as·sist'ance, *n.* the act of helping. —as·sist'ant, *n.* a helper.

associate (2) [əsow'šiyeyt`], *v.* 1. connect in thought. **Ex.** *He associated the cake with his mother.* 2. join as a companion or partner. **Ex.** *She likes to associate with people who are her age.*

associate (2) [əsow'šiyət], *n.* each of two or more owners of a business; fellow-worker; companion. **Ex.** *The two men are business associates.*

association (2) [əsow'šiyey'šən], *n.* 1. group of people organized for a common purpose. Ex. *He is a member of the lawyers' association.* 2. fellowship; partnership. Ex. *The two men formed a business association.* 3. the act of associating or the fact of being associated. Ex. *His association with criminals is known to the police.*

assorted (5) [əsɔr'təd], *adj.* of different kinds. Ex. *She received a box of assorted cheeses.* —as·sort'ment, *n.* variety. Ex. *The store had a large assortment of styles.*

assume (2) [əsuwm'], *v.* 1. believe or accept as a fact; suppose. Ex. *I assume that you can do the work.* 2. take a responsibility. Ex. *She will assume care of the child during the mother's illness.* 3. pretend to be or to have. Ex. *Although he was excited, he assumed the appearance of a calm man.* —as·sump'tion, *n.*

assure (2) [əšu:r'], *v.* 1. say with certainty; satisfy, as by a promise; give confidence to. Ex. *He assured them that he was able to do the work.* 2. make something certain and sure. Ex. *The warm weather assured the success of our trip to the seashore.* —as·sur'ance, *n.* —as·sured', *adj.*

astonish (3) [əstan'iš], *v.* cause to wonder; surprise greatly. Ex. *The size of the elephant astonished the little boy.* —as·ton'ish·ment, *n.* —as·ton'ish·ing, *adj.* —as·ton'ish·ing·ly, *adv.*

astronaut (5) [æs'trɔnɔt], *n.* A person who is trained to operate a space ship; one who makes a flight into space. Ex. *We watched the astronauts journey to the moon on television.*

astronomy (5) [əstran'əmiy], *n.* the science of stars, the moon, the planets, and other heavenly bodies. —as·tron'o·mer, *n.* one who is an expert in astronomy. —as·tro·nom'i·cal, *adj.* 1. connected with astronomy. 2. very large, like the numbers used in astronomy. Ex. *The rich man's salary is astronomical.*

at (1) [æt'], *prep.* present on, in, or near to. Ex. *I met him at the station.* 2. to or toward. Ex. *The dog rushed at the stranger.* 3. occupied with; busy with. Ex. *The family was at dinner.* 4. in a situation or condition of. Ex. *They seemed at ease with one another.* 5. because of; caused by. Ex. *She was frightened at the sight of blood.* 6. in a series; in relation to the value or cost of. Ex. *At last she saw him.* —at once, now; immediately. Ex. *Do the work at once.*

ate (2) [eyt'], *v.* past tense of *eat.* Ex. *I ate breakfast this morning.*

-ate (3) [ət], *suffix.* become or cause to become. Exs. *Active, activate; origin, originate; valid, validate.* 2. having the character of. Exs. *Affection, affectionate; fortune, fortunate.*

athlete (4) [æθ'liyt'], *n.* a person trained in a sport that requires strength, speed, and skill. Ex. *The young athlete was much admired for his speed.*

athletic (4) [æθlet'ik], *adj.* 1. concerning athletes or sports. Ex. *The game was played on the athletic field.* 2. strong; skillful in sports. —**ath·let'i·cal·ly,** *adv.* —**ath·let'ics,** *n.* the games and sports of athletes.

atmosphere (3) [æt'məsfi:r'], *n.* 1. the air surrounding the earth; the gases surrounding a planet or star. 2. the air in a certain place. Ex. *Mountain atmosphere is usually dry and cool.* 3. the general feeling of a place or thing. Ex. *The old house had an atmosphere of neglect.* —**at'mos·pher'ic,** *adj.*

atom (3) [æt'əm], *n.* a bit of matter so small that anything smaller is not the same matter. —**a·tom'ic,** *adj.* of or concerning atoms. Ex. *Atomic energy is created when atoms are split.*

attach (3) [ətæč'], *v.* 1. bind; fasten; tie; connect. Ex. *A card was attached to the gift.* 2. bring close together by feelings of love. Ex. *My uncle is very attached to my brother.* 3. assign to as if connected. Ex. *He attaches great importance to the report.* —**at·tach'ment,** *n.*

attack (2) [ətæk'], *v.* 1. start a fight with. Ex. *When do you expect to attack the enemy?* 2. direct unfavorable words against; blame violently. Ex. *The writer attacked crime in his newspaper articles.* 3. go to work with energy. Ex. *They attacked the work in order to finish it quickly.* 4. begin to act upon injuriously. Ex. *Acid attacks metal.* —*n.* 1. act of attacking. 2. a military action which aims at destroying the enemy. 3. being seized by disease. Ex. *He had a heart attack.*

attain (3) [əteyn'], *v.* 1. accomplish or reach by effort; gain. Ex. *She attained fame.* 2. arrive at. Ex. *My father has attained the age of sixty-five.* —**at·tain'able,** *adj.* —**at·tain'ment,** *n.*

attempt (1) [ətempt'], *v.* make an effort; try. Ex. *The doctor attempted to save the dying man.* —*n.* an effort; a try. Ex. *This is his second attempt to win a prize.*

attend (2) [ətend'], *v.* 1. be present at; go to. Ex. *They attend school five days a week.* 2. care for. Ex. *She is at-*

tended by a nurse. —at·tend'ance, *n.* the act of attending. —at·tend'ant, *n.* one who attends.

attention (2) [əten'šən], *n.* 1. the act of keeping one's mind on a subject. Ex. *They listened with great attention.* 2. care; consideration. Ex. *Your request will receive my personal attention.* 3. act of kindness. Ex. *Small attentions are appreciated by everyone.*

attentive (3) [əten'tiv], *adj.* 1. listening closely; observant. Ex. *He is a very attentive student.* 2. polite; kind; thoughtful. Ex. *He is always attentive toward his wife.* —at·ten'tive·ly, *adv.* —at·ten'tive·ness, *n.*

attic (4) [æt'ik], *n.* a room or rooms in the part of a house directly under the roof. Ex. *We store trunks in the attic of our house.*

attire (4) [ətayr'], *v.* dress. Ex. *She was attired in a beautiful silk gown for the dance.* —*n.* clothes, especially rich or splendid garments. Ex. *The bride's attire was especially lovely.*

attitude (2) [æt'ətuwd`, æt'ətyuwd`], *n.* 1. a manner; a way of looking or feeling toward someone or something. Ex. *He took a sympathetic attitude toward my problems.* 2. position of the body in relation to a person or thing. Ex. *The madman assumed a threatening attitude.*

attorney (4) [ətər'niy], *n.* lawyer; one who has been given the right to act for another. Ex. *The court appointed an attorney for the accused man.*

attract (3) [ətrækt'], *v.* cause to come closer; pull toward one's self. Ex. *The .eautiful girl attracted much attention.* —at·trac'tion, *n.* —at·trac'tive, *adj.* —at·trac'tive·ly, *adv.* in a way that attracts.

attribute (4) [ətrib'yət], *v.* regard something as coming from a particular person or thing. Ex. *This poem is attributed to Shakespeare.*

attribute (4) [æt'rəbyuwt`], *n.* a characteristic or quality which is part of the nature of a person or a thing. Ex. *A sense of justice should be an attribute of a judge.* —at`tri·bu'tion, *n.*

auction (5) [ɔk'šən], *n.* a public sale of property to the highest bidder. —*v.* sell at auction. Ex. *The furniture was auctioned*

---

a, far; æ, am; e, get; ey, late; i, in; iy, see; ɔ, all; ow, go; u, put; uw, too; ə, but, ago; ər, fur; aw, out; ay, life; oy, boy; ŋ, ring; θ, think; ð, the; ž, measure; š, ship; j, edge; č, child.

at a good price. —**auc·tion·eer**[1], *n.* one who conducts an auction.

audience (3) [ɔ:'diyəns], *n.* 1. a group of people watching or listening to a speaker or a performance. 2. an interview with a high-ranking person. **Ex.** *The ambassador had an audience with the queen.*

August (1) [ɔ:'gəst], *n.* the eighth month of the year.

aunt (1) [ænt][1], *n.* the sister of one's father or mother; also, an uncle's wife.

austere (5) [ɔsti:r[1]], *adj.* 1. severe or stern in appearance or manner. **Ex.** *The judge had an austere look on his face as he spoke to the criminal.* 2. simple in manner of living or acting. **Ex.** *The old man's life was very austere.* 3. plain; without decorations. **Ex.** *The austere room seemed dark and cold.* —**aus·tere·ly**, *adv.* —**aus·ter·i·ty**, *n.*

authentic (5) [ɔθen'tik], *adj.* 1. worthy of acceptance; true. **Ex.** *We need an authentic report of his activities.* 2. of the authorship or origin claimed; real; genuine. **Ex.** *This is an authentic tenth-century painting.* —**au·then·ti·cate**, *v.* prove to be real. —**au·then·tic·i·ty**, *n.*

author (2) [ɔ:'θər], *n.* 1. a person who writes a novel, poem, play, etc. 2. the beginner or creator of anything. **Ex.** *She was the author of the plan to improve the schools.*

authority (2) [əθ'rcər'ətiy], *n.* 1. the right to control, command, or order. **Ex.** *By what authority do you order me to do this?* 2. a person with such rights or powers. **Ex.** *The judge is the authority in this case.* 3. a person or book considered as the correct source of information or advice. **Ex.** *The dictionary is my authority for the meaning of this word.*

authorize (3) [ɔ:'θərayz[1]], *v.* 1. give someone the power or right to do something. **Ex.** *The president of the company authorized the manager to hire new workmen.* 2. give permission to do something. **Ex.** *They authorized the construction of the building.* —**au·thor·i·za·tion**, *n.*

autobiography [ɔ'təbayag'rəfiy], *n.* the story of a person's life written by himself. **Ex.** *The explorer's autobiography was an exciting story.*

automatic (4) [ɔ'təmæt'ik], *adj.* 1. having the power of moving by itself, especially used to describe machinery or mechanical devices. **Ex.** *An automatic timer turns the street ⌐hts on at night and off in the morning.* 2. done without

conscious thought or effort. **Ex.** *Breathing is automatic.*
—au'to·mat'i·cal·ly, *adv.*

automation (4) [ɔ'təmey'šən], *n.* a system or process of producing goods or information in which much or all of the
work is done by automatically controlled machines.

automobile (2) [ɔ'təməbiyl'], *n.* a motor car
especially for passengers. —au'to·mo'tive,
adj. concerning automobiles.

AUTOMOBILE

autumn (2) [ɔ'təm], *n.* the season between summer and winter; fall.

avail (4) [əveyl'], *v.* be of use; benefit; help. **Ex.** *In times of
sorrow, words do not avail us.* —*n.* use or benefit. **Ex.** *She
cried, but her tears were to no avail.* —**avail oneself of,**
make use of. **Ex.** *You must avail yourself of every opportunity to improve.*

available (3) [əveyl'əbəl], *adj.* obtainable; ready for use or
service. **Ex.** *Use every available remedy to save the child.*
—a·vail'a·bil'i·ty, *n.*

avenue (2) [æv'ənuw', æv'ənyuw'], *n.* 1. a wide street. **Ex.**
The avenue was lined with trees. 2. a way or opening to
something. **Ex.** *Hard work is an avenue to success.*

average (2) [æv'(ə)rij], *adj.* normal; ordinary. **Ex.** *She is an
average student.* —*n.* 1. the number produced by adding
two or more quantities and then dividing by the number of
quantities added. **Ex.** *The average of 3, 4, and 5 is 4 (3 +
4 + 5 = 12 ÷ 3 = 4).* 2. the ordinary, normal, or typical
amount. —*v.* find an average of. **Ex.** *Average these numbers for me.*

avert (5) [əvərt'], *v.* 1. turn aside or away. **Ex.** *She averted
her glance from the corpse.* 2. prevent. **Ex.** *He averted an
automobile accident by stopping quickly.* —a·ver'sion, *n.*
strong feeling of dislike. **Ex.** *He felt an aversion to the man.*

aviation (5) [ey'viyey'šən], *n.* the art or science of flying airplanes. **Ex.** *He hopes to have a career in aviation.* —a'vi·a·
tor, *n.* a man who flies airplanes. —a'vi·a·trix, *n.* a woman
who flies airplanes.

avoid (2) [əvoyd'], *v.* keep away from. **Ex.** *He avoids me because he owes me money.* —a·void'a·ble, *adj.* —a·void'·
ance, *n.*

awake [əweyk'], *adj.* not sleeping. **Ex.** *He was already aw⌍
when I went to call him.*

award (4) [əwɔrd'], *v.* give after careful consideration. **Ex.** *He was awarded first prize.* —*n.* the thing given; a prize. **Ex.** *He received an award for his fine work.*

aware (3) [əwe:r'], *adj.* informed; conscious; understanding. **Ex.** *He drove carefully, aware of the danger of the icy road.* —a·ware'ness, *n.*

away (1) [əwey'], *adv.* 1. aside; out of one's possession. **Ex.** *Either give the clothes away or throw them away.* 2. from this or that place. **Ex.** *We are going away.* —*adj.* 1. absent. **Ex.** *He will be away for two days.* 2. at a distance. **Ex.** *He lives far away from me.*

awe (4) [ɔ:'], *n.* respectful fear or wonder inspired by what is grand. **Ex.** *Looking up at the mountain, they were filled with awe.* —*v.* inspire with awe. **Ex.** *They were awed by the sight of the beautiful gardens.*

awful (2) [ɔ:'fəl], *adj.* terrible; frightening. **Ex.** *It was an awful storm.* —aw'ful·ly, *adv.*

awkward (4) [ɔk'wərd], *adj.* 1. lacking in ease, grace, or skill. **Ex.** *He had many accidents because he was awkward.* 2. not convenient; difficult to use. **Ex.** *The chair was placed in an awkward position.* —awk'ward·ly, *adv.* —awk'ward·ness, *n.*

ax, axe (2) [æks'], *n.* a tool used for cutting, chopping, or splitting wood.

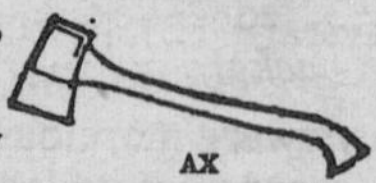

axis (5) [æk'səs], *n.* the real or imaginary straight line about which something turns. **Ex.** *The earth turns on its axis.*

axle (5) [æk'səl], *n.* the rod or bar on which a wheel turns or which turns with the wheel.

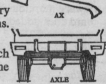

AX

AXLE

B

�, *n.* the second letter of the English alphabet.

baby (1) [bey'biy], *n.* 1. very young child; infant. **Ex.** *The baby is only two weeks old.* 2. youngest member of a family. **Ex.** *The baby of the family is already ten years old.* —*adj.* like, of, or for a baby. **Ex.** *She prefers to make baby clothes rather than buy them.*

bachelor (3) [bæč'ələr], *n.* 1. a man who has not married. 2. one who has received the first or lowest degree given by a university. Ex. *He is a bachelor of arts.*

back (1) [bæk'], *n.* 1. the rear of the human body. Ex. *He lay on his back looking at the sky.* 2. in most animals, the upper part of the body from the neck to the end of the backbone. Ex. *He rode on the horse's back.* 3. the part of anything which is opposite the front. 4. something at or on the back for support. Ex. *He leaned against*  BACK *the back of the chair.* —*adv.* to or at a former place, time, or condition. Ex. *We are going back home.* —*adj.* rear; away from the front. Ex. *Shut the back door.* —*v.* move backward or to the rear. Ex. *Back the truck away from the door.* —**back and forth,** one way and then the opposite way. Ex. *He went back and forth between the houses.* —**in back of,** behind.

background (4) [bæk'grawnd'], *n.* 1. the parts of a scene or picture that are or seem to be behind something else. 2. anything that happened before and helps explain. Ex. *In order to understand the war, they are studying its background.* 3. education and experience. Ex. *He does not have the background for the job.*

backward (3) [bæk'wərd], *adv.* 1. away from the front; toward the rear. Ex. *Looking backward, he saw a man following him.* 2. other than the usual way; wrongly. Ex. *This part of the machine was put in backward.* —*adj.* 1. directed toward the back or past. Ex. *She gave a backward glance at the house behind her.* 2. slow in learning. Ex. *Backward children need special lessons to help them to read.*

bacon (4) [bey'kən], *n.* meat from the back or sides of a pig, salted and smoked. Ex. *He had bacon and eggs for breakfast.*

bacteria (5) [bæk'tir'iyə], *n. pl.* one-celled living things, too small to be seen without a microscope, which cause rot, souring, etc. Ex. *Bacteria are everywhere; some are helpful, and some produce disease.* —**bac·te'ri·al,** *adj.*

bad (1) [bæd'], *adj.* 1. not good; useless; unpleasant. Ex. *The bad food made him ill.* 2. wicked. Ex. *The bad man was*

punished. 3. faulty; incorrect. **Ex.** *His spelling is bad.*
—**bad'ly,** *adv.*

badge (5) [bæǰ'], *n.* a special mark or pin worn to show membership or authority. **Ex.** *The policeman's badge was a silver
star.*

baffle (5) [bæf'əl], *v.* puzzle; confuse. **Ex.** *The student's failure baffled the teacher.*

bag (1) [bæg'], *n.* 1. container made of paper, cloth, or other
soft material. **Ex.** *She carried the food in a large bag.* 2. a
woman's purse. 3. a suitcase. —**bag'gy,** *adj.* like a bag;
loose. **Ex.** *His trousers were baggy at the knees.*

baggage (4) [bæg'iǰ], *n.* suitcases, boxes, etc. used in traveling. **Ex.** *I need a man to carry my baggage onto the train.*

bait (4) [beyt'], *n.* 1. food used as a lure to catch fish or trap
animals. 2. anything used to attract a person. **Ex.** *A diamond
ring, left on the table, was used as bait to catch the thief.*
—*v.* prepare a hook or a trap with bait. **Ex.** *He baited the
fish hook with meat.*

bake (2) [beyk'], *v.* 1. cook by dry heat, usually in an oven.
Ex. *My mother bakes bread every week.* 2. dry or harden
by heat. **Ex.** *Bricks are baked in the sun or by fire.* —**bak'er,**
n. one who bakes. —**bak'er·y,** *n.* a place where bread,
cakes, etc. are made; a place where bread and cakes are
sold. **Ex.** *I stopped at the bakery to buy some bread.*

balance (2) [bæl'əns], *n.* 1. equality in amount, weight, importance, or value between two things. **Ex.** *The artist tried
to keep a balance of light and dark in his paintings.* 2. equal
distribution of weight which keeps one steady. **Ex.** *You must
learn to keep your balance to ride a bicycle.* 3. an amount
of money in a bank account. **Ex.** *My bank balance is very
small.* 4. the amount of money still owed on a bill. **Ex.** *When
can you pay the balance?* —*v.* 1. keep or make steady by
equal weight distribution. **Ex.** *She balanced the book on her
head.* 2. mentally weigh two things to learn which is of more
value, more importance, etc. **Ex.** *He balanced his chances
of winning or losing.* 3. find the difference, if any, between
what one has or is owed and what one has spent or owes;
to make such amounts equal. **Ex.** *He balances his accounts
every month.*

balcony (5) [bæl'kəniy], *n.* 1. a platform with a railing, built out from the wall of a building. 2. upper floor in a theater or hall that extends out over the floor below. Ex. *Do you prefer theater seats on the main floor or in the balcony?*

BALCONY 1

bald (5) [bɔːld'], *adj.* lacking hair on the head. Ex. *His bald head is smooth.* —**bald'ness,** *n.*

bale (5) [beyl'], *n.* a large bundle of some material, closely pressed for storage or shipping. Ex. *The men loaded the bales of cotton onto the ship.* —*v.* make into bales.

balk (5) [bɔːk'], *v.* 1. refuse to move or do. Ex. *The horse balked when he had a heavy load.* 2. stop from doing something. Ex. *He was balked in his efforts to obtain the land.* —**balk'y,** *adj.*

ball (1) [bɔːl'], *n.* 1. a round or egg-shaped object, used in a game. Ex. *The children were playing with the ball.* 2. any round shape. Ex. *The earth is a ball.*

BALL 1

ball (1) [bɔːl'], *n.* a large dancing party. Ex. *She danced at the President's ball.*

ballad (5) [bæl'əd], *n.* a poem or song that tells a story.

balloon (4) [bəluwn'], *n.* 1. a bag of strong, light material that rises and floats in the air when filled with a gas lighter than air. 2. a rubber bag that can be filled with air, used as a child's toy. —*v.* fill up and swell out like a balloon. Ex. *The sails ballooned out in the wind.*

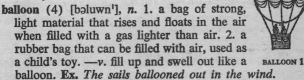

BALLOON 1

ballot (4) [bæl'ət], *n.* 1. a piece of paper used in voting. Ex. *They counted the ballots to see who had won the election.* 2. a method of secret voting in which printed sheets of paper are used. Ex. *They voted by ballot.*

balmy (5) [baːm'iy], *adj.* soft and gentle; mild. Ex. *A balmy breeze was blowing.*

bamboo (5) [bæm'buw'], *n.* a tropical, woody, treelike grass, with hollow jointed stems, used for making furniture, poles, etc.

ban (5) [bæn'], *v.* not allow; forbid; prohibit. Ex. *The sale of liquor to children is banned.* —*n.* an official prohibition against something. Ex. *There is a ban on smoking in the theater.*

banana (3) [bənæn'ə], *n.* a large plant that grows in hot climates and bears bunches of yellow fruit; also the fruit itself.

BANANA

band (2) [bænd'], *n.* 1. a group of persons united for a common purpose. Ex. *A band of thieves broke into the house.* 2. a group of persons who play music together. Ex. *A band played for the dance.* 3. a thin, flat strip of material for binding or decorating. Ex. *Her hat was trimmed with a velvet band.* —*v.* 1. join together in a group. Ex. *The settlers banded together for protection.* 2. place a band around. Ex. *They banded the pieces of wood together.*

bandage (4) [bæn'dij], *n.* a strip of cloth or other material used for covering and binding a wound. Ex. *The bandage on his leg was changed every day.*

bandit (5) [bæn'dət], *n.* a robber; an outlaw. Ex. *Bandits robbed the train.*

bang (4) [bæŋ'], *n.* a loud sudden noise, as the shooting of a gun or the violent closing of a door. Ex. *The wind blew the door closed with a bang.* —*v.* 1. strike violently or noisily. Ex. *He banged on the door.* 2. make a loud noise. Ex. *We heard the guns bang in the distance.*

banish (4) [bæn'iš], *v.* 1. officially require a person to leave a country as a punishment. Ex. *The king banished him for his crimes.* 2. dismiss; send away. Ex. *The widow attempted to banish her grief.* —**ban'ish·ment,** *n.*

bank (1) [bæŋk'], *n.* 1. a place where money is kept for safe-keeping and where other money business is done. Ex. *He went to the bank for money.* 2. a place where supplies are stored for later use. Ex. *The Red Cross operates a blood bank.* —*v.* place money in a bank. Ex. *He banked part of his money every week.*

bank (1) [bæŋk'], *n.* 1. the high ground on the edges of a river or stream. Ex. *He sat on the bank with his feet in the water.* 2. any pile. —*v.* 1. form into a bank. Ex. *The snow was banked on each side of the road.* 2. cover a fire with ashes so that it will burn slower.

banker (1) [bæŋk'ər], *n.* a person who directs the work of or owns a bank.

bankrupt (5) [bæŋk'rəpt'], *n.* any person who is found by a court to be unable to pay his debts and whose remaining money is divided among those to whom he owes money.

—*adj.* of or like a bankrupt in some way. Ex. *He is bankrupt of ideas.* —*v.* make poor; make bankrupt. Ex. *His own generosity bankrupted him.*

banner (4) [bæn'ər], *n.* 1. flag of a country, state, or organization. 2. piece of cloth, paper, or other material, with writing or symbols on it. Ex. *The marchers in the parade carried banners that said "peace."*

banquet (4) [bæŋ'kwət], *n.* a feast conducted with great ceremony and often followed by speeches. Ex. *A banquet was given in honor of the mayor.*

bar (2) [ba:r'], *n.* 1. a long piece of wood or metal used to stop, enclose, support, fasten, lift, etc. Ex. *The iron bars of the prison windows were two inches apart.* 2. anything that blocks the way and stops action. Ex. *The law is a bar to crime.* 3. a long, high table or counter at which liquor or food is served; the place in which there is such a table. Ex. *Your friends are having drinks at the bar.* 4. a law court. Ex. *He was called to the bar to answer the judge's questions.* —*v.* 1. provide or secure with a bar. Ex. *The door was barred.* 2. shut out, prevent, or block. Ex. *They barred the way to strangers.*

barbarian (5) [barber'iyən], *n.* a rough, uncivilized person. Ex. *People who behave like barbarians are not welcome at this hotel.* —**bar·bar'ic,** *adj.*

barber (3) [bar'bər], *n.* one whose work is to cut hair.

bare (2) [be:r'], *adj.* 1. without clothing or covering. Ex. *The children walked on the sand with bare feet.* 2. empty. Ex. *The room was bare of furnishings.* 3. plain; without additions. Ex. *What are the bare facts of the matter?* 4. just sufficient; mere. Ex. *The settlers had only the bare necessities of life.* —**bare'ly,** *adv.*

bargain (3) [bar'gən], *n.* 1. a businesslike agreement between persons. Ex. *He made a bargain to lend his neighbor a horse in return for the use of his plow.* 2. something bought or offered for sale at less than the usual cost. Ex. *Mother always shops for bargains.* —*v.* try to buy or sell something at a good price. Ex. *He bargained with the merchant for an hour before he bought the rug.* —**bargain for,** seek; expect. Ex. *He received more letters than he bargained for.*

---

a, far; æ, am; e, get; ey, late; i, in; iy, see; ɔ, all; ow, go; u, put; uw, too; ə, but, ago; ər, fur; aw, out; ay, life; oy, boy; ŋ, ring; θ, think; ð, that; ž, measure; š, ship; ǰ, edge; č, child.

barge (4) [barĵ'], *n.* a large, flat-bottomed boat without a motor, used for carrying goods on waterways. Ex. *The barge was loaded with coal.*

bark (2) [bark'], *n.* the hard, outside covering of a tree.

bark (2) [bark'], *n.* the sudden, sharp cry of a dog or other animal. —*v.* 1. make a sudden sharp cry or series of cries, as a dog. 2. speak or shout roughly. Ex. *The captain barked his orders.*

barley (5) [bar'liy], *n.* 1. a grasslike plant that produces seed or grain. 2. the seeds of this plant, which are used in making some liquors, put in soup, and fed to animals.

barn (2) [barn'], *n.* a farm building for storing crops, housing farm animals, etc. Ex. *The cows are in the barn.*

barracks (5) [bær'əks, ber'əks], *n.* a building or buildings for housing soldiers. Ex. *Two hundred soldiers live in this barracks.*

barrel (3) [bær'əl, ber'əl], *n.* 1. a large container made of curved strips of wood that are held together with wooden or steel bands. 2. the tubelike part of a gun from which the shot comes. Ex. *He cleaned the long barrel of his gun.*

BARREL 1

barren (4) [bær'ən], *adj.* 1. unable to produce young. Ex. *The woman was barren.* 2. unproductive. Ex. *The barren land could produce little food.*

barricade (5) [bær'əkeyd`, ber'əkeyd`], *n.* 1. anything built or serving to bar passage, especially something built roughly and hurriedly, as in a street or entrance. Ex. *The cars were stopped at the police barricade.* 2. any barrier to entry. —*v.* shut in or defend with a barricade.

barrier (4) [bær'iyər, ber'iyər], *n.* 1. anything that prevents approach or attack. Ex. *Countries can no longer depend on mountain barriers for protection.* 2. anything that prevents progress or causes difficulty. Ex. *High tariffs are a barrier to international trade.*

barter (5) [bar'tər], *v.* exchange or trade articles or services without the use of money. Ex. *She bartered eggs for wool.* —*n.* the act of bartering.

base (2) [beys'], *n.* 1. the bottom or support on which a thing stands or rests. Ex. *The base of the lamp was made of wood.* 2. the main part on which the rest depends or from which

the rest began. **Ex.** *The ship returned to its base for sup-*
plies. —*v.* 1. make or form a foundation for. 2. place or
establish on a foundation. **Ex.** *He based his request for re-*
election on his past performance. —*adj.* at the base of.

base (2) [beys'], *adj.* 1. morally bad; mean; selfish. **Ex.** *His*
base character caused the people to dislike him. 2. poor in
quality; low in value compared to something else. **Ex.**
Brass and iron are base metals. —**base'ly,** *adv.* —**base'**
ness, *n.*

baseball (5) [beys'bɔ:l'], *n.* 1. an American game played with
a bat and ball by two teams of nine persons each, on a
playing field shaped like a diamond. 2. the ball used in
playing this game.

basement (2) [beys'mənt], *n.* the lowest level of a building,
partly or completely underground. **Ex.** *The basement was*
dark and wet.

basic (2) [bey'sik], *adj.* of or forming a base; main. **Ex.** *You*
must obey the basic rules.

basin (3) [bey'sən], *n.* 1. a shallow bowl for holding water or
other liquid. **Ex.** *He washed his hands and face in a basin*
of water. 2. land drained by a river. **Ex.** *The basin of a river*
usually has rich farm land.

basis (3) [bey'səs], *n.* essential facts or reasons; foundation
which supports something. **Ex.** *What is the basis for your*
opinion?

basket (1) [bæs'kət], *n.* any container made of
grasses, thin strips of wood, or other material.

bat (4) [bæt'], *n.* a strong, solid stick or club,
especially one used for hitting a ball in games.
—*v.* strike or hit, as with a bat. **Ex.** *He batted*
stones with a stick.

BASKET

bat (4) [bæt'], *n.* a furry, winged animal that looks like a
mouse. **Ex.** *Bats usually fly in the dark.*

bath (2) [bæθ'], *n.* 1. act of washing or cleaning the body with
water. **Ex.** *Give yourself a hot bath before going to*
bed. 2. water for washing the body. **Ex.** *The bath was too*
cold. 3. a room equipped for bathing; the bathroom. **Ex.**
Each room in this hotel has a bath.

bathe (3) [beyð'], *v.* 1. wash; go swimming. **Ex.** *Most people* *bathe in hot water.* 2. wet or moisten with liquid. **Ex.** *The doctor told him to bathe the wound with hot water.*

batter (4) [bæt'ər], *v.* 1. break to pieces by pounding. **Ex.** *The police battered the door with their clubs.* 2. damage by rough use. **Ex.** *The boys soon battered the furniture.* —*n.* 1. the beaten mixture of flour and liquid used for making bread, cake, etc. 2. a person who strikes, or bats, a ball in games.

battery (4) [bæt'(ə)riy], *n.* a small container or connected group of containers which retains electric current and is capable of discharging the current when needed. **Ex.** *The battery could not start the car.*

battle (1) [bæt'əl], *n.* 1. a fight between opposing armed forces. **Ex.** *We won the battle on the second day.* 2. war or armed fighting in general. **Ex.** *He was wounded in battle.* 3. any fight or struggle. **Ex.** *That editor fought many battles for a free press.* —*v.* fight; struggle. **Ex.** *The seamen battled the storm.*

bay (1) [bey'], *n.* a large area of water formed by a deep cut into the shore of a sea or ocean. **Ex.** *Chesapeake Bay is near Washington. D.C.*

be (1) [biy'], *v.* (These are the common forms of *be.* In the present: I *am;* you, we, they *are;* he, she, it *is.* In the past: I, he, she, it *was;* you, we, they *were.* In the future: I, you, he, she, it, we, they *will.*) 1. equal in meaning. **Ex.** *That man is my teacher.* 2. have a noted quality or character. **Ex.** *Your sister is kind.* 3. exist; live. **Ex.** *Many years ago a house was on the corner of that street.*

beach (2) [biyč'], *n.* a smooth area of sand and small stones on the shore of an ocean or lake. **Ex.** *Two boys walked in the sand on the beach.*

bead (3) [biyd'], *n.* a small piece of glass, stone, etc., with a small hole in it so that it can be put on a string. **Ex.** *She usually wore a string of beads around her neck.*

beak (4) [biyk'], *n.* the long, horny points extending out from a bird's mouth; a bill. **Ex.** *The mother bird held the worm in her beak.*

beam (3) [biym'], *n.* 1. any long, heavy piece of wood or metal cut for use, especially in the structure or supports of a building or ship. 2. a ray of light. **Ex.** *Sunbeams came* *through the open window.* 3. a continuous radio or other electrical signal. **Ex.** *The airplane followed the radio beam.* —*v.* 1. shine; send forth light. **Ex.** *The sun beamed brightly.* 2. smile broadly. **Ex.** *The teacher beamed at the students.* 3. aim radio signals. **Ex.** *The Voice of America programs are beamed around the world.*

bean (1) [biyn'], *n.* 1. the seed of certain plants grown in a case and used for food. 2. a plant that produces beans. 3. bean-like seed. **Ex.** *Coffee is made from a bean.*

BEAN 1

bear (2) [be:r'], *v.* 1. support. **Ex.** *The beams bear the weight of the roof.* 2. carry. **Ex.** *They came bearing gifts.* 3. be equipped, furnished, or marked with. **Ex.** *Soldiers bear arms.* 4. bring forth; produce; yield; give birth to. **Ex.** *These trees bear good apples.* 5. endure; suffer. **Ex.** *I cannot bear his shouting.* —**bear down,** push down or against. **Ex.** *Bear down on the lid and the box will close.* —**bear out,** confirm; prove. **Ex.** *His actions bear out what I said about him.* —**bear up,** continue bravely. **Ex.** *How can she bear up under all her troubles?*

bear (2) [be:r'], *n.* a large, wild animal with a short tail.

BEAR

beard (3) [bi:rd'], *n.* the hair that grows on a man's chin and face. —**bearded,** *adj.* having a beard. —**beard'less,** *adj.* without a beard. **Ex.** *The man has a long beard; the boy is beardless.*

bearing (5) [ber'iŋ], *n.* 1. manner of carrying one's self; behavior. **Ex.** *She was a woman of graceful bearing.* 2. reference or relation to. **Ex.** *Do these facts have any bearing on your problem?* 3. direction or relative position. **Ex.** *He looked at his map to get his bearings.*

beast (2) [biyst'], *n.* 1. any four-footed animal. **Ex.** *The ox and the horse are beasts of burden.* 2. a person who acts cruelly, like an animal. **Ex.** *The beast hit his gentle wife.* —**beast'ly,** *adj.* —**beast'li·ness,** *n.*

beat (2) [biyt'], *v.* 1. strike or hit repeatedly. **Ex.** *We heard* *the rain beating against the window.* 2. move or make a sound in an even, regular manner. **Ex.** *Her heart was beating rapidly.* 3. defeat. **Ex.** *Our team beat the visiting team in a ball game.* —*n.* 1. a stroke or blow. 2. the sound made by a stroke or blow. —**beat about** or **around the bush**, approach indirectly. **Ex.** *He should stop beating around the bush and tell us what he wants.* — **beat a retreat**, retreat. **Ex.** *The soldiers beat a retreat to their camp.*

beaten (2) [biyt'ən], *adj.* 1. made smooth by continuous walking on. **Ex.** *A beaten path led to his door.* 2. hammered thin or fine into a required shape. **Ex.** *The temple roof was covered with beaten gold.* 3. hit by many blows; whipped. **Ex.** *A beaten dog fears a stick.* 4. defeated. **Ex.** *The beaten team returned home.* —*v.* past participle of *beat.*

beauty (1) [byuw'tiy], *n.* 1. the appearance or sound of any object or person that is pleasant; loveliness. **Ex.** *The city was famous for the beauty of its flower gardens.* 2. a person or thing who has beauty. **Ex.** *That girl is a beauty.* —**beau'ti·ful**, *adj.* —**beau'ti·fy**, *v.* make beautiful. **Ex.** *He beautified the land with flowers.*

beaver (5) [biy'vər], *n.* an animal that can live on land or in water and that has valuable brown fur, a broad, flat tail, and strong teeth able to cut wood.

BEAVER

became (1) [bikeym'], *v.* past tense of *become.* **Ex.** *Their son became a doctor.*

because (1) [bikə:z', bikəz'], *conj.* for the reason that; since. **Ex.** *We did not go because it rained.* —*adv.* as a result of; on account of. **Ex.** *He was absent because of illness.*

become (1) [bikəm'], *v.* 1. come to be. **Ex.** *The seeds will become flowers in the summer.* 2. be right or suitable for. **Ex.** *That dress becomes her.* —**be·com'ing**, *adj.* suitable. **Ex.** *That color is becoming to you.* —**become of**, happen to. **Ex.** *We asked what had become of his sister.*

bed (1) [bed'], *n.* 1. a piece of furniture to sleep or rest in or on. 2. a piece of ground used for growing plants. **Ex.** *They have many kinds of flower beds in their garden.* 3. the ground at the bottom of a body of water. **Ex.** *The bed of the stream was dry.*

BED 1

bee (2) [biy'], *n.* a small insect that often lives in organized groups and stings to protect itself.

BEE

beef (3) [biyf'], *n.* 1. meat from a bull, cow, or ox. Ex. *They ate roast beef for dinner.* 2. the full-grown bull, cow, or ox raised for meat.

been (1) [bin'], *v.* past participle of *be.* Ex. *Where have you been for the past two days?*

beer (4) [bi:r'], *n.* an alcoholic drink with a slightly bitter taste, made from cereals. Ex. *Many people drink cold beer on a hot day.*

beetle (4) [biy'təl], *n.* an insect with four wings, the outer two of which are hard and protect the inner wings when folded.

BEETLE

before (1) [bifɔ:r'], *prep.* 1. earlier than, or ahead of, in time, place, worth, etc. Ex. *He arrived before noon.* 2. in the presence or sight of. Ex. *He stood before the king.* —*conj.* 1. earlier than the time that. Ex. *Think before you speak.* 2. rather than. Ex. *They would starve before they would ask for help.* —*adv.* 1. in front; in advance; ahead. Ex. *The boy walked along the road, while the dog ran before.* 2. in a past time. Ex. *I never saw that book before.* 3. at an earlier time; sooner. Ex. *I can meet you at noon, but not before.*

beg (2) [beg'], *v.* 1. ask that something be given without payment. Ex. *A very poor boy stood on the corner begging for food.* 2. ask for humbly and earnestly. Ex. *The captured soldier begged for mercy.* —**beg'gar,** *n.* one who lives by begging; one who is poor.

began (1) [bigæn'], *v.* past tense of *begin.* Ex. *He began his new job yesterday.*

begin (1) [bigin'], *v.* start; take the first step toward doing. Ex. *When does school begin?* —**be·gin'ner,** *n.* —**be·gin' ning,** *n.*

begun (2) [bigən'], *v.* past participle of *begin.* Ex. *I am already tired, and the day has just begun.*

behalf (4) [bihæf'], *n.* support; part. Ex. *My employer spoke in my behalf.*

behave (3) [biheyv'], *v.* 1. conduct oneself or itself; act; do.

Ex. *That man behaves as if he were ill.* 2. act properly. **Ex.** *Good children behave themselves in public.*

behavior (3) [biheyv'yər], *n.* act or manner of behaving oneself; conduct. **Ex.** *His unkind behavior offended other people.*

behind (1) [bihaynd'], *prep.* 1. at the back of; in back of. **Ex.** *There is a garden behind the house.* 2. after; later than. **Ex.** *The train arrived behind time.* 3. less advanced than. **Ex.** *He is behind his class in history.* —*adv.* back in place or time. **Ex.** *He came, but his family stayed behind in the city.* —*adj.* at the back of. **Ex.** *He is in the car behind.*

being (1) [biy'iŋ], *n.* 1. a person, animal, or other living thing. **Ex.** *We do not know if there are beings on other planets.* 2. existence; life. **Ex.** *The town came into being about two hundred years ago.*

belief (3) [biliyf'], *n.* 1. that which is believed. **Ex.** *I do not like to discuss my religious beliefs.* 2. anything believed or accepted as true; opinion. **Ex.** *It is my belief that we should go ahead with the plan.* 3. faith; trust; confidence. **Ex.** *Nothing can change my belief in his honesty.*

believe (1) [biliyv'], *v.* 1. accept as true. **Ex.** *I believe what you say.* 2. have faith, trust, confidence in. **Ex.** *Many people believe there is a God.* 3. think. **Ex.** *I believe he has returned.*

bell (1) [bel'], *n.* 1. an object that rings when hit. **Ex.** *I heard the door bell ring.* 2. anything that looks or sounds like a bell. **Ex.** *Each blossom was a tiny white bell.*

BELL 1

bellow (4) [bel'ow], *v.* make a loud cry, like that of a bull; roar. **Ex.** *He bellowed forth his reply.* —*n.* the act or sound of bellowing. **Ex.** *He answered with a bellow.*

belly (5) [bel'iy], *n.* 1. the lower front part of a person's body; the stomach. **Ex.** *The belly of the starving child was swollen.* 2. the underpart of an animal's body.

belong (1) [bilɔ:ŋ'], *v.* 1. be suited to; have a place or position which is correct for it. **Ex.** *The lamp belongs on this table.* 2. be owned by; be the property of. **Ex.** *This house belongs to me.* 3. be part of; be connected to. **Ex.** *The garden belongs to this house.* —**be·long'ings,** *n.* possessions; the things one owns. **Ex.** *She packed all her belongings in a box and took them with her.*

beloved (3) [biləvd', biləv'əd], *adj.* greatly loved. **Ex.** *He grieved at the death of his beloved wife.* —*n.* one who is greatly loved. **Ex.** *She is his beloved.*

below (1) [bilow'], *adv.* under; in a lower place. **Ex.** *Read the note written below.* —*prep.* lower than in position, rank, amount, etc. **Ex.** *The first floor is below the second.*

belt (2) [belt'], *n.* 1. a band or strip of leather, cloth, etc., worn around the middle of the body. **Ex.** *She wore a belt that matched her dress.* 2. a broad loop placed around two wheels, so that the wheels will turn together.

BELT 2

bench (3) [benč'], *n.* 1. a long metal, wooden, or stone seat for two or more people. 2. the seat on which a judge sits in court; the position or office of a judge. **Ex.** *He was appointed to the bench.*

bend (2) [bend'], *v.* 1. force into a different or particular shape, especially a curved shape. **Ex.** *The strong man was able to bend the bar of iron.* 2. stoop; lean over. **Ex.** *You must bend down to see the marks on the floor.* 3. cause to submit, bow, or yield. **Ex.** *The father could not bend the boy to his will.* —*n.* 1. act of bending. 2. something curved. **Ex.** *They turned at the bend in the road.*

beneath (2) [biniyθ'], *prep.* 1. below; under and covered by; in a lower place than. **Ex.** *The floor is beneath the rug.* 2. unworthy of. **Ex.** *It is beneath you to lie.* —*adv., adj.* below something; in a lower place. **Ex.** *He lives on the floor beneath.*

benefit (2) [ben'əfit], *n.* help; act of kindness. **Ex.** *The students had the benefit of a fine library.* —*v.* do good; be of service to; help. **Ex.** *The new hospital will benefit all the people.*

benevolent (5) [bənev'ələnt], *adj.* desiring or doing good for others; kind. **Ex.** *The free food was given by a benevolent person.* —be·nev'o·lence, *n.* —be·nev'o·lent·ly, *adv.*

bent (2) [bent'], *v.* past tense and participle of *bend.* **Ex.** *He* *bent the stick until it broke.* —*adj.* curved; no longer straight. Ex. *A bent pin can be used for a fishhook.*

berry (3) [ber'iy], *n.* any soft, juicy fruit, small in size.

beside (1) [bisayd'], *prep.* 1. at or by the side of; near. Ex. *We live beside a lake.* 2. compared by putting by the side of. Ex. *My fingers are small beside yours.* —**beside oneself,** very troubled; upset. Ex. *She was beside herself when she saw the broken dish.*

besides (2) [bisaydz'], *adv.* also; in addition. Ex. *We are too tired to go; besides, it is raining.* —*prep.* in addition to; other than. Ex. *Besides your teacher, who else was with you?*

besiege (5) [bisiyǰ'], *v.* 1. surround with armed forces. Ex. *The army besieged the town.* 2. surround; make many requests. Ex. *The students besieged the teacher with questions.*

best (1) [best'], *adj.* better than any others in quality, results, position, etc. Ex. *These are the best books on the subject.* —*adv.* in a way that is better than any other. Ex. *The boy who writes best wins the prize.* —*n.* that which is better than any other person or thing. Ex. *My school is the best in the city.* —**at best,** at most. Ex. *At best, your money is returned.* —**get the best of,** beat; defeat. Ex. *I got the best of him in this game.* —**make the best of,** do as well as one can under unfavorable circumstances. Ex. *He made the best of his illness by studying for his examination.*

bestow (4) [bistow'], *v.* give; present to; confer on. Ex. *The president of the college bestowed honors on the best students.* —**be·stow'al,** *n.*

bet (4) [bet'], *n.* 1. an agreement that if someone is proved wrong about something he will pay money or other penalty to the person who is right. Ex. *I made a bet with my friend that it would rain before noon today.* 2. the thing which is promised. Ex. *Our bet was a good dinner.* —*v.* make such an agreement. Ex. *He bet a week's salary on a horse in the third race.* —**bet'ter, bet'tor,** *n.* one who bets.

betray (3) [bitrey'], *v.* 1. assist or support an enemy of one's country or friends. Ex. *He betrayed us by telling the enemy where we were.* 2. reveal intentionally or unintentionally. Ex. *Her eyes betrayed her real feelings.* —**be·tray'al,** *n.* act of betraying. —**be·tray'er,** *n.* one who betrays.

better (1) [bet'ər], *adj.* 1. more valuable; more desirable; finer in quality; etc. Ex. *This is a better house than mine.* 2.

improved in health. **Ex.** *She was very ill, but she is better today.* —*adv.* in a more excellent manner or higher degree. **Ex.** *The teacher knows the lesson better than I do.* —*v.* make more desirable or valuable; improve. **Ex.** *Rest will better the sick child's health.* —*n.* 1. that which is finer. **Ex.** *This painting is the better of the two.* 2. advantage; victory. **Ex.** *The big dog got the better of the little one.* —**better off,** in an improved condition. **Ex.** *He is better off without a car.* —**for the better,** in the direction of improvement. **Ex.** *His health changed for the better.* —**get the better of,** beat; defeat. **Ex.** *He got the better of his enemies.*

between (1) [bitwiyn'], *prep.* 1. in the space or time that separates. **Exs.** *The lunch hour is between twelve and one o'clock. The table is between the door and the window.* 2. connecting. **Ex.** *There is a bus line between the two cities.* 3. involving two. **Ex.** *Why must there be quarrels between people?* —*adv.* being in or doing some action in the space separating two things. **Ex.** *They saw two large buildings with a small house between.* —**in between,** in the space or time that separates. **Ex.** *I walked in between the buildings.*

beverage (5) [bev'ərij], *n.* a drink of any kind. **Ex.** *Coffee, milk, wine, and beer are all beverages.*

beware (4) [biwe:r'], *v.* be on guard against. **Ex.** *Beware of the big dog.*

bewilder (4) [biwil'dər], *v.* puzzle or confuse greatly. **Ex.** *The busy streets of the city bewildered the country boys.* —**be·wil'der·ment,** *n.*

beyond (1) [biyand'], *prep.* 1. on or to the far side of; farther than. **Ex.** *The sea is beyond the mountains.* 2. outside or past the limits, understanding, or reach of. **Ex.** *He was beyond the doctor's help and died.* 3. superior to; better than. **Ex.** *He received a fortune beyond his expectations.*

bias (5) [bay'əs], *n.* 1. a mental inclination, especially one which prevents the fair consideration of a question. **Ex.** *He liked old-fashioned ways and had a bias against progress.* 2. a line cut or sewn across the weave of cloth. —*v.* influence or be influenced strongly, especially unfairly or against. **Ex.** *Many people are biased against moneylenders.*

BIAS 2

Bible (3) [bay'bəl], *n.* the sacred book of some world religions.

bicycle (1) [bay'sik'əl], *n.* a machine for riding, with two wheels, one behind the other. —**bi'cy·clist**, *n.* one who rides a bicycle.

BICYCLE

bid (4) [bid'], *v.* 1. command. Ex. *Do as you are bid.* 2. say, as a greeting. Ex. *We always bid our friends good morning.* 3. offer as a price, usually at a public sale. Ex. *What am I bid for this painting?* —*n.* an offer or that which is offered. Ex. *His bid was higher than any other.* 2. an attempt or effort to win or attract. Ex. *With his sad story, he made a bid for our sympathy.* —**bid'der**, *n.*

bide (5) [bayd'], *v.* remain or wait. —**bide one's time**, wait for a favorable opportunity. Ex. *He may get a good job if he can bide his time.*

big (1) [big'], *adj.* 1. large in size or amount. Ex. *He is a big man.* 2. important. Ex. *The boy's first birthday was a big event in the family.* —**big'ness**, *n.*

bill (2) [bil'], *n.* 1. a paper showing money owed for goods or services supplied; the amount owed. Ex. *He gave them a bill for the food they bought in the shop.* 2. in government, a law being considered by the lawmakers. Ex. *Congress will vote today on a bill to increase taxes.* 3. a piece of paper money. Ex. *I was paid with a ten-dollar bill.* —*v.* send a paper showing money owed and requesting payment. Ex. *The store will bill me later for the dresses I bought.*

bill (2) [bil'], *n.* the long horny points extending out from a bird's mouth.

billion (4) [bil'yən], *n.* and *adj.* American: a thousand million (1,000,000,000); British: a million million (1,000,000,000,000).

BILL

billow (5) [bil'ow], *n.* 1. a large wave of water. Ex. *The ship was tossed by the ocean billows.* 2. any large rolling mass like a wave, such as of smoke or flame. —*v.* rise and swell in large waves. Ex. *The smoke billowed from the burning house.* —**bil'low·y**, *adj.*

bind (2) [baynd'], *v.* 1. tie together or fasten with a band or cord. Ex. *Please bind these papers in one package.* 2. place under obligation by a promise or agreement. Ex. *This agreement binds you to pay the full amount.* 3. treat a wound by putting a cloth or bandage on it. Ex. *The doctor* *will bind that wound.* —**bind'er,** *n.* the person or thing that binds.

biography (5) [bayag'rəfiy], *n.* the story of one person's life written by another. **bi·og'ra·pher,** *n.* the writer of a biography. —**bi`o·graph'i·cal,** *adj.*

biology (3) [bayal'əjiy], *n.* the science of life or living things in all their shapes and forms. —**bi`o·log'i·cal,** *adj.* concerning the science of biology. —**bi·ol'o·gist,** *n.* a person who studies and works in biology.

birch (4) [bərč'], *n.* 1. a hardwood tree with a smooth white outer bark that peels off in thin layers. 2. the wood itself.

bird (1) [bərd'], *n.* any warm-blooded, egg-laying, feathered animal that has wings and can fly.

birth (2) [bərθ'], *n.* 1. act of being born. Ex. *The birth of their first child was a happy time.* 2. origin; family background. Ex. *He returned to the land of his birth.* 3. beginning. Ex. *The birth of the United Nations occurred in the city of San Francisco in 1945.*

biscuit (4) [bis'kət], *n.* a kind of bread baked in small, soft cakes. Ex. *She served hot biscuits with the chicken.*

bishop (3) [biš'əp], *n.* a minister or priest in charge of a district of several churches.

bit (2) [bit'], *n.* a small piece or quantity. Ex. *She gave him a bit of cake.*

bit (2) [bit'], *v.* past tense of *bite.* Ex. *The dog bit the man.*

bite (2) [bayt'], *v.* cut into, usually with the teeth. Ex. *My dog will bite strangers.* —*n.* 1. the act of biting. Ex. *The bite of an animal should be treated by a doctor.* 2. a mouthful; a little. Ex. *Please have a bite of cake.*

bitten (2) [bit'ən], *v.* past participle of *bite.* Ex. *The man had been badly bitten by the lion.*

bitter (2) [bit'ər], *adj.* 1. having a sharp, unpleasant taste. Ex. *The coffee was so strong that it tasted bitter.* 2. hard to receive or bear. Ex. *They learned a bitter lesson from the unpleasant experience.* 3. causing pain; stinging. Ex. *The day was bitter cold.* 4. showing great dislike. Ex. *He felt bitter hatred against his enemy.* —**bit'ter·ly,** *adv.* —**bit'ter·ness,** *n.*

a, far; æ, am; e, get; éy, late; i, in; iy, see; ɔ, all; ow, go; u, put; uw, too; ə, but, ago; ər, fur; aw, out; ay, life; oy, boy; ŋ, ring; θ, think; ð, that; ž, measure; š, ship; ǰ, edge; č, child.

black (1) [blæk'], *adj.* the darkest color. Ex. *It is black outside the house at night.* —**black'ness,** *n.*

blackboard (3) [blæk'bɔrd'], *n.* a dark, smooth surface used for writing on with chalk. Ex. *The teacher wrote the questions on the blackboard.*

blacksmith (3) [blæk'smiθ'], *n.* a man who shapes iron or other metals into various things. Ex. *The blacksmith made shoes for the farmer's horses.*

blade (3) [bleyd'], *n.* 1. the sharp, cutting part of an instrument, especially of a knife. 2. narrow leaf of a plant. Ex. *A blade of grass is green.*

blame (2) [bleym'], *v.* regard as responsible for a mistake; consider guilty of. Ex. *They blamed the driver for the accident.* —*n.* the responsibility for what is wrong. Ex. *I will accept the blame.*

blank (2) [blæŋk'], *adj.* 1. not written or printed on. Ex. *A blank sheet of paper has no writing on it.* 2. showing no attention or interest. Ex. *The student gave the teacher a blank look.* —*n.* an empty space to be filled on a written or printed form. Ex. *Write your name in the blank on this form.* —**blank'ly,** *adv.* —**blank'ness,** *n.*

blanket (2) [blæŋ'kət], *n.* 1. a large piece of soft material, often wool, used as a covering for warmth. Ex. *In the winter, I sleep with two blankets on my bed.* 2. any thin, large covering like a blanket. Ex. *A blanket of flowers covered the grave.* —*v.* cover with, or as with, a blanket. Ex. *Snow blanketed the earth.*

blast (3) [blæst'], *n.* 1. a sudden blowing, or rush, of wind. 2. the sound made by blowing any wind instrument. Ex. *The blast of horns was heard over the hill.* 3. the sound made by anything exploding. Ex. *We heard a blast from the burning building.* —*v.* tear to pieces, or destroy, by exploding something. Ex. *The engineers are blasting the mountainside in order to build a new road.*

blaze (3) [bleyz'], *n.* 1. a brightly burning flame or fire. Ex. *We could see the blaze for miles.* 2. a strong, bright light. Ex. *We were blinded for a moment by the blaze of the car's lights.* —*v.* burn with a bright flame or light. Ex. *The fire blazed.*

bleach (5) [bliyč'], *v.* make white, colorless, or stainless. Ex. *The sun will bleach the cloth and make it whiter.* —*n.* any product, usually a chemical, used to bleach.

bleak (5) [bliyk'], *adj.* 1. bare, cold, and usually open to winds. **Ex.** *The climbers reached a bleak mountain top.* 2. cold and sharp. **Ex.** *A bleak wind was blowing.* 3. cheerless. **Ex.** *The jobless man had a bleak view of life.* —**bleak'ly,** *adv.* —**bleak'ness,** *n.*

bleat (5) [bliyt'], *n.* a thin, high cry, as that of a sheep or goat. —*v.* make such a cry. **Ex.** *Lambs bleat when they are hungry.*

bled (2) [bled'], *v.* past tense and participle of *bleed.* **Ex.** *His wound bled for an hour.*

bleed (2) [bliyd'], *v.* lose blood. **Ex.** *His wounded leg began to bleed.*

blend (4) [blend'], *v.* 1. mix completely together so that the things mixed cannot be separated. **Ex.** *Yellow and blue blend to make green.* 2. prepare varieties of wine, tobacco, coffee, etc., by mixing several together. 3. mix pleasantly. **Ex.** *The children's voices blended in song.* —*n.* a mixture of different kinds. **Ex.** *We like this blend of tea.*

bless (3) [bles'], *v.* 1. make or pronounce holy by prayer. **Ex.** *They asked the minister to bless the food.* 2. make happy or fortunate. **Ex.** *God blessed them with many children.*

blew (3) [bluw'], *v.* past tense of *blow.* **Ex.** *The wind blew outside the house.*

blight (5) [blayt'], *n.* 1. any widespread disease which destroys plants. **Ex.** *Blight ruined the potato crop.* 2. anything which destroys or damages. **Ex.** *Bad housing is a blight on a big city.* —*v.* damage; destroy. **Ex.** *Insects blighted the fruit trees.*

blind (2) [blaynd'], *adj.* 1. unable to see. **Ex.** *He helped the blind man across the street.* 2. unable or unwilling to understand or judge. **Ex.** *He was blind to his own faults.* —*v.* cause to be unable to see. **Ex.** *For a moment, the sun blinded him.* —**blind'ly,** *adv.* —**blind'ness,** *n.*

blink (4) [blink'], *v.* 1. open and close the eyes often and quickly. **Ex.** *She blinked at the sun.* 2. shine unsteadily. **Ex.** *The light blinked on and off.*

bliss (5) [blis'], *n.* a great gladness or happiness. **Ex.** *She felt bliss when she heard the good news.* —**bliss'ful,** *adj.*

blister (5) [blis'tər], *n.* a raised place in the skin with water underneath, caused by a burn or other injury. —*v.* cause a blister to form. **Ex.** *He blistered his hands in the fire.*

block (2) [blak'], *n.* 1. a solid mass of wood, stone, ice, etc. with some flat surface. Ex. *Blocks of ice floated down the river.* 2. in the United States, a portion of a town or city enclosed by four streets; a square block. Ex. *Many people live on this block.* 3. the length or distance of one side of this square. Ex. *He lives eight blocks from school.* 4. anything which stops movement or progress. Ex. *The police formed a road block to catch the criminal.* —*v.* hold back to prevent passage or progress. Ex. *The automobile accident blocked traffic, and cars could not move.*

blond or **blonde.** (3) [bland'], *adj.* light-colored; almost white. Ex. *My daughter has blond hair.* —*n.* a person whose hair is blond. Ex. *Both she and her sister are blondes.*

blood (1) [bləd'], *n.* 1. the red fluid which flows through the body, carrying oxygen and other needed materials to the parts of the body and taking away wastes. Ex. *He was sick from loss of blood.* 2. family line. Ex. *The prince was of royal blood.*

bloom (3) [bluwm'], *n.* 1. flower of a plant. 2. state of having flowers. Ex. *The roses are in bloom.* —*v.* produce or yield blossoms. Ex. *With enough water the plant will bloom.*

blossom (3) [blas'əm], *n.* 1. a flower, especially of a plant which bears fruit. Ex. *Orange blossoms have a sweet smell.* 2. the state of having flowers. Ex. *The apple trees are in blossom.* —*v.* 1. flower; bloom. Ex. *The tree blossomed.* 2. develop. Ex. *The girl's beauty blossomed as she grew.*

blot (4) [blat'], *n.* 1. spot or stain. Ex. *The spilled ink left a blot on the paper.* 2. a stain on character or reputation; shame. Ex. *The boy's arrest was a blot on the family's good name.* —*v.* 1. make a spot or stain on. 2. dry with a special paper that absorbs moisture. —**blot out,** eliminate; destroy. Ex. *She tried to blot out the unhappy memory.* —**blot'ter,** *n.* a paper that absorbs moisture.

blouse (5) [blaws'], *n.* outer clothing, like a shirt, worn by women and children.

BLOUSE

blow (1) [blow'], *v.* 1. move with force; be in motion. Ex. *A strong wind began to blow.* 2. carry or be carried by blowing. Ex. *The wind blows the papers off my desk.* 3. cause to make a sound by forcing air through. Ex. *Blow your horn.* 4. force air out or in to clear. Ex. *Use your handkerchief to blow your* *nose.* —**blow up,** 1. fill with air. **Ex.** *He used a small pump to blow up the bicycle tire.* 2. explode or cause to explode. **Ex.** *A bomb blew up the bridge.* —**blown,** *v.* past participle of *blow.*

blow (1) [blow'], *n.* 1. a hard hit with the hand or some instrument. **Ex.** *He was knocked to the ground by a blow on the head.* 2. a shock. **Ex.** *His sudden death was a great blow to the family.*

blue (1) [bluw'], *n.* a color like that of a clear sky. **Ex.** *Blue is my favorite color.* —*adj.* having the color of a clear sky. **Ex.** *She is wearing a blue dress.*

bluff (4) [bləf'], *n.* a high, steep cliff or hill. **Ex.** *The house on the bluff had a fine view of the ocean.* —*adj.* rough and unusual in speech but good-natured. **Ex.** *The bluff sailor was well liked by the villagers.* —**bluff'ness,** *n.*

bluff (4) [bləf'], *v.* fool; deceive by pretense. **Ex.** *He bluffed them into thinking he was brave.* —*n.* 1. act of bluffing. **Ex.** *His threat was just a bluff.* 2. a person who bluffs. **Ex.** *He is known as a bluff.*

blunder (4) [blən'dər], *n.* a careless or stupid mistake. **Ex.** *His failure to lock the door was a serious blunder.* —*v.* make a careless or stupid mistake. **Ex.** *She blundered and told them our secrets.*

blunt (5) [blənt'], *adj.* 1. having a thick or dull edge or point. **Ex.** *A blunt knife cuts poorly.* 2. plain, almost rude, in speech or manner; impolite. **Ex.** *His blunt answer to my request was "no."* —*v.* make dull. **Ex.** *Constant use blunts the knife.*

blur (5) [blə:r'], *v.* make less clear or readable. **Ex.** *Water spilled on the letter and blurred the writing.* —*n.* 1. a stain or spot that makes something unclear. **Ex.** *There is a blur in the first line.* 2. something unclear or confused. **Ex.** *The memory of the evening was just a blur to him.* —**blur'ry,** *adj.*

blush (3) [bləš'], *v.* redden in the face, as from shame. **Ex.** *She blushed when she saw her mistake.* —*n.* a reddening of the cheeks.

---

a, far; æ, am; e, get; ey, late; i, in; iy, see; ɔ, all; ow, go; u, put; uw, too; ə, but, ago; ər, fur; aw, out; ay, life; oy, boy; ŋ, ring; θ, think; ð, that; ž, measure; š, ship; j, edge; č, child.

board (1) [bɔrd¹], *n.* 1. a long, wide piece of wood, cut thin. Ex. *Many houses have floors made of boards.* 2. a group of persons chosen to manage a business, group, etc. Ex. *The board of directors of the bank meets today.* 3. food, especially meals, served for payment. Ex. *He receives room and board for very little money.* —*v.* 1. cover with boards. Ex. *They boarded the windows of their house during the storm.* 2. receive or provide meals for pay. Ex. *He boards at that house.*

board (1) [bɔrd¹], *v.* go on, as a ship, plane, or train. Ex. *You can board the ship at two o'clock.* —**on board,** on a ship, train, or plane.

boast (3) [bowst¹], *v.* 1. praise oneself, one's family, or one's possessions too much. Ex. *He boasted about his skills.* 2. possess or display with deserved pride. Ex. *The town boasts an excellent new school.* —*n.* a thing boasted of. Ex. *It was his boast that he was the best student in the school.* —**boast¹ful·ly, boast¹ing·ly,** *adv.* —**boast¹ful·ness,** *n.*

boat (1) [bowt¹], *n.* a small vessel for travel on water.

BOAT

body (1) [bad¹iy], *n.* 1. the whole physical structure of an animal or person. Ex. *He exercised every day to keep his body strong.* 2. the physical remains of a dead person or animal. Ex. *The body was lowered into the grave.* 3. the main part of an animal or person, not including the head, arms, and legs; the main or central part of anything. Ex. *He liked the body of the car.* 4. a group considered as a single thing. Ex. *The people went to the meeting in a body.* 5. a separate part of anything. Ex. *He saw a body of land.* —**bod¹i·ly,** *adv., adj.*

boil (2) [boyl¹], *v.* 1. heat a liquid until steam and bubbles form. Ex. *The water for the tea is boiling.* 2. cook by boiling in water. Ex. *Boil the rice for dinner.* —*n.* 1. act or state of boiling. Ex. *The water came to a boil.* 2. hard, swelling sore on the body. Ex. *The boil on my arm is painful.* —**boiler,** *n.* a metal tank in which water is boiled.

bold (3) [bowld¹], *adj.* 1. ready to face danger; unafraid. 2. rude; not respectful. Ex. *They did not like his bold manners.*

bolt (3) [bowlt'], *n*. 1. a threaded metal rod onto which a small metal piece, a nut, can be screwed. Ex. *Parts of many machines are held together by bolts.* 2. a movable bar that slides into an opening to fasten a door, gate, window, etc. 3. a sudden flash of lightning. Ex. *A bolt of lightning struck the old tree.* —*v*. 1. fasten with bolts; lock. Ex. *Be sure to bolt the door.* 2. leave suddenly. Ex. *He bolted from the room when he saw the policeman.*

BOLT AND NUT

bomb (3) [bam'], *n*. a steel container filled with material that explodes with great force. Ex. *Bombs were dropped from the planes.* —*v*. attack or destroy with bombs. Ex. *The airplanes bombed the city.*

bond (4) [band'], *n*. 1. anything that ties or fastens. Ex. *They loosened the prisoner's bonds and set him free.* 2. something that unites people and holds them together. Ex. *The bond of friendship between them was very strong.* 3. a printed or written promise to pay, given by a business, firm, or government, in return for a loan of money. Ex. *The government sold bonds to get money for a new school.*

bone (1) [bown'], *n*. the hard material of which the frame, or skeleton, of the body is made; pieces of this material. Ex. *He broke a bone in his finger.* —**bon'y**, *adj*. 1. full of bones. Ex. *The fish is bony.* 2. having large bones; without much flesh on the bones. Ex. *He had a thin, bony face.*

bonus (5) [bow'nəs], *n*. something given or paid in addition to what is usual or due. Ex. *Every worker received a five-dollar bonus at Christmas.*

book (1) [buk'], *n*. a fairly long, written or printed work or record. Ex. *He is writing a book about the history of this country.* —**notebook**, a number of sheets of blank paper bound together at one side within a cover, used for writing notes. Ex. *I need a notebook for school.*

bookend [buk'end], *n*. a device that supports a row of books.

boom (4) [buwm'], *v*. 1. make a long, deep sound. Ex. *The big guns boomed.* 2. grow or develop rapidly. Ex. *The town boomed after gold was discovered.* —*n*. 1. a deep hollow sound. 2. sudden, rapid growth.

boom (4) [buwm'], *n*. a pole attached to the lower end of a sailboat's mast and used to stretch and hold the lower end of the sail.

boot (3) [buwt¹], *n.* a covering for the foot and leg.
—*v.* kick. Ex. *He booted the ball.*

booth (4) [buwθ¹], *n.* a small, often enclosed space used for a special purpose. Ex. *He went into the telephone booth to call his wife.*

border (2) [bɔr'dər], *n.* 1. the line between two countries; frontier. Ex. *The Rio Grande river is the border between the United States and Mexico.* 2. the outer part or edge. Ex. *There was a border of flowers along the path to the house.* —*v.* touch at the edge or limits. Ex. *Both Canada and Mexico border on the United States.*

BOOT

bore (2) [bɔ:r¹], *v.* 1. cause to tire by dullness. Ex. *People who talk about themselves all the time bore me.* 2. make a hole in, as by drilling. Ex. *The carpenter bored holes in a board.* —*n.* a person or thing that tires by dullness. Ex. *She is a bore.* —**bored,** *adj.*

born (1) [bɔrn¹], *v.* past participle of *bear* (give birth). Ex. *The baby was born yesterday.* —*adj.* 1. brought into existence. Ex. *The newly born child cried loudly.* 2. possessing from birth the quality stated. Ex. *He is a born leader.*

borne (4) [bɔrn¹], *v.* past participle of *bear* (carry). Ex. *He has borne the burden much too long.*

borough (5) [bər'ow], *n.* 1. a town or village that governs itself. 2. one of the five political divisions of New York City.

borrow (1) [bar'ow], *v.* 1. obtain the use of something by promising to return it or its equal. Ex. *He borrowed enough money to buy a house.* 2. copy; imitate. Ex. *All the ideas in his book are borrowed from other writers.*

bosom (4) [buz'əm], *n.* 1. the breast of a human being. 2. the breast, considered as the location of feelings and emotions. Ex. *News of the accident struck fear in her bosom.* —*adj.* intimate; dear. Ex. *They were bosom friends.*

boss (3) [bɔ:s¹], *n.* one who directs the work of others; a manager. Ex. *He was the boss of fifty men.*

both (1) [bowθ¹], *adj., pron.* the two together. Ex. *Both men are here.* —*conj., adv.* as well; not only; equally. Ex. *She was both young and pretty.*

bother (3) [bað'ər], *v.* give trouble to; worry; disturb; annoy. Ex. *I have some questions to ask, but I do not want to bother you now.* —*n.* trouble; inconvenience. Ex. *Insects are a bother when it is hot.*

bottle (1) [bat'əl], *n.* 1. a container usually made of glass, with a narrow opening and no handles. 2. the contents of a bottle. **Ex.** *He drank a bottle of water.*

bottom (1) [bat'əm], *n.* 1. the lowest part of something. **Ex.** *The water must be raised from the bottom of a well.* 2. the base or underside; the part under and supporting the rest. **Ex.** *There is a mark on the bottom of the dish.* 3. the ground under a body of water. **Ex.** *The bottom of the river is sandy.*

BOTTLE

bough (3) [baw'], *n.* branch of a tree, usually a large limb. **Ex.** *The bough bent under the weight of the snow.*

bought (2) [bɔ:t'], *v.* past tense and participle of *buy.* **Ex.** *He bought that book yesterday.*

boulder (5) [bowl'dər], *n.* a large, round, smooth rock. **Ex.** *The boulder was too heavy to move.*

bounce (4) [bawns'], *v.* 1. throw an object against something to make it return. **Ex.** *The little girl is bouncing her rubber ball.* 2. leap suddenly. **Ex.** *She bounced out of the chair.* —*n.* 1. ability to spring back. **Ex.** *This ball does not have enough bounce.* 2. spring or leap. **Ex.** *He jumped to his feet with a bounce.*

bound (2) [bawnd'], *n.* limit; boundary. **Ex.** *Her joy knew no bounds.* —*v.* form the boundary of. **Ex.** *The Atlantic Ocean bounds the United States on the east.*

bound (2) [bawnd'], *v.* past tense and participle of *bind.* **Ex.** *They bound him with a rope.* —*adj.* 1. tied. **Ex.** *They released the bound feet of the prisoner.* 2. required. **Ex.** *You are bound by law to pay this tax.* 3. sure. **Ex.** *He is bound to succeed.*

bound (2) [bawnd'], *n.* a jump; a leap onward or upward. **Ex.** *He was on the train with one bound.* —*v.* move by sudden leaps; jump. **Ex.** *He bounded from the train.*

bound (2) [bawnd'], *adj.* traveling in the direction of; on the way to. **Ex.** *This airplane is bound for New York.*

boundary (3) [bawn'd(ə)ry], *n.* border; a limiting line. **Ex.** *High mountains are the boundary between the two countries.*

bounty (5) [bawn'tiy], *n.* 1. generosity in giving. **Ex.** *The*

---

a, far; æ, am; e, get; ey, late; i, in; iy, see; ɔ, all; ow, go; u, put; uw, too; ə, but, ago; ər, fur; aw, out; ay, life; oy, boy; ŋ, ring; θ, think; ð, that; ž, measure; š, ship; ǰ, edge; č, child.

bounty of nature is seen at harvest time. 2. whatever is given
generously. Ex. *The orphans were grateful for the woman's
bounty.* 3. a reward given for killing dangerous or destruc-
tive animals. Ex. *A bounty was offered for rats.* **—boun'ti·
ful,** *adj.*

bouquet (5) [buw‘key', bow‘key'], *n.* a bunch of flowers. Ex.
She carried a bouquet of roses.

bourgeois (5) [bur‘žwa:', bur‘žwa:'], *n.* a member of the middle class such as a property owner or businessman; one
neither very rich nor very poor. **—adj.** belonging to or like
the middle class.

bout (5) [bawt'], *n.* 1. a contest; a conflict. Ex. *He won the
first bout.* 2. a term; a period of time. Ex. *He had a long
bout of illness.*

bow (2) [baw'], *v.* 1. bend the body, head, or knee in greeting
or to show respect. Ex. *They bowed to each other as they
passed in the street.* 2. submit. Ex. *We must bow to authority.* 3. curve; bend. Ex. *The old man was bowed by age.*

bow (2) [bow'], *n.* 1. a weapon used to
shoot an arrow, made of a curved strip
of wood with a cord connecting the two
ends. 2. anything bent or curved. Ex.
*A rainbow is a curve of many colors in
the sky after a rain.* 3. a type of knot
with two or more open loops. Ex. *She
fastened her hair with a bow of ribbon.*

BOW AND ARROW

bowl (2) [bowl'], *n.* 1. a deep, round dish. 2. the quantity a
bowl contains. Ex. *He ate only one bowl of rice.*

box (1) [baks'], *n.* a blow with the palm of the hand or with
the fist. Ex. *She gave the boy a box on the ear.* **—v.** 1. fight
with the fists. 2. strike with the hand or fist. **—box'ing,** *n.*
the sport of fistfighting, wearing large gloves.

box (1) [baks'], *n.* 1. a container made of firm
material, usually with a removable cover or
lid. 2. the quantity contained in a box. Ex.
The child ate the whole box of candy.

boy (1) [boy'], *n.* a male child. **—boy'ish,** *adj.*

brace (4) [breys'], *n.* anything that supports
something firmly or holds parts together or
in place. Ex. *She wore a brace to support her weak leg.* **—v.**
1. provide a support to make stronger. Ex. *The carpenter
braced the leg of the chair.* 2. prepare oneself for a shock.

BOX 1

Ex. *Seeing her worried expression, he braced himself for the bad news.*

bracelet (4) [breys'lət], *n.* an attractive band or chain worn about the arm. Ex. *Her bracelet is made of gold.*

bracket (5) [bræk'ət], *n.* 1. an L-shaped support fastened to a wall under a shelf to support the shelf. 2. one of two marks [ ] used in writing to enclose certain words or phrases. [These words are between brackets.]

brag (5) [bræg'], *v.* praise one's own ability, possessions, or actions too much. Ex. *She is always bragging about her children.*

braid (4) [breyd'], *v.* divide into three or more parts and weave together, as hair, ribbon, etc. —*n.* 1. a length of hair woven together. 2. a narrow, woven band or tape used to decorate. Ex. *The army general had much gold braid on his uniform.*

brain (2) [breyn'], *n.* 1. the soft, gray matter which fills the head of man and animals and is the center of feeling and thinking. 2. understanding; intelligence. Ex. *She had both brains and beauty.*

brake (4) [breyk'], *n.* mechanical device for stopping the motion of a wheel or wheels. —*v.* slow the motion by using a brake. Ex. *He braked his car to a full stop.*

branch (1) [brænč'], *n.* 1. smaller parts growing out from the main part of a tree; a limb. Ex. *There are several new branches on the tree this year.* 2. any division extending from a main part like a branch. Ex. *This branch of the river flows between the mountains.* 3. a member or part of a larger group or organization. Ex. *The Air Force is a branch of the military service.* —*v.* put forth branches; separate into branches.

brand (4) [brænd'], *n.* 1. a particular kind or make. Ex. *What brand of cigarette do you smoke?* 2. a trade name or mark put on a product by a particular manufacturer or producer. Ex. *What brand of coffee do you use?* —*v.* 1. mark with a particular sign. Ex. *They branded the cow with their mark.* 2. mark or point out a person as shameful. Ex. *He was branded a thief by the newspaper.*

brandy (5) [bræn'diy], *n.* a liquor made from wine or from the juice of a fruit. Ex. *He drank too much apple brandy and has a headache.*

brass (3) [bræs'], *n.* a yellow metal made by melting copper and zinc together. —**brasses,** *n.* in music, the instruments made of brass. **Ex.** *The brasses in the orchestra consisted of horns and trumpets.*

brave (2) [breyv'], *adj.* possessing or showing courage. **Ex.** *The brave young boy saved the child from the burning house.* —*v.* meet or face with courage. **Ex.** *The early settlers braved cold, hunger, and violence.* —**brav'er·y,** *n.* courage. **Ex.** *His bravery saved the child.*

brawl (5) [brɔ:l'], *n.* noisy quarrel or fight. **Ex.** *The brawl in the street could be heard in the houses nearby.* —*v.* fight angrily and noisily. **Ex.** *The two men were brawling in the street.*

bray (5) [brey'], *n.* the loud cry of a mule or donkey. —*v.* make a sound like that of a mule or donkey. **Ex.** *The donkey brayed his anger.*

brazen (5) [brey'zən], *adj.* 1. made of or like brass in appearance or sound. **Ex.** *Inside the temple was a great brazen figure.* 2. shameless. **Ex.** *The brazen woman laughed loudly at the judge who sentenced her.*

breach (5) [briyč'], *n.* 1. the act or result of breaking; a break. **Ex.** *Strong disagreement produced a breach between the business partners.* 2. an opening made by breaking. **Ex.** *The pounding of the sea made a breach in the stone wall along the shore.* 3. a breaking of a law or of any promise. **Ex.** *His failure to pay was a breach of contract.* —*v.* make a breach in. **Ex.** *The soldiers breached the enemy lines.*

bread (1) [bred'], *n.* 1. an article of food made by mixing flour, water, yeast, etc., and baking. 2. the food needed to live. **Ex.** *One must work to earn one's bread.*

breadth (4) [bredθ'], *n.* 1. distance from one side of a thing to the other; width. **Ex.** *They measured the length and breadth of the field.* 2. largeness; extent. **Ex.** *The wise man has a great breadth of understanding.*

break (1) [breyk'], *v.* 1. cause to become pieces by hitting or placing a strain on. **Ex.** *He had to break the window to enter the house.* 2. fail to do or follow. **Ex.** *Those who break the law will be punished.* —*n.* 1. a crack or opening. **Ex.** *The dog escaped through a break in the fence.* 2. the action of forcing a way in or out. **Ex.** *The prisoner made a break for freedom.* —**break away, in,** or **out,** move away, into, or out with force. **Ex.** *The dog can easily break out of the cage.* —**break down,** stop operating or functioning as usual. **Ex.** *If the car breaks down, we will walk.* —**break off,** stop. **Ex.**

He will break off their friendship. **—break up,** cause to become pieces; cause to stop. **Ex.** *Will he break up the game?*

breakfast (2) [brek'fəst], *n.* the first meal of the day. **—v.** eat the first meal of the day. **Ex.** *She breakfasted in bed.*

breast (2) [brest'], *n.* 1. one of the parts of the body of human or animal females from which their babies get milk. **Ex.** *The mother's breasts were full of milk.* 2. the chest or upper part of the front of the body.

breath (2) [breθ'], *n.* air drawn into the body through the nose and mouth and then let out. **Ex.** *They smelled onions on his breath.*

breathe (2) [briyð'], *v.* draw in and let out air. **Ex.** *Open the windows wide and breathe the fresh air.*

bred (5) [bred'], *v.* past tense and participle of *breed.* **Ex.** *These horses were bred on my father's farm.*

breed (4) [briyd'], *v.* 1. produce young by the mating of animals. **Ex.** *Rabbits breed frequently.* 2. raise animals such as cattle, sheep, and horses. **Ex.** *He breeds race horses.* 3. produce. **Ex.** *Dirt breeds disease.* **—n.** a particular kind of animal or plant. **Ex.** *What breed of cattle do they raise on this farm?*

breeze (3) [briyz'], *n.* a light, gentle wind. **Ex.** *There is usually a cool breeze in the evening.*

brew (5) [bruw'], *v.* 1. make beer. 2. prepare a beverage or a liquid by placing the ingredients in water that has come to a boil. **Ex.** *Please brew me some tea.* 3. be forming or beginning. **Ex.** *Trouble is brewing when crowds gather in anger.* **—n.** that which is brewed. **Ex.** *If you are making tea, I like a strong brew.*

bribe (4) [brayb'], *n.* a gift or favor given or promised to influence a person to do something that he should not, or may not want to, do. **Ex.** *The judge was accused of taking a bribe to free the prisoner.* **—v.** give a bribe to; influence by a bribe. **Ex.** *He was bribed to keep silent.* **—brib'er·y,** *n.* the act of giving or accepting bribes.

brick (3) [brik'], *n.* a block of clay hardened by baking in the sun or fire and used as a building material. **—v.** cover with brick.

---

a, far; æ, am; e, get; ey, late; i, in; iy, see; ɔ, all; ow, go; u, put; uw, too; ə, but, ago; ər, fur; aw, out; ay, life; oy, boy; ŋ, ring; θ, think; ð, that; ž, measure; š, ship; j, edge; č, child.

bride (3) [brayd'], *n.* a woman newly married or about to be married. **Ex.** *The bride looked beautiful.* —**brid'al**, *adj.*

bridge (1) [brij'], *n.* 1. a structure built over a river, road, railroad, etc., used as a path or road. 2. anything shaped like a bridge. —*v.* build or make a bridge on or over.

BRIDGE 1

bridle (4) [bray'dəl], *n.* 1. the leather bands and metal pieces that are put about the head of a horse and used to control and guide it. 2. anything that slows down or controls. —*v.* 1. put a bridle on. 2. control. **Ex.** *You must learn to bridle your temper.*

brief (2) [briyf'], *adj.* short; using few words. **Ex.** *He had time only to give a brief report.* —*v.* instruct on how to do a piece of work. **Ex.** *He briefed the men on their duties.* —**brief'ly**, *adv.*

brier (5) [bray'ər], *n.* 1. a woody plant with thorns on its stem. 2. a thorn. **Ex.** *He scratched his leg on a brier.*

bright (1) [brayt'], *adj.* 1. shining; giving or having much light. **Ex.** *The sun is bright today.* 2. happy. **Ex.** *Her bright eyes showed her pleasure.* 3. of a brilliant color. **Ex.** *The box was painted a bright red.* 4. intelligent; quick-witted. **Ex.** *His school record shows he is bright.* —**bright'en**, *v.* —**bright'ly**, *adv.* —**bright'ness**, *n.*

brilliant (3) [bril'yənt], *adj.* 1. shining very brightly. **Ex.** *The lightning flashed a brilliant light.* 2. very intelligent. **Ex.** *The young lawyer has a brilliant mind.* —**bril'liance**, *n.*

brim (4) [brim'], *n.* 1. the upper edge of anything hollow. **Ex.** *The cup was filled to the brim.* 2. an edge which extends out. **Ex.** *The wide brim of her hat protected her from the sun.* —*v.* be full to the brim. **Ex.** *The cup is brimming over.* —**brim'ful**, *adj.* full up to the brim.

bring (1) [briŋ'], *v.* cause to come to a place by carrying or leading. **Ex.** *Bring me a glass.* —**bring about**, cause to happen. **Ex.** *He will bring about many changes.* —**bring around**, persuade; convince. **Ex.** *I will bring him around to my view.* —**bring to**, revive a person who has fainted. **Ex.** *The fresh air may bring him to.* —**bring up**, raise. **Ex.** *His mother will bring him up.*

brink (5) [briŋk'], *n.* 1. the edge of a steep place. **Ex.** *He fell over the brink of the cliff.* 2. the point just before. **Ex.** *The scientists were at the brink of discovery.*

brisk (5) [brisk'], *adj*. 1. active; lively. **Ex**. *The busy man took a brisk walk.* 2. sharp and cool. **Ex**. *The brisk winter weather made us hungry.* —**brisk'ly**, *adv*. —**brisk'ness**, *n*.

bristle (4) [bris'əl], *n*. one of the short, stiff, coarse hairs of certain animals, used especially to make brushes. —*v*. 1. rise or stand stiff or erect. **Ex**. *He was so frightened that his hair seemed to bristle.* 2. be roused up or stirred. **Ex**. *He bristled with anger.* —**brist'ly**, *adj*.

brittle (5) [brit'əl], *adj*. easily broken. **Ex**. *Glass is very brittle.* —**brit'tle·ness**, *n*.

broad (1) [brɔ:d], *adj*. 1. very wide. **Ex**. *We watched the boats on the broad river.* 2. covering a large area. **Ex**. *The farmer planted broad fields of wheat.* 3. general; not limited. **Ex**. *He is a man of broad views about politics.* —**broad'ly**, *adv*. —**broad'en**, *v*.

broadcast (3) [brɔ:d'kæst'], *v*. send messages, speeches, music, etc., by radio. **Ex**. *That radio station broadcasts educational programs.* —*n*. a radio or television program. **Ex**. *We listened to the news broadcast.* —**broad'cast·er**, *n*.

broad-minded [brɔ:d'mayn'ded], *adj*. willing to listen to the ideas of others; tolerant. **Ex**. *A broad-minded person does not oppose dancing.*

broil (5) [broyl'], *v*. cook under or over a flame or other high heat. **Ex**. *Many people broil meat over charcoal.* —**broil'er**, *n*. the part of a stove used for broiling. —**broiled'**, *adj*.

broke (1) [browk'], *v*. past tense of *break*. **Ex**. *The boy fell and broke his arm.*

broken (1) [brow'kən], *v*. past participle of *break*. **Ex**. *The boy has broken his arm.* —*adj*. 1. not whole; in pieces. **Ex**. *The broken dish could not be used.* 2. not kept. **Ex**. *A broken promise ended their friendship.* 3. not working or operating as intended. **Ex**. *The broken radio needs to be repaired.*

bronze (4) [branz'], *n*. a reddish-brown metal made by melting copper and tin together. **Ex**. *That statue is made of bronze.* —*adj*. the color of bronze. —*v*. give a bronze color to something.

brood (4) [bruwd'], *n*. young birds hatched or cared for together. **Ex**. *How many chickens are in the brood?* —*v*. think steadily and moodily about something. **Ex**. *She brooded on her past mistakes so much that she became ill.*

brook (2) [bruk¹], *n.* a small stream of water. **Ex.** *Children like to play in the brook.*

broom (3) [bruwm¹], *n.* a device for sweeping, with a stiff brush and a long handle.

brother (1) [brəð'ər], *n.* 1. a boy or man with the same parents as another person. **Ex.** *She has two older brothers and one younger brother.* 2. one of the same race or group or of the human race. **Ex.** *All men are brothers.* —**broth'er·ly,** *adj.*

BROOM

brother-in-law [brəð'ərənlɔ:¹], *n.* the husband of one's sister; the brother of one's husband or wife.

brought (1) [brɔ:t¹], *v.* past tense and participle of *bring.* **Ex.** *They brought the wheat from the fields.*

brow (3) [braw¹], *n.* 1. hair growing above the eye. 2. the forehead. **Ex.** *His cap covered his brow.*

brown (1) [brawn¹], *n.* the color made by mixing red, black, and yellow; the color of coffee. —*adj.* having the color

BROW

brown. **Ex.** *He has brown eyes.* —*v.* to make brown by cooking. **Ex.** *The meat is browning in the oven.* —**brown'ish,** *adj.* brownlike.

bruise (4) [bruwz¹], *v.* 1. injure by striking, without breaking the skin, often causing a black and blue mark. **Ex.** *He bruised his arm when he hit it on the stone.* 2. injure or hurt other than physically. **Ex.** *That sharp answer bruised her feelings.* —*n.* the injury; the mark left by such an injury. **Ex.** *The bruise became black and blue.* —**bruis'ing,** *adj.*

brush (2) [brəš¹], *n.* 1. a device consisting of stiff hairs attached to a handle, used for painting, cleaning, scrubbing, etc. 2. low, brushlike growth of wild plants. —*v.* 1. sweep, rub, clean, or polish with a brush. **Ex.** *Girls usually brush their hair carefully.* 2. touch lightly in passing. **Ex.** *The cat brushed against her leg.*

brute (4) [bruwt¹], *n.* 1. a beast. **Ex.** *The bear was a great brute.* 2. a cruel, unfeeling person. **Ex.** *Unfortunately, she married a brute.* —*adj.* 1. of or like a beast. 2. purely physical. **Ex.** *He pulled the tree out of the ground by brute force.* —**bru'tal, brut'ish,** *adj.* like a brute; cruel. **Ex.** *He is a brutal man.* —**bru·tal'i·ty,** *n.* savageness; cruelty.

bubble (3) [bəb'əl], *n*. 1. a small ball of air or gas in a liquid. Ex. *Many bubbles appeared in the boiling water.* 2. a small ball of air or gas in a thin liquid cover. Ex. *Children like to make bubbles with soap and water.* —*v*. rise in or form bubbles; foam. Ex. *When a liquid boils, it bubbles.* —**bub'bling,** *adj*.

buck (4) [bək'], *n*. the male of a deer, goat, rabbit, and certain other animals. Ex. *The deer hunters had shot a fine buck.* —*v*. suddenly jump upward, with the head low. Ex. *The horse bucked, but the rider managed to stay on its back.*

bucket (4) [bək'ət], *n*. a vessel for holding or carrying water or other liquid; a pail. —**buck'et·ful,** *n*. the amount contained in a bucket.

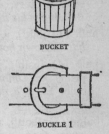

BUCKET

buckle (5) [bək'əl], *n*. 1. a fastening, usually of metal, for holding together the ends of a belt. 2. a similar device used as an ornament, as on women's shoes. —*v*. fasten with a buckle. Ex. *He buckled his belt.*

BUCKLE 1

bud (3) [bəd'], *n*. a blossom or leaf of a plant before it opens. Ex. *The rose already has a few pink buds.* —*v*. form buds. Ex. *The trees are budding early this spring.* —**bud'ding,** *adj*.

budget (4) [bəj'ət], *n*. a plan or estimate of expected income and expense for a period of time. Ex. *They planned a monthly budget for their family.* —*v*. make a plan for using money, time, goods, etc. Ex. *If you wish to get all of your work done, you must budget your time.*

buffalo (5) [bəf'əlow], *n*. any of many kinds of wild ox, including the tamed water buffalo and the American wild buffalo.

buffet (5) [bəf'ət], *n*. a blow with the hand; any blow. Ex. *The buffets of fate were almost more than he could bear.* —*v*. hit; strike repeatedly. Ex. *The ship was buffeted by the waves.*

buffet (5) [bəfey'], *n*. 1. a piece of furniture for holding dishes, silver, etc. 2. dishes of food placed on a table or buffet, so

---

a, far; æ, am; e, get; ey, late; i, in; iy, see; ɔ, all; ow, go; u, put; uw, too; ə, but, ago; ər, fur; aw, out; ay, life; oy, boy; ŋ, ring; θ, think; ð, that; ž, measure; š, ship; ǰ, edge; č, child.

that guests may serve themselves. —*adj.* served in buffe
style. **Ex.** *They were invited to a buffet supper.*

bug (1) [bəg'], *n.* an insect. **Ex.** *A bug was
crawling on the wood.*

bugle (4) [byuw'gəl], *n.* a brass horn used especially for military signals. —**bu'gler,** *n.*

BUGLE

build (1) [bild'], *v.* 1. join materials together to
make something. **Ex.** *They used wood to
build the house.* 2. establish; develop. **Ex.** *It
took several years to build the business.*
—**build'er,** *n.*

building (1) [bil'diŋ], *n.* 1. anything built for use as a house,
store, factory, etc. 2. the work of one who builds. **Ex.**
Building is his trade.

built (1) [bilt'], *v.* past tense and participle of *build.* **Ex.** *He
built his own house.*

bulb (4) [bəlb'], *n.* 1. a thick, ball-shaped root of certain
plants. **Ex.** *Onions are bulbs.* 2. something in the shape of a
bulb. **Ex.** *We need a new electric light bulb.* —**bul'bous,**
adj.

bulge (5) [bəlj'], *n.* a part that swells out. **Ex.** *The bag of
candy made a bulge in the child's pocket.* —*v.* extend;
swell out. **Ex.** *The bag bulged in several places.* —**bulg'ing,**
adj.

bulk (3) [bəlk'], *n.* 1. greatness of size. **Ex.** *It was a ship of
great bulk.* 2. the greatest or major part. **Ex.** *The bulk of
the debt was already paid.* 3. large quantities of some product not packaged or bottled. **Ex.** *Sugar in bulk is cheaper
than boxed sugar.* —**bulk'y,** *adj.* extremely large; large and
of awkward shape.

bull (3) [bul'], *n.* the male animal of the ox family. **Ex.** *The
bull protected the cows.*

bull's-eye [bulz'ay`], *n.* the center of a target used in practice
shooting; any shot that hits it. **Ex.** *A good shooter often hits
the bull's-eye.*

bullet (4) [bul'it], *n.* a small piece of metal that is shot from a
gun. **Ex.** *He was killed by a bullet.*

bulletin (4) [bul'ətən], *n.* 1. a brief public notice or announcement of news. **Ex.** *A bulletin on the radio warned of the
spread of the forest fire.* 2. a magazine or paper published

by an organization. **Ex.** *Many large business companies issue a monthly bulletin for their employees.*

bully (4) [bul'iy], *n.* a person who is cruel to persons weaker than himself. —*v.* try to control others by threats. **Ex.** *He bullies his younger brother unmercifully.*

bulwark (5) [bul'wərk], *n.* 1. a solid, wall-like structure of any material built around a place for purposes of defense. **Ex.** *The soldiers kept their heads down behind the bulwark.* 2. anything that protects. **Ex.** *Health insurance is a bulwark against the expense of illness.*

bump (4) [bəmp'], *v.* come suddenly into contact with something; jolt against. **Ex.** *He bumped into the wall.* —*n.* 1. a blow made by striking against something or someone. **Ex.** *The airplane landed with a bump.* 2. a swelling, often sore, resulting from a heavy blow. **Ex.** *She has a large bump on her head.* 3. a raised place. **Ex.** *The bump in the road caused many traffic accidents.* —**bump'y,** *adj.* —**bump'er,** *n.* a bar across the front or back of a car to protect it from damage when bumped.

bunch (3) [bənč'], *n.* a collection of similar things grouped together. **Ex.** *She picked a bunch of flowers.* —*v.* collect or gather in a group. **Ex.** *The cows were bunched together under the tree.*

bundle (3) [bən'dəl], *n.* a number of things tied or rolled together. **Ex.** *She carried a bundle of clothes.* —*v.* tie or wrap in a bundle. **Ex.** *Please bundle these newspapers.* —**bundle up,** dress warmly. **Ex.** *They bundled up to protect themselves from the cold.*

bungalow (5) [bəŋ'gəlow], *n.* a small house, usually with no upper floors.

burden (3) [bər'dən], *n.* 1. a load; that which is carried. **Ex.** *A horse can carry a heavy burden.* 2. difficulty, worry, or responsibility a person must endure. **Ex.** *Supporting his family was a great burden for him.* —*v.* load heavily; load too heavily. **Ex.** *I am sorry to burden you with these packages.*

bureau (3) [byur'ow], *n.* 1. a government department or office. **Ex.** *The weather bureau says there will be rain tonight.* 2. a business office. **Ex.** *He found work through an employment bureau.* 3. a chest of drawers for holding clothes. —**bu·reau'cra·cy,** *n.* system of government administration noted for many, often complicated rules which are rigidly followed. —**bu·reau·crat`**, *n.* government official or worker in a bureaucracy. —**bu`reau·crat'ic,** *adj.* rigid in following rules; like a bureaucrat.

burglar (5) [bər'glər], *n.* a person who forcibly enters a house or a store to steal. **Ex.** *The burglar was caught by the police.*

burial (5) [ber'iyəl], *n.* act of burying. **Ex.** *The burial of the dead sailor was performed at sea.*

burn (1) [bərn'], *v.* 1. be on fire. **Ex.** *Hard wood burns a long time.* 2. destroy by fire or heat. **Ex.** *The house was completely burned.* 3. be injured by heat. **Ex.** *She burned her hand on the stove.* 4. give light. **Ex.** *The electric lights burned all night.* —*n.* 1. a burned place. **Ex.** *There was a burn in the carpet.* 2. an injury caused by burning or by extreme cold, chemicals, gas, electricity, etc. **Ex.** *He suffered a burn on his hand.*

burrow (5) [bər'ow], *n.* a tunnel in the ground made by an animal as a place to live. **Ex.** *Rabbits live in burrows.* —*v.* dig a tunnel in the earth. **Ex.** *Rats burrowed under the floor of the house.*

burst (2) [bərst'], *v.* 1. break open or into pieces suddenly. **Ex.** *The bubble burst.* 2. come, enter, appear, start, etc., suddenly and with force. **Ex.** *The angry man burst into the room.* —*n.* 1. act of bursting. 2. a sudden display of activity. **Ex.** *He passed the other man with a burst of speed.*

bury (2) [ber'iy], *v.* 1. put into the ground and cover with earth. **Ex.** *Dogs like to bury bones.* 2. put a dead body into the ground, or into the sea, often with a ceremony. **Ex.** *He was buried in the cemetery.*

bus (1) [bəs'], *n.* a motor coach. —**bus'es, bus'ses,** *n.* more than one bus.

bush (2) [buš'], *n.* a low plant with many branches. —**bush'y,** *adj.*

BUS

bushel (3) [buš'əl], *n.* 1. a dry measure equal to 32 dry quarts. **Ex.** *He bought a bushel of apples from the farmer.* 2. a container which holds this quantity. **Ex.** *The farmer put the apples into a bushel.* See **Weights and Measures.**

business (1) [biz'nəs], *n.* 1. one's work; an occupation. **Ex.** *His business is farming.* 2. buying and selling; trade; commerce. **Ex.** *Business was good last year, and the company made money.* 3. a commercial or industrial establishment or enterprise. **Ex.** *He and his father own the business.* 4.

one's personal concern. **Ex.** *My affairs are none of your business.* —**busi·ness·like,** *adj.*

bust (4) [bəst'], *n.* 1. the head, neck, and shoulders of a person, shaped in clay, wood, metal, etc. 2. a woman's bosom.

bustle (4) [bəs'əl], *v.* move about busily and with a great show of energy. **Ex.** *During the busy lunch hour, the servants bustled about serving the guests.* —*n.* noisy activity; stir. **Ex.** *In the bustle of their departure, one lady forgot her coat.*

busy (1) [biz'iy], *adj.* 1. doing something; not idle. **Ex.** *The mother was busy cleaning the house.* 2. full of activity. **Ex.** *The busy street was full of cars, bicycles, and people.* —**bus'i·ly,** *adv.*

but (1) [bət'], *conj.* 1. however; yet. **Ex.** *He went, but I did not.* 2. except. **Ex.** *I will go anywhere but to the mountains.* —*prep.* except; other than. **Ex.** *No one knows this but me.* —*adv.* only; just. **Ex.** *There is but one answer to your question.*

butcher (3) [buč'ər], *n.* 1. one whose work is preparing animals for use as food. **Ex.** *A butcher needs sharp knives.* 2. one who sells meat. —*v.* kill and cut up, as a butcher does.

butt (5) [bət'], *n.* the thicker end of anything. **Ex.** *He struck him with the butt of his gun.*

butt (5) [bət'], *v.* strike or hit with force, especially with the head or horns. **Ex.** *The goat butted the boy and knocked him down.*

butter (1) [bət'ər], *n.* the solid, yellow fat gotten by beating cream. **Ex.** *He spread butter on his bread.* —*v.* put butter on. **Ex.** *He buttered his bread.*

butterfly (4) [bət'ərflay'], *n.* an insect with large, broad wings, usually bright in color.

button (2) [bət'ən], *n.* 1. a small, usually round, piece of metal, glass, etc. pushed through an opening to fasten clothing parts together. 2. a small device like a button. **Ex.** *Press the button to start the machine* —*v.* fasten clothing. **Ex.** *Button your coat.*

BUTTON 1

buy (1) [bay'], v. get by paying a price, usually money. **Ex.** *I will buy a new coat when I have enough money.* —**buy'er,** *n.* —**buy out** or **up,** buy all. **Ex.** *He plans to buy up the available meat.*

buzz (4) [bəz'], v. make a long, low, steady sound like that made by bees; murmur or whisper excitedly. **Ex.** *The whole town is buzzing about their marriage.* —*n.* a long, low, steady sound like that made by bees. —**buz'zer,** *n.* that which makes a buzzing sound.

by (1) [bay'], *prep.* 1. near; at. **Ex.** *He sat by my side.* 2. during. **Ex.** *They traveled by night.* 3. according to a fixed measurement. **Ex.** *They bought oranges by the dozen.* 4. not later than. **Ex.** *They were home by midnight.* 5. through the means of. **Ex.** *The rug was made by several people.* 6. in area measurement. **Ex.** *The piece of wood was two by four by twenty inches.* —**by and by,** after some time. **Ex.** *He will be home by and by.* —**by the way,** also; in passing. **Ex.** *By the way, I am going too.*

C

C, c, [siy'], *n.* third letter of the English alphabet.

cab (4) [kæb'], *n.* an automobile in which the passengers pay a fare; a taxicab. **Ex.** *He took a cab to the airport.*

cabbage (4) [kæb'ij], *n.* a vegetable with many curved leaves forming a round, firm head.

CABBAGE

cabin (3) [kæb'en], *n.* 1. a small house; a hut. **Ex.** *The pioneers built a log cabin.* 2. a private room on a ship for officers or passengers.

cabinet (3) [kæb'ənət], *n.* 1. a piece of furniture with shelves or drawers for storing articles. 2. a group of advisers, especially of a chief executive. **Ex.** *The President is meeting with his Cabinet.*

cable (3) [key'bəl], *n.* 1. a strong, thick rope, often made of wire. 2. a waterproof bundle of wires used for sending electricity. 3. a message sent under the ocean by means of these bundles of wires. **Ex.** *They sent a cable from London to*

New York. —*v.* send a message by cable. **Ex.** *They cabled us the news.* —**ca'ble·gram**, *n.* a cable.

café (3) [kæ`fey'], *n.* a coffeehouse, restaurant, or bar. **Ex.** *They stopped at a sidewalk café for lunch.*

cage (3) [keyǰ'], *n.* a boxlike room or space, with sides made of wire or bars, in which animals are kept. **Ex.** *The bird escaped from its cage.* —*v.* put or confine in a cage.

cagey [keyǰ'iy], *adj.* cunning; tricky. **Ex.** *His cagey answers do not tell us much.*

cake (1) [keyk'], *n.* 1. a sweet food, made of flour, sugar, eggs, and milk and baked in an oven. 2. any mass, usually one shaped like a cake. **Ex.** *Great cakes of ice were cut from the pond.*

calamity (5) [kəlæm'ətiy], *n.* bad fortune, either personal or public. **Ex.** *Floods, fires, and illness are great calamities.*

calcium (5) [kæl'siyəm], *n.* a soft, white chemical element found in bone, chalk, marble, etc. **Ex.** *Calcium is needed by the body to build bones and teeth.*

calculate (4) [kæl'kyəleyt`], *v.* 1. add, subtract, multiply, or divide to obtain information. **Ex.** *They calculated how much it had cost to build the house.* 2. plan in advance. **Ex.** *His remarks were calculated to win their confidence.* 3. estimate. **Ex.** *He calculated that the cost would be high.* —**cal'cu·lat`ing**, *adj.* 1. that performs calculations. **Ex.** *Our office has a calculating machine.* 2. shrewd; scheming. **Ex.** *Do not trust a calculating person.* —**cal'cu·la'tion**, *n.* the use of mathematics in solving a problem. —**cal'cu·la`tor**, *n.* a person or machine that calculates.

calendar (3) [kæl'əndər], *n.* a chart showing the days, weeks, months, and years. **Ex.** *Here is a calendar for the coming year.*

calf (4) [kæf'], *n.* 1. the young of the cow and of certain other animals. **Ex.** *The calf soon learned to drink milk from a pail.* 2. the fleshy part at the back of the human leg below the knee.

call (1) [kɔ:l'], *v.* 1. cry out in a loud voice. **Ex.** *He called my name.* 2. give a name to; name. **Ex.** *We have decided we will call the baby "Mary."* 3. telephone. **Ex.** *I called her on the telephone.* —*n.* 1. a cry or shout. **Ex.** *We heard a call in the night.* 2. a summons or signal. **Ex.** *That is the first call for dinner.* 3. a telephone conversation. **Ex.** *We have been expecting your call.* —**call for**, request. —**call off**,

decide against doing, having, etc. **Ex.** *He called off the trip.*
—**call on,** 1. visit. **Ex.** *We called on them at their home.*
2. ask to do. **Ex.** *We called on him to finish the work.* —**call
up,** telephone. **Ex.** *Call her up tonight.* 2. order one to come
for military duty. **Ex.** *During the emergency, I was called up
by the army.*

calm (2) [ka:m'], *n.* a period of quiet and stillness. **Ex.** *A
great calm followed the storm.* —*adj.* 1. peaceful; quiet.
Ex. *It was a calm evening with no wind.* 2. undisturbed by
passion or emotion; not excited. **Ex.** *She spoke in a calm
voice.* —*v.* make peaceful or quiet; soothe. **Ex.** *She calmed
the weeping girl.* —**calm'ly,** *adv.* —**calm'ness,** *n.*

calves (4) [kævz'], *n.* more than one *calf.* **Ex.** *The farmer has
two calves.*

came (1) [keym'], *v.* past tense of *come.* **Ex.** *They came to
our house.*

camel (4) [kæm'əl], *n.* a large animal used
in many desert regions for carrying goods.

camera (4) [kæm'(ə)rə], *n.* a device for taking photographs. **Ex.** *I need some film for
my camera.*

camp (2) [kæmp'], *n.* a place where soldiers
or other people live in tents or simple
buildings placed close together. **Ex.** *The young soldiers left
home and went to camp.* —*v.* 1. establish a camp. **Ex.** *The
army camped for the night.* 2. live for a short time in a tent
or out of doors. **Ex.** *The children camped in the woods.*
—**camp'er,** *n.*

CAMEL

campaign (3) [kæm`peyn'], *n.* 1. a connected series of military
actions in a war, to gain a certain result. **Ex.** *The old general had seen many campaigns.* 2. the competition by opposing political candidates for public office. **Ex.** *The President's
campaign to get reelected began several months ago.* —*v.*
serve in or go on a campaign. **Ex.** *He campaigned by visiting
the home of each voter.*

campus (5) [kæm'pəs], *n.* the main buildings and grounds of
a college or school. **Ex.** *Many students live on the campus.*

can (1) [kæn'], *v.* used with another verb to show: 1. know
how to; be able to. **Ex.** *She can swim very well.* 2. have the
right to. **Ex.** *He can vote.* 3. may; have permission. **Ex.** *You
can go now.*

can (1) [kæn'], *n.* 1. a small, sealed, metal container for food, milk, etc. **Ex.** *She opened a can of corn.* 2. a large metal container for water, waste material, etc. **Ex.** *The men carried the ash can.* —*v.* preserve food in cans. **Ex.** *That factory buys and cans fruit.* —**canned'**, *adj.* preserved in cans. **Ex.** *They ate canned food.*

canal (3) [kənæl'], *n.* a man-made waterway used by boats or ships. **Ex.** *The Suez Canal joins the Mediterranean and Red Seas.*

cancel (5) [kæn'səl], *v.* 1. strike or cross out with lines or marks. **Ex.** *The stamps on a letter are canceled to show they have been used.* 2. decide not to join in planned activity or not to have such an activity take place. **Ex.** *The singer canceled his concert.* —**can'cel·la'tion**, *n.*

cancer (5) [kæn'sər], *n.* a dangerous disease in which cells grow at a rapid rate and destroy healthy parts of the body. **Ex.** *Her father, who died of cancer, had been a heavy smoker.*

candidate (3) [kæn'dədeyt], *n.* one who seeks or is suggested for an office or an honor. **Ex.** *He was a candidate for president three times.* —**can'di·da·cy**, *n.* the state or fact of being a candidate.

candle (3) [kæn'dəl], *n.* a stick of wax or similar material, with a string running through it, which gives light when burned. **Ex.** *The garden was lit by candles.*

candy (2) [kæn'diy], *n.* a sweet food made mostly of sugar, often with the addition of flavoring, nuts, fruits, etc. **Ex.** *Children love candy.*

cane (4) [keyn'], *n.* 1. a stick used as an aid in walking. 2. a plant having a hollow, jointed stem. **Ex.** *Sugar is made from the juice of sugar cane.*

cannon (4) [kæn'ən], *n.* a large gun fastened to a base or wheels.

CANNON

canoe (3) [kənuw'], *n.* a light, narrow boat moved by paddles. —*v.* ride in a canoe. **Ex.** *The boys canoed on the lake.*

CANOE

can't (1) [kænt'], short form of *cannot*. **Ex.** *I can't go now.*

canvas (4) [kæn'vəs], *n*. 1. a strong, heavy cloth made of cotton or other fibers used for tents, sails, oil paintings, etc. 2. an oil painting. **Ex.** *The artist showed us three of his canvases.*

canyon (5) [kæn'yən], *n*. a deep valley with high, steep sides and often with water flowing through it.

cap (2) [kæp'], *n*. 1. a small, closely fitting covering for the head, often with a projecting edge in front. 2. like a cap, such as a top or lid. **Ex.** *Put the cap on the milk bottle.* —*v*. put a cap on. **Ex.** *The trees were capped with snow.*

capable (3) [key'pəbəl], *adj*. having skill; fit; able to do something well. **Ex.** *She is a capable teacher.* —**ca'pa·bil'i·ty**, *n*. —**ca'pa·bly**, *adv*. **capable of**, able or ready to. **Ex.** *He is capable of doing good work.*

capacity (3) [kəpæs'ətiy], *n*. 1. the space for receiving or containing. **Ex.** *The capacity of this bottle is one gallon.* 2. ability to do or become. **Ex.** *He has the capacity to become a doctor.* 3. position. **Ex.** *She worked in the capacity of nurse.*

cape (3) [keyp'], *n*. 1. a sleeveless garment that fastens at the neck and hangs over the shoulders. **Ex.** *She wore a long cape over her dress.* 2. a narrow piece of land that extends out into the sea. **Ex.** *The fisherman lived on the cape.*

capital (2) [kæp'ətəl], *n*. 1. the city or town in which the government is located. **Ex.** *Washington, D.C., is the capital of the United States.* 2. money, buildings, land, and machines owned and used by businesses, people, or the government to make more money. **Ex.** *He saved his money and used it as capital to start his own business.* —**cap'i·tal·ism**, *n*. an economic system in which most of the means for producing goods and services are owned and operated for profit by individuals or private companies. —**cap'i·tal·ist**, *n*. a person who owns much capital or supports capitalism. —**cap'i·tal·is'tic**, *adj*.

capital (2) [kæp'ətəl], *adj*. 1. referring to the large letters. **Ex.** *You must begin a sentence with a capital letter.* 2. punishable by death. **Ex.** *Murder is a capital offense.* —**cap'i·tal·ize**, *v*. write in capital letters. **Ex.** *In "Mary," the letter "M" is capitalized.*

captain (1) [kæp'tən], *n*. 1. one in authority over others; a chief; leader. **Ex.** *That boy is the captain of the team.* 2. the rank of an army officer above a first lieutenant. 3. the rank of a navy officer just above a commander. 4. the commander or master of a ship. **Ex.** *The captain ordered every-one to leave the ship.*

captive (4) [kæp'tiv], *n.* a prisoner, especially in war. —**cap·tiv'i·ty**, *n.* state of being held or of not being free. **Ex.** *Animals in the zoo are in captivity.*

capture (3) [kæp'čər], *v.* take by force or by surprise; take prisoner; seize. **Ex.** *The hunters captured the wild animal with a net.* —*n.* the act of capturing. **Ex.** *The capture was made at dawn.*

car (1) [ka:r'], *n.* 1. an automobile. **Ex.** *Four of us are going in his car.* 2. anything on wheels used for carrying passengers, goods, etc., especially over rails. **Ex.** *There were 55 freight cars in that train.*

caravan (5) [kær'əvæn`, ker'əvæn`], *n.* 1. a company of persons traveling together for safety, as across a desert or through dangerous country. 2. a covered wagon in which people travel and live.

carbon (4) [kar'bən], *n.* 1. a non-metallic chemical element found in all living matter. **Ex.** *Diamonds are pure carbon; coal is a form of carbon that is not pure.* 2. a kind of paper coated with carbon, which is placed between sheets of paper so that what is written on the top sheet also appears on the other sheets; the copy itself. **Ex.** *Bring me the original and two carbons of the letter.*

carcass (5) [kar'kəs], *n.* the body of a dead animal.

card (2) [kard'], *n.* 1. a piece of heavy, stiff paper, either blank or printed. **Ex.** *Hold up the card so we can see what is written on it.* 2. one of a set of cards with spots, figures, pictures, etc., used in playing games. **Ex.** *Bridge is a popular game of cards.* 3. a piece of stiff paper bearing a greeting. **Ex.** *She received many birthday cards.*

cardboard [kard'bɔrd`], *n.* a heavy paper used to make boxes, signs, etc. **Ex.** *The box was made of cardboard.* —*adj.* made of cardboard.

cardinal (5) [kar'dənəl], *n.* 1. a high-ranking church official. 2. an American songbird with red feathers. —*adj.* of highest importance; chief; principal. **Ex.** *Exercise is of cardinal importance to health.*

care (1) [ke:r'], *n.* 1. serious attention. **Ex.** *She took good care of the baby.* 2. worry; anxiety. **Ex.** *The doctor told her to forget her cares.* 3. protection; charge. **Ex.** *She is under a doctor's care.* —*v.* 1. wish; like. **Ex.** *Would you care to go*

to the theater? 2. feel anxiety, worry, or interest. **Ex.** *I do
not care where we go this evening.* 3. watch; take charge of.
Ex. *They cared for the children during the parents' absence.*
4. love. **Ex.** *They care very much for each other.* —**care'ful**,
adj. acting so as not to harm, make mistakes, etc. **Ex.** *Be
careful when you walk.* —**care'ful·ness**, *n.* —**care'ful·ly**, *adv.*
—**care'less**, *adj.* acting without care. —**care'less·ly**, *adv.*
—**in care of**, at the address of. **Ex.** *I do not have a place of
my own; send my mail in care of my mother.*

career (3) [kəriːr'], *n.* profession; life's work; progress in a
profession or public life. **Ex.** *He prepared for a career in
law.*

caress (4) [kəres'], *n.* a gentle touch, kiss, or embrace. **Ex.** *His
caresses told her of his love.* —*v.* touch or stroke tenderly.
Ex. *Soft music caresses the ear.* —**ca·ress'ing**, *adj.* —**ca·ress'
ing·ly**, *adv.*

caretaker [keːr'teyk`ər], *n.* one who cares for a building or
place. **Ex.** *The caretaker unlocked the apartment door.*

careworn [keːr'wɔrn`], *adj.* tired from worry and concern. **Ex.**
She looked careworn.

cargo (4) [kar'gow`], *n.* a load of articles carried by a ship or
plane. **Ex.** *A cargo of tea arrived from Ceylon.*

carpenter (3) [kar'pəntər], *n.* a workman who builds or repairs wooden structures, such as houses. **Ex.** *The carpenter
built a porch on the house.*

carpet (3) [kar'pət], *n.* 1. a thick, heavy material used as a
floor covering. **Ex.** *The carpet on the hall floor is red.* 2. a
carpetlike covering. **Ex.** *The grass was a green carpet.* —*v.*
1. cover with a carpet. **Ex.** *They want to carpet the hall.*
2. cover like a carpet. **Ex.** *Snow carpeted the ground.*

carriage (2) [kær'ij, ker'ij], *n.* any
wheeled vehicle for carrying people,
usually one drawn by horses.

CARRIAGE

carrot (5) [kær'ət, ker'ət], *n.* a plant with
a long, pointed, orange-colored root,
eaten as a vegetable. **Ex.** *She served
peas and carrots with the roast beef.*

carry (1) [kær'iy, ker'iy], *v.* take from one place and put in
another; move while supporting. **Ex.** *Two men carried the
heavy box into the house.* —**car'ri·er**, *n.* —**carry on**, do
or continue. **Ex.** *Carry on the work while I am away.*

—**carry out**, accomplish. Ex. *Carry out the work in the way I asked you to.*

cart (3) [kart'], *n.* a light, small wagon used for transporting articles, or carrying people. Ex. *The farmer took his vegetables to market in a cart.* —*v.* carry in a cart. Ex. *The farmer carted the hay to the barn.*

carton (5) [kar'tən], *n.* a box made of heavy, stiff paper. Ex. *They bought a carton of eggs.*

cartridge (5) [kar'triǰ], *n.* 1. a case, usually of metal, for holding the gunpowder and the bullet, for a rifle, gun, etc. Ex. *The soldier placed a cartridge in his gun.* 2. a case or holder like this.

carve (3) [karv'], *v.* 1. shape by cutting. Ex. *He carved the figure out of stone.* 2 cut meat. Ex. *His father carved the meat for us.* —**carv'er,** *n.*

case (1) [keys'], *n.* 1. a particular instance; a single happening. Ex. *Only one case of stealing was reported to the police.* 2. a problem to be tried in a court of law. Ex. *The judge decided the case in our favor.* 3. someone with a problem. Ex. *The doctor is treating several cases of this disease.* —**in case,** in the event that. Ex. *Wear your raincoat in case it rains.*

case (1) [keys'], *n.* 1. a container. Ex. *Goods shipped by train are packed in cases.* 2. a box with its contents. Ex. *Stores buy whole cases of canned fruit at one time.*

cash (2) [kæš'], *n.* coins or paper money. Ex. *I paid by check because I did not have any cash with me.* —*v.* give or get money for. Ex. *Please cash this check for me.*

cashier (5) [kæ'ši:r'], *n.* a person who receives and pays money. Exs. *He works as a cashier at a bank. Pay the cashier, not the waiter.*

cast (4) [kæst'], *v.* 1. throw away, out, or down. Ex. *He cast stones into the water.* 2. direct; send in a certain direction. Ex. *The lamp cast a light on the table.* 3. shape melted metal by pouring into a hollow form. —*n.* the actors in a play. —**cast one's vote,** vote.

castle (2) [kæs'əl], *n.* a large, strong building or group of buildings; the home of a nobleman. Ex. *A king once lived in the mountain castle.*

casual (4) [kæž'uwəl, kæž'ul], *adj.* 1. happening by chance; not planned. Ex. *It was not a business appointment, just a casual meeting with a friend.* 2. without a definite purpose. Ex. *He gave the book a casual glance but did not study it.* —**cas'u·al·ty**, *n.* one hurt or killed.

cat (2) [kæt'], *n.* a small, furry animal kept as a pet and useful for catching rats and mice.

CAT

catalog, catalogue (4) [kæt'əlɔg'], *n.* 1. a paper or book, usually containing descriptions and pictures of items for sale. Ex. *In the United States, many people buy things from a catalog.* 2. an alphabetical record on cards of the books in a library or of things in other collections. Ex. *You can find the name of the book you want in the card catalog.*

catastrophe (5) [kətæs'trəfiy'], *n.* a sudden happening that causes great damage, loss, or suffering. Ex. *The flood was a catastrophe.* —**cat'a·stroph'ic**, *adj.*

catch (1) [kæč', keč'], *v.* 1. seize after a chase; capture. Ex. *The cat will catch the mouse.* 2. stop the motion of and seize in the hands. Ex. *Catch the ball.* 3. get by a hook or trap. Ex. *How many fish did you catch?* 4. get an illness. Ex. *I catch a cold easily.* —*n.* 1. the act of taking, holding, or seizing. Ex. *The ballplayer made a good catch.* 2. something taken or captured. Ex. *The fishermen said their catch was large today.* —**catch up**, 1. reach those ahead. Ex. *Walk slowly, and I will catch up with you.* 2. become current. Ex. *I must catch up on my work.*

caterpillar (4) [kæt'ərpil'ər], *n.* the worm-like stage in the life of an insect such as the butterfly.

CATERPILLAR

cathedral (5) [kəθiy'drəl], *n.* an important large church. Ex. *France has many famous cathedrals.*

cattle (2) [kæt'əl], *n.* members of the cow family. Ex. *Cows, bulls, steers, and oxen are cattle.*

caught (1) [kɔ:t'], *v.* past tense of *catch.* Ex. *The boy caught the ball with both hands.*

cause (1) [kɔ:z'], *n.* 1. the thing or person that produces a result. Ex. *What was the cause of the fire?* 2. a reason for an action. Ex. *You have good cause to be angry.* 3. an aim or purpose. Ex. *They fought for the cause of freedom.* —*v.*

make happen; be the cause of. **Ex.** *He did not want to cause trouble.*

caution (3) [kɔːˈšən], *n.* 1. watchfulness in regard to danger; carefulness. **Ex.** *Proceed with caution when crossing the street.* 2. a warning against danger or evil. **Ex.** *Let his experience serve as a caution to you.* —*v.* give warning; advise of danger. **Ex.** *The lifeguards cautioned the swimmers to be careful.*

cautious (3) [kɔːˈšəs], *adj.* careful to avoid danger or trouble. **Ex.** *He was a cautious driver.* —**cau'tious·ly,** *adv.*

cavalry (4) [kævˈəlriy], *n.* soldiers who fight on horseback. **Ex.** *The cavalry rode into the city.*

cave (3) [keyvˈ], *n.* a hollow place in the earth, usually in a hill or mountain. **Ex.** *Pictures were painted on the walls of the cave.* —**cave in,** sink or fall in. **Ex.** *The roof caved in because of the heavy snow.*

caveman [keyvˈmænˈ], *n.* a human who lived long ago in caves.

cavern (5) [kævˈərn], *n.* a large cave. **Ex.** *The children were lost in the cavern.* —**cav'ern·ous,** *adj.* large, like a cavern.

cavity (5) [kævˈətiy], *n.* hole; hollow place. **Ex.** *She had the cavity in her tooth filled.*

cease (2) [siysˈ], *v.* stop; end. **Ex.** *She ceased crying.* —**cease' less,** *adj.* going on without end. —**cease'less·ly,** *adv.*

cedar (4) [siyˈdər], *n.* an evergreen tree with sweet-smelling wood. **Ex.** *Cedar chests are used to store clothes.*

ceiling (3) [siyˈliŋ], *n.* the overhead surface of a room, opposite the floor. **Ex.** *A light hung from the middle of the ceiling.*

celebrate (4) [selˈəbreytˈ], *v.* honor an event with special activity. **Ex.** *I will celebrate my birthday tomorrow.* —**ce·leb' ri·ty,** *n.* a famous or well-known person.

celery (5) [selˈ(ə)riy], *n.* a green vegetable that grows in stalks with a leafy top.

cell (2) [selˈ], *n.* 1. a room in a prison. **Ex.** *The prisoner was locked in a cell.* 2. the basic part of the stucture of all living matter. **Ex.** *Every plant and animal is made of one or more cells.*

CELERY

cellar (3) [selˈər], *n.* an underground area,

usually under a building, often used for storage. **Ex.** *The potatoes were stored in the cellar.*

cement (4) [siment¹], *n.* a powdered substance which, when mixed with water and allowed to dry, becomes hard like stone. **Ex.** *Cement is used to make floors, walls, and sidewalks.*

cemetery (3) [sem¹əterˈiy], *n.* a burial ground; graveyard.

censure (5) [sen¹šər], *n.* act of finding fault or condemning as wrong. **Ex.** *His actions deserve severe censure.* —*v.* find fault with; condemn as wrong. **Ex.** *You must not censure him until you know the whole story.*

census (5) [sen¹səs], *n.* an official count of the population of a country, city, or town, that usually includes details about age, sex, occupation, etc. **Ex.** *In the United States there is a census every ten years.*

cent (1) [sent¹], *n.* 100th part of a dollar or other units of money; a penny. See **Weights and Measures.**

center (2) [sen¹tər], *n.* 1. the middle point; a place in the middle. **Ex.** *This building is at the center of town.* 2. a place that is the main point of some kind of activity. **Ex.** *The public library was a center of interest for everyone in the town.* 3. the middle point of a circle or sphere. —*v.* 1. place on or near a center. **Ex.** *He centered the picture on the wall.* 2. concentrate. **Ex.** *Their interests centered on their home.*

central (3) [sen¹trəl], *adj.* 1. in, at, or near the center. **Ex.** *They lived in the central area of the city.* 2. main; principal. **Ex.** *Nearly every story has a central idea.* —**cen¹tral·ize,** *v.* bring to or put in a center or one place. **Ex.** *Many powers are centralized in the government.*

century (1) [sen¹čəriy], *n.* a period of 100 years.

cereal (4) [sir¹(i)yəl], *n.* 1. any grass yielding grain used for food; the grain produced from such grass. **Ex.** *Wheat and rice are cereals.* 2. a food made from grain. **Ex.** *In the United States cereals are often eaten for breakfast.*

ceremony (3) [ser¹əmowˈniy], *n.* 1. an act or series of acts done in a particular way established by custom. **Ex.** *The wedding ceremony was performed in the morning.* 2. very polite formal behavior. **Ex.** *They were received with great ceremony.* —**cerˈe·moˈni·al,** *adj.* —**cerˈe·moˈni·ousˈly,** *adv.*

certain (2) [sərt¹ən], *adj.* 1. having no doubt; confident. **Ex.** *I am certain that my information is correct.* 2. sure to happen.

Ex. *Spring is certain to follow winter*. 3. definite but not named. Ex. *Certain people are aware of the facts in the case*. —cer'tain·ly, *adv*. surely. —cer'tain·ty, *n*.

certificate (4) [sərtif'əkət], *n*. an official statement declaring that something is true. Ex. *A birth certificate proves one's age*.

chaff (5) [čæf'], *n*. the worthless, outside leaves of grains and grasses separated from the seed. Ex. *They separated the wheat from the chaff*.

chain (2) [čeyn'], *n*. 1. a connected series of rings or links, usually of metal. Ex. *They pulled the automobile with a heavy chain*. 2. a series of connected things. Ex. *That incident was the first in a chain of events*. 3. bondage. Ex. *The prisoner was in chains*. —*v*. fasten or secure with a chain. Ex. *The dog was chained to the fence*.

chair (1) [če:r'], *n*. a piece of furniture for one person to sit on.

chairman (4) [čer'mən], *n*. a person in charge of a meeting or any organized group. Ex. *He was asked to be the chairman of the committee*.

CHAIR

chalk (4) [čɔ:k'], *n*. a soft, white, powdery material, sometimes made from shells. Ex. *A piece of chalk is used for writing on a blackboard*. —chalk'y, *adj*.

challenge (3) [čæl'ənǰ], *n*. a call to a contest of skill or strength. Ex. *He thought of his new job as a challenge*. —*v*. 1. call or summon to a contest. Ex. *He challenged his enemy to fight*. 2. question. Ex. *She challenged her friend's decision*.

chamber (5) [čeym'bər], *n*. 1. a room. 2. a group of people organized for a business purpose. Ex. *A chamber of commerce encourages people to visit its city*.

champion (3) [čæm'piyən], *n*. 1. the winner; one who holds first place. Ex. *He is a boxing champion*. 2. one who fights for or defends a person or cause. Ex. *The major is a champion of the poor*. —*adj*. victorious over all others; the best of its kind. Ex. *That is a champion race horse*.

chance (1) [čæns'], *n*. 1. an opportunity. Ex. *Now is your* *chance to escape.* 2. unknown cause of an event; fortune; luck. **Ex.** *Chance played a part in his success.* 3. how possible or probable it is something will happen. **Ex.** *The doctor said the patient had a good chance to recover.* 4. a happening resulting from an unknown cause. **Ex.** *We met by chance.* —*adj.* due to chance; accidental. **Ex.** *A chance remark helped solve the problem.*

change (1) [čeynǰ'], *v.* 1. put or take another in place of. **Ex.** *He changed into a clean shirt before dinner.* 2. become or make different; vary. **Ex.** *If you do not like this picture, it can be changed.* 3. exchange. **Ex.** *They changed seats.* —*n.* 1. act of changing; alteration. **Ex.** *He suggested several changes in the plan of the house.* 2. variety; substitution. **Ex.** *The change in jobs was good for him.* 3. the amount returned when payment is more than the amount owed. **Ex.** *The cashier gave him his change.* 4. small coins. —**change'a·ble**, *adj.* —**change'less**, *adj.*

channel (5) [čæn'əl], *n.* 1. a narrow body of water that joins two larger bodies of water. 2. a long cut, groove, tube, or other path through which something may flow, pass, etc. **Ex.** *Can your television set receive that channel?* —*v.* 1. make a channel. 2. direct toward or into some particular course. **Ex.** *He channeled all of his energy into fixing his house.*

chant (4) [čænt'], *n.* a song, especially a short, simple tune in which many words are sung in one tone. **Ex.** *Chants are often used in religious services.* —*v.* say or sing in a chant. **Ex.** *The worshipers chanted a prayer.*

chaos (5) [key'as'], *n.* lack of order; complete confusion. **Ex.** *The thieves left the house in chaos.* —**cha·ot'ic**, *adj.*

chap (5) [čæp'], *v.* crack or roughen and redden the skin. **Ex.** *My hands are chapped from the cold.*

chapel (5) [čæp'əl], *n.* a small or private place of prayer or worship. **Ex.** *The wedding was held in the chapel.*

chapter (2) [čæp'tər], *n.* any of the main divisions of a book. **Ex.** *This novel has ten chapters.*

character (1) [kær'əktər, ker'əktər], *n.* 1. all the qualities by which a person is judged; his strengths and weaknesses. **Ex.** *As he grew older, his character changed greatly.* 2. those qualities in a person considered to be morally good. **Ex.** *A person dealing with the money of others must have character.* 3. the qualities that distinguish one person or thing from others. **Ex.** *The character of the country changed as we traveled south.* 4. person in a play or story. **Ex.** *The most important character in the story is a young doctor.* —**char'ac·ter·i·za'tion,** *n.* —**char'ac·ter·ize`,** *v.*

characteristic (3) [kærˋəktərisˈtik, kerˋəktərisˈtik], *adj.* belonging to a person or thing as part of its nature; typical. **Ex.** *Burning leaves have a characteristic smell.* —*n.* a distinguishing feature or quality. **Ex.** *A red color is a characteristic of that type of apple.*

charcoal (5) [čarˈkowlˋ], *n.* 1. a black, coal-like material made from burning wood in a container that has no air. **Ex.** *We cooked our food over burning charcoal.* 2. a stick for drawing made of this material.

charge (1) [čarǰˈ], *v.* 1. set a price for. **Ex.** *How much do you charge for this bread?* 2. delay payment until a later date. **Ex.** *She was able to charge the furniture she bought.* 3. rush toward. **Ex.** *He charged toward the door to escape.* 4. put the blame upon; accuse. **Ex.** *They charged him with murder.* —*n.* 1. an accusation. **Ex.** *A criminal charge has been made against him.* 2. care; management. **Ex.** *He has charge of the horses.* 3. price; cost. **Ex.** *Their charge for the work was high.* 4. a quantity of electricity. **Ex.** *What electric charge is carried by that battery?* —**in charge of,** have control of or responsibility for. **Ex.** *He is in charge of the office.*

charity (3) [čærˈətiy], *n.* 1. help or money given to those in need. **Ex.** *The poor family depended upon charity.* 2. kindness; willingness to forgive. **Ex.** *They treated even their enemies with charity.* 3. an organized fund or institution for giving money. **Ex.** *The Red Cross is a well-known charity.* —**char'i·ta·ble,** *adj.* —**char'i·ta·bly,** *adv.*

charm (2) [čarmˈ], *n.* 1. some quality or feature which delights or attracts. **Ex.** *Her lovely voice had great charm.* 2. an act, thing, or word which is believed to have magic power to do good or evil. **Ex.** *He believed a charm could prevent him from becoming ill.* —*v.* please greatly. **Ex.** *She charmed them with her dancing.* —**charm'er,** *n.*

chart (4) [čartˈ], *n.* 1. an arrangement of facts in the form of a list or drawing so that it may be read at a glance. **Ex.** *This sales chart shows how many sales were made last week.* 2. a map used to show distances at sea, military operations, or weather conditions. **Ex.** *The course of the ship was marked* *on the chart.* —*v.* 1. draw or show on a chart. 2. plan a course of action.

charter (4) [čar'tər], *n.* 1. an official paper giving rights or privileges to a person or business group. **Ex.** *The charter permits the bank to open an office here.* 2. an official paper which contains the aims of a group or organization. **Ex.** *He had a copy of the United Nations Charter in his office.* —*v.* 1. establish by charter. **Ex.** *The university was chartered two hundred years ago.* 2. hire for private use. **Ex.** *The group chartered a boat for the day.*

chase (3) [čeys'], *v.* 1. pursue in order to seize. **Ex.** *The police chased the thief.* 2. cause to run away. **Ex.** *The dog chased them from the house.* —*n.* act of chasing; pursuit.

chaste (5) [čeyst'], *adj.* virtuous; pure in matters relating to sex. **Ex.** *She was a chaste young woman.* —**chas'ti·ty,** *n.* state of being chaste; virginity.

chat (4) [čæt'], *v.* talk informally, in a light, familiar manner. **Ex.** *The women chatted on the telephone for an hour.* —*n.* a relaxed conversation. **Ex.** *They had a nice chat at lunch.*

chatter (5) [čæt'ər], *v.* 1. make a series of rapid, speechlike sounds that cannot be understood. **Ex.** *The squirrels chattered among themselves.* 2. talk idly and rapidly. **Ex.** *She chattered on foolishly.* —*n.* 1. light, quick noises or voices. 2. idle or foolish talk. —**chat'ter·er,** *n.*

chauffeur (5) [šow'fər, šow'fə:r'], *n.* the paid operator of a private automobile. **Ex.** *They rented a car with a chauffeur for the day.*

cheap (2) [čiyp'], *adj.* 1. inexpensive; bought or sold at a low price. **Ex.** *These are good shoes and were very cheap.* 2. poor in quality; of no great value. **Ex.** *Cheap material was used in the building.* 3. unworthy of respect. **Ex.** *He felt cheap when he considered his actions.* —**cheap'en,** *v.*

cheat (3) [čiyt'], *n.* one who does not act honestly or who deceives. **Ex.** *The boy was a cheat because he copied another student's work.* —*v.* deceive; obtain something by a trick. **Ex.** *The man was cheated out of his money by a stranger.* —**cheat'er,** *n.*

check (2) [ček'], *n.* 1. a written order, usually on a printed form, directing a bank to pay money from an account. **Ex.** *He wrote a check for the amount he owed me.* 2. a paper which shows how much is owed in a café or restaurant. **Ex.** *Ask the waiter for our check, so we can pay and leave.*

3. a mark (√) put before each thing on a list as it is examined. Ex. *He put a check before our names when he saw we were present.* —*v.* 1. examine; compare. Ex. *Check your list to see if you have forgotten anything.* 2. control; stop. Ex. *The dam checked the flow of water.* 3. leave in the care of another, in a public place. Ex. *Check your hat at the door, please.* —**check in,** place your name on a list as a guest, a member, etc. Ex. *He checked in at a good hotel.* —**check out,** pay one's bill at a hotel and leave. Ex. *He checked out of the hotel last night.*

checkbook [ček'buk'], *n.* a book of printed forms used for writing orders to a bank.

checkroom [ček'ruwm'], *n.* a room in a public place where one can leave one's hat, coat, etc.

checkup [ček'əp'], *n.* an examination to establish the condition of someone or something. Ex. *He went to his doctor for a checkup.*

cheek (3) [čiyk'], *n.* either side of the face below the eye. Ex. *She kissed him on the cheek.*

cheer (2) [či:r'], *n.* 1. a shout of approval or joy. Ex. *A cheer rose from the crowd as they heard the news.* 2. that which gives joy or gladness. Ex. *His words of cheer brought relief to the anxious people.* —*v.* 1. greet with shouts or other sounds of approval. Ex. *The crowd cheered at the football game.* 2. make glad. Ex. *His friends cheered the sick man with visits.* —**cheer'ful,** *adj.* full of cheer. —**cheer'ful·ly,** *adv.* —**cheer up,** make happy. Ex. *His funny stories cheered us up.*

cheese (3) [čiyz'], *n.* a solid food made from the thick, soft substance that separates from milk when it becomes sour. Ex. *He ate bread and cheese for lunch.*

chemical (3) [kem'ikəl], *n.* a substance made by, or used in, the science of chemistry. —*adj.* concerned with chemistry. Ex. *Creation of salt is a chemical process.* —**chem'i·cal·ly,** *adv.*

chemistry (3) [kem'əstriy], *n.* the science in which substances are studied to discover what they are made of, how they act under different conditions, and how they combine or separate to form other substances. Ex. *Plastics were developed*

a, far; æ, am; e, get; ey, late; i, in; iy, see; ɔ, all; ow, go; u, put; uw, too; ə, but, ago; ər, fur; aw, out; ay, life; oy, boy; ŋ, ring; θ, think; ð, that; ž, measure; š, ship; ǰ, edge; č, child.

through chemistry. —**chem'ist**, *n.* a person who studies and works in chemistry.

cherish (4) [čer'iš], *v.* 1. treat with love and tenderness. **Ex.** *He cherished his wife.* 2. keep in mind. **Ex.** *She cherished the memory of her parents.*

cherry (3) [čer'iy], *n.* 1. a small, round fruit, usually red, that has a small seed at its center. 2. the tree on which the fruit grows. **Ex.** *Their favorite dessert is cherry pie.*

chest (2) [čest'], *n.* 1. the upper front part of the body within the ribs. **Ex.** *With your hand on your chest, you can feel your heart beating.* 2. a box with a lid, often large and strong. **Ex.** *The carpenter took a hammer from his tool chest.*

chew (3) [čuw'], *v.* bite and crush with the teeth. **Ex.** *Dogs like to chew bones.* —**chew'y**, *adj.*

chicken (2) [čik'ən], *n.* the common farm bird raised for its eggs and meat.

CHICKEN

chief (1) [čiyf'], *n.* the head or leader of a group of people. **Ex.** *The oldest man in the tribe was the chief.* —*adj.* 1. highest in rank or authority. **Ex.** *The chief clerk will see that the work is done.* 2. most important. **Ex.** *What are the chief merits of this plan?* —**chief'ly**, *adv.* almost entirely. —**chief'tain**, *n.* a chief.

child (1) [čayld'], *n.* a baby; a young boy or girl. **Ex.** *The child is just learning to talk.* —**child'ish**, *adj.* like a child. **Ex.** *The man's behavior was childish.* —**child'ish·ness**, *n.* —**child'less**, *adj.*

childhood (1) [čayld'hud'], *n.* state or time of being a child. **Ex.** *She had a happy childhood.*

children (1) [čil'drən], *n.* more than one child. **Ex.** *All of her children are in school.*

chill (3) [čil'], *n.* feeling of coldness. **Ex.** *There is a chill in the air as winter approaches.* —*adj.* 1. rather cold. **Ex.** *A chill wind blew.* 2. without warmth of feeling. **Ex.** *He received only a chill greeting.* —*v.* 1. cool; make cold. **Ex.** *Chill the wine before serving it.* 2. cause to feel a chill. **Ex.** *The thought of the battle chilled the soldier.* —**chill'y**, *adj.*

chimney (3) [čim'niy], *n.* an outlet for smoke from a stove or furnace, especially an outlet on the roof of a building. **Ex.** *The chimney of the factory produced much smoke.*

chin (3) [čin'], *n.* the part of the face below the mouth; the point of the lower jaw. **Ex.** *Your chin moves when you speak.*

chip (4) [čip'], *n.* 1. a small piece broken or cut off something. **Ex.** *She swept up the chips from the broken cup.* 2. a place where a small piece has been broken off. **Ex.** *There is a chip on his front tooth.* —*v.* break off small pieces. **Ex.** *Do not chip the dishes when you wash them.* —**chipped,** *adj.*

chirp (5) [čərp'], *v.* make a short, sharp sound, as small birds and some insects. **Ex.** *As the sun rose, the birds began to chirp.* —*n.* a short, sharp sound.

chisel (5) [čiz'əl], *n.* a long, flat tool with a sharp edge used for cutting or shaping wood or stone. —*v.* cut with a chisel.

chivalry (5) [šiv'əlriy], *n.* the ideal qualities of a gentleman, such as honor, generosity, and bravery. **Ex.** *He was admired for his chivalry.* —**chiv'al·rous,** *adj.*

chocolate (3) [čɔk'lət], *n.* 1. a dark brown food substance made from the ground beans of a certain tree, often used in sweets and desserts. 2. candy made of chocolate. **Ex.** *He bought a box of chocolates.* —*adj.* a reddish-brown color.

choice (2) [čoys'], *n.* 1. act of selecting; the right to select. **Ex.** *The students had a choice of languages to study.* 2. thing or person selected. **Ex.** *He married the girl of his choice.*

choir (5) [kwayr'], *n.* a group of trained singers, usually in a church.

choke (3) [čowk'], *v.* 1. cause to be unable to breathe, by pressing the throat or by stopping the supply of air. **Ex.** *The murderer choked his victim.* 2. have difficulty breathing. **Ex.** *He was choking on a piece of meat.* 3. stop the growth of. **Ex.** *Weeds were choking the garden.* —**choke back,** hold back. **Ex.** *He choked back his tears and tried to smile.* —**choke up,** come close to crying. **Ex.** *He choked up but did not cry.*

choose (1) [čuwz'], *v.* make a choice; select. **Ex.** *In a democracy, the people choose their leaders.*

chop (3) [čap'], *v.* cut by striking with something sharp, as an ax. **Ex.** *He chopped down the tree.* —*n.* 1. act of chopping. 2. a slice of meat with a piece of bone in it. **Ex.** *We had lamb chops for dinner.* —**chop'py,** *adj.* rough. **Ex.** *During the storm, the sea was choppy.*

chorus (4) [kɔr'əs], *n*. 1. a group of people singing together. 2. the part of a song repeated after each verse.

chose (2) [čowz'], *v*. past tense of *choose*. **Ex.** *The teacher chose four boys to represent the class.*

chosen (2) [čow'zən], *v*. past participle of *choose*. **Ex.** *He was chosen to be leader.*

chronic (5) [kran'ik], *adj*. continuing for a long time. **Ex.** *An old person often has a chronic illness.*

chuckle (5) [čək'əl], *v*. laugh quietly. **Ex.** *He chuckled at the amusing way things were happening. —n.* soft, quiet laugh. **Ex.** *His chuckle was barely heard.*

church (1) [čərč'], *n*. a building for public worship. **Ex.** *That is the church we attend on Sunday.*

cigar (3) [sigar'], *n*. tightly packed roll of tobacco leaves for smoking.

cigarette (1) [sig'əret', sig'ərət'], *n*. finely cut tobacco in a long, thin paper tube for smoking.

cinder (5) [sin'dər], *n*. a partly burned piece of coal, wood, etc.

circle (1) [sər'kəl], *n*. 1. a closed curve that has all of its points at an equal distance from its center. 2. a group of people having the same interests. **Ex.** *She has a wide circle of friends. —v.* surround; move around in a circle. **Ex.** *The group of dancers joined hands and circled the leader.*

CIRCLE 1

circuit (4) [sər'kət], *n*. 1. act of moving, or revolving around, as in a circle. **Ex.** *The moon makes a complete circuit around the earth each month.* 2. a regular movement from place to place, as a part of one's occupation. **Ex.** *The judge made his circuit from one court to another throughout his district.* 3. the path through which an electric current flows.

circular (4) [sərk'yələr], *adj*. round like a circle; of a circle. **Ex.** *He made a circular motion with his hand. —n.* a notice or letter written or printed for general distribution. **—cir'cu·lar·ize,** *v*. send circulars to. **Ex.** *He circularized us to ask our views.*

circulate (5) [sərk'yəleyt'], *v*. 1. move in a circle or move around a path returning to the starting point. **Ex.** *The blood circulates through the body.* 2. pass from place to place or person to person. **Ex.** *The story circulated quickly.* —cir`cu·la'tion, *n.*

circumference (5) [sərkəm'f(ə)rəns], *n.* the outside line of, or distance around, a circle or any area. **Ex.** *They walked around the circumference of the lake.*

circumstances (2) [sər'kəmstæns`ez], *n.* 1. the conditions, facts, or events connected with another fact or event. **Ex.** *He explained the circumstances that caused him to be late.* 2. financial condition. **Ex.** *He lived in very comfortable circumstances.* —cir`cum·stan'tial, *adj.* having to do with the circumstances of a situation.

circus (4) [sər'kəs], *n.* a traveling show staged in a large, level space, often in a tent. **Ex.** *The children enjoyed seeing the trained animals at the circus.*

cite (5) [sayt'], *v.* 1. refer to as a proof, an example, or an illustration of an argument. **Ex.** *To prove your statement you must cite your references.* 2. summon to appear before a court. **Ex.** *He was cited for drunken driving.* 3. give honorable mention to. **Ex.** *The soldier was cited for bravery.* —ci·ta'tion, *n.*

citizen (2) [sit'əzən], *n.* a member of a country or state by birth or by law. **Ex.** *A citizen of a country enjoys certain rights and owes certain duties to it.* —cit'i·zen·ship`, *n.* having the rights and duties of a citizen.

city (1) [sit'iy], *n.* any important, large town. **Ex.** *Paris is the largest city in France.*

city hall [sit'iy hɔ:l'], *n.* the building in which a city government is located.

civil (3) [siv'əl], *adj.* 1. of or relating to citizens and to their rights and affairs. **Ex.** *Exercising civil rights is important in a democracy.* 2. well-mannered; gentlemanly. **Ex.** *He received a civil answer to his question.* —ci·vil'ian, *n.* a person not in the military forces. —**civil service**, that group of non-military people who work for the government. —**civil war**, war within a country between groups of citizens.

civilization (3) [siv`ələzey'šən], *n.* 1. culture and manner of living of a people, period, or nation. **Ex.** *Modern civilization is strongly influenced by science.* 2. the relative progress in government, art, education, etc., that a nation or

a, far; æ, am; e, get; ey, late; i, in; iy, see; ɔ, all; ow, go; u, put; uw, too; ə, but, ago; ər, fur; aw, out; ay, life; oy, boy; ŋ, ring; θ, think; ð, that; ž, measure; š, ship; ǰ, edge; č, child.

people has made. **Ex.** *The ancient Romans reached a high degree of civilization.* —**civ'i·lize,** v. bring to a higher state of culture.

claim (2) [kleym'], v. 1. ask for or demand something as belonging to one. **Ex.** *He claimed a share of the family property.* 2. state as fact. **Ex.** *She claimed that she was the best student in the class.* —n. 1. a demand for something that belongs to one. **Ex.** *He submitted a claim to his insurance company.* 2. a title or right to something. **Ex.** *He has no claim to special attention.* 3. something claimed, especially land. **Ex.** *The settler put a wooden marker at each corner of his claim.* —**claim'ant,** n.

clam (5) [klæm'], n. an animal from the sea enclosed in a hard double shell. **Ex.** *Some clams are good to eat, either raw or cooked.*

clamor (5) [klæm'ər], n. continual shouting and noise. **Ex.** *The speaker could hardly be heard above the clamor of the crowd.* —v. demand noisily. **Ex.** *The children clamored for candy.*

clan (5) [klæn'], n. a group of families related by blood. **Ex.** *The people living in that valley are all members of one clan.* —**clan'nish,** adj. acting as if of one clan. **Ex.** *The families on the street are very clannish.*

clang (5) [klæŋ'], n. a loud, ringing sound like that of a bell. **Ex.** *We heard the clang of the dinner bell.*

clap (4) [klæp'], v. 1. strike the hands together to show approval or enjoyment. **Ex.** *The audience clapped after the speech.* 2. put or place suddenly. **Ex.** *She clapped her hand over her mouth.* —n. 1. the striking of the hands together. 2. a loud noise. **Ex.** *A clap of thunder followed the lightning.*

clarify (5) [klær'əfay`, kler'əfay`], v. make or become clearer. **Ex.** *The answer to his question helped to clarify the problem.* —**clar'i·fi·ca'tion,** n.

clash (4) [klæš'], n. 1. a loud, unpleasant noise, often of metal striking against metal. **Ex.** *A clash was heard as the cars crashed.* 2. opposition; conflict. **Ex.** *There is a clash of views about the election.* —v. 1. hit with a clash. 2. conflict. **Ex.** *Their opinions always clashed.*

clasp (3) [klæsp'], n. 1. a grasping of hands in a handshake; an embrace. 2. a hook or catch used to fasten two things together. **Ex.** *The clasp on her string of pearls is made of* *silver.* —*v.* hold tightly in the arms; hold hands tightly. **Ex.** *The dancers clasped hands and formed a circle.*

class (1) [klæs'], *n.* 1. a group of persons or things similar to one another. **Ex.** *He is a member of the working class.* 2. a group of students taught together. **Ex.** *He and she were in the same English class.* 3. a division based on grade or quality. **Ex.** *Very few of the passengers are traveling first class.* —*v.* put in a group; classify.

classic (4) [klæs'ik], *n.* a work, especially of music, literature, or art, of great excellence. **Ex.** *That book is considered to be a classic.* —**clas'si·cal,** *adj.*

classify (5) [klæs'əfay'], *v.* arrange in classes or groups. **Ex.** *They classified the children according to age.* —**clas`si·fi·ca' tion,** *n.*

clatter (5) [klæt'ər], *n.* crashing, clashing sounds. **Ex.** *The clatter of dishes was heard from the kitchen.* —*v.* move with or make a clatter. **Ex.** *The horse's shoes clattered on the stones.*

clause (5) [klɔ:z'], *n.* 1. a part of a sentence which has a subject and verb of its own. **Ex.** *In the sentence, "I knew him when he was a boy," the clause, "when he was a boy," depends on the clause "I knew him."* 2. a separate article in a contract, law, etc. **Ex.** *The first clause in the law explained its purpose.*

claw (4) [klɔ:'], *n.* a sharp, hooked nail on the foot of a bird or animal. **Ex.** *The cat scratched the chair with her claws.* —*v.* tear or scratch. **Ex.** *The lion clawed its trainer.*

clay (3) [kley'], *n.* a kind of stiff, muddy earth that hardens after drying. **Ex.** *Clay is used to make bricks.*

clean (1) [kliyn'], *adj.* free from dirt. **Ex.** *The windows were very clean.* —*v.* make free from dirt. **Ex.** *She cleaned the floor with soap and water.* —**clean'er,** *n.* a person or thing that cleans.

clear (1) [kli:r'], *adj.* 1. easily understood; plain. **Ex.** *His explanation was clear.* 2. bright; uncloudy. **Ex.** *The sky is clear today.* 3. free from doubt; certain. **Ex.** *It was a clear case of murder.* 4. free of anything that might block. **Ex.** *The road is clear.* —*v.* 1. remove persons or things; empty. **Ex.** *She clears the table after meals.* 2. prove or declare innocent. **Ex.** *The lawyer's defense cleared the accused man.* 3. become clear. **Ex.** *The weather will clear in the after-*

noon. —**clear'ance, clear'ness,** *n.* —**clear'ly,** *adv.* —**clear'ing,** *n.* land where there are no trees. —**clear out,** make a cleared place. **Ex.** *He cleared out the room.* —**clear up,** 1. make clear or plain. **Ex.** *He cleared up the mystery.* 2. make neat. **Ex.** *He cleared up the room.*

clench (5) [klenč'], *v.* press closely together. **Ex.** *She clenched her teeth in pain.*

clergy (4) [klər'jiy], *n.* the men who serve a church as ministers or priests. **Ex.** *Members of the clergy are serious students of religion.* —**cler'i·cal,** *adj.* relating to the clergy.

clerk (3) [klərk'], *n.* an office worker who keeps records, writes letters, etc.; a salesman or saleswoman in a store. **Ex.** *The file clerk put the papers in the cabinet.* —*v.* act of work as a clerk, especially in a store. **Ex.** *She clerks in a department store.* —**cler'i·cal,** *adj.* relating to office clerks or their work.

clever (2) [klev'ər], *adj.* 1. quick-thinking; intelligent. **Ex.** *The clever boy quickly understood the problem.* 2. skillful. **Ex.** *I wish I were clever enough to make my own furniture.* —**clev'er·ly,** *adv.* —**clev'er·ness,** *n.*

click (4) [klik'], *n.* a light, sharp sound like that of a key turning in a lock. **Ex.** *We heard the click of a woman's shoes on the sidewalk.* —*v.* make or cause to click.

client (4) [klay'ənt], *n.* one who employs the services of a professional man, especially of a lawyer. **Ex.** *The lawyer advised his client to complain.*

cliff (4) [klif'], *n.* high, steep rock. **Ex.** *He was hurt in a fall from a cliff.*

climate (2) [klay'mət], *n.* The general weather conditions of a place over a period of time. **Ex.** *The doctor advised a move to a warm, dry climate.* —**cli·mat'ic,** *adj.*

climax (5) [klay'mæks'], *n.* the strongest idea or event in a series; the point of most interest or excitement in a story. **Ex.** *The climax of the story occurred when the hero died.*

climb (2) [klaym'], *v.* 1. go up or down something by using the feet and sometimes the hands. **Ex.** *To reach the roof he climbed a ladder.* 2. grow upward. **Ex.** *The vine climbed the wall.*

cling (4) [kliŋ'], *v.* stick to; hold tightly. **Ex.** *Mud is clinging to your shoes.*

clip (4) [klip'], *v.* cut short; cut off or out. **Ex.** *The barber* *clipped the boy's hair.* —**clip'pers,** *n.* a tool for cutting or trimming. —**clip'ping,** *n.* that which is cut off or out.

clip (4) [klip'], *n.* a device used to fasten things together. **Ex.** *The papers were fastened together with a clip.* —*v.* fasten or clasp together.

cloak (5) [klowk'], *n.* 1. a long, loose outer garment with or without sleeves. 2. that which hides or conceals like a cloak. **Ex.** *He used fine words as a cloak for his bad actions.*

clock (1) [klak'], *n.* a device which measures and shows time. —**clock'wise,** in the direction clock hands move.

CLOCK

close (1) [klows'], *adj.* near in space, time, or thought. **Ex.** *The school is close to my house.* —*adv.* in a close position or manner. **Ex.** *We walked close to the wall.* —**close call,** something that almost happened. **Ex.** *He had a close call when the wall fell near him.*

close (1) [klowz'], *v.* 1. shut. **Ex.** *Close the door.* 2. come to an end. **Ex.** *The store closed because it sold very few things.* —*n.* the end. **Ex.** *At the close of the meeting, everyone left.*

closet (3) [klaz'ət], *n.* an enclosed space for storing things. **Ex.** *He kept all his clothes in one closet.*

cloth (1) [klɔ:θ'], *n.* material made from the threads of cotton, wool, silk, etc. **Ex.** *She bought cloth for a dress.*

clothe (2) [klowð'], *v.* provide with clothes. **Ex.** *The Red Cross helps to clothe people in need.*

clothes (1) [klowz', klowðz'], *n., pl.* garments for the body. **Ex.** *Suits, coats, etc. are clothes.* —**cloth'ing,** *n.* garments of any type. **Ex.** *He needs winter clothing.*

cloud (1) [klawd'], *n.* 1. a mass of tiny drops of water floating in the air. **Ex.** *The sun is hidden by a cloud.* 2. mass of steam, smoke, or dust. **Ex.** *A cloud of dust arose as the horseman passed.* —**cloud'y, cloud'less,** *adj.* —**cloud'i·ness,** *n.*

clover (5) [klow'vər], *n.* small, low-growing plant with three leaves. **Ex.** *Cows like clover.*

club (2) [kləb'], *n.* 1. a group of persons associated for a common purpose. **Ex.** *She belongs to the garden club.* 2. a heavy wood stick; a weapon. **Ex.** *A policeman usually carries a club.* —*v.* beat with a club.

a, far; æ, am; e, get; ey, late; i, in; iy, see; ɔ, all; ow, go; u, put; uw, too; ə, but, ago; ər, fur; aw, out; ay, life; oy, boy; ŋ, ring; θ, think; ð, that; ž, measure; š, ship; ǰ, edge; č, child.

clue (5) [kluw'], *n.* anything that leads to the solution of a problem or a mystery. *Ex. The police found no clues.*

clumsy (4) [kləm'ziy], *adj.* awkward; without grace. *Ex. The boy was a clumsy dancer.* —**clum'si·ly,** *adv.* —**clum'si·ness,** *n.*

cluster (4) [kləs'tər], *n.* similar things growing or grouped together. *Ex. A cluster of men and women waited at the door.* —*v.* gather together. *Ex. They clustered around the fire.*

clutch (4) [kləč'], *v.* 1. seize or grip tightly. *Ex. He clutched the knife.* 2. try to reach and grasp. *Ex. She clutched at the railing as she fell.* —**clutch'es,** *n., pl.,* control or power. *Ex. The man was in the clutches of a moneylender.*

co- (3) [kow], *prefix.* 1. together with; at the same time. *Ex. He is a co-worker.* 2. equal. *Ex. He is a co-owner of the house.*

coach (3) [kowč'], *n.* 1. a large, closed carriage, usually pulled by horses. *Ex. The king came to the ceremony in a coach.* 2. a railroad passenger car. 3. a teacher of sports. —*v.* teach. *Ex. His father coached him in English.*

coal (2) [kowl'], *n.* 1. a black, hard substance that burns and gives off heat. 2. a piece of burning substance. *Ex. A coal fell from the stove and burned the rug.*

coarse (3) [kɔrs'], *adj.* 1. relatively large pieces; not fine. *Ex. The path was covered with coarse sand.* 2. rough to the touch. *Ex. Her dress was made of coarse wool.* 3. lacking good manners; indelicate. *Ex. His conversation was coarse.* —**coars'en,** *v.* make coarse; become coarse. *Ex. Hard work coarsened her hands.*

coast (2) [kowst'], *n.* the seashore; the land next to the sea. *Ex. His house is on the coast.* —*v.* slide or glide down a hill. —**coast'al,** *adj.* near the seashore.

coat (1) [kowt'], *n.* 1. an outer garment with sleeves. 2. the hair or fur of an animal. *Ex. The dog's coat was dirty.* 3. a covering or outside layer. *Ex. The house needs a coat of paint.* —*v.* cover with something. *Ex. The table is coated with dust.*

coax (4) [kowks'], *v.* ask gently and repeatedly for something. *Ex. The children coaxed their parents to let them play.* —**coax'ing,** *adj.* —**coax'ing·ly,** *adv.*

cock (5) [kak'], *n.* the male of various birds, especially of chickens. *Ex. The cock crows at dawn.* —*v.* tilt to one side. *Ex. His hat was cocked over one eye.*

cockpit [kak'pit], *n.* in a small plane, the place where the pilot and sometimes passengers sit; in a large plane, the place where the pilot, co-pilot, and crew sit.

cocktail [kak'teyl], *n.* a mixed drink made with liquor.

cocoa (5) [kow'kow`], *n.* 1. a powder made from the ground beans of a certain tree and having a chocolate flavor. 2. a hot drink made by mixing this powder with milk, water, and sugar.

code (4) [kowd'], *n.* 1. any system of laws or rules. **Ex.** *The city building code limits the height of new buildings.* 2. a system of signals for sending messages. **Ex.** *The sailors used flags to send a message in code.* 3. a system of words used to send secret messages. —*v.* put into the symbols of a code.

coffee (2) [kɔ:f'iy], *n.* a drink made from the roasted and ground seeds of a certain plant. **Ex.** *He likes to drink hot coffee.*

coffin (5) [kɔ:f'ən], *n.* a box in which a dead person is buried. **Ex.** *They lowered the coffin into the grave.*

coil (4) [koyl'], *v.* wind in the shape of circles. **Ex.** *The snake coiled itself around the man's arm.* —*n.* circle, or series of circles, made by winding something around and around. **Ex.** *The sailor made a coil of rope.*

COIL

coin (2) [koyn'], *n.* a piece of metal marked and issued by government authority for use as money. **Ex.** *She had several coins in her purse.* —**coin'age,** *n.* act of making coins.

coincide (5) [kow`insayd], *v.* 1. correspond exactly; agree. **Ex.** *Their stories of what happened coincide.* 2. occur at the same time or occupy the same place. **Ex.** *His arrival and my departure coincided.* —**co·in'ci·dence,** *n.* a chance occurrence of two or more events at the same time. —**co·in`ci·den'tal,** *adj.*

cold (1) [kowld'], *adj.* 1. low in temperature; not warm. **Ex.** *Winter nights are cold.* 2. experiencing a feeling of cold. **Ex.** *He was cold without his coat.* 3. unemotional; unfriendly. **Ex.** *He is a cold person.* —*n.* 1. low temperature; lack of heat. **Ex.** *She suffered from the cold.* 2. a common illness that affects the throat and nose. —**cold'ly,** *adv.* —**cold'ness,** *n.*

cold-blooded [kowld`bləd'əd], *adj.* lacking in feeling. **Ex.** *He is a cold-blooded killer.*

cold war [kowld' wɔ:r'], strong differences between countries, without actual war.

collapse (4) [kəlæps'], v. 1. fall to pieces; fall down. Ex. *The roof of the house collapsed.* 2. fold into a smaller space. Ex. *He collapsed the umbrella when the rain stopped.* —n. act of collapsing; failure. Ex. *The collapse of the company ruined him.* —**col·laps'i·ble**, adj.

collar (3) [kal'ər], n. 1. the part of a shirt, coat, or dress that is around the neck. Ex. *He buttoned his collar.* 2. a leather neckpiece worn by a dog or horse. Ex. *He tied a rope to the dog's collar.*

colleague (5) [kal'iyg'], n. an associate in office or professional work. Ex. *His colleagues gave him a gift when he retired.*

collect (2) [kəlekt'], v. 1. bring together. Ex. *The teacher always collects the homework.* 2. demand and obtain payment of. Ex. *Income taxes are collected yearly.* 3. come together. Ex. *The people collected in the market place.* —**col·lec'tion**, n. the things collected. —**col·lec'tor**, n. a person who collects. —**col·lec'tive**, adj. as a group. Ex. *We made a collective effort to finish the work.* —**col·lec'tive·ly**, adv.

college (1) [kal'ij], n. an educational institution beyond high school, often one of several schools forming a university. Ex. *He has been to high school but not to college.* —**col·le'gi·an**, n. a college student. —**col·le'gi·ate**, adj.

colonel (3) [kər'nəl], n. an army officer above the rank of major and below the rank of general. Ex. *While the colonel was away, the major was in charge of the men.*

colony (2) [kal'əniy], n. 1. a group of people who form a settlement in a new land but remain under the rule of their native country. Ex. *In 1607, the English established a colony in North America.* 2. a group of people in the same occupation or with the same interests. Ex. *There is a colony of artists near the seashore.* 3. a group of animals, plants, etc. living in one place. —**col'o·nist**, n. —**col'o·nize**, v. —**co·lo'ni·al**, adj.

color (1) [kəl'ər], n. 1. the effect of light on the eye. Ex. *Everything we see has color.* 2. appearance; look. Ex. *He had a healthy color after his vacation.* 3. coloring matter; paint. Ex. *You have a pleasing color on your walls.* —v. put color on; paint. Ex. *The child was coloring a picture book.* —**col'or·ful, col'or·less**, adj.

color-blind [kəl'ərblaynd`], *adj.* not able to see color or certain colors.

colossal (5) [kəlas'əl], *adj.* huge; enormous. **Ex.** *There are colossal mountains in the north.*

colt (4) [kowlt'], *n.* a young horse. **Ex.** *The colt followed its mother.*

column (3) [kal'əm], *n.* 1. an upright support or decoration for a building. 2. anything suggesting an upright support. **Ex.** *A column of smoke rose from the campfire.* 3. a line of soldiers or ships, one behind another. 4. the printed sections of a page of a book, newspaper, or magazine. 5. articles appearing regularly in a newspaper, usually by the same author. **Ex.** *That writer has an interesting daily column.* —**col'um·nist**, *n.* one who writes a column for a newspaper.

COLUMN 1

comb (2) [kowm'], *n.* an instrument used for smoothing and arranging the hair. —*v.* arrange the hair with a comb. **Ex.** *The girl combed her hair.*

combat (4) [kəm'bæt'], *v.* fight; struggle; oppose. **Ex.** *The candidate for mayor promises to combat crime.*

COMB

combat (4) [kam'bæt`], *n.* a battle. **Ex.** *The soldier was wounded in combat.* —**com·bat'ant**, *n.* one who fights.

combine (2) [kəmbayn'], *v.* mix; bring together. **Ex.** *The color blue can be combined with yellow to make green.* —**com·bi·na'tion**, *n.* something made by mixing two or more things together.

come (1) [kəm'], *v.* 1. move toward; approach. **Ex.** *Come here.* 2. arrive. **Ex.** *When did you come to this town?* 3. take or have its place in a series. **Ex.** *Six comes after five.* 4. be related to. **Ex.** *Jack comes from a good family.* 5. be caused by; the result of. **Ex.** *Success often comes from hard work.* 6. available. **Ex.** *This hat comes in three colors.* 7. extend; reach. **Ex.** *Her dress comes to her ankles.* —**come about,** happen. **Ex.** *How did it come about?* —**come over,** happen to. **Ex.** *What came over you?* —**come to**, become conscious. **Ex.** *The water helped him to come to.* —**come up**, be mentioned. **Ex.** *The matter came up as we talked.*

comedy (4) [kam'ədiy], *n.* a light and amusing play or movie with a happy ending. —**co·me'di·an**, *n.* 1. an actor in a comedy. 2. a performer who amuses people by doing or saying funny things.

comet (5) [kam'ət], *n.* a bright body seen in the sky, usually with a tail of light. **Ex.** *Comets move around the sun.*

comfort (2) [kəm'fərt], *v.* cheer; give strength and hope. **Ex.** *The mother comforted her crying child.* —*n.* 1. consolation. **Ex.** *Her children were a great comfort to the widow.* 2. freedom from pain or worries. **Ex.** *She lived in comfort with her parents.* —**com'fort·a·ble**, *adj.*

command (2) [kəmænd'], *v.* 1. order. **Ex.** *He commanded the soldiers to fire.* 2. have authority over. **Ex.** *That officer commands a ship.* —*n.* 1. order; direction. **Ex.** *The soldiers obeyed commands.* 2. control. **Ex.** *He is in command of the situation.* —**com·mand'ment**, *n.* a law.

commence (4) [kəmens'], start; begin. **Ex.** *The school day commences with physical exercises.* —**com·mence'ment**, *n.* 1. a beginning. 2. the ceremony at which a school or college gives degrees.

commend (5) [kəmend'], *v.* praise. **Ex.** *The student was commended for his good work.* —**com·mend'a·ble**, *adj.* —**com'·men··da'tion**, *n.*

comment (3) [ka'ment'], *n.* words spoken or written, that express an opinion or explain. **Ex.** *His comments about the book were favorable.* —*v.* make remarks. **Ex.** *Everyone commented on her new dress.* —**com'men·ta'tor**, *n.* one who comments.

commerce (3) [ka'mərs], *n.* trade; buying and selling, especially on a large scale and between different places. **Ex.** *He is engaged in commerce.* —**com·mer'cial**, *adj.* —**com·mer'cial·ize**, *v.*

commission (3) [kəmiš'ən], *n.* 1. a group of individuals entrusted with certain business or public duties. **Ex.** *He was appointed to the commission studying health problems.* 2. the authority by which one holds, or acts in, a position of responsibility. **Ex.** *He has received a commission as a naval officer.* —*v.* give a commission or appoint to do. **Ex.** *The artist was commissioned to paint a picture.*

commissioner (3) [kəmiš'ənər], *n.* the chief of a government department of public service. **Ex.** *The commissioner of education was once a schoolteacher.*

commit (3) [kəmit'], *v.* 1. give in trust; place in the charge of. **Ex.** *The boy was committed to the care of his aunt.* 2. do something bad. **Ex.** *He committed a robbery.* —**com·mit' ment**, *n.* a promise; pledge.

committee (2) [kəmit'iy], *n.* a group of people appointed to do a certain thing. **Ex.** *A committee was formed to plan the new school.*

commodity (4) [kəmad'ətiy], *n.* a thing that is useful or of value, especially an article of commerce or trade. **Ex.** *Rice and sugar are commodities.*

common (2) [kam'ən], *adj.* 1. shared by all of a group. **Ex.** *Our common interest in art brought us together.* 2. often found or experienced. **Ex.** *White flowers are very common.* 3. ordinary; not special. **Ex.** *The package was wrapped in common brown paper.* —**com'mon·ly**, *adv.* —**commonplace**, *adj.* usual; frequent; ordinary. —**common sense**, practical intelligence.

communicate (3) [kəmyuwn'əkeyt'], *v.* 1. make known; give information. **Ex.** *Radio, television, and newspapers quickly communicate news to all parts of the world.* 2. pass from one person to another. **Ex.** *How is this disease communicated?* —**com·mu'ni·ca·ble**, *adj.* readily passed to others. **Ex.** *A cold is a very communicable disease.*

communication (3) [kəmyuwn'əkey'šən], *n.* 1. exchange of information, ideas, etc. **Ex.** *Communication is difficult when people do not speak the same language.* 2. the news, message, or information sent. **Ex.** *We received your communication.* 3. the various means, or ways, of communicating. **Ex.** *Communications were interrupted by the storm.*

communism (4) [kam'yaniz'am], *n.* a system and program of common ownership of the means for producing goods and services and governmental control of economic and political activities. **Ex.** *Communism is the system of the Soviet Union.* —**com'mu·nist**, *n.* one who believes in communism. —**com' mu·nist, com·mu·nis'tic**, *adj.*

community (2) [kəmyuwn'ətiy], *n.* a group of people living in a particular city, town, etc. **Ex.** *Our community has its own library.*

compact (4) [kəmpækt', kam'pækt'], *adj.* 1. packed tightly together. **Ex.** *The saleswoman tied the customer's purchases into a compact bundle.* 2. brief; without unnecessary words. **Ex.** *His report was clear and compact.*

companion (2) [kəmpæn'yən], *n.* a person who goes with another; a friend; an associate. **Ex.** *They were companions on the journey.* —**com·pan'ion·ship,** *n.* friendship.

company (1) [kəm'pəniy], *n.* 1. a business. **Ex.** *He is the president of a manufacturing company.* 2. the state or condition of being companions. **Ex.** *The boy was good company on the long trip.*

compare (2) [kəmpe:r'], *v.* 1. examine similarities or differences. **Ex.** *She compared the ideas to see if they agreed.* 2. consider or describe as the same or equal to. **Ex.** *The quality of these two coats cannot be compared.* —**com'pa·ra·ble,** *adj.* of approximately the same kind; equal to. **Ex.** *This metal is comparable to steel in strength.* —**com·par'a·tive,** *adj.* relative; nearly the same. **Ex.** *After many hardships, he now lives in comparative ease.*

comparison (2) [kəmper'əsən], *n.* an examination to learn similarities or differences. **Ex.** *A comparison was made between the two machines to learn which would be more effective.*

compass (3) [kəm'pəs], *n.* 1. an instrument for determining directions, having a needle which always points north. 2. an instrument for drawing circles and for measuring distances.

COMPASS 2

compel (2) [kəmpel'], *v.* force. **Ex.** *My sense of duty compels me to do this.*

compensate (4) [kam'pənseyt'], *v.* 1. repay; substitute for. **Ex.** *Nothing can compensate for the loss of his mother.* 2. pay. **Ex.** *We will compensate you for your work.* —**com'pen·sa'tion,** *n.*

compete (3) [kəmpiyt'], *v.* be in rivalry for. **Ex.** *The three men competed for the prize.* —**com'pe·ti'tion,** *n.* the act of competing for. —**com·pet'i·tor,** *n.* one who competes. —**com·pet'i·tive,** *adj.*

competence (3) [kam'pətəns], *n.* ability. **Ex.** *Her competence as a teacher is known to everyone at the school.*

competent (3) [kam'pətənt], *adj.* capable; skillful. **Ex.** *He is a competent doctor.* —**com'pe·tent·ly,** *adv.*

complain (2) [kəmpleyn'], *v.* 1. express pain, dissatisfaction, annoyance, etc. **Ex.** *He complains about having to work late.*

2. report a wrong. Ex. *He complained to the police about the noise in his neighborhood.* —**com·plaint'**, *n.* **com·plain' ant**, *n.* one who makes a complaint, as in court.

complete (1) [kəmpliyt'], *adj.* 1. whole; full. Ex. *We bought a complete set of dishes.* 2. ended or finished. Ex. *The book is not complete.* 3. absolute. Ex. *We have complete trust in you.* —*v.* finish; bring to an end. Ex. *They completed the journey.* —**com·plete'ly**, *adv.* —**com·plete'ness**, **com·ple' tion**, *n.*

complex (3) [kəmpleks', kam'pleks`], *adj.* made of many parts that are difficult to understand; not simple; complicated. Ex. *The engine of an airplane is very complex.* —**com· plex'ity**, *n.*

complexion (5) [kəmplek'šən], *n.* 1. appearance and color of the skin, in particular of the face. Ex. *He had a healthy complexion.* 2. general appearance; nature. Ex. *Machines have changed the complexion of modern life.*

complicate (3) [kam'pləkeyt`], *v.* make or become complex or difficult. Ex. *Machines improve but also complicate life.* —**com'pli·ca'tion**, *n.* —**com'pli·cat`ed**, *adj.*

compliment (4) [kam'pləmənt], *n.* an expression of praise or admiration. Ex. *The girl enjoyed the compliment.* —*v.* praise or express approval. Ex. *He complimented her on her voice.* —**com`pli·men'tary**, *adj.* praising or admiring.

compose (3) [kəmpowz'], *v.* 1. combine to form. Ex. *This substance is composed of many chemicals.* 2. calm oneself. Ex. *He composed himself after the accident.* 3. write; create. Ex. *He composes beautiful music.* —**com·pos'er**, *n.* the one who composes. —**com'po·si'tion**, *n.* that which is composed, especially a piece of writing or music.

compound (3) [kam'pawnd`], *n.* 1. a mixture; anything made of two or more parts. 2. a chemical substance of two or more elements. Ex. *Salt is a compound of two chemical elements.* —*adj.* made of two parts or more. Ex. *"Horseback" is a compound word.*

comprehend (5) [kam`prihend'], *v.* understand. Ex. *She cannot comprehend the problem.* —**com`pre·hen'si·ble**, *adj.* capable of being understood. Ex. *This poem is not comprehensible.* —**com`pre·hen'sive**, *adj.* complete; including much.

---

a, far; æ, am; e, get; ey, late; i, in; iy, see; ɔ, all; ow, go; u, put; uw, too; ə, but, ago; ər, fur; aw, out; ay, life; oy, boy; ŋ, ring; θ, think; ð, that; ł, measure; š, ship; ǰ, edge; č, child.

Ex. *He gave a comprehensive description of the criminal.*
—com`pre·hen'sion, *n.*

compress (5) [kəmpres'], *v.* press into a small size. Ex. *The clay was compressed into brick.* —com·pres'sion, *n.* —com·pres'sor, *n.*

compromise (4) [kam'prəmayz`], *n.* the settlement of an argument by each side yielding some of what it wants. Ex. *The disagreement about the boundary between the two countries was settled by compromise.* —*v.* resolve by compromise.

compute (5) [kəmpyuwt'], *v.* determine by mathematics. Ex. *He is computing his yearly taxes.* —com·pu'ter, *n.* 1. a person who determines an amount by mathematics. 2. a machine which performs mathematical operations, especially by electricity and at a high speed. Ex. *He used a computer to solve the problem.*

comrade (3) [kam'ræd`], *n.* companion; good friend. Ex. *They were comrades at school.*

conceal (3) [kənsiyl'], *v.* 1. hide. Ex. *He concealed himself behind a large tree.* 2. keep secret. Ex. *Nothing could conceal the facts.* —con·ceal'ment, *n.*

concede (5) [kənsiyd`], *v.* 1. admit as true or just in a dispute. Ex. *We concede your rights to this property.* 2. yield. Ex. *The employer conceded to the workers' demand for more pay.* —con·cess'ion, *n.*

conceit (5) [kənsiyt'], *n.* flattering judgment of oneself. Ex. *Her conceit about her beauty angered many people.* —con·ceit'ed, *adj.*

conceive (3) [kənsiyv'], *v.* 1. invent; think of and develop an idea. Ex. *The criminal conceived a plan for stealing the money.* 2. understand. Ex. *I cannot conceive how he did such a foolish thing.* —con·ceiv'a·ble, *adj.*

concentrate (4) [kan'səntreyt`], *v.* 1. give one's whole attention to. Ex. *You must concentrate on your work.* 2. gather together closely. Ex. *Large numbers of people concentrate in cities.* —con`cen·tra'tion, *n.* deep thought and close attention.

concept (4) [kan'sept`], *n.* a notion; an idea. Ex. *The judge had a clear concept of justice.* —con·cep'tion, *n.* 1. the act of conceiving an idea. 2. an idea concerning. Ex. *He has no conception of what it is like to be a doctor.* 3. beginning of pregnancy.

concern (2) [kənsərn'], v. 1. relate to; interest. **Ex.** *The election of officials should concern every citizen.* 2. trouble; worry. **Ex.** *Their son's trouble concerned them greatly.* —n. 1. matter or affair of importance to one. **Ex.** *The situation is of great concern to me.* 2. anxiety; great care. **Ex.** *She expressed concern for their safety.* 3. a business firm. **Ex.** *From what concern do you usually buy farm equipment?* —con·cer'ning, *prep.* regarding.

concert (3) [kan'sərt], n. a musical performance. **Ex.** *We listened to a piano concert.*

concerted (3) [kənsərt'ed], *adj.* agreed upon; together. **Ex.** *They all made a concerted effort to win.*

concession (5) [kənseš'ən], n. the act of yielding or admitting as true. **Ex.** *To reach agreement, both sides must make concessions.*

conclude (2) [kənkluwd'], v. 1. finish; end. **Ex.** *The president concluded the meeting with an announcement.* 2. arrange; settle; reach an agreement. **Ex.** *The two countries concluded an economic agreement.* 3. decide. **Ex.** *He concluded that they had gone.*

conclusion (3) [kənkluw'žən], n. 1. the end; the final part. **Ex.** *At the conclusion of the talk, we asked questions.* 2. a reasoned judgment. **Ex.** *He thought about the problem carefully before reaching a conclusion.* —con·clu'sive, *adj.*

concrete (4) [kan'kriyt`], n. building material made by mixing crushed stone, cement, and water. **Ex.** *The workmen poured the concrete for the road.* —adj. 1. real; specific. **Ex.** *The professor supported each statement with a concrete example.* 2. made of concrete.

condemn (3) [kəndem'], v. 1. say a person or thing is bad. **Ex.** *Do not condemn me just because I do not agree with you.* 2. judge guilty; sentence. **Ex.** *The judge condemned the man to ten years in prison.* 3. declare not suitable or fit for use. **Ex.** *The building was condemned as too dangerous to occupy.* —con`dem·na'tion, *n.*

condense (3) [kəndens'], v. 1. reduce to fewer words. **Ex.** *Many books are condensed to save the reader time.* 2. concentrate; make more compact. **Ex.** *They condensed the work of three days into two.* 3. reduce from a gas or vapor to a liquid. **Ex.** *The cold condensed the steam into water.* —con`den·sa'tion, *n.*

condition (1) [kəndiš'ən], n. 1. state of a person or thing. **Ex.**

The road was in good condition. 2. state of affairs or circumstances. **Ex.** *Economic conditions are not favorable now.* —*v.* put into order or good condition for use. **Ex.** *Please condition the car for a long trip.* —**on condition that,** provided that.

conduct (2) [kan'dəktˋ], *n.* the way one acts; behavior. **Ex.** *Her conduct in school was poor.*

conduct (2) [kəndəktˈ], *v.* 1. behave; act. **Ex.** *He conducted himself well.* 2. guide; lead. **Ex.** *The teacher conducted his students through the museum.* 3. manage; direct. **Ex.** *He conducted the meeting well.* 4. serve as a channel for heat, electricity, etc. **Ex.** *Pipes conducted heat through the building.* —**con·duc'tor,** *n.* 1. leader of an orchestra, chorus, band, etc. 2. person who collects fares on a train or streetcar. 3. something through which heat or electricity will pass.

cone (5) [kownˈ], *n.* 1. a form that narrows from a circular base to a point. 2. anything cone-shaped. **Ex.** *Children like ice cream cones.* 3. the fruit of the pine tree and some other trees which is shaped like a cone.

CONE 1

confer (3) [kənfə:rˈ], *v.* 1. grant; give. **Ex.** *The school conferred a high honor upon the scientist.* 2. meet to discuss; exchange opinions. **Ex.** *The principal conferred with the teachers.* —**conˈfer·ence,** *n.* a meeting for discussion purposes. **Ex.** *The President met with newsmen for a conference.*

confess (3) [kənfesˈ], *v.* 1. admit a crime or tell one's faults. **Ex.** *He confessed that he had stolen the money.* 2. admit what one really thinks. **Ex.** *I confess I do not like this city.* —**con·fes'sion,** *n.* 1. act of confessing. 2. a statement, especially written, of something confessed.

confide (5) [kənfaydˈ], *v.* 1. tell in trust. **Ex.** *He confides in his wife.* 2. entrust or commit to. **Ex.** *He confided the child to his mother's care.*

confidence (2) [kan'fədəns], *n.* 1. complete trust. **Ex.** *She has confidence in her daughter.* 2. self-reliance; a belief in one's own ability. **Ex.** *She has confidence in herself.* —**con'fi·denˈtial,** *adj.* secret. —**in confidence,** in secret. **Ex.** *I told him that in confidence.*

confident (2) [kan'fədənt], *adj.* sure; certain. **Ex.** *He is confident he will succeed.*

confine (3) [kənfaynˈ], *v.* keep within limits. **Ex.** *Confine your-*

self to the facts when you tell the story. —con·fine'ment, *n.*

confirm (3) [kənfərm'], *v.* 1. strengthen; make sure. **Ex.** *The new facts confirmed his opinion.* 2. assure the truth of. **Ex.** *He would not confirm the report.* —con·firmed', *adj.* established in one's habits. **Ex.** *He was a confirmed smoker.* —con`fir·ma'tion, *n.*

conflict (3) [kənflikt'], *v.* be in opposition to. **Ex.** *His ideas conflict with mine.*

conflict (3) [kan'flikt`], *n.* 1. a fight; a battle, especially a long one. 2. a sharp contest of opposing opinions or ideas. **Ex.** *The conflict was over who should lead the people.*

conform (5) [kənfɔrm'], *v.* 1. obey. **Ex.** *A citizen is expected to conform to the laws of his country.* 2. become or make similar; agree. **Ex.** *Children like to conform to the customs of their group.* —con·form'i·ty, *n.*

confuse (3) [kənfyuwz'], *v.* 1. produce a mental condition in which one is unable to decide or act. **Ex.** *The complicated directions confused me.* 2. mistake one person or thing for another. **Ex.** *He confused me with my brother.* —con·fu'sion, *n.*

congratulate (4) [kəngræč'əleyt`], *v.* express pleasure to a person on his success or good fortune. **Ex.** *Friends congratulated him on his success.* —con·grat`u·la'tion, *n.*

congregation (5) [kaŋ`grəgey'šən], *n.* a group of people gathered for religious worship. —con'gre·gate, *v.* gather. **Ex.** *A crowd congregated in the street.*

Congress (2) [kaŋ'grəs], *n.* the group of persons elected by the people of each state to make the laws of the United States of America. **Ex.** *The Congress of the United States meets in Washington, D.C.* —con·gres'sion·al, *adj.*

conjunction (4) [kənjəŋk'šən], *n.* a word that joins together sentences, phrases, or groups of words. **Ex.** *In the sentence "She and I will go, but he will not," "and" and "but" are conjunctions.*

connect (2) [kənekt'], *v.* 1. join or unite one thing to another; put together. **Ex.** *Connect the two wires.* 2. associate mentally. **Ex.** *I do not wish to be connected with him in any way.* —con·nec'tion, *n.*

---

a, far; æ, am; e, get; ey, late; i, in; iy, see; ɔ, all; ow, go; u, put; uw, too; ə, but, ago; ər, fur; aw, out; ay, life; oy, boy; ŋ, ring; θ, think; ð, that; ž, measure; š, ship; j, edge; č, child.

conquer (3) [kaŋ'kər], *v.* 1. get by using force. **Ex.** *They quickly conquered the new territory.* 2. overcome; defeat. **Ex.** *She was able to conquer her fear.* —**con'quer·or,** *n.*

conquest (5) [kaŋ'kwest`], *n.* 1. the act of gaining by force. **Ex.** *Rockets made possible the conquest of space.* 2. that which is gained by force or conquered.

conscience (3) [kan'šəns], *n.* a sense of what is right and wrong; a feeling of obligation to do right or be good. **Ex.** *His conscience kept him from stealing.* —**con·sci·en'tious,** *adj.*

conscious (3) [kan'šəs], *adj.* 1. aware of oneself and the people and things around one. **Ex.** *She was conscious of someone's presence.* 2. awake; mentally active. **Ex.** *The injured man was still conscious.* 3. with purpose; deliberate. **Ex.** *He made a conscious effort to improve his work.* —**con'scious·ly,** *adv.* —**con'scious·ness,** *n.*

consent (2) [kənsent'], *n.* agreement; permission. **Ex.** *Her parents gave their consent to the marriage.* —*v.* agree; give approval. **Ex.** *He consented to let me go.*

consequence (3) [kan'səkwens`], *n.* result. **Ex.** *The consequences of his acts were serious.* —**con'se·quent,** *adj.*

conservative (4) [kənsər'vətiv`], *adj.* 1. opposed to change; wanting to preserve existing conditions. **Ex.** *He is conservative in his views about government.* 2. careful about taking risks; not extreme. **Ex.** *He is very conservative in his dress.* —**con·serv'a·tism,** *n.*

conserve (5) [kənsərv'], *v.* preserve; keep from being wasted. **Ex.** *Conserve your strength for the difficult work ahead.* —**con·ser·va'tion,** *n.* a conserving or protecting from waste, loss, or harm. **Ex.** *We have a program for the conservation of our national forests.*

consider (1) [kənsid'ər], *v.* 1. think carefully about; examine. **Ex.** *Consider all the costs before you buy a house.* 2. believe to be; regard as. **Ex.** *They consider him a good teacher.* 3. be thoughtful of. **Ex.** *She considers others before herself.* —**con·sid'er·ate,** *adj.* —**con·sid·er·a'tion,** *n.*

considerable (1) [kənsid'ərəbəl], *adj.* 1. much; rather large. **Ex.** *We had considerable rain this summer.* 2. worth regarding as important. **Ex.** *He was a man of considerable talent.* —**con·sid'er·a·bly,** *adv.*

consist (2) [kənsist'], *v.* be made of. **Ex.** *This plan consists of* *three parts.* —**con·sis'tent**, *adj.* state of being or acting the same way. Ex. *He was consistent in his views.*

console (3) [kənsowl'], *v.* comfort. Ex. *The grieving woman was consoled by her friends.* —**con·so·la'tion**, *n.*

conspicuous (5) [kənspik'yuwəs], *adj.* noticeable; attracting attention. Ex. *He was conspicuous because of his great size.* —**con·spic'u·ous·ly**, *adv.*

conspire (5) [kənspayr'], *v.* 1. plot; plan together in secret to do something unlawful or evil. Ex. *The two men conspired to rob a bank.* 2. act together. Ex. *All things conspired to make the day a happy one.* —**con·spir'a·tor**, *n.* one who conspires.

constant (3) [kan'stənt], *adj.* 1. unchanging; always present. Ex. *There is a constant flow of water from the river.* 2. firm in belief; faithful. Ex. *He was a constant friend.* —*n.* something that never changes. —**con'stant·ly**, *adj.* always.

constitute (3) [kan'stətuwt`, kan'stətyuwt'], *v.* 1. compose; form. Ex. *The farm and the cattle constitute his entire fortune.* 2. appoint. Ex. *He constituted himself their guide.* 3. establish a law, a government, etc. Ex. *These rules were constituted by lawful authority.*

constitution (2) [kan'stətuw'šən, kan'stətyuw'šən], *n.* 1. the structure or form of a person, animal, or thing. Ex. *People with strong constitutions are not often sick.* 2. the fundamental principles, often written, according to which a nation, state, or group is governed. Ex. *There are procedures for amending the Constitution of the United States.* —**con·sti·tu'tion·al**, *adj.* of or from a constitution. Ex. *He has a constitutional right to speak.* —**con·sti·tu`tion·al'i·ty**, *n.* agreement with the Constitution.

construct (3) [kənstrəkt'], *v.* build. Ex. *The workmen are constructing a road* —**con·struc'tion**, *n.* —**con·struc'tive**, *adj.* helping to build. Ex. *He made constructive suggestions.*

consul (5) [kan'səl], *n.* an official appointed by a government to live in a foreign city to look after the interests of his own country. —**con'su·lar**, *adj.* —**con'su·late**, *n.* the office of the consul.

consult (3) [kənsəlt'], *v.* 1. seek information or advice from. Ex. *He consulted a lawyer about his problem.* 2. confer with. Ex. *Two doctors consulted about the patient.* —**con·sult'ant**, *n.* a specialist who gives advice. —**con'sul·ta'tion**, *n.* the act of consulting.

consume (4) [kənsuwm', kənsyuwm'], *v.* 1. use up. **Ex.** *Business consumed his time.* 2. eat or drink. **Ex.** *The family consumes a lot of food.* 3. destroy, as by fire. **Ex.** *Fire consumed the house.* —**con·sum'er**, *n.* one who consumes. —**con·sump'tion**, *n.* act or process of consuming.

contact (3) [kan'tækt'], *n.* 1. a touching. **Ex.** *The contact of the two electric wires caused the fire.* 2. a meeting or association. **Ex.** *I have few contacts with him, though we work in the same building.*

contain (1) [kənteyn'], *v.* 1. hold; include. **Ex.** *This book contains ten short stories.* 2. control. **Ex.** *She was so angry that she could hardly contain her feelings.* —**con·tain'er**, *n.* a box, barrel, bottle, etc. used to contain something.

contemplate (4) [kan'təmpleyt'], *v.* 1. think about seriously. **Ex.** *It is well to contemplate one's past before making decisions for the future.* 2. intend; have as a purpose. **Ex.** *They do not contemplate building a house this year.* —**con·tem·pla'tion**, *n.*

contemporary (4) [kəntem'pərer'iy], *adj.* 1. living or happening in the same era. 2. belonging to the present. **Ex.** *Some people do not understand contemporary art.* —*n.* a person living during the same time as another. **Ex.** *He was a contemporary of my grandfather.* —**con·tem'po·ra·ne·ous**, *adj.*

contempt (4) [kəntempt'], *n.* scorn; the feeling a person has for that which is unworthy. **Ex.** *He looked at the thief with contempt.* —**con·tempt'i·ble**, *adj.* deserving scorn. —**con·temp'tu·ous**, *adj.* scornful.

contend (5) [kəntend'], *v.* 1. struggle against. **Ex.** *Early settlers in America had to contend with many hardships.* 2. argue; claim. **Ex.** *He contends that he is innocent.* —**con·tend'er**, *n.* —**con·ten'tion**, *n,* the act of contending.

content (2) [kan'tent], *n.* the amount contained. **Ex.** *The metallic content of this rock is high.* —**con'tents**, *n.* 1. all that is contained. **Ex.** *We examined the contents of the box.* 2. things with which written material is concerned. **Ex.** *He looked at the table of contents of the magazine.*

content (2) [kəntent'], *adj.* satisfied; pleased with one's position or circumstances. **Ex.** *He is content to live in a small house.* —*v.* satisfy; make happy. **Ex.** *The baby contented herself with the new toy.* —**con·tent'ed·ly**, *adv.* —**con·tent'ment**, *n.*

contest (3) [kan'test'], *n.* a competition or a game in which the players struggle to win. **Ex.** *We held a contest to see who could run fastest.*

contest (3) [kantest¹], *v.* dispute; try to prove the opposite. **Ex.** *He contested our claim that we own the house.* —**con·test¹ant**, *n.* a person who takes part in a contest.

continent (2) [kan¹tənənt], *n.* any of the great land divisions of the earth. **Ex.** *North America, South America, Europe, Asia, Africa, and Australia are all continents.* —**con·ti·nen¹tal**, *adj.* —**the Continent**, Europe.

continue (1) [kəntin¹yuw], *v.* 1. keep doing or being. **Ex.** *The rain continued all week.* 2. proceed after an interruption. **Ex.** *We will continue our meeting after lunch.* 3. last; endure. **Ex.** *The government was not able to continue in power.* —**cor·tin¹u·al**, *adj.* —**con·tin¹u·al·ly**, *adv.* happening again and again. —**con·tin¹u·ous**, *adj.* —**con·tin¹u·ous·ly**, *adv.* without a break in space or time. —**con·tin¹u·ance, con·tin·u·a¹tion, con·tin·u¹i·ty**, *n.*

contract (2) [kan¹trækt⁾], *n.* an agreement, especially one that is written and legally binding. **Ex.** *They signed a contract to buy the house.*

contract (2) [kantrækt¹], *v.* 1. agree by contract. **Ex.** *They contracted to pay cash for the house.* 2. reduce in size or become smaller. **Ex.** *Most metals contract when they cool.* 3. get; acquire. **Ex.** *He contracted a fatal disease.*

contrary (3) [kan¹trer⁾iy], *adj.* opposite; not agreeing with. **Ex.** *My opinion is contrary to yours.* —*n.* the opposite. **Ex.** *He said that no one is hungry, but the contrary is true.*

contrast (3) [kan¹træst⁾], *v.* 1. compare so that the differences are shown. **Ex.** *The teacher contrasted the hot climate of one country witʰ the cold climate of another.* 2. exhibit differences when compared. **Ex.** *The heights of the boys contrasted with the heights of the girls.* —*n.* 1. a difference between things which are compared. **Ex.** *The contrast between his words and actions is disappointing.* 2. a person or thing that shows a difference when compared. **Ex.** *The tall man is a contrast to his short brother.*

contribute (3) [kəntrib¹yət], *v.* 1. give to some fund or charity. **Ex.** *They contributed money to the Red Cross.* 2. write articles, stories, etc., for a newspaper or magazine. **Ex.** *My*

a, far; æ, am; e, get; ey, late; i, in; iy, see; ɔ, all; ow, go; u, put; uw, too; ə, but, ago; ər, fur; aw, out; ay, life; oy, boy; ŋ, ring; θ, think; ð, that; ž, measure; š, ship; ǰ, edge; č, child.

favorite author contributes regularly to this magazine.
—**con·trib'u·tor,** *n.* one who contributes. —**con·tri·bu'tion,**
n. that which is contributed. —**con·trib'u·tor·y,** *adj.*

contrive (5) [kəntrayv'], *v.* plan; scheme; plot. **Ex.** *The prisoner contrived to escape.*

control (1) [kəntrowl'], *v.* 1. manage or direct. **Ex.** *The lights controlled the traffic.* 2. keep in check; have command over. **Ex.** *Control your temper.* —*n.* 1. power to manage or direct. **Ex.** *He lost control of the car, and it went off the road.* 2. act of keeping in check. **Ex.** *She brought her temper under control.*

controversy (5) [kan'trəvər`siy], *n.* dispute or argument. **Ex.** *There was a controversy about the location of the new school.* —**con·tro·ver'sial,** *adj.*

convenience (2) [kənviyn'yəns], *n.* anything that makes work or life easier. **Ex.** *A car is a great convenience.*

convenient (2) [kənviyn'yənt], *adj.* 1. easy to use or reach. **Ex.** *Put the table in a convenient place.* 2. causing little trouble. **Ex.** *Is it convenient for you to meet me?* —**con·ven'ient·ly,** *adv.*

convent (4) [kan'vent`], *n.* a community of women devoted to a religious life; the place where they live.

convention (4) [kənven'šən], *n.* 1. a large meeting for a particular purpose. **Ex.** *He is attending the national convention of his party.* 2. a custom or general rule which is accepted because of common usage. **Ex.** *It is the convention in many countries for people to shake hands when they meet.* —**con·ven'tion·al,** *adj.*

conversation (2) [kan`vərsey'šən], *n.* talk between two or more people. **Ex.** *I enjoyed the conversation we had this afternoon.*

converse (2) [kənvərs'], *v.* talk. **Ex.** *We will converse in English.*

convert (3) [kənvərt'], *v.* 1. change from one substance or state to another. **Ex.** *In that factory, iron is converted into steel.* 2. adopt one belief or religion and leave another. **Ex.** *He was converted to a new educational theory by his teacher.* —**con·ver'sion,** *n.* —**con·ver'ti·ble,** *adj.*

convey (4) [kənvey'], *v.* 1. carry or bear from one place to another. **Ex.** *A truck conveyed my furniture to my new home.* 2. make known; give. **Ex.** *This book conveys the* *author's meaning very well.* —**con·vey'ance,** *n.* anything used to convey, such as a car or train. —**con·vey'er,** *n.*

convict (5) [kənvikt'], *v.* prove or declare guilty of a crime. **Ex.** *The prisoner was convicted of robbery.*

convict (5) [kan'vikt], *n.* a person sent to prison for committing a crime. **Ex.** *The convict was locked in a cell.*

convince (3) [kənvins'], *v.* persuade by argument; satisfy by proof. **Ex.** *You have convinced me that I should go.* —**con·vinc'ing,** *adj.* —**con·vinc'ing·ly,** *adv.*

cook (1) [kuk'], *v.* prepare food by using heat. **Ex.** *The rice was cooked in a large pot.* —*n.* one who prepares food to be eaten.

cookie (2) [kuk'iy], *n.* a small, crisp, sweet cake. **Ex.** *The child wanted cookies for dessert.*

cool (1) [kuwl'], *adj.* 1. somewhat cold; not too hot. **Ex.** *A cool breeze was blowing.* 2. comfortable. **Ex.** *The house is cool in summer.* 3. calm. **Ex.** *He stayed cool during the argument.* 4. unfriendly. **Ex.** *He was cool toward us.* —*v.* make or become cool. **Ex.** *The evening breeze cooled the room.* —**cool'ly,** *adv.* —**cool'ness,** *n.*

cooperate (2) [kowap'əreyt'], *v.* act or work together to accomplish something. **Ex.** *All members must cooperate to make the group a success.* —**co·op·er·a'tion,** *n.*

coordinate (5) [kowɔr'dəneyt'], *adj.* equal in importance, rank, etc. —*v.* bring into proper relation; cause to agree in timing, manner of performance, etc. for greater efficiency. **Ex.** *Have you coordinated these plans with all the people concerned?* —**co·or·di·na'tion,** *n.*

copper (3) [kap'ər], *n.* a reddish metal, one of the best conductors of heat and electricity. **Ex.** *The lamp wire is made of copper.*

copy (2) [kap'iy], *n.* 1. an imitation or likeness of an original work. **Ex.** *That is a copy of a famous painting.* 2. one of a number of the same, book, newspaper, magazine, etc. **Ex.** *I bought a copy of the book.* —*v.* 1. make a copy of. **Ex.** *Copy this letter.* 2. imitate. **Ex.** *She copies her sister's style of dress.*

coral (5) [kɔr'əl], *n.* a hard, shell-like substance, usually white or red, formed in the sea from the bones of very small sea animals. **Ex.** *Coral is used to make beads.* —*adj.* made of coral; like coral in color.

cord (3) [kɔrd'], *n.* 1. a string or small rope. **Ex.** *Tie cord around the box.* 2. a rubber-covered wire used to conduct electricity.

cordial (4) [kɔr'jəl], *adj.* warm and friendly. **Ex.** *He gave us a cordial welcome.* —**cor'dial·ly**, *adv.*

core (5) [kɔ:r'], *n.* 1. the tough center part containing the seeds of apples, pears, and some other fruits. 2. the most important part of anything. **Ex.** *The core of the city's problem is housing.*

cork (5) [kɔrk'], *n.* the outer bark of a type of oak tree; a piece of this bark used to fill the opening of a bottle. —*v.* fill a hole of a bottle with a cork. **Ex.** *He corked the bottle after pouring a drink.*

corn (1) [kɔrn'], *n.* a common grain grown in America and eaten by people and animals.

corner (1) [kɔr'ner], *n.* 1. the place where two sides or surfaces of a thing meet. **Ex.** *There is a chair in one corner of the room.* 2. the place where two streets come together. **Ex.** *He was standing on the street corner.* —*adj.* at, on, or in a corner. —**cut corners,** save time or money.

CORN

corporation (3) [kɔr'pərey'šən], *n.* a group of persons permitted by law to act as one person when managing a business. **Ex.** *Those men are organizing a corporation to sell machines.*

corps (5) [kɔ:r'], *n.* 1. a special branch or section of a service, usually the military. **Ex.** *He is a member of the Marine Corps.* 2. a group of persons working together. **Ex.** *The corps of dancers traveled from city to city.*

corpse (5) [kɔrps'], *n.* the dead body of a human being.

correct (2) [kərekt'], *adj.* 1. free from mistakes; true. **Ex.** *He gave the correct answer.* 2. agreeing with what is considered proper. **Ex.** *His manners are always correct.* —*v.* 1. change to what is right; rid of mistakes. **Ex.** *You must correct your grammar.* 2. direct attention to the mistake of; punish for mistakes. **Ex.** *Some parents do not like to correct their children.* —**cor·rect'ness,** *n.* —**cor·rec'tion,** *n.* a correcting. **Ex.** *He made corrections in what he had written.* —**cor·rec'tive,** *adj.*

correspond (3) [kɔr'əspand'], *v.* 1. match; agree with. **Ex.** *Your words do not correspond with your actions.* 2. be equal or similar to. **Ex.** *A captain in the Navy corresponds to a colonel in the Army.* 3. communicate with someone by letters. **Ex.** *They correspond with each other regularly.* —cor·re·spond'ence, *n.*

corridor (4) [kɔr'ədər], *n.* a passageway or long hall that connects rooms or parts of a building.

corrupt (4) [kərəpt'], *adj.* dishonest, usually to gain money. **Ex.** *The corrupt judge accepted money to let the prisoner go unpunished.* —*v.* cause to be dishonest, usually by giving money. **Ex.** *He was corrupted by evil companions.* —cor·rup'tion, *n.*

cost (1) [kɔ:st'], *n.* 1. the amount paid or asked for something. **Ex.** *The cost of the hat was high.* 2. loss; sacrifice. **Ex.** *The father saved his son's life at the cost of his own.* —*v.* be priced at. **Ex.** *That house costs a lot of money.* —cost'ly, *adj.* expensive; not cheap. **Ex.** *She was wearing costly furs.* —at all costs, by whatever means necessary. **Ex.** *Stop them from leaving at all costs.*

costume (3) [ka'stuwm`, ka'styuwm`], *n.* 1. clothing characteristic of a class, time, or place. **Ex.** *The guides at the museum were dressed in 18th-century costumes.* 2. the clothes actors and actresses wear in a play.

cot (4) [kat'], *n.* a light, narrow bed, especially a folding one.

cottage (3) [kat'iǰ], *n.* a small house.

cotton (2) [kat'ən], *n.* 1. soft, white threadlike substance that grows around the seeds of the cotton plant. 2. thread or cloth made of this substance. **Ex.** *Shirts made of cotton are comfortable.*

couch (3) [kawč'], *n.* a sofa; a piece of furniture to sit or lie on.

cough (3) [kɔ:f'], *v.* force air through the throat noisily. —*n.* 1. the act or sound of coughing. **Ex.** *The boy's cough attracted the girl's attention.* 2. a condition of frequent coughing. **Ex.** *The boy had a bad cough.*

COUCH

could (1) [kud'], *v.* 1. past tense of the verb *can.* **Ex.** *Last year only two people could go.* 2. should be or would be able. **Ex.** *He could help you if he wanted to.*

council (4) [kawn'səl], *n.* 1. people meeting together to give advice or make plans. **Ex.** *The political party held a council to decide on future actions.* 2. a group of people chosen or elected to make laws or rules. **Ex.** *The city council is in conflict with the mayor.* —**coun'ci·lor,** *n.*

counsel (4) [kawn'səl], *n.* 1. advice; opinion. **Ex.** *I sought the lawyer's counsel.* 2. a lawyer who is handling a case. **Ex.** *He is the counsel for the defense.* —*v.* give advice; advise. **Ex.** *The adviser counseled him very wisely.* —**coun'se·lor,** *n.* 1. an adviser. 2. a lawyer.

count (1) [kawnt'], *v.* 1. say numbers in regular order. **Ex.** *The child can count to ten.* 2. get the total by numbering. **Ex.** *The teacher counted the students in the room.* 3. be important; have value. **Ex.** *Everything you do counts in this world.* 4. take or be taken into account. **Ex.** *Because he cheated, his score will not count.* —*n.* a counting. **Ex.** *A count showed that thirty people were present.* —**count on,** rely on; depend upon. **Ex.** *Can I count on your help?* —**count up,** add. **Ex.** *Count up what I owe you.*

countenance (5) [kawn'tənəns], *n.* 1. face; features; expression showing one's nature or feelings. **Ex.** *The old man had a noble countenance.* 2. approval or support. —*v.* support; approve. **Ex.** *I cannot countenance such behavior.*

counter (4) [kawn'tər], *n.* a long table in a store at which business is done. **Ex.** *The clerk stood behind the glove counter.*

counter- (4) [kawn'tər], *prefix.* against; opposite; in response. **Ex.** *He refused my offer and made a counterproposal.*

country (1) [kən'triy], *n.* 1. the territory of a nation. **Ex.** *Canada is a very large country.* 2. land with farms and very small towns; land outside of the large cities. **Ex.** *Do you prefer to live in the city or in the country?* 3. a particular area of land. **Ex.** *That country is very hilly.* 4. the entire nation, especially the people. **Ex.** *The President asked the country to make sacrifices.*

countryside (2) [kən'triysayd'], *n.* land outside the city. **Ex.** *We will drive out into the countryside.*

county (4) [kawn'tiy], *n.* in the United States, one of the parts into which a state is divided for purposes of government.

couple (2) [kəp'əl], *n.* 1. two things of the same kind together. **Ex.** *He ate a couple of eggs for breakfast.* 2. a man and a woman together. **Ex.** *They are a handsome couple.*

courage (2) [kər'ij], *n.* bravery; the ability to face danger or difficulties without fear. **Ex.** *Courage is needed to try again after a defeat.* —**cou·ra'geous,** *adj.* —**cou·ra'geous·ly,** *adv.*

course (1) [kɔrs'], *n.* 1. moving from one point to the next; progress. **Ex.** *In the course of my life, I have seen many strange things.* 2. a way or direction in which something moves. **Ex.** *Our ship was off its course because of bad weather.* 3. an entire series of studies or any one of these studies. **Ex.** *What course are you taking at the university?* —**in the course of,** while; during. —**of course,** certainly. **Ex.** *Of course, I will go with you.*

court (2) [kɔrt'], *n.* 1. a place where disputes are settled according to law. **Ex.** *The man accused of the crime was brought to the court.* 2. judges and officials of the court. 3. the palace of a ruler. 4. the attendants and relatives of a ruler. —*v.* seek the affection or favor of. **Ex.** *He courted her for a year before they were married.*

courtesy (4) [kər'təsiy], *n.* 1. good manners; polite way of acting. **Ex.** *He was admired for his courtesy.* 2. a favor; polite act. **Ex.** *Please do me the courtesy of answering my letter promptly.* —**cour'te·ous,** *adj.* —**cour'te·ous·ly,** *adv.*

courthouse [kɔrt'haws'], *n.* building in which courts of law meet.

courtroom [kɔrt'ruwm'], *n.* room in which a court of law meets.

courtship [kɔrt'šip'], *n.* the courting of a woman for marriage.

cousin (2) [kəz'ən], *n.* the child of one's uncle or aunt.

cover (1) [kəv'ər], *v.* 1. put a layer of something on. **Ex.** *She covered the table with a cloth.* 2. hide. **Ex.** *He covered the coin with his hand.* 3. extend over. **Ex.** *His farm covers several miles.* 4. get news. **Ex.** *The reporter covered the fire.* —*n.* 1. anything which covers, such as a lid or blanket. **Ex.** *She liked warm covers on her bed.* 2. shelter; protection. **Ex.** *The prisoner escaped under cover of the night.*

cow (2) [kaw'], *n.* a large farm animal that gives milk.

coward (4) [kaw'ərd], *n.* a person who lacks courage. **Ex.** *No one wishes to be thought a coward.* —**cow'ard·ly,** *adj., adv.*

cow

cowboy [kaw'boy'], *n.* a man who works with cattle in the American West.

cowhide [kaw'hayd'], *n.* the skin of a cow; leather made from cowskin.

crack (3) [kræk¹], v. 1. break, with or without separating, into parts. Ex. *The cup was cracked.* 2. make a sharp, sudden sound as of something breaking. Ex. *The driver cracked the whip over the horses' heads.* —n. 1. a break without complete separation. Ex. *There was a crack in the mirror.* 2. a sharp, sudden sound, as of something breaking. —**cracked¹**, adj.

cracker (5) [kræk¹ər], n. a thin, crisp biscuit.

cradle (4) [kreyd¹əl], n. a baby's bed. —v. hold in the arms and rock as in a cradle. Ex. *She cradled the child in her arms.*

craft (4) [kræft¹], n. 1. any kind of skilled work done with the hands. Ex. *The arts and crafts of any people are an important part of their culture.* 2. cunning; skill in tricking others. Ex. *By his craft he got the property away from his brothers and sisters.* —**craft¹y**, adj. —**craft¹i·ly**, adv.

crank (5) [kræŋk¹], n. a handle that forms a right angle and is fastened to the shaft of a machine in order to turn it. Ex. *Turn the crank to start the motor.* —v. turn a crank.

crash (2) [kræš¹], n. 1. a hitting against something with force by which damage is caused. Ex. *Many people died in the airplane crash.* 2. a loud noise like something breaking. Ex. *He heard the crash of a falling tree.* —v. 1. hit. Ex. *The two cars crashed into each other.* 2. make a sudden loud noise. Ex. *Thunder crashed in the sky.*

crave (5) [kreyv¹], v. 1. want very much. Ex. *A child craves candy.* 2. beg. Ex. *He craved forgiveness.* —**crav¹ing**, n.

crawl (3) [krɔ:l¹], v. 1. move slowly on one's hands and knees. Ex. *The wounded soldier crawled to safety.* 2. move slowly. Ex. *The cars crawled through the traffic.*

crazy (2) [krey¹ziy], adj. 1. sick in mind. Ex. *She has gone crazy from grief.* 2. not practical; very foolish. Ex. *He has crazy ideas.*

creak (5) [kriyk¹], v. make a sharp, thin, high sound. Ex. *The floor creaked as he stepped on a loose board.* —n. the sound of a creak. —**creak¹y**, adj.

cream (2) [kriym¹], n. 1. the rich, buttery part of milk that rises to the top. Ex. *Do you like cream in your coffee?* 2. any soft, thick substance which resembles cream. Ex. *She uses face cream to soften her skin.* —v. make into a smooth mixture like cream. —**cream¹y**, adj.

create (2) [kriy`eyt¹], v. 1. bring into being; make; form. Ex.

Several new jobs were created. 2. produce as a work of thought or imagination. **Ex.** *The artist created many beautiful pictures.* —**cre·a'tion,** *n.* that which is created. —**cre·a'tor,** *n.* one who creates. —**cre·a'tive,** *adj.*

creature (2) [kriy'čər], *n.* any living being; any animal or person.

credit (3) [kred'ət], *n.* 1. belief that something is true; trust. **Ex.** *He put no credit in the statement.* 2. honor; recognition. **Ex.** *The boy received credit for his hard work.* 3. reputation for paying one's bills. **Ex.** *My credit is very good at this store.* 4. an amount of money in a bank account. **Ex.** *His bank balance shows a credit.* —*v.* 1. believe; accept as the truth. **Ex.** *The woman did not credit the boy's story.* 2. add to an account. **Ex.** *The bank credited the deposit to his account.* 3. regard as owing to or caused by. **Ex.** *The old man credited his long life to his regular habits.* —**cred'i·ble,** *adj.* believable. —**cred·i·bil'i·ty,** *n.* —**cred'it·a·ble,** *adj.* deserving praise. —**cred'i·tor,** *n.* one to whom money is owed. —**credit with,** recognize or honor someone for. **Ex.** *We credited him with loyalty.* —**do credit to,** bring recognition to. **Ex.** *The painting would do credit to a great artist.* —**on credit,** a promise to pay later. **Ex.** *They bought their car on credit.*

creed (5) [kriyd'], *n.* 1. a statement of the principal beliefs of a religion. 2. guiding principles in science, politics, etc.

creek (3) [kriyk', krik'], *n.* stream of water smaller than a river. **Ex.** *The boys like to play in the creek during the summer.*

creep (3) [kriyp'], *v.* 1. crawl; move with the body close to the ground. **Ex.** *A baby creeps before it walks.* 2. move slowly, quietly, and carefully. **Ex.** *The thief was creeping in the dark.* 3. grow along the ground or over a wall. **Ex.** *The vine creeps up the side of the house.* —**creep'y,** *adj.* causing fear. **Ex.** *They heard creepy noises.*

crept (3) [krept'], *v.* past tense and participle of *creep.* **Ex.** *The boy crept quietly through the dark house.*

crest (4) [krest'], *n.* 1. a bunch of hair, feathers, or fur on the head of a bird or animal. 2. anything like a crest. **Ex.** *The crest of the mountains rose above us.*

crew (3) [kruw'], *n.* 1. the men working on a ship, plane, o
train. **Ex.** *The ship had a small crew.* 2. a group of person
working together. **Ex.** *A crew of workmen painted th*
building.

crime (2) [kraym'], *n.* a wrong act forbidden by law. **Ex**
Murder is a very serious crime.

criminal (2) [krim'ənəl], *n.* a person who has committed
crime. **Ex.** *The criminal was sent to jail.* —*adj.* relating t
crime. **Ex.** *He studied criminal law.*

crimson (5) [krim'zən], *n., adj.* deep red color. **Ex.** *His hand*
were crimson with blood.

cripple (4) [krip'əl], *n.* a person or animal that is without th
normal use of some part of the body. **Ex.** *That cripple los*
his leg in an accident. —*v.* damage; take away the use o
any part. **Ex.** *The accident crippled him.*

crisis (4) [kray'səs], *n.* 1. a decisive or extremely importan
stage in a series of events. **Ex.** *The sick man passed th*
crisis and began to regain his strength. 2. a time of difficult
or danger. **Ex.** *Scarcity of food caused a crisis in the nation*

crisp (4) [krisp'], *adj.* 1. hard but easily broken. **Ex.** *He ha*
crisp, buttered toast for breakfast. 2. firm and fresh. **Ex**
The salad vegetables were crisp. 3. sharp; clear. **Ex.** *She ha*
a crisp manner of speaking. 4. pleasantly cool. **Ex.** *The ai*
was crisp. —**crisp'ly,** *adv.* —**crisp'ness,** *n.*

critic (3) [krit'ik], *n.* 1. a person skilled in judging books
music, plays, art, etc. **Ex.** *I saw the music critic of the news*
paper at the concert. 2. a person who objects or complain
without reason. **Ex.** *He is a critic of everyone's actions bu*
his own. —**crit'i·cism,** *n.* the judgment expressed. —**crit'i**
cize, *v.*

critical (3) [krit'ikəl], *adj.* 1. tending to complain about an
other's actions or to judge severely. **Ex.** *I do not like peopl*
who are too critical. 2. extremely dangerous; at a very im
portant stage. **Ex.** *The most critical battle of the wa*
occurred near that town. —**crit'i·cal·ly,** *adj.*

crooked (4) [kruk'əd], *adj.* 1. bent; not straight; curved
twisted. **Ex.** *It was hard to drive along the crooked roa*
in the dark. 2. not honest. **Ex.** *He was involved in some ver*
crooked business.

crop (2) [krap'], *n.* produce of the soil such as grain, fruit, o
vegetables. **Ex.** *The farmer raised a wheat crop.* —*v.* cu
or bite short. **Ex.** *The cattle cropped the grass in the field*

cross (1) [krɔːsˈ], v. 1. go across; extend from one side to the other side. **Ex.** *We crossed the street.* 2. draw a line through. **Ex.** *Be sure to cross your "t's" when you write.* —n. 1. a structure made with an upright post with a bar across it close to the top. 2. any mark made by putting one line directly across another. —adj. mean; angry. —**crossˈing,** n. a place at which to cross a street.

cross-examine [krɔsˈigzæmˈən], v. examine one already examined for further information. **Ex.** *The lawyer cross-examined the witness.*

cross-purpose [krɔsˈpərˈpəs], n. an opposite purpose or reason. **Ex.** *Instead of working together, we are working at cross-purposes.*

cross-reference [krɔsˈ refˈrəns], n. a referral to another part of a book, paper, etc. **Ex.** *The cross-references helped him to learn more about the subject.*

cross section [krɔsˈ sekˈšən], 1. a section or part of something that shows what the whole thing is like. **Ex.** *He spoke with a cross section of the group.* 2. a flat section made by cutting an object at right angles to its length; such a section or a picture of it.

crouch (4) [krawčˈ], v. stoop low with bent knees. **Ex.** *The hunter crouched in the long grass.* —n. act of stooping or bending low.

crow (4) [krowˈ], n. 1. a large bird, usually black, with shiny feathers and an unpleasant shrieking cry. 2. the loud cry made by a rooster. —v. make such a cry. **Ex.** *The rooster crowed at dawn.*

crowd (1) [krawdˈ], n. a large number of people in a group. **Ex.** *A crowd collected to hear the speaker.* —v. 1. push together. **Ex.** *People crowded into the bus.* 2. gather together in crowds. **Ex.** *People crowded to see the President.*

crown (2) [krawnˈ], n. 1. a head covering for a king or queen. **Ex.** *The gold crown was covered with jewels.* 2. royal power. 3. anything like a crown. **Ex.** *Walk up to the crown of the hill.* 4. a ring of flowers or leaves for the head worn as a sign of victory or honor. —v. place a crown upon. **Ex.** *He was crowned king.*

crude (3) [kruwdˈ], adj. 1. looking or acting unfinished; lacking grace. **Ex.** *His manners were crude.* 2. in a natural state, raw; not ready for use. **Ex.** *Crude oil is pumped through pipes.* —**crudeˈly,** adv. —**crudeˈness,** n.

cruel (2) [kruw'əl], *adj.* 1. liking to cause pain for others; without mercy or pity. **Ex.** *The cruel boy threw stones at the children.* 2. causing suffering. **Ex.** *The cruel heat of the desert sun prevented them from traveling during the day.* —**cru'el·ly,** *adv.* —**cru'el·ty,** *n.*

cruise (5) [kruwz'], *v.* go on a long boat trip for pleasure. **Ex.** *They cruised through the Mediterranean.* —*n.* a ship voyage, especially one for pleasure and with stops at many ports.

crumb (4) [krəm'], *n.* a very small bit of bread, cake, etc. **Ex.** *She fed crumbs to the birds.* —*v.* break into crumbs, as bread.

crumble (5) [krəm'bəl], *v.* break into small pieces; fall into decay. **Ex.** *Their house crumbled from lack of repair.* —**crum'bly,** *adj., adv.*

crusade (5) [kruw'seyd'], *n.* 1. any campaign or fight for a good cause or against a bad cause. **Ex.** *The citizens are having a crusade for better housing.* 2. any of the religious wars fought during the 11th, 12th, and 13th centuries. —*v.* engage in a crusade. **Ex.** *Women in the United States crusaded for the right to vote.* —**cru·sad'er,** *n.*

crush (2) [krəš'], *v.* 1. press together with force so as to break, hurt, or change the shape of. **Ex.** *She crushed her hat when she sat on it.* 2. break into fine pieces as by pounding. **Ex.** *The machine crushed the stones into a fine powder.* 3. defeat completely. **Ex.** *The revolt was crushed.* —*n.* 1. the act of crushing; strong pressure. 2. many people or things crowded together. **Ex.** *We lost sight of each other in the crush of people at the door.*

crust (4) [krəst'], *n.* 1. the hard outer part of bread. **Ex.** *He had only a crust of bread for supper.* 2. the shell or covering of a pie. 3. any hard outer shell. **Ex.** *He walked over the crust of the snow.* —**crus'ty,** *adj.*

crutch (5) [krəč'], *n.* 1. a support used by a lame person to help in walking. 2. any support or help.

cry (1) [kray'], *v.* 1. call in a loud voice; shout. **Ex.** *They cried for help.* 2. weep. **Ex.** *The child cried because he was hurt.* —*n.* 1. a loud call or shout. **Ex.** *He heard the cry, "Fire! Fire!"* 2. weeping; sound made by one in pain or grief. **Ex.** *We heard the cry of the injured boy.* 3. call

CRUTCH 1

of an animal or bird. **Ex.** *The hunter heard the cry of the wounded animal.* 4. appeal. **Ex.** *The cry of the people was for food.*

crystal (3) [kris'təl], *n.* 1. a hard, clear, glasslike rock; also a piece of this material used as an ornament. 2. glass of superior brilliancy; articles made of this glass. **Ex.** *Crystal was sparkling on the table.* 3. the shapes of many substances when they become solid. **Ex.** *The crystals of snow were beautiful.* —*adj.* made of or like crystal; clear. **Ex.** *The crystal water was icy cold.* —**crys'tal·lize,** *v.* 1. form into crystals. **Ex.** *The melted sugar crystallized on the fruit.* 2. give form to something. **Ex.** *His plans crystallized into action.*

cub (5) [kəb'], *n.* the young of some animals, such as the fox, bear, and lion.

cube (5) [kyuwb'], *n.* a solid having six square sides, all equal in size. —**cu'bic,** *adj.*

CUBE

cuff (4) [kəf'], *n.* 1. a band around the lower part of a sleeve. 2. the turned-up fold around the bottom of the legs of trousers.

cultivate (3) [kəl'təveyt'], *v.* 1. loosen the soil around plants to help them grow; prepare and use land for raising crops. **Ex.** *The farmer cultivated his land.* 2. help and protect the growth of; improve; develop, as by education. **Ex.** *He cultivated his mind by reading good books.* —**cul·ti·va'tion,** *n.*

culture (3) [kəl'čər], *n.* 1. the ideas, arts, and way of life of a people or nation at a certain time. **Ex.** *We have learned much from the culture of ancient Greece.* 2. a specially prepared material in which bacteria and cells will grow, used in scientific experiments. —**cul'tur·al,** *adj.* —**cul'tur·al·ly,** *adv.*

cunning (3) [kən'iŋ], *adv.* 1. clever in cheating. **Ex.** *He is as cunning as a fox.* 2. clever; skillful. **Ex.** *This clock was made by a cunning workman.* —*n.* skill in tricking others. **Ex.** *He used cunning to take the land away from his partner.* —**cun'ning·ly,** *adv.*

---

cup (1) [kəp'], *n.* 1. a small container with a handle, usually in the shape of a bowl, used for drinking. 2. a unit of measure equal to eight ounces; the amount a cup will hold. **Ex.** *I have used two cups of flour to make the cake.* —*v.* form a cup shape. **Ex.** *He cupped his hands and dipped water from the brook.*

CUP 1

cupboard (3) [kə'bərd], *n.* a closet or piece of furniture with shelves for storing food, dishes, etc.

curb (4) [kərb'], *n.* 1. the raised edging of stone or concrete along a street. 2. that which controls. **Ex.** *He resolved to put a curb on his spending.* —*v.* control. **Ex.** *He was told to curb his temper.*

cure (2) [kyu:r'], *n.* 1. any remedy or method of treatment that makes a sick person healthy. **Ex.** *The doctors searched for a cure for the disease.* 2. restoration to health. **Ex.** *The child's cure was immediate.* —*v.* 1. restore to health; make well. **Ex.** *The medicine cured her cold.* 2. stop from doing or remove something bad. **Ex.** *Her burned finger cured her of playing with matches.* —**cur'a·ble,** *adj.*

curious (2) [kyur'iəs], *adj.* 1. strange; odd; unusual; peculiar. **Ex.** *We saw some curious birds today.* 2. eager to learn; desiring knowledge. **Ex.** *He has the curious mind of a student.* 3. interested in things which do not concern one. **Ex.** *The curious girl listened to our private conversation.* —**cu·ri'os'i·ty,** *n.* 1. a desire to know. 2. a curious thing. **Ex.** *He brought home many curiosities from his travels.* —**cu'ri·ous·ly,** *adv.*

curl (2) [kərl'], *v.* 1. form or twist into rings. **Ex.** *She curls her hair.* 2. bend into curves. **Ex.** *Smoke curled from the chimney.* —*n.* 1. arrangement of the hair in rings. 2. anything in the shape of curves or rings. **Ex.** *Curls of smoke rose from the chimney.* —**curl'y,** *adj.*

currency (4) [kər'ənsiy], *n.* money in use in a country, both coins and paper. **Ex.** *The currency of the country is sound.*

current (2) [kər'ənt], *adj.* belonging to the present time. **Ex.** *This is the current issue of the magazine.* —*n.* the flow of water or air. **Ex.** *The current carried the boat downstream.* 2. movement of electricity in a wire.

curse (2) [kərs'], *n.* 1. a wish that evil might happen to another. **Ex.** *He placed a curse upon his enemy.* 2. something that causes evil or trouble. **Ex.** *His jealousy was a curse to him.* 3. evil words; bad language. —*v.* 1. use evil language. 2. wish evil or harm on. **Ex.** *He cursed his enemies.*

curtain (2) [kər'tən], *n.* a cloth which is hung at a window or in front of a stage to decorate, hide, cover, or separate one place from another. **Ex.** *She made curtains for the kitchen windows.*

curve (2) [kərv'], *n.* a bending line, as in part of a circle. **Ex.** *The road had many curves.* —*v.* bend in a curve. **Ex.** *The road curved away from the river.*

cushion (4) [kuš'ən], *n.* a soft pillow to sit on or lean against. **Ex.** *Here is a cushion for your chair.*

custom (2) [kəs'təm], *n.* 1. a long-established habit or habits having almost the force of law. **Ex.** *They were strangers and did not know our customs.* 2. a usual action; habit. **Ex.** *It was his custom to take a bath before going to bed.* —**cus'toms**, *n.* taxes paid to the government on things brought from a foreign country; the government agency collecting these taxes. —**cus'tom·ar·y**, *adj.* usual.

customer (3) [kəs'təmər], *n.* a person who buys from another. **Ex.** *This store has thousands of customers.*

cut (1) [kət'], *v.* 1. make a hole, narrow opening, wound, etc. with a knife or other sharp-edged tool. **Ex.** *While shaving, he cut himself.* 2. divide into parts using such a tool; carve. **Ex.** *Please cut me a slice of bread.* 3. make or form by cutting. **Ex.** *She cut out a dress.* 4. shorten by trimming. **Ex.** *He cut the grass.* 5. lower; reduce. **Ex.** *They had to cut expenses.* —*n.* 1. the act of cutting. 2. the result of cutting; a wound. **Ex.** *He received a cut on his hand.* 3. a reduction. **Ex.** *There was a cut in prices.* —**cut back,** shorten; reduce. —**cut down,** reduce; lessen. **Ex.** *I must cut down on what I eat.* —**cut in,** move between; interrupt. **Ex.** *He cut in on their conversation.* —**cut short,** stop without finishing. **Ex.** *He cut short his visit.*

-cy (3) [siy], *suffix.* 1. quality; condition; state. **Exs.** *Hesitant, hesitancy; frequent, frequency.* 2. rank; position. **Exs.** *President, presidency; captain, captaincy.*

cylinder (5) [sil'əndər], *n.* a round object with two flat ends; a roller-shaped object which may be hollow or solid.

CYLINDER

D

D, d [diy'], *n.* fourth letter of the English alphabet.

dad (3) [dæd'], *n.* a familiar term for father. —**dad'dy**, *n.* a child's word for father.

dagger (5) [dæg'ər], *n.* a short knife with a pointed blade used as a weapon. **Ex.** *The warrior was armed with a dagger.*

daily (1) [dey'liy], *adj.* every day. **Ex.** *That newspaper is a daily newspaper.*

dainty (4) [deyn'tiy], *adj.* of delicate beauty and charm. **Ex.** *The tea was served in dainty little cups.* —**dain'ti·ly,** *adv.*

dairy (4) [de:r'iy], *n.* 1. a place where milk and cream are made into butter and cheese. 2. a store or company which sells milk, butter, and cheese.

dam (4) [dæm'], *n.* a wall built across a river to hold back flowing water. **Ex.** *Dams are essential in any flood control program.* —*v.* hold back by means of a dam. **Ex.** *Engineers are going to dam the river to save the water.*

damage (2) [dæm'ij], *n.* harm; hurt; loss due to injury. **Ex.** *Disease and fire cause much damage.* —*v.* harm; hurt; injure. **Ex.** *The fire damaged everything in the store.* —**dam'a·ges,** *n.pl.* money asked or paid for harm or damage done. **Ex.** *The judge ordered him to pay the damages asked.*

damn (4) [dæm'], *v.* 1. condemn as bad, not legal, or wicked. **Ex.** *The critics damned his new play.* 2. curse. **Ex.** *In his anger, he damned his friend.* —*n.* the use of the word *damn* as a curse. —**dam·na'tion,** *n.*

damp (3) [dæmp'], *adj.* slightly wet; moist. **Ex.** *She put a damp cloth on his head.* —*n.* a small amount of wetness; moisture. —**damp'en,** *v.* 1. make moist. **Ex.** *The light rain dampened our clothes.* 2. slow; decrease; make dull. **Ex.** *The bad news dampened their enthusiasm.* —**damp'ly,** *adv.* —**damp'ness,** *n.*

dance (1) [dæns'], *v.* 1. move the feet and body, usually to music or the beat of a drum, either alone or with others. 2. move in a lively way. **Ex.** *She danced with joy at the good news.* —*n.* 1. a series of steps, usually in time to music. **Ex.** *Everyone wants to learn the latest dance.* 2. a party where people dance. —**danc'er,** *n.* a person who dances.

danger (1) [deyn'jər], *n.* 1. a situation in which great harm, injury, or loss is possible. **Ex.** *The ship was in danger of sinking during the storm.* 2. something which may cause harm. **Ex.** *There is great danger to life in a fire.* —**dan'gerous,** *adj.*

dare (1) [de:r'], *v.* 1. have courage; be bold; meet bravely. **Ex.** *Do you dare climb that mountain alone?* 2. tell someone to do something to show he is not afraid; challenge. **Ex.** *He dared his brother to jump from the tree.* —*n.* a challenge. **Ex.** *His brother accepted the dare.* —**dar'ing,** *adj.* brave; fearless.

dark (1) [dark'], *adj.* 1. without light. **Ex.** *The room was completely dark.* 2. not light-colored. **Ex.** *The dress was dark blue, not light blue.* —*n.* lack of light; a dark place or time. **Ex.** *The child did not like the dark.* —**dark'en,** *v.* make dark or darker. **Ex.** *The sky darkened before the storm.* —**dark'ly,** *adv.* —**dark'ness,** *n.*

darling (3) [dar'liŋ], *n.* one who is dearly loved. **Ex.** *Their only child is their darling.* —*adj.* dearly loved. **Ex.** *He is a darling baby.*

darn (4) [darn'], *v.* fix a hole in cloth by sewing threads over it. **Ex.** *His wife darned the hole in his suit.* —*n.* the place fixed in this way. **Ex.** *The darn could hardly be seen.*

dart (3) [dart'], *n.* a short, pointed weapon, either shot or thrown. —*v.* suddenly begin to run fast. **Ex.** *The child darted away from his mother.*

dash (3) [dæš'], *n.* 1. a mark (—) used in writing or printing. 2. a small amount. **Ex.** *The soup needs a dash of pepper.* 3. a short race. **Ex.** *He won the 100-yard dash.* —*v.* 1. run fast. **Ex.** *The boy dashed for the bus.* 2. throw or scatter a liquid. **Ex.** *The waves dashed against the rocks.* 3. break or throw with violence. **Ex.** *In her anger, she dashed the glass to the floor.* —**dash'ing,** *adj.* colorful; lively. **Ex.** *They are a dashing couple.*

data (5) [dey'ta, dæt'e], *n.* facts or information, often expressed in numbers, used in reaching conclusions, making decisions, etc. **Ex.** *He is gathering data about birds for a scientific study.*

date (1) [deyt'], *n.* 1. a statement of time. Ex. *The date of the meeting was set for next Friday.* 2. an agreement to see a friend at a certain time. Ex. *I have a date with my friend tomorrow.* —*v.* 1. note the time of writing or doing. Ex. *Please date all of your letters.* 2. give the date at which something happened or existed. Ex. *Historians date the event as occurring in the 11th century.* 3. belong to a specific time. Ex. *This house dates back to 1800.*

date (1) [deyt'], *n.* the sweet fruit of a type of palm tree.

daughter (1) [dɔ:'tər], *n.* a female child considered in relation to her father, her mother, or both parents. Ex. *She is the older daughter.*

daughter-in-law (3) [dɔ:'tərənlɔ:'], *n.* the wife of one's son.

daunt (5) [dɔ:nt'], *v.* frighten; discourage. Ex. *He was not daunted by the threat to his life.* —**daunt'less,** *adj.* fearless. —**daunt'less·ly,** *adv.*

dawn (2) [dɔ:n'], *n.* 1. sunrise. Ex. *We started our trip at dawn.* 2. the beginning. Ex. *Since the dawn of time, man has had to struggle with nature.* —*v.* become light. Ex. *The day dawned bright and sunny.*

day (1) [dey'], *n.* 1. a 24-hour period. Ex. *He will be gone for three days.* 2. the time of light; the time between sunrise and dark.

daydream [dey'driym'], *n.* a time of dreamy thinking, while awake. —*v.* have daydreams.

daze (5) [deyz'], *v.* confuse or stun by a blow or shock. Ex. *He was dazed by the fall.* —*n.* condition of being dazed. Ex. *The injured girl was in a daze after the accident.*

dazzle (5) [dæz'əl], *v.* 1. confuse with a very bright light. Ex. *Coming out of the dark theater, we were dazzled by the bright sunlight.* 2. surprise or cause admiration. Ex. *He was dazzled by the girl's beauty.* —**daz'zling,** *adj.*

de- (1) [diy], *prefix.* 1. do the reverse; undo. Exs. *Frost, defrost; form, deform.* 2. take away. Exs. *Vein, devein; inflate, deflate.*

dead (1) [ded'], *adj.* 1. no longer alive. Ex. *The patient is dead.* 2. not now in use. Ex. *Dead languages are still studied in school.* —*n.* a dead person or persons. Ex. *We put flowers on the graves of the dead.* —**dead'en,** *v.* make dead; lessen feeling. Ex. *The doctor gave him medicine to deaden his pain.* —**dead'ly,** *adj.* 1. able to cause death. Ex. *A deadly* *poison is made from this plant.* 2. like death. **Ex.** *Her face grew deadly pale.*

deadline [ded'layn`], *n.* the time by which it is necessary that something be done. **Ex.** *The deadline for buying tickets to the theater is twelve o'clock.*

deadlock [ded'lak`], *n.* a point in a dispute, struggle, etc., at which both sides are equally strong and cannot win. **Ex.** *The two leaders were at a deadlock in their discussion, and neither would make any concessions.*

deaf (3) [def'], *adj.* 1. unable to hear or unable to hear properly. **Ex.** *He was deaf and could not hear the noise.* 2. unwilling to hear. **Ex.** *He was deaf to my pleading.* —**deaf'en**, *v.* —**deaf'ness**, *n.*

deal (1) [diyl'], *v.* 1. treat; be concerned with; give attention to. **Ex.** *We must learn to deal with our problems.* 2. act or behave. **Ex.** *That lawyer deals honorably with everyone.* 3. do business in or with; buy or sell. **Ex.** *We deal directly with the farmers for our vegetables.* 4. deliver; give. **Ex.** *The fighters dealt each other severe blows.* —**deal'er**, *n.* a person whose business it is to buy and sell. **Ex.** *Buy your car from a good automobile dealer.*

dean (5) [diyn'], *n.* an official of a college or school who is in charge of students or teachers. **Ex.** *He is dean of men.*

dear (1) [di:r'], *adj.* 1. loved very much. **Ex.** *He is a dear friend of mine.* 2. highly respected; a polite form of address. **Ex.** *He began the letter with the words "dear sir."* —*n.* a person who is loved. **Ex.** *Your mother is a dear.* —**dear'ly**, *adv.*

death (2) [deθ'], *n.* the ending of life; act of dying. **Ex.** *After his death, his body was sent home to be buried.* —**death'ly**, *adj., adv.*

debate (4) [dibeyt'], *v.* give arguments for or against something. **Ex.** *The people of the town debated whether to build a new road.* —*n.* a public argument for and against a question; a discussion. **Ex.** *The high school students are having a debate today.* —**de·bat'a·ble**, *adj.* —**de·bat'er**, *n.*

debt (2) [det'], *n.* 1. something that is owed. **Ex.** *His debts are more than he can pay.* 2. the obligation to pay; the condition of owing. **Ex.** *He is in debt to his brother.* —**debt'or**, *n.* one who owes a debt.

decay (3) [dikey'], *v.* 1. rot; spoil; become bad. **Ex.** *Apples* *decay rapidly.* 2. lose health and strength; pass gradually from a condition of quality to the opposite condition. **Ex.** *Our physical powers decay in old age.* —*n.* 1. a gradual decline; a falling into ruin. **Ex.** *The beautiful old house had fallen into decay.* 2. state of being rotten. **Ex.** *There were no signs of decay in the tooth.*

deceit (5) [disiyt¹], *n.* the act or practice of deceiving or lying. **Ex.** *The merchant used deceit in his business dealings.* —**de·ceit'ful,** *adj.*

deceive (3) [disiyv¹], *v.* lead into error; cause someone to believe what is not true. **Ex.** *He deceived his friends about his income.* —**de·ceiv'er,** *n.* —**de·ceiv'ing,** *adj.*

December (1) [disem'bər], *n.* the twelfth and last month of the year.

decent (3) [diy'sənt], *adj.* 1. proper; respectable; modest. **Ex.** *He always uses decent language.* 2. moderate but sufficient. **Ex.** *He earns a decent salary.* —**de'cen·cy,** *n.* —**de'cent·ly,** *adv.*

deception (5) [disep'šən], *n.* that which deceives; the act of deceiving. **Ex.** *His deception caused us to believe he had gone.*

decide (1) [disayd¹], *v.* 1. choose to do after thinking for a while. **Ex.** *He decided to leave home.* 2. end a contest by selecting one side the victor; settle; judge. **Ex.** *The jury will decide the case tomorrow.*

decision (3) [disiž'ən], *n.* 1. a settling; resolving of a problem by giving judgment on the matter; the conclusion arrived at. **Ex.** *I made a decision to accept the job offer.* 2. firmness; determination. **Ex.** *He is a man of decision.*

deck (2) [dek¹], *n.* 1. the floor or floors of a ship. **Ex.** *The ship had three decks.* 2. a set of playing cards. **Ex.** *There are 52 cards in the deck.*

declare (2) [dikle:r¹], *v.* say positively; cause to be known; proclaim. **Ex.** *"I refuse to go," he declared.* —**dec'la·ra¹ tion,** *n.*

decline (2) [diklayn¹], *v.* 1. refuse. **Ex.** *They declined the invitation.* 2. become less, as in strength, power, value. **Ex.** *His health is declining.* —*n.* 1. a lessening in power, health, value, etc.; the period when this is happening. **Ex.** *There was a decline in the number of automobiles sold.* 2. a descending slope. **Ex.** *The car rolled down the decline.*

decorate (3) [dek'əreyt`], v. 1. put ornaments on; make more pleasing by addition. **Ex.** *We decorated the hall with flags.* 2. select the colors and furnishings of a house. **Ex.** *They decorated their house in a Spanish style.* 3. give a medal or a ribbon, etc., as an honor. **Ex.** *The soldier was decorated for his heroism.* —**dec'o·ra·tor,** n. one who decorates. —**dec`o·ra'tion,** n. anything used to decorate.

decrease (3) [dikriys'], v. cause to become less; gradually become smaller in size, number, etc. **Ex.** *We will decrease the size of the group from 30 to 20.* —n. 1. a lessening. **Ex.** *There was a decrease in sales this week.* 2. amount of lessening. **Ex.** *The decrease in price was ten percent.*

decree (5) [dikriy'], n. an official government or court order or decision. **Ex.** *By decree all stores were closed for two days.* —v. decide or order by decree. **Ex.** *The judge decreed that a divorce be granted.*

dedicate (4) [ded'əkeyt`], v. 1. devote to a special or sacred purpose. **Ex.** *The statue was dedicated to the soldiers who had died in battle.* 2. give or devote. **Ex.** *A good doctor dedicates his life to serving others.* 3. honor a person by putting his name at the beginning of a book, poem, etc. **Ex.** *The author's latest book was dedicated to his father.* —**ded`i·ca'tion,** n.

deed (2) [diyd'], n. 1. an act; that which is done. **Ex.** *His words do not agree with his deeds.* 2. a paper which shows ownership of property. **Ex.** *After he had paid for the house, he was given a deed to it.*

deem (5) [diym'], v. believe; think; judge. **Ex.** *He deems it wise to remain silent.*

deep (1) [diyp'], adj. 1. going far down. **Ex.** *The ocean is deep here.* 2. going from front to back. **Ex.** *The box is 3 feet wide and 4 feet deep.* 3. extreme. **Ex.** *He is in deep trouble.* 4. low in tone. **Ex.** *He has a deep voice.* 5. strong and dark in color. **Ex.** *Blood is a deep red in color.* 6. feel strongly. **Ex.** *You have my deep sympathy.* 7. greatly absorbed. **Ex.** *They were in deep conversation.* —n. 1. deep thing or place. 2. the most extreme part. **Ex.** *The cold is most severe in the deep of winter.* —adv. to or at a depth.

---

a, far; æ, am; e, get; ey, late; i, in; iy, see; ɔ, all; ow, go; u, put; uw, too; ə, but, ago; ɔr, fur; aw, out; ay, life; oy, boy; ŋ, ring; θ, think; ð, that; ž, measure; š, ship; ǰ, edge; č, child.

Ex. *They must dig deep for water.* —**deep'en,** *v.* —**deep'ly,** *adv.*

deer (3) [di:r'], *n.* a wild animal with hoofs and horns.

DEER

defeat (2) [difiyt'], *v.* 1. overcome; cause to lose in a battle or struggle. Ex. *We defeated the enemy.* 2. make hopeless. Ex. *Our plans for the trip were defeated by the weather.* —*n.* failure; state of having lost. Ex. *After his defeat in the elections, he returned to his former business.*

defect (4) [diy'fekt`, difekt'], *n.* a fault; a weakness; something not perfect. Ex. *The car was unsafe because of a defect in construction.* —*v.* to leave one's cause, group, or country for another. Ex. *He defected because he no longer believed in the policies of his government.*

defend (2) [difend'], *v.* 1. protect; keep safe; guard. Ex. *The dog defended his master from harm.* 2. act, speak, or write in favor of something under attack. Ex. *He wrote a letter to the newspaper defending his actions.* —**de·fend'ant,** *n.* a person against whom legal action is brought. —**de·fend'er,** *n.* one who defends.

defense (3) [difens'], *n.* 1. act of defending; resistance against attack. Ex. *The army's defense of the city was successful.* 2. argument in support of one's actions. Ex. *The President gave a speech in defense of his policies.* 3. that which is used to protect. Ex. *High walls were their only defense against the enemy.*

defer (5) [difər'], *v.* delay until a later time. Ex. *The ship deferred its sailing because of bad weather.* —**de·fer'ment,** *n.*

defer (5) [difər'], *v.* yield to the judgment or opinion of another. Ex. *Youth is expected to defer to old age.* —**def'er·ence,** *n.*

defiance (5) [difay'əns], *n.* the act of defying. Ex. *He showed his defiance by walking away.* —**de·fi'ant,** *adj.*

defile (5) [difayl'], *v.* 1. make dirty or impure. Ex. *The river was defiled by the wastes poured into it.* 2. bring dishonor upon. Ex. *His evil acts defiled his family's name.*

define (4) [difayn'], *v.* 1. give the meaning of; explain. Ex. *A dictionary defines words.* 2. fix the limits of. Ex. *The treaty defined the boundary between the two countries.*

—**def'i·ni'tion,** *n.* meaning. **Ex.** *What is the definition of that word?*

efinite (3) [def'ənət], *adj.* 1. clear; exact. **Ex.** *His meaning is very definite.* 2. limiting; determining; fixed. **Ex.** *This work must be completed within a definite period of time.* —**def'i·nite·ly,** *adv.*

efy (4) [difay'], *v.* 1. dare; challenge to do something that is difficult or not possible. **Ex.** *I defy you to solve this problem.* 2. refuse to obey; pay no attention to. **Ex.** *The driver of the car was defying the law by speeding.* 3. be too difficult to do. **Ex.** *Some beauty defies description.*

egree (1) [dəgriy'], *n.* 1. a step or stage in a series. **Ex.** *The country reached a high degree of civilization.* 2. a unit used in measuring temperature. 3. the 360th part of a circle. (The sign for degree in temperature measurements or parts of a circle is °. **Ex.** *90°.*) 4. the rank given by a university to a student who fulfills certain requirements or to a person as an honor.

elay (2) [diley'], *v.* 1. decide to do at a later time. **Ex.** *He delayed his trip for two weeks.* 2. cause to be late; stop for a time. **Ex.** *The accident delayed the train.* —*n.* a wait; a length of time before something happens or someone appears. **Ex.** *There will be a delay of two hours because of engine trouble.*

elegate (3) [del'əgeyt], *n.* one sent to act for another; one who represents another. **Ex.** *Delegates have been sent by three countries.* —*v.* 1. send to represent. **Ex.** *We delegated one of our most able men to go.* 2. transfer authority or responsibility to another. **Ex.** *He delegated some of the work to his assistant.* —**del'e·ga'tion,** *n.* a group of one or more delegates.

eliberate (4) [dəlib'ərət], *adj.* 1. intentional; for a specific purpose. **Ex.** *The man gave me a deliberate push.* 2. slow and careful in deciding what to do. **Ex.** *She was very deliberate in her actions.* —**de·lib'er·ate·ly,** *adv.* —**de·lib'er·a'tion,** *n.*

eliberate (4) [dəlib'əreyt'], *v.* consider carefully before deciding. **Ex.** *The jury deliberated for several hours before declaring the criminal guilty.*

elicate (2) [del'əkət], *adj.* 1. pleasing because of fineness. **Ex.** *The wine has a delicate flavor.* 2. finely made; fine in quality. **Ex.** *The box was decorated with delicate carvings.*

3. easily broken; not strong. **Ex.** *They drank from delic[.]
glasses.* 4. requiring careful handling. **Ex.** *The teach[.]
handled the delicate problem with understanding.* —**del[.]
cate·ly,** *adv.* —**del'i·ca·cy,** *n.* 1. condition of being delica[.]
2. fine or unusual food.

delicious (3) [dəliš'əs], *adj.* very pleasing to the taste; deligl[.]
ful. **Ex.** *The food was delicious.*

delight (1) [dilayt'], *n.* 1. great joy or pleasure. **Ex.** *She f[.]
great delight at meeting her old friends again.* 2. somethi[.]
that gives pleasure. **Ex.** *A flower garden can be a consta[.]
delight.* —*v.* 1. please greatly. **Ex.** *Their gift delighted h[.]
2. feel great pleasure. **Ex.** *They were delighted to hear t.
good news.* —**de·light'ful,** *adj.*

deliver (2) [diliv'ər], *v.* 1. carry and give to someone. F[.]
Please deliver this package to my mother. 2. speak. **Ex.** *[.]
delivered an excellent speech.* 3. strike. **Ex.** *The fighter d[.]
livered a blow to the head.* 4. help to give birth. **Ex.** *T[.]
doctor delivered the child.* —**de·liv'er·ance,** *n.* the act [.]
delivering; the state of being delivered; rescue. **Ex.** *Th[.]
prayed for the deliverance of the trapped miners.* —[.]
liv'er·y, *n.* the act of delivering.

delusion (5) [diluw'žən], *n.* a mistaken belief, usually a si[.]
of mental illness. **Ex.** *He suffered under the delusion th[.]
he was a king.*

demand (1) [dimænd'], *v.* 1. request as a right. **Ex.** *He d[.]
manded to be heard.* 2. request with authority. **Ex.** *T[.]
policeman demanded our names.* 3. require; need. **Ex.** *T[.]
man's wound demanded immediate attention.* —*n.* 1. act [.]
demanding. **Ex.** *He stated his demand in a loud voice.* 2. [.]
expressed desire for ownership or use. **Ex.** *The gre[.]
demand for cotton cloth raised the price.*

democracy (2) [dəmak'rəsiy], *n.* a system of government [.]
which the people hold the ruling power by electing certa[.]
persons to make the laws and to do the work of th[.]
government.

democrat (2) [dem'əkræt], *n.* 1. a person who believes th[.]
a country should be governed by and for the people. 2. [.]
member of the Democratic party, one of the two ma[.]
political parties in the United States. —**dem'o·crat'ic,** *a[.]

demolish (5) [dimal'iš], *v.* destroy; tear down; ruin. **Ex.** *T[.]
building was demolished by the wreckers.* —**dem'o·li'tio[.]
n. the act of destroying.

demonstrate (4) [dem'ənstreyt'], *v.* 1. prove by facts. **Ex.** *The scientist demonstrated the correctness of his theory.* 2. explain by using examples. **Ex.** *The teacher demonstrated by showing the students pictures.* 3. make a public show of opinions or feelings. **Ex.** *Hundreds demonstrated to protest the tax.* —**dem'on·stra'tion,** *n.* —**de·mon'stra·ble,** *adj.* provable. —**de·mon'stra·tive,** *adj.* showing feelings openly.

den (5) [den'], *n.* 1. a place where a wild animal lives. **Ex.** *The hunter followed the lion to its den.* 2. a small private room used for reading or studying. **Ex.** *The professor worked until midnight in his den.*

denial (5) [dinay'əl], *n.* 1. refusal of a request, right, opportunity, etc. **Ex.** *The denial of her request to leave early upset her.* 2. act of declaring that a statement is not true. **Ex.** *He made a denial of any connection with the crime.*

denounce (5) [dinawns'], *v.* 1. state a dislike for. **Ex.** *He denounced the man as a coward.* 2. inform against; accuse. **Ex.** *She denounced him to the police.*

dense (4) [dens'], *adj.* thick; crowded; close together. **Ex.** *Dense smoke filled the room.* —**dense'ly,** *adv.* —**dense'ness, den'si·ty,** *n.*

dental (5) [den'təl], *adj.* concerning teeth or dentistry. **Ex.** *He needs dental attention.* —**den'tist,** *n.* a doctor whose work is caring for teeth. —**den'tis·try,** *n.* the work of dentists.

deny (2) [dinay'], *v.* 1. declare to be untrue. **Ex.** *I deny that he took the book.* 2. refuse to fulfill a request, allow an opportunity, etc. **Ex.** *His employer denied him an increase in salary.*

depart (4) [dipart'], *v.* 1. leave; go away. **Ex.** *He said good-by and departed.* 2. make a change. **Ex.** *The radio station departed from its usual program.* —**de·par'ture,** *n.*

department (2) [dipart'mənt], *n.* a separate part of a government, business, or other organization. **Ex.** *This college has an excellent history department.* —**de'part·men'tal,** *adj.*

department store [dipart'mənt stɔ:r'], *n.* a large store, organized into departments, selling many different things and services.

depend (2) [dipend'], *v.* 1. rely on for help or support. **Ex.**

ɑ, far; æ, am; e, get; ey, late; i, in; iy, see; ɔ, all; ow, go; u, put; uw, too; ə, but, ago; ər, fur; aw, out; ay, life; oy, boy; ŋ, ring; θ, think; ð, that; ž, measure; š, ship; j, edge; č, child.

Children depend on their parents for food and shelter. be controlled by. **Ex.** *Whether we will go on the trip d* *pends on the weather.* —**de·pend'ent,** *adj.* —**de·pend'ent,** one who depends upon another. —**de·pend'ence,** *n.* sta of being dependent.

deport (2) [dipɔrt'], *v.* force to leave the country. **Ex.** *He w* *deported from the United States.* —**de'por·ta'tion,** *n.*

deposit (3) [dipaz'ət], *v.* 1. put down; place. **Ex.** *Deposit tl* *package on the table.* 2. place in a bank account. **Ex.** *H* *deposited part of his salary in the bank.* 3. give as part c total payment. **Ex.** *He deposited a small amount of mone* *toward the purchase of the car.* —*n.* 1. money in a ban account. 2. a part payment on a purchase. 3. a quantity c a mineral, such as oil or gas, found in nature. **Ex.** *Tl* *country has large oil deposits.* —**de·pos'i·tor'y,** *n.* a plac to deposit things for safekeeping. **Ex.** *The library is a d* *pository for books.*

depression (3) [dipreš'ən], *n.* 1. a place lower than tl surface around it. **Ex.** *The heavy rains filled the depressic* *in the road.* 2. low spirits. **Ex.** *The man had feelings c* *depression because of his illness.* 3. period of reduced bus ness activity during which many people lose their jobs. **E** *There was a severe depression in the 1930's.* —**de·press',** cause to feel unhappy. **Ex.** *The news depressed him.* —**d** **press'ing,** *adj.*

deprive (5) [diprayv'], *v.* keep from using, having, enjoying take away from. **Ex.** *Death deprived the children of the* *parents.* —**dep'ri·va'tion,** *n.*

depth (3) [depθ'], *n.* 1. measurement down from the surfac deepness. **Ex.** *The depth of the river at this point is 20 fee* 2. measurement from the front to the back. **Ex.** *What* *the depth of that box?*

deputy (4) [dep'yuwtiy], *n.* a person appointed to act in plac of another; an assistant. **Ex.** *The sheriff appointed a deputy* —**dep'u·tize,** *v.*

derive (3) [dirayv'], *v.* take; get; obtain; receive. **Ex.** *H* *derives pleasure from books.* —**der'i·va'tion,** *n.* the sourc of something. —**de·riv'a·tive,** *adj.* derived from. —*n.* tha which is derived.

descend (3) [disend'], *v.* go or come down. **Exs.** *The woma* *descended the stairs. The business will descend to my sor* —**descend from,** have as an ancestor. **Ex.** *He is descende* *from a famous writer.* —**de·scend'ant**, *n.* one who is related to a particular ancestor. —**de·scent'**, *n.* act of descending.

describe (2) [diskrayb'], *v.* give an account of. **Ex.** *He described his sister to me.* —**de·scrip'tion**, *n.* written or spoken words used to tell about a person, place, happening, etc. **Ex.** *His description of the child's grief saddened everyone.* —**de·scrip'tive**, *adj.*

desert (2) [dez'ərt], *n.* a dry area, usually sandy, with little or no plant life. **Ex.** *The Arabian desert is very hot.*

desert (2) [dizərt'], *v.* 1. abandon; fail when needed. **Ex.** *He deserted his wife.* 2. leave military duty when not permitted to. **Ex.** *The soldier deserted and fled to a nearby town.* —**de·sert'er**, *n.* —**de·ser'tion**, *n.*

deserve (2) [dizərv'], *v.* be worthy of; merit; earn. **Ex.** *Their efforts deserve to be rewarded.* —**de·serv'ed·ly**, *adv.*

design (2) [dizayn'], *v.* 1. plan; intend; scheme. **Ex.** *Her questions were designed to make me angry.* 2. make plans for. **Ex.** *The girl designed a dress.* —*n.* 1. a sketch or plan; a design for a house, a bridge, etc. 2. an artistic arrangement; a pattern. **Ex.** *The dress has a beautiful design of flowers.*

desire (1) [dizayr'], *v.* want very much. **Ex.** *They desire peace more than anything else.* —*n.* a want; the thing wanted. **Ex.** *His greatest desire is to sleep.* —**de·sir'a·ble**, *adj.* worthy of wanting; valuable. **Ex.** *The house is in a desirable location.*

desk (2) [desk'], *n.* a piece of furniture like a table, usually with drawers, which is used for writing, studying, etc.

desolate (4) [des'ələt], *adj.* 1. not lived in; deserted; ruined. **Ex.** *A few desolate houses stood in the former mining town.* 2. unhappy; miserable; lonely. **Ex.** *She has led a desolate life since his death.* —*v.* ruin; lay waste. **Ex.** *The fire desolated a large part of the city.* —**des'o·late·ly**, *adv.* —**des'o·la'tion**, *n.*

despair (2) [dispe:r'], *n.* state of hopelessness. **Ex.** *He was in despair when his father died.* —*v.* lose hope; be without hope. **Ex.** *They despaired of being rescued.*

desperate (3) [des'pərət], *adj.* 1. despairing; almost without hope. **Ex.** *The enemy attack left them in a desperate situation.* 2. reckless; extreme. **Ex.** *He took a desperate chance.* —**des'per·ate·ly**, *adv.* —**des'per·a'tion**, *n.*

despise (3) [dispayz'], *v.* dislike very much; scorn. **Ex.** *He despises people who lie.* —**des·pi'ca·ble**, *adj.*

despite (3) [dispayt'], *prep.* in spite of; regardless. **Ex.** H
went despite my warning.

dessert (3) [dəzərt'], *n.* a course of sweets or fruits at th
end of a meal. **Ex.** *Apple pie is a favorite American desser*

destine (4) [des'tən], *v.* be fated for. **Ex.** *He was destined t*
become a great president. —**destined for,** going toward a
planned. **Ex.** *The ship was destined for South America*
—**des'ti·na'tion,** *n.*

destiny (4) [des'təniy], *n.* 1. that which is certain to happen
Ex. *It was his destiny to die young.* 2. a course of event
often thought of as determined in advance and impossibl
to change. **Ex.** *Destiny directed him toward the life of*
soldier.

destroy (1) [distroy'], *v.* 1. break into pieces; ruin. **Ex.** *Fir*
destroyed his house. 2. kill. **Ex.** *They destroyed the enemy*
—**de·stroy'er,** *n.* 1. one who destroys. 2. small, speedy shi
of war.

destruction (3) [distrək'šən], *n.* the act of destroying or bein;
destroyed; ruin. **Ex.** *The destruction of their house left then*
no place to live.

detach (5) [ditæč'], *v.* part; separate. **Ex.** *The engine was de*
tached from the rest of the train. —**de·tach'a·ble,** *adj.* —**de
tached',** *adj.* —**de·tach'ment,** *n.* 1. a separation. 2. a grou
of soldiers separated from the others for a special purpose
Ex. *He took a detachment up on the hill.*

detail (2) [diy'teyl', di'teyl'], *n.* one small part of a whole
Ex. *Each detail of the picture was carefully painted.*

detain (5) [diteyn'], *v.* delay; keep from proceeding. **Ex.** *Th*
accident detained us for an hour.

detect (4) [ditekt'], *v.* 1. discover the true character of. **Ex**
He detected a slight degree of fear in her manner. 2. sens
the presence, existence, or fact of. **Ex.** *We detected an odo*
of food in the room. —**de·tec'tion,** *n.* the act of detecting

determine (2) [ditər'mən], *v.* 1. decide. **Ex.** *The judge wil*
determine who is telling the truth. 2. resolve. **Ex.** *I am*
determined to go. 3. establish accurately. **Ex.** *We mus*
determine the boundaries of our property. —**de·ter'mi·na**
tion, *n.* —**de·ter'mined,** *adj.*

develop (2) [divel'əp], *v.* 1. cause to grow by gradual change.
Ex. *Sun and rain develop plants.* 2. make or become larger,

better, more advanced, more knowledgeable. **Ex.** *He developed his mind by study.*

device (1) [divays'], *n.* 1. a tool or machine designed for a special purpose. **Ex.** *The steering device on my car is broken.* 2. a plan or scheme used to produce a certain result. **Ex.** *The child's tears were a device to get attention.*

devil (2) [dev'əl], *n.* an evil spirit or the chief evil spirit. **Ex.** *The Devil appeared to him in a dream.* —**dev'il·ish**, *adj.*

devise (4) [divayz'], *v.* plan; invent. **Ex.** *He devised a new method of doing work.*

devote (2) [divowt'], *v.* give one's time completely to some person, purpose, or service. **Ex.** *The mother devoted herself to caring for her sick child.* —**de·vo'tion**, *n.*

devour (4) [divawr'], *v.* 1. eat hungrily or greedily. **Ex.** *The starving man devoured the food.* 2. destroy; ruin. **Ex.** *Fire devoured the city.* 3. take in eagerly by the senses or the mind. **Ex.** *His eyes devoured the contents of the letter.*

dew (3) [duw', dyuw'], *n.* water from the air which condenses on cool surfaces, especially at night. **Ex.** *There was a heavy dew on the grass early this morning.* —**dew'y**, *adj.*

diamond (2) [day'mənd], *n.* 1. a crystallized mineral; one of the hardest substances known. **Ex.** *A clear, pure diamond is a jewel of great value.* 2. a figure with four equal sides but with unequal angles.

DIAMOND 2

diary (5) [day'əriy], *n.* a daily record, especially of personal observations and experiences. **Ex.** *The traveler kept a diary of his trip.*

dictate (4) [dik'teyt'], *v.* 1. read or say something for another to write. **Ex.** *The president of the company dictated a letter to his secretary.* 2. command with authority; order. **Ex.** *Terms were dictated to the conquered.* —*n.* a command; a rule. **Ex.** *He followed the dictates of his heart.* —**dic·ta'tion**, *n.* —**dic'ta·tor**, *n.* a ruler who has unlimited power. **Ex.** *The country was ruled by a dictator for many years.* —**dic·ta·to'ri·al**, *adj.*

dictionary (3) [dik'šəner'iy], *n.* a reference book in which the words of a language are arranged from *A* to *Z* and for which meanings are given. Ex. *You are now using The New Horizon Ladder Dictionary.*

did (1) [did'], *v.* past tense of *do.* Ex. *He did the work yesterday.*

die (1) [day'], *v.* 1. cease living. Ex. *My father died two years ago.* 2. decrease; become less. Ex. *The music died away.*

diet (3) [day'ət], *n.* 1. usual daily food and drink. Ex. *Bread is an important part of my diet.* 2. a special selection of food eaten for one's health. Ex. *The doctor recommended a diet without salt.* —*v.* be on a diet, especially to lose weight. Ex. *She has been dieting for two weeks.* —di'e·tar`y, *adj.*

differ (3) [dif'ər], *v.* 1. be different. Ex. *She differs from her sister in character.* 2. do not agree. Ex. *Their opinions about politics differ.*

difference (1) [dif'rəns], *n.* the way in which things are not alike. Ex. *One difference between my brother and me is that I like sports.* —**make a difference,** cause a change in a situation; be important. Ex. *Liking your work makes a difference in how you do it.*

different (1) [dif'rənt], *adj.* 1. partly or totally unlike. Ex. *His ideas were different from mine.* 2. not the same. Ex. *Three different people came to see you while you were away.* 3. unusual. Ex. *His style of painting is different.* —dif'fer·ent·ly, *adv.* —dif'fer·en'ti·ate, *v.* see or describe a difference. Ex. *He could not differentiate one color from another.*

difficult (1) [dif'əkəlt`], *adj.* not easy. Ex. *Sewing is difficult for me.* —dif'fi·cul`ty, *n.* 1. that which is not easy to do or understand. 2. trouble. Ex. *He is in difficulty with the law.*

dig (2) [dig'], *v.* 1. open or loosen earth; make a hole in the ground. Ex. *The boys were digging a hole.* 2. bring to the surface. Ex. *Miners dig coal.*

digest (3) [dijest'], *v.* change food in the stomach into a form that the body can use. Ex. *Food must be chewed well to be digested properly.* —*n.* a short form of a long book, story, etc. —di·gest'i·ble, *adj.* able to be digested. Ex. *Soft food is more digestible.* —di·ges'tion, *n.*

dignify (4) [dig'nəfay`], *v.* cause to seem honorable, worthy, and admirable. Ex. *They dignified her job by giving her a special title.* —dig'ni·fied, *adj.* having dignity or honor; noble and serious in manner.

dignity (2) [dig'nətiy], *n.* 1. a quality of goodness that is admired and deserves respect. Ex. *His deeds revealed his dignity.* 2. nobleness of manner or style. Ex. *He walked with the dignity of a king.*

dim (3) [dim'], *adj.* 1. not bright; not clear. Ex. *There was only a dim light.* 2. unclear in seeing or understanding. Ex. *The old man's eyes were dim with tears.* —*v.* make or become less bright. Ex. *He dimmed his lights as he approached another car.* —**dim'ly,** *adv.* —**dim'ness,** *n.*

dime (5) [daym'], *n.* a United States coin worth ten cents; the tenth part of a dollar.

dimension (5) [dimen'šən], *n.* 1. a measurement in length, width, or height. Ex. *What are the dimensions of the room?* 2. extent; importance. Ex. *A project of large dimensions is being discussed by the government.* —**di·men'sion·al,** *adj.*

diminish (4) [dimin'iš], *v.* make less; become smaller in size, amount, or importance; lessen; reduce. Ex. *As their food supply diminished, their hopes were diminished, too.* —**di·min'ish·ing,** *adj.*

dine (2) [dayn'], *v.* 1. eat dinner. Exs. *We always dine at seven. They invited their friends to dine with them.* —**din'er,** *n.* 1. one who dines. 2. a car on a railroad train where meals are served; a lunchroom built to look like this.

dinner (1) [din'ər], *n.* 1. the large meal of the day. Ex. *We always eat dinner at night, but he eats it at noon.* 2. a special meal in honor of some person or occasion. Ex. *This evening we are going to a dinner to honor our doctor.*

dip (3) [dip'], *v.* 1. plunge into any liquid, completely or partly, and lift out. Ex. *She dipped her hand in the cool water.* 2. lift liquid, as with a spoon or cup. Ex. *He dipped soup from the pot with a spoon.* —*n.* 1. the act of dipping; a brief plunge. Ex. *They went for a dip in the ocean.* 2. a liquid into which something is dipped. —**dip'per,** *n.* a container with a long handle used for dipping.

diplomatic (5) [dip'ləmæt'ik], *adj.* 1. relating to the management of affairs between two countries. Ex. *The diplomatic service represents our government in foreign capitals.* 2. having the ability to deal with others without giving offense. Ex. *His diplomatic remarks satisfied everyone.* —**dip'lo·mat,** *n.* a person who represents his country in dealing with another country. —**di·plo'ma·cy,** *n.*

direct (1) [dərekt'], *v.* 1. manage; control. **Ex.** *The policeman directed traffic.* 2. command; order. **Ex.** *The teacher directed us to sit quietly.* 3. point or aim toward. **Ex.** *He directed his eyes at the girl.* 4. tell or show the way or road. **Ex.** *Can you direct me to the hotel?* —*adj.* 1. not through some other person or thing; personal; immediate. **Ex.** *He was in direct contact with the President.* 2. proceeding in a straight line or by the shortest course. **Ex.** *This is the most direct road to the city.* 3. frank; honest. **Ex.** *Please give me a direct answer.* —**di·rec'tion,** *n.* the way in which or the place toward which someone or something is directed. **Ex.** *He went in that direction.* —**di·rec'tor,** *n.* one who directs. —**di·rec' tory,** *n.* a book which lists names and addresses, etc. —**di· rect'ly,** *adv.* straight; immediately; **Ex.** *Go directly home.*

dirt (2) [dərt'], *n.* 1. anything that is not clean, such as dust, mud, etc. **Ex.** *She washed the dirt from her hands.* 2. loose or packed earth; soil. **Ex.** *He was in the garden digging in the dirt.*

dirty (2) [dər'tiy], *adj.* not clean; soiled by dirt. **Ex.** *He wore a dirty shirt.* —*v.* make dirty; soil. **Ex.** *Try not to dirty your new clothes.*

dis- (2) [dis], *prefix.* 1. reversal or undoing of an act. **Exs.** *Belief, disbelief; appear, disappear.* 2. stop; refuse to. **Exs.** *Agree, disagree; obey, disobey.*

disappear (2) [dis'əpi:r'], *v.* 1. become unseen. **Ex.** *The ship disappeared in the distance.* 2. be lost; cease to exist. **Ex.** *The old houses have all disappeared from this street.* —**dis\ ap·pear'ance,** *n.*

disappoint (2) [dis'əpoynt'], *v.* fail to satisfy the hopes, expectations, or wishes of. **Ex.** *The boy's failure at school disappointed his parents.* —**dis'ap·point'ment,** *n.* —**dis'ap· point'ing,** *adj.* **Ex.** *His work was disappointing.*

disaster (4) [dizæs'tər], *n.* sudden and extraordinary bad fortune. **Ex.** *The flood was a disaster for the village.* —**dis·as' trous,** *adj.* causing disaster.

discern (5) [disərn'], *v.* see or understand clearly through the senses or mental powers; distinguish; recognize. **Ex.** *In the darkness I could not discern his face.* —**dis·cern'i·ble,** *adj.* —**dis·cern'ment,** *n.*

discharge (3) [dis'čarǰ', dis'čarǰ], *v.* 1. relieve from work or responsibility. **Ex.** *He was discharged from his job.* 2. un-

load. Ex. *The bus discharged the children at the school.*
3. shoot; fire a gun. Ex. *The gun discharged with a loud
noise.* 4. set at liberty. Ex. *The patient was discharged from
the hospital.* —*n.* act of discharging. Ex. *His discharge from
the army left him free to return to school.*

discipline (4) [dis'əplin], *n.* 1. strict training of mind and body
to obey rules and control one's behavior. Ex. *Military
schools are known for their discipline.* 2. orderly conduct;
self-control. Ex. *A poorly organized paper shows lack of
discipline.* —*v.* 1. train in obedience and control. Ex. *He
disciplined himself by walking two miles every day.* 2. punish. Ex. *They disciplined the children by sending them to
bed early.* —**dis'ci·pli·nar'y,** *adj.*

disclose [dis'klowz'], *v.* show; reveal; open. Ex. *He disclosed
to us that he was leaving.* —**dis·clo'sure,** *n.*

discord (5) [dis'kɔrd'], *n.* 1. lack of agreement; conflict. Ex.
There was discord over what should be done. 2. an unpleasant combination of sounds.

discount [dis'kawnt'], *n.* the amount by which a price is lowered. Ex. *Buy now and get a ten-percent discount from the
usual price.* —*v.* 1. give an amount off. Ex. *We are discount-
ing the price ten percent today.* 2. believe only in part. Ex.
Discount half of what he says.

discourage [diskər'ij], *v.* cause to give up hope or lose confidence. Ex. *His father's criticism discouraged the boy.*

discourse (5) [dis'kɔrs'], *n.* 1. an orderly expression of ideas
in speech or writing. Ex. *The judge's talk was a discourse
on the need for law.* 2. conversation; talk. Ex. *In their discourse after dinner, they talked about politics.* —*v.* talk;
express ideas in an orderly way. Ex. *They discoursed on the
subject of the election.*

discover (1) [diskəv'ər], *v.* find or learn something for the
first time. Ex. *Columbus discovered America in 1492.*
—**dis·cov'er·y,** *n.*

discreet (5) [diskriyt'], *adj.* showing good judgment in conduct, especially in speech; careful in action and speech. Ex.
Bankers are usually very discreet. —**dis·creet'ly,** *adv.* —**dis·
creet'ness,** *n.*

a, far; æ, am; e, get; ey, late; i, in; iy, see; ɔ, all; ow, go; u, put; uw, too;
ə, but, ago; ər, fur; aw, out; ay, life; oy, boy; ŋ, ring; θ, think; ð, that;
ž, measure; š, ship; j, edge; č, child.

discuss (2) [diskəs'], v. consider by presenting various ideas and opinions; talk about. **Ex.** *The business partners discussed their plans for the coming year.* —**dis·cus'sion,** *n.*

disdain (5) [disdeyn'], v. regard as unworthy; scorn. **Ex.** *He disdains work of any kind.* —*n.* scorn. **Ex.** *She spoke to the poor young man with disdain.* —**dis·dain'ful,** *adj.*

disease (2) [diziyz'], *n.* sickness; illness. **Ex.** *A person with that disease will have a fever.*

disgrace (4) [disgreys'], *n.* 1. loss of honor and respect; shame. **Ex.** *His bad conduct led to his disgrace.* 2. cause of shame; that which makes one lose honor. **Ex.** *His actions were a disgrace to his family.* —*v.* cause to be shamed. **Ex.** *The young man disgraced his family by his marriage.* —**dis·grace'ful,** *adj.* —**dis·grace'ful·ly,** *adv.*

disguise (4) [disgayz'], v. 1. change the dress or appearance in order not to be known or in order to appear as someone else. **Ex.** *He was disguised as an old man.* 2. hide the true nature or character of. **Ex.** *He disguised his greed with generous words.* —*n.* 1. clothing or costume that changes appearance. **Ex.** *No one recognized him in his disguise.* 2. that which conceals the real nature or character of a person or thing. **Ex.** *His smiling face was a disguise for a very unfriendly nature.*

disgust (4) [disgəst'], *n.* a very strong feeling of dislike. **Ex.** *The smell of the rotten meat filled her with disgust.* —*v.* cause to feel disgust. **Ex.** *Her bad behavior disgusted him.* —**dis·gust'ing,** *adj.*

dish (1) [diš'], *n.* 1. a plate, bowl, or cup in which food is served at the table. 2. the food served in a dish; any particular food. **Ex.** *Fried chicken is his favorite dish.*

dismal (5) [diz'məl], *adj.* dark and cheerless; sorrowful. **Ex.** *The rain made the autumn day dismal.* —**dis'mal·ly,** *adv.*

dismay (4) [dismey'], v. cause fear or dread so that one is unable to act; frighten; alarm. **Ex.** *He was dismayed by the sight of the burning house.* —*n.* sudden loss of courage. **Ex.** *The sight of the damaged car filled her with dismay.*

dismiss (4) [dismis'], v. send someone away; allow to go. **Ex.** *The children at the school were dismissed and told to go home.* 2. discharge; remove from office, service, or employment. **Ex.** *He was dismissed because he was always late for work.* 3. refuse to consider further. **Ex.** *The matter was so* *unimportant that she dismissed it from her thoughts.* **—dis· miss'al,** *n.*

disorder [disɔr'dər], *n.* 1. confusion; absence of order. **Ex.** *His papers were in disorder.* 2. disturbance; riot. **Ex.** *Police quieted the disorder.* **—dis·or'der·ly,** *adj.*

dispatch (4) [dispæč], *v.* 1. send off quickly. **Ex.** *They dispatched a telegram.* 2. get something done quickly. **Ex.** *He dispatched his business in a few hours.* **—n.** 1. promptness; speed. **Ex.** *He did his work with dispatch.* 2. a written message. **Ex.** *The dispatch contained important news.* **—dis· patch'er,** *n.* a person who dispatches.

dispense (5) [dispens'], *v.* give out in portions; distribute. **Ex.** *The nurse was dispensing medicine.* **—dis·pen'sa·ry,** *n.* a place where medicines are prepared and distributed. **—dis· pense with,** do without; do away with. **Ex.** *We can dispense with further discussion.*

disperse (5) [dispərs'], *v.* 1. cause to break apart and go different ways; scatter. **Ex.** *The crowd dispersed when the rain fell.* 2. spread. **Ex.** *Daily papers disperse the news quickly.* 3. cause to disappear or vanish. **Ex.** *The hot sun will disperse the fog.* **—dis·pers'al,** *n.*

display (2) [displey'], *v.* 1. spread out; exhibit. **Ex.** *They display their flag on national holidays.* 2. show or reveal. **Ex.** *When questioned, they displayed their ignorance.* **—n.** an exhibit; a show. **Ex.** *We enjoyed the interesting displays at the fair.*

dispose (3) [dispowz'], *v.* 1. get rid of; do away with. **Ex.** *They disposed of the paper by burning it.* 2. arrange or settle matters finally. **Ex.** *We were not able to dispose of the problem.* **—dis·pos'a·ble,** *adj.* **—dis·pos'al,** *n.* the disposing of something.

dispute (3) [dispyuwt'], *v.* 1. oppose by argument; quarrel. **Ex.** *The villagers are disputing the building of a new road.* 2. doubt the truth of; question. **Ex.** *He disputed my word.* **—n.** an argument; a quarrel. **Ex.** *They had a bitter dispute about money.*

disrupt (4) [disrəpt'], *v.* create a disturbance; cause a speech, a meeting, a plan, etc. to be interrupted in a disorderly way. **Ex.** *The noisy students disrupted the class.*

dissolve (3) [dizalv'], *v.* 1. mix evenly in a liquid. **Ex.** *He dis-*

solved some sugar in his coffee. 2. end. **Ex.** *The two men dissolved their partnership.* 3. disappear; fade away. **Ex.** *Their fears dissolved with the coming of day.*

distance (1) [dis'təns], *n.* the amount of space between two locations or objects. **Ex.** *The distance from my house to yours is two miles.*

distant (1) [dis'tənt], *adj.* 1. separated; away. **Ex.** *The town is two miles distant.* 2. not near; far; separated in space, time, or other scale. **Ex.** *The moon is distant from the earth.* —**dis·tant·ly,** *adv.*

distinct (3) [distiŋkt'], *adj.* 1. unlike; different; individual. **Ex.** *A dog has characteristics distinct from those of a cat.* 2. clear; plain. **Ex.** *His handwriting was very distinct.* —**dis·tinct'ly,** *adv.* —**dis·tinc'tion,** *n.*

distinguish (3) [distiŋ'gwiš], *v.* 1. recognize one thing from, or among, others; recognize as different. **Ex.** *I was able to distinguish my friend in the crowd.* 2. perceive clearly. **Ex.** *The night was too dark to distinguish the man's face.* 3. make oneself famous or well-known. **Ex.** *The man distinguished himself as an author.* —**dis·tin'guish·a·ble,** *adj.*

distract (5) [distrækt'], *v.* 1. have one's mind or attention drawn away from what one is doing. **Ex.** *She was distracted from her work by a noise.* 2. confuse to the point that one is unable to think. **Ex.** *He was distracted by the many instructions he received.* —**dis·trac'tion,** *n.* anything which distracts, either pleasantly or unpleasantly.

distress (3) [distres'], *n.* 1. physical or mental suffering; pain; trouble. **Ex.** *The sick woman was in great distress.* 2. a state of danger. **Ex.** *The ship was in distress and called for help.* —*v.* cause suffering or worry. **Ex.** *The bad news distressed them.* —**dis·tress'ing,** *adv.*

distribute (3) [distrib'yət], *v.* divide among many. **Ex.** *Please distribute the books to the students.* —**dis'tri·bu'tion,** *n.*

district (2) [dis'trikt], *n.* 1. a definite portion of a city or state. **Ex.** *He was elected to represent his district.* 2. any portion of territory; region. **Ex.** *They live in a farming district.*

disturb (3) [distərb'], *v.* 1. bother; interrupt. **Ex.** *The doctor is busy; you must not disturb him.* 2. make uneasy; worry; trouble. **Ex.** *His unfriendly manner disturbs me.* 3. change the correct or normal condition of. **Ex.** *The wind disturbed* *the papers on the desk.* —**dis·turb'ance,** *n.* —**dis·turb'ing,** *adj.*

ditch (3) [dič'], *n.* a narrow channel, usually long, dug in the earth. **Ex.** *The workmen dug a ditch beside the road to drain the water away.*

dive (4) [dayv'], *v.* 1. jump into water, especially headfirst. **Ex.** *The swimmers dived from the side of the boat.* 2. plunge into, physically or mentally. **Ex.** *The rabbit dived into the hole.* 3. plunge downward. **Ex.** *The plane dived toward the earth.* —*n.* 1. a plunge into water. 2. a plunge down or a sudden plunge. —**div'er,** *n.*

divert (5) [divərt'], *v.* 1. turn aside or in a different direction. **Ex.** *The river was diverted from its channel by the engineers.* 2. turn away from business or study; amuse; entertain. **Ex.** *The children diverted themselves by playing games.* —**di·vert'ing,** *adj.* —**di·ver'sion,** *n.*

divide (1) [divayd'], *v.* 1. separate; keep apart. **Ex.** *A fence divided his property from mine.* 2. share; separate into portions and distribute. **Ex.** *The four men divided the money among themselves.* 3. separate by feelings or ideas. **Ex.** *A difference of opinion divided the family.*

divine (3) [divayn'], *adj.* 1. of a god. **Ex.** *People thought that the storm was a divine punishment.* 2. holy; religious. **Ex.** *Divine services were held once a week.*

division (3) [diviž'ən], *n.* 1. the act of dividing. 2. one of the parts into which something is divided. **Ex.** *The work is handled by another division of the business.*

divorce (3) [divɔrs'], *n.* the legal ending of marriage. **Ex.** *His wife asked him for a divorce.* —*v.* 1. separate by divorce. **Ex.** *She has been divorced for a year.* 2. separate. **Ex.** *It is difficult to divorce politics from government.*

dizzy (4) [diz'iy], *adj.* affected with a spinning or unsteady feeling. **Ex.** *She became dizzy from the heat and fainted.* —**diz'zi·ly,** *adv.* —**diz'zi·ness,** *n.*

do (1) [duw'], *v.* 1. perform. **Ex.** *They do their work well.* 2. put forth effort. **Ex.** *Do your best.* 3. take care of. **Ex.** *My sister and I do the housework.* 4. be satisfactory. **Ex.** *This coat will not do for the winter.* 5. bring about; cause.

a, far; æ, am; e, get; ey, late; i, in; iy, see; ɔ, all; ow, go; u, put; uw, too; ə, but, ago; ər, fur; aw, out; ay, life; oy, boy; ŋ, ring; θ, think; ð, that; ž, measure; š, ship; j, edge; č, child.

Ex. *A rest will do you good.* 6. fare; prosper. **Ex.** *How do you do?* (The verb *do* has some special uses which have no definite meaning: 1. in asking questions. **Ex.** *Do you like English?* 2. in emphasizing a verb. **Ex.** *You say you do not have the book, but you do have it.* 3. in taking the place of a verb, to avoid repeating it. **Ex.** *She walks the way I do.*) —**do away with,** get rid of. **Ex.** *We can do away with these old papers.* —**have to do with,** be about; be on the subject of. —**make do,** manage. **Ex.** *We will make do with the money we have.*

dock (4) [dak'], *n.* 1. a platform built along the shore or out over the water, at which ships load or unload. 2. a space between two piers for a ship. —*v.* come into a dock. **Ex.** *The ship docked early in the morning.*

doctor (1) [dak'tər], *n.* 1. a person trained in medicine to treat sick or injured people. 2. the holder of an advanced academic degree. **Ex.** *He is a Doctor of Philosophy.*

doctrine (5) [dak'trən], *n.* that which is taught as a principle in any branch of knowledge. **Ex.** *Every religion has its own doctrine.* —**doc'tri·nal,** *adj.*

document (4) [dak'yəmənt], *n.* an original or official paper relied upon as proof or support of something. **Ex.** *The Declaration of Independence is an important document of American history.* —*v.* provide or prove with documents. **Ex.** *The lawyer's arguments were well documented.* —**doc'u·men'ta·ry,** *adj.* having, using, or being documents. —**doc'u·men·ta'tion,** *n.*

dodge (4) [daj'], *v.* 1. move quickly to one side. **Ex.** *The man jumped aside to dodge the car.* 2. avoid some duty or responsibility by a trick. **Ex.** *He dodged the question by pretending not to hear it.* —*n.* 1. the action of dodging. 2. a skillful trick. —**dodg'er,** *n.*

does (1) [dəz'], present tense of the verb *do,* used with nouns in the singular and he, she, and it. **Ex.** *The boy does his work well.*

dog (1) [dɔ:g'], *n.* a meat-eating animal often kept as a pet.

DOG

dole (5) [dowl'], *n.* giving of food, money, etc., to the poor. —*v.* give in small bits. **Ex.** *He doled out the money* money, etc. to the poor. —*v.* give in

doll (2) [dal¹], *n.* a small figure of a baby or child used as a toy. **Ex.** *Little girls like to play with dolls.*

dollar (1) [dal¹ər], *n.* a unit of money in the United States equal to 100 cents. (The sign for dollar is $. **Ex.** *$1.00.*) **Ex.** *That book will cost you one dollar.*

-dom (2) [dəm], *suffix.* 1. rank; office; area. **Ex.** *King, kingdom.* 2. state of being. **Ex.** *Free, freedom.*

domain (5) [dow˅meyn¹], *n.* 1. a territory under the rule of; an estate. **Ex.** *The king was respected throughout his domain.* 2. a field of thought or action. **Ex.** *Chemistry is that scientist's domain.*

dome (4) [dowm¹], *n.* a round roof shaped like an upside-down bowl.

domestic (3) [dəmes¹tik], *adj.* 1. of the household and family. **Ex.** *Cooking and sewing are domestic tasks.* 2. of or manufactured in one's own country; not foreign. 3. accustomed to living with people. **Ex.** *Cats and dogs are domestic animals.* —**do·mes'ti·cal·ly,** *adv.*

DOME

—**do˅mes'ti·cate,** *v.* tame or train an animal to live with people. —**do˅mes·ti'ci·ty,** *n.* life at home.

dominate (4) [dam¹əneyt˅], *v.* 1. rule or control by power or authority; govern. **Ex.** *The weak are dominated by the strong.* 2. hold a commanding position over. **Ex.** *The building on the hill dominates the city.* —**dom˅i·na'tion,** *n.*

dominion (4) [dəmin¹yən], *n.* 1. supreme authority; power of governing. **Ex.** *Few countries now hold dominion over distant lands.* 2. the territory governed.

done (1) [dən¹], *v.* past participle of the verb *do.* **Ex.** *He has done his work well.*

donkey (4) [dɔŋ¹kiy], *n.* an animal somewhat like a small horse with long ears.

don't (1) [downt¹], short form, or contraction, of *do not.* **Ex.** *Don't be late.*

DONKEY

doom (4) [duwm¹], *n.* 1. fate or destiny, especially an unhappy or tragic one; ruin; death. **Ex.** *Her car carried her over the cliff to her doom.* 2. a judgment; a sentence to punishment. **Ex.** *The prisoner heard his doom pronounced.* —*v.* sentence to some fate. **Ex.** *The criminal was doomed to death.*

door (1) [dɔ:r'], *n.* a piece of wood or metal for opening or closing an entrance to a building or room.

doorway [dɔ:r'wey'], *n.* the opening in which a door is located. **Ex.** *I could see a young girl standing in the doorway of the kitchen.*

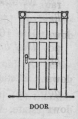

DOOR

dot (2) [dat'], *n.* 1. a very small mark (·). **Ex.** *He made a dot on the paper with his pencil.* 2. a small spot, usually round. **Ex.** *Her dress is red with white dots.* —*v.* mark with or as with a dot or many dots. **Ex.** *The grass was dotted with tiny flowers.*

double (1) [dəb'əl], *adj.* 1. twice in size, quantity, etc. **Ex.** *The bigger boys received double portions of food.* 2. consisting of two parts or layers. **Ex.** *The double doors led to the dining room.* —*n.* twice as much; twice as many. **Ex.** *He is earning double your salary.* —*v.* make or become double in size, quantity, etc. **Ex.** *The merchant doubled his last month's sales.* —**dou'bly,** *adv.* —**double over,** fold or bend over. **Ex.** *He doubled over because of the pain.* —**double up,** 1. fold over or bend. **Ex.** *The pain caused him to double up.* 2. form into twos. **Ex.** *Double up that line of men.*

doubt (1) [dawt'], *v.* be uncertain about; not trust; question. **Ex.** *I doubt that he will come.* —*n.* a condition of being uncertain or unsure. **Ex.** *We are in doubt about the results.*

dough (5) [dow'], *n.* a mixture of flour, water or milk, and other materials for baking.

down (1) [dawn'], *adv.* 1. at, in, or toward a lower position. **Ex.** *He lay down on the bed.* 2. to a lesser quantity or amount. **Ex.** *The price of food is down this month.* 3. from a past time to the present. **Ex.** *Down through the years, the styles have changed.* 4. in cash, usually a part payment. **Ex.** *You can buy it for five dollars down and five dollars each week.* —*prep.* 1. from a higher to a lower place. **Ex.** *Water runs downhill.* 2. along. **Ex.** *We walked down the road.* —**down and out,** poor; having bad luck. **Ex.** *It is nice to have friends when you are down and out.*

downcast [dawn'kæst'], *adj.* 1. very sad. **Ex.** *He seems downcast today.* 2. toward the ground. **Ex.** *His downcast eyes made him seem shy.*

downfall [dawn'fɔ:l'], *n.* 1. a loss of position or power. **Ex.**

Excessive drinking led to his downfall. 2. a heavy fall of rain or snow, often sudden. Ex. *He was soaked when the light rain turned into a downfall.*

downgrade [dawn'greyd'], *v.* lower the value of or the importance of; lower the regard for. Ex. *They downgraded his job.*

downhearted [dawn'har'təd], *adj.* unhappy. Ex. *He seems so downhearted today.*

downpour [dawn'pɔ:r'], *n.* a heavy rain.

downtown (3) [dawn'tawn'], *adv.* to, toward, or in the business center of a town. Ex. *My father goes downtown every day.*

dozen (2) [dəz'ən], *n.* a set of twelve. Ex. *We need a dozen eggs.*

draft (3) [dræft'], *n.* 1. a current of air. Ex. *He sat in a draft between two open doors.* 2. the choosing of people for military service. Ex. *He was not accepted for the draft because of poor eyesight.* 3. a plan or sketch of something to be done; an outline or a rough version of a piece of writing. Ex. *He is reworking the first draft of his novel.* —*v.* 1. make a plan or sketch of; write out. Ex. *He drafted plans for a house.* 2. select for some special purpose, as for military service. Ex. *He was drafted into the army.* —**draft'y**, *adj.* having a current of air.

drag (2) [dræg'], *v.* slowly pull a heavy thing. Ex. *The little boy dragged the large box up the hill.*

drain (3) [dreyn'], *v.* 1. draw off a liquid gradually; draw off completely. Ex. *The wet land was drained of water so houses could be built on it.* 2. empty of wealth, strength, etc. by drawing from it gradually; exhaust. Ex. *Her energy was drained away by overwork.* 3. empty into. Ex. *This river drains into the sea.* —*n.* a pipe or other means of draining. Ex. *The drain in the kitchen sink is not working.* —**drain'er, drain'age,** *n.*

drama (4) [dra'mə, dræm'ə], *n.* a story written, sometimes in verse, to be acted on a stage; a play. —**dra·mat'ic,** *adj.* exciting, like a drama. Ex. *He spoke in a dramatic way.* —**dram'a·tist,** *n.* one who writes dramas. —**dram'a·tize,** *v.*

1. make into a drama. **Ex.** *The writer dramatized the book.*
2. present in a dramatic way. **Ex.** *Pictures of the children dramatized the need for food.*

drank (2) [dræŋk¹], *v.* past tense of *drink.* **Ex.** *He drank a glass of water and asked for another.*

draw (2) [drɔ:¹], *v.* 1. form a picture with a pencil, paint, etc. **Ex.** *That artist draws beautiful flowers.* 2. pull. **Ex.** *A horse was needed to draw the wagon.* 3. attract. **Ex.** *This speaker always draws a large crowd.* —**draw¹ing,** *n.* a picture that has been made with a pencil or pen. —**draw out,** make more lengthy. **Ex.** *He draws out his speeches so much that people get tired.* —**draw up,** prepare in written form. **Ex.** *I will draw up legal papers that will give you ownership of the house.*

drawback [drɔ:¹bæk¹], *n.* a thing or condition that halts or holds back. **Ex.** *His poor speaking voice is a drawback to his success.*

drawer (3) [drɔ:r¹], *n.* 1. a boxlike container, part of a larger piece of furniture, that slides in and out and is used for storage. 2. one who draws.

DRAWER 1

drawn (2) [drɔ:n¹], *v.* past participle of *draw.* **Ex.** *The cart was drawn by two horses.* —*adj.* looking very tired; pale.

dread (3) [dred¹], *v.* fear greatly; look forward to with fear and terror. **Ex.** *He dreaded the day he would have to leave home.* —*n.* great fear. **Ex.** *Some people have a dread of snakes.*

dream (1) [driym¹], *n.* 1. a series of thoughts, pictures, or emotions that occur during sleep. **Ex.** *I had a disturbing dream last night.* 2. something like a dream which one keeps in mind when awake. **Ex.** *It was her dream to live on an island someday.* —*v.* have a dream. —**dream¹er,** *n.* —**dream¹i·ly,** *adv.* —**dream¹y,** *adj.*

dreary (4) [drir¹iy], *adj.* cheerless; without joy; dull. **Ex.** *The rain made the house seem dreary.* —**drear¹i·ly,** *adv.* —**drear¹i·ness,** *n.*

dress (1) [dres¹], *n.* 1. the outer garment worn by women or girls. **Ex.** *She wore a pretty dress.* 2. clothing in general. **Ex.** *I knew that he was a stranger by his unusual dress.* —*v.* 1. put on clothes. **Ex.** *The mother dressed her children* *quickly.* 2. put on medicine and bandages. **Ex.** *The doctor dressed her sore arm.* —**dress'y,** *adj.*

dressing [dres'iŋ], *n.* 1. a cloth placed on a sore. **Ex.** *The doctor put on a new dressing.* 2. a sauce, usually for salads. 3. a mixture placed inside a chicken, duck, etc., when roasting. 4. the act of putting on clothing.

drew (2) [druw'], *v.* past tense of *draw.* **Exs.** *The boy drew a picture of a horse. The horse drew the wagon along the street.*

dried (1) [drayd'], *v.* past tense and participle of *dry.* **Ex.** *She dried the wet boy.*

drift (3) [drift'], *v.* 1. carry or be carried by currents. **Ex.** *The boat drifted toward the shore.* 2. going along without knowing or caring where one is going. **Ex.** *He drifted from one town to another.* 3. heap or be heaped up by the wind. **Ex.** *The snow drifted across the road.* —*n.* 1. the act of drifting; the amount of drift. **Ex.** *They mapped the drift of the ocean current.* 2. anything that has been piled up or driven by wind or water. **Ex.** *They built walls to control the drifts of sand.* —**drift'er,** *n.*

drill (4) [dril'], *n.* 1. a tool for making holes. 2. the act or exercise of training soldiers, especially in marching. **Ex.** *The troops had a drill in the street.* —*v.* 1. make a hole using a drill. **Ex.** *He drilled a hole in the board.* 2. go through exercises, physical or mental, to learn. 3. train soldiers.

drink (1) [driŋk'], *v.* 1. swallow water or any liquid. **Ex.** *We drink coffee with our dinner.* 2. take alcoholic liquors. **Ex.** *What will you have to drink? I am having wine.* —*n.* 1. any liquid swallowed. **Ex.** *She wants a drink of water.* 2. liquor containing alcohol. **Ex.** *He went into the bar for a drink.* —**drink'er,** *n.* —**drink to,** drink as an offering of good wishes. **Ex.** *I drink to your health.*

drip (4) [drip'], *v.* fall or let fall in drops. **Ex.** *When the roof leaked, water dripped from the ceiling.* —*n.* the falling of a liquid drop by drop. **Ex.** *We heard the drip of water outside the window.* —**drip'pings,** the liquid that falls from cooking meat.

drive (1) [drayv'], *v.* 1. go, or take, in a motor car. **Ex.** *They drive to work in their car every morning.* 2. push or urge forward, back, or away from. **Ex.** *The boy drives the sheep to the shed.* 3. control and direct the movement of an automobile, wagon, etc. **Ex.** *He drives a bus.* —*n.* 1. a journey in an automobile. **Ex.** *They would like to go for a drive.* 2. a road to drive on. **Ex.** *The road is called Riverside Drive because it follows the river.* 3. an organized effort by a group of people; a campaign. **Ex.** *They had a drive to raise money for charity.* —**driv'er,** *n.* —**drive at,** mean; intend. **Ex.** *I know what he is driving at when he says that.*

droop (3) [druwp'], *v.* 1. hang, sink, or bend down from hunger, exhaustion, etc. **Ex.** *Flowers droop when they need water.* 2. be low in spirits or sad. **Ex.** *Our spirits drooped when we heard we could not go.* —*n.* a sloping down; a drooping. **Ex.** *The droop of his shoulders showed his despair.*

drop (1) [drap'], *n.* 1. the small quantity of liquid that falls in one round mass. **Ex.** *A drop of rain struck his cheek.* 2. a sudden fall. **Ex.** *The child's drop from the roof injured him.* 3. the distance of the fall. **Ex.** *It was a drop of five feet.* —*v.* 1. fall; let fall. **Ex.** *The man dropped to the ground.* 2. go lower; sink. **Ex.** *Prices dropped sharply.* —**drop in,** visit. —**drop out,** stop being part of; quit. **Ex.** *He dropped out of school.*

drought (5) [drawt', drɔ:t'], *n.* a prolonged period of dry weather, with little or no rain. **Ex.** *Many trees died during the long drought.*

drove (2) [drowv'], *v.* past tense of *drive.* **Ex.** *He drove the car down the road.* —*n.* a group moving together or being driven. **Ex.** *A drove of cattle blocked the road.*

drown (3) [drawn'], *v.* die or kill by keeping the head under water or other liquid. **Ex.** *They were drowned when the ship sank.*

drowsy (5) [draw'ziy], *adj.* sleepy; half-asleep. **Ex.** *Put the drowsy child to bed.* —**drowse',** *v.* —**drow'si·ly,** *adv.* —**drow'si·ness,** *n.*

drug (3) [drəg'], *n.* 1. anything used as a medicine or in making medicines. **Ex.** *Drugs should be used only at the direction of a doctor.* 2. a substance used to relieve pain or bring about sleep. —*v.* put to sleep or make dull by the use of drugs. **Ex.** *He walked as if he were drugged.* —**drug'gist,** *n.* one who makes or sells drugs.

drum (2) [drəm'], *n.* a hollow musical instrument that is played by beating upon the flat ends with sticks or with the hands, —*v.* beat or play on a drum. —**drum'mer,** *n.* one who plays a drum.

drumstick [drəm'stik`], *n.* 1. a stick for playing a drum. 2. the leg of a chicken or other bird, when cooked.

drunk (4) [drəŋk`], *v.* past participle of *drink*. Ex. *He said he had drunk too much.* —*adj.* overcome by or behaving as if overcome by alcoholic liquor. Ex. *He was drunk and did not know what he was doing.* —**drunk, drunk'ard,** *n.* one who is frequently drunk. —**drunk'en,** *adj.* —**drunk'en·ly,** *adv.*

dry (1) [dray`], *adj.* 1. not wet. Ex. *The clothes are dry.* 2. thirsty. Ex. *His throat was very dry after working in the sun.* 3. not interesting; dull. Ex. *His lecture was dry.* —*v.* make or become dry. Ex. *He hung his clothes on the line to dry.* —**dry'ly, dri'ly,** *adv.* —**dry'ness,** *n.* —**dry up,** become dry; lose water. Ex. *The well has dried up, and so we have no water.*

dry-clean [dray'kliyn`], *v.* clean clothes with something other than water. —**dry cleaning,** the cleaning of materials without water. —**dry cleaner,** one whose business is to clean clothes. Ex. *Silk dresses should be sent to a dry cleaner.*

dryer [dray'ər], *n.* a machine that dries by the use of heat or forced air. Ex. *She put the wet clothes in the dryer.*

dry measure [dray' mež'ər], a measure of dry things. See **Weights and Measures.**

duck (1) [dək`], *n.* a flat-billed, swimming bird with a short neck and legs, often raised for its meat. Ex. *She prepared the roast duck with an orange sauce.* —**duck'ling,** *n.* a baby duck.

duck (1) [dək`], *v.* move or lower the head or body, usually to avoid being hit, seen, etc. Ex. *He ducked when I tried to hit him.*

due (1) [duw`], *adj.* 1. owed as a debt. Ex. *This money is due me for the work I did.* 2. expected. Ex. *The plane is due any minute now.* —*n.* that which is owed. Ex. *Give the man his due.* —*adv.* directly. Ex. *The ocean is due east of us.* —**due to,** caused by. Ex. *The closing of school was due to the snow.*

dug (3) [dəg`], *v.* past tense and participle of *dig*. Ex. *The dog dug up the bone.*

dull (2) [dəl'], *adj.* 1. tiring; boring; uninteresting. **Ex.** *That is a dull book.* 2. not cheerful; not colorful. **Ex.** *A rainy day is likely to be dull.* 3. not sharp. **Ex.** *The knife is so dull that it will not cut.* 4. stupid; slow to understand. **Ex.** *He is a dull child.* —**dull'ness**, *n.*

dumb (3) [dəm'], *adj.* unable to speak. **Ex.** *The child was born dumb.* —**dumb'ly**, *adv.* **Ex.** *The girl stared at the man dumbly.*

dump (4) [dəmp'], *v.* throw down; unload. **Ex.** *The workmen dumped the dirt into the hole.* —*n.* a place for dumping things that are not wanted.

dump truck [dəmp' trək'], *n.* a truck with a back end that moves up and down to permit dumping.

dumpy [dəmp'iy], *adj.* short and fat.

dungeon (5) [dən'jən], *n.* a dark prison or cell, usually underground.

during (1) [dur'iŋ, dyur'iŋ], *prep.* 1. through the whole time. **Ex.** *He studied hard during his college years.* 2. in the course of. **Ex.** *Come sometime during the evening.*

dusk (1) [dəsk'], *n.* 1. the time just before dark. **Ex.** *He always works in the garden until dusk.* 2. shadowy darkness. **Ex.** *The old man sat in the dusk of his room.* —**dusk'y**, *adj.*

dust (2) [dəst'], *n.* fine, dry, powdery earth; fine powder of any kind. **Ex.** *Dust from the road covered the car.* —*v.* remove or wipe dust from. **Ex.** *We dust the furniture every day.* —**dust'y**, *adj.*

duty (1) [duw'tiy, dyuw'tiy], *n.* 1. what one does because it is moral, right, or just. **Ex.** *We have a duty to help our country.* 2. the respect one should show parents, older people, etc. **Ex.** *He recognized his duty to his parents.* 3. that which one has to do as part of one's work. **Ex.** *What are your duties as a teacher?* —**du'ti·ful**, *adj.* —**du'ti·ful·ly**, *adv.*

dwarf (5) [dwɔrf'], *n.* animal, human being, or plant much smaller than the normal size of its kind. —*adj.* of unusually small size. **Ex.** *A dwarf apple tree grew in the flower pot.*

dwell (5) [dwel'], *v.* live. **Ex.** *Some bats dwell in caves.* —**dwell'ing**, *n.* a house in which people live. —**dwell on**, think, write, or speak about continually. **Ex.** *Please do not dwell on unimportant matters.*

dye (4) [day'], *n.* coloring matter used to color cloth, hair, etc. —*v.* color with a dye. **Ex.** *She dyed her hair red.*

E

E, e [iyˈ], *n.* the fifth letter of the English alphabet.

each (1) [iyčˈ], *adj.* every one by itself of two or more. **Ex.** *Each man has his own opinion.* —*pron.* every one. **Ex.** *Each will be asked one question.* —*adv.* to, of, by, or for every person or thing. **Ex.** *They gave the boys an apple each.* —**each other**, *adv.* each the cther. **Ex.** *The man and woman love each other.*

eager (2) [iyˈgər], *adj.* want very much. **Ex.** *He is eager to open the box to see what is inside.* —**eaˈger·ness**, *n.*

eagle (3) [iyˈgəl], *n.* a large bird noted for its strength, keenness of sight, and power of flight.

EAGLE

ear (1) [iːrˈ], *n.* either of the two parts of the body with which human beings and animals hear.

EAR

early (1) [ərˈliy], *adj.* 1. at or near the beginning of. **Ex.** *They discovered the disease in its early stages.* 2. before the usual or set time. **Ex.** *He was early for his appointment.* —*adv.* 1. near the beginning. **Ex.** *He left early in the morning.* 2. before the usual or set time. **Ex.** *He arrived fifteen minutes early.*

earn (2) [ərnˈ], *v.* 1. receive as pay for work or service. **Ex.** *He earns money by working in the factory.* 2. deserve or get. **Ex.** *The fearless soldier earned a medal for bravery.* —**earnˈings**, *n.* wages; salary.

earnest (3) [ərˈnist], *adj.* serious; not joking. **Ex.** *The scientist has an earnest attitude toward his work.* —**earˈnest·ness**, *n.* —**earˈnest·ly**, *adv.*

earth (1) [ərθˈ], *n.* 1. the planet on which man lives. **Ex.** *The earth travels around the sun.* 2. ground; soil; dirt. **Ex.** *He planted the seeds in the earth.* —**earthˈly**, *adj.* concerning the earth, not heaven. **Ex.** *All the poor man's earthly possessions were the clothes he wore.* —**earthˈy**, *adj.* 1. of or like the earth. 2. not refined; natural. 3. worldly. —**earthˈen**, *adj.* made of earth or baked clay.

earthquake (5) [ərθˈkweykˈ], *n.* a shaking of the earth's surface caused by changes in the position of rocks or other disturbances underground. **Ex.** *Many buildings were damaged by the earthquake.*

ease (2) [iyz'], *n.* 1. state of being comfortable; freedom from pain, want, or discomfort. **Ex.** *The rich family lived a life of ease.* 2. without difficulty; naturalness. **Ex.** *The famous actor spoke with ease.* —*v.* make less painful, difficult, etc. **Ex.** *This medicine will ease your pain.*

east (1) [iyst'], *n.* 1. the direction to the right of one facing north; one of the four points of the compass. **Ex.** *The sun rises in the east.* 2. regions or countries lying to the east; that part of the United States lying east of the Mississippi. **Ex.** *He spent several years in the East.* —*adv.* toward the east. **Ex.** *This train goes east.* —*adj.* 1. toward, in, or at the east. **Ex.** *He lives on the east side of the island.* 2. from the east. **Ex.** *An east wind is blowing.* —**east'ern,** *adj.* in, of, to, or from the east; characteristic of the east. —**east'ern·er,** *n.* one from the east.

easy (1) [iy'ziy], *adj.* 1. not difficult. **Ex.** *The easy work is done quickly.* 2. comfortable; not hurried. **Ex.** *When he retires, he expects to lead an easy life.* —**eas'i·ly,** *adv.* without difficulty. **Ex.** *He did the work easily.*

eat (1) [iyt'], *v.* take food into the body; have a meal. **Ex.** *Children like to eat cake.* —**eat'a·ble,** *adj.* suitable to eat. —**eat'er,** *n.* one who is eating.

echo (3) [ek'ow], *n.* a sound heard a second time as a result of reflected sound waves. **Ex.** *He heard the echo of his voice from the other side of the valley.* —*v.* sound again. **Ex.** *The room echoed with his voice.*

economic (2) [ek'ǝnam'ik, iy'kǝnam'ik], *adj.* of or concerned with the economy. —**e·co·nom'ics,** *n.* the science concerned with the production, distribution, and use of income and wealth.

economy (2) [iykan'ǝmiy, ǝkan'ǝmiy], *n.* 1. the management of the money and other resources of a nation, community, etc. **Ex.** *The development of railroads had a tremendous effect on the country's economy.* 2. the doing of something so as not to waste. **Ex.** *Her economies in preparing meals cut family expenses.* —**e·co·nom'i·cal,** *adj.* —**e·co·nom'i·cal·ly,** *adv.* —**e·con'o·mize,** *v.*

ecstasy (5) [ek'stǝsiy], *n.* a strong emotion, especially of joy

or delight. **Ex.** *The beautiful music filled them with ecstasy.*
—**ec·stat·ic** [ekstæt'ik], *adj.*

-ed (1) [əd, d, t], *suffix.* 1. past action of a verb. **Ex.** *We walked two miles yesterday.* 2. past participle ending. **Exs.** *Fade, faded; load, loaded.* 3. characterized by. **Exs.** *Beard, bearded; wing, winged.*

edge (1) [ej'], *n.* 1. the line at which something ends or begins. **Ex.** *He sat at the edge of the river and put his feet in the water.* 2. the thin cutting side of the blade of an instrument. **Ex.** *He sharpened the edge of his ax.* —*v.* 1. put a border on. **Ex.** *She edged the neck of the dress with white.* 2. move sideways, little by little. **Ex.** *The man edged his way through the crowd.* —**edg'y**, *adj.* tense; nervous. —**on edge**, tense; nervous. **Ex.** *He acts on edge today.*

edible (3) [ed'ibəl], *adj.* suitable for eating because not harmful to people. **Ex.** *The meat is too old and no longer edible.*

edit (3) [ed'it], *v.* 1. prepare a piece of writing to be published by making changes, corrections, etc. **Ex.** *He corrected errors in grammar and spelling when he edited the manuscript.* 2. manage and direct the preparation of a newspaper, magazine, etc. **Ex.** *He edits the village newspaper.* —**ed'i·tor**, *n.*

edition (4) [ədiš'ən], *n.* 1. the form in which a literary work is published. **Ex.** *He bought an illustrated edition of the book.* 2. one of several printings of the same work, issued at different times and differing from the others by changes or additions. **Ex.** *I prefer this edition of the book to the earlier one.*

editorial (4) [ed'ɔtɔr'iyəl], *n.* an article in a newspaper or magazine giving the opinions or views of the editor or publishers. **Ex.** *The editorial was critical of the court's ruling.* —*adj.* of or relating to an editor. **Ex.** *How large is the editorial staff?*

educate (2) [ej'əkeyt'], *v.* develop the mind or character by training; teach. **Ex.** *He was educated in good schools.* —**ed'u·ca`tor**, *n.* one who educates. —**ed`u·ca'tion**, *n.* the act of educating; the things learned from being educated. —**ed`u·ca'ti·n·al**, *adj.*

effect (2) [əfekt'], *n.* 1. a result caused by something. **Ex.** *The effects of the storm could be seen in the morning.* 2. a mental impression. **Ex.** *The drums had an effect on the animals like that of thunder.* —*v.* cause; accomplish. **Ex.** *He effected many changes.* —**ef·fec'tive,** *adj.* successful in producing an effect intended or desired. **Ex.** *Water is effective in stopping some fires.* —**ef·fec'tive·ness,** *n.*

efficient (4) [əfiš'ənt], *adj.* producing the desired result with the least waste. **Ex.** *An automobile is more efficient for rapid travel than a horse.* —**ef·fi'cient·ly,** *adv.* —**ef·fi'cien·cy,** *n.*

effort (1) [ef'ərt], *n.* 1. the work required to do something; struggle. **Ex.** *With great effort, they pulled the car out of the mud.* 2. an attempt. **Ex.** *He will make an effort to visit you.*

egg (1) [eg'], *n.* 1. the roundish body containing the unborn young produced by female birds, fish, etc. 2. the hen's egg eaten as food.

EGG

eight (1) [eyt'], *n., adj.* the number between seven and nine; the number 8. —**eighth',** *n., adj.* coming after seven others. —**eight'een,** *n., adj.* the number *18.* —**eight'eenth,** *n., adj.* coming after seventeen others. —**eight'y,** *n., adj.* the number *80.* —**eight'i·eth,** *n., adj.* coming after seventy-nine others.

either (1) [iy'ðər], *adj.* 1. one of two but not the other. **Ex.** *Take either book.* 2. each of two. **Ex.** *There are seats on either side of the room.* —*pron.* one or the other of two. **Ex.** *Either of the dresses is suitable.* —*conj.* one or the other of two. **Ex.** *Either give it back to him or pay him for it.*

elaborate (4) [əlæb'ərət], *adj.* complicated; with much detail; developed with great care. **Ex.** *Elaborate plans were made for the party.*

elaborate (4) [əlæb'əreyt], *v.* 1. develop carefully and in detail. **Ex.** *He elaborated his theory in the book he wrote.* 2. explain with more details. **Ex.** *He refused to elaborate on his original statement.* —**e·lab'o·rate·ly,** *adv.*

elastic (5) [əlæs'tik], *adj.* able to return to its original shape or size after being stretched. **Ex.** *A rubber ball bounces because it is elastic.* —*n.* a material containing rubber or similar threads that make it stretchable. **Ex.** *She used elastic in the waist of the skirt.* —**e·las'tic'i·ty,** *n.*

elbow (2) [el'bow], *n.* the joint between the upper and lower arm. **Ex.** *The arm bends at the elbow.*

elder (3) [el'dər], *adj.* older. **Ex.** *My elder brother is three years older than I am.* —*n.* a person who is older. **Ex.** *The children listened to the advice of their elders.* —**eld'er·ly,** *adj.* rather old.

elect (2) [əlekt', ilekt'], *v.* select or choose for an office by v . **Ex.** *The people elected him President.* —**e·lec'tion,** *n.* the act of choosing or selecting by vote. **Ex.** *There is a presidential election every four years.*

electric (1) [əlek'trik, ilek'trik], *adj.* concerned with electricity. —**e·lec'tri·cal,** *adj.* —**e·lec'tri·cal·ly,** *adv.* —**e·lec'tri'cian,** *n.* one who places in position for use, repairs, or operates electrical equipment.

electricity (1) [əlek'tris'ətiy, iy'lektris'ətiy], *n.* a form of power which travels through wires to produce light, heat, etc. **Ex.** *That lamp uses very little electricity.*

elegant (3) [el'əgənt], *adj.* 1. having the qualities of richness, fineness, and dignity combined in a pleasing effect. **Ex.** *The furnishings of the palace were elegant.* 2. having good manners and showing that one can appreciate what is beautiful. **Ex.** *The queen was always elegant in her behavior.* —**el'e·gant·ly,** *adv.* —**el'e·gance,** *n.*

element (2) [el'əmənt], *n.* 1. one of the 103 basic substances known to scientists that cannot be separated into substances of other kinds. **Ex.** *Iron is an element.* 2. one of the basic principles or necessary parts of something. **Ex.** *He has mastered the elements of the English language.* —**el'e·men'tal,** *adj.* simple; basic.

elementary (3) [el'əmen't(ə)riy], *adj.* dealing with the first, most simple facts about a subject. **Ex.** *The elementary principles of mathematics are taught in the lower grades at school.*

elementary school [el'əmen't(ə)riy skuwl'], a school of the first six or eight years of education.

elephant (2) [el'əfənt], *n.* a huge, heavy, gray-skinned animal with a long tube-like nose or trunk.

elevate (4) [el''əveyt'], *v.* lift up; raise. **Ex.** *The platform was elevated to a height of five feet.* —**el'e·va'tion,** *n.* a raised place or high piece of ground.

ELEPHANT

elevator (5) [el'əvey'tər], *n.* a cage or platform for carrying persons or goods from one level to another in a building. **Ex.** *This elevator stops at the sixth floor.*

eleven (2) [əlevʹən, ilevʹən], *n., adj.* the number between ten and twelve; the number *11.* —e·levʹenth, *n., adj.* coming after ten others.

eliminate (4) [əlimʹəneyt`, ilimʹəneyt`], *v.* remove; get rid of; leave out. Ex. *Part of the program was eliminated to save time.* —e·limʹi·na·tion, *n.*

elm (5) [elmʹ], *n.* a tall, leafy, shade tree with a spreading top.

eloquence (5) [elʹəkwəns], *n.* language used with grace and force so that it influences the thinking and feeling of people. Ex. *The speaker was noted for his eloquence.* —elʹo·quent, *adj.* —elʹo·quent·ly, *adv.*

else (1) [elsʹ], *adj.* 1. instead of; in the place of; other. Ex. *He cannot go; someone else must go.* 2. in addition to. Ex. *I am going; who else is going?* —*adv.* 1. in a different place, time, or manner. Ex. *How else could he have done it?* 2. otherwise. Ex. *Dress warmly, or else you will be cold.*

elsewhere [elsʹhwe:r`], *adv.* at, to, or in some other place. Ex. *It may be quieter elsewhere.*

embarrass (4) [embærʹəs, emberʹəs], *v.* cause to feel uncomfortable about one's appearance or actions. Ex. *They were embarrassed because there was not enough food for all the guests.* —em·barʹrass·ment, *n.*

embrace (3) [embreysʹ], *v.* hold in one's arms to show love or fondness. Ex. *The groom embraced the bride.*

emerge (4) [əmərǰʹ, imərǰʹ], *v.* come into view; appear; become known. Ex. *After the rain, the sun emerged from the clouds.* —e·merʹgence, *n.*

emergency (3) [əmərʹǰənsiy, im`erʹǰənsiy], *n.* an unexpected circumstance or occurrence requiring immediate action. Ex. *The fire created a serious emergency.*

emigrate (5) [emʹəgreyt`], *v.* leave one's own country or region to settle in another. Ex. *In the 19th century many Europeans emigrated to America.* —emʹi·graʹtion, *n.*

eminent (5) [emʹənənt], *adj.* ranking above many others in talent, worth, etc.; famous; distinguished. Ex. *An eminent scientist is teaching at our university.* —emʹi·nent·ly, *adv.* —emʹi·nence, *n.*

emotion (2) [imowʹšən], *n.* a strong feeling of any kind; a particular feeling. Ex. *Love, hate, and fear are all emotions.* —e·moʹtion·al, *adj.* —e·moʹtion·al·ly, *adv.*

emperor (3) [emʹpərər], *n.* the ruler of an empire.

emphasis (3) [em'fəsəs], *n.* 1. special attention given because of importance. **Ex.** *There is great emphasis on mathematics in studies for engineers.* 2. stress given to particular words or parts of words or phrases in speaking. **Ex.** *In pronouncing the word "travel," the emphasis is on the syllable "trav."* —**em'pha·size,** *v.* —**em·phat'ic,** *adj.* spoken or performed with emphasis.

empire (2) [em'payr], *n.* a group of countries or states controlled by a single ruler. **Ex.** *The United States was once part of the British Empire.*

employ (2) [employ'], *v.* 1. give work to for wages; hire. **Ex.** *That store employs many people.* 2. use. **Ex.** *The methods he employed were very practical.* —**em·ploy'ment,** *n.* 1. the state of being employed. 2. that on which one is employed.

employee, employe (5) [employ'iy, employ'iy'], *n.* one who works for wages or salary in the service of another. —**em·ploy'er,** *n.* one who employs another. **Ex.** *That employer pays his employees good wages.*

empty (2) [emp'tiy], *adj.* having nothing inside. **Ex.** *I need an empty box for packing the dishes.* —*v.* 1. make or become empty; pour out; take out. **Ex.** *She emptied the water from the pail.* 2. discharge; flow out or into. **Ex.** *That stream empties into the river.* —**emp'ti·ness,** *n.*

en- (1) [in, en], *prefix.* 1. put on or into; surround; close in. **Exs.** *Case, encase; circle, encircle.* 2. make. **Exs.** *Able, enable; large, enlarge.* 3. add strength to a meaning. **Exs.** *Liven, enliven; snare, ensnare.*

-en (1) [ən], *suffix.* 1. make or become. **Exs.** *Deep, deepen; sick, sicken; fat, fatten.* 2. made of; like. **Exs.** *Gold, golden; wool, woolen; wood, wooden.* 3. gain; cause to have. **Exs.** *Haste, hasten; strength, strengthen; length, lengthen.*

enamel (5) [inæm'əl], *n.* 1. a hard, shiny substance baked on the surface of metal. **Ex.** *The kitchen sink is covered with enamel.* 2. a paint used to give a surface a smooth, shiny finish.

-ence (2) [əns], *suffix.* act of, state of, or quality of. **Exs.** *Prefer, preference; differ, difference; excel, excellence.*

enchant (5) [enčænt'], *v.* charm; delight greatly. **Ex.** *The audi-*

---

a, far; æ, am; e, get; ey, late; i, in; iy, see; ɔ, all; ow, go; u, put; uw, too; ə, but, ago; ər, fur; aw, out; ay, life; oy, boy; ŋ, ring; θ, think; ð, that; ž, measure; š, ship; j, edge; č, child.

ence was enchanted by the grace of the dancer. —**en·chan'ter**, *n.* —**en·chant'ress**, *n. fem.* —**en·chant'ment**, *n.* —**enchant'ing**, *adj.*

encounter (3) [enkawn'tər], *v.* meet, often unexpectedly. **Ex.** *While out walking, we encountered an old friend.* —*n.* 1. a meeting, often unexpected. **Ex.** *The encounter surprised him.* 2. a battle. **Ex.** *The bloody encounter was the beginning of the war.*

encourage (2) [enkər'ij], *v.* 1. give hope, courage, or confidence to. **Ex.** *The teacher's praise encouraged the boy to study.* 2. help the development of; aid. **Ex.** *The sun encouraged the growth of the plants.* —**en·cour'age·ment**, *n.* the giving of hope or confidence.

end (1) [end'], *n.* 1. the part which comes last. **Ex.** *The end of the story was more interesting than the beginning.* 2. the furthest point. **Ex.** *My house is at the end of the road.* —*v.* bring or come to an end; stop; finish. **Ex.** *The road ended at the river.*

endeavor (3) [endev'ər], *v.* make an effort; try very hard. **Ex.** *They endeavored to find a home for him.* —*n.* an effort; an attempt. **Ex.** *He made an endeavor to save the drowning girl.*

endow (4) [endaw'], *v.* 1. give money or property to provide continuing support for. **Ex.** *The rich man endowed a new school for special studies in medicine.* 2. provide with a quality or ability. **Ex.** *She was endowed with great charm.* —**en·dow'ment**, *n.*

endure (2) [endyu:r', indu:r'], *v.* 1. suffer patiently; bear. **Ex.** *The early settlers endured great hardships.* 2. continue for a long time; last. **Ex.** *Those ancient buildings have endured for centuries.* —**en·dur'ance**, *n.* —**en·dur'ing**, *adj.* long-lasting. —**en·dur'a·ble**, *adj.* capable of being endured.

enemy (1) [en'əmiy], *n.* 1. an unfriendly person; one who is opposed to an idea, cause, etc. **Ex.** *The quarrel made them enemies.* 2. a person or persons opposed to one in war. **Ex.** *The enemy attacked during the night.* —*adj.* of or about the enemy.

energy (2) [en'ərjiy], *n.* 1. strength or force of action. **Ex.** *He used his energy to work for peace.* 2. the capacity of certain natural forces to do work. **Ex.** *Sunlight and electricity are both forms of energy.* —**en'er·get'ic**, *adj.* full of energy; active. **Ex.** *He is an energetic worker.*

engage (2) [engeyǰ'], *v.* 1. occupy the attention or time of. Ex. *She is engaged in writing a book.* 2. promise to marry. Ex. *They became engaged yesterday.* 3. employ; hire. Ex. *They engaged workmen to paint the house.* —**en·gage'ment,** *n.* 1. an agreement to marry. Ex. *Their engagement was announced.* 2. an appointment to meet at a particular time and place. Ex. *He could not see me because he had another engagement.*

engine (2) [en'ǰən], *n.* 1. a machine that uses energy to cause motion or to do work. Ex. *Most cars have gasoline engines.* 2. the car of a railroad train that pulls the load. Ex. *The engine pulling the railroad cars used electricity for power.*

engineer (2) [en`ǰəni:r'], *n.* one who is trained to plan and build engines, roads, bridges, etc. Ex. *Many engineers work together to design a bridge.* —**en`gi·neer'ing,** *n.* the science of designing and building engines, roads, bridges, etc.

English (1) [iŋ'gliš], *n.* 1. the main language spoken in England, the United States, Canada, Australia, and other countries. 2. the people of England. —*adj.* of or having to do with England, its people, or its language.

enjoy (1) [enǰoy'], *v.* receive pleasure from. Ex. *She enjoyed her vacation.* —**en·joy'ment,** *n.* —**en·joy'able,** *adj.* —**enjoy oneself,** have an enjoyable time. Ex. *He enjoyed himself at the party.*

enlighten [enlayt'ən], *v.* inform; provide knowledge. Ex. *The book enlightened him.*

enlist (5) [enlist'], *v.* 1. join a cause or group, especially by one's own wish. Ex. *He enlisted in the army.* 2. secure the help or support of. Ex. *May we enlist your help?* —**en·list'ment,** *n.* —**en·list'ed man,** *n.* soldier; any man in the armed forces except commissioned officers and warrant officers.

enormous (3) [ənɔ:r'məs, inɔ:r'məs], *adj.* extremely large; huge. Ex. *The enormous building was over 100 stories high.* —**e·nor'mous·ly,** *adv.*

enough (1) [ənəf', inəf'], *adj.* as many or as much as required or desired; sufficient. Ex. *We have enough chairs to seat everyone.* —*n.* the amount required or desired. Ex. *Did you have enough?* —*adv.* as much as necessary or desired. Ex. *Is the water hot enough to make the tea?*

enroll [enrowl'], *v.* become a member, usually by writing one's name. Ex. *He is enrolled to attend college this year.*

ensue (5) [ɛnsuw'], v. 1. follow; come afterward. **Ex.** *We met and a long conversation ensued.* 2. happen as a consequence. **Ex.** *After some angry words, a fight ensued.*

-ent (3) [ənt], *suffix.* 1. being or acting in a particular way. **Exs.** *Differ, different; urge, urgent.* 2. one who, or that which, acts in a particular way. **Exs.** *Depend, dependent; preside, president.*

enter (1) [en'tər], v. 1. come or go into. **Ex.** *He entered the house.* 2. become a member; join. **Ex.** *He entered the army last week.*

enterprise (3) [en'tərprayz'], n. 1. a business or project, especially one that requires boldness and hard work. **Ex.** *Building the steel factory was a great enterprise.* 2. the quality or character that leads one to begin new and difficult projects. **Ex.** *The man who built the steel factory was a man of enterprise.* —**en'ter·pris'ing,** *adj.*

entertain (3) [en'tərteyn'], v. 1. hold the attention of; amuse. **Ex.** *Her jokes and stories entertained everyone.* 2. have as a guest. **Ex.** *We entertained friends for lunch.* —**en·ter·tain'er,** *n.* one who entertains. —**en·ter·tain'ing,** *adj.* —**en·ter·tain'ment,** *n.* the act of entertaining or the thing that entertains.

enthusiasm (3) [enθuw'ziyæz'əm], n. keen interest; strong liking. **Ex.** *He does work he likes with enthusiasm.* —**en·thu'si·as'tic,** *adj.*

entire (2) [entayr'], *adj.* whole; complete; all. **Ex.** *The walls supported the entire weight of the roof.* —**en·tire'ly,** *adv.* —**en·tire'ty,** *n.*

entitle (3) [entay'təl], v. give a right or claim to. **Ex.** *This ticket entitles you to attend the concert without charge.*

entrance (2) [en'trəns], n. 1. a place through which one enters; door; gate. **Ex.** *We went into the house through the front entrance.* 2. act of entering. **Ex.** *Everyone in the courtroom rose at the entrance of the judge.*

entreat (5) [entriyt'], v. earnestly plead; beg. **Ex.** *He entreated her to marry him.* —**en·treat'y,** *n.*

entry (4) [en'triy], n. 1. act of entering. **Ex.** *The general made a grand entry into the city.* 2. a passage or hallway through which one enters. **Ex.** *The front door is located in the entry.* 3. each item entered in a list. **Ex.** *The accountant checked the entries in the account books.*

envelope (3) [en'vəlowpˋ, an'vəlowpˋ], *n.* a folded piece of paper in which a letter is placed for mailing. **Ex.** *Please put a stamp on this envelope.*

environment (4) [envay'rənmənt], *n.* all the surrounding things, conditions, and influences that affect the development of a person, animal, or plant. **Ex.** *The teacher blamed the boy's poor manners on his environment.* —en·vi'ron·men'tal, *adj.*

envy (3) [en'viy], *n.* 1. dislike or jealousy caused by something another person has or can do. **Ex.** *His sudden wealth filled me with envy.* 2. the person or thing that causes such feeling. **Ex.** *His new bicycle was the envy of his friends.* —*v.* feel envy at, toward, or because of. **Ex.** *He envied his friend's success in business.* —en'vi·able, *adj.* of a quality that is envied. **Ex.** *He has an enviable talent.* —en'vi·ous, *adj.* full of envy.

episode (5) [ep'əsowdˋ], *n.* an important happening or incident in a story or history. **Ex.** *The episode of the rescue was the most exciting part of the book.*

equal (1) [iy'kwəl], *adj.* 1. the same in amount, size, number, etc. **Ex.** *One half is equal to the other.* 2. having the same rights, abilities, etc. **Ex.** *All men are equal before the law.* —*n.* a thing or person that is equal. **Ex.** *It will be hard to find his equal as a teacher.* —*v.* be equal to; match. **Ex.** *The runner equaled the world's record.* —e·qual'i·ty, *n.* —e'qual·ly, *adv.*

equator (2) [ikwey'tər], *n.* an imaginary line around the world which is equal in distance from the North and South Poles; 0 degrees latitude. **Ex.** *Quito, Ecuador is a little south of the equator.* —e'qua·tor'i·al, *adj.* of, near, or like the equator.

equip (3) [ikwip'], *v.* provide or furnish what is needed. **Ex.** *He equipped himself for a hunting trip.* —e·quip'ment, *n.* the things needed for some special purpose. **Ex.** *Guns are hunting equipment.*

equivalent (4) [ikwiv'ələnt], *adj.* equal or same in quantity, value, or meaning. **Ex.** *One half dozen is equivalent to six.* —*n.* that which is equal to something else. **Ex.** *You may pay me in cash or give me the equivalent in merchandise.* —e·quiv'a·lence, *n.*

a, far; æ, am; e, get; ey, late; i, in; iy, see; ɔ, all; ow, go; u, put; uw, too; ə, but, ago; ər, fur; aw, out; ay, life; oy, boy; ŋ, ring; θ, think; ð, that; ž, measure; š, ship; j, edge; č, child.

-er (1) [ər], *suffix*. 1. a person or thing that does something. **Exs.** *Listen, listener; teach, teacher; read, reader.* 2. a person concerned with. **Exs.** *Law, lawyer; bank, banker; engine, engineer.* 3. a person who resides in or on. **Exs.** *Island, islander; New York, New Yorker.* 4. more. **Exs.** *Cold, colder; fast, faster.*

era (4) [i:r'ə], *n.* a period of history associated with an important event. **Ex.** *We are living in the atomic era.*

erase (5) [ireys'], *v.* rub out; wipe clean; remove. **Ex.** *The student erased his mistake on the examination paper.* —**e·ras'er,** *n.* something that erases. —**e·ras'ure,** *n.* something that has been erased.

erect (3) [irekt'], *adj.* straight up; not leaning or slanted. **Ex.** *Flagpoles and trees are erect.* —*v.* 1. build; construct. **Ex.** *They will erect a building here.* 2. put in an upright position. **Ex.** *They erected a flagpole.* —**e·rec'tion,** *n.*

err (4) [ə:r'], *v.* make an error; do or be wrong. **Ex.** *He erred when he said that the earth was flat.*

errand (4) [e:r'ənd], *n.* a trip to perform a special task, usually for someone else. **Ex.** *Her mother sent her on an errand to buy bread.*

error (2) [e:r'ər], *n.* 1. an incorrect act or belief; a mistake. **Ex.** *He made an error in addition.* 2. the condition of believing or doing what is not correct. **Ex.** *You are in error about her age.* —**er·ro'ne·ous,** *adj.* —**er·ro'ne·ous·ly,** *adv.*

-ery (2) [əriy], *suffix*. 1. place where something is done. **Ex.** *Bake, bakery.* 2. act, art, or occupation of. **Ex.** *Rob, robbery.* 3. quality or condition collectively. **Ex.** *Slave, slavery.*

escape (1) [əskeyp', iskəyp'], *v.* 1. get free; run away from. **Ex.** *The prisoner escaped from prison.* 2. keep from being harmed or injured; avoid. **Ex.** *He escaped being hurt in the fall.* 3. come gradually out of a closed place. **Ex.** *Gas was escaping from the pipe.* —*n.* 1. act or fact of escaping. **Ex.** *The prisoner's escape was not noticed until morning.* 2. the leaking or flowing out of something. **Ex.** *The escape of so much gas was dangerous.*

escort (4) [es'kɔrt], *n.* a person or group accompanying another or others to protect or show honor. **Ex.** *An escort was waiting for the distinguished visitor.*

escort (4) [eskɔrt'], *v.* accompany to protect or show honor. **Ex.** *He escorted her home.*

-ese (2) [iyz], *suffix*. of or from a certain place. **Ex.** *Japan, Japanese.*

especially (1) [əspeš'əliy], *adv*. unusually; particularly. **Ex.** *He is an especially good student in history.*

-ess (1) [əs], *suffix*. female. **Exs.** *Lion, lioness; actor, actress.*

essay (5) [es'ey], *n*. a short piece of writing on a single subject which gives the writer's personal ideas. **Ex.** *The students wrote essays about the importance of education.* —**es'say·ist**, *n*. one who writes essays.

essence (5) [es'əns], *n*. the essential quality of a thing; the most important quality or part. **Ex.** *The essence of his success in teaching is patience.*

essential (3) [əsen'čəl], *adj*. 1. extremely important; necessary. **Ex.** *Food and water are essential to life.* 2. of, belonging to, or constituting the inner character of something; basic. **Ex.** *Sympathy is an essential part of her personality.* —*n.* something important, necessary, or basic. **Ex.** *We took only essentials on the trip.* —**es·sen'tial·ly**, *adv*.

-est (2) [əst], *suffix*. most. **Exs.** *Warm, warmest; pretty, prettiest; soon, soonest.*

establish (2) [əstæb'liš], *v*. 1. make permanent; settle; set firmly. **Ex.** *They established themselves in the community.* 2. begin a school, group, or nation, etc. **Ex.** *He plans to establish a new business.* 3. prove to be true. **Ex.** *They established their ownership of the property.* —**es·tab'lish·ment**, *n*. 1. act of establishing. 2. the thing established.

estate (3) [əsteyt'], *n*. 1. everything owned by a person, including land, money, and other property. **Ex.** *He left a small estate when he died.* 2. a large area of land with a big, luxurious house. **Ex.** *The rich man lived on a large estate.* —**real estate**, *n*. land with its natural resources and any manmade improvements.

esteem (4) [əstiym'], *v*. respect; consider highly; value greatly. **Ex.** *His writing is much esteemed.* —*n.* respect. **Ex.** *They held him in high esteem.* —**es'ti·ma·ble**, *adj*. deserving respect.

estimate (3) [es'təmeyt'], *v*. make a careful guess about value, amount, size, etc. **Ex.** *They estimated that the trip would take two hours.*

estimate (3) [es'tamit'], *n*. a careful guess about the value, amount, size, etc. **Ex.** *They submitted an estimate of build-*

ing costs. —es`ti·ma'tion, *n.* 1. the act of estimating. 2. opinion; estimate. 3. good opinion; respect. **Ex.** *He is held in high estimation by his fellow students.*

et cetera (3) [etset'ərə], a Latin phrase meaning "and other things of that kind." **Ex.** *The hammers, nails, et cetera, which you ordered, have arrived.* Et cetera is frequently shortened to *etc.* in writing.

eternal (3) [itər'nəl], *adj.* 1. with neither beginning nor end; never ending. **Ex.** *He said that his religion is based on eternal truths.* 2. seeming to continue forever. **Ex.** *His years as a prisoner of war seemed eternal.* —e·ter'nal·ly, *adv.* —e·ter'ni·ty, *n.*

evaporate (5) [ivæp'əreyt`], *v.* 1. change from a liquid into a vapor. **Ex.** *Water evaporates when boiled.* 2. vanish; disappear. **Ex.** *When she saw that her children were safe, her fears for them evaporated.* —e·vap`o·ra'tion, *n.*

eve (4) [iyv'], *n.* evening or day before some special day or event. **Ex.** *December thirty-first is New Year's Eve.*

even (1) [iy'vən], *adj.* 1. not higher or lower; level; smooth; flat. **Ex.** *The top of the table has an even surface.* 2. equal in size, number, or quantity. **Ex.** *Each of the children got an even share of the candy.* —*adv.* 1. just or exactly. **Ex.** *Even as he spoke, the clock struck twelve.* 2. unlikely as it may seem. **Ex.** *Even his brother hated him.* 3. still; in comparison. **Ex.** *It was even later than we thought.* —e'ven·ly, *adv.* —e'ven·ness, *n.* —**get even with,** obtain revenge. **Ex.** *I got even with him by not going to his party.*

evening (1) [iyv'niŋ], *n.* the time of the day between sunset and the early part of night. **Ex.** *Children usually go to bed early in the evening.*

event (2) [ivent'], *n.* 1. that which happens, especially a happening of importance. **Ex.** *The party was an important social event.* 2. an item or contest in a program of sports. **Ex.** *My brother is running in the next event.* —e·vent'ful, *adj.* full of events. —**in any event,** regardless of what happens. **Ex.** *We will go in any event.* —**in the event of,** if a particular event occurs. **Ex.** *In the event of a fire, leave quickly.*

eventual (5) [iven'čuwəl], *adj.* coming after the passing of time or as a result of. **Ex.** *They hoped for the eventual success of their plans.* —e·ven'tu·al·ly, *adv.* —e·ven`tu·al'i·ty, *n.* something that might happen.

ever (1) [ev'ər], *adv.* at any time. **Ex.** *Have you ever seen him before?*

evermore [ev'ərmɔ:r'], *adv.* always; forever. **Ex.** *He will regret it evermore.*

every (1) [ev'riy], *adj.* each one, not leaving out any. **Ex.** *Every time I saw him, he smiled.* —**every other,** every second one. **Ex.** *Every other book in the row was red.*

everybody [ev'riybəd'y, ev'riybad'iy], *pron.* all persons. **Ex.** *Everybody in the school came to the party.*

everywhere [ev'riyhwe:r'], *adv.* to or in every place. **Ex.** *We looked everywhere for you.*

evidence (2) [ev'ədəns], *n.* indication; a reason for believing; proof. **Ex.** *From the evidence, the police believe two people committed the crime.*

evident (3) [ev'ədənt], *adj.* not difficult to understand or see; clear; plain. **Ex.** *It was evident they were brothers.* —**ev'i·dent·ly,** *adv.*

evil (2) [iy'vəl], *n.* anything which results in harm or suffering. **Ex.** *Although he treated me badly, I wish him no evil.* —*adj.* 1. not good; harmful; injurious. **Ex.** *Smoking is an evil habit.* 2. morally bad; sinful. **Ex.** *The criminal led an evil life.*

evolve (5) [ivalv'], *v.* develop gradually. **Ex.** *Their plan evolved by trial and error.* —**ev'o·lu'tion,** *n.* gradual development.

ex- (1) [eks], *prefix.* earlier; former. **Exs.** *President, ex-president; teacher, ex-teacher.*

exact (2) [igzækt'], *adj.* without error; having no mistakes; correct. **Ex.** *Make an exact copy of this letter.* —**ex·act'ly,** *adv.* in a way which is exact. **Ex.** *You have done this job exactly as I wanted it done.*

exaggerate (4) [igzæj'əreyt'], *v.* speak of something as larger, more important, or greater than it is. **Ex.** *The fisherman exaggerated the size of the fish.* —**ex·ag'ger·a'tion,** *n.*

exalt (5) [igzɔ:lt'], *v.* 1. raise in rank, honor, etc.; praise. **Ex.** *The hero was exalted in song.* 2. fill with pride or joy. **Ex.** *They were exalted by their son's success.* —**ex'al·ta'tion,** *n.*

examine (2) [igzæm'ən], *v.* 1. look at with care. **Ex.** *The doctor examined my sore eye.* 2. test the truth or knowledge of.

Ex. *The teacher examined the students on the previous lesson.* —ex·am'in·er, *n.* one who examines. —ex·am'i·na'tion, *n.* 1. the act of looking at closely and carefully. 2. a test of what one has learned.

example (2) [igzæm'pəl], *n.* 1. a part that shows what the rest of a thing or group is like. **Ex.** *This painting is an example of the artist's work.* 2. model or pattern to be followed. **Ex.** *His essay was used as an example for the class.*

exceed (3) [iksiyd'], *v.* 1. be or go beyond the limit of. **Ex.** *Don't exceed the speed limit.* 2. be greater or better than. **Ex.** *His skill exceeds that of the other carpenters.* —ex·ceed'ing·ly, *adv.*

excellent (2) [ek'sələnt], *adj.* better than others; of great worth. **Ex.** *He is an excellent student.* —ex·cel', *v.* be better. **Ex.** *He excels at sports.* —ex'cel·lence, *n.*

except (1) [iksept'], *prep.* other than; but. **Ex.** *He works every day except Sunday.* —ex·cep'tion, *n.* 1. the act of leaving out. **Ex.** *Everyone must be here; there will be no exceptions.* 2. something or someone that is left out or is different. **Ex.** *That case is an exception to the rule.* – ex·cep'tion·al, *adj.* different; unusual. —**take exception,** object to; argue against. **Ex.** *I took exception to what he said.*

excess (4) [ek'ses`, ikses'], *adj.* more than necessary, allowed, or desirable. **Ex.** *She must eat less to lose her excess weight.* —*n.* extra amount; the amount over that needed. —ex·ces'sive, *adj.* beyond the limit. —ex·ces'sive·ly, *adv.*

exchange (2) [iksčeynj'], *v.* give or receive one thing for another; trade. **Ex.** *He exchanged the box for another which is larger.* —*n.* 1. a giving of one thing for another; a trade. **Ex.** *He gave two pictures in exchange for a book.* 2. the act of exchanging. **Ex.** *There was an exchange of ideas between the two leaders.* 3. a place of business where things are bought and sold. **Ex.** *He lost a fortune on the stock exchange.*

excite (2) [iksayt'], *v.* cause strong feelings or mental or physical activity. **Exs.** *The remark excited his anger. The fire excited the animals.* —ex·cit'ing, *adj.* —ex·cite'ment, *n.*

exclaim (3) [ikskleym'], *v.* cry out or speak suddenly with emotion. **Ex.** *"She is hurt!" he exclaimed.* —ex·cla·ma'tion, *n.* word or sentence which exclaims. —**exclamation mark** or **point,** the mark (!) used after words or sentences to show strong or sudden feeling.

exclude (4) [ikskluwd'], *v.* keep out; shut out; refuse to consider or think about. Exs. *He was excluded from the meeting. I excluded that idea from my thoughts.* —**ex·clu'sion,** *n.* the act or state of being excluded.

exclusive (5) [ikskluw'siv], *adj.* limited or belonging to a particular individual or group. Ex. *I have the exclusive right to sell these houses.* —**ex·clu'sive·ly,** *adv.*

excuse (2) [ikskyuwz'], *v.* 1. pardon or forgive; overlook a fault. Ex. *Please excuse me for being late.* 2. be a reason or explanation for. Ex. *His illness excused his absence.* 3. release from a duty or promise. Ex. *The teacher excused him from attending class.* —*n.* a reason, real or pretended, given for being excused. Ex. *He had a good excuse for being late.* —**ex·cus'a·ble,** *adj.*

execute (4) [ek'səkyuwt'], *v.* 1. complete; put into effect. Ex. *The lawyer executed the dead man's will.* 2. put to death according to law. Ex. *The spy was executed this morning.* —**ex'e·cu'tion,** *n.* —**ex'e·cu'tion·er,** *n.* one who kills those sentenced by law to die.

executive (3) [igzek'yətiv], *n.* 1. any of the persons who manage and direct a business or organization. Ex. *He is an executive in a steel company.* 2. any of the persons who put the laws of a nation into effect. Ex. *The President is the chief executive of the United States.* —*adj.* concerning the operation or management of a company or the governing of a country. Ex. *The new manager is noted for his executive ability.*

exercise (2) [ek'sərsayz'], *n.* 1. physical effort for the purpose of improving the body or staying healthy. Ex. *He enjoys walking for exercise.* 2. a series of movements done regularly to strengthen muscles. Ex. *He does exercises every morning.* 3. problems done for training or improving the mind. Ex. *The class did a written exercise each day.* —*v.* use physical effort or do a series of regular movements to improve or train the body. Ex. *He exercised his muscles every day.*

exert (4) [igzərt'], *v.* use. Ex. *He exerted his strength to lift the heavy trunk.* —**ex·er'tion,** *n.*

exhale (4) [eksheyl'], *v.* force air out from the lungs; breathe out. Ex. *He held his breath for a moment before he exhaled.*

exhaust (3) [igzɔ:st'], *v.* 1. tire very much. Ex. *The hard work exhausted him.* 2. use completely. Ex. *They had exhausted* *all their money.* —*n.* the hot gas produced by a gasoline engine. —**ex·haus'tion,** *n.*

exhibit (3) [igzib'ət], *v.* 1. show; display. **Ex.** *The paintings were exhibited at the art gallery.* 2. reveal. **Ex.** *Some people never exhibit their emotions.* —*n.* the act of showing; a display. **Ex.** *We attended an exhibit of photographs.* —**ex'hi·bi'tion,** *n.* a display. —**ex·hib'i·tor,** *n.* one who exhibits something.

exile (4) [eg'zayl`, ek'sayl`], *v.* force a person to leave his home and country. **Ex.** *The political leaders were exiled to an island.* —*n.* 1. a person who is exiled. **Ex.** *The exile lived a lonely life.* 2. state of being exiled. **Ex.** *While in exile, he wrote long letters.*

exist (2) [igzist'], *v.* 1. be; have material being. **Ex.** *These mountains have existed for ages.* 2. live. **Ex.** *We need air and water to exist.* —**ex·ist'ence,** *n.* —**ex·ist'ent,** *adj.*

exit (5) [eg'zet, ek'sət], *n.* 1. a place through which to go out. **Ex.** *He left the building through the rear exit.* 2. the act of going out. **Ex.** *The thief made a quick exit through the window.*

expand (4) [ikspænd'], *v.* 1. make or grow larger. **Ex.** *The balloon expanded as it was filled with air.* 2. develop the details of. **Ex.** *He expanded his short story into a book.* —**ex·pan'sion,** *n.*

expect (1) [ikspekt'], *v.* look forward to; look for confidently; anticipate. **Ex.** *He expects her to come on Friday.* —**ex·pect'ant,** *adj.* —**ex'pec·ta'tion,** *n.*

expedition (3) [ek`spədiš'ən], *n.* 1. a journey for some special purpose, such as trade, exploration, or war. **Ex.** *The boy dreamed of going on an expedition to discover an unknown land.* 2. The group of people, ships, etc. that makes such a journey. **Ex.** *There were twenty-five people in the expedition.*

expel (5) [ikspel'], *v.* 1. drive or force out. **Ex.** *They used pumps to expel water from the ship.* 2. force to leave as punishment. **Ex.** *The student was expelled from college.*

expend (4) [ikspend'], *v.* spend; use. **Ex.** *He had expended much time and effort on the experiment.* —**ex·pen'di·ture,** *n.* a using. —**ex·pend'a·ble,** *adj.* that can be consumed in use without concern. **Ex.** *The paper is expendable, but the books are not.*

expense (2) [ikspens'], *n.* 1. the cost; the money paid out. **Ex.**

He could not afford the expense of a new car. 2. the cause
of spending. **Ex.** *Food and rent were his chief expenses.*
—ex·pen'sive, *adj.* costing much; very high-priced. **Ex.** *The
gold watch is more expensive than the silver one.*

experience (1) [ikspir'iyəns], *n.* 1. the act of living through an
event or events; something that one has done or lived
through. **Ex.** *His first ride in an airplane was an exciting
experience.* 2. the knowledge or skill gained from work or
practice. **Ex.** *He is a teacher of wide experience.* **—v.** live
through; feel. **Ex.** *He experienced many troubles when he
was younger.*

experiment (2) [iksper'əmənt], *n.* a test or trial made to prove
a theory true or false or to discover something. **Ex.** *The
purpose of the experiment is to determine whether this
material will burn.* *v.* test or make a trial in order to find
out. **Ex.** *The doctors are experimenting with a new medicine.* **—ex·per'i·men'tal,** *adj.* **—ex·per'i·men'tal·ly,** *adv.*
—ex·per'i·men·ta'tion, *n.* act of experimenting.

expert (3) [ek'spərt], *n.* a person who has special skill or
knowledge in some particular subject; an authority. **Ex.** *He
is an expert on law.* **—adj.** 1. very skillful; having much
training, knowledge, and experience. **Ex.** *He is an expert
driver.* 2. coming from an expert. **Ex.** *He gave us expert advice.* **—ex·pert'ly,** *adv.*

expire (5) [ikspayr'], *v.* cease; die; terminate. **Ex.** *The agreement expired yesterday.* **—ex'pi·ra'tion,** *n.*

explain (1) [ikspleyn'], *v.* 1. tell what the meaning is. **Ex.**
*After the teacher explained the lesson, the children under-
stood it.* 2. make plain; make clear; tell about. **Ex.** *He explained how the machine worked.* 3. give reasons for. **Ex.**
Please explain your lateness. **—ex'plan·a'tion,** *n.* **—ex·plan'
a·to'ry,** *adj.*

explode (2) [iksplowd'], *v.* burst with a loud noise. **Ex.** *A
bomb exploded and killed many people.* **—ex·plo'sion,** *n.*
—ex·plo'sive, *adj.*

exploit (4) [eks'ployt], *n.* a bold, heroic act or deed. **Ex.** *The
soldier was decorated for his exploits.*

exploit (4) [eksployt'], *v.* 1. use in a practical way; get the
full value from. **Ex.** *The new dam did much to exploit the*

a, far; æ, am; e, get; ey, late; i, in; iy, see; ɔ, all; ow, go; u, put; uw, too;
ə, but, ago; ər, fur; aw, out; ay, life; oy, boy; ŋ, ring; θ, think; ð, that;
ž, measure; š, ship; j, edge; č, child.

water power resources of the area. 2. make unfair use of; use for one's own advantage or profit. **Ex.** *Slaves were exploited by their masters.* —ex`ploi·ta'tion, *n.*

explore (2) [iksplɔːr'], *v.* 1. travel in a place that is not well known to discover more about it. **Ex.** *Man is now exploring the moon.* 2. make a careful search; examine closely. **Ex.** *He explored every possibility before making a decision.* —ex`plo·ra'tion, *n.* the act of exploring. —ex·plor'er, *n.* one who explores.

export (3) [ek'spɔrt`, ikspɔrt'], *v.* send goods made in one country to be sold in another. **Ex.** *Japan exports a large number of cameras to the United States.* —*n.* 1. the act of sending goods from one country for sale in another. **Ex.** *Japan manufactures cameras for export.* 2. the article exported. **Ex.** *Machinery is one of our most important exports.* —ex`por·ta'tion, *n.* —ex·port'er, *n.* one who exports.

expose (3) [ikspowz'], *v.* 1. leave unprotected. **Ex.** *The child was exposed to the sun's rays too long.* 2. uncover; make known; reveal. **Ex.** *The crime of the official was exposed.* —ex·pos'ure, *n.*

express (2) [ikspres'], *v.* 1. say clearly; state. **Ex.** *He expressed his ideas very well.* 2. reveal; show one's feelings. **Ex.** *He expressed his anger by shouting.* —*adj.* 1. for one purpose only. **Ex.** *He went for the express purpose of seeing his friend.* 2. in the quickest or shortest way; without stopping. **Ex.** *The express train does not stop at any station between here and the city.* —ex·pres'sion, *n.* 1. an outward sign of how one feels or thinks. **Ex.** *Their cheers were an expression of their approval.* 2. a putting into words. **Ex.** *This story is an expression of the author's ideas.* —ex·pres'sive, *adj.*

expressway [ikspres'wey`], *n.* a divided road built for fast driving.

exquisite (5) [eks'kwizət, ikskwiz'ət], *adj.* 1. made with great care and skill; of rare and delicate beauty. **Ex.** *The exquisite diamond pin was a work of art.* 2. of the finest quality; excellent. **Ex.** *The queen's table was set with exquisite dishes and silver.* —ex·qui'site·ly, *adv.*

extend (2) [ikstend'], *v.* 1. be stretched out in area or in length. **Ex.** *The railroad has been extended for another twenty miles.* 2. continue for a longer time. **Ex.** *They extended their visit for two more days.* 3. give; offer. **Ex.** *May*

I extend my sympathy on the death of your mother? —**ex·ten'sion**, *n.* —**ex·ten'sive**, *adj.* covering a large area; including much or many.

extent (3) [ikstent'], *n.* 1. size, amount, length, etc. to which a thing is extended. **Ex.** *The extent of the new railroad line is ten miles.* 2. degree; measure. **Ex.** *The extent of his knowledge increased after he studied in the university.*

exterior (5) [ikstir'iyər], *adj.* outer. **Ex.** *The exterior surface of the house was bleached by the sun.* —*n.* the outer surface or part. **Ex.** *The exterior of the house was brick.*

external (4) [ikstər'nəl], *adj.* 1. on, coming from, or applied to the outside; outer. **Ex.** *This medicine is for external use only.* 2. relating to foreign nations. **Ex.** *The country's external problems concerned its frontiers with neighboring countries.* —**ex·ter'nal·ly**, *adv.*

extinct (5) [ikstinkt'], *adj.* no longer living or in existence. **Ex.** *Many animals that lived thousands of years ago are now extinct.* —**ex·tinc'tion**, *n.*

extra (2) [eks'trə], *adj.* greater than ordinary, expected, or necessary; additional. **Ex.** *He received more money for the extra work he did.* —*adv.* more than usually. **Ex.** *Such a big man needs extra-large clothes.*

extract (5) [ikstrækt'], *v.* pull out, usually with effort. **Ex.** *He had two teeth extracted.* —**extraction**, *n.* 1. the act of extracting. **Ex.** *The extraction of his tooth was very painful.* 2. origin; line of descent. **Ex.** *He is of Italian extraction.*

extract (5) [iks'trækt], *n.* 1. a substance taken out which is the essential part. **Ex.** *She flavored the cake with lemon extract.* 2. a section taken from a written work, often for the purpose of quoting. **Ex.** *She read an extract from my favorite poem.*

extraordinary (3) [ikstrɔr'dəne:r'iy], *adj.* not ordinary; not usual. **Ex.** *A genius has extraordinary talents.* —**ex'tra·or·di·nar'i·ly**, *adv.*

extravagance (5) [ikstræv'əgəns], *n.* wastefulness; spending more money than is necessary. **Ex.** *Buying a second car was an extravagance.* —**ex·trav'a·gant**, *adj.*

extreme (3) [ikstriym'], *adj.* 1. greatest; to the utmost. **Ex.** *He uses extreme care when driving in the rain.* 2. farthest away. **Ex.** *He lives in the house at the extreme end of the street.* 3. going beyond the usual or accepted. **Ex.** *The radical candidate has very extreme political ideas.* —*n.* either of two things as different or as far apart as possible. **Ex.** *The weather went from one extreme to the other.* —**ex·treme'ly**, *adv.* —**ex·trem'ist**, *n.* one who has extreme ideas. —**ex·trem'i·ty**, *n.* the point farthest removed; the end. —**ex·trem'i·ties**, *n.* the feet and hands.

eye (1) [ay'], *n.* 1. the part of the body with which people and animals see. 2. power of seeing; sight; vision. **Ex.** *He has a good eye for color.* 3. something that looks like an eye. **Ex.** *I need a needle with a large eye.* —**eye'less**, *adj.* without eyes; blind. —**catch one's eye**, attract one's attention. —**keep an eye on** or **out**, watch closely. **Ex.** *Keep an eye out for cars when crossing the street.*

EYE 1

eyeball [ay'bɔ:l'], *n.* the whole of an eye inside the eyelid.

eyebrow [ay'braw'], *n.* the curved line of hair above each eye.

eyeglass [ay'glæs'], *n.* a piece of special glass used to improve vision. —**eye'glass·es**, *n.* two of such glasses in a frame.

eyelash [ay'læš'], *n.* each of the hairs growing on the eyelid.

EYEGLASSES

eyelid [ay'lid'], *n.* the skin that covers and un-covers the eyeball as one opens or closes one's eyes.

eyesore [ay'sɔ:r'], *n.* anything not pleasant to look at. **Ex.** *The old houses were eyesores.*

eyewitness [ay'wit'nəs], *n.* a person who saw something him-self, not someone who was only told about it. **Ex.** *He was an eyewitness to the accident.*

F

F, f [ef'], *n.* the sixth letter of the English alphabet.

fable (4) [fey'bəl], *n.* a short story that explains a moral, especially one in which animals speak and act like people. **Ex.** *He read to the child from an old book of fables.*

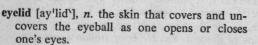

fabric (4) [fæb'rik], *n*. cloth; material. **Ex.** *Clothes are made of fabric.* —**fab'ri·cate**, *v*. 1. make by assembling parts. **Ex.** *He fabricated a car with the parts he had.* 2. invent. **Ex.** *He fabricated the story.*

face (1) [feys'], *n*. 1. the front part of the head, from the forehead to the chin. **Ex.** *She has a pretty face.* 2. something resembling a face. **Ex.** *It is too dark to see the face of the clock.* —*v*. 1. look toward; be turned toward. **Ex.** *The teacher faced the class.* 2. meet with courage. **Ex.** *They could not face their accusers.* —**fa'cial**, *adj*. —**in the face of,** 1. in the presence of. **Ex.** *He showed his courage in the face of danger.* 2. despite. **Ex.** *He completed the work in the face of many difficulties.* —**make a face,** twist one's face to show feeling. **Ex.** *When he tasted the bitter medicine, he made a face.* —**on the face of it,** from what can be seen or known. **Ex.** *On the face of it, your plan seems good.*

facility (4) [fəsil'ətiy], *n*. 1. ease or skill in doing, acting, working, etc. **Ex.** *We admired his facility in playing the piano.* 2. that which makes it easier to do something. **Ex.** *This kitchen has the latest facilities for cooking.* —**fa·cil'i·tate**, *v*. make easier.

fact (1) [fækt'], *n*. 1. a thing known to be true or to have really happened. **Ex.** *He told the police all the facts.* 2. truth; reality. **Ex.** *In fact, he just left.* 3. something said to be true or supposed to have happened. **Ex.** *Are you sure of the facts?* —**fac'tu·al**, *adj*.

faction (5) [fæk'šən], *n*. a group of people within, and often in opposition to, a larger group. **Ex.** *He belongs to the liberal faction of his political party.*

factor (5) [fæk'tər], *n*. any one of the causes of a result. **Ex.** *Mechanical failure was the chief factor in causing the wreck.*

factory (2) [fæk't(ə)riy], *n*. a building, or group of buildings, where goods are manufactured. **Ex.** *We have a shoe factory in our town.*

faculty (4) [fək'əltiy], *n*. 1. any of the physical powers of the body, such as hearing, sight, etc.; any special ability or talent. **Ex.** *The old man still had all his faculties.* 2. all those who teach in a school or college; all the persons who teach in a department of a college or university. **Ex.** *He is a member of the college faculty.*

fade (3) [feyd'], *v.* 1. lose or cause to lose color or brightness. **Ex.** *The sun has faded the curtains.* 2. die away. **Ex.** *The sound faded as he walked away.* 3. lose strength and freshness. **Ex.** *Flowers will fade without water.*

fail (1) [feyl'], *v.* 1. not succeed; not reach. **Ex.** *He failed in his schoolwork.* 2. not do; neglect. **Ex.** *She failed to answer the letter.* 3. be of no use or help; disappoint. **Ex.** *He failed us when we needed him most.* 4. become weaker. **Ex.** *His health has been failing.* —**fail'ure,** *n.* —**without fail,** certainly; surely. **Ex.** *He will come without fail.*

faint (2) [feynt'], *adj.* weak; without brightness, strength, etc. **Exs.** *We heard a faint cry for help. She felt faint.* —*v.* lose consciousness. **Ex.** *She fainted when she heard the news.* *n.* loss of consciousness. **Ex.** *She fell in a faint.* —**faint'ly,** *adv.*

fainthearted [feynt'har'təd], *adj.* not brave; lacking confidence. **Ex.** *He was too fainthearted to ask her to marry him.*

fair (1) [fe:r'], *adj.* 1. just; honest. **Ex.** *They received a fair share of the money.* 2. ordinary; average; not very good or very bad. **Ex.** *He is a fair student.* 3. not dark; light-colored. **Ex.** *She has blond hair and very fair skin.* 4. sunny; not stormy. **Ex.** *The weather is fair today.* —**fair'ly,** *adv.*

fair (1) [fe:r'], *n.* a gathering of people to buy and sell goods, show products, etc. **Ex.** *A fair is held in the village every Saturday.*

fairy (3) [fer'iy], *n.* an imaginary being in children's stories that is supposed to look like a tiny human with wings and to have powers of magic. **Ex.** *The fairy promised to grant the child's wish.*

faith (2) [feyθ'], *n.* 1. believing without proof; trust. **Ex.** *He has complete faith in his lawyer.* 2. religion or belief. **Ex.** *There are people of many faiths in the United States.* —**faith'ful,** *adj.* loyal; honest. —**faith'ful·ly,** *adv.* —**faith'ful·ness,** *n.*

fall (1) [fɔ:l'], *v.* 1. drop; go down; descend. **Ex.** *The snow started to fall last night.* 2. suddenly drop or come down from a standing position. **Ex.** *Be careful on the ice or you* *will fall.* 3. be killed or wounded. **Ex.** *I saw him fall in battle.* 4. hit; land; strike. **Ex.** *Where did the blow fall?* 5. become less in number or lower in degree; decrease. **Ex.** *In summer, the price of fresh fruit will fall.* 6. pass suddenly into a new state or condition; become. **Ex.** *I often fall asleep while reading.* —*n.* the act of falling or dropping. **Ex.** *The fall hurt the child's leg.* —**fall'en,** *adj.* —**fall back,** retreat. —**fall back on,** turn to or go to for help. **Ex.** *She fell back on her family.* —**fall behind,** 1. drop back as in a race or other effort. **Ex.** *He fell behind in his work.* 2. be late in paying. —**fall off,** drop or decrease. —**fall out,** 1. get out of a line. 2. quarrel. —**fall through,** fail to develop; fail. **Ex.** *Her plan fell through.*

false (2) [fɔːlsˈ], *adj.* 1. not true; incorrect. **Ex.** *She had a false idea of what she was to be paid.* 2. dishonest; lying. **Ex.** *She made a false statement.* 3. not real. **Ex.** *He has false teeth.* —**false'ly,** *adv.* —**fal'si·fy,** *v.*

falter (5) [fɔlˈtər], *v.* 1. be unsteady or unsure; stumble; hesitate. **Ex.** *She began to falter in her beliefs.* 2. stumble or hesitate in moving. **Ex.** *The old man faltered as he walked.*

fame (2) [feymˈ], *n.* public reputation, especially a very favorable one. **Ex.** *His fame as an honest man spread everywhere.* —**famed',** *adj.*

familiar (2) [fəmilˈyər], *adj.* 1. well-known; common. **Ex.** *His voice is familiar to radio listeners.* 2. well-acquainted; friendly. **Ex.** *He was familiar with my family.* —**fa·mil'i·ar'i·ty,** *n.* 1. a thorough knowledge of. 2. friendliness, usually not wanted. —**fa·mil'i·ar·ize,** *v.* make well-known; become acquainted. **Ex.** *He familiarized himself with the strange city.*

family (1) [fæmˈ(ə)liy], *n.* 1. the group consisting of children and their parents. **Ex.** *There are seven in my family.* 2. a group of people related to each other. **Ex.** *The whole family, including my cousins, came to my wedding.* 3. a group of related animals or plants. **Ex.** *The lion and the tiger belong to the same family.*

famine (4) [fæmˈən], *n.* a great scarcity of food resulting in starvation. **Ex.** *If the crops fail, there will be a famine this year.*

famous (1) [feyˈməs], *adj.* very well-known. **Ex.** *He is a famous writer.*

fan (3) [fæn¹], *n.* a device used to create currents of air, usually to cool. **Ex.** *In the summer, we use an electric fan.* —*v.* make a current of air, as with a fan; blow air toward. **Ex.** *He fanned the fire until it grew stronger.*

FAN

fancy (1) [fæn¹siy], *n.* 1. the power of forming mental pictures of things that are not present; imagination. **Ex.** *The idea of travel appealed to her fancy.* 2. the things imagined; an image. **Ex.** *She had wild fancies of fame and wealth.* 3. a liking. **Ex.** *He took a fancy to her.* —*adj.* 1. of better than ordinary quality. **Ex.** *They bought some fancy fruits for their sick friend.* 2. having complicated design and much ornament; not plain. **Ex.** *She wore a fancy dress to the party.* —*v.* 1. imagine; picture to oneself. **Ex.** *The boy fancied himself a great statesman.* 2. like. **Ex.** *She fancied the dress and bought it.*

fantastic (5) [fæn¹tæs¹tik], *adj.* 1. beyond belief. **Ex.** *She gave fantastic reasons for her absences.* 2. wildly fanciful. **Ex.** *The wall was covered with fantastic designs.* —**fan¹ta·sy**, *n.* imagination; unreal dreams, stories, etc. **Ex.** *In his fantasy, he imagined he was a king.*

far (1) [fa:r¹], *adv.* 1. at, to, or from a great distance. **Ex.** *He lives far from here.* 2. to or at a certain distance or degree. **Ex.** *How far up did the plane go?* 3. very much or a great deal. **Ex.** *He is a far better writer than his brother.* —*adj.* 1. distant; not near. **Ex.** *He came from a far country.* 2. farther away. **Ex.** *He lives on the far side of the mountain.* —**as far as, so far as,** to the extent or degree that. **Ex.** *As far as I know, he has not come.* —**by far, far and away,** greatly. **Ex.** *He is far and away the better writer.* —**so far, thus far,** to this place, time, etc. **Ex.** *He has not arrived so far.*

faraway [fa:r¹əwey¹], *adj.* distant; seeming to be distant. **Ex.** *As she read his letter, she had a faraway look in her eyes.*

fare (3) [fe:r¹], *n.* 1. the price of a ride. **Ex.** *How much is the fare on this train?* 2. a person who pays to use transportation. **Ex.** *The taxi picked up two fares at the corner.* 3. food. **Ex.** *The fare we tasted was good.* —*v.* get along; manage; do. **Ex.** *How did you fare on your trip?*

farewell (3) [fe:r¹wel¹], *interj.* good-by. **Ex.** *Farewell, my* *friends. —n.* leave-taking; departure; good wishes at departure. **Ex.** *Their farewell was sad. —adj.* parting. **Ex.** *They gave him a farewell party.*

farm (1) [farm'], *n.* land used for raising crops or animals. **Ex.** *They grew very good corn on their farm. —v.* raise crops or animals. **Ex.** *He farmed the land himself.* **—farm'er,** *n.* one who farms.

farsighted [fa:r'sayt`d], *adj.* 1. able to see things at a distance. 2. able to plan wisely for the future.

farther (2) [far'ðǝr], *adv.* 1. at or to a greater distance. **Ex.** *I can swim farther than you can.* 2. to a greater degree or extent; more. **Ex.** *He has not developed his idea any farther.* **—adj.** more distant. **Ex.** *The farther hill is ten miles away.*

fascinate (5) [fæs'ǝneyt`], *v.* 1. attract strongly; charm. **Ex.** *Her beauty fascinated him.* 2. hold motionless by a strong power, such as fear. **Ex.** *The child was fascinated by the snake.* **—fas`ci·na'tion,** *n.*

fashion (2) [fæš'ǝn], *n.* 1. manner; way. **Ex.** *He talked in a childish fashion.* 2. dress, way of living, etc. that is popular. **Ex.** *She always knew the latest dress fashions. —v.* make; shape; form. **Ex.** *He fashioned a figure out of clay.* **—fash'ion·a·ble,** *adj.* in style. **Ex.** *She wears fashionable clothes.*

fast (1) [fæst'], *adj.* 1. moving or working at high speed; quick; rapid. **Ex.** *The boy is a fast runner.* 2. indicating a time ahead of the correct time. **Ex.** *His watch is fast. —adv.* 1. quickly; rapidly. **Ex.** *His car will not go fast.* 2. tightly. **Ex.** *Hold fast to my hand.* 3. completely. **Ex.** *He is fast asleep.*

fast (1) [fæst'], *v.* go without food. **Ex.** *Some people fast on certain days of the year. —n.* a time of fasting. **Ex.** *During his fast, he ate no solid food.*

fasten (3) [fæs'ǝn], *v.* 1. attach securely to something; join. **Ex.** *He fastened the papers together.* 2. fix firmly in place by closing or locking. **Ex.** *Fasten the doors before you go to bed.* **—fas'ten·er,** *n.* that which fastens. **—fas'ten·ing,** *n.* anything used to fasten.

fat (1) [fæt'], *n.* an oily substance, white or yellowish, found especially in animals. **Ex.** *She melted the fat and fried potatoes in it.* —*adj.* 1. fleshy; heavy. **Ex.** *He is a fat but healthy baby.* 2. thick; broad. **Ex.** *He was carrying a fat book.* —**fat'ten**, *v.* —**fat'ty**, *adj.*

fatal (3) [fey'təl], *adj.* 1. deadly. **Ex.** *He was in a fatal accident.* 2. causing ruin or destruction. **Ex.** *The delay was fatal to their plan.* —**fa·tal·ly**, *adv.* —**fa·tal'i·ty**, *n.* a death.

fate (2) [feyt'], *n.* 1. a force or power thought to determine in advance what is going to happen. **Ex.** *He blamed fate for his failure in life.* 2. the events that happen as though controlled by this force or power. **Ex.** *It was their fate to meet and marry.* —**fat'ed**, *adj.* decided in advance by fate. **Ex.** *He was fated to lead his country.* —**fate'ful**, *adj.*

father (1) [fa'ðər], *n.* 1. male parent. **Ex.** *That man is my father.* 2. founder; creator. **Ex.** *George Washington was the father of his country.* 3. priest. —*v.* be the father of. **Ex.** *He fathered eight children.* —**fa'ther·ly**, *adj.*

father-in-law [fa'ðərənlɔ:'], *n.* the father of one's wife or husband.

fatigue (4) [fətiyg'], *n.* weariness. **Ex.** *After a hard day's work, they were overcome by fatigue.* —*v.* make or become weary or tired. **Ex.** *Working in the hot kitchen fatigued her.*

fault (2) [fɔ:lt'], *n.* 1. imperfection. **Ex.** *His greatest fault is laziness.* 2. blame. **Ex.** *Whose fault is it that the window is open?* —**fault'y**, *adj.* —**find fault with**, point to the weaknesses of. **Ex.** *She finds fault with everything he does.*

favor (1) [fey'vər], *n.* 1. liking; approval. **Ex.** *He is in favor of your plan.* 2. a kind, helpful action. **Ex.** *He did me a favor.* 3. special treatment. **Ex.** *The teacher showed some favor to the younger children.* —*v.* 1. like; approve. **Ex.** *The President favored a small tax.* 2. show preference; give special treatment. **Ex.** *That teacher favors the boys.*

favorable (3) [fey'v(ə)rəbəl], *adj.* 1. approving; friendly. **Ex.** *He is favorable to our plan.* 2. giving help. **Ex.** *We will leave as soon as we have favorable weather.* —**fa'vor·a·bly**, *adv.*

favorite (3) [fey'v(ə)rət], *n.* a person or thing liked best or preferred. **Ex.** *She is her father's favorite.* —*adj.* preferred; liked best. **Ex.** *Blue is my favorite color.* —**fa'vor·it·ism**, *n.* act of showing preference for one person.

fawn (5) [fɔ:n'], *n.* a deer less than one year old.

fawn (5) [fɔ:n'], *v.* try to win favor or notice by acting in a humble and flattering way. **Ex.** *He fawned on her only to borrow money.*

FAWN

fear (1) [fi:r'], *n.* 1. a distressing feeling one has when danger, trouble, evil, etc. is close. **Ex.** *He felt fear when he heard a sudden noise.* 2. an uneasy or anxious feeling; anxiety. **Ex.** *Fear for the future kept her awake.* 3. a particular cause of fear. **Ex.** *Her greatest fear was being alone.* —*v.* 1. be afraid. **Ex.** *He fears nothing.* 2. feel anxious. **Ex.** *I fear that he may be hurt.* —**fear'ful,** *adj.* causing fear; feeling fear.

feast (2) [fiyst'], *n.* a large meal with many dishes, prepared for some special occasion. **Ex.** *We enjoyed the wedding feast.* —*v.* eat much food. **Ex.** *They feasted for three days during the king's visit.*

feat (5) [fiyt'], *n.* a deed of great courage, skill, or strength. **Ex.** *The first flight into space was a brilliant feat.*

feather (2) [feð'ər], *n.* a light, thin outgrowth from a bird's skin that forms a covering. —*v.* supply or cover with feathers. **Ex.** *The bird feathered a nest for its young.* —**feath'er·y,** *adj.* like feathers.

FEATHER

feature (2) [fiy'čər], *n.* 1. a part of the face such as the eyes, nose, mouth, or chin. **Ex.** *Her mouth is her best feature.* 2. a notable quality. **Ex.** *Light is a necessary feature in a house.* 3. the main attraction of a program; a special article or story in a newspaper or magazine. **Ex.** *There is an interesting feature about world peace in this magazine.* —*v.* present as especially important. **Ex.** *They featured him as the writer of the year.*

February (1) [feb'ruwer`iy], *n.* the second month of the year.

fed (2) [fed'], *v.* past tense and participle of *feed.* **Ex.** *The children were fed first.*

federal (3) [fed'(ə)rəl], *adj.* of or relating to a union of states which give up some of their individual powers to a central government. **Ex.** *The United States has a federal government.* —**fed'er·al·ism,** *n.* the principle of such a union. —**fed'er·al·ist,** *n.* one who supports the federal principle. **Ex.** *Federalists wanted the central government to be strong.* —**fed'er·ate,** *v.* form a union of states.

fee (4) [fiy'], *n.* a payment required for a service or privilege. **Ex.** *The fee for a visit by the doctor was small.*

feeble (4) [fiy'bəl], *adj.* weak; without strength. **Ex.** *He was too feeble to lift the chair.* —**fee'ble·ness,** *n.* —**fee'bly,** *adv.*

feed (1) [fiyd'], *v.* 1. give food to. **Ex.** *Feed the baby first.* 2. eat. **Ex.** *The chickens are feeding in the yard.* —*n.* food, especially for animals. **Ex.** *The farmer is carrying a bag of feed.*

feel (1) [fiyl'], *v.* 1. experience an emotion. **Ex.** *She feels happy because of his success.* 2. think; believe. **Ex.** *He feels you should go.* 3. know or be aware of through the sense of touch. **Ex.** *She felt rain on her cheeks.* 4. examine by touching; test. **Ex.** *Feel his forehead to see if he has a fever.* —**feel,** *n.* sense of touch; becoming aware of by the sense of touch. **Ex.** *This material has a silky feel.* —**feel'ing,** *n.* 1. an emotion; pleasure, pain, etc. experienced within oneself. **Ex.** *She saw the jewel and had a sudden feeling of envy.* 2. attitude; belief. **Ex.** *My feeling is that he will make a good president.* 3. the act of being aware by touch; the sense of touch. **Ex.** *Since his injury, he has no feeling in his arm.* —**feel'ing·ly,** *adv.* —**feel'ings,** *n.* the capacity for being affected by outside influences. **Ex.** *Her feelings were hurt by what he said.*

feet (1) [fiyt'], *n.* plural of foot. **Ex.** *We heard the sound of marching feet.*

fell (1) [fel'], *v.* past tense of *fall.* **Ex.** *He fell from the tree.*

fell (1) [fel'], *v.* 1. knock down. **Ex.** *He was felled by one blow.* 2. cut down. **Ex.** *A woodsman will fell the tree for us.*

fellow (1) [fel'ow], *n.* a male; a companion. **Ex.** *He went with two other fellows.* —*adj.* being a comrade, associate, etc. **Ex.** *We are fellow students.*

fellowship [fel'owšip'], *n.* 1. friendliness; comradeship. 2. money given to a good student to help pay for graduate studies.

felt (1) [felt'], *v.* past tense and participle of *feel.* **Ex.** *Yesterday he felt better.*

felt (1) [felt'], *n.* cloth made by rolling and pressing together a mass of wool, hair, or fur. **Ex.** *His winter hat is made of felt.*

female (2) [fiy'meyl'], *n.* 1. woman or girl. **Ex.** *Only one female works in our office.* 2. an animal of the sex that brings forth young or lays eggs. **Ex.** *Hens and cows are females.* —*adj.* 1. of a woman or girl. 2. of an animal of the sex that brings forth young or lays eggs.

feminine (5) [fem'ənən], *adj.* of or like a woman or a girl. **Ex.** *The pink lace dress was very feminine.* —**fem'i·nin'i·ty,** *n.*

fence (1) [fens'], *n.* railing, wall, or other means of keeping people or animals in or out or of marking a boundary. **Ex.** *They have a fence around their house.* —*v.* put a fence around. **Ex.** *They fenced the field.* —**on the fence,** not on one side or the other. **Ex.** *He is on the fence about this question.*

fend (5) [fend'], *v.* resist; force away. **Ex.** *She fended off the dog with a stick.* —**fend'er,** *n.* the metal guard over each wheel of a car. —**fend for oneself,** take care of oneself without help.

FENDER

fern (5) [fərn'], *n.* a plant which has delicate, feathery leaves but no flowers. **Ex.** *He put green ferns in the bunch of roses.*

ferry (4) [fer'iy], *v.* carry or be carried from place to place, usually over a small body of water. **Ex.** *We ferried the goods across the river.* —*n.* a boat which carries goods or people across a river or other small body of water; a ferryboat. **Ex.** *We go by ferry to work every day.*

FERN

fertile (4) [fər'təl], *adj.* 1. producing plentiful crops; rich. **Ex.** *His land is fertile.* 2. able to produce seeds, fruit, or young. **Ex.** *The rabbit is a very fertile animal.* —**fer'til'i·ty,** *n.* —**fer'ti·lize,** *v.* make fertile. —**fer'ti·liz·er,** *n.* anything which, when added to the soil, increases fertility.

festive (4) [fes'tiv], *adj.* joyous; gay; merry; suitable for a feast. **Ex.** *His birthday was a festive occasion.* —**fes'tiv·al, fes·tiv'i·ty,** *n.*

fetch (3) [feč'], *v.* go and get; bring. **Ex.** *Please fetch me a* *glass of water.* —**fetch'ing,** *adj.* pleasing; attractive. **Ex.** *She wore a fetching hat.*

feud (5) [fyuwd'], *n.* a long and deadly quarrel, especially between families. **Ex.** *Because of the feud, they did not speak when they met.* —*v.* carry on a feud. **Ex.** *They were still feuding.*

feudal (5) [fyuw'dəl], *adj.* of or having to do with the way of life when kings and lords owned all land and granted the use of it to others in return for goods and services. **Ex.** *Under the feudal system, ordinary men could not own land.*

fever (2) [fiy'vər], *n.* 1. a high body temperature, usually due to illness. **Ex.** *Her high fever indicated she was sick.* 2. an excited, restless condition. **Ex.** *The man was in a fever of excitement over the news.* —**fe'ver·ish,** *adj.*

few (1) [fyuw'], *adj.* not many. **Ex.** *A few friends came early.* —*n.* a small number of. **Ex.** *The few who came early were friends.*

fiber (4) [fay'bər], *n.* the threadlike structures of a plant or animal. **Ex.** *The fibers of cotton make strong cloth.*

fiction (5) [fik'šən], *n.* 1. a piece of writing about imaginary persons and events. **Ex.** *His novels are fiction at its best.* 2. something imagined or invented. **Ex.** *What he told us was pure fiction.* —**fic'tion·al,** *adj.*

field (1) [fiyld'], *n.* 1. a piece of open land with few or no trees, especially land on which crops can be grown or animals fed. **Ex.** *The farmer is plowing his fields.* 2. a piece of land used for some special purpose or yielding some special product. **Ex.** *This ball field is part of the school playground.* 3. a range of activity, interest, or opportunity. **Ex.** *Science is his field of study.*

fiend (5) [fiynd'], *n.* 1. a devil; an evil spirit. **Ex.** *The fiends in his dreams frightened him.* 2. a very wicked, cruel person. **Ex.** *Catch the fiend who committed these murders.* —**fiend' ish,** *adj.*

fierce (2) [firs'], *adj.* 1. savage; furious in anger or cruelty; of a nature to inspire terror. **Ex.** *The fierce dog frightened the neighbors away.* 2. raging; violent. **Ex.** *The fierce fire destroyed several houses.* 3. eager; very strong. **Ex.** *A fierce ambition drove him on.* —**fierce'ly,** *adv.* —**fierce'ness,** *n.*

fifteen (1) [fif'tiyn'], *n., adj.* the number between fourteen and sixteen; the number *15.* —**fif'teenth',** *n., adj.* coming after fourteen others.

fifth (1) [fifθ'], *n.*, *adj.* coming after four others.

fifty (1) [fif'tiy], *n.*, *adj.* the number between forty-nine and fifty-one; the number *50*. —**fif'tieth,** *n.*, *adj.* coming after forty-nine others.

fig (4) [fig'], *n.* a small, soft, sweet fruit with many seeds; the tree that figs grow on. **Ex.** *Figs are delicious fresh or dried.*

FIG

fight (1) [fayt'], *v.* 1. struggle with, using force; attempt to defeat or destroy an enemy; battle. **Ex.** *He was fighting with his brother.* 2. try to overcome. **Ex.** *He has been fighting his illness for a long time.* —*n.* 1. use of force to gain victory; battle. **Ex.** *The fight was long and hard.* 2. struggle; contest. **Ex.** *The fight against that disease will someday be won.*

figure (1) [fig'yər], *n.* 1. a symbol for a number. **Ex.** *"1" is the figure for "one."* 2. amount. **Ex.** *The cost figure he gave for the work was too high.* 3. pattern; design; drawing. **Ex.** *Her dress was made of blue cloth with figures in red.* 4. form; outline; shape. **Ex.** *She saw the figure of a man ahead of her.* 5. a person or character. **Ex.** *He is one of the great figures in history.* 6. a carved, painted, or drawn representation. **Ex.** *In the garden were many stone figures.* —*v.* use numbers to find the answer to a problem. **Ex.** *He figured the cost to be low.* —**figure out,** find an answer or solution to. **Ex.** *I figured out a way of doing it.*

figurehead [fig'yərhed'], *n.* a person in an important position controlled by someone else who has the real power. **Ex.** *The king can't help. He is only a figurehead.*

file (3) [fayl'], *n.* 1. a place for keeping papers in order; a set of papers kept in order. **Ex.** *The lawyer had a separate file on each of his cases.* 2. a row of people or things. **Ex.** *A long file of people waited for the bus.* —*v.* 1. put away in order. **Ex.** *The clerk filed the cards in order.* 2. march or move in a line. **Ex.** *The children filed out of the classroom.*

file (3) [fayl'], *n.* a steel tool with many small ridges for smoothing rough surfaces. —*v.* rub smooth with a file. **Ex.** *The workman filed the rough edges of the lock.*

fill (1) [fil'], *v.* 1. put or pour into until no more can be contained; make full; become full. **Ex.** *He filled the pail with water.* 2. supply what is needed; satisfy. **Ex.** *They filled the order.* 3. occupy or put someone into an office or job. **Ex.** *No one was found to fill that job.* —*n.* a complete supply;

satisfaction. **Ex.** *He has had his fill of cake.* —**fill in,** 1. make complete. **Ex.** *Fill in all the spaces on the form.* 2. act as a substitute. **Ex.** *Will you fill in for me at the office today?* —**fill out,** 1. become rounder or fatter. **Ex.** *The good food filled him out.* 2. make complete by writing. **Ex.** *Please fill out this form.* —**fill up,** make full. **Ex.** *Fill up the bottle with water.*

filling station [fil'iŋ stey'šən], a place to buy gas, oil, etc. for the car.

film (2) [film'], *n.* 1. a roll or sheet covered with a coating that is changed by light and used in making photographs. **Ex.** *He took the roll of film out of his camera.* 2. a motion picture; a movie. **Ex.** *There is a new film being shown at the theater.* 3. a very thin surface. **Ex.** *There is a film of ice on the lake.* —*v.* make a motion picture. **Ex.** *They are filming a famous play.*

filter (5) [fil'tər], *n.* a device using a substance such as cloth or sand through which water, air, etc. is passed to remove something not wanted. **Ex.** *The filter cleaned the water that flowed through it.* —*v.* pass through a device or substance in order to strain out something. **Ex.** *They filtered the water through a cloth to remove the dirt.*

filth (5) [filθ'], *n.* a foul or dirty substance. **Ex.** *The old house was full of filth.* —**filth'y,** *adj.*

final (2) [fay'nəl], *adj.* 1. at the end; last. **Ex.** *The final test was the hardest one of the year.* 2. not to be changed. **Ex.** *The ruling of the highest court is final.* —**fi'nal·ly,** *adv.*

finance (3) [fay'næns, fənæns'], *n.* the management of money. **Ex.** *He studied banking and finance at the university.* —*v.* provide money for. **Ex.** *The bank financed his purchase of a house.* —**fi'nan·ces,** *n.* funds; money; income. —**fi·nan'cial,** *adj.* **fin'an·cier,** *n.* a manager of large amounts of money.

find (1) [faynd'], *v.* 1. discover by accident. **Ex.** *Did she find some money on the street?* 2. discover by searching. **Ex.** *Did you find your lost book?* 3. observe; declare as being. **Ex.** *We find it impossible to do.* 4. arrive at; reach. **Ex.** *Water finds its own level.* —*n.* something of value that is found. **Ex.** *That painting is an important find.* —**find'er,** *n.* one who or that which finds. —**find out,** learn; discover. **Ex.** *I can find out what they are doing.*

fine (1) [fayn'], *adj.* 1. very good; excellent; **Ex.** *He goes to a fine school.* 2. very small; not coarse; very thin. **Ex.** *The* *beach is covered with fine sand.* 3. made with care. Ex. *Such fine sewing must be the work of an artist.* —fine'ly, *adv.* —fine'ness, *n.*

fine (1) [fayn'], *n.* money paid as a punishment for an offense. Ex. *There is a fine for driving too fast.* —v. cause to pay money as punishment. Ex. *The judge fined him ten dollars for speeding.*

finger (1) [fiŋ'gər], *n.* 1. one of the five end parts of the hand. Ex. *Her second finger was cut.* 2. anything shaped or used like a finger. Ex. *The fingers of the glove are torn.* —v. touch or feel with the fingers. Ex. *She fingered the soft material.*

FINGERPRINT

fingernail [fiŋ'gərneyl'], *n.* the hard covering at the end of each finger.

fingerprint [fiŋ'gərprint'], *n.* the mark made by pressing the end of a finger to a flat surface.

finish (1) [fin'iš], *v.* 1. end; complete. Ex. *She finished the work she was doing.* 2. use all. Ex. *We finished the cake at supper.* 3. give a surface to. Ex. *He finished the table with red paint.* —n. 1. the end. Ex. *We saw the finish of the race.* 2. the way in which the surface is prepared. Ex. *The chair had a dark finish.* —finish off, 1. end. 2. kill. —finish up, 1. end. 2. use all. Ex. *Finish up the candy, and I will buy more.*

fir (5) [fə:r'], *n.* a tree belonging to the pine family. Ex. *The fir remains green all year.*

fire (1) [fayr'], *n.* 1. the fact of burning, as shown by light and heat; something burning, as in a stove. Ex. *They built a fire to keep warm.* 2. the discharge from a gun. Ex. *We could hear the gunfire of the hunters.* 3. strong spirit or feeling. Ex. *The young actor spoke his lines with fire.* —v. shoot. Ex. *The soldiers fired their guns.* —catch fire, start burning. —on fire, burning. —open fire, start shooting. —set fire to, cause to burn. —under fire, being attacked.

FIR

firearm [fayr'arm`], *n.* any weapon that fires or shoots bullets and can be carried; a gun.

firecracker [fayr'kræk`ər], *n.* paper with powder inside that explodes when burned. **Ex.** *They exploded many firecrackers on the holiday.*

fire engine [fayr' en'jən], *n.* a truck used by firemen.

fireman [fayr'mən], *n.* a man hired, usually by a government, to fight fires as his regular work.

fireplace [fayr'pleys`], *n.* an open place at the bottom of a chimney for a fire; any structure in or on which a fire is built inside the wall of a house. **Ex.** *They lit a fire in the fireplace.*

fireproof [fayr'pruwf`], *adj.* not easily burned. **Ex.** *The school was built of fireproof materials.* —*v.* make fireproof by treating with chemicals or other methods.

fire station [fayr' stey'šən], a place where fire engines and firemen stay when not fighting fires.

firetrap [fayr'træp`], *n.* a building that is dangerous because it would burn easily.

fireworks [fayr'wərks`], *n.* a series of firecrackers and other explosive devices making a loud noise or a display of light. **Ex.** *Fireworks lighted the night sky with brilliant color.*

firm (1) [fərm'], *adj.* 1. not easily moved or changed. **Ex.** *He has very firm ideas.* 2. strong and steady in character. **Ex.** *He is firm, yet kind.* 3. solid and unyielding. **Ex.** *The house is on firm ground.*

first (1) [fərst'], *adj.* coming before any other. **Ex.** *The first letter received was from him.* —*adv.* 1. before any other person or thing. **Ex.** *He always arrives first.* 2. the first time. **Ex.** *When did you first meet?* 3. rather; before. **Ex.** *I will not pay the money; I will go to jail first!* —*n.* 1. that which is first. **Ex.** *He is the first on the list.* 2. the beginning; start. **Ex.** *I liked him at first.*

first aid [fərst' eyd'], treatment given to injured or sick people while waiting for the doctor.

firsthand [fərst`hænd'], *adj., adv.* direct from the person who saw or did something. **Ex.** *We heard a firsthand account of the meeting from a man who attended it.*

first person [fərst' pər'sən], *pronoun* or *verb* form referring to the speaker. Ex. *"I," "me," and "we" are first-person pronouns.*

first-rate [fərst'reyt'], *adj.* best quality; very good. Ex. *The book is first-rate.*

fish (1) [fiš'], *n.* an animal, usually with scales, that lives and can breathe in water. —*v.* catch or attempt to catch fish. Ex. *They fished from a boat.* —**fish'y,** *adj.*

FISH

fist (3) [fist'], *n.* the hand closed tightly, as it is in fighting. Ex. *He raised his fist and threatened to hit me.*

fit (1) [fit'], *adj.* 1. suited to or suitable for a special purpose; right; proper. Ex. *Is that book fit for young people to read?* 2. ready; prepared. Ex. *The soldiers are fit for battle.* 3. in good health. Ex. *You are looking fit.* —*v.* 1. be the proper size, shape, or quality. Ex. *These shoes fit my feet.* 2. make a person ready or qualified. Ex. *Training will fit you for this work.* 3. make the right size. Ex. *The dressmaker fitted the coat.* 4. provide with; equip. Ex. *The doors are fitted with new locks.* —*n.* the manner in which a thing fits. Ex. *That suit is a perfect fit.*

fit (1) [fit'], *n.* 1. a sudden attack of a disease. Ex. *He fell to the floor in a fit.* 2. a sudden expression of emotion or feeling. Ex. *She had a fit of anger.*

fitting [fit'iŋ], *adj.* proper; suitable. Ex. *Flowers were a fitting gift for her birthday.* —*n.* trying on clothes to see if they are the right size. Ex. *I had two fittings by the dressmaker before the clothes were right.*

five (1) [fayv'], *n., adj.* the number between four and six; the number 5.

fix (1) [fiks'], *v.* 1. attach firmly. Ex. *They fixed the sign to the wall.* 2. settle definitely; determine. Ex. *Fix a date for the meeting.* 3. repair. Ex. *He will fix the broken table.* 4. prepare; get ready. Ex. *My wife will fix dinner.* 5. direct and hold steady. Ex. *Fix your eyes on that sign.*

flag (2) [flæg'], *n.* a piece of cloth with colored designs used as a symbol of a country, group, etc. —*v.* signal with, or as if with, a flag. Ex. *They flagged the train.* —**flag down,** cause to stop by waving something. Ex. *He flagged down a passing car.*

FLAG

flake (4) [fleyk¹], *n.* a small, very thin piece. **Ex.** *The snow was falling in large flakes.* —*v.* break away or split into small, thin pieces. **Ex.** *The paint flaked from the ceiling.* —**flak¹y,** *adj.*

flame (2) [fleym¹], *n.* 1. the brightly colored light of a fire. **Ex.** *The flame of the burning candle was yellow.* 2. a state of burning brightly and strongly. **Ex.** *The building fell in flames.* 3. a strong passion or emotion. **Ex.** *The flames of love had died.* —*v.* blaze; burn brightly. **Ex.** *Fire flamed from the burning house.* —**flam¹ing,** *adj.* burning with a flame. **Ex.** *He threw water on the flaming papers.* —**flam¹ ma·ble,** *adj.* easy to burn. **Ex.** *Paper is very flammable.*

flank (4) [flæŋk¹], *n.* 1. the side of an animal between the ribs and the upper part of the legs. **Ex.** *The horse's flanks were wet.* 2. the right or left side of anything. **Ex.** *The enemy attacked both our flanks.* —*v.* go around; stand or be placed at the side or sides. **Ex.** *Trees flanked the garden.*

flap (4) [flæp¹], *v.* 1. swing loosely and noisily. **Ex.** *The curtain flapped and waked me.* 2. move up and down as in beating. **Ex.** *Birds flap their wings when flying.* —*n.* 1. anything broad, flat, and thin that hangs loosely, attached at one side only. **Ex.** *She sealed the flap of the envelope.* 2. the motion or sound produced by something that flaps. **Ex.** *We heard the flap of the wings.*

flare (4) [fle:r¹], *v.* 1. burn with an unsteady, swaying flame or with a sudden burst of flame. **Ex.** *The candle flared in the wind.* 2. spread out in a bell shape. **Ex.** *Her full skirt flared as she walked.* 3. become excited or angry. **Ex.** *His temper flared at their remarks.* —*n.* 1. a short, bright, swaying flame. **Ex.** *We saw a flare of light.* 2. a flaming light used as a signal. **Ex.** *They placed flares by the hole to warn of the danger.*

flash (2) [flæš¹], *n.* 1. a sudden, brief light. **Ex.** *There was a flash of lightning in the sky.* 2. a sudden, brief show of emotion, wit, etc. **Ex.** *There was a flash of anger in her eyes.* 3. the time occupied by a flash of light; an instant. **Ex.** *He returned in a flash.* —*v.* 1. light suddenly. **Ex.** *The electric sign flashed on and off.* 2. move quickly. **Ex.** *The car flashed past us.* 3. gleam; sparkle. **Ex.** *His eyes flashed with anger.*

flat (2) [flæt¹], *adj.* 1. not curved; smooth and level, or nearly so. **Ex.** *His farm is on flat land.* 2. at full length or spread out. **Ex.** *Put the map flat on the table.* 3. thin; not deep. **Ex.** *Put the cake on a flat plate.* 4. not interesting. **Ex.** *The food tasted flat.* —*n.* the flat surface or part of anything. **Ex.** *She set it on the flat of her hand.* —**flat'ten,** *v.* cause to become flat.

flatter (3) [flæt'ər], *v.* 1. seek to please by attention, false praise, or by more praise than deserved. **Ex.** *He flatters those who can help him.* 2. make to appear better than it is. **Ex.** *This picture flatters her.* 3. be pleased. **Ex.** *I am flattered that you came.* —**flat'ter·er,** *n.* one who flatters. —**flat'ter·y,** *n.* act of flattering.

flavor (3) [fley'vər], *n.* 1. taste, especially distinct in character. **Ex.** *What gives the soup this good flavor?* 2. something which has its own special taste. **Ex.** *I like the lemon flavor of this cake.* 3. the special quality of a thing. **Ex.** *The story has the flavor of city life.* —*v.* give flavor to. **Ex.** *His colorful style flavors the story.* —**fla'vor·ing,** *n.* something which is added to give a special taste.

flax (5) [flæks'], *n.* a plant with blue flowers, the stems of which are used to make linen thread and cloth. **Ex.** *Some of the farmers grew flax.*

fled (3) [fled'], *v.* past tense and participle of *flee.* **Ex.** *They fled from the burning house.*

flee (3) [fliy'], *v.* run away from something. **Ex.** *People flee from a burning building.*

fleece (5) [fliys'], *n.* the coat of wool that covers a sheep or a similar animal; the wool cut from such a coat. **Ex.** *His warm coat was made from the fleece of a sheep.* —*v.* 1. cut the wool from a sheep or similar animal. **Ex.** *In the spring, we fleece the sheep.* 2. take money or possessions by a trick. **Ex.** *He was fleeced of his savings by two strangers.*

fleet (2) [fliyt'], *n.* 1. a number of war vessels under a single command; the navy of a country. **Ex.** *The fleet is in the harbor.* 2. any group, such as vessels and airplanes, which moves together or operates under one control. **Ex.** *He owns a fleet of trucks.*

fleet (2) [fliyt'], *adj.* swift in motion; fast. **Ex.** *The deer is fleet-footed.* —**fleet'ness,** *n.*

---

a, far; æ, am; e, get; ey, late; i, in; iy, see; ɔ, all; ow, go; u, put; uw, too; ə, but, ago; ər, fur; aw, out; ay, life; oy, boy; ŋ, ring; θ, think; ð, that; ž, measure; š, ship; j, edge; č, child.

flesh (2) [fleš'], *n.* 1. the soft parts of the body of a person or an animal. **Ex.** *The knife cut into the flesh of his arm.* 2. meat; those parts of an animal which are eaten. 3. the soft parts of fruits and vegetables. **Ex.** *The flesh of the apple was sweet.* —**flesh'y,** *adj.* fat.

flew (2) [fluw'], *v.* past tense of *fly.* **Ex.** *The bird flew away.*

flexible (5) [flek'səbəl], *adj.* 1. able to bend or be bent easily. **Ex.** *Rubber is used when a very flexible tube is needed.* 2. ready to yield to influence; easily led; easily changed. **Ex.** *He had a flexible nature.* —**flex`i·bil'i·ty,** *n.*

flicker (4) [flik'ər], *v.* 1. burn unsteadily; shine with an unsteady light. **Ex.** *The fire flickered and died.* 2. move like a flame. **Ex.** *The shadows flickered on the wall.* —*n.* 1. an unsteady light or flame. **Ex.** *They saw the flicker of candles.* 2. a brief movement or feeling. **Ex.** *A flicker of hope showed in her eyes.*

flier (1) [flay'ər], *n.* 1. something that flies. 2. one who flies an airplane. **Ex.** *That flier has been up in every kind of plane.*

flight (2) [flayt'], *n.* 1. movement through the air; the act or manner of flying. **Ex.** *We watched the robins in flight.* 2. the distance covered or the course followed in flying. **Ex.** *The plane made a flight over the ocean.* 3. a stairway or set of steps. **Ex.** *His room is two flights above us.*

flight (2) [flayt'], *n.* the act of running away. **Ex.** *The dog put the robbers to flight.* —**flight'y,** *adj.* not serious; not responsible.

fling (4) [fliŋ'], *v.* throw. **Ex.** *Boys love to fling stones into water.* —*n.* 1. the act of throwing. **Ex.** *He gave the box a fling into the air.* 2. a time of fun and pleasure. **Ex.** *After his fling, he settled down to study.*

flint (5) [flint'], *n.* a hard kind of stone which produces a spark when it is hit by steel. **Ex.** *The spark from the flint was used to start a fire.*

flip (5) [flip'], *v.* throw or toss with a sudden, sharp movement. **Exs.** *She flipped herself over on her back. He flipped a coin to decide what to do.*

flirt (5) [flərt'], *v.* 1. play at love. **Ex.** *She flirted with many men but loved only one.* 2. consider lightly. **Ex.** *He flirted with the idea of living abroad.* —*n.* a person who flirts. **Ex.** *She had a reputation as a flirt.*

flit (5) [flit'], *v.* fly or move lightly and swiftly. **Ex.** *The bee flits from flower to flower.*

float (2) [flowt'], *v.* 1. be on a liquid without sinking into it. **Ex.** *Wood floats on water.* 2. move or be moved gently, as on water or through the air. **Ex.** *The falling leaves floated to the ground.* —*n.* an object that rests on the surface of a liquid or holds something up in a liquid. **Ex.** *He climbed out of the water and rested on the float.*

flock (2) [flak'], *n.* a number of birds or animals, usually of one kind, that travel or are herded together. **Ex.** *The flock of birds all flew to one tree.*

flood (2) [fləd'], *n.* 1. flowing of water from a river, lake, etc. over the land along the banks. **Ex.** *The flood destroyed many homes on the shore.* 2. any great outpouring. **Ex.** *A flood of memories came back to her.* —*v.* 1. overflow; cover with water. **Ex.** *The river flooded the town.* 2. fill to overflowing. **Ex.** *The sunlight flooded the room.* —**flood'ed,** *adj.* covered by or filled with. **Ex.** *Her eyes were flooded with tears.*

floor (1) [flɔːr'], *n.* 1. the bottom or lower part of a room. **Ex.** *He walked across the floor.* 2. a level of a building. **Ex.** *He lives on the third floor.* 3. the lowest surface of anything. **Ex.** *We are discovering many things about the ocean floor.* —*v.* 1. cover with a floor. **Ex.** *He floored the house with good wood.* 2. knock down. **Ex.** *A single blow floored his attacker.*

flour (2) [flaw'ər], *n.* a finely ground grain, usually white and powdery, such as wheat flour. **Ex.** *Flour is used to make bread.*

flourish (3) [flər'iš], *v.* 1. grow in a strong, healthy way; be healthy or successful. **Ex.** *Flowers flourish in good soil.* 2. make bold and sweeping movements; wave. **Ex.** *He flourished a gun at us.* —*n.* a bold, sweeping movement. **Ex.** *The officer made a flourish with his sword.*

flow (2) [flow'], *v.* 1. move like a liquid. **Ex.** *The river flows to the sea.* 2. fall or hang loose. **Ex.** *Her long hair flowed down over her shoulders.* —*n.* 1. the act, manner, or quantity of flowing. **Ex.** *They could not stop the flow of blood from the wound.* 2. anything that moves steadily and easily like a stream of liquid. **Ex.** *The flow of mail is heaviest during holidays.*

flower (1) [flaw'ər], *n.* 1. the blossom or part of any plant bearing the seed. **Ex.** *The bees are flying from flower to flower.* 2. state of being in bloom. **Ex.** *Her garden is in flower.* —*v.* produce flowers. **Ex.** *The rose bushes are flowering.*

FLOWER 1

flown (2) [flown'], *v.* past participle of *fly.* **Ex.** *The birds have flown away.*

fluid (2) [fluw'id], *n.* anything that can flow such as water, gas, or air. **Ex.** *Blood is an important body fluid.* —*adj.* 1. able to flow in the form of a liquid or gas. **Ex.** *He poured two fluid ounces of the medicine.* 2. changing easily; not fixed. **Ex.** *Our plans are fluid enough to be changed quickly.*

flung (3) [fləŋ'], *v.* past tense and participle of *fling.* **Ex.** *He flung his coat onto the floor.*

flush (4) [fləš'], *n.* 1. a red coloring of the skin. **Ex.** *A flush of shame colored her cheeks.* 2. a sudden flow or rush of emotion. **Ex.** *She experienced a flush of pleasure on seeing him.* —*v.* 1. to glow or redden. **Ex.** *Her face flushed.* 2. flood with water in order to clean. **Ex.** *Water trucks flush the streets every morning.*

flush (4) [fləš'], *adj.* even or level; making an even surface with. **Ex.** *The door is flush with the wall.*

flute (5) [fluwt'], *n.* a musical instrument in the shape of a long, thin tube with a series of holes along the side and an opening at one end through which one blows. —**flut'ist,** *n.* one who plays the flute.

FLUTE

flutter (3) [flət'ər], *v.* 1. move back and forth quickly; wave. **Ex.** *The flag fluttered in the breeze.* 2. move wings rapidly without flying. **Ex.** *The little bird fluttered its wings.* 3. tremble; shake. **Ex.** *Her heart fluttered when she saw him.* —*n.* a rapid movement back and forth; a quivering. **Ex.** *They heard a flutter of wings.*

fly (1) [flay'], *v.* 1. move through the air on wings, as a bird or an airplane. **Ex.** *He is flying home tomorrow.* 2. operate an airplane. **Ex.** *He is learning to fly.* 3. wave in the air. **Ex.** *The flag flies in the wind.* 4. move or pass rapidly. **Ex.** *How time flies!* 5. run from danger. **Ex.** *He was forced to* *fly from his home.* **—fly into,** pass suddenly into some condition. **Ex.** *She is likely to fly into a temper if you disagree with her.*

fly (1) [flay¹], *n.* a winged insect, especially the common housefly.

FLY

foam (4) [fowm¹], *n.* white mass of bubbles formed on liquids. **Ex.** *The wind whipped the waves into foam.* **—v.** gather or form bubbles. **Ex.** *The fresh milk foamed in the pail.*

focus (5) [fow'kəs], *n.* a central point; a center of activity, attention, etc. **Ex.** *The pretty girl was the focus of all eyes.* **—v.** 1. center the mind on one thing or subject. **Ex.** *Please focus your attention on the speaker.* 2. bring into clear view by adjusting the focus of the eye or of a camera. **Ex.** *He was so tired he could not focus his eyes on the book.* **—in focus,** clear. **—out of focus,** unclear.

foe (4) [fow¹], *n.* an enemy; one who holds ill feelings against a person, idea, etc. **Ex.** *He is a foe of evil.*

fog (3) [fag¹, fɔ:g¹], *n.* 1. a cloud lying near the ground. **Ex.** *A heavy fog stops planes from landing.* 2. a state of mental confusion. **Ex.** *She was in a fog about what to do.* **—v.** 1. surround with fog. **Ex.** *Steam fogged his glasses.* 2. confuse. **Ex.** *Doubts fogged his mind.* **—fog'gy,** *adj.*

foil (5) [foyl¹], *v.* prevent the success of; stop. **Ex.** *The police foiled his evil scheme.*

foil (5) [foyl¹], *n.* 1. a very thin sheet of metal, such as gold or tin. **Ex.** *Some kinds of foil are used for wrapping food.* 2. any person or thing that serves to set off another thing to advantage by contrast. **Ex.** *The black dress was a foil for her diamond pin.*

fold (2) [fowld¹], *v.* 1. double or bend over upon itself. **Ex.** *She folded the paper.* 2. bring together and clasp. **Ex.** *She folded her arms and waited.* **—n.** a part that is doubled or bent over another part. **Ex.** *The tablecloth had six folds.* **—fold'er,** *n.* 1. one who folds. 2. a folded heavy paper or cardboard used to hold other papers.

-fold (2) [fowld¹], *suffix.* 1. having a stated number of parts. **Ex.** *There was a threefold screen in the living room.* 2. multiplied by. **Ex.** *His wealth was increased tenfold.*

a, far; æ, am; e, get; ey, late; i, in; iy, see; ɔ, all; ow, go; u, put; uw, too; ə, but, ago; ɔr, fur; aw, out; ay, life; oy, boy; ŋ, ring; θ, think; ð, that; ž, measure; š, ship; ǰ, edge; č, child.

foliage (5) [fow'liyij], *n.* the leaves of a plant or tree or of a number of plants or trees. **Ex.** *In summer the house next door is hidden by foliage.*

folk (2) [fowk'], *n.* 1. a group of related people forming a tribe or nation. **Ex.** *The folk who settled this valley came from the north.* 2. people; persons. **Ex.** *Folks around here are friendly.* —*adj.* having to do with the customs of a people or country. **Ex.** *We enjoyed watching the folk dances and hearing folk songs and tales.*

follow (1) [fal'ow], *v.* 1. come after in natural order. **Ex.** *Night follows day.* 2. accept the authority of; obey. **Ex.** *He followed his father's advice.* 3. engage in or observe an occupation, profession, activity, etc. **Ex.** *He followed the law.* 4. pursue. **Ex.** *He followed and caught the thief.* 5. travel on or along. **Ex.** *Follow this road for four miles.* —**fol'low·er,** *n.* one who follows. —**fol'low·ing,** *n.* 1. a body of followers. **Ex.** *That doctor has a large following.* 2. things that follow. **Ex.** *I need the following: eggs, sugar, butter, and milk.* —*adj.* coming after; next after. **Ex.** *He is leaving the following week.*

folly (3) [fal'iy], *n.* 1. condition of being unwise or foolish; lack of good sense. **Ex.** *If you are careless about your health, you will pay for your folly.* 2. a foolish act or idea. **Ex.** *It is folly to drive fast on icy roads.*

fond (3) [fand'], *adj.* 1. having an affection or liking for. **Ex.** *He is fond of horses.* 2. affectionate; tender and loving. **Ex.** *He gave her a fond glance.* —**fond'le,** *v.* touch in a fond way. —**fond'ly,** *adv.* —**fond'ness,** *n.*

food (1) [fuwd'], *n.* 1. what is taken in by an animal or plant to supply the material for strength and growth. **Ex.** *Milk is the baby's chief food.* 2. that which is taken in as a solid rather than a liquid. **Ex.** *They offered us food and drink.* 3. anything that sustains or develops. **Ex.** *Those ideas are food for thought.*

fool (1) [fuwl'], *n.* 1. a person who is silly or lacks sense; a person who is made to appear this way. **Ex.** *He acted like a fool.* 2. a person who amuses or entertains people by silly actions. **Ex.** *He enjoyed playing the fool.* —*v.* trick; deceive. **Ex.** *He fooled them with a false story.* —**fool'ish,** *adj.*

foot (1) [fut'], *n.* 1. a measurement of length. **Ex.** *There are 12 inches in a foot.* (See **Weights and Measures.**) 2. that part of the leg below the ankle on which a person or animal stands and walks. **Ex.** *He put his right foot in the water.* 3. something like a foot in position or use; the bottom; the lowest part. **Ex.** *Wait for me at the foot of the stairs.* —**on foot,** walking or standing. **Ex.** *He came in the car; I came on foot.* —**underfoot,** in the way. **Ex.** *The children are underfoot when I want to work.*

football (3) [fut'bɔːl`], *n.* a leather ball filled with air; a game using such a ball and played on a long field. **Ex.** *In American football, the ball is egg-shaped.*

foothill [fut'hil`], *n.* a low hill near the bottom of mountains.

foothold [fut'howld`], *n.* a place for the foot which is safe, as in climbing. **Ex.** *I found a foothold on the side of the hill.*

footnote [fut'nowt`], *n.* a note, usually at the bottom of a page, that gives an explanation of something on the page or refers to another page, book, etc.

for (1) [fɔːr'], *prep.* 1. in order to gain or attain the object or purpose in mind. **Ex.** *He is saving money for a car.* 2. in place of; instead of; in exchange. **Ex.** *I gave him ten cents for an apple.* 3. in the interest of; to the benefit or support of. **Ex.** *He is working for himself.* 4. obliging someone to do; requiring action. **Ex.** *I have work for him to do.* 5. showing the cause or reason. **Ex.** *He was punished for being late.* 6. intending to be used or received by; intending to go to. **Ex.** *He is leaving for the city.* 7. extending or lasting. **Ex.** *We waited for an hour.* 8. in respect to; in regard to; concerning. **Ex.** *It is warm for this time of year.*

forbid (3) [fərbid'], *v.* command someone not to do something; prohibit. **Ex.** *I forbid you to see him again.* —**for·bid'den,** *adj.* not permitted. **Ex.** *Smoking is forbidden in this room.*

force (1) [fɔrs'], *n.* 1. power; strength; energy. **Ex.** *The force of the wind closed the door.* 2. strength used against a person or object. **Ex.** *He entered the house by force.* 3. military power of a nation; large groups of soldiers; any group of men prepared to do some special work. **Ex.** *He hopes to become a member of the police force.* —*v.* 1. compel to do something; make do something by the use of strength or power. **Ex.** *He forced me to give him the money.* 2. break open, into, or through; obtain; get; etc. by using strength. **Ex.** *We forced our way through the crowd.* —**for·ci·ble,** *adj.* —**for'ci·bly,** *adv.* in a compelling manner; using strength; with force. **Ex.** *The angry man was forcibly removed from the room.*

ford (5) [fɔrd'], *n.* a place in a river or stream where the water is shallow enough so that one may cross by walking or riding. **Ex.** *The ford in the river is a busy place.* —*v.* cross a river at a shallow spot by walking or riding. **Ex.** *Cars can ford the river at this point.*

fore (3) [fɔːr'], *adj.* situated at or toward the front. **Ex.** *A horse has two forefeet and two hind feet.* —*n.* the front. **Ex.** *The idea of space travel came to the fore in the 1950's.*

fore- (3) [fɔːr'], *prefix.* before; in advance; front. **Ex.** *Warn, forewarn; paw, forepaw.*

forearm [fɔːr'arm'], *n.* the arm from elbow to wrist.

forefather [fɔːr'fa'ðər], *n.* ancestor. **Ex.** *His forefathers came from Africa.*

forefinger [fɔːr'fiŋ'gər], *n.* the finger next to the thumb.

forefront [fɔːr'frənt'], *n.* the very front; the most important or active place. **Ex.** *He was always in the forefront of the battle.*

foregoing [fɔːr'gow'iŋ, fɔːr'gow'iŋ], *adj.* appearing before. **Ex.** *See the foregoing page for an explanation.*

foreground [fɔːr'grawnd'], *n.* the front part of a scene or picture. **Ex.** *In the foreground, there is a large tree.*

forehead (2) [fɔːr'hed', fɔːr'əd], *n.* the part of the face above the eyes and below the hair. **Ex.** *When he frowns, his forehead wrinkles.*

foreign (1) [fɔːr'ən], *adj.* 1. outside of one's own place or country. **Ex.** *He often travels to foreign countries.* 2. not from one's own place or country. **Ex.** *He enjoys foreign wines.* 3. relating to or dealing with other countries. **Ex.** *That company is engaged in foreign trade.* —**for'eign·er,** *n.* a person from another country.

foreman [fɔːr'mən], *n.* one in charge of a group of workers.

foremost (3) [fɔːr'mowst'], *adj.* first in place, order, time, etc. **Ex.** *He is the foremost statesman of the nation.*

forerunner [fɔːr'rən'ər], *n.* someone or something that goes before; a sign of something to come or happen later. **Ex.** *He was a forerunner of today's pilots.*

forest (1) [fɔːr'əst], *n.* a large area of land with many trees; the trees themselves. **Ex.** *The farmers cut down the forest and planted crops.* —**for'est·ry,** *n.* science of growing forests.

forever (1) [fərev'ər], *adv.* for an unlimited time. **Ex.** *I will not live forever.* 2. always. **Ex.** *He is forever talking.*

forge (4) [fɔrǰ'], *n.* a furnace or a place with a furnace in which metal is shaped by heating and hammering. **Ex.** *The children watched horseshoes being made at the forge.* —*v.* 1. form by heating and hammering; force into shape. **Ex.** *The settlers forged a new nation.* 2. copy or imitate to deceive, especially handwriting. **Ex.** *He forged my name on the letter.* —**forg'er,** *n.* —**for'ger·y,** *n.* the crime of copying and pretending the copy is the original.

forget (1) [fərget'], *v.* 1. not remember. **Ex.** *Who is he? I forget his name.* 2. neglect. **Ex.** *He keeps forgetting to stop there.* —**for·get'ful,** *adj.*

forgive (2) [fərgiv'], *v.* pardon; stop feeling anger or a desire to punish. **Ex.** *He will forgive you if you apologize.* —**for·give'ness,** *n.*

forgo [fɔːr'gow'], *v.* go without; not take. **Ex.** *I will forgo dessert.*

forgot (2) [fərgat'], *v.* past tense of *forget.* **Ex.** *He forgot to lock the door.* —**for·got'ten,** *v.* past participle of *forget.* **Ex.** *I had forgotten he was coming.*

fork (3) [fɔrk'], *n.* 1. an instrument with two or more long points used to pick up food. 2. a farming tool which looks like the eating fork. **Ex.** *He picked up the hay with a pitchfork.* 3. division of anything into two or more parts; place where such a division occurs. **Ex.** *He turned left at the fork in the road.* —*v.* divide into two or more branches. **Ex.** *The river forks a mile north of here.*

FORK 1

form (1) [fɔrm'], *n.* 1. kind; sort; way. **Ex.** *Ice and snow are forms of water.* 2. shape; figure. **Ex.** *The form of a man appeared in the doorway.* 3. a card or sheet of paper with blank spaces to be filled out with required information. **Ex.** *He was given several forms to complete.* 4. any of the different uses or spellings into which a word is changed. **Ex.** *"Broke" is the past form of the verb "break."* —*v.* 1. take the shape of; make. **Ex.** *Form a circle and join hands.* 2. train; develop. **Ex.** *Teachers help form* *the minds of children.* —**for·ma'tion,** *n.* —**for'ma·tive,** *adj.*

formal (4) [fɔr'məl], *adj.* 1. following society's rules or customs exactly; according to a fixed form. **Ex.** *You must write a formal acceptance to this invitation.* 2. ceremonial; concerned with form or appearance. **Ex.** *Guests at the wedding wore formal clothes.* —**for·mal'i·ty,** *n.* —**for'mal·ly,** *adv.*

former (2) [fɔr'mər], *adj.* 1. previously but not now; earlier in time. **Ex.** *He is a former teacher.* 2. the first of two. **Ex.** *I like the red coat and the blue coat, but I prefer the former.* —**for'mer·ly,** *adv.*

formidable (4) [fɔr'mədəbəl], *adj.* 1. causing fear or dread; alarming. **Ex.** *The army made a formidable show of strength.* 2. very difficult. **Ex.** *They had a formidable job to do.*

formula (4) [fɔr'myələ], *n.* 1. a special combination of words or symbols used to express a rule, fact, or principle. **Ex.** H_2O *is the chemical formula for water.* 2. a method or set of directions for doing something. **Ex.** *He could give no easy formula for success.*

formulate (5) [fɔr'myəleyt'], *v.* organize in exact form. **Ex.** *Formulate your ideas before you begin to write.*

forsake [fərseyk'], *v.* stop helping; desert. **Ex.** *His friends will not forsake him.*

fort (3) [fɔrt'], *n.* a place with strong walls protected by guns; any armed place surrounded by walls or other means of defense and occupied by troops. **Ex.** *There was a fort at the mouth of the river.*

forth (2) [fɔrθ'], *adv.* 1. forward; onward. **Ex.** *The army marched forth to battle.* 2. out of concealment. **Ex.** *The rabbit jumped forth from behind the bush.*

forthright [fɔrθ'rayt'], *adv.* honest and direct. **Ex.** *He is a forthright speaker.*

forthwith [fɔrθ'wiθ', fɔrθ'wið'], *adj.* immediately; without delay. **Ex.** *He gave his answer forthwith.*

fortify (5) [fɔr'təfay'], *v.* strengthen; make stronger. **Exs.** *A hot meal fortified him against the cold. They fortified the town against an attack.*

fortune (2) [fɔr'čən], *n.* 1. chance; luck. **Ex.** *Fortune did not favor him.* 2. the future; one's fate. **Ex.** *He had his fortune told.* 3. a large amount of wealth. **Ex.** *He received a large fortune when his uncle died.* —**for'tu·nate,** *adj.* lucky. —**for'tu·nate·ly,** *adv.*

forty (1) [fɔr'tiy], *n., adj.* the number between thirty-nine and forty-one; the number *40.* —**for'ti·eth**, *adj.* coming after thirty-nine others.

forward (1) [fɔr'wərd], *adj.* 1. near, at, or of the front part of anything. **Ex.** *The forward cars of the train are already in the station.* 2. bold; rude; not modest. **Ex.** *That child is too forward.* —*adv.* toward the front. **Ex.** *They slowly moved forward.* —*v.* send onward. **Ex.** *Please forward my mail to my new home.*

fought (2) [fɔ:t'], *v.* past tense and participle of *fight.* **Ex.** *They fought a battle.*

foul (3) [fawl'], *adj.* 1. dirty; offending the senses. **Ex.** *The room had a foul smell.* 2. choked up with dirt. **Ex.** *The old well was foul with leaves.* 3. hateful; evil. **Ex.** *He was guilty of a foul crime.* 4. not favorable; stormy. **Ex.** *Foul weather prevented them from leaving.* 5. not permitted by the rules of the game. **Ex.** *The batter hit a foul ball.* —**foul'ly**, *adv.*

found (1) [fawnd'], *v.* past tense and participle of *find.* **Ex.** *He found money in the street.*

found (1) [fawnd'], *v.* 1. start or establish. **Ex.** *He helped to found the university.* 2. base; build on a base. **Ex.** *He founded his career on honesty.* —**found'er**, *n.* one who starts.

foundation (2) [fawn'dey'šən], *n.* 1. the act of founding or establishing. **Ex.** *The foundation of a college was his dream.* 2. that on which something rests or is built; a base. **Ex.** *The foundation of the house was stone.* 3. an institution which is established to spend money, pay for research, etc. **Ex.** *The work of the Ford Foundation is known everywhere.*

fountain (2) [fawn'tən], *n.* a place or device from which water rises or is forced to rise. **Exs.** *There is a drinking fountain in the hall. Visitors admire the beautiful display of lighted fountains in the park.*

FOUNTAIN

four (1) [fɔ:r'], *n., adj.* the number between three and five; the number *4.* —**fourth'**, *n., adj.* coming after three others. —**four'teen'**, *n., adj.* the number *14.* —**four'teenth'**, *n., adj.* coming after thirteen others.

fowl (4) [fawl'], *n.* birds, especially farm birds, such as chickens raised for eating; the meat of such birds. **Ex.** *I prefer the taste of chicken to that of other kinds of fowl.*

fox (3) [faks'], *n.* 1. a flesh-eating wild animal of the dog family, similar to a wolf but smaller. 2. the fur of a fox. **Ex.** *Her coat is trimmed with fox.* —**fox'y,** *adj.* tricky like a fox. **Ex.** *His answers were very foxy.*

FOX 1

fraction (4) [fræk'šən], *n.* 1. a part of anything, especially a small part. **Ex.** *He saves only a fraction of his salary.* 2. one of several parts of a whole. **Ex.** ½ and ⅔ *are both fractions.* —**frac'tion·al,** *adj.*

fracture (5) [fræk'čər], *n.* a break or crack, especially of a bone. **Ex.** *She suffered a fracture of the leg.* —*v.* crack or break. **Ex.** *She fractured her heel.*

fragile (5) [fræj'əl], *adj.* easily broken; delicate. **Ex.** *That glass dish is very fragile.* —**fra·gil'i·ty,** *n.*

fragment (3) [fræg'mənt], *n.* 1. a part broken off or separated. **Ex.** *She was cut by a fragment of glass.* 2. a part that is incomplete. **Ex.** *He read me a fragment of the letter.* —**frag'men·tar'y,** *adj.*

fragrance (4) [frey'grəns], *n.* a sweet or pleasant smell. **Ex.** *The fragrance of baking bread reminds me of home.* —**fra'grant,** *adj.*

frail (4) [freyl'], *adj.* weak; easily damaged or broken. **Ex.** *He was too frail to play games.* —**frail'ty,** *n.*

frame (2) [freym'], *n.* 1. a border which encloses something such as a picture or mirror. **Ex.** *The mirror has a silver frame.* 2. the part of anything that gives it shape and holds it up; an open structure. **Ex.** *The brick house was built around a wood frame.* 3. the structure of the body. **Ex.** *He had a large frame.* —*v.* 1. put in a frame. **Ex.** *I am going to frame this picture.* 2. imagine, as ideas; plan; compose. **Ex.** *The Founding Fathers framed the Constitution of the United States.* —**fram'er,** *n.* —**frame of mind,** a particular mental state; a mood. **Ex.** *She is in a bad frame of mind.*

frank (3) [fræŋk'], *adj.* unreserved and honest in speech. *He liked the boy's frank way of speaking.* —**frank'ly,** *adv.* —**frank'ness,** *n.*

frantic (4) [fræn'tik], *adj.* wild with excitement, fear, pain, etc. **Ex.** *Frantic efforts were made to escape the sinking ship.* —**fran'ti·cal·ly,** *adv.*

fraud (4) [frɔːd'], *n.* an act of trickery, lying, or cheating. **Ex.** *They took his property from him by fraud.* —**fraud'u·lent,** *adj.*

free (1) [friy'], *adj.* 1. having political and civil rights; not enslaved; not imprisoned. **Ex.** *They were fighting to make their country free.* 2. permitted or able to do something at will; not limited by rules. **Ex.** *You are free to leave when you choose.* 3. without cost or charge. **Ex.** *These books are free.* 4. not tied down; not fastened; loose. **Ex.** *He took the free end of the line.* 5. not burdened, worried, blocked, etc. **Ex.** *The road is free from snow.* —*v.* release; make free. **Ex.** *I shall free the bird from the cage.* —*adv.* without paying. **Ex.** *The children were admitted to the theater free.* —**free'dom,** *n.* —**free'ly,** *adv.*

freeway [friy'wey'], *n.* a wide road for fast driving and with few stops.

freeze (2) [friyz'], *v.* 1. harden by cold into ice or a similar solid. **Ex.** *The river freezes in the winter.* 2. cause to be or become very cold. **Ex.** *Please close the window before I freeze.* 3. make or become very still as a result of fear, horror, etc. **Ex.** *The sight of the wreck made her freeze with horror.* —**freez'er,** *n.* a place to freeze food or to keep frozen food.

freight (3) [freyt'], *n.* 1. transportation of goods by truck, train, or plane. **Ex.** *Send the furniture by freight.* 2. goods that are transported. **Ex.** *This train carries no freight.* 3. the price paid for transporting goods. **Ex.** *The freight was more than I could pay.* —**freight'er,** *n.* a ship which transports goods.

frenzy (5) [fren'ziy], *n.* an uncontrolled outburst of emotion. **Ex.** *He was in a frenzy because he missed his plane.* —**fren'zied,** *adj.*

frequent (2) [friy'kwənt], *adj.* occurring often. **Ex.** *The train made frequent stops.* —*v.* visit often. **Ex.** *The actors frequent an eating place near the theater.* —**fre'quen·cy,** *n.* —**fre'quent·ly,** *adv.*

fresh (1) [freš'], *adj.* 1. newly made or gathered; recent. **Ex.** *These eggs are fresh.* 2. not salty. **Ex.** *The sailor was glad* *to wash in fresh water again.* 3. rested; looking healthy and young. **Ex.** *Do that work while you are still fresh.* 4. new; different. **Ex.** *This writer has fresh ideas about the problem.* 5. having just arrived; not experienced. **Ex.** *He is just fresh from college.* 6. pure and cool. **Ex.** *The country air is fresh.* —**fresh'en,** *v.* —**fresh'ly,** *adv.* —**fresh'ness,** *n.*

freshman [frešˈmən], *n.* a person in his first year at high school or college; a beginner at anything. **Ex.** *He is a freshman in the Senate.*

fret (5) [fretˈ], *v.* make or become worried and restless. **Ex.** *She fretted at the delay.* —**fret'ful,** *adj.*

Friday (1) [frayˈdiy], *n.* the day between Thursday and Saturday; the sixth day of the week.

friend (1) [frendˈ], *n.* 1. a person one likes and is close to. **Ex.** *This friend is almost like a brother.* 2. a person who believes in and supports a group, cause, etc. **Ex.** *He is a friend of labor.* —**friend'ly,** *adj.* kindly.

fright (2) [fraytˈ], *n.* sudden great fear. **Ex.** *Fright caused her to run.* —**fright'en,** *v.* —**fright'ful,** *adj.* —**fright'ful·ly,** *adv.*

fringe (4) [frinǰˈ], *n.* 1. a border of lengths of cord, thread, etc. **Ex.** *The fringe of the rug is badly worn.* 2. anything which suggests a border or edge. **Ex.** *They live on the fringe of town.* —*v.* 1. furnish with a fringe. **Ex.** *I fringed this handkerchief with lace.* 2. serve as fringe for. **Ex.** *Forests fringed the town.*

FRINGE 1

FROG

frog (3) [fragˈ, frɔːgˈ], *n.* a small animal without a tail that lives on land 'or in water.

frolic (5) [fralˈik], *n.* a gay occasion; a time of making merry. **Ex.** *After the harvest they had a frolic.* —*v.* play merrily. **Ex.** *The children love to frolic on the grass.*

from (1) [frəmˈ], *prep.* 1. having some person, place, or thing as its beginning, source, or cause. **Ex.** *Where is the note from your teacher?* 2. at a place distant; not near; separated. **Ex.** *We are far from home.* 3. because of. **Ex.** *He is suffering from a cold.* 4. out of. **Ex.** *He took money from his pocket.*

front (1) [frəntˈ], *n.* 1. the forward part; the opposite of *back.*

Ex. *The front of the house faces the park.* 2. the beginning; the first part. **Ex.** *The writer's picture is in the front of the book.* 3. a place before a person or thing. **Ex.** *A tree is growing in front of the house.* —*v.* face in some direction. **Ex.** *The house fronted on the river.* —**fron'tal,** *adj.* of the front.

frontier (4) [frən'ti:r'], *n.* 1. that part of a country which borders another country. **Ex.** *There are not many guards along the frontier.* 2. the outer area of a settled region, lying next to a wilderness. **Ex.** *There are few frontiers remaining in the United States.* 3. a new or not completely developed field of knowledge. **Ex.** *There are many frontiers in science to be explored.*

frost (3) [frɔ:st'], *n.* 1. temperature cold enough to cause freezing. **Ex.** *There is frost in the air.* 2. light covering of ice formed by dew or water vapor freezing on a surface. **Ex.** *There was frost on the window.* —*v.* 1. cover with frost. **Ex.** *The windows are frosted.* 2. cover a cake with a topping made of sugar, butter, flavoring, etc. —**frost'y,** *adj.*

frostbite [frɔst'bayt'], *n.* damage to a part of the body caused by freezing. **Ex.** *The skier suffered from frostbite.*

frown (3) [frawn'], *v.* 1. draw the eyebrows together as in worry or anger. **Ex.** *She frowned as she heard the news.* 2. show that one does not like or disapproves of something. **Ex.** *His employer frowned upon his plan to leave early.* —*n.* the look one has when frowning. **Ex.** *There was a frown on her face.*

froze (2) [frowz'], *v.* past tense of *freeze.* **Ex.** *The water froze last night.* —**fro'zen,** *v.* past participle of *freeze.* **Ex.** *The water in the pool had frozen during the night.* —*adj.* 1. caused to become ice or covered with ice. **Ex.** *They skated on the frozen lake.* 2. preserved by freezing. **Ex.** *She bought a package of frozen vegetables.* 3. made completely motionless; shocked. **Ex.** *She was frozen with fear at the sound of footsteps.*

frugal (5) [fruw'gəl], *adj.* 1. without waste; thrifty. **Ex.** *She is frugal in managing her money.* 2. cheap; very simple. **Ex.** *They could afford only a frugal meal.* —**fru'gal·ly,** *adv.* —**fru·gal'i·ty,** *n.*

fruit (1) [fruwt'], *n.* 1. the eatable parts of some trees and plants, consisting of the seeds and the surrounding flesh. **Ex.** *Apples, oranges, and bananas are fruit.* 2. the product of any plant, work, or effort, etc. **Ex.** *The worker grew rich from the fruits of his labor.*

frustrate (3) [frəs'treyt`], *v.* 1. cause to have no effect. **Ex.** *He frustrated our plans.* 2. keep from doing or obtaining. **Ex.** *We were frustrated in our efforts to climb the mountain.* —**frus·tra'tion,** *n.*

fry (3) [fray'], *v.* cook in fat over a flame. **Ex.** *She will fry eggs for our breakfast.*

fuel (4) [fyuw'əl], *n.* 1. any substance that is burned to make heat or power. **Ex.** *Gasoline is fuel for an automobile.* 2. anything that causes an emotion to become stronger. **Ex.** *Her unkind words added fuel to his anger.* —*v.* supply with or take in fuel. **Ex.** *The cook fueled the fire with more wood.*

fugitive (5) [fyuw'jətiv], *n.* one in the act of running away. **Ex.** *He is a fugitive from the police.* —*adj.* escaping; fleeing. **Ex.** *The fugitive criminal was captured.*

-ful (1) [fəl], *suffix.* 1. full of. **Exs.** *Care, careful; beauty, beautiful.* 2. tending or likely to. **Exs.** *Wake, wakeful; harm, harmful.* 3. a quantity sufficient to fill. **Exs.** *Hand, handful; cup, cupful.*

fulfill (2) [fəlfil'], *v.* do; cause to happen; complete. **Ex.** *By completing college, he fulfilled his mother's dreams.*

full (1) [ful'], *adj.* 1. filled with as much as a thing or person can hold. **Ex.** *I drank a full glass of water.* 2. containing a plentiful supply; enough for one's need. **Ex.** *He always has a pocket full of money.* 3. with something or someone occupying it. **Ex.** *Every seat is full.* 4. being at its greatest size or highest development. **Ex.** *The moon is full tonight.* 5. complete in number, quantity, length, etc. **Ex.** *We waited for a full hour.* 6. filled out; rounded. **Ex.** *With her sails full, the ship moved rapidly.* —*n.* the greatest extent or highest degree. **Ex.** *He enjoyed his vacation to the full.* *adj.* entirely; completely. **Ex.** *He turned full around to face us.* —**in full,** entirely; completely. **Ex.** *He paid his debt in full.*

full-blown [ful'blown'], *adj.* in full bloom; fully developed. **Ex** *The plain little girl had become a full-blown beauty.*

full dress [ful' dres'], formal dress. **Ex.** *Full dress is required at the ball.*

fullface [ful'feys'], *adv.* with the face toward. **Ex.** *He turned fullface toward us.*

fumble (5) [fəm'bəl], *v.* feel about for or handle with a lack of skill or ease. **Ex.** *He fumbled for the lock in the dark.*

fume (5) [fyuwm'], *n.* strong-smelling smoke or smokelike gas. **Ex.** *The gasoline fumes made her sick.* —*v.* 1. throw off fumes. **Ex.** *The chimney was fuming.* 2. show anger. **Ex.** *He fumed because he had missed the train.*

fun (2) [fən'], *n.* 1. pleasure; amusement. **Ex.** *The young people had fun at the dance.* 2. playfulness. **Ex.** *He is always happy and full of fun.* —**make fun of,** joke about. **Ex.** *They made fun of the way he spoke.*

function (3) [fəŋk'šən], *n.* 1. the natural or special action or activity of a person or thing. **Ex.** *The function of a watch is to keep time.* 2. any public ceremony, gathering, etc. **Ex.** *The mayor must attend many political functions.* —*v.* act; operate; carry out normal work. **Ex.** *His car does not function as it should.* —**func'tion·al,** *adj.*

fund (3) [fənd'], *n.* 1. a sum of money set aside for a special purpose. **Ex.** *That fund pays the medical expenses of the poor people.* 2. a store or stock of something. **Ex.** *He has a fund of information about famous people.* —**funds,** available money. **Ex.** *His funds for food are limited.*

fundamental (3) [fən`dəmen'təl], *adj.* of or relating to a foundation; basic; essential. **Ex.** *They had fundamental differences of opinion.* —*n.* a principle, rule, or law that serves as a basis of a system. **Ex.** *He studied the fundamentals of government.* —**fun`da·men'tal·ly,** *adv.*

funeral (2) [fyuw'n(ə)rəl], *n.* services, often religious, held after a person has died. **Ex.** *People came from great distances to attend his funeral.*

funny (2) [fən'iy], *adj.* amusing; causing laughter. **Ex.** *Everyone laughed at his funny stories.*

fur (2) [fə:r'], *n.* 1. the skin of an animal, covered with soft, thick hair. **Ex.** *The fur of a bear is very warm.* 2. an article of clothing made of fur. **Ex.** *This store sells furs.* —*adj.* made of fur. **Ex.** *She has two fur coats.* —**fur'ry,** *adj.*

furious (4) [fyur'iyəs], *adj.* 1. full of fury or rage. **Ex.** *He was* *furious when he heard the news.* 2. violent; fierce. **Ex.** *A furious storm sank the boat.* —**fur'i·ous·ly,** *adv.*

furnace (3) [fər'nəs], *n.* a closed structure in which heat is produced for warming a house, melting metals, etc. **Ex.** *An oil furnace heats our school building.*

furnish (2) [fər'niš], *v.* 1. supply with furniture or equipment. **Ex.** *It took months to furnish their house.* 2. provide or supply. **Ex.** *The hotel furnished clean sheets and towels every day.* —**fur'nish·ings,** *n.* furniture and equipment in a house, office, etc.

furniture (2) [fər'nicər], *n.* the movable things such as tables, chairs, beds, and desks in a house, office, store, etc. **Ex.** *Their furniture fits comfortably in the new house.*

furrow (5) [fər'ow], *n.* 1. a long, narrow cut made in the earth by a plow for the purpose of planting. **Ex.** *The farmer was proud of his straight furrows.* 2. a long, narrow depression in any surface. **Ex.** *There were deep furrows on the old man's forehead.* —*v.* make furrows; plow land. **Ex.** *Care furrowed his brow.*

further (1) [fər'ðər], *adj.* 1. at a greater distance. **Ex.** *He is at the further end of the field.* 2. added or more. **Ex.** *We are waiting for further word about the weather.* —*adv.* 1. at or to a greater distance; farther. **Ex.** *He will go further in life than his brother.* 2. to a greater degree or extent; more. **Ex.** *He questioned the teacher further.* —*v.* help forward; advance; promote. **Ex.** *To further peace, we need better understanding between nations.*

furthermore [fər'ðərmɔ:r'], *adv.* also; in addition. **Ex.** *I cannot go, and furthermore I will not go.*

fury (3) [fyur'iy], *n.* 1. rage or wild anger. **Ex.** *He was in a terrible fury.* 2. violence; fierceness. **Ex.** *The fury of the storm frightened the children.*

fuse (5) [fyuwz'], *n.* 1. the string or similar material which is lighted to make something explode. **Ex.** *Twenty seconds after he lit the fuse, the bomb burst.* 2. a safety device containing a wire that melts when the electric current becomes too strong and thus stops the flow of electricity. **Ex.** *When he replaced the fuse, the light went on again.*

fuse (5) [fyuwz'], *v.* combine by melting together; melt. **Ex.** *The two metals fused into one.*

fuss (4) [fəs'], *n.* an unnecessary worry or bother; nervous action about something unimportant. **Ex.** *She made a big* *fuss about a spot on her dress.* —*v.* worry about unimportant things. **Ex.** *He fusses about everything.* —**fuss'y,** *adj.*

futile (5) [fyuw'təl], *adj.* 1. useless; not possible of success. **Ex.** *He made futile efforts to rescue the child.* 2. not important; valueless. **Ex.** *He wasted his time in futile talk.* —**fu-til'i·ty,** *n.*

future (1) [fyuw'čər], *n.* 1. the time that is to come. **Ex.** *They are planning for the future.* 2. a condition in the time to come; chance for success. **Ex.** *His future in business seemed promising.* —*adj.* 1. in the time that is to come. **Ex.** *I am looking forward to seeing you on a future day.* 2. expressing the time to come. **Ex.** *"Will go" is the future tense of the verb "go."*

-fy (3) [fay], *suffix.* 1. make; become. **Exs.** *Clear, clarify; intense, intensify.* 2. cause to feel or have. **Exs.** *Terror, terrify; glory, glorify.*

G

G, g [ǰiy'], *n.* the seventh letter of the English alphabet.

gain (1) [geyn'], *v.* 1. obtain; win; earn. **Ex.** *Her kindness gained her many friends.* 2. obtain or add as an increase. **Ex.** *He gained weight.* 3. become better; improve. **Ex.** *The patient is gaining strength.* —*n.* 1. money made in business; profit. **Ex.** *His gains were greater than his losses.* 2. increase; improvement. **Ex.** *Good schools bring gains in education.* —**gain'er,** *n.* one who gains. —**gain'ful,** *adj.* —**gain'ful·ly,** *adv.*

gale (4) [geyl'], *n.* 1. a strong wind. **Ex.** *The gale blew down a tree.* 2. a sudden loud burst, as of sound. **Ex.** *His funny story caused a gale of laughter from the audience.*

gallant (4) [gæl'ənt], *adj.* 1. brave; noble. **Ex.** *The gallant soldier died to save his friend.* 2. polite and attentive. **Ex.** *The handsome gentleman was gallant to all the ladies.* —**gal'lant·ly,** *adv.*

gallery (3) [gæl'(ə)riy], *n.* a room or building where works of art are shown. **Ex.** *We visited a gallery of modern art.*

gallon (3) [gæl'ən], *n.* a measure of liquids. **Ex.** *Four quarts equal one gallon.* See **Weights and Measures.**

gallop (3) [gæl'əp], v. ride or run very fast. Ex. *The horse galloped to victory.* —n. 1. the fastest manner in which a horse runs, when all four feet are off the ground at the same time. Ex. *The race horse had a beautiful gallop.* 2. a ride at this speed. Ex. *We went for a gallop.*

GALLOP 1

gallows (5) [gæl'owz], n. a high wooden frame with a rope from which criminals are hanged. Ex. *The murderer died on the gallows.*

gamble (4) [gæm'bəl], v. 1. play any game of chance for money or other things of value; bet. Ex. *He gambled away a fortune at the horse races.* 2. risk anything of value; take a chance. Ex. *Drive carefully and don't gamble with your life.* —n. a matter involving risk. Ex. *Putting money into that failing business is a gamble.* —**gam'bler**, n. one who gambles.

game (1) [geym'], n. 1. any contest played according to rules in which persons or teams compete against each other. Ex. *She enjoys a game of cards.* 2. any form of amusement or play. Ex. *What games did the children play at the party?* 3. wild animals that are hunted. Ex. *He is hunting game in the forest.* —adj. of animals, including fish and birds, that are hunted. Ex. *A forest fire destroyed the game birds.*

gang (3) [gæŋ'], n. 1. a group of people gathered together for some reason. Ex. *The gang of small boys was playing ball.* 2. a group of criminals. Ex. *A gang of robbers broke into the store.*

gangplank [gæŋ'plæŋk'], n. a movable walk used to go on or off a ship.

gangster (5) [gæŋ'stər], n. a person in a criminal gang. Ex. *The gangster was arrested by the police.*

gap (4) [gæp'], n. 1. a break or opening, as in a wall; a mountain pass. Ex. *The cows went through a gap in the fence.* 2. a vacant space or interval. Ex. *The mother's death left a gap in the lives of her children.*

garage (4) [gəra:ž', gəra:ǰ'], n. a building for sheltering, servicing, or repairing automobiles, trucks, etc. Ex. *My car is in the garage for repairs.*

garbage (5) [gar'biǰ], n. waste; unwanted or spoiled food. Ex. *Leave your garbage in a can outside your door.*

garden (1) [gar'dən], *n.* a piece of ground where plants are grown for beauty or for food. **Ex.** *They have a rose garden behind their house.* —*v.* work in a garden. **Ex.** *She likes to garden.* —**gar'den·er,** *n.* one who gardens.

garment (3) [gar'mənt], *n.* any article of clothing. **Ex.** *Her best garment was a red dress.*

garrison (4) [gær'əsən, ger'əsən], *n.* a fort or town which has soldiers stationed there for protection; also the body of troops stationed there. **Ex.** *The garrison is on the hill.*

gas (2) [gæs'], *n.* 1. any substance that is neither solid nor liquid. **Ex.** *Air is a gas.* 2. any such substance which burns and provides heat or light. **Ex.** *Our home is heated by gas.* 3. gasoline. **Ex.** *The car needed ten gallons of gas.*

gash (5) [gæš'], *n.* a deep, long cut. **Ex.** *He was taken to the hospital with a gash in his head.* —*v.* make a deep, long cut. **Ex.** *She gashed her hand with a knife.*

gasoline (3) [gæs'əliyn`, gæs`əliyn'], *n.* the liquid used as fuel for automobiles and other engines. **Ex.** *His car drives 20 miles on a gallon of gasoline.*

gasp (3) [gæsp'], *n.* a sudden, sharp intake of air, made with the mouth open. **Ex.** *She gave a gasp of surprise when she saw him.* —*v.* 1. struggle to get air, with the mouth open. **Ex.** *He gasped for air as he ran from the smoke-filled room.* 2. speak with gasps. **Ex.** *She gasped out her story.*

gate (1) [geyt'], *n.* the part of a fence, wall, or passageway that opens and closes like a door; entrance. **Ex.** *There was a guard at the gate of the factory.*

gather (1) [gæð'ːr], *v.* 1. bring together into one group or place; assemble. **Ex.** *The guests gathered around the fire.* 2. collect, as a harvest. **Ex.** *The farmer gathered the crops.* 3. learn from observation. **Ex.** *I gather that he did not like my ideas.* —**gath'er·ing,** *n.* a crowd; a coming together.

gave (1) [geyv'], *v.* past tense of *give.* **Ex.** *He gave me the book.*

gay (2) [gey'], *adj.* 1. full of joy; expressing happiness. **Ex.** *The orchestra played gay dance music.* 2. bright and colorful. **Ex.** *Gay flags decorated the hall.* —**gai'e·ty,** *n.* —**gai'ly,** *adv.*

gaze (2) [geyz¹], v. look long and steadily; look with wonder. **Ex.** *He gazed lovingly into her eyes.* —n. a long, steady look. **Ex.** *Her gaze was fixed on the moon.*

gear (5) [gi:r¹], n. 1. in a mechanical device, a wheel with teeth that fit together with similar parts of another wheel, so that the movement of one wheel causes the other to move; a particular arrangement of such wheels. **Ex.** *When a car is in gear, the motor begins to turn the wheels.* 2. the equipment used for a particular occupation. **Ex.** *Several pieces of the sailor's gear were missing.*

GEAR 1

geese (3) [giys¹], n. plural of *goose.* **Ex.** *The wild geese were flying high above us.*

gem (3) [jem¹], n. 1. a rare and beautiful stone; a jewel. **Ex.** *The crown sparkled with gems.* 2. something as rare and valuable as a gem. **Ex.** *That painting is the gem of the collection.*

general (1) [jen¹(ə)rəl], adj. 1. not detailed; not definite. **Ex.** *I have a general idea of what he means.* 2. not local; widespread. **Ex.** *A general election will be held this fall.* 3. affecting or including all. **Ex.** *These rules are for the general good.* 4. not specialized. **Ex.** *He is taking a course in general science.* —n. any army officer ranking above a colonel. —gen¹er·al·ly, adv. —gen¹er·al¹i·ty, n. —gen¹er·al·ize, v. —in general, usually.

generate (3) [jen¹əreyt`], v. produce; make. **Ex.** *The motor generated steam.* —gen¹er·a`tor, n. a machine that produces power. —gen`er·a¹tion, n. the act of producing, making, or bringing into being. **Ex.** *The generation of electric power is important to modern industry.*

generation (3) [jen`ərey¹šən], n. 1. all persons born about the same time. **Ex.** *This generation could be called the space age generation.* 2. the average period of a generation, commonly accepted as 30 years. **Ex.** *It happened two generations ago.*

generous (2) [jen¹ərəs], adj. 1. ready to give; willing to share. **Ex.** *He is generous to his friends.* 2. free from meanness of character; noble of mind. **Ex.** *It was generous of him to admit his mistake.* 3. plentiful; large. **Ex.** *They always serve generous portions of food.* —gen`er·ous·ly, adv. —gen`er·os¹i·ty, n.

genius (3) [jiyn'yəs], *n.* 1. extraordinary natural mental ability; any great ability. **Ex.** *The teacher recognized the boy's musical genius.* 2. a person who has a great ability. **Ex.** *She is recognized as a genius.*

gentle (1) [jen'təl], *adj.* 1. not rough or violent. **Ex.** *He has a gentle manner.* 2. moderate; mild. **Ex.** *A gentle breeze was blowing.* —**gen'tle·ness**, *n.* —**gent'ly**, *adv.*

gentleman (1) [jen'təlmən], *n.* 1. a man of culture, good manners, and honor. **Ex.** *A gentleman would not have behaved that way.* 2. any man. **Ex.** *It belongs to the gentleman in the brown suit.*

genuine (4) [jen'yuwən], *adj.* 1. not imitation; real. **Ex.** *It is a genuine gold ring.* 2. sincere; true. **Ex.** *He proved himself a genuine friend.* —**gen'u·ine·ly**, *adv.* —**gen'u·ine·ness**, *n.*

geography (4) [jiyag'rəfiy], *n.* 1. the science of the areas of the earth, in regard to nations, climate, plants, people, etc. **Ex.** *Schoolchildren need maps to study geography.* 2. the hills, lowlands, etc., of a particular area or place. **Ex.** *We are studying the geography of our town.* —**ge·og'ra·pher**, *n.* one who studies geography. —**ge'o·graph'ic**, *adj.*

germ (4) [jərm'], *n.* a plant or animal so tiny that it cannot be seen by the eye alone, especially such a plant or animal which produces disease. **Ex.** *The wound must be kept clean so that germs do not infect it.*

gerund (5) [jeir'ənd], *n.* a verb form which is used as a noun. **Exs.** *In the sentence, "Winning the race was important to him," "winning" is a gerund. In the sentence, "He angered his friend by speaking rudely," "speaking" is a gerund.*

gesture (3) [jes'čər], *n.* 1. a movement of the body, hands, face, etc. which expresses a feeling or thought. **Ex.** *She held out her hand in a gesture of welcome.* 2. something done only to be polite. **Ex.** *His offer of help was only a gesture.* —*v.* make gestures. **Ex.** *She gestured to attract our attention.*

get (1) [get'], *v.* 1. obtain, gain, or acquire. **Ex.** *I expect to get some money soon.* 2. go and bring back. **Ex.** *Get some bread at the store.* 3. carry; take; remove. **Ex.** *We could not get the tree out of the road.* 4. prepare; make ready. **Ex.** *I have to get dinner now.* 5. cause to happen. **Ex.** *When can you get this finished?* 6. persuade. **Ex.** *Can I get you to do something for me?* 7. be; become. **Ex.** *He gets sick very* *easily.* 8. arrive; reach. Ex. *When will we get to town?* **—get along,** 1. be friendly; work well with. Ex. *He gets along well with young people.* 2. progress; succeed. Ex. *How are you getting along in business?* 3. grow older. Ex. *He is getting along in years.* **—get by,** 1. pass. Ex. *The faulty work did not get by the inspector.* 2. just manage. Ex. *I'll get by, with your help.* **—get down to,** start. Ex. *After lunch, he got down to work.* **—get in,** enter; receive; arrive. Ex. *When does the bus get in?* **—get off,** 1. come off of. Ex. *Get off the rug while I clean it.* 2. leave. Ex. *I want to get off to the country early.* **—get over,** recover from. Ex. *He is getting over his illness.* **—get through,** finish. Ex. *Hurry and get through with your work.* **—get up,** rise. Ex. *He got up as she entered the room.*

ghastly (5) [gæst'liy], *adj.* 1. causing horror or terror. Ex. *The murder was a ghastly crime.* 2. ghostlike; without color. Ex. *After a sleepless night, she looked ghastly.* **—ghast'li·ness,** *n.*

ghost (3) [gowst'], *n.* 1. the soul of a dead person, imagined as wandering about among living persons in the form of a pale shadow. Ex. *Ghosts are said to appear in the cemetery at night.* 2. a shadow or slight suggestion of something. Ex. *He does not have a ghost of a chance.* **—ghost'ly,** *adj.*

giant (2) [jay'ənt], *n.* 1. an imaginary being of human form but of unusual size and power. Ex. *Children like stories about giants.* 2. a person or thing of unusual importance, ability, etc. Ex. *He is one of the giants of the newspaper world.* **—adj.** very large. Ex. *The child dreamed of a giant cat.*

gift (1) [gift'], *n.* 1. a present; something that is given without cost. Ex. *Her gift to him was a book.* 2. a special ability. Ex. *He has a gift for music.* **—gift'ed,** *adj.*

gigantic (4) [jay`gæn'tik], *adj.* very large; huge in size. Ex. *That football player is gigantic.*

giggle (5) [gig'əl], *v.* laugh in a light, silly way. Ex. *The young girls giggled among themselves.* **—n.** a light, silly laugh. Ex. *The teacher heard a giggle in the back of the room.*

gin (5) [jin'], *n.* an alcoholic liquor, flavored with berries and usually like water in color. Ex. *He likes drinks made with gin.*

gin (5) [jin'], *n.* a machine for separating cotton from its seeds. Ex. *The cotton gin was invented in 1793.*

ginger (4) [jin'jər], *n.* a sharply flavored plant root, used for seasoning food and drinks and for medicinal purposes. **Ex.** *My favorite cake is one flavored with ginger.*

gingerly [jin'jərliy], *adv.* very carefully. **Ex.** *She opened the door gingerly.*

girdle (5) [gər'dəl], *n.* 1. a woman's lightweight undergarment which supports the abdomen. **Ex.** *The doctor told her to wear a girdle.* 2. any encircling band, especially a belt or cord worn about the waist. **Ex.** *She wore a girdle with a silver clasp.* —*v.* encircle as with a belt. **Ex.** *The mountain peak was girdled with clouds.*

girl (1) [gərl'], *n.* a female child; a young unmarried woman. **Ex.** *The girls were playing with their dolls.*

give (1) [giv'], *v.* 1. hand to another to keep. **Ex.** *I want to give you this book.* 2. grant; state; make public. **Ex.** *Give me your opinion, please.* 3. perform; do. **Ex.** *He gave a shake of his head.* 4. hand; pass to; lend. **Ex.** *Please give me your pencil.* 5. yield to pressure. **Ex.** *We pushed until the door began to give.* 6. be the cause or source of; produce. **Ex.** *The new system gave good results.* 7. sacrifice; pay. **Ex.** *He was willing to give his life for his friends.* —**give in**, stop opposing. **Ex.** *He gave in to her requests and bought the car.* —**give off**, send out. **Ex.** *What is giving off that terrible smell?* —**give out**, make known; distribute. **Ex.** *He gave out the information.* —**give up**, 1. stop. **Ex.** *He is trying to give up smoking.* 2. hand over; surrender. **Ex.** *He gave himself up to the police.*

given [giv'ən], *v.* past participle of *give.* **Ex.** *What has he given you?*

given name [giv'ən neym'], *n.* one's first name. **Ex.** *John F. Kennedy's given name was John.*

glad (1) [glæd'], *adj.* 1. pleased; happy. **Ex.** *We were glad to see her.* 2. showing or causing pleasure. **Ex.** *He brought us glad news.* 3. willing. **Ex.** *We will be glad to help.* —**glad'den**, *v.* —**glad'ly**, *adv.* —**glad'ness**, *n.*

glamour (5) [glæm'ər], *n.* strong attraction; charm; fascination. **Ex.** *The glamour of the life of an actress made other careers seem dull to her.*

glance (2) [glæns'], *v.* 1. look quickly or briefly. **Ex.** *She glanced in the mirror as she passed.* 2. strike and go off in a slanting direction. **Ex.** *The stone struck the car and glanced off.* —*n.* a quick or brief look. **Ex.** *She cast a glance in his direction.*

glare (3) [gle:r'], *n.* 1. a steady, brilliant light. **Ex.** *The glare of the sun was almost blinding.* 2. a staring, angry look. **Ex.** *Her glare silenced him.* 3. smooth, glassy surface. **Ex.** *The road was a glare of ice.* —*v.* 1. shine with a strong, almost blinding light. **Ex.** *The electric sign glared through my window.* 2. look at with anger in one's eyes. **Ex.** *The old woman glared at the noisy children.* —**glar'ing**, *adj.*

glass (1) [glæs'], *n.* 1. a hard, easily broken material through which one can see. **Ex.** *Windows are made of glass.* 2. something made of glass, such as a window pane or mirror. **Ex.** *She looked at herself in the glass.* 3. the quantity contained in a drinking glass. **Ex.** *He drank a glass of wine before dinner.* —**glass'es**, *n.* eyeglasses. —**glass'y**, *adj.* like glass; hard, clear, and shiny.

glaze (5) [gleyz'], *v.* 1. cover with glass or with something which looks like glass. **Ex.** *The road was glazed with a thin coat of ice.* 2. produce a glassy surface on dishes, baked goods, etc. **Ex.** *The cook glazed the cake with sugar.* —*n.* a glassy surface. **Ex.** *The glaze on these dishes does not crack easily.*

gleam (3) [gliym'], *n.* 1. a slight or brief glow, ray, or beam of light. **Ex.** *A gleam of light shone through the partly open door.* 2. a soft shining light reflected from a polished surface. **Ex.** *The gleam of copper pans brightened the kitchen.* 3. a faint suggestion or hint. **Ex.** *There was a gleam of laughter in her eyes.* —*v.* send out a gleam. **Ex.** *A light gleamed in the distance.*

glide (3) [glayd'], *v.* move smoothly and easily along. **Ex.** *They glided across the ice.* —*n.* act of gliding. —**glid'er**, *n.* an airplane with no engines that glides on air.

glimpse (3) [glimps'], *n.* 1. a brief view; a quick look. **Ex.** *We had a glimpse of the lake as we flew over it.* 2. a faint idea; a suggestion. **Ex.** *We see glimpses of other writers in his book.* —*v.* look briefly or glance at; see only briefly. **Ex.** *We glimpsed a running figure.*

glisten (4) [glis'ən], *v.* shine with a sparkling light; glitter. **Ex.** *The snow glistened in the sunlight.*

glitter (3) [glit'ər], *v.* sparkle with a brilliant light. **Ex.** *The diamonds in her ring glittered.* —*n.* brilliant, sparkling light;

splendor. **Ex.** *They prefer the quiet of their home to the glitter of society.*

globe (3) [glowb¹], *n.* 1. the earth. **Ex.** *They have traveled around the globe.* 2. a round ball with a map of the earth on it. **Ex.** *The teacher pointed to the continents on the globe.* 3. a round or ball-shaped object. **Ex.** *An electric globe hung from the ceiling.* —**glo¹bal,** *adj.*

gloom (4) [gluwm¹], *n.* 1. darkness; dimness; deep shade. **Ex.** *They dreaded the gloom of approaching night.* 2. low spirits; sadness. **Ex.** *Gloom descended upon the family when they heard the bad news.* —**gloom¹y,** *adj.*

glory (2) [glɔ:r¹iy], *n.* 1. praise or honor given for doing something good and special. **Ex.** *His acts of courage brought him glory.* 2. beauty; that which is splendid. **Ex.** *They stood silent before the glory of the sunset.* —**glor¹i·fy,** *v.* —**glor¹i·ous,** *adj.*

glossary (1) [glas¹(ə)riy, glɔ:s¹(ə)riy], *n.* a list of words and terms with an explanation of their meaning. **Ex.** *The author has provided a glossary at the end of the book.*

GLOVE

glove (2) [gləv¹], *n.* a covering for the hand, with a separate place for each finger.

glow (2) [glow¹], *n.* 1. light that comes from a heated substance. **Ex.** *The glow of the fire lighted the room.* 2. brightness of color. **Ex.** *There was a rosy glow in her cheeks.* 3. warm feeling; emotion. **Ex.** *There was a glow of happiness in his eyes.* —*v.* 1. give bright light because of heat. **Ex.** *The dying coals glowed.* 2. shine. **Ex.** *The headlights of the car glowed in the distance.* 3. show strong, bright color. **Ex.** *The children's faces glowed as they played in the snow.* 4. show emotion. **Ex.** *They glowed with excitement when they heard the news.*

glue (3) [gluw¹], *n.* a thick substance used for sticking things together. **Ex.** *He used glue to repair the book.* —*v.* join or fasten with glue. **Ex.** *The carpenter glued the legs to the chair.*

gnaw (4) [nɔ:¹], *v.* 1. wear away or remove by biting little by little; chew. **Ex.** *The dog gnawed the bone.* 2. make by chewing. **Ex.** *The rat gnawed a hole in the door.*

go (1) [gow¹], *v.* 1. move from one location to another. **Ex.** *We go that way to town.* 2. leave; depart from. **Ex.** *You*

should go now. 3. move about, be, or do in a certain way.
Ex. *It is too cold to go without a coat.* 4. be or remain in a
particular condition. **Ex.** *She let the children go hungry.* 5.
move for some purpose. **Ex.** *She has to go and get dinner
ready.* 6. do at a future time; intend to do. **Ex.** *He is going
to come here tomorrow.* 7. reach; reach a certain state; become. **Ex.** *He will go mad.* 8. be in operation; run; work.
Ex. *Can you make this clock go?* 9. fit; be suited to. **Ex.**
Those colors go well together. —**go on,** continue. —**go by,**
1. pass. **Ex.** *We go by the house every morning.* 2. obey;
follow. **Ex.** *I will go by the rules in doing the work.* —**go
out,** 1. cease; end. **Ex.** *The fire will go out without fuel.* 2.
attend a party, dinner, etc. **Ex.** *Are you going out tonight?*
—**go off,** 1. leave. **Ex.** *Don't go off without me.* 2. explode;
fire. **Ex.** *Did you hear the gun go off?* —**go over,** look at
closely. **Ex.** *Go over the work and see if it is correct.* —**go
through,** experience. **Ex.** *I will not go through that trouble
again.* —**go through with,** finish. **Ex.** *I will go through with
what I promised.* —**go without,** deprive oneself; sacrifice.
Ex. *The mother goes without food sometimes so the children can eat.* —**let oneself go,** express one's true self. **Ex.**
At the party, he let himself go and danced.

goal (4) [gowl'], *n.* 1. aim or end; that toward which effort is
directed. **Ex.** *His goal in life is to be a good doctor.* 2. the
end of the journey or race. **Ex.** *The goal of our trip was the
city.* 3. the line or net a ball must reach in certain games.
Ex. *In football, one scores when he crosses the goal.*

goat (3) [gowt'], *n.* a horned animal related
to the sheep.

god (1) [gad'], *n.* a spirit that is worshiped
for the special powers he is believed to
have. **Ex.** *They prayed to God for help.*

GOAT

goes (1) [gowz'], *v.* present tense of *go* used
with he, she, it, and singular nouns. **Exs.** *He goes to work
early. If she goes to the store, I will go with her.*

gold (1) [gowld'], *n.* 1. a precious yellow metal. **Ex.** *The rings
were made of gold.* 2. coins made from gold; money. **Ex.** *He
cares more for gold than for what it will buy.* 3. something
compared to this metal in value, brightness, color, etc. **Ex.**
She has a heart of gold. —*adj.* of or like gold. **Ex.** *He had a
gold watch.* — **gold'en,** *adj.* 1. made of or having the color
of gold; bright yellow. **Exs.** *The child had golden hair. The*

prize was a golden apple. 2. very useful; very good. **Ex.** *This is a golden opportunity to travel.*

golf (5) [gɔ:lf¹], *n.* a game, played on a grassy field, in which a small ball is hit with special clubs into a series of holes. **Ex.** *Do you like golf better than swimming?* —*v.* play the game of golf. **Ex.** *He golfs every Wednesday.* —**golf¹er,** *n.* one who plays golf.

GOLFER

gone (1) [gɔ:n¹], *v.* past participle of *go.* **Ex.** *The train has gone.*

good (1) [gud¹], *adj.* 1. better than average. **Ex.** *Her school work is always good.* 2. suitable; qualified. **Ex.** *He is a good man for this job.* 3. generous; friendly; kind. **Ex.** *His parents were very good to him.* 4. agreeable; pleasant. **Ex.** *We had a good time during our vacation.* 5. morally proper; well behaved. **Ex.** *She was always a good child.* 6. honorable; well regarded. **Ex.** *He has a good name in business.* 7. strong; sound. **Ex.** *You must have good eyes to read such small print.* 8. considerable; fairly great in amount. **Ex.** *He has read a good many books.* —*n.* 1. that which is good. **Ex.** *He is not old enough to know good from bad.* 2. benefit; advantage. **Ex.** *She is doing it for your own good.* —*interj.* an expression of agreement or being satisfied. **Ex.** *Good! I am glad you can go.* —**good¹ness,** *n.* —**as good as,** almost. **Ex.** *The work is as good as done.* —**for good,** forever. **Ex.** *He has gone for good.* —**good for,** will continue or last for. **Ex.** *The food supply is good for three days.* —**make good,** succeed. **Ex.** *He made good in business.*

good-by (1) [gudˋbay¹], *interj.* an expression used when parting; farewell. —*n.* **Ex.** *I just had time to say good-by.* —**good af¹ter·noon, good morn¹ing, good night,** *interj.* greetings or farewells proper for the times of day stated.

goods (2) [gudz¹], *n.* 1. things one owns that can be moved. **Ex.** *Are these all of your household goods?* 2. things offered for sale. **Ex.** *I examined all of the goods in the store.* 3. cloth. **Ex.** *Do you sell cotton goods?*

good turn [gud¹ tərn¹], a helpful act. **Ex.** *He did me a good turn by carrying that box.*

good will [gud' wil'], a friendly feeling. **Ex.** *By helping with the work, we gained her good will.*

goose (2) [guws'], *n.* a bird that swims and is similar to but larger than a duck.

gorge (5) [gorj'], *n.* a narrow passageway through hills, with high walls of rock on each side. **Ex.** *The boat trip through the river gorge is difficult.* —*v.* eat too much food. **Ex.** *He gorged himself at dinner.*

GOOSE

gorgeous (4) [gor'jəs], *adj.* splendid in appearance or coloring. **Ex.** *They watched the gorgeous sunset.* —**gor'geous·ly,** *adv.*

gossip (4) [gas'əp], *n.* 1. useless and sometimes harmful talk about other people which may not be true. **Ex.** *Her letter was filled with gossip about her neighbors' troubles.* 2. a person who gossips. **Ex.** *A gossip often damages people's reputations.* —*v.* talk in a useless and sometimes harmful way about others. **Ex.** *She gossips about her neighbors.*

got (1) [gat'], *v.* past tense and participle of get. **Ex.** *He got some water from the well.* —**got'ten,** *v.* past participle of get.

govern (1) [gəv'ərn], *v.* 1. rule by authority. **Ex.** *The President governed the country.* 2. be guided by; influence. **Ex.** *He was governed by his father's ideas.* —**gov·ern'or,** *n.* one who governs, usually a state. **Ex.** *The governor proposed new taxes.*

government [gəv'ərnmənt], *n.* 1. the people and organization in power; the rulers. **Ex.** *The government has just increased taxes.* 2. the act or art of governing. **Ex.** *Government of a large city is difficult.* 3. the form of government. **Ex.** *Our country has a democratic government.*

gown (3) [gawn'], *n.* a woman's dress or robe. **Ex.** *She bought an evening gown for the party.* 2. a long, loose outer garment worn at official events. **Ex.** *The students received their university degrees wearing cap and gown.*

grab (4) [græb'], *v.* take hold of suddenly; seize. **Ex.** *She grabbed the stair rail when she slipped.* —*n.* the act of taking hold of suddenly. **Ex.** *The thief made a grab for the woman's purse.*

GOWN

grace (3) [greys¹], *n.* 1. beauty of form or motion. **Ex.** *She danced with grace.* 2. charm; a pleasing manner. **Ex.** *His speech was full of grace and wit.* —**grace'ful,** *adj.* —**gra'cious,** *adj.* charming. —**in the good graces of,** liked by; favored.

grade (2) [greyd¹], *n.* 1. a step or degree in an order or series, according to quality, progress, etc. **Ex.** *That store sells only the best grade of meat.* 2. a division of a school, according to the progress of the students, usually one year long. **Ex.** *He is in the eleventh grade.* 3. score showing the quality of work done, as on a test at school. **Ex.** *All his grades were high.* 4. the slope or slant of a road. **Ex.** *That road has a steep grade.* —*v.* 1. arrange in grades. **Ex.** *The farmer graded the eggs from the largest to smallest.* 2. give a score to. **Ex.** *The teacher graded the test papers.*

grade school [greyd¹ skuwl¹], a school of the first six or eight years of study.

gradual (2) [græj¹uwəl, græj¹ul], *adj.* happening or changing by small degrees. **Ex.** *The doctor noticed a gradual improvement in his patient.* —**grad'u·al·ly,** *adv.*

graduate (3) [græj¹uwət], *n.* one who has completed a course of study. **Ex.** *He is a university graduate.* —*adj.* having been graduated; of or for a graduate. **Ex.** *He is working for a graduate degree.* —*v.* 1. give or receive a degree upon completion of a course of study. **Ex.** *He graduated from college last year.* 2. divide into degrees or a series. **Ex.** *The rate of the income tax is graduated according to the amount of income.* —**grad`u·a'tion,** *n.*

graft (5) [græft¹], *n.* the part of a plant or tree put into a cut in another plant or tree to grow there; the portion of living skin, bone, etc. removed from one part of the body and put into another. **Ex.** *The badly burned boy was given a skin graft.* —*v.* put a graft on a plant or part of the body. **Ex.** *The doctor grafted new skin onto the boy's leg.*

graft (5) [græft¹], *n.* the dishonest use of one's position to get money; money obtained in this way. **Ex.** *The mayor went to prison because of graft.*

grain (1) [greyn¹], *n.* 1. the seed of certain plants, such as wheat and corn, which may be eaten; the plants themselves. **Ex.** *The farmers are harvesting the grain.* 2. a very small piece. **Ex.** *A few grains of sugar fell on the floor.* 3. a very small amount. **Ex.** *There is not a grain of truth in what he* *says.* 4. a pattern of natural markings, such as those in wood, marble, leather, etc. **Ex.** *This piece of wood has a beautiful grain.*

gram (5) [græm'], *n.* a unit of weight. See **Weights and Measures.**

grammar (3) [græm'ər], *n.* 1. a study of words, their form, and their use in sentences; the rules for using a language. **Ex.** *He is studying English grammar.* 2. a book describing rules of language. **Ex.** *This grammar is easy to understand.* 3. speaking or writing, considered in relation to rules of language. **Ex.** *She uses poor grammar.*

grammatical [grəmæt'ikəl], *adj.* concerning or in agreement with rules of grammar. —**gram·mat'i·cal·ly,** *adv.* **Ex.** *He always speaks grammatically correct English.*

grand (2) [grænd'], *adj.* 1. large; expensive; splendid. **Ex.** *They lived in a grand house.* 2. having great dignity; fine; noble. **Ex.** *He was a grand old man.* 3. most important; main; principal. **Ex.** *They had dinner in the grand dining room of the hotel.* —**grand'ly,** *adv.* —**grand'ness,** *n.*

grandchild [græn(d)'čayld'], *n.* one's grandson or grand-daughter.

granddaughter [græn(d)'dɔ:t'ər], *n.* daughter of one's son or daughter.

grandfather [græn(d)'fa'ðər], *n.* father of one's father or mother.

grandmother [græn(d)'məð'ər], *n.* mother of one's father or mother.

grandparent [græn(d)'per'ənt], *n.* one's grandmother or grand-father.

grandson [græn(d)'sən'], *n.* son of one's son or daughter.

granite (4) [græn'ət], *n.* a very hard, usually gray or pink rock. **Ex.** *That building is faced with polished granite.*

grant (2) [grænt'], *v.* 1. give that which is requested; agree to. **Ex.** *He granted their request to hold a meeting.* 2. agree as to truth. **Ex.** *I grant that he was there.* —*n.* the act of giving; that which is given; a gift. **Ex.** *The university received a large grant of money from a former student.* —**take for granted,** 1. regard as true; expect confidently. **Ex.** *He took it for granted that I knew the answer.* 2. undervalue. **Ex.** *They took their brother's help for granted.*

grape (2) [greyp'], *n.* a juicy, smooth-skinned, small fruit that grows in bunches; the vine which bears this fruit. Ex. *He made wine from the grapes.*

grasp (2) [græsp'], *v.* 1. seize and hold with the fingers, hand, etc.; try to seize. Ex. *The drowning man grasped at the rope.* 2. understand. Ex. *The child heard the words but did not grasp their meaning.* —*n.* 1. a firm, strong hold. Ex. *His grasp hurt my arm.* 2. understanding. Ex. *That teacher has a good grasp of his subject.*

GRAPES

grass (2) [græs'], *n.* a plant with long, narrow, green, blade-like leaves. Ex. *The cattle were eating the grass in the field.*

grasshopper (5) [græs'hap`ər], *n.* a winged insect that can hop or leap a long distance.

grateful (2) [greyt'fəl], *adj.* thankful; appreciative. Ex. *We are grateful for your help.* —**grate'ful·ly**, *adv.*

GRASSHOPPER

gratify (4) [græt'əfay`], give pleasure to; satisfy. **Exs.** *The speaker was gratified by the large audience. Her wishes were gratified when he returned.*

gratitude (5) [græt'ətuwd`, græt'ətyuwd`], *n.* the feeling of being grateful for a gift, help, or kindness. Ex. *They showed their gratitude by sending her flowers.*

grave (1) [greyv'], *adj.* 1. thoughtful; dignified. Ex. *He had a grave look on his face.* 2. serious; important. Ex. *We have some grave matters to discuss.* 3. dangerous. Ex. *The condition of the patient was grave.* —**grave'ly**, *adv.*

grave (1) [greyv'], *n.* a place where a dead person is buried. Ex. *We put flowers on her grave.*

gravel (4) [græv'əl], *n.* small stones, often mixed with coarse sand. Ex. *The path to the house was covered with gravel.*

gravity (4) [græv'ətiy], *n.* 1. the force that pulls things toward the center of the earth and prevents objects on the earth from being thrown into space. Ex. *The space ship needed tremendous power to escape the force of gravity.* 2. seriousness; importance; state of being grave. **Ex.** *The hush in the room indicated the gravity of the situation.* —**grav'i·tate,** *v.* move or be attracted toward. **Ex.** *We gravitated toward the speaker.*

gravy (5) [grey'viy], *n.* a sauce made by mixing flour with the juices that come from cooking meat. **Ex.** *The boy liked gravy on his potatoes.*

gray (1) [grey'], *adj.* 1. of a color made by mixing black and white. **Ex.** *She wore a gray dress.* 2. cheerless; dull. **Ex.** *It is a gray day.* —*n.* a color made by mixing black and white. **Ex.** *Gray is not a cheerful color.*

graze (4) [greyz'], *v.* feed on grass and other growing plants. **Ex.** *The cows are grazing in the field.*

graze (4) [greyz'], *v.* touch or scratch in passing. **Ex.** *The ball grazed my arm as it went by me.*

grease (4) [griys'], *n.* 1. the melted fat from an animal body. **Ex.** *She spilled the grease on the stove while cooking.* 2. any fatty, oily matter. **Ex.** *His clothes were stained with grease from the car.* —*v.* put grease on; oil. **Ex.** *Grease the pan well before frying eggs in it.* —**greas'y,** *adj.*

great (1) [greyt'], *adj.* 1. very large or more than usual in size, number, etc. **Ex.** *Eight million people live in the great city.* 2. important; famous; remarkable. **Ex.** *The country's first President was a great man.* 3. extreme; much more than the usual. **Ex.** *He is a great friend of mine.* 4. older or younger by a generation, used with a (-) mark. **Ex.** *My great-grandfather is the father of my grandfather.* **great'ness,** *n.* —**great'ly,** *adv.*

greed (2) [griyd'], *n.* a great desire to take and have things for oneself without thinking of others. **Ex.** *Although he had many toys, his greed made him want more.* —**greed'y,** *adj.* —**greed'i·ly,** *adv.*

green (1) [griyn'], *adj.* 1. of a color made by mixing blue and yellow; the color of growing leaves and grass. **Ex.** *She bought a green hat.* 2. not ripe; not ready to be eaten. **Ex.** *Green apples made the little boy sick.* 3. not experienced; untrained. **Ex.** *The new workmen were too green to do a good job.* —*n.* the color green. —**green'ish,** *adj.* like the color green. —**greens,** *n.pl.* green leafy vegetables.

greenhouse [griyn'haws'], *n.* a building made mostly of glass in which flowers and plants are grown.

greet (2) [griyt'], *v.* 1. speak to upon meeting; welcome. **Ex.**

She opened the door and greeted me by saying "hello." 2. receive in a special way. **Ex.** *The angry man greeted him with insults.* —**greet'ing,** *n.* the act or words of someone who greets.

grew (1) [gruw'], *v.* past tense of *grow.* **Ex.** *The trees grew tall.*

grief (2) [griyf'], *n.* great sorrow or sadness, such as one feels when a loved one dies. **Ex.** *The death of her father caused her grief.*

grieve (3) [griyv'], *v.* feel or cause to feel grief. **Ex.** *She grieved over the death of her father.* —**griev'ance,** *n.* a wrong about which one feels troubled or angry. **Ex.** *Long hours of work without extra pay was their grievance.* —**griev'ous,** *adj.* —**griev'ous·ly,** *adv.*

grim (4) [grim'], *adj.* 1. severe; stern; not yielding. **Ex.** *The judge had a grim look on his face.* 2. shocking; frightful; cruel. **Ex.** *The dead men were a grim sight.* —**grim'ly,** *adv.* —**grim'ness,** *n.*

grin (4) [grin'], *v.* smile broadly, by drawing back the lips to show the teeth. **Ex.** *The boy grinned when he saw the dog.* —*n.* a big smile. **Ex.** *The boy's broad grin showed his delight.*

grind (4) [graynd'], *v.* 1. reduce to small, fine pieces by crushing. **Ex.** *We buy coffee beans and grind them ourselves.* 2. sharpen; make smooth; shape by rubbing. **Ex.** *The old man made his living by grinding scissors.* 3. press or rub two things against each other. **Ex.** *He grinds his teeth in his sleep.* —**grind'er,** *n.*

grindstone [grayn(d)'stown'], *n.* a round stone used for sharpening.

grip (3) [grip'], *n.* 1. a firm hold, as with the hands. **Ex.** *He had a grip on my shoulder.* 2. a small suitcase. **Ex.** *He packed his grip for a trip.* —*v.* seize firmly. **Ex.** *He gripped the boy by the arm.*

groan (3) [grown'], *n.* a low, sad sound of pain or grief. **Ex.** *We could hear the groans of the injured man.* —*v.* make such a sound. **Ex.** *The sick woman groaned.*

grocery (3) [grows'(ə)riy, growš'riy], *n.* a store where food and other supplies for home use are sold. **Ex.** *We bought sugar and flour at the grocery.* —**gro'cer·ies,** *n.* the items sold at a grocery. **Ex.** *I bought enough groceries for all of us.* —**gro'cer,** *n.* owner, manager, or clerk at a grocery.

groom (4) [gruwm¹], *n.* 1. a person who tends horses. **Ex.** *The groom was brushing the horse.* 2. a man newly married or about to be married. **Ex.** *The groom looked happy at the wedding.* —*v.* 1. make clean and neat. **Ex.** *The boy groomed himself carefully.* 2. get one ready; prepare. **Ex.** *He was groomed to run for mayor.*

groove (5) [gruwv¹], *n.* a long, thin depression or cut in a surface. **Ex.** *He cut a groove in the wood with a chisel.*

grope (5) [growp¹], *v.* feel about with the hands, as in the dark; search for blindly. **Ex.** *He groped for the light switch.*

gross (4) [grows¹], *n.* twelve dozen; 144. **Ex.** *He ordered a gross of pencils.* —*adj.* 1. very noticeable; extreme. **Ex.** *The accident was caused by gross negligence.* 2. improper; indelicate; coarse. **Ex.** *No gentleman uses gross language.*

ground (1) [grawnd¹], *n.* land; the earth's surface; soil. **Ex.** *They planted the seeds in the ground.* —*adj.* on, at, or near the surface of the earth. **Ex.** *He lives on the ground floor of the building.* —*v.* 1. place, put, or keep on the ground. **Ex.** *The airplane was grounded by bad weather.* 2. fix firmly; establish. **Ex.** *Her statements were grounded in truth.* 3. run onto the ground. **Ex.** *The boat is grounded on the sand and cannot move.* —**cover ground,** travel a considerable distance; make progress. **Ex.** *He had only fifteen minutes but covered much ground in his speech.* —**gain** or **lose ground,** move forward or fall back.

ground (4) [grawnd¹], *v.* past tense and participle of *grind.* **Ex.** *The butcher ground the meat.*

groundless [grawnd¹ləs], *adj.* without cause or basis in fact. **Ex.** *The rumor proved to be groundless.*

grounds [grawn(d)z¹], *n.* 1. land for private or special use. **Ex.** *The grounds of their property are very large.* 2. reason; basis in fact. **Ex.** *She had grounds for leaving him.*

groundwork [grawnd¹wərk`], *n.* foundation. **Ex.** *Education is the groundwork of success.*

group (1) [gruwp¹], *n.* 1. a gathering of persons or things taken as a unit; a collection. **Ex.** *There were ten people in the group.* 2. a number of similar persons or things placed or considered together. **Ex.** *That is an interesting group of paintings.* —*v.* place together in a group. **Ex.** *The children grouped themselves around their parents.*

grove (3) [growv¹], *n.* a small woods or group of trees. **Ex.** *There are one hundred orange trees in the grove.*

grow (1) [grow¹], *v.* 1. become larger in size, number, etc. **Ex.** *The boy is growing rapidly.* 2. develop; become older. **Ex.** *Plants need water to grow.* 3. gradually become. **Ex.** *The children are growing tired.* 4. cultivate; raise. **Ex.** *The farmer grows potatoes in this field.* —**growth¹**, *n.* act of growing; increase. —**grow on,** become more likable. **Ex.** *The boy's charm grows on you.* —**grow up,** become an adult.

growl (4) [grawl¹], *v.* 1. make a deep threatening sound in the throat. **Ex.** *The dog growled at the stranger.* 2. talk low and angrily. **Ex.** *The angry man growled an answer to the question.* —*n.* the act of growling. **Ex.** *The growls of the dog frightened the children.*

grown (1) [grown¹], *adj.* having reached one's full growth. **Ex.** *He does not look like a grown man.* —*v.* past participle of *grow.* **Ex.** *The boy has grown rapidly.*

grownup [grown'əp¹], *n.* an adult. **Ex.** *The grownups watched the children play.* —**grown`up¹,** *adj.* of or for adults. **Ex.** *He acts grownup.*

grudge (4) [grəj¹], *n.* a feeling of resentment toward someone because of a past wrong. **Ex.** *He had a grudge against his noisy neighbor.* —*v.* give or allow unhappily. **Ex.** *He grudged his landlord the rent.* —**grudg'ing,** *adj.* —**grudg'ing·ly,** *adv.*

grumble (4) [grem'bəl], *v.* 1. complain in a low unpleasant manner or voice. **Ex.** *He is always grumbling about his boss.* 2. make low, unpleasant sounds. **Ex.** *His stomach grumbled with hunger.* —**grum'bler,** *n.*

grunt (4) [grənt¹], *v.* 1. make a deep noise, as the sound of a pig. **Ex.** *Pigs grunt as they eat.* 2. express with a grunt. **Ex.** *The sullen man grunted a reply.* —*n.* the sound of a pig; a sound like this.

guarantee (4) [gær`əntiy¹, ger`əntiy¹], *n.* a promise that something will satisfy in a certain way. **Ex.** *This guarantee lets me return the radio within ten days if it does not perform well.* —*v.* promise satisfaction, according to terms agreed upon. **Ex.** *The merchant guaranteed that the color of the material would not fade.*

guard (1) [gard¹], *v.* 1. watch a person, place, or thing to

a, far; æ, am; e, get; ey, late; i, in; iy, see; ɔ, all; ow, go; u, put; uw, too; ə, but, ago; ər, fur; aw, out; ay, life; oy, boy; ŋ, ring; θ, think; ð, that; ž, measure; š, ship; ǰ, edge; č, child.

make sure no one enters, steals, or harms; protect. **Ex.** *The dog guards the house.* 2. act so as to prevent, control, etc. **Ex.** *They tried to guard against illness.* —*n.* 1. the act of guarding. **Ex.** *He was on guard all night.* 2. a person, group, or thing that guards or protects. **Ex.** *There is an armed guard at the gate of the army camp.* —**guard'ian,** *n.* —**on guard,** careful; alert. **Ex.** *He was told to be on guard against strangers.*

guess (1) [ges'], *v.* 1. form an opinion without many facts. **Ex.** *He guessed that it would rain.* 2. form an opinion which is correct but which was arrived at by chance. **Ex.** *You guessed my age correctly.* 3. think; believe. **Ex.** *I guess you will want to rest after your long trip.* —*n.* an opinion formed by guessing.

guest (2) [gest'], *n.* 1. a person invited to go somewhere or do something at the expense of the inviter. **Ex.** *We are having guests at our house for dinner tonight.* 2. a person who pays for food at an eating place or for a room at a hotel. **Ex.** *How long was he a guest at the hotel?*

guide (1) [gayd'], *v.* 1. lead; direct; show the way. **Ex.** *He guided them around the city.* 2. direct the opinions or acts of; influence. **Ex.** *Let his words guide you.* —*n.* 1. one who shows the way. **Ex.** *A guide led us through the mountains.* 2. that which guides or directs. **Ex.** *The book was a helpful guide to the sights of the city.*

guild (5) [gild'], *n.* a group organized for some purpose. **Ex.** *The ladies' guild raised money for the hospital.*

guilt (2) [gilt'], *n.* the fact or feeling of having done something wrong, bad, or not legal. **Ex.** *His guilt was proven by his fingerprints.* —**guilt'y,** *adj.* 1. having committed a wrong. **Ex.** *He is guilty of breaking the window.* 2. judged in court to have committed a crime. **Ex.** *The jury decided the man was guilty of stealing.* 3. showing or caused by a feeling one has done wrong. **Ex.** *He had a guilty look on his face.* —**guilt'i·ly,** *adv.*

gulf (2) [gəlf'], *n.* 1. a large part of an ocean or sea extending into the land. **Ex.** *Fishing boats were out in the gulf.* 2. a wide separation, as of wealth, education, etc. **Ex.** *There is a great gulf between the very rich and the very poor.*

gulp (5) [gəlp'], *v.* 1. swallow eagerly or too quickly. **Ex.** *The thirsty man gulped the cold water.* 2. hold back with a swallowing motion. **Ex.** *She tried to gulp back her tears.*

—*n.* the amount swallowed at one time. **Ex.** *The dog ate the meat in one gulp.*

gum (3) [gəm¹], *n.* 1. a gluelike substance or liquid that comes from some plants and trees. **Ex.** *The gum from rubber trees has many uses.* 2. a substance suitable for long chewing, flavored and sweetened. **Ex.** *The boy asked for a piece of chewing gum.* —*v.* cover something with gum or glue to make it stick to something; stick together with gum or glue. **Ex.** *He gummed the labels on the packages.* —**gum'my,** *adj.* sticky; like gum.

gum (3) [gəm¹], *n.* the fleshy part of the mouth that covers the roots of the teeth. **Ex.** *The gum hurt after the tooth was pulled out.*

gun (1) [gən¹], *n.* 1. a large metal tube from which a ball of lead or similar object is shot by an explosion of gunpowder; a cannon; a shotgun, rifle, or pistol. **Ex.** *The guns destroyed the enemy's buildings across the river.* 2. any device that sprays liquid in a fine mist. **Ex.** *They used a spray gun to kill the insects.* —*v.* hunt or shoot with a gun. **Ex.** *They gunned down the escaped lion.*

gush (5) [gəš¹], *v.* flow or pour suddenly and in great amounts. **Ex.** *Blood gushed from the wound.* —**gush'ing,** *adj.*

gust (5) [gəst¹], *n.* a brief, sudden rush of air, wind, smoke, etc. **Ex.** *A gust of wind blew his hat off.* —**gust'y,** *adj.*

gutter (5) [gət¹ər], *n.* 1. a narrow ditch along the side of a street which drains the water from the street. **Ex.** *The gutters filled with water in the heavy rain.* 2. narrow metal or tile channels fastened to the lower edges of a roof for guiding off water. **Ex.** *The leaves must be taken from the gutters several times a year.*

gymnasium (5) [jim\ney¹ziyəm], *n.* a place for physical exercise and sports. **Ex.** *On rainy days the students play games in the gymnasium.*

H

H, h [eyč¹], *n.* the eighth letter of the English alphabet.

habit (2) [hæb¹ət], *n.* 1. an act repeated so often that it is difficult to change or stop. **Ex.** *Smoking cigarettes was a* *habit he could not stop.* 2. custom; a regular practice. **Ex.** *He has a habit of rising early.* —**ha·bit'u·al,** *adj.*

habitation (5) [hæb'ətey'šən], *n.* 1. the act of inhabiting or occupying a dwelling place. **Ex.** *That old house is not suitable for habitation.* 2. a place where people live; a dwelling. **Ex.** *He walked for miles and saw no habitation.* —**hab'it·a·ble,** *adj.*

had (1) [hæd'], *v.* past tense and participle of *have.* **Ex.** *He had no money.*

haggard (5) [hæg'ərd], *adj.* having a thin, worn, ungroomed look in the face, as from suffering or anxiety. **Ex.** *He looked haggard after a sleepless night.* —**hag'gard·ly,** *adj.* —**hag'gard·ness,** *n.*

hail (3) [heyl'], *v.* greet with shouts; praise. **Ex.** *The king was hailed by his people.*

hail (3) [heyl'], *n.* small pieces of ice that fall during a storm. **Ex.** *For a short time the ground was covered with hail.* —*v.* fall as hail. **Ex.** *Suddenly stones began to hail down on us.*

hair (1) [he:r'], *n.* fine, threadlike growths forming the fur of animals or growing from the skin of human beings, especially from the head; also one of these threadlike growths. **Ex.** *The girl's hair is long and pretty.* —**hair'y,** *adj.*

HAIR

half (1) [hæf'], *n.* one of the parts of anything divided equally in two. **Ex.** *Each of the two brothers received half of the money.* —*adj.* forming one of two equal parts. **Ex.** *He owns a half share of this land.* —*adv.* partly. **Ex.** *This meat is only half cooked.*

half-wit [hæf'wit'], *n.* a person who is stupid or mentally slow.

hall (1) [hɔːl'], *n.* 1. a passage at the doorway of a building or between rooms in a building. **Ex.** *The kitchen is at the end of this hall.* 2. a large room or building for public meetings. **Ex.** *The lecture was held in the town hall.*

halt (3) [hɔːlt'], *v.* come or cause to come to a stop for a short time. **Ex.** *The marching soldiers halted.* —*n.* a stop. **Ex.** *They came to a halt at the corner and looked both ways.*

ham (4) [hæm¹], *n.* one of the rear legs of a pig, either fresh or salted and smoked, eaten as meat.

hammer (3) [hæm'ər], *n.* a tool with a head set on a handle and used for pounding nails. —*v.* 1. pound with a hammer. **Ex.** *He hammered a nail into the piece of wood.* 2. beat on something. **Ex.** *She hammered on the door until someone heard her.* —**hammer away,** work to complete. **Ex.** *He hammered away at the problem.*

HAMMER

hamper (5) [hæm'pər], *v.* hold back; make difficult; get in the way of. **Ex.** *Heavy clothing hampered the movements of the climbers.* —*n.* a basket, usually with a cover. **Ex.** *They took a hamper of food with them on their journey.*

hand (1) [hænd¹], *n.* 1. the part of the body at the end of the arm, including the fingers and thumb. 2. something similar to a hand in shape or use. **Ex.** *The hands of the clock pointed to twelve.* 3. control; care. **Ex.** *The child is in the hands of the nurse.* —*v.* give by hand; pass. **Ex.** *The nurse handed the doctor the instrument.*

HAND 1

—**at hand,** near. **Ex.** *She was at hand when he needed her.* —**by hand,** with the hands rather than by a machine. **Ex.** *She sewed the seam by hand.* —**change hands,** change ownership. —**from hand to mouth,** without anything such as food or money to spare. **Ex.** *During the depression, many people lived from hand to mouth.* —**hand down,** 1. pass along as from older to younger. 2. give a legal decision. **Ex.** *The judge handed down his ruling Monday.* —**hand in hand,** together; closely. **Ex.** *They walked hand in hand.* —**hand to hand,** very close, in fighting. —**in hand,** under control. **Ex.** *The firemen have the fire in hand.* —**on hand,** available. **Ex.** *They keep extra food on hand.* —**upper hand,** position of advantage. **Ex.** *They have the upper hand in this fight.*

handbag [hænd'bæg¹], *n.* a purse; a small suitcase. **Ex.** *She took money from her handbag.*

a, far; æ, am; e, get; ey, late; i, in; iy, see; ɔ, all; ow, go; u, put; uw, too; ə, but, ago; ər, fur; aw, out; ay, life; oy, boy; ŋ, ring; θ, think; ð, that; ž, measure; š, ship; j, edge; č, child.

handbill [hænd'bil`], *n.* a printed notice or advertisement distributed by hand. **Ex.** *The handbill said there was a special sale.*

handbook [hænd'buk`], *n.* a small book of instructions. **Ex.** *The handbook told him how to fix the car.*

handicap (4) [hænd'ikæp`], *n.* anything that is a disadvantage or that makes success difficult. **Ex.** *Lack of education can be a handicap all through life.* —*v.* make things more difficult for. **Ex.** *His illness handicaps him.*

handily [hænd'əliy], *adv.* easily. **Ex.** *He won the race handily.*

handiness [hænd'inəs], *n.* skill in using the hands. **Ex.** *Her handiness at sewing was useful to us.*

handiwork [hænd'iwərk`], *n.* work produced by using the hands. **Ex.** *Her home was filled with examples of her handiwork.*

handkerchief (2) [hæŋ'kərčəf], *n.* a square piece of cloth carried on the person for wiping the nose. **Ex.** *Do you have a clean handkerchief?*

handle (2) [hæn'dəl], *n.* that part of an object by which it is held in the hand. **Ex.** *The handle of the pot is hot.* —*v.* 1. touch or feel with the hand. **Ex.** *Handle this delicate silk carefully.* 2. control; manage. **Ex.** *She knows how to handle children.*

handout [hænd'awt`], *n.* something given free, as to the poor.

handsome (2) [hæn'səm], *adj.* 1. of fine or admirable appearance; good-looking, especially referring to men and boys. **Exs.** *He is a handsome boy. That is a handsome piece of furniture.* 2. large; generous. **Ex.** *He left a handsome fortune.* —**hand·some·ly,** *adv.* generously; in a proper manner. **Ex.** *They were handsomely rewarded for their efforts.*

handwriting (3) [hænd'rayt`iŋ], *n.* 1. writing done by hand rather than typed or printed. **Ex.** *Printing is easier to read than handwriting.* 2. the way a person writes. **Ex.** *His handwriting is improving.*

handy [hæn'diy], *adj.* 1. easily reached; not far away. **Ex.** *The store is handy.* 2. helpful; easy to use. **Ex.** *The can opener was very handy.*

hang (1) [hæŋ'], *v.* 1. fasten to a nail, hook, rope, etc., and let fall loosely. **Ex.** *Hang your coat on that hook.* 2. put or be put to death by swinging from a rope around the neck.

Ex. *The criminal was hanged in the prison yard.* —**hang'er,** *n.* a shaped support of wire or wood for hanging a garment. —**hang back,** be reluctant to go forward. **Ex.** *The others are eager to go, but she hangs back for some reason.* —**hang on,** continue to hold. **Ex.** *Hang on to this rope, and I will pull you up with it.* —**hang out,** extend out. **Ex.** *The boy was hanging out of the window.* —**hang up,** 1. put on a hanger. 2. end a telephone conversation.

happen (1) [hæp'ən], *v.* 1. occur; take place. **Ex.** *They told us everything that happened on their trip.* 2. occur by chance rather than by plan. **Ex.** *They happened to meet on the street.* —**hap'pen·ing,** *n.*

happy (1) [hæp'iy], *adj.* 1. pleased; contented; joyful. **Ex.** *We are happy to see you.* 2. fortunate; lucky. **Ex.** *He made a happy decision when he went into business.* —**hap'pi·ly,** *adv.* —**hap'pi·ness,** *n.*

harbor (2) [har'bər], *n.* a place where ships may safely anchor; a port. **Ex.** *The ship docked in the harbor.* —*v.* give shelter to. **Ex.** *They were harboring a thief.*

hard (1) [hard'], *adj.* 1. firm and solid; not soft. **Ex.** *The bread was too hard to eat.* 2. difficult. **Ex.** *This is a hard problem to solve.* 3. working steadily and with energy. **Ex.** *He is a hard worker.* 4. severe; stern. **Ex.** *He has a hard face.* —*adv.* with great energy or force. **Ex.** *He works hard.* —**hard and fast,** not changeable. **Ex.** *There are hard and fast rules.* —**hard of hearing,** not able to hear well.

hardly (2) [hard'liy], *adv.* 1. almost none. **Ex.** *There is hardly any bread in the house.* 2. possible but not likely. **Ex.** *They would hardly start on a trip in this rain.*

hardship (3) [hard'šip`], *n.* anything that causes suffering, such as hunger or pain. **Ex.** *Not having enough water was a hardship.*

hardware [hard'we:r`], *n.* objects made of metal; nails; tools; etc. **Ex.** *He bought a hammer and other hardware at the store.*

hardy (5) [har'diy], *adj.* able to live under bad conditions; strong. **Ex.** *Only hardy plants will survive the desert heat.*

harm (2) [harm'], *n.* 1. damage; hurt. **Ex.** *His delay did great harm to our plans.* 2. evil; wrong. **Ex.** *He meant no harm by* *going to see her.* —*v.* injure; damage. **Ex.** *This medicine will not harm you.* —**harm'ful,** *adj.*

harmony (4) [har'məniy], *n.* 1. agreement in feelings, ideas, or manners. **Ex.** *There was always harmony in the family.* 2. pleasing combination of parts, sounds, or colors. **Ex.** *The colors of the room were in harmony.* —**har·mo'ni·ous,** *adj.* —**har'mo·nize,** *v.*

harness (3) [har'nis], *n.* a device made of long pieces of leather and metal rings with which a horse or other work animal is fastened to a wagon or plow. —*v.* 1. put such a device on. 2. control to make use of the power of. **Ex.** *The dam harnessed the water power of the river.*

harp (4) [harp'], *n.* a stringed musical instrument, played with the fingers. —**harp'ist,** *n.* one who plays the harp.

harsh (4) [harš'], *adj.* 1. rough, unpleasant, or sharp to one of the senses. **Ex.** *He has a harsh voice.* 2. cruel; severe; stern. **Ex.** *Her parents were very harsh.* —**harsh'ly,** *adv.* —**harsh'ness,** *n.*

HARP

harvest (2) [har'vəst], *n.* 1. the gathering in of crops. **Ex.** *Many men were needed to help with the harvest.* 2. the crop itself. **Ex.** *The harvest was plentiful this year.* —*v.* gather crops. **Ex.** *The farmer harvested his wheat.* —**har'vest·er,** *n.* 1. one who harvests. 2. a machine for harvesting.

has (1) [hæz'], *v.* present tense of *have* used with he, she, it, and singular nouns. **Ex.** *The girl has more interesting ideas than he has.*

haste (3) [heyst'], *n.* a hurry; a rush. **Ex.** *They left in haste for the airport.* —**hast'en,** *v.* move or act quickly; hurry. **Ex.** *He hastened to the train station.* —**hast'y,** *adj.* —**hast'i·ly,** *adv.* —**make haste,** hurry. **Ex.** *Make haste, or we will be late.*

hat (1) [hæt'], *n.* a covering for the head. —**pass the hat,** ask for money. **Ex.** *He passed the hat for the poor people.* —**take one's hat off to,** admire; express approval. **Ex.** *I take off my hat to those who won the race.*

HAT

hatch (4) [hæč'], *v.* bring forth young from the egg. **Ex.** *The hen hatched ten chickens.* —**hatch'er·y,** *n.* a place for hatching. **Ex.** *He received baby chicks from the hatchery.*

hatch (4) [hæč'], *n.* an opening in the deck of a ship. Ex. *Close the hatches during the storm.*

hatchet (5) [hæč'ət], *n.* a small, short-handled ax which can be used with one hand.

HATCHET

hate (2) [heyt'], *v.* 1. have strong feelings against; regard as an enemy. Ex. *Most people hate war.* 2. be unwilling; not like. Ex. *I hate to trouble you with my problems.* —*n.* a strong feeling against. Ex. *There was nothing but hate in his heart.* —**ha'tred,** *n.* a strong hate.

haughty (5) [hɔ:'tiy], *adj.* having too much pride; thinking little of others and too much of oneself. Ex. *She gave him a haughty look.* —**haugh'ti·ly,** *adv.* —**haugh'ti·ness,** *n.*

haul (4) [hɔ:l'], *v.* 1. move by pulling or dragging with force. Ex. *They hauled the small boat up on the beach.* 2. move or carry from one place to another in a truck, wagon, etc. Ex. *That company hauls furniture at a reasonable rate.*

haunt (3) [hɔ:nt'], *v.* 1. visit often, especially as a ghost. Ex. *That house is said to be haunted by a ghost.* 2. return often to a place or to the mind. Ex. *Memories of poverty haunted her.* —*n.* a place where one spends or has spent much time. Ex. *The museum is his favorite haunt.*

have (1) [hæv'], *v.* 1. possess; own; hold. Ex. *I have a car.* 2. contain. Ex. *A day has twenty-four hours.* 3. get; receive; take. Ex. *Will you have dinner now?* 4. experience; engage in; perform. Ex. *We had a good time at the party.* 5. hold in the mind or memory; feel. Ex. *We have some doubts about him.* —**have on,** be wearing. Ex. *The clothes I have on are dirty.*

hawk (4) [hɔ:k'], *n.* any of a large family of birds that lives by eating other birds and animals.

hay (3) [hey'], *n.* grass cut and dried for use as feed for animals. Ex. *The hay was stored in the barn.*

hazard (5) [hæz'ərd], *n.* danger; peril; risk. Ex. *The ice on the roads is a hazard for driving.* —*v.* 1. dare to offer. Ex. *May I hazard a suggestion?* 2. risk. Ex. *The pilot hazarded his life for the safety of the passengers.* —**haz'ard·ous,** *adj.*

---

a, far; æ, am; e, get; ey, late; i, in; iy, see; ɔ, all; ow, go; u, put; uw, too; ə, but, ago; ər, fur; aw, out; ay, life; oy, boy; ŋ, ring; θ, think; ð, that; ž, measure; š, ship; j, edge; č, child.

he (1) [hiy'], *pron.* a male person or animal that has already been mentioned or that is understood. **Ex.** *My brother is not here. He is at work.*

head (1) [hed'], *n.* 1. the upper part of the human body and of most animals containing the brain, mouth, eyes, ears, etc., and joined to the lower part of the body by the neck. 2. a position of leadership or command; chief. **Ex.** *He is the head of the school.* 3. the top part of anything. **Ex.** *Hit the nail on the head.* 4. the front; the highest position. **Ex.** *She is at the head of her class.* 5. mind; intelligence. **Ex.** *He has a good head for science.* —*v.* 1. lead; command. **Ex.** *He heads the city government.* 2. go to or be at the front, head, or top of. **Ex.** *Your name heads the list.* —**head off**, get ahead of and stop. **Ex.** *Head him off before he falls in the hole.* —**keep one's head** or **lose one's head**, keep or lose control of one's thoughts and actions. **Ex.** *He lost his head during the fire.* —**over one's head,** too difficult to understand. **Ex.** *This problem is over my head.* —**turn one's head,** make one feel too proud. **Ex.** *Their flattery turned her head.*

headlight [hed'layt'], *n.* light on the front of a car, truck, etc. **Ex.** *Turn on your headlights during the rain.*

headline [hed'layn'], *n.* large words printed at the top of a story in a newspaper. **Ex.** *He reads the headlines first.*

headlong [hed'lɔːŋ'], *adj., adv.* with the head first. **Ex.** *He jumped headlong into the water.*

head-on [hed'an', hed'ɔːn'], *adj., adv.* with the front part forward. **Ex.** *The cars hit each other head-on.*

headquarters (5) [hed'kwɔr'tərz], *n.* any center from which orders are issued. **Ex.** *Many policemen work at police headquarters.*

headstrong [hed'strɔːŋ'], *adj.* doing what one wants to do despite what others advise. **Ex.** *He is so headstrong that he is often in trouble.*

headway [hed'wey'], *n.* forward movement; progress. **Ex.** *Because of the snow, we made little headway.*

heal (2) [hiyl'], *v.* 1. return to good health; cure. **Ex.** *The doctor healed the sick man.* 2. become well. **Ex.** *The cut healed quickly.*

health (1) [helθ'], *n.* 1. the condition of being free from sickness. **Ex.** *He has regained his health.* 2. general condition of the body and mind. **Ex.** *She is in poor health.* —**health'y,** *adj.* having or showing good health.

heap (3) [hiyp¹], *n.* a number of things lying one on top of another; a pile. **Ex.** *A heap of stones blocked the road.* —*v.* 1. gather, put, or throw in a heap; pile. **Ex.** *She heaped the clothes together.* 2. give in great quantities. **Ex.** *The mother heaped the child's plate with food.*

hear (1) [hi:r¹], *v.* 1. notice or perceive by ear. **Ex.** *Do you hear a strange sound?* 2. listen to; pay attention to. **Ex.** *He does not hear my explanation.* 3. receive news or information. **Ex.** *Did you hear about the fire?*

heard (1) [hərd¹], *v.* past tense and participle of *hear.* **Ex.** *We heard about your accident.*

heart (1) [hart¹], *n.* 1. an organ that pumps blood to all parts of the body. 2. this organ considered as the center of life, thought, and honest feeling. **Ex.** *He spoke from the heart.* 3. the breast. **Ex.** *She pressed the child to her heart.* 4. the center or middle part of anything. **Ex.** *They lived in the heart of town.* 5. the most important part. **Ex.** *Your words go to the heart of the matter.* —**heart'i·ly,** *adv.* —**heart'y,** *adj.* —**at heart,** in the center of one's feelings. **Ex.** *At heart, he was still a child.* —**by heart,** by memorizing; from memory. **Ex.** *He knew the words of the song by heart.* —**change of heart,** change of mind or view. **Ex.** *He had a change of heart and went with us.* —**take heart,** receive encouragement; become hopeful. **Ex.** *We took heart when we heard you were coming.* —**take to heart,** be very serious about. **Ex.** *We took his advice to heart.*

hearth (4) [harθ¹], *n.* 1. the floor of a fireplace, usually brick or stone. **Ex.** *A fire was burning on the hearth.* 2. home; the fireside. **Ex.** *They spent the holidays at the family hearth.*

heat (1) [hiyt¹], *n.* 1. great warmth. **Ex.** *The heat of the sun dried the wet clothes.* 2. very warm weather or climate. **Ex.** *They do not mind the summer heat.* 3. warmth of feeling. **Ex.** *He said sharp words in the heat of the argument.* 4. warmth supplied for a room or house. **Ex.** *We use gas for heat.* —*v.* cause to be hot; become hot. **Ex.** *The water heated rapidly.*

heat wave [hiyt¹ weyv¹], a period of very hot weather. **Ex.** *The heat wave lasted two weeks this summer.*

heave (4) [hiyv¹], *v.* 1. raise or lift with great effort. **Ex.** *The fat man heaved himself to his feet.* 2. utter with great effort or painfully. **Ex.** *She heaved a sigh of relief.* 3. rise and fall, as does the chest in heavy breathing. **Ex.** *Her breast heaved with sobs.*

heaven (1) [hev'ən], *n.* in some religions, the place where gods and spirits are said to dwell. —**heav'en·ly,** *adj.* —**the heavens,** the sky. **Ex.** *Millions of stars shone in the heavens.*

heavy (1) [hev'iy], *adj.* 1. of great weight; not easy to lift. **Ex.** *He carried a heavy load.* 2. of great amount or force. **Ex.** *A heavy rain fell today.* 3. burdensome. **Ex.** *Our taxes are heavy.* 4. full of sorrow. **Ex.** *Her heart was heavy because of her loss.* —**heav'i·ly,** *adv.* —**heav'i·ness,** *n.*

hedge (4) [hej'], *n.* a row of bushes which forms a fence. **Ex.** *There was a hedge in front of the house.* —*v.* avoid being honest and direct. **Ex.** *She hedged when I asked her age.*

heel (2) [hiyl'], *n.* 1. the part of the foot which is below and in back of the ankle. 2. that part of the sock, stocking, or shoe that covers the heel. **Ex.** *There is a hole in the heel of his sock.*

height (1) [hayt'], *n.* 1. distance upward from the ground; distance from bottom to top. **Ex.** *His height is six feet three inches.* 2. state of being high. **Ex.** *Some people are afraid of great height.* 3. highest point; peak. **Ex.** *He died at the height of his career.*

heir (4) [e:r'], *n.* the person who receives or has the right to receive another person's property when that person dies. **Ex.** *When he died, his son was his only heir.*

held (1) [held'], *v.* past tense and participle of *hold.* **Ex.** *He held her hand tightly.*

hell (2) [hel'], *n.* 1. in some religions, a place or state of punishment of the wicked after death; a place where evil spirits are thought to dwell. 2. any state of great pain or suffering. **Ex.** *It is hell on earth to live with a guilty conscience.* —**hell'ish,** *adj.*

hello (1) [helow', həlow'], *interj.* a word used to greet someone or to attract attention. **Ex.** *Hello, sir; I am glad to see you.*

helmet (4) [hel'mət], *n.* a covering to protect the head, often made of metal or other strong material.

help (1) [help'], *v.* 1. aid; assist. **Ex.** *Please help me with the work.* 2. give relief to. **Ex.** *This medicine will help to cure your illness.* 3. prevent; avoid. **Ex.** *He could not help arriving*

late. 4. serve; wait on. **Ex.** *The waiter helped us to the meat.*
—*n.* aid or assistance. **Ex.** *I came to offer my help.*
—**help'er,** *n.* —**help out,** assist. **Ex.** *She helped out when
we were very busy.*

hem (4) [hem'], *n.* a folded edge on a garment made by turning back the material and sewing it in place. —*v.* 1. make
a hem in. **Ex.** *The dress was hemmed by hand.* 2. block on
all sides; surround. **Ex.** *His car was hemmed in by traffic.*

hen (3) [hen'], *n.* a female chicken. **Ex.** *We raised hens to
get eggs.*

her (1) [hə:r'], *pron.* 1. form of *she* used as the object of a
verb or preposition. **Ex.** *She is not home now; please come
to visit her later.* 2. form of *she* used to show ownership.
Ex. *That is her book.*

herb (4) [ərb', hərb'], *n.* one of a group of plants used in
medicine or in flavoring food. **Ex.** *We like to use herbs in
cooking.*

herd (3) [hərd'], *n.* a number of large animals gathered
together. **Ex.** *We saw a herd of cattle.* —*v.* 1. cause to move
in a group. **Ex.** *He herds his sheep from one place to
another.* 2. go in a herd. **Ex.** *The people herded together
for safety.*

here (1) [hi:r'], *adv.* 1. in this place. **Ex.** *The book is right
here.* 2. to this place. **Ex.** *Please come here.* —*n.* this place.
Ex. *It is hot in here.*

hereabout [hi:r'əbawt'], *adv.* near here. **Ex.** *They have been
seen hereabout.*

hereafter [hi:r'æf'tər], *adv.* after this time. **Ex.** *Hereafter, I
will do the work myself.*

hereby [hi:r'bay', hi:r'bay'], *adv.* by means of this letter, these
words, etc. **Ex.** *I hereby give you my permission.*

heretofore [hi:r'təfɔr'], *adv.* until now. **Ex.** *Heretofore, I did
all the work.*

herewith [hi:r'wiθ', hi:r'wið'], *adv.* with this letter, message,
etc. **Ex.** *I send you the money herewith.*

heritage (5) [he:r'ətij], *n.* that received from one's ancestors,
such as traditions, ideals, and rights. **Ex.** *Free education is
an American heritage.*

---

a, far; æ, am; e, get; ey, late; i, in; iy, see; ɔ, all; ow, go; u, put; uw, too;
ə, but, ago; ər, fur; aw, out; ay, life; oy, boy; ŋ, ring; θ, think; ð, that;
ž, measure; š, ship; j, edge; č, child.

hermit (4) [hər'mət], *n.* one who leaves society and lives alone, especially for reasons of religion. **Ex.** *A hermit lives in that forest.*

hero (2) [hi:r'ow, hiy'row], *n.* 1. a man of great courage; a man who has done a brave deed. **Ex.** *He was a war hero.* 2. one greatly admired by others; one looked upon as a model. **Ex.** *The father was a hero to his son.* 3. the principal male character in a story, poem, or play. **Ex.** *The hero of this novel is a doctor.* —**he·ro'ic**, *adj.* —**her'o·ism**, *n.*

herring (5) [her'iŋ], *n.* a small fish caught in the North Atlantic and used for food.

hers (1) [hərz'], *pron.* belonging to her. **Ex.** *This book is hers.*

herself (2) [hərself'], *pron.* 1. her own self. **Ex.** *She fell and hurt herself.* 2. her usual self. **Ex.** *She is behaving strangely; she is not herself today.*

hesitate (2) [hez'əteytˑ], *v.* wait, as if uncertain; pause because of doubts. **Ex.** *He hesitated before crossing the street.* —**hes'i·tant**, *adj.* —**hes'i·ta'tion**, *n.*

hid (2) [hid'], *v.* past tense of *hide.* **Ex.** *He hid the money in a book.* —**hid'den**, *v.* past participle of *hide.* **Ex.** *The treasure had been hidden long ago.*

hide (2) [hayd'], *v.* 1. place something where it cannot be seen or found; conceal. **Ex.** *The child was hiding under the bed.* 2. keep secret. **Ex.** *She tried to hide her feelings from everyone.*

hide (2) [hayd'], *n.* the skin of an animal. **Ex.** *Fur coats are made of animal hides.*

hideous (4) [hid'iyəs], *adj.* extremely ugly; frightful; morally shocking. **Ex.** *That was a hideous crime.* —**hid'e·ous·ly**, *adv.* —**hid'e·ous·ness**, *n.*

high (1) [hay'], *adj.* 1. tall; extending far upward. **Ex.** *This is a high building.* 2. at some distance above the ground. **Ex.** *The plane is high above the city.* 3. sharp; raised in tone. **Ex.** *She spoke in a high voice.* 4. of superior rank, character, kind. **Exs.** *He is a high official. He has very high ideals.* 5. more than usual; greater in degree. **Exs.** *The child has a high fever. The automobile was traveling at a high speed.* 6. very serious; grave. **Ex.** *The official was removed for high crimes against the state.* 7. expensive. **Ex.** *He paid a high price for the car.* —*adv.* at or to a high place, level, rank, or degree. **Ex.** *The airplane flew high above the clouds.*

—**high'ly,** *adv.* 1. in or to a high degree; greatly. **Ex.** *Her story was highly unlikely.* 2. with high praise. **Ex.** *They spoke highly of his work.* 3. at or in a high position, rank, price, etc. **Exs.** *He is a highly placed officer. He is a highly paid writer.*

highhanded [hay'hæn'dəd], *adj.* without concern for others. **Ex.** *He acted in a very highhanded way.*

highlight [hay'layt'], *v.* point out; feature. **Ex.** *He highlighted the picture by placing it in the window.* —*n.* the important or best part. **Ex.** *He described the highlights of the book.*

high school [hay' skuwl'], a school of the tenth, eleventh, and twelfth years of study, and sometimes the ninth.

high seas [hay' siyz'], *n.* that part of the sea or ocean that does not belong to any country.

high-strung [hay'strəŋ'], *adj.* nervous; alert; tense.

highway (3) [hay'wey'], *n.* an important road. **Ex.** *That highway crosses the entire country.*

high time [hay' taym'], a time that is almost too late. **Ex.** *It is high time you arrived.*

hike (4) [hayk'], *v.* walk a great distance, especially in the woods or country. **Ex.** *The boys hiked through the woods.* —*n.* a walk of some distance, especially in the woods or the country. —**hik'er,** *n.* one who hikes.

hill (1) [hil'], *n.* high rounded land that is not as high as a mountain. **Ex.** *The mountain was surrounded by low hills.* —**hill'y,** *adj.* having many hills.

him (1) [him'], *pron.* form of *he* used as the object of a verb or preposition. **Ex.** *He was away at the time we wanted to see him.*

himself (2) [himself'], *pron.* 1. his own self. **Ex.** *He looked at himself in the mirror.* 2. his usual self. **Ex.** *He is very unhappy today; he is not himself.*

hind (3) [haynd'], *adj.* located toward or in the back or rear. **Ex.** *The horse rose on its hind legs.*

hinder (4) [hin'dər], *v.* 1. interrupt; delay. **Ex.** *The constant ringing of the telephone hinders my work.* 2. stop; prevent from acting. **Ex.** *There is nothing to hinder you from leaving now.* —**hin'drance,** *n.*

hindsight [hayn(d)'sayt'], *n.* knowing what should have been done when it is too late. **Ex.** *Hindsight did not help him to recover the money he had lost.*

hinge (4) [hinĵ'], *n.* a joint, usually of metal, used on a door to enable it to open and shut, and on a box, trunk, etc. to allow the top or lid to be raised and lowered. —*v.* furnish with a hinge or hinges.

HINGE

hint (3) [hint'], *n.* 1. indirect suggestion. **Ex.** *He ignored her hint that he leave.* 2. slight trace; slight suggestion. **Ex.** *There was a hint of winter in the air.* —*v.* make an indirect suggestion. **Ex.** *He hinted that he needed money.*

hip (4) [hip'], *n.* that part of the human body projecting on both sides just below the waist and above the upper legs.

hire (2) [hayr'], *v.* obtain the services of a person or the use of a thing for pay. **Ex.** *They hired several new workers.*

his (1) [hiz'], *pron.* belonging to him. **Ex.** *That brown hat is his.*

history (1) [his't(ə)riy], *n.* 1. the written record of the past. **Ex.** *Abraham Lincoln is a famous person in history.* 2. the branch of knowledge that records and explains past events. **Ex.** *She is studying history.* 3. a long story or tale. **Ex.** *He told us the history of that old house.* —**his·tor'ic**, *adj.* —**his·to'ri·an**, *n.* one who writes or is an expert in history.

hit (1) [hit'], *v.* 1. strike; give a blow. **Ex.** *The boy hit his little brother.* 2. strike with force. **Ex.** *The car hit the tree.* 3. reach or strike by throwing or shooting. **Ex.** *The bursting shell hit his shoulder.* —*n.* a blow, especially one that reaches the object aimed at. —**hit it off**, work well together; like each other.

hitch (5) [hič'], *v.* tie; fasten, as with a rope. **Ex.** *He hitched the horse to the post.*

hive (5) [hayv'], *n.* 1. a box or cover for honeybees. 2. a colony of honeybees living in such a box or cover. **Ex.** *The farmer had three hives of bees.*

hoard (5) [hord'], *n.* a supply for future use, especially a secret one. **Ex.** *He had a hoard of food in his cellar.* —*v.* pile up; keep for future use. **Ex.** *When sugar, coffee, and other foods were scarce, many people hoarded them.* —**hoard'er**, *n.*

hoarse (5) [hors'], *adj.* rough and deep in sound, as the voice of a person with a cold. **Ex.** *He shouted until he was hoarse.* —**hoarse'ly**, *adv.* —**hoarse'ness**, *n.*

hobby (5) [hab'iy], *n.* an activity done in one's spare time for pleasure. **Ex.** *Stamp collecting was his hobby.*

hoe (5) [how'], *n.* a long-handled tool with a flat blade at one end for digging in the garden. —*v.* use the hoe.

hog (4) [hag', hɔːg'], *n.* a large, fully grown pig, raised for its meat.

hoist (4) [hoyst'], *v.* raise or lift, especially by a mechanical device. **Ex.** *The ship hoisted anchor.* —*n.* a mechanical device for lifting. **Ex.** *We need a hoist to lift the boat out of the water.*

HOE

hold (1) [howld'], *v.* 1. grasp and keep in the hands or arms. **Ex.** *Please hold this package.* 2. keep in a certain position. **Ex.** *Please hold the door open.* 3. possess; keep. **Ex.** *I will hold this land for my children.* 4. contain. **Ex.** *This bottle holds one quart of oil.* 5. possess; occupy. **Ex.** *He holds the rank of captain.* 6. engage in; conduct. **Ex.** *They are holding a meeting.* 7. keep with an effort. **Ex.** *The soldiers held the fort against attack.* —*n.* 1. the act of holding or grasping. **Ex.** *Get a good hold on this rope.* 2. a controlling force; a strong influence. **Ex.** *The general has a powerful hold on the country.* 3. the lower part of a ship in which the load is carried. —**hold forth,** talk for a long time. **Ex.** *He held forth about guns for an hour.* —**hold off,** keep away. **Ex.** *The soldiers held off the enemy.* —**hold on,** continue to hold; keep in one place. **Ex.** *Hold on to him for an hour if you can.* —**hold up,** 1. prevent from falling. 2. rob. **Ex.** *The robbers held us up with guns and took our money.*

holdings [howld'iŋz], *n.* anything one owns such as land, stocks and bonds, etc. **Ex.** *He has large holdings in that country.*

hole (1) [howl'], *n.* 1. a torn or broken place in something; a tear. **Ex.** *There is a hole in your dress.* 2. a hollow place in the ground. **Ex.** *The rabbit went into his hole.*

holiday (2) [hal'ədey'], *n.* 1. any day on which one does not work; vacation. **Ex.** *We spent our holiday at the seashore.* 2. a day on which no business is done in memory of some event or person. **Ex.** *New Year's Day is a legal holiday in* *the United States. —adj.* joyful; gay. **Ex.** *People were in a holiday mood.*

hollow (2) [hal'ow], *adj.* 1. having a hole within; empty. **Ex.** *The fox hid in the hollow tree.* 2. having a depression or low place. **Ex.** *The car bumped over the hollow spot in the road.* 3. having a dull sound; empty sounding. **Ex.** *The barrel made a hollow sound when tapped.* 4. with no real meaning; empty; false. **Ex.** *She gave her enemy hollow praise.* **—hollow out,** *v.* make or become hollow. **Ex.** *He hollowed out a stick of wood to make a whistle.*

holy (2) [how'liy], *adj.* 1. reserved for purposes of religion or worship. **Ex.** *This building is a holy place.* 2. pure in heart; saintly. **Ex.** *He is a holy man.* **—ho'li·ness,** *n.*

homage (5) [ham'ij, am'ij], *n.* respect or honor, shown or given to another. **Ex.** *Our homage is due the men who died for us in battle.*

home (1) [howm'], *n.* 1. the place where a person lives. **Ex.** *Do you own your home?* 2. the family group. **Ex.** *He came from a happy home.* 3. one's native country or place; the place where one was born or brought up. **Ex.** *His home is the United States.* **—adj.** connected with the home; domestic. **Ex.** *He enjoyed home life after living in a hotel.* **—adv.** to, toward, or at home. **Ex.** *He will be home all evening.*

homely (4) [howm'liy], *adj.* 1. not good-looking; ugly. **Ex.** *She is a homely woman.* 2. plain; simple. **Ex.** *The food was homely but filling.* **—home'li·ness,** *n.*

homesick (3) [howm'sik'], *adj.* longing for home. **Ex.** *They were homesick for their own country.* **—home'sick·ness,** *n.*

honest (2) [an'əst], *adj.* 1. truthful; able to be trusted. **Ex.** *He is an honest person.* 2. having or giving full worth or value. **Ex.** *He did an honest day's work.* 3. open and frank. **Ex.** *The boy had an honest face.* **—hon'est·ly,** *adv.* **—hon'es·ty,** *n.*

honey (2) [hən'iy], *n.* 1. a sweet, thick fluid produced by bees from the liquid they gather from flowers. 2. darling; a term of affection. **Ex.** *He always called her "Honey."*

honeymoon [hən'iymuwn'], *n.* a trip taken by newly married persons soon after the wedding. **Ex.** *They went to the mountains for their honeymoon.*

honor (1) [an'ər], *n.* 1. fame; glory; public respect. **Ex.** *He* *held a place of honor in his town.* 2. something given as a sign or mark of respect. **Ex.** *The soldier was given a medal of honor.* 3. good reputation. **Ex.** *He was a man of honor.* 4. source of credit; glory. **Ex.** *She was an honor to the school.* 5. a title of respect given to public officials. **Ex.** *His Honor, the Judge, is entering the courtroom.* 6. a strong sense of right to which one is true. **Ex.** *Her honor kept her from accepting the gift.* —*v.* 1. hold in high respect. **Ex.** *We should honor our parents.* 2. give honor to. **Ex.** *They honored the returning hero.* —**hon'or·a·ble,** *adj.* —**hon'or·ar`y,** *adj.* given as an honor.

hood (4) [hud'], *n.* 1. a soft covering for the head and neck, sometimes attached to a coat. 2. anything that covers. **Ex.** *He lifted the hood of the car engine to see what was wrong.*

-hood (2) [hud], *suffix.* 1. members of a group. **Ex.** *Priest; priesthood.* 2. state of being. **Ex.** *Mother; motherhood.*

hoof (3) [huf'], *n.* the foot or hard covering on the feet of horses, cattle, pigs, and some other animals.

hook (2) [huk'], *n.* a curved piece of metal, wood, etc. for catching or holding something. —*v.* fasten or catch with a hook. **Ex.** *He hooked a big fish out of the stream.*

HOOK

hop (3) [hap'], *v.* 1. make short leaps on one foot. **Ex.** *The children hopped down the street.* 2. move by jumps. **Ex.** *The bird hopped about on the ground.* —*n.* a short leap.

hope (1) [howp'], *n.* 1. a desire that one expects will be fulfilled. **Ex.** *He has great hopes of success.* 2. a person or thing on which one bases hope. **Ex.** *This plan is our last hope for an agreement.* 3. the thing hoped for. **Ex.** *His hope is to go to college.* —*v.* desire something with confidence that it will happen; expect. **Ex.** *I hope you will come again soon.* —**hope'ful,** *adj.* feeling or causing hope.

horizon (3) [həray'zən], *n.* 1. the line where the sky and earth appear to meet. **Ex.** *We saw a ship on the horizon.* 2. the limit of knowledge; experience. **Ex.** *Young people seek new horizons.*

horizontal (3) [hɔr`əzan'təl], *adj.* on the same line as the horizon; sideways; not up and down. **Ex.** *The horizontal lines on the paper are an inch apart.* —**hor`i·zon'tal·ly,** *adv.*

horn (2) [hɔrn'], *n.* 1. hard, bonelike growths, which are often curved and pointed, on the heads of cattle, goats, and some other animals. 2. anything made of horn. **Ex.** *His eyeglass frames are made of horn.* 3. a musical instrument, usually made of brass, played by blowing air through it. 4. any device that makes a loud noise as a warning. **Ex.** *We stepped back as we heard the automobile horn.*

HORN 1

HORN 3

horrible (3) [hɔːr'əbəl, har'əbəl], *adj.* causing great fear; ugly. **Ex.** *He has a horrible cut on his face.*

horrid (5) [hɔːr'əd, har'əd], *adj.* terrible; dreadful; shocking; causing horror. **Ex.** *The accident was a horrid experience.*

horror (3) [hɔːr'ər, har'ər], *n.* 1. a painful feeling of great fear. **Ex.** *She drew back in horror at the sight.* 2. anything that causes such a feeling. **Ex.** *He had not forgotten the horrors of war.* 3. a painful or very strong feeling of not liking. **Ex.** *He had a horror of great heights.*

horse (1) [hɔrs'], *n.* a large animal used by man for working and riding.

horsepower [hɔrs'pawr'], *n.* a measure of the power of engines. One horsepower will raise 33,000 pounds one foot in a minute. **Ex.** *This car has a 200-horsepower engine.*

HORSE

hose (5) [howz'], *n.* 1. an easily bent tube, usually of rubber or plastic, through which liquid can flow. **Ex.** *Water from the fire hoses poured into the burning house.* 2. a covering for the legs and feet; stockings. **Ex.** *She bought a pair of black hose.* —*v.* water or wash by means of a hose. **Ex.** *The boy hosed the garden.*

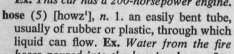

hospital (2) [has'pitəl], *n.* a place where sick or injured people are given medical care. **Ex.** *The sick man was sent to the hospital.* —**hos'pi·tal·ize'**, *v.* put in a hospital.

hospitality (5) [has'pətæl'ətiy], *n.* kind and generous treatment of guests. **Ex.** *He is known for his hospitality.* —**hos·pi'ta·ble,** *adj.*

host (3) [howst'], *n.* 1. one who receives guests in his home. **Ex.** *He was a wonderful host.* 2. a man in charge of a hotel or eating place. —**hos'tess,** *n.* a female host.

hostile (4) [has'təl], *adj.* 1. ready for war; in a warlike man-

ner. Ex. *A hostile attack was expected during the night.*
2. unfriendly. Ex. *The student was hostile to the teacher.*
—hos'tile·ly, *adv.* —hos·til'i·ty, *n.*

hot (1) [hat'], *adj.* 1. extremely warm. Ex. *The tea is too hot
for me to drink.* 2. burning to the taste. Ex. *Pepper is hot.*
3. quick; excited; full of passion. Ex. *He has a hot temper.*

hotbed [hat'bed'], *n.* a place or conditions which favor growth
or much activity. Ex. *Areas of poor housing are hotbeds of
crime.*

hotel (2) [howtel'], *n.* an establishment or building that provides room and food to travelers for pay. Ex. *We stayed at
some nice hotels on our trip.*

hotheaded [hat'hed'əd], *adj.* quick to anger. Ex. *He is so hotheaded that he is always in a fight.* —hot'head, *n.* one who
is quick to anger.

hothouse [hat'haws'], *n.* a building made mostly of glass in
which plants and flowers are grown.

hound (4) [hawnd'], *n.* 1. a dog with a sharp sense of smell,
used in hunting. 2. any dog. Ex. *He is just a hound.* —*v.*
hunt with hounds or as with hounds; pursue without stopping. Ex. *His creditors were hounding him for money.*

hour (1) [awr'], *n.* 1. 60 minutes. Ex. *The trip is two hours
long.* 2. a particular or appointed time. Ex. *At what hour
did you see him?* 3. the time. Ex. *The hour was late when
he returned.* —hour'ly, *adv.*

house (1) [haws'], *n.* 1. a building in which people live. Ex.
They live in a large house. 2. a structure for sheltering or
storing something such as goods or animals. Ex. *The boys
are building a dog house.* —*v.* provide with shelter. Ex. *The
horses were housed in a new stable.*

housebreaking [haws'breyk'iŋ], *n.* the act of entering the house
of another for the purpose of robbing or committing some
other crime. Ex. *He was sent to prison for housebreaking.*
—house'break'er, *n.*

household (2) [haws'howld'], *n.* all of the people, as a group,
who live together in one house. Ex. *The household was
awake at seven in the morning.* —*adj.* referring to things of

a, far; æ, am; e, get; ey, late; i, in; iy, see; ɔ, all; ow, go; u, put; uw, too;
ə, but, ago; ər, fur; aw, out; ay, life; oy, boy; ŋ, ring; θ, think; ð, that;
ž, measure; š, ship; j, edge; č, child.

the house; domestic. **Ex.** *The household expenses were high.*
—**house'hold`er**, *n.* one who lives in a house.

housekeeper [haws'kiyp`ər], *n.* one who is hired to take care of a house. **Ex.** *Since the mother worked in an office, she hired a housekeeper for her home.*

House of Representatives [haws' əv rep`rizen'tətivz], the lower and larger branch of the American Congress and legislative groups of other governments.

housewife [haws'wayf`], *n.* the female head of a household; a woman who manages her own home. **Ex.** *She is an excellent housewife.*

housing [hawz'iŋ], *n.* 1. the act of providing a place to live. **Ex.** *The housing of such a large group will be difficult.* 2. houses; a place to live. **Ex.** *Housing is expensive in this city.*

how (1) [haw'], *adv.* 1. in what way or manner. **Ex.** *Do you know how to swim?* 2. to what extent, degree, or amount. **Ex.** *How much time do we have?* 3. in what condition. **Ex.** *How are you?*

however (1) [haw`ev'ər], *conj.* nevertheless; yet; in spite of that. **Ex.** *He does not think he will succeed; however, he will try.* —*adv.* in what way; by what means. **Ex.** *However can I repay you?*

howl (3) [hawl'], *v.* 1. make a long, loud, sad cry, as the cry of a wolf or a dog. **Ex.** *The dogs were howling at the moon.* 2. make a similar cry in anger, pain, etc. **Ex.** *The baby howled for food.* 3. make a sound like an animal or human howling. —*n.* a long, loud, sad cry. **Ex.** *We heard the howl of a wolf in the distance.*

huddle (5) [həd'əl], *v.* 1. crowd together. **Ex.** *Four people were huddled under one umbrella.* 2. draw oneself in as though to make oneself small. **Ex.** *She was huddled in the corner of a big chair.* —*n.* a confused heap or crowd. **Ex.** *There was a huddle of people at the entrance.*

hue (5) [hyuw'], *n.* a color or shade of color. **Ex.** *The room was decorated in various hues of blue, ranging from light to dark.*

hug (4) [həg'], *v.* hold tightly in the arms; embrace. **Ex.** *The mother hugged her lost child.* —*n.* a tight hold with the arms; a close embrace. **Ex.** *She gave him a sisterly hug.*

huge (2) [hyuwj'], *adj.* of great size. **Ex.** *The huge buildings seem to touch the sky.*

hum (4) [həm'], *v.* 1. make a low, steady sound like a bee fly-ing. Ex. *The sewing machine hummed as she sewed.* 2. sing with closed lips and without forming words. Ex. *She hummed as she worked.* —*n.* wordless murmur; low, steady sound. Ex. *We heard the hum of voices in the next room.*

human (1) [hyuw'mən], *adj.* 1. of, like, or referring to man. Ex. *The human body needs care.* 2. being a man; consisting of men. Ex. *The human race includes all men.* —**hu'man·ly,** *adv.* —**hu·man'i·ty,** *n.* 1. all human beings; the human race. 2. kindness. Ex. *They treated the prisoners with humanity.* —**hu·man'i·tar'i·an,** *n.* one who is concerned with and tries to improve the welfare of human beings. —*adj.*

human being [hyuw'mən biy'iŋ], a person.

humble (2) [həm'bəl], *adj.* 1. of low rank or position; plain; simple. Ex. *He came from a humble home.* 2. modest; with-out false pride; not proud. Ex. *He was a humble man.* —*v.* bring low; lower oneself in importance, dignity, or condi-tion. Ex. *She humbled herself to ask forgiveness.* —**hum'bly,** *adv.*

humiliate (5) [hyuwmil'iyeyt'], *v.* cause to lose pride and self-respect, especially in the presence of others. Ex. *She was humiliated by her daughter's rudeness.* —**hu·mil'i·a'tion,** *n.*

humor (2) [hyuw'mər], *n.* 1. the quality of causing amuse-ment. Ex. *This story is full of humor.* 2. the way one feels; mood. Ex. *He is in a bad humor today.* 3. the ability to understand, enjoy, or express what is funny or amusing. Ex. *It takes a sense of humor to be able to laugh at oneself.* —*v.* agree with every wish of a person. Ex. *It is often best to humor sick people.* —**hu'mor·ist,** *n.* —**hu'mor·ous,** *adj.*

hundred (1) [hən'drəd], *n., adj.* the number which comes after 99; the number *100.* —**hun'dredth,** *adj.* coming after ninety-nine others.

hung (2) [həŋ'], past tense and participle of *hang.* Ex. *He has hung his coat in the closet.*

hunger (1) [həŋ'gər], *n.* 1. the unpleasant feeling or weakness caused by the need for food. Ex. *He was so aware of his hunger that he could not study.* 2. the need for food. Ex. *He died of hunger.* 3. a strong desire. Ex. *She felt a hunger for good music.* —*v.* 1. need food; be hungry. Ex. *They hun-gered for a good meal.* 2. have an eager desire. Ex. *He* *hungered for fame.* —**hun'gry,** *adj.* 1. needing food; feeling hunger. Ex. *The child is hungry.* 2. desiring strongly; eager. Ex. *They are hungry for knowledge.* —**hun'gri·ly,** *adv.*

hunt (1) [hənt'], *v.* 1. search for wild animals or birds to catch or kill them. Ex. *The men are hunting deer.* 2. try to find; search for; seek. Ex. *They hunted for the lost child.* —*n.* the act of hunting wild animals; the act of searching. —**hunt'er,** *n.*

hurl (4) [hərl'], *v.* 1. cast with great force. Ex. *A rock was hurled at the car.* 2. say with great force. Ex. *She hurled insults at him.*

hurrah (4) [hərɑ:'], *interj.* an exclamation of joy; a cheer. Ex. *Hurrah for our team!*

hurry (1) [hə:r'iy], *v.* 1. move or act quickly or rapidly. Ex. *They hurried home.* 2. cause to move or act more rapidly. Ex. *We tried to hurry them on their way.* —*n.* act of hurrying; haste; need for hurrying. Ex. *Don't bother me now; I am in a hurry.*

hurt (1) [hərt'], *v.* 1. cause bodily injury, pain, or suffering. Ex. *He hurt himself when he fell.* 2. damage or harm. Ex. *Nothing will hurt this plastic tabletop.* 3. cause mental pain; distress. Ex. *I don't want to hurt her feelings.* —*n.* pain; injury; harm.

husband (1) [həz'bənd], *n.* a man who is married. Ex. *They are husband and wife.*

hush (3) [həš'], *v.* become quiet or still; make quiet. Ex. *The children hushed their voices.* —*n.* silence or quiet, especially after noise. Ex. *A hush fell upon the city at midnight.*

hustle (5) [həs'əl], *v.* 1. push along quickly; crowd roughly or rudely. Ex. *The crowd hustled into the train.* 2. force roughly or quickly. Ex. *The guards hustled the man off to prison.* —*n.* much activity. Ex. *The hustle of the crowd caused a great noise.*

hut (5) [hət'], *n.* a small, rough house; a cabin. Ex. *They passed a hut in the forest.*

hydrogen (5) [hay'drəʲən], *n.* a gas that has no color or smell and that burns with a very hot flame. Ex. *Hydrogen combines chemically with oxygen to form water.*

hymn (4) [him'], *n.* a song in honor or praise of a god or a nation. Ex. *The people joined together in singing a hymn.*

I

I, i [ay'], *n.* the ninth letter of the English alphabet.

I (1) [ay'], *pron.* the person speaking, thinking, or acting. **Ex.** *I want to leave now.*

-ible (1) [əbəl], *suffix.* that is possible; that can be done. **Exs.** *Eat, edible; divide, divisible.*

-ic (1) [ik], *suffix.* 1. of the nature of; like. **Ex.** *Metal, metallic.* 2. in the manner of. **Ex.** *Artist, artistic.* 3. consisting of; containing. **Ex.** *Crystal, crystallic.*

ice (1) [ays'], *n.* frozen water. **Ex.** *Is the ice thick enough to walk on?* —**i'cy,** *adj.* very cold; like ice.

ice cream (3) [ays' kriym'], a frozen food made of cream or milk, eggs, sugar, and flavoring. **Ex.** *We like to have ice cream for dessert.*

idea (1) [aydiy'ə], *n.* 1. a thought; mental picture. **Ex.** *She has a strange idea of happiness.* 2. opinion; belief; plan. **Ex.** *He has definite ideas on every subject.*

ideal (3) [aydiy'əl], *n.* 1. an idea of something that is perfect. **Ex.** *Peace and justice are ideals.* 2. something or someone thought of as perfect. **Ex.** *The pilot was the boy's ideal.* —*adj.* perfect. **Ex.** *The seashore is an ideal spot for a vacation.* —**i·de'al·ly,** *adv.* —**i·de'al·ism,** *n.* the practice of forming ideals; a strong belief in ideals. —**i·de'al·ist,** *n.* a person who believes in and lives by ideals. —**i·de'al·ize,** *v.* to act or plan as if a person, thing, or action is perfect. **Ex.** *He idealized his wife.*

identify (3) [ayden'təfay'], *v.* 1. recognize as being a particular person or thing; prove as the same. **Ex.** *She identified the things that were stolen from her house.* 2. associate closely; consider as the same. **Ex.** *She identifies wealth with generosity.*

identity [ayden'tətiy], *n.* the qualities taken as a whole by which a person or thing is known or recognized. **Ex.** *The identity of the body has not yet been determined.* 2. the personality. **Ex.** *He felt that he would lose his identity if he worked for such a large company.* 3. sameness; the equality of one thing to another. —**i·den'ti·cal,** adj.

idiot (5) [id'iyət], *n.* 1. a very foolish or very stupid person. **Ex.** *He is behaving like an idiot.* 2. one who is not able to learn much, often because of the condition of the brain. —**id'i·ot'ic,** *adj.*

idle (3) [ay'dəl], *adj.* 1. doing nothing; not busy. **Ex.** *He spent an idle hour watching the river.* 2. lazy. **Ex.** *The idle boy did not prepare his class assignment.* —*v.* 1. do nothing. **Ex.** *Although there was a great deal of work to be done, they were idling.* 2. operate a motor at low speed, so that the machine does not actually move or expend much energy. **Ex.** *He idled the motor while waiting for his wife.* —**i'dle· ness,** *n.* —**i'dly,** *adv.*

idol (4) [ay'dəl], *n.* 1. an image or object which people worship. **Ex.** *A stone idol stood at the entrance to the village.* 2. any person admired to the point of worship. **Ex.** *Her idol is a movie actor.* —**i'dol·ize,** *v.* adore; worship.

if (1) [if'], *conj.* 1. on condition that; provided. **Ex.** *I will help you if you come early.* 2. in case that; in the event that. **Ex.** *He will come if you need him.* 3. supposing that; granted that. **Ex.** *If both suits cost the same, I will take the blue one.* 4. whether. **Ex.** *We wondered if you were ill.* —**even if,** though; although. **Ex.** *We will go even if it rains.*

-ify (3) [əfay], *suffix.* make; form into; cause to become. **Exs.** *Class, classify; solid, solidify.*

ignore (3) [ignɔ:r'], *v.* refuse to notice or recognize. **Ex.** *He ignored the danger.* —**ig'no·rant,** *adj.* lacking in knowledge. **Ex.** *He was ignorant of the danger.*

il- (3) [il], *prefix.* **Exs.** *Literate, illiterate; legal, illegal.*

ill (1) [il'], *adj.* 1. not well; sick. **Ex.** *He is very ill.* 2. bad. **Ex.** *Her ill manners lost her many friends.* —*n.* sickness; trouble; harm; evil. **Ex.** *He suffered all the ills of the tropics.* —**ill' ness,** *n.*

ill- (1) [il], *prefix.* poorly; badly. **Exs.** *Kept, ill-kept; mannered, ill-mannered.*

illegal (5) [iliy'gəl], *adj.* not legal; unlawful. **Ex.** *He was arrested for the illegal sale of guns.* —**il·le'gal·ly,** *adv.* —**il' le·gal'i·ty,** *n.*

illuminate (4) [iluw'məneyt'], *v.* 1. supply with light. **Ex.** *The lamp illuminated the room.* 2. explain; enlighten, as with knowledge. **Ex.** *The professor illuminated the problem for his students.* —**il·lu'mi·na'tion,** *n.*

illusion (4) [iluw'žən], *n.* 1. something which seems to be real but is not. **Ex.** *Riding in the open car gave them the illusion of moving at great speed.* 2. a false impression or idea. **Ex.** *She had illusions about her chances for a career in the movies.* —**il·lu'sive**, *adj.*

illustrate (3) [il'əstreyt`, iləs'treyt`], *v.* 1. explain by examples, figures, etc. **Ex.** *He illustrated his point with a story about his youth.* 2. provide with pictures, as in a book or magazine. **Ex.** *The book was illustrated with drawings and maps.* —**il'lus·tra`tor**, *n.* one who makes illustrations for a book, magazine, etc. —**il`lus·tra'tion**, *n.* the act of illustrating; that which illustrates.

ill will [il' wil'], bad feeling. **Ex.** *His actions produced much ill will toward him.*

im- (2) [im], *prefix.* 1. not. **Ex.** *Mature, immature.* 2. into. **Ex.** *Part, impart.*

image (3) [im'iĵ], *n.* 1. a likeness of a person or thing, in the form of a painting, drawing, or especially a statue. **Ex.** *The artist carved an image in stone.* 2. the picture reflected by a mirror. **Ex.** *In the mirror he saw an image of himself.* 3. a mental picture; an idea. **Ex.** *He tried to create in people's minds an image of himself as a friendly, generous man.* 4. a copy; a person or thing closely resembling another. **Ex.** *He is the image of his father.*

imagine (2) [imæĵ'ən], *v.* 1. form a picture or idea in the mind. **Ex.** *He tried to imagine life abroad.* 2. think, suppose, or guess. **Ex.** *I imagine you are tired after your trip.* —**i·mag'in·a·ble**, *adj.* —**i·mag'i·nar·y**, *adj.* not real. —**i·mag`i·na'tion**, *n.* the ability to imagine. **Ex.** *He has a good imagination.*

imitate (3) [im'əteyt`], *v.* 1. copy in action or manner. **Ex.** *Boys often imitate their sports heroes.* 2. resemble. **Ex.** *The wood was painted to imitate marble.* —**im`i·ta'tion**, *n.* 1. a product or result of imitating. **Ex.** *These pearls are only imitations.* 2. the act of copying. —**im'i·ta`tive**, *adj.* like someone or something else. **Ex.** *His style is imitative of other artists.*

immediate (2) [imiy'diyit], *adj.* 1. without delay; instant. **Ex.** *We must have an immediate reply.* 2. very near in time or place. **Ex.** *Our immediate plans are to sell the store.* 3. direct; directly related. **Ex.** *Heart failure was the immediate cause of death.* —**im·me'di·ate·ly**, *adv.* —**im·me'di·a·cy**, *n.*

immense (3) [imens'], *adj*. 1. very large; vast; huge; big. **Ex.** *He was left an immense fortune*. 2. boundless; not able to be measured. **Ex.** *The heavens are immense*. —**im·men' si·ty,** *n*.

immigrant (4) [im'əgrənt], *n*. a person from a foreign land who enters another country for the purpose of making his home there. —**im'mi·grate,** *v*. —**im`mi·gra'tion,** *n*. the act of immigrating.

immortal (5) [imɔr'təl], *adj*. not mortal; never dying; everlasting. **Ex.** *The work of great artists is immortal*. —*n*. a person whose fame is enduring. **Ex.** *His writings have made him an immortal*. —**im`mor·tal'i·ty,** *n*. unending life.

impact (4) [im'pækt], *n*. the striking of one object or body against another; the act of coming together with force. **Ex.** *The force of the impact threw the driver out of the car*.

imperial (4) [impi:r'iyəl], *adj*. of or suitable to an empire or the rulers of an empire. **Ex.** *There was a ceremony to welcome His Imperial Majesty*.

implement (4) [im'pləmənt], *n*. an object; a tool; an instrument used in performing work. **Ex.** *A plow is a farm implement*. —*v*. fulfill; complete. **Ex.** *Money is needed to implement the program*.

implore (5) [implɔ:r'], *v*. ask for earnestly and with feeling, as for help or mercy; beg. **Ex.** *We implored him to act before it was too late*. —**im·plor'ing,** *adj*.

imply (4) [implay'], *v*. say indirectly; hint; suggest something without actually saying it. **Ex.** *Your manner implies that you are not pleased with me*.

import (3) [impɔrt', im'pɔrt], *v*. bring commercial goods in from a foreign country. **Ex.** *That merchant imports wine*. —*n*. 1. a product or products brought in from another country. **Ex.** *Imports during the year were greater than exports*. 2. meaning. **Ex.** *What is the import of the President's remarks?* —**im·port'er,** *n*. one who brings in goods from a foreign country. —**im`por·ta'tion,** *n*. the act of importing.

important (1) [impɔr'tənt], *adj*. 1. having great meaning or value. **Ex.** *It was an important date*. 2. of great power or authority. **Ex.** *He has an important position with his company*. —**im·por'tance,** *n*. greatness; value. **Ex.** *The President is a man of importance*.

impose (4) [impowz'], *v.* 1. subject to a tax, penalty, or other burden. **Ex.** *The judge imposed a heavy fine on the law-breaker.* 2. force oneself or one's company upon others; take advantage of. **Ex.** *He imposed on his friends by visiting them too often.* —**im'po·si'tion**, *n.* that which imposes; the act of imposing. —**im·pos'ing**, *adj.* grand in size, manner, appearance, etc. **Ex.** *The most imposing buildings are in the center of town.*

impossible (2) [impas'əbəl], *adj.* not possible; that cannot be, exist, or happen. **Ex.** *It is impossible for an apple tree to grow oranges.* —**im·pos'si·bil'i·ty**, *n.*

impress (2) [impres'], *v.* 1. have a deep effect on the thinking or feelings; influence. **Ex.** *My talk with the President impressed me deeply.* 2. produce a mark by pressing. **Ex.** *The writing paper is impressed with the school seal.* —**im·pres'sive**, *adj.* —**im·pres'sion**, *n.* 1. a deep effect on the mind or feelings. **Ex.** *The boy made a good impression by his hard work.* 2. a general feeling; an uncertain belief. **Ex.** *It is my impression that they have met before.* 3. mark made by pressing. **Ex.** *The impression of the seal on the wax was very clear.* —**im·pres'sion·a·ble**, *adj.* easily impressed. **Ex.** *The child was very impressionable.*

improve (2) [impruwv'], *v.* 1. become better. **Ex.** *His health is improving.* 2. make better. **Ex.** *She improved her reading by practice.* —**im·prove'ment**, *n.*

impulse (3) [im'pəls], *n.* 1. a sudden desire to do something. **Ex.** *Acting on impulse, she quit her job.* 2. the force that starts an action. **Ex.** *An electrical impulse started the motor.* —**im·pul'sive**, *adj.*

in (1) [in'], *prep.* 1. held by; contained by; surrounded by; covered by. **Ex.** *They walked home in the rain.* 2. during. **Ex.** *He will be away in April.* 3. within the limits of; not beyond. **Ex.** *They are visiting in the city.* 4. showing; affected by; influenced by. **Ex.** *In her haste, she forgot the money.* 5. according to; with regard to. **Ex.** *In her mind, he is guilty.* 6. by means of; by the use of. **Ex.** *The design was done in colored wool.* 7. belonging to; being a part of. **Ex.** *There are three girls in the group.* 8. having as a location; affecting. **Ex.** *He has a pain in his stomach.* 9. working at;

a, far; æ, am; e, get; ey, late; i, in; iy, see; ɔ, all; ow, go; u, put; uw, too; ə, but, ago; ər, fur; aw, out; ay, life; oy, boy; ŋ, ring; θ, think; ŏ, that; ž, measure; š, ship; j, edge; č, child.

occupied by. **Ex.** *He is now in business.* —*adv.* inside; toward the inside. **Ex.** *Bring your friend in.*

in- (2) [in], *prefix*. 1. in; into; within; toward. **Exs.** *Come, income; born, inborn.* 2. not; without. **Exs.** *Attention, inattention; action, inaction; correct, incorrect; definite, indefinite.*

inasmuch [in'əzməč'], because. **Ex.** *Inasmuch as they are going, I will not go.*

inaugurate (5) [inɔ:'gyureyt`, inɔ:'gəreyt`], *v.* 1. begin. **Ex.** *A French language course was inaugurated in school this year.* 2. place in office with ceremony. **Ex.** *The President of the United States is elected in November and inaugurated in January of the following year.* —**in·au·gu·ra'tion,** *n.* —**in·au'gu·ral,** *adj.*

incense (4) [in'sens], *n.* a substance producing a pleasing odor when burned. **Ex.** *Some churches use incense during their religious services.*

incense (4) [insens'], *v.* enrage; fill with anger. **Ex.** *The official was incensed at the lack of respect shown him.*

incessant (5) [inses'ənt], *adj.* continuous; apparently endless; unceasing. **Ex.** *The incessant barking of the dog kept him awake.* —**in·ces'sant·ly,** *adv.*

inch (1) [inč'], *n.* a unit of length which is ¹⁄₁₂ of a foot. **Ex.** *The ribbon is three inches wide.* See **Weights and Measures.**

incident (3) [in'sədənt], *n.* something that happens or takes place; an event. **Ex.** *He told of many incidents that had occurred when he was in the army.* —**in'ci·dence,** *n.* the regularity with which something happens. **Ex.** *The incidence of car accidents is increasing.* —**in'ci·den'tal,** *adj.* of lesser importance; secondary. **Ex.** *Taxi fare from the station was an incidental expense of the trip.* —**in'ci·den'tal·ly,** *adv.*

incline (3) [inklayn'], *v.* 1. slope; lean. **Ex.** *The two trees inclined toward each other.* 2. bend toward, as the head or body. **Ex.** *The mother inclined her head to hear the child's words.* 3. have a preference for; tend. **Ex.** *He inclines to carelessness.*

incline (3) [in'klayn], *n.* an inclined surface; a slope. **Ex.** *They had to walk up a steep incline.* —**in'cli·na'tion,** *n.* 1. a preference; choice. **Ex.** *He went to school against his inclination.* 2. a sloping, bending, or leaning position. **Ex.** *He recognized her with an inclination of the head.*

include (1) [inkluwd'], *v.* 1. contain as part of a whole. **Ex.** *This book includes all his poems.* 2. place with others in a

group. **Ex.** *We shall include his name on the list of guests.*
—**in·clu'sion,** *n.*

income (3) [in'kəm], *n.* money received as salary, earnings,
profit from business, etc. **Ex.** *He has a very high income.*

increase (1) [inkriys'], *v.* 1. make greater, larger, more numerous; add to. **Ex.** *He increased his efforts.* 2. become
greater or more numerous; grow. **Ex.** *The number of people
living in the city is increasing rapidly.*

increase (1) [in'kriys], *n.* growth in size, number, or amount.
Ex. *There has been an increase in the taxes we must pay.*
—**in·creas'ing,** *adj.* —**in·creas'ing·ly,** *adv.*

incredible (5) [inkred'əbəl], *adj.* not believable. **Ex.** *He told
me an incredible story.* —**in·cred'i·bil'i·ty,** *n.* —**in·cred'i·bly,**
adv.

indeed (1) [indiyd'], *adv.* really; in fact; in truth; very much.
Ex. *It is indeed a pleasure to be here.*

independence (3) [in'dəpən'dəns], *n.* freedom from the rule
or the control of others. **Ex.** *Many countries have recently
gained their independence.* —**in'de·pend'ent,** *adj.* not influenced by, controlled by, or dependent upon others; separate.
Ex. *He is an independent thinker.*

index (4) [in'deks], *n.* an alphabetical list or table of subjects,
names, etc. in a book, telling on what pages they may be
found. **Ex.** *The teacher taught the children how to use the
index of their textbook.* —*v.* provide with an index. **Ex.** *He
is indexing a history book.*

index finger [in'deks fiŋ'gər], *n.* the finger next to the thumb.

indicate (2) [in'dəkeyt'], *v.* 1. be a sign of. **Ex.** *The red traffic
light indicates "stop."* 2. show; point. **Ex.** *Please indicate the
city on the map.* 3. make known. **Ex.** *He indicated that he
wanted to go.* —**in'di·ca'tion,** *n.* a sign or signal. —**in·dic'**
a·tive, *adj.*

indignant (4) [indig'nənt], *adj.* full of anger about an unjust
action or unfair treatment. **Ex.** *He was indignant at the man
who treated him so badly.* —**in·dig'nant·ly,** *adv.* —**in'dig·
na'tion,** *n.* anger caused by that which is unfair. —**in·dig'**
ni·ty, *n.* the unfair act.

individual (2) [in'dəvij'uwəl], *adj.* 1. single; one; separate
from others. **Ex.** *They each received individual letters.* 2. of
a single person; different from others. **Ex.** *The students'
rooms reflected their individual interests.* 3. about, by, or
for one person. **Ex.** *The members of the committee gave*

individual reports. —*n.* a single human being. **Ex.** *She is a happy individual.* —**in·di·vid'u·al·ly,** *adv.* —**in·di·vid'u·al· ism,** *n.* 1. the idea or belief that individuals and their inter- ests are more important than the group or common inter- ests. 2. individuality. —**in·di·vid·u·al'i·ty,** *n.* the quality or qualities of a person or thing which are different from another.

indoors (5) [in'dɔrz', in'dɔrz'], *adv.* in or into a building. **Ex.** *They play indoors during bad weather.* —**in'door, in·door',** *adj.* **Ex.** *There are many indoor games we can play during the rain.*

induce (4) [induws', indyuws'], *v.* 1. lead into doing some- thing; persuade. **Ex.** *Nothing would induce him to change his mind.* 2. effect; cause. **Ex.** *His poor health was induced by lack of proper food.* —**in·duce'ment,** *n.* that which per- suades. **Ex.** *Better earnings are an inducement to change jobs.*

indulge (4) [indəlj'], *v.* 1. yield to. **Ex.** *He indulged his desire for cigarettes to a harmful extent.* 2. grant the wishes of. **Ex.** *Those parents indulge their children too much.* —**in·dul' gence,** *n.* —**in·dul'gent,** *adj.* —**in·dul'gent·ly,** *adv.*

industrious (3) [indəs'triyəs], *adj.* hard-working; busy. **Ex.** *He is an industrious student.* —**in·dus'tri·ous·ly,** *adv.* —**in·dus' tri·ous·ness,** *n.*

industry (1) [in'dəstriy], *n.* 1. any business that produces goods or services. **Ex.** *He works in the automobile industry.* 2. business and manufacturing as a whole. **Ex.** *The Presi- dent asked the leaders of industry for advice.* 3. hard work. **Ex.** *Not only ability but industry is needed for success.* —**in·dus'tri·al,** *adj.* —**in·dus'tri·al·ize',** *v.* form industries. —**in·dus'tri·al·ist,** *n.* an owner or manager of an important industry.

inevitable (4) [inev'ətəbəl], *adj.* not avoidable or escapable; certain. **Ex.** *An increase in taxes was inevitable.* —**in·ev'i· ta·bly,** *adv.*

infamous [in'fəməs], *adj.* of very bad reputation; known as very bad. **Ex.** *He is an infamous liar.*

infant (4) [in'fənt], *n.* a very young child; a baby. **Ex.** *The woman was carrying an infant in her arms.* —*adj.* 1. of or referring to infants. **Ex.** *The shop sells infant clothes.* 2. in a very early stage of growing up or development. **Ex.** *Infant*

industries sometimes need government help. —**in'fan·cy,** *n.*
—**in'fan·tile,** *adj.* childish.

infantry (4) [in'fəntriy], *n.* soldiers who fight on foot; the
branch of the army consisting of these soldiers. **Ex.** *Men in
the infantry often march long distances.*

infect (5) [infekt'], *v.* 1. make ill with something that produces
disease. **Ex.** *His wound was infected by dirt.* 2. spread one's
feelings or moods to others. **Ex.** *They were all infected by
her enthusiasm.* —**in·fec'tion,** *n.* condition produced in the
body by entry of a disease. —**in·fec'tious,** *adj.* caused by or
causing infection; spreading easily.

inferior (4) [infi:r'iyər], *adj.* 1. lower in rank, importance, etc.
Ex. *The rank of captain is inferior to the rank of major.* 2.
poor or poorer in quality when compared to someone or
something else. **Ex.** *The builder used inferior material in
that house.* —*n.* one lower in rank or importance. **Ex.** *A
good superior uses the practical experience of his inferiors.*
—**in·fe`ri·or'i·ty,** *n.*

infinite (4) [in'fənit], *adj.* 1. too great to measure; vast. **Ex.**
The sky is infinite in size. 2. endless; without limit. **Ex.** *His
father has infinite patience.* —**in'fi·nite·ly,** *adv.* —**in·fin'i·ty,**
n. that which is without end.

infinitive (5) [infin'ativ], *n.* simple form of a verb, having no
tense and usually preceded by "to." **Exs.** *In the sentence, "I
want to see," "see" is an infinitive. In the sentence, "He had
me wait," "wait" is an infinitive.*

inflammation (5) [in`fləmey'šən], *n.* a painful, hot, red swell-
ing of some part of the body. **Ex.** *The inflammation of his
knee made it difficult for him to walk.* —**in·flame',** *v.* 1.
swell and become hot, red, and painful. **Ex.** *His right eye
was inflamed.* 2. anger or excite. **Ex.** *His speech inflamed
the people to rebel.* —**in·flam'ma·ble,** *adj.* easily excited;
quick to begin hurting. —**in·flam'ma·tor`y,** *adj.* causing
anger or excitement. **Ex.** *He made inflammatory speeches.*

inflate (5) [infleyt'], *v.* 1. cause to swell by filling wit.. air or
gas. **Ex.** *He inflated the life preserver.* 2. make larger or
greater than is proper or usual. **Ex.** *Scarcity has inflated the
price of fruit.* —**in·fla'tion,** *n.* 1. the act of filling with air or
gas. 2. a period in which there is a general rise in prices; a

a, far; **æ,** am; **e,** get; **ey,** late; **i,** in; **iy,** see; **ɔ,** all; **ow,** go; **u,** put; **uw,** too;
ə, but, ago; **ər,** fur; **aw,** out; **ay,** life; **oy,** boy; **ŋ,** ring; **θ,** think; **ð,** that;
ž, measure; **š,** ship; **ǰ,** edge; **č,** child.

lessening of the buying power of money. Ex. *Because of inflation, they had to spend more money for food.*

inflict (5) [inflikt'], *v.* 1. give, as a blow; cause to suffer pain, wounds, etc. Ex. *The enemy artillery inflicted many wounds upon our soldiers.* 2. put on as a punishment, tax, etc. Ex. *The government inflicted heavy taxes on the people.*

influence (2) [in'fluwəns], *n.* 1. the act or power to persuade someone or affect something. Ex. *He had a great influence upon his students.* 2. a thing or person that persuades or affects. Ex. *He is an influence for good among his classmates.* 3. the power that comes from wealth, authority, etc. Ex. *The mayor is a man of influence in this city.* —*v.* have an effect upon; affect; change. Ex. *He was not influenced by promises of riches.* —**in'flu·en'tial**, *adj.* of or having influence.

inform (2) [infɔrm'], *v.* 1. tell; give knowledge to. Ex. *The repairman informed me that the work was completed.* 2. give evidence or information, especially against another. Ex. *The spy informed on his companions.* —**in·form'er**, *n.* one who gives information against others.

information (2) [in'fərmey'šən], *n.* 1. knowledge; facts; news. Ex. *He got the information he needed from the library.* 2. the act of informing. Ex. *For your information, I will be away on Friday.* —**in·form'a·tive**, *adj.* providing knowledge. Ex. *This book is very informative.*

-ing (1) [iŋ], *suffix.* 1. continuing action of a verb. Ex. *When I came, he was eating.* 2. the act of one who does what the verb describes. Exs. *Fish, fishing; dream, dreaming.* 3. product or result of an action. Exs. *Draw, drawing; offer, offering.* 4. material for. Exs. *Roof, roofing; flavor, flavoring.*

ingenious (5) [inǰiyn'yəs], *adj.* 1. showing cleverness of planning or design. Ex. *The door was fastened with an ingenious lock.* 2. talented or clever. Ex. *The ingenious boy won a prize for his invention.* —**in·gen'ious·ly**, *adv.* —**in'ge·nu'i·ty**, *n.*

ingredient (4) [ingriy'diyənt], *n.* one of the parts of a mixture or combination. Ex. *Flour is one of the ingredients needed to make a cake.*

inhabit (3) [inhæb'it], *v.* have as a home; live in. Ex. *Wild animals once inhabited much of this land.* —**in·hab'it·a·ble**, *adj.* suitable for living in. —**in·hab'it·ant**, *n.*

inhale (4) [inheyl'], v. draw into the lungs; breathe in. **Ex.** *He stood at the open window and inhaled deeply.*

inherit (4) [inher'it], v. 1. receive something upon the death of the former owner. **Ex.** *He inherited land and money from his uncle.* 2. have at birth from one's parents. **Ex.** *The baby inherited his mother's blue eyes.* —**in·her'i·tance,** n.

initial (4) [iniš'əl], adj. first; of the beginning. **Ex.** *He failed in his initial attempts.* —n. the first letter of each word in a person's name. **Ex.** *President John Fitzgerald Kennedy's initials were J.F.K.* —v. sign with initials. **Ex.** *He initialed the correction to show that he had approved it.* —**i·ni'tial·ly,** adv.

initiative (5) [iniš'ətiv], n. 1. an introductory act or step. **Ex.** *She took the initiative in getting acquainted with her neighbors.* 2. willingness and ability to get things started. **Ex.** *In the absence of his superior, he showed his initiative.*

injure (3) [in'jər], v. harm; hurt; wound. **Ex.** *He injured his leg when he fell.* —**in·ju'ri·ous,** adj. —**in'ju·ry,** n. damage or harm done or received. **Ex.** *His injury prevented him from participating in sports that summer.*

ink (4) [iŋk'], n. a fluid used for writing or printing. **Ex.** *His pen has no ink.* —v. mark with ink.

in-law (3) [in'lɔ:'], n. a relative by marriage. **Ex.** *My wife's brother is my brother-in-law.*

inlet [in'let'], n. a narrow body of water going into the land or between islands. **Ex.** *They entered the inlet in a boat.*

inmate [in'meyt'], n. a person held in a prison or mental hospital. **Ex.** *The inmates received visitors on Sundays.*

inn (5) [in'], n. a place that provides food and a place to sleep for travelers; a small hotel. **Ex.** *The village has only an inn.*

inner [in'ər], adj. nearest to the center; the farthest in. **Ex.** *They went to the inner rooms of the house.*

innocent (3) [in'əsənt], adj. 1. not guilty, especially legally; free from moral wrong; pure. **Ex.** *A person is innocent until proven guilty.* 2. not intending to do wrong; harmless. **Ex.** *They joined in the innocent pleasures of the country people.* 3. simple; knowing no evil. **Ex.** *She was an innocent young girl.* —**in'no·cent·ly,** adv. —**in'no·cence,** n.

inquire (2) [inkwayr'], v. ask; request information. **Ex.** *They inquired about his past experience.* —**in·quir'ing,** adj. —**in·qui'ry,** n. a question.

insane (5) [inseyn'], *adj.* 1. not sane; mentally very ill. **Ex.** *Insane people are treated in special hospitals.* 2. very foolish; senseless. **Ex.** *The idea of a trip to the moon was once considered insane.* —in·san'i·ty, *n.*

inscription (5) [inskrip'šən], *n.* something written, especially in a lasting and important manner. **Ex.** *The inscription on the ancient monument was hard to read.*

insect (2) [in'sekt], *n.* a very small animal, usually with three pairs of legs and two pairs of wings.

insert (5) [insərt'], *v.* put in. **Ex.** *The secretary inserted the letter in the envelope.* —in'sert, *n.* that which is inserted. —in·ser'tion, *n.* act of inserting.

INSECT

inside (1) [in'sayd', in'sayd'], *n.* the inner side; the surface, part, etc. that is within. **Ex.** *The inside of the box is painted red.* —adj. 1. on or in the inside. **Ex.** *He preferred an inside job to an outside one.* 2. private; secret. **Ex.** *He has inside information about the company's plans.* —prep. within; in or into the interior. **Ex.** *Have you been inside the new theater?* —adv. on the inside; within. —in·sid'er, *n.* a person who is inside, as inside a group, and has special knowledge. **Ex.** *Insiders say the President will come.*

insight [in'sayt'], *n.* special understanding. **Ex.** *He has a good insight into the problem.*

insist (2) [insist'], *v.* 1. demand firmly. **Ex.** *I insist that you go.* 2. be firm in holding an opinion or a position. **Ex.** *She insisted that she was right.* —in·sis'tent, *adj.* —in·sis'tence, *n.*

insofar [in'sowfa:r'], *adv.* to the extent. **Ex.** *Insofar as I know, he has gone home.*

inspect (4) [inspekt'], *v.* 1. view closely; examine. **Ex.** *They inspected the new car models before buying.* 2. view officially. **Ex.** *The mayor inspected the new waterworks.* —in·spec'tion, *n.* the act of inspecting. —in·spec'tor, *n.* one who inspects.

inspire (3) [inspayr'], *v.* 1. have an influence upon; cause to act. **Ex.** *His brother's success inspired the boy to work harder.* 2. produce a feeling. **Ex.** *His words inspired confidence in us.* —in'spi·ra'tion, *n.* —in'spi·ra'tion·al, *adj.*

install (4) [instɔ:l'], *v.* place in position for service or use. **Ex.** *Electric wiring was installed in the new house.* —in'stal·la'tion, *n.* the act of putting in place.

instance (2) [in'stəns], *n.* 1. an occasion or case. Ex. *New instances of courage were reported every day.* 2. example; something given as proof. Ex. *Can you give an instance of the boy's ability?*

instant (2) [instənt'], *n.* 1. a moment; a very short period of time. Ex. *It was done in an instant.* 2. a particular moment or point in time. Ex. *Come here this instant! —adj.* 1. happening in a moment or without delay. Ex. *The play was an instant success.* 2. ready for quick preparation. Ex. *She prefers instant coffee.*

instead (1) [insted'], *adv.* 1. in the place of; taking the place of. Ex. *They came by plane instead of by train.* 2. in its place; rather. Ex. *They ordered coffee but were served tea instead.*

instinct (3) [in'stiŋkt], *n.* 1. a natural tendency or feeling in persons or animals from birth. Ex. *Fear of the unknown is a common instinct.* 2. natural ability or talent. Ex. *She has an instinct for avoiding bad company.* —in·stinc'tive, *adj.*

institution (2) [in'stətuw'šən, in'stətyuw'šən], *n.* 1. an organization, such as a school, hospital, or church, for doing some special work. Ex. *Colleges and universities are educational institutions.* 2. established law, custom, etc. Ex. *Marriage is a basic institution in most societies.* 3. the act of starting or establishing. Ex. *The children benefited from the institution of a new playground.* —in'sti·tute, *v.* start or establish. Ex. *They instituted new rules.* —in'sti·tu'tion·al, *adj.*

instruct (2) [instrəkt'], *v.* 1. teach; train; educate. Ex. *He instructed the students in history.* 2. direct or command. Ex. *The doctor instructed his patient to remain in bed.* —in·struc'tion, *n.* —in·struc'tor, *n.*

instrument (2) [in'strəmənt], *n.* 1. a tool or device, especially for exact work. Ex. *A doctor's instruments must be kept absolutely clean.* 2. a device for producing musical sounds. Ex. *He prefers to play a wind instrument, such as the flute, rather than a stringed instrument, such as the violin.*

insult (3) [in'səlt], *n.* an act or remark which is rude or injures another's feelings. Ex. *Your refusal to believe my story is an insult.*

---

a, far; æ, am; e, get; ey, late; i, in; iy, see; ɔ, all; ow, go; u, put; uw, too; ə, but, ago; ər, fur; aw, out; ay, life; oy, boy; ŋ, ring; θ, think; ð, that; ž, measure; š, ship; j, edge; č, child.

insult (3) [insəlt'], *v.* act or speak rudely; offend. **Ex.** *He insulted the speaker by leaving before the lecture was ended.* —in·sult'ing, *adj.*

insure (3) [inšu:r'], *v.* 1. make sure; make certain. **Ex.** *They sent a car for him in order to insure his presence at the meeting.* 2. protect or secure against damage or loss. **Ex.** *They insured their money against theft by depositing it in a bank.* 3. buy or obtain insurance. —in·sur'ance, *n.* 1. a contract giving protection against loss. 2. the amount for which something or someone is insured. **Ex.** *The insurance on his house is $30,000.* —in·sured', *n.* that which is protected by insurance.

integrate (5) [in'təgreyt'], *v.* 1. open to the use of all races; do away with segregation. **Ex.** *The schools in this city are integrated.* 2. bring together to form a whole. **Ex.** *He integrated ideas from several philosophers into his own philosophy.*

integrity (5) [integ'rətiy'], *n.* soundness; freedom from faults or defects; strict honesty. **Ex.** *The judge's integrity was never doubted.*

intellect (5) [in'təlekt'], *n.* 1. the power of the mind by which one knows and reasons; understanding. **Ex.** *His ease in solving that problem showed the power of his intellect.* 2. a person possessing great powers of the mind. **Ex.** *He is one of this century's great intellects.* —in'tel·lec'tu·al, *adj., n.*

intelligence (3) [intel'əǰəns], *n.* 1. great mental ability; the ability to think. **Ex.** *Man's intelligence has enabled him to overcome many of his natural handicaps.* 2. information; news. **Ex.** *No intelligence about the flood victims has reached us.* —in·tel'li·gent, *adj.* having intelligence. —in·tel'li·gent·ly, *adv.* in a wise way.

intend (2) [intend'], *v.* 1. plan; have as a purpose. **Ex.** *I intend to buy a new suit today.* 2. design for a particular purpose. **Ex.** *We intended this room for you.*

intense (4) [intens'], *adj.* 1. very strong; great. **Ex.** *The intense heat exhausted him.* 2. earnest; serious. **Ex.** *He is an intense worker.* —in·tense'ly, *adv.* —in·ten'si·ty, *n.*

intent (3) [intent'], *n.* purpose; aim. **Ex.** *What is your intent in asking these questions?* —*adj.* 1. giving full attention. **Ex.** *He was so intent upon his reading that he did not hear* *the bell.* 2. firmly decided; determined. **Ex.** *They were intent on revenge.* —**in·tent'ly,** *adv.* with full attention. —**in·ten'tion,** *n.* purpose; plan. **Ex.** *It was his intention to invite her to dinner.* —**in·ten'tion·al,** *adj.* —**in·ten'tion·al·ly,** *adv.* with purpose.

inter- (2) [intər], *prefix.* 1. among; between; together. **Ex.** *Mix, intermix.* 2. between the parts. **Exs.** *Continental, intercontinental; American, inter-American.*

intercourse (5) [in'tərkɔrs'], *n.* 1. activity or action between persons or nations; exchange of ideas, products, etc. **Ex.** *There was much commercial intercourse between the two countries.* 2. physical relations between the sexes.

interest (1) [in't(ə)rəst], *n.* 1. a desire to give special attention to someone or something; attraction toward. **Ex.** *He had a great interest in music.* 2. the ability to cause such a desire. **Ex.** *The question of the origin of man is of unending interest to mankind.* 3. the object of one's attention or feelings. **Ex.** *Gardening is one of her many interests.* 4. benefit or advantage. **Ex.** *It will be to your interest to get more education.* 5. a share in ownership of a business. **Ex.** *They bought an interest in the shoe factory.* 6. regular payments for the use of money borrowed. **Ex.** *They pay interest on the loan monthly.* —*v.* 1. draw or excite the attention or curiosity of. **Ex.** *Foreign stamps interest him.* 2. cause to be concerned in; involve. **Ex.** *He interested his friend in outdoor sports.* —**in'ter·est·ed,** *adj.* having or being interested. **Ex.** *He is an interested reader.* —**in'ter·est·ing,** *adj.* of interest. **Ex.** *That is an interesting book.*

interfere (4) [in'tərfi:r'], *v.* 1. get in the way of; work against. **Ex.** *The noise interfered with his sleep.* 2. take a part in the affairs of others, especially when not asked to do so. **Ex.** *It is best not to interfere in other people's arguments.* —**in·ter·fer'ing,** *adj.* —**in'ter·fer'ence,** *n.*

interior (3) [inti:r'iyər], *n.* 1. the inside; the inner part. **Ex.** *The interior of the house is cool.* 2. the inland part of a country; any place located at a distance from the coast or border. **Ex.** *The hunters went deep into the interior.* —*adj.* 1. being within something; referring to the inside. **Ex.** *He is studying interior decorating.* 2. far from the boundaries or shores of a country; inland. **Ex.** *The interior regions have not been explored.*

interjection (5) [in'tərjek'sən], *n.* a word used to show feeling or emotion, usually one without grammatical meaning or structure. **Exs.** *Oh!; Ah!; Well!; Alas!*

internal (4) [intər'nəl], *adj.* 1. inner; of or for the interior. **Ex.** *This medicine is not for internal use.* 2. within a country; domestic. **Ex.** *His office is concerned with internal affairs.* —**in'ter'nal·ly,** *adv.*

international (3) [in'tərnæš'(ə)nəl], *adj.* concerning relations among nations. **Ex.** *Six nations have signed an international trade agreement.* —**in·ter·na'tion·al·ly,** *adv.*

interpret (4) [intər'prət], *v.* 1. tell or explain the meaning of something. **Ex.** *Please interpret this message for me.* 2. translate. **Ex.** *She interpreted for the foreign visitors.* —**in·ter' pre·ta'tion,** *n.* the act of interpreting. —**in·ter'pre·ter,** *n.* one who interprets.

interrupt (2) [in'tərəpt'], *v.* 1. stop for a short time. **Ex.** *They interrupted the meeting for lunch.* 2. break into; prevent. **Ex.** *The quiet was interrupted by a shot.* 3. stop another's actions, conversation, etc. temporarily, especially with questions or remarks. **Ex.** *Their conversation was interrupted by a telephone call.* —**in'ter·rup'tion,** *n.*

interval (3) [in'tərvəl], *n.* the time between two events. **Ex.** *In the interval between his departure and return, many things changed in his country.* —**at intervals,** 1. occasionally. 2. with spaces in between. **Ex.** *Trees were planted at intervals of twenty feet.*

intervene (5) [in'tərviyn'], *v.* 1. come or happen between. **Ex.** *Only an instant intervened between the flash of lightning and the thunder.* 2. come between in order to settle or solve. **Ex.** *He intervened in the quarrel between the two brothers.* —**in'ter·ven'tion,** *n.*

interview (3) [in'tərvyuw'], *n.* 1. a meeting of two persons to discuss something. **Ex.** *Every new student has an interview with a guidance counselor.* 2. a conversation between a journalist or a writer and another person to obtain information to be published or broadcast. **Ex.** *The President granted a personal interview.* —**in'ter·view·er,** *n.* one who interviews.

intimate (3) [in'təmit], *adj.* 1. very close or familiar. **Ex.** *They are intimate friends.* 2. private; very personal. **Ex.** *We do not discuss intimate matters with strangers.* 3. resulting from a thorough study of or a familiarity with. **Ex.** *He has an intimate knowledge of the problem.* —**in'ti·mate·ly,** *adv.*

intimate (3) [in'təmeyt'], *v.* suggest; hint. Ex. *He intimated by a glance at his watch that it was time to leave.* —**in'ti·ma'tion,** *n.*

into (1) [in'tuw], *prep.* 1. from being outside toward being within a place or thing. Ex. *Come into the house.* 2. showing a change of state from one kind of thing or condition to another. Ex. *Spring changed into summer.*

intoxicate (5) [intak'səkeyt'], *v.* 1. lose or cause to lose mental and physical control as a result of the use of alcohol or drugs. Ex. *The whiskey intoxicated him, and he could not drive his car.* 2. excite. Ex. *They were intoxicated by the bright lights and music.* —**in·tox'i·ca'tion,** *n.* a condition of being intoxicated. —**in·tox'i·cant,** *n.* that which causes one to be intoxicated.

intra- (2) [intrə], *prefix.* within; inside. Exs. *State, intrastate; group, intragroup.*

intrigue (5) [intriyg'], *v.* 1. plan in a secret way; plot; scheme. Ex. *They are intriguing against the government.* 2. excite the curiosity or interest of. Ex. *The story of your adventures intrigues me.* —*n.* a plot or scheme. Ex. *They were accused of political intrigues.* —**in·tri'guing,** *adj.*

introduce (2) [in'trəduws', in'trədyuws'], *v.* 1. make known; present; acquaint. Ex. *She introduced her friend to her mother.* 2. bring into notice or use. Ex. *New electrical products are continually being introduced.* 3. bring forward for consideration; purpose. Ex. *Several plans were introduced at the meeting.* 4. bring a person or persons to a first knowledge of something; make familiar with. Ex. *The children were introduced to a foreign language in the fifth grade.* —**in'tro·duc'tion,** *n.*

intrude (5) [intruwd'], *v.* push or force in or come in without being asked or wanted. Ex. *Their friends intruded upon them during dinner.* —**in·trud'er,** *n.* one who intrudes. —**in·tru'sion,** *n.* act of intruding.

invade (4) [inveyd'], *v.* 1. enter in order to seize or conquer. Ex. *Enemy troops invaded the country.* 2. rush in; crowd into. Ex. *On the first day of the season, thousands of city*

---

a, far; æ, am; e, get; ey, late; i, in; iy, see; ɔ, all; ow, go; u, put; uw, too; ə, but, ago; ər, fur; aw, out; ay, life; oy, boy; ŋ, ring; θ, think; ð, that; ž, measure; š, ship; j, edge; č, child.

dwellers invaded the beach. **—in·vad'er,** *n.* one who invades. **—in·va'sion,** *n.* act of invading.

invent (2) [invent'], *v.* 1. plan and make something never made before. **Ex.** *Who invented the telegraph?* 2. create in the mind. **Ex.** *He invented an excuse for not doing his work.* **—in·ven'tion,** *n.* 1. the act of inventing. 2. the thing invented. **—in·ven'tor,** *n.* one who invents.

invest (4) [invest'], *v.* 1. put money into a business enterprise in order to earn a profit. **Ex.** *He invested his money in a store.* 2. expend something of value to earn a return. **Ex.** *He invested his time in learning to paint.* 3. put in office with ceremony. **Ex.** *The judge was invested with the robes of office.* **—in·vest'ment,** *n.* act of investing. **—in·ves'tor,** *n.* one who invests.

investigate (3) [inves'təgeyt'], *v.* examine officially; search or inquire into. **Ex.** *The police investigated the murder.* **—in·ves'ti·ga'tion,** *n.* the act of investigating. **—in·ves'ti·ga·tor,** *n.* one who investigates.

invite (2) [invayt'], *v.* 1. ask as one's guest, especially to a meal or social gathering. **Ex.** *They invited us to go to the theater.* 2. attract; tend to cause. **Ex.** *Don't invite danger by being careless.* **—in'vi·ta'tion,** *n.* an act of inviting. **Ex.** *His invitation to dinner was beautifully printed.* **—in·vit'ing,** *adj.* having a quality which attracts. **Ex.** *The hot food looked inviting.*

involve (3) [invalv'], *v.* 1. include as a necessary part. **Ex.** *His work involves a great deal of travel.* 2. bring into difficulty or trouble. **Ex.** *He is involved with the police.* 3. make more difficult, confused, or complicated. **Ex.** *His explanation was too involved for us to understand.* 4. be highly interested in; be much occupied with. **Ex.** *He was so involved in his work that he refused to go home.* **—in·volve'ment,** *n.*

-ion (1) [ən], *suffix.* act, condition, or result of. **Exs.** Collect, *collection; correct, correction.*

-ior (3) [iyər], *suffix.* 1. state or quality of. **Ex.** *Behave, behavior.* 2. doer; one who. **Ex.** *Save, savior.*

-ious (2) [yəs, əs, iyəs], *suffix.* having or characterized by; full of. **Exs.** *Space, spacious; victory, victorious.*

ir- (3) [ir], *prefix.* not. **Exs.** *Regular, irregular; rational, irrational.*

iron (1) [ay'ərn], *n.* 1. a strong, hard metal used in making tools and machines. Ex. *The plow was made.of iron.* 2. something hard, strong, and unyielding. Ex. *He has a grip of iron.* 3. an electrical device used for pressing or smoothing cloth. Ex. *The iron is hot.* —*adj.* 1. made of iron. Ex. *There is an iron fence around the building.* 2. like iron; strong. Ex. *Because of his iron fists, he seldom loses a fight.* —*v.* press; make smooth with an iron. Ex. *Please iron this shirt.*

IRON 3

ironing board [ay'ərniŋ bord'], a board on which clothing, linens, etc. are placed in order to iron.

irregular (5) [ireg'yulər], *adj.* 1. not having a regular or even shape, arrangement, or order. Ex. *Train schedules were irregular during the flood.* 2. occurring at an uneven rate or unequal rate. Ex. *The sick man's heartbeat was irregular.* 3. not according to the usual rule or to the accepted principle or method. Ex. *He kept irregular accounts.* —**ir·reg'u·lar·ly,** *adv.* —**ir`reg·u·lar'i·ty,** *n.*

irritate (4) [i:r'əteyt`], *v.* 1. make nervous, impatient, or angry. Ex. *When she has a headache, the slightest noise irritates her.* 2. cause to become red or sore. Ex. *The rough cloth irritated the child's tender skin.* —**ir'ri·ta·ble,** *adj.* easily irritated. —**ir`ri·ta'tion,** *n.*

is (1) [iz'], *v.* present tense of *be* used with he, she, it, and singular nouns. Ex. *He is a doctor.*

-ish (2) [iš], *suffix.* 1. like. Exs. *Devil, devilish; girl, girlish.* 2. somewhat; rather. Exs. *Tall, tallish; yellow, yellowish.* 3. of; belonging to. Exs. *England, English; Spain, Spanish.*

island (1) [ay'lənd], *n.* a section of dry land entirely surrounded by water. Ex. *The island can be reached only by boat.*

isle (3) [ayl'], *n.* a very small island. Ex. *There are many isles at the mouth of this river.*

-ism (3) [izəm], *suffix.* 1. the act or result of. Exs. *Terrorize, terrorism; organize, organism.* 2. the state, condition, or quality of. Exs. *Defeat, defeatism; hero, heroism.* 3. theory; belief. Exs. *National, nationalism; real, realism.*

isolate (4) [ay'səleyt`], *v.* set apart; separate; cause to be alone. Ex. *He isolated himself in order to study.* —**i·so·la'tion,** *n.*

—i'so·la'tion·ist, *n.* one who favors his country keeping apart from international involvements.

issue (2) [iš'uw, iš'yuw], *n.* 1. printed material, usually part of a series, such as a magazine or newspaper. **Ex.** *The latest issue of the newspaper contains the story of my accident.* 2. a matter of interest or discussion. **Ex.** *Increasing taxes are a current issue.* —*v.* 1. send out; publish. **Ex.** *That magazine is issued once a month.* 2. give out; distribute. **Ex.** *Food and clothing were issued to the flood victims.* —is'su·ance, *n.* act of issuing. —at issue, being discussed or argued about. **Ex.** *Where to go was the question at issue.*

-ist (2) [ist], *suffix.* 1. one who practices; one whose profession is. **Exs.** *Art, artist; science, scientist.* 2. one who believes in; one who is a student of. **Exs.** *Nationalism, nationalist; socialism, socialist.*

it (1) [it'], *pron.* 1. a thing, place, happening, or idea that has already been mentioned or that is understood. **Ex.** *He saw a house and bought it.* 2. a reference to a general condition or action. **Exs.** *Weather: it rains, it is cold; event: it happens.*

item (3) [ay'təm], *n.* 1. a separate article or thing in a list or group. **Ex.** *Meat, salad, and potatoes were three of the items on her shopping list.* 2. a piece of news or information. **Ex.** *He read an item about his friend in the newspaper.* —i'tem·ize, *v.* list things, one by one. **Ex.** *Please itemize your expenses.*

its (1) [itš], *pron.* of or belonging to it. **Ex.** *The cat is playing with its ball.*

itself (2) [itself'], *pron.* 1. its own self. **Ex.** *The dog hurt itself.* 2. a form of emphasis. **Ex.** *Death itself held no greater terror.*

-ity (2) [ətiy, itiy], *suffix.* state; quality. **Exs.** *Real, reality; regular, regularity; active, activity.*

-ive (2) [iv], *suffix.* 1. having the quality of. **Ex.** *Affirm, affirmative.* 2. likely to; tending to. **Ex.** *Express, expressive.*

-ize (3) [ayz], *suffix.* 1. make into or like; become. **Exs.** *Human, humanize; crystal, crystallize.* 2. act in a certain way; treat; engage in. **Exs.** *Theory, theorize; sympathy, sympathize.* 3. treat; combine with; subject to the action of. **Ex.** *Critic, criticize.*

J

J, j [ǰey¹], *n.* the tenth letter of the English alphabet.

jacket (2) [ǰæk¹it], *n.* 1. an outer garment worn on the upper part of the body; a short coat. **Ex.** *A man's suit consists of a pair of trousers and a jacket.* 2. an outer covering, such as the skin of a potato.

JACKET 1

jail (4) [ǰeyl¹], *n.* a prison for those awaiting a trial or for those who have committed crimes that are not serious. **Ex.** *The judge sent him to jail for sixty days.* —*v.* take into or hold in jail. **Ex.** *He was jailed for stealing a car.* —**jail'er,** *n.* person in charge of a jail.

jam (4) [ǰæm¹], *v.* 1. push; crowd in together. **Ex.** *The returning workers jammed into the buses.* 2. cause to become stuck; force in so that something will not move. **Ex.** *The key is jammed in the lock.* —*n.* a crowding together or a being crowded together. **Ex.** *There is a traffic jam in the city streets every morning.*

jam (4) [ǰæm¹], *n.* a food made of fruit and sugar cooked together until thick. **Ex.** *He spread jam on his bread.*

January (1) [ǰæn¹yuwe:r`iy], *n.* the first month of the year.

jar (2) [ǰa:r¹], *n.* a round container, usually made of glass, with a wide opening at the top.

JAR

jar (2) [ǰa:r¹], *v.* cause to shake; shock. **Ex.** *He was jarred by a loud noise.*

jaw (4) [ǰɔ:¹], *n.* one of the two bones which hold the teeth and form the frame of the mouth. **Ex.** *The meat was so tough his jaws hurt from chewing it.*

jealous (3) [ǰel¹əs], *adj.* 1. fearful of losing love or favor to another. **Ex.** *The little boy was jealous of his baby sister.* 2. angry or sad because someone else has what one wants. **Ex.** *He was jealous of his neighbor's good fortune.* —**jeal'ous·ly,** *adv.* —**jeal'ous·y,** *n.*

jelly (4) [jĕl'iy], *n.* a food, usually sweet, made by boiling sugar and fruit juice together until it is thick and partly clear. Ex. *We had toast and jelly at breakfast.* —**jell'**, *v.* cause to become semi-solid like jelly.

jerk (4) [jərk'], *n.* a quick, sharp movement. Ex. *He stopped the car with a jerk, and we were thrown to the floor.* —*v.* give a sudden push, pull, or twist to. Ex. *He jerked open the door.* —**jerk'y**, *adj.* —**jerk'i·ly**, *adv.* with sudden starts and stops.

jet (3) [jĕt'], *n.* 1. a burst of liquid or gas forced from a small opening. Ex. *A jet of water came from the hole in the pipe.* 2. an airplane powered by streams of hot air and gases that are forced out through the rear of the engine.

jewel (2) [ju̇w'əl], *n.* gem; a valuable stone, such as a diamond. Ex. *The jewel in her ring was a diamond.* —**jew'el·er**, *n.* a person who makes, sells, or repairs jewels. —**jew'el·ry**, *n.* a valuable ornament, often made with jewels.

job (1) [jäb'], *n.* 1. work; employment. Ex. *His job pays him enough money to buy food and clothes.* 2. a piece of work; a duty. Ex. *A mother has many different jobs to do every day.*

join (1) [joyn'], *v.* 1. become a member of. Ex. *He joined the Boy Scouts.* 2. bring or put together; combine. Ex. *The carpenter joined the two pieces of wood with glue.* —**join'er**, *n.* a person who joins.

joint (3) [joynt'], *n.* 1. the place at which two things are joined. Ex. *The joints of the chair were loose.* 2. the place where two bones of the body are joined. Ex. *The elbow and the knee are joints.* —*adj.* shared by two or more; affecting two or more. Ex. *The men were joint owners of the land.* —**joint'ed**, *adj.* having joints. —**joint'ly**, *adv.*

joke (2) [jowk'], *n.* 1. something done or said to cause laughter or amusement. Ex. *The jokes he told made everybody laugh.* 2. a thing or person that causes laughter. Ex. *We thought his threat was only a joke.* —*v.* speak or act in an amusing or playful way. Ex. *The funny man joked about his accident and everyone laughed.* —**jok'er**, *n.* —**jok'ing·ly**, *adv.*

jolly (4) [jäl'iy], *adj.* gay; joyful; in good spirits. Ex. *Everyone at the party was very jolly.* —**jol'li·ty**, *n.*

jolt (5) [jowlt'], v. shake roughly. **Ex.** *The car jolted over the rocky road.* —n. a rough movement; a sudden shock. **Ex.** *The bad news gave us a jolt.*

journal (3) [jər'nəl], n. 1. a written account of what happened daily. **Ex.** *During his trip, he kept a journal of his experiences.* 2. a newspaper published daily; any regular publication. **Ex.** *He writes for a business journal.* —**jour'nal·ism**, n. the business of managing or writing news for a journal, radio, etc. —**jour'nal·ist**, n. one who writes for a newspaper, radio, etc. **Ex..** *The President was asked questions by several journalists.*

journey (1) [jər'niy], n. a trip. **Ex.** *We are making a journey abroad this summer.*

joy (1) [joy'], n. 1. great delight, pleasure, or happiness. **Ex.** *They were filled with joy at the good news.* 2. that which causes joy. **Ex.** *Their daughter is their pride and joy.* —**joy'ful**, adj. feeling happy. —**joy'ful·ly**, adj. —**joy'ous**, adj. happy. —**joy'ous·ly**, adv.

judge (1) [jəj'], n. 1. a public official who settles problems of law in a court. **Ex.** *The judge sentenced the thief to two years in prison.* 2. a person appointed to decide the winner of a contest. **Ex.** *The judges could not agree on who had won the race.* —v. 1. form an opinion about; estimate the quality of. **Ex.** *The critics judge the play to be a success.* 2. think; believe. **Ex.** *We judge the problem to be serious.* —**judg'ment**, n. 1. a judge's decision. 2. the ability to decide wisely. **Ex.** *He used good judgment in returning to school.* 3. opinion. **Ex.** *In my judgment, he should not be allowed to go.*

jug (5) [jəg'], n. a container with a handle, used to hold liquids. **Ex.** *She filled the jug with water.*

JUG

juice (2) [juws'], n. the fluid part of fruit, vegetables, or meat. **Ex.** *He drank a glass of orange juice at breakfast.* —**juic'y**, adj. having much juice.

July (1) [julay'], n. the seventh month of the year.

jump (1) [jəmp'], v. 1. leap or spring into the air. **Ex.** *He jumped up to catch the ball.* 2. leap or spring down from. **Ex.** *The people jumped from the burning building.* 3. **pass**

from one place to another by a leap. **Ex.** *He jumped over the hole in the street.* —*n.* 1. a leap; the act of jumping. 2. a sudden rise, as of price or amount. —**jump'er,** *n.* one who jumps. —**jump'y,** *adj.* nervous.

junction (5) [jənk'šən], *n.* 1. the act of joining; the state of being joined. **Ex.** *The two rivers make their junction near the sea.* 2. the place of joining or crossing. **Ex.** *There is a store at the junction of the two roads.*

June (1) [juwn'], *n.* the sixth month of the year.

jungle (4) [jəŋ'gəl], *n.* land covered with a tangled growth of trees, vines, and bushes. **Ex.** *Many wild animals live in the jungle.*

junior (3) [juwn'yər], *adj.* 1. younger of two, usually written "Jr." **Ex.** *Thomas Smith, Jr., is the son of Thomas Smith.* 2. of lower rank. **Ex.** *This training course is for junior officers.* —*n.* 1. a person younger in age or rank. **Ex.** *He is my junior by two years.* 2. a student in the second year of a three-year high school or the third year of a four-year high school or college. **Ex.** *He is a junior in school this year.*

junior college [juwn'yər kal'ij], a college giving courses of the first two years of college study. **Ex.** *After junior college, I will go to the university.*

junior high school [juwn'yər hay' skuwl'], a school of the seventh, eighth, and ninth years of study.

junk (5) [jəŋk'], *n.* old or worthless material, such as old metal, paper, broken glass, etc. **Ex.** *They took the junk to the city dump.*

jury (3) [ju:r'iy], *n.* 1. a group of persons who promise to decide what is true in a law trial. **Ex.** *The jury decided the man was guilty.* 2. a group of persons who decide winners, what is best, etc. in a contest. **Ex.** *The jury gave prizes to two of his paintings.*

just (1) [jəst'], *adv.* 1. at the same time. **Ex.** *He left just as I came in.* 2. barely. **Ex.** *The coat is just big enough for you.* 3. only. **Ex.** *Help me for just a minute.* 4. very shortly before or after the present moment. **Ex.** *He just left.* 5. exactly. **Ex.** *That is just what I want.*

just (1) [jəst'], *adj.* 1. fair; acting from fair and truthful motives. **Ex.** *A good judge is a just man.* 2. fair and right. **Ex.** *He has a just claim to the property.* —**just'ly,** *adv.*

justice (2) [jəs'tis], *n.* 1. the quality of being fair, just, or

honest. *Ex. In the interest of justice, a new trial was ordered.*
2. proper punishment or reward. **Ex.** *The injured man demanded justice.* 3. a judge. **Ex.** *The justices wore black robes.*

justify (5) [jəs'təfay`], *v.* 1. prove to be just. **Ex.** *The results justify the expense.* 2. excuse; free from blame. **Ex.** *The accused man tried to justify himself.* —**jus'ti·fi`a·ble,** *adj.* capable of being proved just. —**jus`ti·fi·ca'tion,** *n.* that which shows something to be just.

K

K, k [key`], *n.* the eleventh letter of the English alphabet.

keen (3) [kiyn`], *adj.* 1. very sharp. **Ex.** *An ax must have a keen blade.* 2. quick to understand, see, or hear. **Exs.** *He has a keen mind. The eagle has keen eyes.* —**keen'ly,** *adv.* —**keen'ness,** *n.*

keep (1) [kiyp`], *v.* 1. have for one's own; possess. **Ex.** *This book is yours to keep.* 2. fulfill. **Ex.** *He always keeps his promise.* 3. prevent. **Ex.** *They could not keep him from going.* 4. remain good; stay as it is. **Ex.** *Cold milk keeps longer.* 5. save for later use. **Ex.** *Keep the cake until tomorrow.* 6. have the care of. **Ex.** *He keeps the lions at the zoo.* —**keep'er,** *n.* one who has the care of people, animals, or things. —**keep company,** associate with; be a friend of. **Ex.** *He kept company with her for six months, and then they became engaged.* —**keep to oneself,** stay away from others. **Ex.** *The quiet boy kept to himself most of the time.* —**keep track,** stay informed. **Ex.** *I kept track of what they were doing.* —**keep up with,** stay equal to or beside; be aware of. **Ex.** *He keeps up with the news.*

kept (1) [kept`], *v.* past tense and participle of *keep.* **Ex.** *The clerk kept us waiting.*

kerosene (5) [ke:r'əsiyn`, ke:r`əsiyn`], *n.* an oil burned in lamps and stoves for cooking or heating; coal oil. **Ex.** *This stove burns kerosene.*

kettle (3) [ket'əl], *n.* 1. a covered container for boiling water used for making tea or for other purposes; a teakettle. 2. a covered container for boiling or cooking; a pot.

KETTLE 1

key (2) [kiy'], *n.* 1. a metal device for opening or closing a lock. 2. that which solves, explains, etc. **Ex.** *The key to success is hard work.* 3. flat piece on a piano, typewriter, etc. which one presses or strikes to operate. **Ex.** *A piano has black keys and white keys.* —*adj.* of chief importance. **Ex.** *The treasurer occupied a key position in his company.*

KEY 1

keyboard [kiy'bɔrd], *n.* a row or rows of many small bars or buttons which are pressed to operate a musical instrument, typewriter, etc. **Ex.** *She sat down at the keyboard and began to play a popular song.*

keynote [kiy'nowt`], *n.* the most important idea of a talk, written article, etc. **Ex.** *The keynote of the President's talk was freedom.*

kick (2) [kik'], *v.* strike or give a blow to with the foot. **Ex.** *The horse kicked the boy.* —*n.* the act of kicking; a blow or thrust with the foot. —**kick'er,** *n.* a person who kicks.

kill (1) [kil'], *v.* take the life of a person, animal, etc.; cause to die. **Ex.** *Many people are killed by guns.* —**kill'er,** *n.*

kin (5) [kin'], *n.* all of one's relatives. **Ex.** *His aunts, uncles, and cousins are his kin.* —**next of kin,** the closest living relative or relatives. **Ex.** *His father is his next of kin.*

kind (1) [kaynd'], *n.* class; sort; type. **Ex.** *What kind of dog is that?*

kind (1) [kaynd'], *adj.* 1. gentle; friendly. **Ex.** *She is kind to her children.* 2. showing goodness. **Ex.** *Helping the old man across the street was a kind thing to do.* —**kind'ly,** *adv.* in a friendly way. **Ex.** *She spoke kindly to the old man.* —**kind'ness,** *n.*

kindle (4) [kin'dəl], *v.* 1. start a fire; cause to burn. **Ex.** *We kindled the fire in the stove.* 2. inflame; excite. **Ex.** *Their interest was kindled by his speech.* —**kin'dling,** *n.* bits of material, such as dry wood, used for starting a fire.

king (1) [kiŋ'], *n*. a male ruler whose position usually passes from father to son. —**king'dom**, *n*. a country ruled by a king or queen. —**king'ly**, *adj*.

kiss (1) [kis'], *v*. touch with the lips in love or respect. **Ex.** *The man kissed his wife good-by.* —*n*. the act of kissing.

kit (5) [kit'], *n*. 1. a set of tools, instruments, supplies, etc. **Ex.** *A kit of tools came with the car.* 2. the case for such equipment or the case with its contents. **Ex.** *He packed a shaving kit in his suitcase.*

kitchen (1) [kič'ən], *n*. a room where food is prepared. **Ex.** *She is in the kitchen cooking dinner.*

kite (4) [kayt'], *n*. a flat frame, usually of light wood, covered with paper or cloth and flown in the wind at the end of a long string.

KITE

kitten (3) [kit'ən], *n*. the young of the cat family. **Ex.** *The cat has six kittens.*

knee (2) [niy'], *n*. the part of the leg that joins the upper leg to the lower leg.

kneel (4) [niyl'], *v*. fall or rest on the knees or on one knee. **Ex.** *He kneeled to pray.* —**knelt'**, past tense and participle.

knew (1) [nuw', nyuw'], *v*. past tense of *know*. **Ex.** *The boy knew his lessons well.*

KNEE

knife (2) [nayf'], *n*. a sharp blade for cutting, attached to a handle. —*v*. cut with a knife. **Ex.** *He was knifed in the back by the robber.*

knit (3) [nit'], *v*. 1. make sweaters, stockings, etc., by locking wool thread together in stitches with special needles. **Ex.** *She knitted her husband a scarf.* 2. grow firmly together; unite. **Ex.** *The broken bones in his leg are knitting nicely.*

KNIFE

knives [nayvz'], *n*. plural of *knife*. **Ex.** *All of her kitchen knives are sharp.*

knob (5) [nab¹], *n.* a rounded handle of a door, drawer, radio, etc. **Ex.** *He turned the door knob to open the door.*

knock (2) [nak¹], *v.* 1. strike a blow with a closed hand on a surface, such as a door, to attract attention. **Ex.** *She heard the visitor knock on the door.* 2. make or do by striking or pounding with tools. **Ex.** *They knocked out a doorway in the wall.* 3. cause to break or fall by striking. **Ex.** *He was knocked down by a horse.* 4. strike against something while moving. **Ex.** *He knocked into the chair in the dark.* —*n.* a loud, sharp blow on a surface, such as a door, to attract attention. **Ex.** *I came when I heard your knock.* —**knock out,** cause to lose consciousness by hitting. **Ex.** *The boxer knocked him out and won the fight.*

knot (3) [nat¹], *n.* the joined ends of a rope, cord, etc.; the point at which there is a tie in ropes, etc. **Ex.** *The knots on your package must be tied tightly.* —*v.* tie knots. **Ex.** *Knot the string tightly.*

knot (3) [nat¹], *n.* a hard swelling or lump on a tree at the point at which a limb or branch connects. **Ex.** *The tree had many knots where limbs had been removed.*

KNOT

know (1) [now¹], *v.* 1. be certain of. **Ex.** *Do you know how much money you have?* 2. recognize; be acquainted with. **Ex.** *Do you know that man?* 3. understand and be able to use. **Ex.** *She knows English.* 4. be able to see that things are different; be able to judge. **Ex.** *We expect him to know right from wrong.* 5. realize; be aware of. **Ex.** *He knows he must study hard.* —**know¹ing,** *adj.* informed; wise. —**know¹ing·ly,** *adv.*

knowledge (2) [nal¹ij], *n.* 1. that which is known; understanding. **Ex.** *To fix a car you need some knowledge of machines.* 2. wide learning or understanding. **Ex.** *The old man was respected for his knowledge.* 3. all that man knows. **Ex.** *Knowledge increases with every generation.*

know-how [now¹haw¹], *n.* expert knowledge and practical ability in doing something. **Ex.** *He has considerable business know-how.*

known (1) [nown¹], *v.* past participle of *know.* **Ex.** *He had known her for several years.*

knuckle (5) [nək'əl], *n.* the joint between sections of a finger and between the fingers and the hand. **Ex.** *Fingers bend at the knuckles.*

L

L, l [el'], *n.* the twelfth letter of the English alphabet.

label (5) [ley'bəl], *n.* a slip of paper or other material fastened to something to show what it is, who owns it, who made it, etc. **Ex.** *She read the label on the jar carefully.* —*v.* 1. put a label on. **Ex.** *The bottle is labeled "poison."* 2. describe as; call. **Ex.** *He was labeled a "thief" because of youthful mistakes.*

labor (1) [ley'bər], *n.* 1. hard work. **Ex.** *He spent the summer doing physical labor.* 2. workers as a group. **Ex.** *Skilled labor is scarce.* —*v.* work; toil. **Ex.** *The men labored from dawn to dark.* —**la'bor·er,** *n.* —**la·bo'ri·ous,** *adj.*

laboratory (3) [læb'(ə)rətɔːr'iy], *n.* a room or a building where experiments in science are made. **Ex.** *That university has a good physics laboratory.*

labor union [ley'bər yuwn'yən], a group of workers united to further their interests, such as better wages.

lace (3) [leys'], *n.* 1. threads made into a delicate patterned cloth with many openings like those in net. 2. cord put through the holes in a shoe to draw the edges together. **Ex.** *Tie your shoelaces.* —*v.* fasten or draw together by a lace. **Ex.** *Lace your shoes.* —**lac'y,** *adj.*

LACE 1

LACE 2

lack (2) [læk'], *n.* a shortage or absence of something needed. **Ex.** *The farmers worried about the lack of rain.* —*v.* be without. **Ex.** *They lacked courage.*

lad (4) [læd'], *n.* a boy or young man. **Ex.** *We lived on a farm when I was a lad.*

ladder (1) [læd'ər], *n.* 1. a structure of metal, wood, or rope consisting of two side pieces between which a series of crosspieces or rungs are set and used for climbing. 2. anything that helps a person to rise or climb higher; the steps or levels one reaches as one climbs. **Ex.** *Education was his ladder to success.*

LADDER 1

lady (1) [ley'diy], *n.* 1. woman of good family; a woman with good manners and a sense of honor. **Ex.** *She is always a lady.* 2. any woman. **Ex.** *He began his speech with the usual, "Ladies and gentlemen. . . ."*

lag (5) [læg'], *v.* move slowly; fall behind. **Ex.** *The child lagged behind the others.* —*n.* a falling behind. **Ex.** *There was a lag in the sale of cars.*

laid (1) [ley'], *v.* past tense and participle of *lay.* **Ex.** *He laid the magazine on the table.*

lain (1) [leyn'], *v.* past participle of *lie.* **Ex.** *He had lain on the bed.*

lake (1) [leyk'], *n.* a large body of water surrounded by land. **Ex.** *They went sailing on the lake.*

lamb (2) [læm'], *n.* 1. a young sheep. **Ex.** *The lambs were playing on the hillside.* 2. the meat of a young sheep. **Ex.** *They had roast lamb for dinner.*

lame (3) [leym'], *adj.* 1. having an injured leg or foot that makes walking difficult. **Ex.** *The lame boy walked slowly.* 2. stiff and sore. **Ex.** *Cold weather bothered his lame back.* 3. not good; poor. **Ex.** *His lame excuse was not accepted.* —**lame'ly,** *adv.* —**lame'ness,** *n.*

lament (4) [ləment'], *v.* mourn; weep; feel or express sorrow. **Ex.** *They lamented the death of their father.* —*n.* sound of grief or sorrow; weeping. **Ex.** *The lament of the mourners was heard during the funeral.* —**lamen'ta·ble,** *adj.*

lamp (2) [læmp'], *n.* a device for making light.

land (1) [lænd'], *n.* 1. the part of the earth's surface not covered by water; the ground. **Ex.** *Some traveled by land and others by sea.* 2. a region or country. **Ex.** *They visited many lands during their travels.* 3. property. **Ex.** *They own land in the west.* —*v.* 1. to arrive on land from the sea or air. **Ex.** *The airplane*

LAMP

landed in the morning. 2. come to the ground. **Ex.** *He was thrown from the horse but landed on his feet.*

landlady [læn(d)'ley`diy], *n.* a female landlord.

landlocked [lænd'lakt`], *adj.* surrounded or nearly surrounded by land; unable to reach the sea by way of water. **Ex.** *The city is landlocked; its nearest port is 100 miles away.*

landlord [læn(d)'lɔrd`], *n.* one who owns and rents land, houses, rooms, etc. to another; a landowner. **Ex.** *The landlord put a new furnace in our house.*

landmark [læn(d)'mark`], *n.* a statue, building, or other object, well-known, by which a person knows where he is. **Ex.** *The White House is a landmark in Washington, D.C.*

lane (3) [leyn'], *n.* 1. a narrow road between fences, trees, houses, etc. **Ex.** *The children were playing in the lane.* 2. part of a highway for traffic moving in one line. **Ex.** *There is a four-lane highway between the two cities.*

language (1) [læŋ'gwij], *n.* 1. speech or the writing that represents speech. **Ex.** *Language must have meaning as well as sound.* 2. the speech of a particular country, nation, or group. **Ex.** *English is the language spoken in the United States.*

lantern (4) [læn'tɔrn], *n.* a container of glass or other material protecting a light-giving flame from the wind, rain, or snow.

lap (3) [læp'], *n.* the front of the body from the waist to the knees when one sits down. **Ex.** *The child sat on his mother's lap.*

lap (3) [læp'], *v.* 1. wash against something with a slapping sound, as water. **Ex.** *The waves lapped gently against the shore.* 2. take up liquid with the tongue. **Ex.** *The cat lapped the milk.*

LANTERN

large (1) [larj'], *adj.* big; being of more than usual size, amount, or number. **Ex.** *He lives in a large city.* —**large'ly**, *adv.* mainly. **Ex.** *He is largely responsible for the change.* —**at large**, free; not held. **Ex.** *The robber escaped and is still at large.*

lash (4) [læš'], *n.* 1. a whip, especially the part which bends on its tip. **Ex.** *The lash made a cracking sound.* 2. a blow with a whip. **Ex.** *The prisoner received ten lashes.* 3. the hair on the lids of the eye; eyelash. **Ex.** *She has long lashes.*

—*v.* 1. beat or drive, usually with a whip. **Ex.** *He lashed the horses until they ran.* 2. beat against. **Ex.** *The waves lashed against the wall.*

lass (5) [læs¹], *n.* a girl or young woman. **Ex.** *She was a pretty lass.*

last (1) [læst¹], *adj.* 1. placed after all others. **Ex.** *December 31 is the last day of the year.* 2. most recent. **Ex.** *These last few days have been rainy.* 3. the only one remaining. **Ex.** *He lost his last friend.* —*adv.* 1. after all others. **Ex.** *The letter "z" comes last in the alphabet.* 2. on the most recent occasion. **Ex.** *She looked well when I last saw her.* —*v.* 1. continue. **Ex.** *The rain lasted all day.* 2. continue in the same condition. **Ex.** *This furniture will last a lifetime.* 3. be enough. **Ex.** *This money must last until next payday.* —*n.* the end; the final part. **Ex.** *She ate the last of the cake.* —**last¹ly,** *adv.* finally; in conclusion. **Ex.** *Lastly, I want to discuss the problem of housing.*

late (1) [leyt¹], *adj.* 1. after the correct time. **Ex.** *He was late in arriving at school.* 2. not early; toward the end. **Ex.** *It happened in the late eighteenth century.* 3. recently dead or ended. **Ex.** *I knew your late father.* —*adv.* 1. not in time. **Ex.** *Help came too late to save the drowning boy.* 2. not early. **Ex.** *He came late in the afternoon.* —**late¹ly,** *adv.* recently; not long ago. **Ex.** *I have not seen her lately.* —**late¹ness,** *n.*

latitude (4) [læt¹ətuwd`, læt¹ətyuwd`], *n.* 1. distance measured in degrees, north or south of the equator. **Ex.** *One degree of latitude on the earth's surface equals almost 70 miles.* 2. freedom from narrow rules or limits. **Ex.** *That girl is given much latitude in her choice of friends.*

latter (2) [læt¹ər], *adj.* 1. near or nearer the end. **Ex.** *He was here in the latter part of May.* 2. being the second of two previously mentioned. **Ex.** *The latter fire was more serious than the former.*

laugh (1) [læf¹], *v.* 1. make sounds that show one is merry, amused, or happy. **Ex.** *The man laughed loudly at the joke.* 2. make fun of; scorn. **Ex.** *They laughed at his mistake.* —*n.* the act or sound which shows happiness or amusement. **Ex.** *He answered with a laugh.* —**laugh¹a·ble,** *adj.* causing laughs.

laughter (1) [læf¹tər], *n.* the act of laughing; the sound of laughing. **Ex.** *Shouts of laughter greeted his remark.*

launch (4) [lɔ:nč'], *n.* a motorboat used to carry people and supplies between a ship and the shore. **Ex.** *The launch came alongside the ship.*

launch (4) [lɔ:nč'], *v.* 1. cause to float. **Ex.** *The new ship was launched as the crowd cheered.* 2. send up into space. **Ex.** *A new spaceship was launched yesterday.* 3. start; begin. **Ex.** *The attack was launched at midnight.* —**launch, laun' ching,** *n.*

launch pad [lɔ:nč' pæd'], the starting place from which a spaceship goes into space. **Ex.** *The launch pad for the moon flight is at Cape Kennedy.*

laundry (5) [lɔn'driy], *n.* a place where clothes and linens are washed, dried, and sometimes ironed. **Ex.** *They sent their dirty clothes to the laundry.* 2. clothes and linens that have been or are to be washed. **Ex.** *She gathered the laundry together.* —**laun'der,** *v.* wash.

law (1) [lɔ:'], *n.* all or any one of the rules made by a government. **Ex.** *Each person is expected to obey the law.* 2. the profession or study of law. **Ex.** He intends to study law. —**law'ful, law'less,** *adj.*

lawn (3) [lɔ:n'], *n.* land covered with grass kept closely cut, as near or around a house. **Ex.** *He is cutting the lawn.*

lawsuit [lɔ:'suwt`, lɔ:'syuwt`], *n.* the claim brought into court for a judge's decision. **Ex.** *In this lawsuit, he is asking to be paid for damage to his car.*

lawyer (2) [lɔ:'yər], *n.* a person trained in the law who practices it as his profession. **Ex.** *I had a lawyer to represent me in court.*

lay (1) [ley'], *v.* 1. put or place so as to rest on or against something. **Ex.** *Lay the book on the table.* 2. put or place. **Ex.** *The story is laid in a foreign country.* 3. put down to be buried. **Ex.** *We saw them lay the body in the grave.* 4. produce and bring forth. **Ex.** *Our hens lay many eggs.* 5. construct as a base. **Ex.** *By studying you are laying a foundation for the future.* —**lay aside, lay away,** save; set aside for later use. —**lay off,** cause a worker to stop being employed for a period of time. **Ex.** *He was laid off until there was more work to do.* —**lay out,** set things where they can be seen, worn, or used. **Ex.** *She laid out his clothes so he* *could find them in the morning.* —**lay over,** stop for a period of time during travel. **Ex.** *On this trip, how long do we have to lay over in New York?*

lay (1) [ley'], *v.* past tense of *lie.* **Ex.** *He lay down and slept.*

lay (1) [ley'], *adj.* not of the clergy or a certain profession. **Ex.** *A layman conducted part of the church service.*

layer (2) [ley'ər], *n.* 1. one thickness or fold. **Ex.** *The cake had three layers.* 2. a thin cover. **Ex.** *There was a layer of dust on the desk.*

lazy (3) [ley'ziy], *adj.* not willing to work or be active. **Ex.** *He is a lazy student.* —**la'zi·ly,** *adv.* slowly, not eagerly. —**la'zi·ness,** *n.*

lead (1) [liyd'], *v.* 1. guide; show the way. **Ex.** *You lead the way and I will follow.* 2. be in first place; be at the head of. 3. command or direct. **Ex.** *The general will lead the army into battle.* 4. live; experience. **Ex.** *He leads an idle life.* —**lead off,** begin. **Ex.** *He will lead off the test with a hard question.* —**lead up to,** get ready for; bring to. **Ex.** *We knew what he was leading up to after his first question.*

lead (1) [led'], *n.* 1. a heavy gray metal which is easily melted. **Ex.** *Lead is often mixed with other metals.* 2. a black substance used in pencils. **Ex.** *The lead in this pencil is too soft.* —*adj.* made of lead. —**lead'en,** *adj.* 1. made of lead. 2. the color of lead. 3. heavy. **Ex.** *He walked with a leaden step.*

leader (1) [liy'dər], *n.* one who guides, directs, or leads. **Ex.** *The President is the leader of our country.*

leaf (3) [liyf'], *n.* one of the green parts that grows from the stems on trees, plants, and bushes. **Ex.** *He picked a leaf from the tree.*

leak (3) [liyk'], *n.* an opening, hole, or crack that accidentally lets something in or out. **Ex.** *There is a leak in the roof.* —*v.* come out through a crack or opening. **Ex.** *Gas is leaking from the stove.* —**leak'y,** *adj.* having leaks. **Ex.** *That gas stove is leaky.*

lean (2) [liyn'], *v.* 1. bend the upper part of the body. **Ex.** *She leaned out of the window and looked at the ground.* 2. rest against; place at a slant. **Ex.** *Lean your umbrella against the wall.*

lean (2) [liyn'], *adj.* without fat. **Ex.** *He ate only lean meat.*

leap (4) [liyp'], *n.* a jump; a springing up. **Ex.** *The boy made a high leap.* —*v.* 1. jump. **Ex.** *He leaped out of bed when* *the bell rang.* 2. jump over. **Ex.** *The dog leaped over the fence.*

leap year [liyp' yi:r'], a year of 366 days that occurs every fourth year.

learn (1) [lərn'], *v.* 1. acquire skill or knowledge of. **Ex.** *She is learning to dance.* 2. come to know a fact or facts. **Ex.** *We have just learned where he lives.* —**learn'ed,** *adj.* having much knowledge. —**learn'ing,** *n.* 1. great knowledge. 2. the gaining of some skill or ability.

lease (4) [liys'], *n.* a written agreement giving the right to use property for a certain length of time in exchange for rent. **Ex.** *They signed a one-year lease for the house.* —*v.* rent under a written agreement. **Ex.** *I leased the house for one year.*

least (1) [liyst'], *adj.* littlest; the smallest in size, quantity, or position. **Ex.** *He did the work without the least difficulty.* —*adv.* to the smallest extent, amount, or degree. **Ex.** *He liked that book least of all.*

leather (2) [leð'ər], *n.* the prepared skin or hide of certain animals. **Ex.** *His shoes are made of leather.* —*adj.* made of leather. **Ex.** *He is wearing a leather belt.*

leave (1) [liyv'], *v.* 1. go away. **Ex.** *Did you see him leave?* 2. go away from. **Ex.** *He leaves home early in the morning.* 3. allow to remain behind or in some place. **Ex.** *You may leave your books here.* 4. let remain in a particular condition. **Ex.** *Leave the window open at night.* 5. let someone else do; trust someone with. **Ex.** *Leave the rest of the work for me.*

leaves (3) [liyvz'], *n.* plural of *leaf.*

lecture (3) [lek'čər], *n.* a speech or a talk given to a class or group. **Ex.** *The professor gave a lecture on modern art.* —*v.* give a speech or talk to a class or group. **Ex.** *The professor lectured in the evening.* —**lec'tur·er,** *n.*

led (1) [led'], *v.* past tense and participle of *lead.* **Ex.** *He has led them out of the forest.*

ledge (4) [lej'], *n.* 1. a flat, narrow projection on which something can be placed. **Ex.** *He put his pipe on the window ledge.* 2. a ridge of rock. **Ex.** *They seated themselves on the ledge facing the lake.*

left (1) [left'], *v.* past tense and participle of *leave.* **Ex.** *He left just a few minutes ago.*

left (1) [left'], *adj.* 1. on or to the side that is toward the west when one is facing north. **Ex.** *Not many people write with their left hand.* 2. desiring radical change or favoring liberal, democratic, socialistic, etc. ideas in politics. —*n.* 1. the direction or side to the left. **Ex.** *When you face the rising sun, the north is on your left.* 2. liberal groups, parties, etc. that favor political ideas which are left. **Ex.** *His ideas are toward the left.* —*adv.* toward the left. **Ex.** *Walk two blocks and turn left.*

leftist [lef'tist], *n., adj.* one who favors the left in politics.

leg (1) [leg'], *n.* 1. one of the lower limbs of the human body. **Ex.** *The legs are used for standing and walking.* 2. one of the limbs of an animal. **Ex.** *Insects have six legs.* 3. anything shaped or used like a leg. **Ex.** *One of the table legs is loose.* 4. The part of a garment that covers the leg. **Ex.** *The leg of his trousers is torn.*

legal (3) [liy'gəl], *adj.* 1. lawful. **Ex.** *In some towns it is not legal to keep stores open on Sundays.* 2. of the law. **Ex.** *Lawyers are members of the legal profession.* —**le'gal·ly,** *adv.* in a way that is lawful. —**le·gal'i·ty,** *n.* —**le'gal·ize,** *v.*

legend (4) [lej'ənd], *n.* 1. a story coming down from the past, which many people believe but which may not be true. **Ex.** *My grandfather knew many old legends.* 2. what is written on a coin, a medal, or below a picture or map. **Ex.** *I could not read the legend on the coin.* —**leg'end·ar`y,** *adj.*

legislate (4) [lej'isleyt`], *v.* make laws. **Ex.** *The Congress of the United States has the power to legislate.* —**leg`is·la'tor,** *n.* member of a lawmaking body. —**leg`is·la'tion,** *n.* 1. the act of making laws. 2. the laws made. **Ex.** *This legislation gives help to education.* —**leg`is·la'ture,** *n.* the lawmaking group. —**leg`is·la'tive,** *adj.*

legitimate (4) [ləjit'əmit], *adj.* 1. right; lawful. **Ex.** *They have a legitimate claim to the property.* 2. born of parents who are married to each other. **Ex.** *He is their legitimate child.* 3. expected; reasonable. **Ex.** *His request was a legitimate one.* —**le·git'i·ma·cy,** *n.*

leisure (4) [liy'žər], *n.* free time in which a person may rest, amuse himself, and do the things he likes to do. **Ex.** *He had no leisure for his favorite sport.* —**lei'sure·ly,** *adj.* taking plenty of time. **Ex.** *He enjoyed a leisurely walk.* —**lei'sure·ly,** *adv.* —**at one's leisure,** slowly; without rush. **Ex.** *Do the work at your leisure.*

lemon (3) [lem'ən], *n.* a sour, juicy fruit, light yellow in color, which grows in warm climates. —*adj.* pale yellow.

lend (2) [lend'], *v.* 1. permit someone else to use a thing for a time. **Ex.** *I asked him to lend me his pencil.* 2. make a loan of money. **Ex.** *The bank lends money as part of its regular business.* —**lend'er,** *n.* —**lend a hand,** help. **Ex.** *Please lend me a hand with this work.* —**lend itself to,** be suitable for. **Ex.** *That chair lends itself to use in many rooms.*

length (1) [leŋkθ', leŋθ'], *n.* 1. the distance from one end to the other. **Ex.** *The length of the rope is ten feet.* 2. the measure of how long a thing lasts. **Ex.** *The length of the school year is ten months.* 3. the longest side of any object. **Ex.** *The length of the table is six feet.* —**length'y,** *adj.* long; too long. —**length'en,** *v.* make longer; become or grow longer. **Ex.** *Her mother lengthened her dress.* —**at length,** for a long time. **Ex.** *He talked at length.* —**go to any lengths,** do everything necessary. **Ex.** *He will go to any lengths to get a new car.*

lens (5) [lenz'], *n.* 1. a specially shaped piece of glass in eyeglasses, cameras, and certain instruments used for viewing. **Ex.** *He needed powerful lenses in his glasses.* 2. the part of the eye through which the light passes, enabling one to see.

lent (2) [lent'], *v.* past tense and participle of *lend.* **Ex.** *He lent me his book.*

less (1) [les'], *adj.* smaller in amount or extent. **Ex.** *He has less land than his brother.* —*adv.* not so much. **Ex.** *The weather is less cold today.* —*n.* a smaller amount or part. **Ex.** *She gave me less than she gave him.* —**less'en,** *v.* become or make less.

-less (1) [ləs, lis], *suffix.* 1. free from; without. **Exs.** *Fear, fearless; home, homeless.* 2. unable to do or to be. **Exs.** *Count, countless; help, helpless.*

lesson (2) [les'ən], *n.* 1. that which must be learned; a part of a course of study. **Ex.** *The teacher explained the history lesson.* 2. a useful piece of wisdom; something learned for one's own good. **Ex.** *The accident was a lesson to him to drive more carefully.*

let (1) [let'], *v.* 1. permit or allow to do or to be. **Ex.** *I let him have the money.* 2. please; do. **Ex.** *Let us go now to the*

a, far; æ, am; e, get; ey, late; i, in; iy, see; ɔ, all; ow, go; u, put; uw, too; ə, but, ago; ər, fur; aw, out; ay, life; oy, boy; ŋ, ring; θ, think; ð, that; ž, measure; š, ship; j, edge; č, child.

theater. **—let alone, 1.** do not bother. **Ex.** *Let him alone; he is reading.* **2.** without reference to; not to mention. **Ex.** *He is doing poorly now, let alone trying to do more work.* **—let down,** disappoint. **Ex.** *She let us down by not coming.* **—let off, let out,** release; permit to go. **Ex.** *We were let off early today at school.*

letter (1) [let'ər], *n.* **1.** one of the symbols of the alphabet. **Ex.** *"A" and "B" are the first two letters of the English alphabet.* **2.** a written or printed message. **Ex.** *He wrote a letter to his friend.*

letterhead [let'ərhed'], *n.* the printing at the top of a sheet of paper used for letter writing.

letter-perfect [let'ərpə:r'fikt], *adj.* completely correct. **Ex.** *He did letter-perfect work.*

lettuce (5) [let'əs], *n.* a garden vegetable with green leaves, used in salads.

level (2) [lev'əl], *adj.* **1.** flat; smooth; even. **Ex.** *The floor is not level.* **2.** even with something else. **Ex.** *The two pictures are not level.* **—n. 1.** the height to which a thing rises or reaches. **Ex.** *The flood water rose to a level of sixty feet.* **2.** a certain position; rank. **Ex.** *This word is on the 2,000-word level.* **—v.** make smooth and flat. **Ex.** *The builder leveled the ground to build the house.*

levy (5) [lev'iy], *v.* force the payment of; collect money by taxing. **Ex.** *A tax was levied on certain goods.* **—n.** a raising or collecting, by authority or force. **Ex.** *A levy was needed to pay for roads.*

liable (4) [lay'əbəl], *adj.* **1.** responsible; required by law to pay. **Ex.** *He stated that he would not be liable for his son's debts.* **2.** likely to happen with unpleasant results. **Ex.** *You are liable to get wet if you go out in this rain.* **—li·a·bil'i·ty,** *n.* **1.** an obligation, especially for payment of a debt. **2.** an unfavorable condition. **Ex.** *Lack of education is a distinct liability.*

liar (1) [lay'ər], *n.* one who tells an untruth, knowing it is not true.

liberal (3) [lib'ərəl], *adj.* **1.** generous; more than enough. **Ex.** *He gave the waiter a liberal tip.* **2.** open to new ideas; not limited. **Ex.** *They want their children to have a liberal education.* **3.** favorable to progress or change. **Ex.** *He is liberal in his views on government.* **—n.** a person of liberal principles or views. **—lib'er·al·ism,** *n.* liberal ideas or policies,

especially regarding political and social questions. —**lib'**
er·al·ize`, *v.*

liberty (2) [lib'ərtiy], *n.* 1. freedom from the will of a master
or from an absolute ruler or government. **Ex.** *He dreamed*
of bringing liberty to his country. 2. freedom from being
confined. **Ex.** *She opened the cage and gave the bird its*
liberty. 3. freedom of choice. **Ex.** *The boy was given the*
liberty of choosing his school. —**lib'er·ate,** *v.* make free.
Ex. *The prisoners of war were liberated.* —**at liberty,** free
to do; permitted. **Ex.** *I am at liberty to go with you.* —**take**
liberties, be too familiar with; use too freely.

library (2) [lay'brer`iy], *n.* a room or building where a col-
lection of books is kept; also, a collection of books. **Ex.** *Our*
school has a large library. —**li·brar'i·an,** *n.* one who is in
charge of a library.

license (4) [lay'səns], *n.* legal written permission to do something. **Ex.** *He always carried his driver's license.* —*v.* permit
by law. **Ex.** *He was licensed to practice medicine.*

lick (4) [lik'], *v.* 1. pass the tongue over. **Ex.** *The dog licked*
my hand. 2. take up with the tongue. **Ex.** *The cat licked the*
milk from the dish.

lid (3) [lid'], *n.* 1. a removable cover; a
top. 2. a cover of skin that is moved
in opening and closing the eye; the
eyelid.

lie (1) [lay'], *v.* 1. have one's body extended on the ground or other surface.
Ex. *They lie down for a rest every after-*

LID 1

noon. 2. rest or remain flat on a surface. **Ex.** *The news-*
papers lie on the floor. 3. be in a certain place. **Ex.** *Europe*
lies north of Africa.

lie (1) [lay'], *v.* say something one knows to be untrue. **Ex.** *He*
lied about the amount of money he had spent. *n.* an untrue
statement. **Ex.** *He told a lie to explain his absence.*

lieutenant (4) [luw`ten'ənt], *n.* 1. an army officer ranking below
a captain. 2. a naval officer two ranks below a commander
(lieutenant, lieutenant commander, commander). 3. one
who acts for or assists a superior. **Ex.** *The lieutenant gover-*
nor attended the meeting in place of the governor.

life (1) [layf'], *n.* 1. the state of living; being alive. **Ex.** *People,*
animals, and plants have life. 2. the time of being alive; the
time between being born and dying. **Ex.** *She worked hard*

all her life. 3. a living being; a person. **Ex.** *Five lives were lost in the fire.* 4. living things of any kind. **Ex.** *There seems to be no life on the moon.* 5. a way of living. **Ex.** *City life is often interesting.* 6. the story of someone's life. **Ex.** *He enjoyed reading the lives of great men.*

life belt [layf' belt'], a special belt made to help people stay afloat in water.

lifeboat [layf'bowt'], *n.* a small boat, carried on a ship, to be used in case the ship is sinking or is in other danger.

LIFE BELT

lifeguard [layf'gard], *n.* an expert swimmer whose duty it is to protect the safety of other swimmers, bathers, etc.

life preserver [layf' prəzər'vər], a device such as a jacket or a ring that helps a person to stay afloat in water. **Ex.** *The passengers were shown how to use the life preservers.*

life-sized [layf'sayzd'], *adj.* same in size as the thing or person represented. **Ex.** *They made a life-sized statue of him.*

lifetime [layf'taym'], *n.* the time that one lives. **Ex.** *Many things happened in his lifetime.*

lift (1) [lift'], *v.* 1. raise; take or bring up to a higher place. **Ex.** *The man lifted the heavy load.* 2. rise and go; go away. **Ex.** *When the fog lifts, we shall try again.*

light (1) [layt'], *n.* 1. a form of energy that affects the eyes so that one is able to see. **Ex.** *The sun is the source of our light.* 2. that which gives light, such as a lamp. **Ex.** *He saw a light in the window.* —*adj.* 1. having light; bright; clear. **Ex.** *The room is light.* 2. pale in color. **Ex.** *The girl has light hair.* —*v.* 1. set fire to; burn. **Ex.** *Please light the fire.* 2. give light to. **Ex.** *The lamp lights the room.* —**light'er,** that which starts a fire. —**in light of,** with knowledge of. **Ex.** *In light of the bad weather report, we should leave early.*

light (1) [layt'], *adj.* 1. not heavy; having little substance. **Ex.** *He was wearing a light coat.* 2. less than usual in amount or force. **Ex.** *We had only a light rain.* 3. not serious. **Ex.** *She enjoyed light reading.* —**light'ness,** *n.* —**light'ly,** *adv.*

lightheaded [layt'hed'id], *adj.* silly; not serious; dizzy. **Ex.** *The drink caused him to feel lightheaded.*

lighthearted [layt'har'təd], *adj.* gay; happy. **Ex.** *The good news made her feel very lighthearted.*

lighthouse [layt'haws`], *n.* a tower, or a structure resembling a tower, with a strong light to warn ships of danger.

lightning (2) [layt'niŋ], *n.* a discharge or flash of electricity in the sky. **Ex.** *Lightning is usually followed by thunder.*

like (1) [layk'], *prep.* 1. almost the same as; similar to. **Ex.** *Our house is like theirs.* 2. showing the same quality; in the same way. **Ex.** *Some other animals bark like dogs.* 3. typical of; with a special quality. **Ex.** *How like her to be late!* 4. almost certain to; as if about to happen. **Ex.** *It looks like snow today.* 5. in the mood for. **Ex.** *I feel like going to the movies.* —**like'ness,** *n.* 1. the fact of being similar. **Ex.** *Her likeness to her mother is very strong.* 2. a picture; a copy. **Ex.** *The painting is a good likeness of the boy.*

like (1) [layk'], *v.* 1. have affection for. **Ex.** *They liked the neighbor's children.* 2. take pleasure in; enjoy. **Ex.** *She likes to swim.* 3. choose; prefer. **Ex.** *What would you like to do?* —**lik'a·ble,** *adj.* —**lik'ing,** *n.* an affection or preference for. **Ex.** *She has a liking for cake.*

-like (3) [layk], *suffix.* similar to. **Exs.** *Life, lifelike; child, childlike.*

likewise [layk'wayz`], *adv.* in a similar way. **Ex.** *She studied the lesson and you must do likewise.*

likely (1) [layk'liy], *adj.* 1. seeming about to be or happen. **Ex.** *A rise in prices seems likely.* 2. probable; believable. **Ex.** *That is not a very likely story.* —*adv.* probably. **Ex.** *Very likely you are right.*

lily (3) [lil'iy], *n.* a tall plant, usually with white flowers, grown from a bulb. —*adj.* like a lily; pure, white, pale, or delicate.

limb (3) [lim'], *n.* 1. an arm or leg. **Ex.** *He lost one of his limbs in the accident.* 2. a branch of a tree. **Ex.** *He cut off the dead limb of the tree.*

limit (2) [lim'it], *n.* 1. the farthest edge; the boundary line. **Ex.** *They lived beyond the city limits.* 2. as far as a person or thing can go. **Ex.** *They stretched the rope to its limit.* 3. the greatest amount, number, etc. permitted. **Ex.** *He was arrested for driving beyond the speed limit.* —*v.* keep within bounds; set a limit to. **Ex.** *She limited her telephone* *conversation to three minutes.* —**lim'i·ta'tion**, *n.* a limiting; something that limits. Ex. *His lack of a college degree was a limitation on his professional advancement.*

limp (4) [limp'], *adj.* lacking stiffness; not firm. Ex. *The flowers were limp from lack of water.* —**limp'ly**, *adv.* —**limp'ness**, *n.*

limp (4) [limp'], *v.* walk unevenly because of an injured leg. Ex. *He limped across the street.* —*n.* an uneven step or walk. Ex. *He walked with a limp.*

line (1) [layn'], *n.* 1. a row of letters, things, words, etc. Ex. *A line of people waited to get on the bus.* 2. a mark drawn by a pencil, pen, etc. Ex. *The child was learning to draw a straight line.* 3. any mark like that made by a pencil or pen. Ex. *The old woman's face was covered with lines.* 4. a division or limit. Ex. *He drove across the county line.* 5. wires or pipes used to carry electricity, gas, or water. Ex. *A telephone line is now being installed.* —*v.* 1. make lines on; mark with lines. Ex. *Care lined the old woman's face.* 2. form a row or line along. Ex. *Crowds lined the streets for the parade.* —**draw a line**, limit. Ex. *With children, one must draw a line as to what is permitted.* —**hold the line**, keep a firm position; resist. Ex. *We must hold the line on prices and keep them from rising.* —**line up**, get into or form a line. Ex. *Boys will line up here.* —**read between the lines**, find hidden meanings in writing or words. Ex. *She wrote that she was fine, but reading between the lines I knew there were problems.*

line (1) [layn'], *v.* place a lining on the inside of. Ex. *She lined her coat with silk.* —**lin'ing**, *n.* an inside covering.

lineman [layn'mən], *n.* one who fixes telephone or electric wires.

linen (3) [lin'ən], *n.* cloth or thread made from the stems of a plant. Ex. *She bought three yards of linen for a tablecloth.* —**lin'ens**, *n.* articles once made of linen, but now made of cotton, such as sheets, pillowcases, and tablecloths. Ex. *We bought some linens on sale.*

-ling (3) [liŋ], *suffix.* 1. small or lesser. Ex. *Duck, duckling.* 2. of. Ex. *Earth, earthling.*

linger (3) [liŋ'gər], *v.* stay as if unwilling to leave; leave or move slowly. Ex. *She told him not to linger on his way home from school.*

link (4) [liŋk'], *n.* 1. one ring or loop of a chain; any of the joined sections of something like a chain. **Ex.** *A chain is only as strong as its weakest link.* 2. anything that joins as a link joins. **Ex.** *The photographs were a link to the past.* —*v.* connect or unite with or as with a link. **Ex.** *The railroad cars were linked together.*

lion (2) [lay'ən], *n.* a large, yellowish-brown, flesh-eating member of the cat family, found in Africa and Asia.

LION

lip (2) [lip'], *n.* 1. either of the two edges of the mouth. 2. anything like a lip. **Ex.** *A drop of water remained on the lip of the cup.*

LIP 1

lip-read [lip'riyd'], *v.* learn what another is saying by watching his lips form the words. **Ex.** *The deaf boy can lip-read what I say.*

liquid (2) [lik'wid], *n.* a substance neither a solid nor a gas. **Ex.** *Water and milk are liquids.* —*adj.* in the form of a liquid. **Ex.** *The sick man could eat only liquid foods.* —**liq'ue·fy,** *v.* change into a liquid.

liquor (2) [lik'ər], *n.* a drink containing alcohol. **Ex.** *Does this restaurant have a license to serve liquor?*

list (1) [list'], *n.* a series of separate items, names, etc. written in order. **Ex.** *He forgot to bring his list of people.* —*v.* make a list of. **Ex.** *She listed the articles she was going to buy.*

listen (1) [lis'ən], *v.* 1. try to hear. **Ex.** *They listened to the radio.* 2. give one's attention to. **Ex.** *You must listen to your teacher.* —**lis'ten·er,** *n.*

lit (4) [lit'], *v.* past tense and participle of *light.* **Ex.** *The fire had been lit before we arrived.*

liter (4) [liy'tər], *n.* See **Weights and Measures.**

literal (4) [lit'ərəl], *adj.* 1. following the exact meaning of the words. **Ex.** *He explained the literal meaning of the phrase.* 2. according to the facts; correct. **Ex.** *The newspaper gave a literal account of the accident.* —**lit'er·al·ly,** *adv.*

literary (3) [lit'ərer'iy], *adj.* 1. of or about literature. **Ex.** *He is a literary critic.* 2. knowing much about literature. **Ex.** *He is a very literary person.* —**lit'er·ate,** *adj.* able to read and write; educated. **Ex.** *What percentage of the people* *are literate?* —**lit'er·a·cy,** *n.* the ability to read and write.

literature (2) [lit'(ə)rəčər, lit'(ə)rəčur], *n.* 1. all of the poems, stories, and writings of a period or country, especially those considered valuable because of their excellence of style or thought. **Ex.** *He was studying American literature.* 2. everything written on a certain subject. **Ex.** *The library has a collection of all the literature on 19th-century French art.*

litter (5) [lit'ər], *n.* 1. things scattered about or carelessly left around. **Ex.** *They collected the litter after the party.* 2. young animals born at the same time. **Ex.** *There were six kittens in the litter.* —*v.* scatter things about. **Ex.** *The grass was littered with paper.*

little (1) [lit'əl], *adj.* 1. not tall or big; small in size. **Ex.** *Theirs is a little house.* 2. a small quantity of; a small degree of. **Ex.** *May I have a little water?* 3. short in time or distance. **Ex.** *They take a little walk after dinner every evening.* —*adv.* in a small quantity or degree. **Ex.** *I feel a little tired.*

live (1) [liv'], *v.* 1. have one's home. **Ex.** *The boy lives with his parents.* 2. be alive; exist. **Ex.** *My father lived seventy years.* 3. spend one's time in a certain manner. **Ex.** *They live quietly.* —**liv'a·ble,** *adj.* 1. suitable for living in. **Ex.** *This is a livable house.* 2. worth living; endurable. **Ex.** *He felt that life was no longer livable.* —**liv'ing,** *adj.* having life. —*n.* the means by or resources with which one supports life. **Exs.** *What does he do for a living? He earns his living by painting.* —**live down,** by actions, cause others to forgive or forget what one has done. **Ex.** *By working hard, he lived down his youthful mistakes.* —**live up to,** live in a way expected of one. **Ex.** *By studying, he lived up to his parents' hopes for him.*

live (1) [layv'], *adj.* having life; alive. **Ex.** *They brought back live animals.* —**live'ly,** *adj.* 1. full of energy. **Ex.** *The band played a lively tune.* 2. exciting. **Ex.** *We had a lively evening at the theater.* —**live'li·ness,** *n.*

livelihood [layv'liyhud'], *n.* the means by or resources with which one supports life. **Ex.** *He earned his livelihood by painting.*

liver (4) [liv'ər], *n.* a large, reddish-brown organ of the body which helps to change the food one eats into body-building material.

living room [liv'iŋ ruwm'], the main room of a house, where guests are received and most activities except eating and sleeping occur.

load (2) [lowd'], *n.* 1. that which is carried or to be carried. **Ex.** *The wagon carried a load of wood.* 2. something which weighs down or burdens. **Ex.** *The load of work was too great for him.* —*v.* 1. fill; put weight on. **Ex.** *They loaded the cart with dirt.* 2. prepare a gun for firing. **Ex.** *He loaded the gun.*

loaf (4) [lowf'], *n.* 1. a shaped mass of bread baked in one piece. **Ex.** *He bought two loaves of bread.* 2. any food baked in bread shape. **Ex.** *We ate a meat loaf for dinner.*

loaf (4) [lowf'], *v.* spend time idly. **Ex.** *He loafs all day.* —**loaf'er,** *n.*

loan (2) [lown'], *n.* 1. a lending; permission to use for a time. **Ex.** *May I have the loan of your book?* 2. that which is lent. **Ex.** *He got a loan from the bank.* —*v.* make a loan; lend. **Ex.** *The bank loaned money to the farmer.*

lobby (5) [lab'iy], *n.* an entrance hall of a building. **Ex.** *He waited for me in the lobby of the theater.*

local (2) [low'kəl], *adj.* 1. concerning or having to do with one place. **Ex.** *We have a local newspaper in our town.* 2. making all or almost all stops. **Ex.** *The local train stops twenty times going to the city.* —**lo'cal·ly,** *adv.*

locate (2) [low'keyt], *v.* 1. find the place or position of. **Ex.** *We located the leak in the gas pipe.* 2. show where something is. **Ex.** *Please locate that city on the map.* —**lo·ca'tion,** *n.* where something is located. **Ex.** *Find the location of the door.*

lock (2) [lak'], *n.* a curl or bunch of hair. **Ex.** *A lock of hair hung from her forehead.*

lock (2) [lak'], *n.* a device for fastening doors, chests, drawers, etc., especially one that operates with a key. —*v.* 1. fasten or be fastened with a lock. **Ex.** *Is the gate locked?* 2. shut inside or outside by means of a lock. **Ex.** *The dog was locked in the house.* —**lock'er,** *n.* a chest, box, etc. which can be locked.

locomotive [low`kəmow'tiv], *n.* an engine which runs on a track and pulls railroad cars; a railroad engine. **Ex.** *The locomotive was pulling a long line of freight cars.*

---

a, far; æ, am; e, get; ey, late; i, in; iy, see; ɔ, all; ow, go; u, put; uw, too; ə, but, ago; ər, fur; aw, out; ay, life; oy, boy; ŋ, ring; θ, think; ð, that; ž, measure; š, ship; ǰ, edge; č, child.

lodge (3) [laǰ'], *n.* 1. a small house or cottage, especially one used in connection with outdoor activities. **Ex.** *On our vacation we stayed at a hunting lodge.* 2. the local branch of a large group. **Ex.** *My lodge meets once each month.* —*v.* 1. live in a rented room or rooms in the house of another, usually for a short time. **Ex.** *He lodged with my family for several weeks.* 2. get stuck in a place. **Ex.** *Our car was lodged in the mud.* —**lodg'er,** *n.* a person who rents a room in the house of another. —**lodg'ing,** *n.* a place to rest or stay for a short time. **Ex.** *His brother offered him lodging while he looked for work.* —**lodg'ings,** *n.* a rented room or rooms in the house of another. **Ex.** *He found lodgings near his work.*

lofty (4) [lɔf'tiy], *adj.* 1. extending or rising very high. **Ex.** *Snow covered the lofty mountain peaks.* 2. high in ideals, spirit, rank, etc. **Ex.** *He was a man of lofty sentiments.* 3. too proud; scornful. **Ex.** *He behaved in a lofty manner toward those working for him.* —**loft'i·ness,** *n.*

log (2) [lɔ:g'], *n.* 1. a length of wood cut from a tree. **Ex.** *His home was a cabin made of logs.* 2. the record of a ship's voyage. **Ex.** *The captain kept the ship's log.* —*adj.* made from logs. **Ex.** *He lives in a log cabin.*

logic (4) [laǰ'ik], *n.* 1. the science of reasoning. **Ex.** *He studied logic in college.* 2. good sense; sound and reliable thinking. **Ex.** *His argument showed logic.* —**log'i·cal,** *adj.*

lone (1) [lown'], *adj.* alone; without company; apart from others. **Ex.** *A lone traveler passed by.* —**lone'ly,** *adj.* 1. feeling oneself alone and longing for company. **Ex.** *The old man led a lonely life.* 2. visited by few or no people. **Ex.** *The house was in a lonely place.* —**lone'li·ness,** *n.*

lonesome [lown'səm], *adj.* having or causing a lonely feeling. **Ex.** *He had a lonesome look on his face.*

long (1) [lɔ:ŋ'], *adj.* 1. measuring more than usual from beginning to end; not short. **Ex.** *She has long hair.* 2. in length. **Ex.** *This board is eight feet long.* —*adv.* 1. for much time. **Ex.** *I have long thought about such a trip.* 2. from the beginning to the end. **Ex.** *He was away at school all winter long.* —**as** or **so long as,** since; as. **Ex.** *As long as you are going, why not take me with you?* —**before long,** soon; in a short time. **Ex.** *We will leave before long.*

longhand [lɔŋ'hænd'], *n.* ordinary handwriting with the words spelled out in full. **Ex.** *He wrote his name in longhand.*

longitude (4) [lɔn'jətuwd`, lɔn'jətyuwd`], *n.* a distance on the earth's surface measured in degrees east or west.

longshoreman [lɔŋ'šŏr`mən], *n.* a man who works at putting cargo on and off a ship in port.

long-winded [lɔŋ'win'did], *adj.* speaking or writing for so long as to be dull. Ex. *The speaker was so long-winded I fell asleep.*

look (1) [luk'], *v.* 1. turn the eyes toward in order to see; turn the attention toward or away from. Ex. *Hearing a noise, he looked toward the door.* 2. search for; hunt for. Ex. *The dog looked for rabbits in the bushes.* 3. seem to be; present an appearance of. Ex. *The woman looked tired.* —*n.* 1. the act of looking or examining. Ex. *After one look, I knew he was someone I had seen before.* 2. appearance. Ex. *She had a sad look on her face.* —**look after**, watch; guard. Ex. *Look after the children for me.* —**look back**, consider past events. Ex. *Don't look back on what you did yesterday.* —**look down on**, think of as less than oneself. Ex. *She looks down on girls who work.* —**look forward to**, wait for eagerly. Ex. *I look forward to resting tomorrow.* —**look over**, examine. Ex. *Look over the books and choose one you like.* —**look on**, 1. regard. Ex. *I look on her as a sister.* 2. watch. Ex. *I looked on while they played.* —**look out**, watch for. Ex. *Look out for falling rocks.* —**look to**, depend on. Ex. *I look to him for help.* —**look up**, search or hunt for in a book, newspaper, etc. Ex. *Look up her number in the telephone book.* —**look up to**, admire. Ex. *She looks up to her older brother.*

looking glass [luk'iŋ glæs'], a miror.

loop (4) [luwp'], *n.* the rounded opening made by curving a thread, cord, rope, etc. back to cross itself. —*v.* form a loop. Ex. *The old road looped around the lake.*

loose (2) [luws'], *adj.* 1. not fastened or tied; free. Ex. *The horse is loose.* 2. not firmly set or fastened in. Ex. *The leg of the table is loose.* 3. not tightly fitting. Ex. *He wore a long, loose coat.* 4. not firm or packed down. Ex. *Most plants grow best in loose soil.* —**loos'en**, *v.* make or become loose; untie. Ex. *He loosened his shoelaces.* —**loose'ly**, *adv.* —**loose'ness**, *n.* —**break loose**, become free. Ex. *He broke loose*

LOOP

from the jail. **—set loose,** turn loose, free. **Ex.** *He set the dog loose to run.*

lord (1) [lɔrd'], *n.* a ruler; a person with power. **Ex.** *He obeyed no lord or king.* **—Lord,** *n.* God. **—lord'ly,** *adj.*

lose (1) [luwz'], *v.* 1. have no longer because of accident or death. **Ex.** *When she died, you lost a good friend.* 2. have no longer and not be able to find. **Ex.** *She is always losing her pen.* 3. fail to keep. **Ex.** *He loses his temper easily.* 4. be defeated. **Ex.** *Our team is losing the game.* 5. suffer a loss. **Ex.** *They are losing money on the sale of their car.* **—lose oneself,** be so interested as not to be aware of what else is happening. **Ex.** *The boy loses himself in his books.*

loss (1) [lɔ:s'], *n.* 1. the act of losing. **Ex.** *The loss of the ship marked the end of the battle.* 2. failure to keep, get, or win. **Ex.** *The loss of the ball game disappointed them.* 3. the person, thing, or amount lost. **Ex.** *Their losses in business were greater than their gains.* **—at a loss,** unsure. **Ex.** *He was at a loss about what he should do.*

lost (1) [lɔ:st'], *v.* past tense and participle of *lose.* **Ex.** *He lost his coat yesterday.* **—adj.** 1. not found; missing. **Ex.** *He was looking for his lost glasses.* 2. no longer possessed. **Ex.** *He often talks about his lost fortune.* 3. not won. **Ex.** *The lost battle ended the general's career.*

lot (1) [lat'], *n.* 1. a great many; a great amount; a great deal. **Ex.** *He has a lot of friends.* 2. a section of land. **Ex.** *He owns a small lot.* **—adv.** to a great extent. **Ex.** *He feels a lot better.*

lotion (4) [low'šən], *n.* a liquid used on the skin to smooth, heal, or cleanse. **Ex.** *She uses lotion on her hands.*

loud (1) [lawd'], *adj.* 1. having a strong, powerful sound. **Ex.** *The firing of the gun made a loud noise.* 2. full of sound or noise. **Ex.** *She has a loud voice.* **—loud'ly,** *adv.* **—loud'ness,** *n.*

loudspeaker [lawd'spiyk'ər], *n.* a device that makes sound louder so that it can be heard, as in a radio.

lounge (5) [lawnǰ'], *v.* stand, walk, sit, or lie easily and lazily. **Ex.** *They lounged on the beach all day.* **—n.** a room in which one can be comfortable and at ease. **Ex.** *They met in the main lounge of the club.*

LOUDSPEAKER

love (1) [ləv¹], *n.* 1. a strong feeling of affection; fond and tender attachment. **Ex.** *They show their love for their children in many ways.* 2. a strong sexual feeling for another. **Ex.** *Their love for each other was obvious.* 3. a strong liking for. **Ex.** *He has always had a love of learning.* —*v.* 1. have love or affection for. **Ex.** *They loved their parents.* 2. have a strong liking for. **Ex.** *He loves music.* —**lov'a·ble, lov'ing,** *adj.* —**lov'er,** *n.* one who loves. —**in love,** in a state of loving. **Ex.** *He has fallen in love with her.* —**make love,** kiss, embrace, etc. as lovers do.

lovely (2) [ləv¹liy], *adj.* 1. beautiful. **Ex.** *Your dress is lovely.* 2. having admirable qualities. **Ex.** *She is a lovely person.* 3. enjoyable. **Ex.** *We had a lovely day.* —**love'li·ness,** *n.*

low (1) [low¹], *adj.* 1. not high or tall. **Ex.** *Their house was a long, low building.* 2. below the normal height; closer to the earth than usual. **Ex.** *The airplane flew very low.* 3. below the usual level; below the general level of the earth's surface. **Ex.** *The land near the mouth of the river was quite low.* 4. smaller than usual in amount, degree, value, or power. **Ex.** *Our supply of flour is very low.* 5. near the bottom of the musical scale; deep in pitch. **Ex.** *He sings the low notes very well.* 6. not loud. **Ex.** *They spoke in low whispers.* 7. not high in rank or position; humble. **Ex.** *He held a very low position.* —*adv.* in a low manner; to a low place or degree. **Ex.** *The sun sank low in the west.*

lower (1) [low¹ər], *v.* 1. reduce in amount, price, resistance, force, etc. **Ex.** *Prices were lowered to sell the goods quickly.* 2. cause loss of respect. **Ex.** *He lowered himself in the eyes of others by his actions.* 3. bring down. **Ex.** *They lowered the flag at sundown.* —*adj.* less than another; below another. **Ex.** *That store charges lower prices.*

loyal (3) [loy¹əl], *adj.* faithful to family, friends, etc. **Ex.** *As a loyal citizen, he supported his government.* —**loy'al·ty,** *n.*

luck (2) [lək¹], *n.* 1. fortune; something that happens by chance. **Ex.** *If my luck does not change, I will not be able to buy a house.* 2. good fortune. **Ex.** *I had the luck of finding a good job.* —**luck'y,** *adj.* —**luck'i·ly,** *adv.*

luggage (3) [ləg¹ij], *n.* the baggage of a traveler, usually suitcases, boxes, etc. **Ex.** *She had four pieces of luggage.*

a, far; æ, am; e, get; ey, late; i, in; iy, see; ɔ, all; ow, go; u, put; uw, too; ə, but, ago; ər, fur; aw, out; ay, life; oy, boy; ŋ, ring; θ, think; ð, that; ž, measure; š, ship; j, edge; č, child.

lull (5) [ləl'], *v.* calm; soothe. **Ex.** *The mother lulled the baby to sleep by singing.* —*n.* a short period of quiet after noise or activity. **Ex.** *There was a lull in the battle.*

lumber (3) [ləm'bər], *n.* wood cut into boards, etc. for building. **Ex.** *They bought some lumber to make a fence.*

lumberyard [ləm'bəryard'], *n.* a place of business where lumber is cut and sold.

lump (5) [ləmp'], *n.* 1. a piece or mass of no particular shape. **Ex.** *He threw some lumps of coal on the fire.* 2. a swelling. **Ex.** *The lump on her head was caused by a fall.* —*v.* form into a lump. **Ex.** *The sugar lumped when it became wet.* —**lump'y**, *adj.* having lumps.

lunch (2) [lənč'], *n.* a light meal usually in the middle of the day. **Ex.** *What did you have for lunch?*

lunchroom [lənč'ruwm'], *n.* a restaurant at which one eats quickly prepared light meals.

lung (4) [ləŋ'], *n.* either of two breathing organs in the chest of man and many other animals.

LUNG

lure (4) [luwr', lyuwr'], *n.* 1. an attraction. **Ex.** *The lure of the sea took him away from home.* 2. something to attract fish. **Ex.** *The fisherman had some bright-colored lures.* —*v.* lead or attract with something that seems desirable. **Ex.** *They lured the dog into the house by offering it meat.*

lust (5) [ləst'], *n.* 1. eagerness to enjoy. **Ex.** *He was possessed by a lust for gold.* 2. a strong desire for sex. **Ex.** *His dreams were full of lust.* —*v.* have a strong desire. **Ex.** *He lusted for fame and fortune.* —**lust'y**, *adj.* full of life and spirit. **Ex.** *The baby gave a lusty yell.* —**lust'i·ly**, *adv.*

luster (4) [ləs'tər], *n.* 1. a bright shine on a surface; brilliance. **Ex.** *He shined his shoes to a high luster.* 2. fame; glory. **Ex.** *The luster of his achievements did not dim with the passing years.*

luxury (3) [lək'šəriy, ləg'žəriy], *n.* 1. comforts and beauties of life beyond what is necessary. **Ex.** *They were wealthy enough to live in luxury.* 2. something which one is not usually able to afford. **Ex.** *They considered fresh meat a great luxury.* —**lux·u'ri·ate**, *v.* 1. live in luxury. 2. enjoy with delight or freedom. —**lux·u'ri·ous**, *adj.* giving a feeling of luxury.

—**lux·u'ri·ant**, *adj.* growing thickly, richly. **Ex.** *He had a luxuriant head of hair.*

-ly (1) [liy], *suffix.* 1. in a certain way. **Exs.** *Happy, happily; gradual, gradually.* 2. each; every. **Exs.** *Week, weekly; year, yearly.* 3. like; similar. **Exs.** *Man, manly; saint, saintly.*

lyric (5) [li:r'ik], *adj.* 1. suitable for singing. **Ex.** *It was a lyric piece of music.* 2. having to do with poems describing inner feelings. **Ex.** *She is a lyric poet.* —*n.* 1. a short poem expressing personal emotion. 2. the words of a song. **Ex.** *The lyrics suit the music.* —**lyr'i·cal**, *adj.*

M

M, m [em'], *n.* the thirteenth letter of the English alphabet.

machine (1) [mašiyn'], *n.* a device with moving parts used to do work. **Ex.** *My mother has a sewing machine.* —*adj.* 1. having to do with machines. **Ex.** *Machine parts are made in this factory.* 2. produced by machines. **Ex.** *These are machine products.* —**ma·chin'ist**, *n.* an expert with machines.

machinery (2) [məšiyn'(ə)riy], *n.* a group of machines. **Ex.** *The machinery in the factory consists of several different kinds of machines.*

mad (1) [mæd'], *adj.* 1. mentally ill; crazy. **Ex.** *The mad person was taken to a doctor.* 2. extremely excited. **Ex.** *At the sight of the fire, the horses became mad with fear.* 3. senseless and foolish. **Ex.** *The girl had a mad desire to become a singer.* —**mad'ly**, *adv.* —**mad'ness**, *n.*

madam (3) [mæd'əm], *n.* a respectful term used in speaking to or of a woman. **Ex.** *The clerk asked, "May I help you, madam?"*

made (1) [meyd'], *v.* past tense and participle of *make.* **Ex.** *She made a cake.*

made-up [meyd'əp'], *adj.* false; invented. **Ex.** *That was simply a made-up story.*

magazine (2) [mæg'əziyn', mæg'əziyn'], *n.* a collection of stories, pictures, and articles published at regular intervals. **Ex.** *I like to read news magazines as well as a daily newspaper.*

magic (3) [mǽj'ik], *n.* 1. the art of seeming to make things happen outside of the laws of nature. **Ex.** *Some people still believe in magic.* 2. any extraordinary influence. **Ex.** *The magic of the singer's voice charmed them all.* 3. the art of performing tricks that deceive the eye. **Ex.** *The children enjoyed watching him perform magic.* —*adj.* as if produced by magic or as if producing magic. **Ex.** *The words of the general had a magic influence on his tired soldiers.* —**mag'i·cal·ly**, *adv.* —**ma·gi'cian**, *n.* one who does magic.

magistrate (4) [mǽj'istreyt`, mǽj'istrit], *n.* the holder of an office with the power to enforce laws. **Ex.** *The magistrate found the prisoner guilty.*

magnet (5) [mǽg'nit], *n.* any substance that has the natural power to attract iron and steel. **Ex.** *She used a magnet to pick up the pins.* —**mag·net'ic**, *adj.* —**mag'net·ism**, *n.* 1. the power of a magnet. 2. the power to attract. —**mag'net·ize**, *v.*

magnificent (2) [mægnif'əsənt], *adj.* splendid; unusually fine; rich. **Ex.** *The house has a magnificent view.* —**mag·nif'i·cent·ly**, *adv.* —**mag·nif'i·cence**, *n.*

magnify (5) [mǽg'nəfay`], *v.* cause to appear larger. **Ex.** *A lens magnifies the size of the words on the paper.*

magnitude (5) [mǽg'nətuwd`, mǽg'nətyuwd`], *n.* 1. greatness of size, quantity, etc. **Ex.** *A crowd of great magnitude attended the President's inauguration.* 2. importance. **Ex.** *He had not realized the magnitude of the problem.*

maid (2) [meyd'], *n.* a girl or woman servant. **Ex.** *The maid cleaned the rooms.*

maiden (3) [meyd'ən], *n.* a girl or young woman who is not married. **Ex.** *She is a pretty maiden of sixteen.* —*adj.* 1. unmarried. **Ex.** *She is my maiden aunt.* 2. first. **Ex.** *It was the ship's maiden voyage.*

maiden name [meyd'ən neym'], a woman's family name before she is married. **Ex.** *After marriage to Mr. Smith, Helen Jones became Helen Smith; Jones is her maiden name.*

mail (1) [meyl'], *n.* letters, papers, parcels, etc. sent through a post office. **Ex.** *Mail is not delivered on Sunday.* —*v.* send by mail. **Ex.** *He mailed the letter yesterday.*

mailbox [meyl'baks`], *n.* a public box on the street into which letters are placed to be delivered by the post office; a box at a home into which the mailman delivers mail.

mailman [meyl'mæn`], *n.* a man who delivers mail.

mail order [meyl' ɔr'dər], an order for goods; a buying and selling of goods through the mail. **Ex.** *That company has a large mail order business.*

main (2) [meyn'], *adj.* most important; largest. **Ex.** *Most of the stores in our town are on the main street.* **—main'ly,** *adv.*

mainland [meyn'lænd`, meyn'lənd], *n.* a single mass of land of a country or continent considered apart from its islands. **Ex.** *The islanders go often to the mainland.*

maintain (5) [meynteyn'], *v.* 1. keep; preserve; continue. **Ex.** *He maintained a steady speed on the highway.* 2. keep in a certain manner or condition. **Ex.** *The city maintains the parks.* 3. provide with means of support. **Ex.** *His salary was too small to maintain a family of five.* 4. declare to be true; say positively. **Ex.** *They maintain that they are innocent.*

maintenance (5) [meyn'tənəns], *n.* 1. support, repair. **Ex.** *Taxes pay for the maintenance of roads.* 2. a means of support. **Ex.** *Insurance provided maintenance for his family during his illness.*

majesty (3) [mæj'əstiy], *n.* 1. dignity; nobility; greatness. **Ex.** *They were inspired by the majesty of the mountains.* 2. a title used in speaking to or of a king or queen. **Ex.** *His Majesty is a guest of the United States.* **—ma·jes'tic,** *adj.* **Ex.** *The high mountains look majestic.*

major (2) [mey'jər], *adj.* greater in size, extent, importance, amount, etc. **Ex.** *He spent the major part of his salary for rent and food.* **—n.** 1. an army officer ranking next above a captain. 2. the main subject that a student studies in college. **Ex.** *The major of most students was science.* **—v.** specialize in studies. **Ex.** *He majored in science.*

majority (3) [məjɔ:r'ətiy], *n.* the greater part of a quantity; more than half. **Ex.** *To win an election, a candidate must receive the majority of the votes.*

make (1) [meyk'], *v.* 1. build; produce; bring into existence. **Ex.** *They will make a camp near the river.* 2. become; have the qualities needed for. **Ex.** *Dry wood makes a good fire.* 3. cause to be or become. **Ex.** *The hot weather makes some people sleepy.* 4. cause to do; force to do. **Ex.** *The rain and* *sun make the grass grow.* 5. do; perform. **Ex.** *He will make a trip to town tomorrow.* 6. think about. **Ex.** *He is making plans to go away.* 7. be equal to; add to. **Ex.** *Two and two make four.* **—make believe,** pretend. **Ex.** *Make believe I am not here.* **—make out,** 1. write on a form. **Ex.** *He made out his application for a license.* 2. see or recognize. **Ex.** *He could make out who the stranger was from the voice.* 3. try to prove. **Ex.** *He made her out to be the one who did wrong.* **—make over,** change, redo. **Ex.** *The new owner made over the house.* **—make up,** 1. invent, tell an untruth. **Ex.** *He made up the story.* 2. form; join. **Ex.** *He made up a group of eight.* 3. pay for a loss. **Ex.** *I will make up for your losses.* 4. become friends again. **Ex.** *We often quarrel, but we always make up.* 5. decide. **Ex.** *He made up his mind to work harder.* 6. prepare one's face with powder, color, etc. **Ex.** *She made up her face.*

mal- (3) [mæl], *prefix.* badly or ill. **Exs.** *Adjusted, maladjusted; content, malcontent.*

malady (5) [mæl'ədiy], *n.* illness; sickness. **Ex.** *He is suffering from a strange malady.*

malaria (5) [məle:r'iyə], *n.* a disease in which there are chills followed by fever. **Ex.** *An attack of malaria made him weak.*

male (2) [meyl'], *n.* a man; a boy. **Ex.** *The male is usually stronger than the female.* 2. an animal belonging to the sex that fathers young. **Ex.** *The males of some bird species have bright feathers.* **—adj.** 1. belonging to the male sex. **Ex.** *We saw the male lion first.* 2. consisting of men or boys. **Ex.** *That is an excellent male singing group.*

mammal (3) [mæm'əl], *n.* animals, the females of which produce milk to feed their young. **Ex.** *Humans, cows, dogs, and cats are mammals.*

man (1) [mæn'], *n.* 1. an adult male person. **Ex.** *The boy became a fine man.* 2. the human race. **Ex.** *Man has a highly developed brain.* 3. a person in general. **Ex.** *Any man would be glad to have this opportunity.* 4. a male employee or follower. **Ex.** *The builder and his men did the work well.* 5. husband. **Ex.** *They are now man and wife.* **—v.** 1. supply with men. **Ex.** *The ship is fully manned.* 2. take one's place for action. **Ex.** *Man the guns!* **—man'ly,** *adj.*

-man (1) [mən, mæn], *suffix.* 1. a person of, from, or born in. **Exs.** *English, Englishman; country, countryman.* 2. a person

working in or at. Exs. *Fire, fireman; business, businessman.*
3. a person who uses. Exs. *Boat, boatman; rifle, rifleman.*

manage (2) [mæn'ij], *v.* 1. direct; lead; supervise. Ex. *He manages a large factory.* 2. control; guide; handle. Ex. *He could
not manage the horses.* 3. succeed in accomplishing. Ex. *He
managed to stay afloat by clinging to a piece of wood.*
—**man'age·a·ble,** *adj.* —**man'age·ment,** *n.* 1. the act or manner of directing or controlling. Ex. *Good management can
solve many problems.* 2. the person or persons managing.
Ex. *Labor and management do not always agree.* —**man'
ag·er,** *n.* one who manages.

mankind (3) [mæn'kaynd', mæn'kaynd'], *n.* the human race;
all human beings. Ex. *The library has several good histories
of mankind.*

manner (1) [mæn'ər], *n.* the way in which something is done
or happens; a way of acting or behaving. Ex. *He spoke in
a friendly manner.* —**man'ners,** *n. pl.* way of behaving.
Ex. *His manners are very bad.* —**man'ner·ly,** *adv.* —**man'
ner·ism,** *n.* a way of doing something that is distinctive. Ex.
He has strange mannerisms.

mansion (5) [mæn'šən], *n.* a very large house, usually that of
a wealthy family. Ex. *That old mansion has more than
twenty rooms.*

manufacture (2) [mæn'yəfæk'čər], *n.* the making of goods in
large quantities, usually by machine. Ex. *The manufacture
of shoes is the chief business in the town.* —*v.* make or produce manufactured goods. Ex. *That factory manufactures
automobiles.* —**man'u·fac'tur·er,** *n.* one who makes or produces manufactured goods. Ex. *He is the largest manufacturer of toys in the country.*

manure (5) [mənuwr', mənyuwr'], *n.* waste matter of animals;
any substance put in soil to provide food for plants and help
them grow. Ex. *The farmer spread manure on the field.*

manuscript (4) [mæn'yəskript'], *n.* a letter, article, or book
in unpublished form, especially an author's copy of his work,
which is sent to an editor or printer. Ex. *The author's manuscript was accepted for publication.*

many (1) [men'iy], *adj.* a large number of; numerous. Ex.
Many people were at the party. —*n.* a large number. Ex.
Many of those people are my friends. —*pron.* many persons
or things. Ex. *Many came who were not invited.*

map (2) [mæp'], *n.* a drawing of the earth's surface or part of it. —*v.* 1. make a map of. Ex. *Most parts of the world have been mapped.* 2. plan carefully. Ex. *He mapped a work program for the week.*

MAP

maple (5) [mey'pəl], *n.* 1. a shade tree, grown for its wood and the sweet liquid that some varieties produce. Ex. *We have a maple in our yard.* 2. the hard, light-colored wood of this tree. Ex. *This table is made of maple.* 3. the flavor of the liquid from the tree. Ex. *We flavored the cake with maple sugar.*

marble (3) [mar'bəl], *n.* 1. a hard stone, either white or colored, that can be highly polished and is used in making statues or in building. Ex. *The front of that building is covered with marble.* 2. a small ball of glass or stone, used in games. Ex. *The boys were trading marbles.* —*adj.* of marble. Ex. *That table has a marble top.*

march (1) [marč'], *v.* 1. walk with measured steps, as soldiers do. Ex. *The boys marched around the playground.* 2. cause to walk in that way. Ex. *The teacher marched the children out of the burning building.* —*n.* 1. the act of marching. Ex. *The troops were on a march.* 2. distance marched; the kind of march. Ex. *They made a 20-mile march.* 3. music to accompany marching. Ex. *The band played a march.* —**march'er,** *n.*

March (1) [marč'], *n.* the third month of the year.

mare (4) [me:r'], *n.* a female horse. Ex. *Their only farm animal was an old mare.*

margin (4) [mar'jin], *n.* 1. the white space around the writing or printing on a page. Ex. *Leave a margin of one inch on the left side of your paper.* 2. an amount allowed or available beyond what is necessary. Ex. *Allow a margin of money for unexpected expenses.* —**mar'gin·al,** *adj.* 1. of, near, or in the margin. 2. of low or minimal value, standard, profit, etc.

marine (4) [məriyn'], *adj.* of the sea; found in the sea. Ex. *Many kinds of marine life are found in this ocean.* —*n.* a soldier trained for duty both on land and at sea. Ex. *The marines landed on the island.* —**mar'i·ner,** *n.* a sailor.

mark (1) [mark'], *n.* 1. a line, spot, scratch, stain, or other impression; an effect upon something. Ex. *Several dirty marks* *were on the wall.* 2. a seal, letter, or number put on by an official or teacher to show quality or approval. **Ex.** *The boy always received high marks for his work.* 3. something which guides or shows the limits or important points. **Ex.** *We could see no landmarks that would help us find our way.* 4. goal; target. **Ex.** *He was able to hit the mark the first time.* —*v.* 1. make a line, spot, effect, etc. **Ex.** *The little girl marked the wall with a pencil.* 2. show approval, price, or quality. **Ex.** *The teacher marked the students' papers.* 3. show clearly. **Ex.** *His manner marked him as a man from the country.* —**make one's mark,** succeed; become known. **Ex.** *He made his mark as a writer.* —**mark down,** 1. lower a price. **Ex.** *The $5 book was marked down to $3.* 2. write something on paper. **Ex.** *Mark down the date.* —**mark time,** 1. move the feet as in marching, but without moving forward. **Ex.** *He marked time to the music.* 2. make no progress. **Ex.** *He is only marking time in his present job.* —**mark up,** raise a price.

market (1) [mar'kit], *n.* 1. a place where goods are bought, sold, or traded. **Ex.** *She bought her vegetables at the farmers' market.* 2. a demand. **Ex.** *There is a good market for fresh fruit in the city.* —*v.* 1. buy in a market. **Ex.** *Mother markets on Friday.* 2. sell. **Ex.** *The farmer markets his vegetables in the city.* —**be in the market for,** want to buy. **Ex.** *I am in the market for a new car.* —**put on the market,** offer to sell. **Ex.** *He put his car on the market.*

marriage (3) [mæ:r'iǰ, me:r'iǰ], *n.* 1. live legally together as husband and wife. **Ex.** *Their marriage is a happy one.* 2. the act of marrying; wedding. **Ex.** *The marriage was performed in the morning.*

marry (1) [mæ:r'iy, me:r'iy], *v.* 1. join as husband and wife. **Ex.** *They asked the judge to marry them.* 2. take as husband or wife. **Ex.** *He hopes to marry her.* 3. become husband and wife. **Ex.** *They will marry in June.*

marsh (4) [marš'], *n.* soft wet land. **Ex.** *Rice is grown in some marshes.* —**marsh'y,** *adj.*

marshal (4) [mar'šəl], *n.* an officer of a United States court, with duties similar to a sheriff. **Ex.** *United States marshals were sent to enforce the decision of the court.* —*v.* 1. arrange in proper order. **Ex.** *The lawyer marshaled the facts in the case.* 2. lead; guide. **Ex.** *He marshaled the troops to safety.*

marvel (2) [mar'vǝl], *n.* something unexpected, wonderful, or astonishing. **Ex.** *Space travel is one of the marvels of our time.* —*v.* be filled with wonder. **Ex.** *They marveled at the speed of the train.* —**mar'vel·ous**, *adj.* surprising and wonderful. **Ex.** *He has a marvelous memory.*

masculine (5) [mæs'kyǝlin], *adj.* 1. strong; brave; manly; having these qualities. **Ex.** *He has a very masculine voice.* 2. for men. **Ex.** *Boxing is a masculine sport.* —**mas`cu·lin'i·ty**, *n.*

mask (4) [mæsk'], *n.* a covering to hide or protect the face. **Ex.** *The workman wore a mask to protect his face from the sparks.* —*v.* hide; conceal. **Ex.** *She masked the real purpose of her visit.*

mass (2) [mæs'], *n.* 1. a quantity of matter of no definite shape, usually of a large size. **Ex.** *A mass of snow blocked the door.* 2. a large number or quantity. **Ex.** *The garden is a mass of flowers.* 3. the majority; the principal part. **Ex.** *The great mass of the people elected him President.* 4. size; bulk. **Ex.** *The mass of the load made it difficult to handle.* —*v.* gather or form in a mass or masses. **Ex.** *The troops were massed for the attack.* —*adj.* 1. of, concerning, or for a large mass of people. **Ex.** *Mass education is a nationwide policy.* 2. produced in great quantities; done on a large scale. **Ex.** *Mass production of cars lowers their price.* —**mass'es**, *n.* ordinary or working people as a group.

massacre (5) [mæs'ǝkǝr], *n.* killing of people in large numbers in a cruel way. **Ex.** *More than a thousand people were killed in the massacre.* —*v.* kill many, especially the helpless. **Ex.** *The enemy massacred the citizens of the town.*

massive (4) [mæs'iv], *adj.* large; weighty. **Ex.** *The house was built on a massive rock.* —**mas'sive·ness**, *n.*

mast (3) [mæst'], *n.* a long pole of wood or steel set upright on a ship, to which sails and ropes are fastened. **Ex.** *The sailor climbed up the mast.*

MAST

master (1) [mæs'tǝr], *n.* 1. a person who rules or commands people, animals, or things. **Ex.** *The dog followed his master.* 2. a man skilled in some work or art. **Ex.** *That carpenter is a master at his work.* —*v.* 1. control; conquer.

Ex. *He tried to master his temper.* 2. become skillful at. **Ex.** *She has mastered several languages.* —**mas'ter·ful,** *adj.* —**mas'ter·ly,** *adv.*

mastermind [mæs'tərmaynd'], *n.* a person of unusual executive ability who plans and leads others in some project. —*v.* plan and direct. **Ex.** *He masterminded the bank robbery.*

masterpiece [mæs'tərpiys`], *n.* something of the greatest excellence; the best one has created. **Ex.** *All of his paintings were considered masterpieces.*

mat (4) [mæt'], *n.* a flat piece of material, often coarse, made of grass, straw, etc., and used for a covering or for protection. **Ex.** *He wiped his shoes on the floor mat near the door.* —*v.* cover as with a mat; stick together in a mass. **Ex.** *The walls were matted with vines.* —**mat'ted,** *adj.*

match (2) [mæč'], *n.* a short, thin piece of wood or heavy paper tipped with a mixture that catches fire when rubbed on a rough surface. **Ex.** *He lit his cigarette with a match.*

match (2) [mæč'], *n.* 1. someone or something that is exactly like, similar to, or equal to another. **Ex.** *She has a button that is a perfect match.* 2. a person or thing that is suitable for another. **Ex.** *His suit, tie, and socks were a good match.* 3. a contest. **Ex.** *He went to a boxing match.* —*v.* 1. find or make something just like another. **Ex.** *She matched the glove she lost.* 2. be alike or equal to. **Ex.** *Her dress matched the color of her eyes.*

MATCH

mate (3) [meyt'], *n.* 1. one of a pair. **Ex.** *He could not find the mate to his shoe.* 2. male or female of a pair. **Ex.** *His wife is a good mate for him.* 3. companion. **Ex.** *They are schoolmates.* —*v.* 1. bring two animals together to make a pair or to breed. **Ex.** *The two horses were mated.* 2. join as a pair; unite in marriage. **Ex.** *They are happily mated.*

material (1) [məti:r'(i)yəl], *n.* 1. the substance, substances, or matter of which something is made or from which something can be made. **Ex.** *Wood is one of the materials from which houses are made.* 2. anything that may be worked upon or developed into something else. **Ex.** *His own life provided the material for his novel.* —*adj.* 1. of or consisting of matter or things of substance. **Ex.** *A hermit has few material needs.* 2. important. **Ex.** *He was a material witness to what had happened.* —**ma·te'ri·al·ly,** *adv.*

mathematics (2) [mæθˈəmætˈiks], *n.* the science concerned with quantities, sizes, shapes, and their relationships, as defined by numbers and signs. —**mathˈeˈmatˈiˈcal,** *adj.*

matter (1) [mætˈər], *n.* 1. something happening; something thought about or talked about. **Ex.** *An important matter caused him to stay in town.* 2. difficulty; trouble. **Ex.** *What is the matter with the sick child?* 3. anything that can be seen or felt; that which things are made of; substance. **Ex.** *Wood and stone are matter.* —*v.* be of importance; having meaning. **Ex.** *What people think matters to him.*

mattress (4) [mæˈtrəs], *n.* a case of cloth stuffed with hair, cotton, straw, etc., and used to sleep on. **Ex.** *She slept on a mattress on the floor.*

mature (4) [mətyu:rˈ, mətu:rˈ], *adj.* 1. ripe; arrived at full growth; fully developed. **Ex.** *He is a mature person.* 2. carefully planned or thought out. **Ex.** *He was not able to give a mature opinion.* —*v.* come to full growth. **Ex.** *He matured more rapidly than his brother.* —**maˈtureˈly,** *adv.* —**maturˈiˈty,** *n.*

maximum (4) [mækˈsəməm], *n.* the greatest quantity allowed or attainable. **Ex.** *His luggage weighed more than the maximum.* —*adj.* the greatest possible or allowed. **Ex.** *He drove at the maximum speed.*

may (1) [meyˈ], *v.* used with another verb to mean: 1. allow; permit. **Ex.** *May I come in?* 2. possible; likely. **Ex.** *The sun may shine again soon.* 3. desire; wish. **Ex.** *May you always be successful.*

May (1) [meyˈ], *n.* the fifth month of the year.

maybe (2) [meyˈbiy], *adv.* perhaps. **Ex.** *Maybe we will go tomorrow.*

mayor (3) [meyˈər], *n.* the chief government official of a city or town. **Ex.** *He was elected mayor.*

me (1) [miyˈ], *pron.* the form of *I* used as the object of a verb or preposition. **Ex.** *Give me the ball.*

meadow (5) [medˈow], *n.* a field where grass is grown for hay. **Ex.** *The cows are in the meadow.*

meal (2) [miylˈ], *n.* 1. the food eaten at one time to satisfy hunger. 2. one of the regular times for eating. **Ex.** *Breakfast is the first meal of the day.*

meal (2) [miylˈ], *n.* grain, roughly ground. **Ex.** *Corn is ground into meal by the mill.*

mean (1) [miyn'], *v.* 1. plan; want to do; intend. Ex. *He did not mean to hurt her.* 2. be a sign of; indicate; say. Exs. *What does this word mean? Those dark clouds mean it will rain soon.* —**mean'ing,** *n.* what is intended by a word or act. Ex. *He did not understand the meaning of the word.*

mean (1) [miyn'], *adj.* bad-mannered; unkind. Ex. *He is mean to his brother.* 2. not generous. Ex. *He was too mean to pay his workers well.* —**mean'ness,** *n.*

mean (1) [miyn'], *n.* the middle point. Ex. *His own views were a mean between the extreme views of the others.* —**means,** *n. pl.* 1. that by which something is done or gained. Ex. *He will use any means to win.* 2. riches; money. Ex. *He has the means with which to buy the car.*

meant (2) [ment'], *v.* past tense and participle of *mean.* Ex. *He meant what he said.*

meantime (3) [miyn'taym'], *n.* the time between. Ex. *He left at four and returned at seven, and she wrote letters in the meantime.* —*adv.* 1. during the time between. Ex. *He was away for three hours; meantime, she was writing letters.* 2. at the same time. Ex. *She set the table; meantime, lunch was cooking.*

meanwhile (3) [miyn'hwayl'], *n., adv.* meantime.

measure (1) [mež'ər], *n.* 1. the extent, size, quantity, or capacity of something. Ex. *The tailor took the man's measure for a suit.* 2. anything used to find size, quantity, etc. Ex. *The farmer filled the measure with grain.* 3. any unit of measure. Ex. *Inches and feet are measures frequently used.* 4. an action intended to accomplish a purpose. Ex. *The city has taken measures to improve the streets.* —*v.* 1. learn the extent, quantity, etc. Ex. *She measured her waist.* 2. be of a certain size, quantity, etc. Ex. *This rug measures 9 feet by 12 feet.* 3. compare with a standard. Ex. *A man's worth cannot be measured by his wealth.* See **Weights and Measures.**

meat (1) [miyt'], *n.* animal flesh, other than fish, considered as food. Ex. *What kind of meat are you serving for dinner?* —**meat'y,** *adj.* of, like, or having meat. Ex. *The soup has a meaty flavor.*

mechanic (3) [mǝkæn'ik], *n.* a worker skilled in repairing or working with machinery. **Ex.** *The mechanic repaired the car.*

mechanical (3) [mǝkæn'ikǝl], *adj.* 1. of, like, or related to machinery. **Ex.** *He is a mechanical engineer.* 2. operated by machinery. **Ex.** *The child has a mechanical toy.* —**me·chan'i·cal·ly,** *adv.*

mechanism [mek'ǝniz`ǝm], *n.* the parts of a machine that cause it to work. **Ex.** *The mechanism needs repair.*

medal (3) [med'ǝl], *n.* a small, distinct piece of metal with a design on it, used to honor or reward. **Ex.** *The professor was given a medal for his discovery.*

medicine (2) [med'ǝsǝn], *n.* 1. a substance, drug, etc. used in treating disease or given to relieve pain. **Ex.** *She took the medicine which the doctor gave her.* 2. the science and art of curing disease or improving health. **Ex.** *He is studying medicine.* —**med'i·cal,** *adj.* of or concerning medicine. **Ex.** *He went to medical school.* —**me·dic'i·nal,** *adj.* having a curing effect. **Ex.** *The sun has a medicinal effect.*

medium (4) [miy'diyǝm], *n.* 1. something not at either extreme of a scale. **Ex.** *He tried to achieve a happy medium between study and play.* 2. that through which something acts, something is done, or an effect is made. **Ex.** *Money is a medium of exchange.* 3. the substance, element, or condition, etc. in which something or someone lives, does his best work, etc. **Ex.** *That author's medium is the writing of novels.* —*adj.* having a position in the middle in degree size, amount, etc. **Ex.** *He usually pays a medium price for his suits.*

meet (1) [miyt'], *v.* 1. see one another; come together. **Ex.** *We often meet in the street.* 2. be introduced to; become acquainted with. **Ex.** *I have not yet had a chance to meet him.* 3. wait for and welcome; come together according to a plan. **Ex.** *We will meet her at the train station.* 4. satisfy **Ex.** *Will anything here meet your needs?*

meeting (1) [miyt'iŋ], *n.* a gathering of people. **Ex.** *A teachers' meeting was held this morning.*

mellow (4) [mel'ow], *adj.* 1. having a good flavor from aging or ripening. **Ex.** *The wine from that old bottle is mellow* 2. made kind and gentle by age. **Ex.** *The years had made him mellow.* 3. not coarse or rough; full and pure. **Ex.** *The flute had a mellow sound.* —*v.* 1. make or become mellow **Ex.** *The wine mellowed with age.* 2. make kind and gentl

by age. **Ex.** *My parents mellowed with the passing years.*
—**mel'low·ness,** *n.*

melody (4) [mel'ədiy], *n.* the musical sounds of a song; a sweet or pleasing arrangement of sounds. **Ex.** *I remember the melody but not the words of that song.* —**me·lod'ic,** *adj.*

melon (3) [mel'ən], *n.* a sweet, juicy fruit that grows on a vine.

melt (2) [melt'], *v.* 1. become liquid by heat. **Ex.** *The sun melted the snow.* 2. dissolve; disappear gradually. **Ex.** *The sugar melted in my tea.* 3. soften. **Ex.** *The child's smile melted her anger.*

MELON

melting point [mel'tiŋ poynt'], the temperature at which a substance melts.

member (1) [mem'bər], *n.* one of a group. **Ex.** *She is a member of our club.* —**mem'ber·ship,** *n.* 1. state of being a member. **Ex.** *She has a membership in our club.* 2. all the members. **Ex.** *The whole membership is at the meeting.*

memory (2) [mem'əriy], *n.* 1. the power to keep in the mind; the ability to remember. **Ex.** *He has a good memory for dates.* 2. the thing remembered. **Ex.** *He has happy memories of his childhood.* —**mem'o·ra·ble,** *adj.* important or enjoyable enough to remember. **Ex.** *It was a memorable day.* —**me·mo'ri·al,** *n.* something to preserve the memory of a person or event.

men (1) [men'], *n.* plural of *man.* **Ex.** *Three men were seated at the table.*

menace (4) [men'is], *n.* a threat; something that could cause harm. **Ex.** *Forest fires are a menace.* —*v.* threaten. **Ex.** *Frost menaced the orange crop.* —**men'ac·ing,** *adj.*

mend (3) [mend'], *v.* 1. make whole; repair. **Ex.** *She is mending the hole in the boy's shirt.* 2. improve; make or become better. **Ex.** *The sick girl is mending under the doctor's care.* —*n.* a part that has been mended. **Ex.** *The mend in the dress can hardly be seen.* —**on the mend,** improving. **Ex.** *He has been sick but is on the mend.*

-ment (1) [mənt], *suffix.* 1. result of; act of. **Exs.** *Develop, development; advance, advancement.* 2. means of; thing used for. **Exs.** *Entertain, entertainment; accompany, accompaniment.* 3. condition; state of being. **Exs.** *Astonish, astonishment; disappoint, disappointment.*

mental (2) [men'təl], *adj.* 1. of or concerning the mind. **Ex.** *He had great mental ability.* 2. having sickness of the mind. **Ex.** *He is a mental patient.* —**men·tal'i·ty,** *n.* mental powers; ability to think. **Ex.** *He has the mentality of a child.* —**men' tal·ly,** *adv.*

mention (2) [men'šən], *v.* refer to briefly; speak about. **Ex.** *Your name was mentioned only once during the conversation.* —*n.* brief reference. **Ex.** *Mention was made of the accident.*

menu (3) [men'yuw], *n.* a list of the food available. **Ex.** *I asked the waiter for a menu so that I could order dinner.*

merchandise (4) [mər'čəndayz`, mər'čəndays`], *n.* goods that are presented for sale. **Ex.** *The store had a large stock of merchandise.* —*v.* present for sale, usually in a special way. **Ex.** *It is easier to sell goods that are attractively merchandised.*

merchant (2) [mər'čənt], *n.* a person who buys and sells goods. **Ex.** *That merchant has enlarged his store.* —*adj.* commercial; used in buying or selling. **Ex.** *Merchant ships crowded the harbor.*

mercy (2) [mər'siy], *n.* 1. kindness toward those who should be punished. **Ex.** *They showed mercy toward their enemies.* 2. the power to be kind or forgive. **Ex.** *They were dependent upon the mercy of the judge.* —**at the mercy of,** be completely in the power of. **Ex.** *They were at the mercy of the storm.*

mere (2) [mi:r'], *adj.* nothing more than; only. **Ex.** *His mother died when he was a mere child.* —**mere'ly,** *adv.*

merit (3) [me:r'it], *n.* 1. excellence; worth; that which deserves praise. **Ex.** *His work has some merit.* 2. the real fact or quality, whether good or bad. **Ex.** *The court will judge the case on its merits.* —*v.* deserve. **Ex.** *He merits the prize that he won.* —**mer'i·to'ri·ous,** *adj.*

merry (2) [me:r'iy], *adj.* gay; joyful; full of fun. **Ex.** *His birthday party was a merry occasion.* —**mer'ri·ly,** *adv.* —**mer'ri·ment,** *n.* —**make merry,** be gay; enjoy oneself. **Ex.** *We made merry at his party.*

mess (4) [mes'], *n.* 1. a condition of being dirty or not neat. **Ex.** *Her room was a mess.* 2. a state of confusion; disorder. **Ex.** *His business affairs were in a mess.* —*v.* make dirty or confused. **Ex.** *The children messed up their playroom.* —**mess'i·ness,** *n.* —**mess'y,** *adv.*

message (2) [mes'iǰ], *n.* news, information, a request, etc., either written or spoken, sent from one person to another. **Ex.** *I received a message from my brother by mail.*

messenger (2) [mes'inǰər], *n.* one who transports a message or goods. **Ex.** *The messenger delivered the dress from the shop.*

met (1) [met'], *v.* past tense and participle of *meet.* **Ex.** *We met where we had met before.*

metal (2) [met'əl], *n.* 1. any chemical element that is shiny when pure or polished, can be fused, and can conduct heat and electricity. **Ex.** *Iron, gold, and silver are well-known metals.* 2. a mixture of these elements. **Ex.** *Brass is a metal made from copper and zinc.* —*adj.* made of metal. **Ex.** *He was drinking from a metal cup.* —**me·tal'lic,** *adj.* of or like metal. **Ex.** *That cloth has a metallic appearance.*

meter (4) [miy'tər], *n.* a measure of length; 39.37 inches. See **Weights and Measures.**

meter (4) [miy'tər], *n.* a device for measuring the amount of something used. **Ex.** *A man came to read the electric meter.*

method (1) [meθ'əd], *n.* 1. a definite way of doing something. **Ex.** *He has his own method for doing his work.* 2. an orderly and regular way of doing something. **Ex.** *Method is needed to do that job well.* —**me·thod'i·cal,** *adj.* orderly; organized. —**me·thod'i·cal·ly,** *adv.* in a careful, organized way. **Ex.** *He did the work methodically.*

metric system [met'rik sis'təm]. *See* **Weights and Measures.**

mice (3) [mays'], *n.* plural of *mouse.* **Ex.** *He caught two mice in the trap.*

microscope (5) [may'krəskowp'], *n.* an instrument with a piece of special glass, or a combination of pieces of glass, that causes very small things to appear larger so that they become visible for study.

mid- (2) [mid], *prefix.* middle of; halfway through. **Exs.** *Winter, midwinter; way, midway.*

MICROSCOPE

middle (1) [mid'əl], *n.* the place or time equally

distant from either end or side; the center. Ex. *The table was in the middle of the room.* —*adj.* 1. in the center; equally distant from both ends. Ex. *The middle window is open.* 2. neither great nor small; between the extremes of size, quantity, etc. Exs. *Our teacher is a man of middle age. The middle class of people is neither rich nor poor.*

midnight (2) [mid'nayt'], *n.* twelve o'clock at night. Ex. *The party ended at midnight.* —*adj.* 1. of or at midnight. Ex. *They took a midnight swim.* 2. like midnight; very dark. Ex. *He bought a midnight blue suit.*

midst (3) [midst'], *n.* the middle; the part in the center. Ex. *There is a small house in the midst of the trees.*

might (1) [mayt'], *v.* less likely or less definite than *may.* Used with another verb to show: 1. possible. Exs. *If she had been stronger, she might have recovered. He might be able to help you.* 2. allow; permit. Ex. *Might I ask your name?*

might (1) [mayt'], *n.* power; force; physical strength. Ex. *He tried with all his might to lift the heavy weight.* —**might'y,** *adj.* large in size; having great power.

migrate (5) [may'greyt], *v.* 1. move from one place in order to settle in another. Ex. *His parents migrated to the United States when he was a child.* 2. go from one region to another with the change in seasons. Ex. *Most birds migrate.* —**mi·gra'tion,** *n.* —**mi'gra·tor'y,** *adj.*

mild (3) [mayld'], *adj.* 1. calm; gentle. Ex. *She is a very mild person.* 2. not cold or stormy. Ex. *The climate here is mild.* 3. not strong or sharp in taste. Ex. *She likes mild cheeses.* —**mild'ly,** *adv.* —**mild'ness,** *n.*

mile (1) [mayl'], *n.* a unit for measuring distance equal to 5,280 feet. Ex. *The nearest village is four miles away.* See **Weights and Measures.**

military (2) [mil'ǝte:r'iy], *adj.* 1. referring to the army, or the affairs of war. Ex. *Military training is offered to most young men.* 2. of, by, or for soldiers. Ex. *The band played a military song.* —*n.* the army; soldiers. Ex. *The military teaches young men to fight.*

milk (1) [milk'], *n.* 1. the white liquid produced by female animals to feed their young. Ex. *The milk of cows and goats is used in making cheese.* 2. any liquid or juice like milk. Ex. *The milk from a rubber tree is used to make rubber.* —*v.* take milk from a cow, goat, etc. Ex. *The farmer* *milks his cows twice a day.* —milk'y, *adj.* having milk; white like milk.

milk shake [milk' šeyk'], *n.* a drink made of milk, ice cream, and flavoring mixed together.

mill (2) [mil'], *n.* 1. a place where grain is made into flour or meal. Ex. *The farmer took his grain to the mill.* 2. a place where goods are manufactured; a factory. Ex. *My father works in a steel mill.* —v. crush, shape, or prepare in a mill. Ex. *The wheat was milled into flour for bread.* —mill'er, *n.* one who keeps or operates a mill where grain is ground.

millimeter [mil'əmiy'tər], *n.* a measure of length. See **Weights and Measures.**

million (1) [mil'yən], *n., adj.* one thousand times one thousand; the number 1,000,000.

millionaire (4) [mil'yəne:r', mil'yəne:r'], *n.* a person who has a million dollars or more. Ex. *That millionaire owns his own ship.*

mind (1) [maynd'], *n.* 1. the thinking, feeling, etc. part or center of a person. Ex. *His mind is busy with many affairs.* 2. that which one thinks, believes, or desires. Ex. *We could not get her to speak her mind.* 3. mental ability, intelligence. Ex. *He has lost his mind.* 4. a person of great intelligence. Ex. *He is one of our great minds.* —v. 1. object to; be offended by. Ex. *Do you mind if I smoke?* 2. pay attention to; observe, be careful of. Ex. *Mind what you are doing.* 3. obey. Ex. *The child will not mind his mother.* —bear in mind, remember. Ex. *Bear in mind that I have already been there.* —have a mind to, be inclined to. Ex. *I have a mind not to go.* —have in mind, be thinking of. Ex. *I have in mind going to the city.* —make up one's mind, decide. Ex. *He made up his mind to go to the city.* —never mind, do not think about it. Ex. *Never mind; I will go myself.* —of one mind, agreed. Ex. *We are of one mind on what to do.* —out of one's mind, mentally ill. Ex. *He acts as if he were out of his mind.*

mine (1) [mayn'], *pron.* that which belongs to me. Ex. *This house is mine.*

mine (1) [mayn'], *n.* 1. a manmade hole in the earth from which useful substances are removed. Ex. *Several new coal mines have been opened.* 2. a bomb placed under the surface of land or water so that it cannot be seen. Ex. *They* *were killed by an enemy mine.* —v. 1. dig in the earth for coal, metals, etc. **Ex.** *The men are mining for gold.* 2. lay military mines. **Ex.** *That land was mined during the war.* —**min'er**, *n.* a worker in a mine. —**min'ing**, *n.* the act of taking metals, coal, etc. from the ground.

mineral (2) [min'(ə)rəl], *n.* a substance with a definite chemical structure found in nature; a substance which is neither animal nor plant. **Ex.** *Coal and iron are important minerals.* —*adj.* of or containing minerals. **Ex.** *Mineral water is good for the health.*

mingle (3) [miŋ'gəl], *v.* 1. combine; mix. **Ex.** *Her happiness was mingled with sadness.* 2. join with or unite. **Ex.** *We mingled with the crowd in the market.*

miniature (5) [min'ičər, min'iyəčər], *n.* 1. a copy in a much smaller size. **Ex.** *The child looks like her mother in miniature.* 2. a very small painting. **Ex.** *He had several miniatures of his parents.* —*adj.* copied in a much smaller size. **Ex.** *A miniature car was on the table.*

minimize (4) [min'əmayz`], *v.* make very small; make seem very small. **Ex.** *He modestly minimized the importance of his work.*

minimum (4) [min'əməm], *n.* the least possible or permitted amount. **Ex.** *Some plants grow well with a minimum of care.* —*adj.* smallest; lowest; least permitted. **Ex.** *Those employees are paid only a minimum wage.*

minister (2) [min'istər], *n.* a person who conducts the services in a church. **Ex.** *The minister lives next door to the church.* 2. a high-ranking official who heads a department of government. **Ex.** *The Indian Minister of Education is on a visit to the United States.* —*v.* take care of; give service, care, aid. **Ex.** *The nurse ministered to the needs of the sick.* —**min'is·te'ri·al**, *adj.* —**min'is·try**, *n.* 1. act of ministering. 2. a department of government.

minor (4) [may'nər], *adj.* small in size, extent, importance, etc. **Ex.** *There were only minor objections to the plan.* —*n.* a person under the legal age of responsibility. **Ex.** *Minors cannot vote.* —**mi·nor'i·ty**, *n.* the smaller number. **Ex.** *We went although a minority voted to stay home.*

mint (5) [mint'], *n.* 1. a place where money is made. **Ex.** *The mint issued a new coin.* 2. a great supply. **Ex.** *He has a mint of ideas.* —*v.* make coins. **Ex.** *They minted a new coin.* —*adj.* new; like new. **Ex.** *The car is in mint condition.*

minus (4) [may'nəs], *prep.* decrease by; subtract. **Ex.** *Six minus two is four.* —*adj.* less than zero; showing subtraction. **Ex.** *The temperature is minus ten degrees.* —**minus sign:** (−)

minute (1) [min'it], *n.* 1. one of the sixty equal parts of an hour; sixty seconds. **Ex.** *He will return in ten minutes.* 2. a short time. **Ex.** *I will see him in a minute.* 3. a particular point of time. **Ex.** *Please give him this message the minute you see him.* —**min'utes,** *n. pl.* an official record of the proceedings of a society, committee, etc. **Ex.** *The secretary read the minutes of the previous meeting.*

minute (1) [maynuwt', minyuwt'], *adj.* 1. very small. **Ex.** *The doctor removed a minute piece of dust from the patient's eye.* 2. including every little fact about a thing. **Ex.** *She described her vacation in minute detail.* —**mi·nute'ly,** *adv.*

miracle (4) [mi:r'əkəl], *n.* 1. an event that is beyond the known laws of nature. **Ex.** *His being able to see again was a miracle.* 2. something marvelous. **Ex.** *We hear about new miracles of science every day.* —**mi·rac'u·lous,** *adj.*

mirror (3) [mi:r'ər], *n.* a coated piece of glass used for looking at oneself. **Ex.** *He shaved in front of a mirror.* —*v.* reflect; reflect as a mirror does. **Ex.** *The stars were mirrored in the still water.*

MIRROR

mirth (5) [mərθ'], *n.* gladness as shown by laughter. **Ex.** *The joke caused a great deal of mirth among the children.* —**mirth'ful,** *adj.* **Ex.** *Her mirthful story made us laugh.*

mis- (3) [mis], *prefix.* wrongly; poorly; bad. **Exs.** *Lead, mislead; spent, misspent; fortune, misfortune.*

miscarry [miskæ:r'iy, miske:r'iy], *v.* 1. not succeed; fail. **Ex.** *His plan miscarried.* 2. lose a baby before it is born. **Ex.** *His wife miscarried because of her illness.* —**mis·car'riage,** *n.*

mischief (4) [mis'čif], *n.* 1. an act, done innocently or in fun, that causes harm or trouble. **Ex.** *Tipping over the table was his latest piece of mischief.* 2. harm or damage. **Ex.** *He apologized for the mischief his false story had caused.* 3. a playful mood. **Ex.** *The children are full of mischief today.* —**mis'chie·vous,** *adj.*

miser (5) [may'zər], *n.* a person who has money but will not spend it. **Ex.** *The old miser starved himself to death.* —**mi'ser·ly,** *adj.*

misery (3) [miz'(ə)riy], *n.* 1. a state of great unhappiness or suffering. **Ex.** *Her illness caused her great misery.* 2. that which causes great unhappiness or suffering. **Ex.** *Poverty is the cause of their misery.* —**mis'er·a·ble,** *adj.*

misgiving (3) [misgiv'iŋ], *n.* feeling of doubt, worry, concern, etc. **Ex.** *The mother had misgivings about letting the child go outside.*

mislay [misley'], *v.* lay in a place and not remember; lose. **Ex.** *I mislaid the book.*

miss (1) [mis'], *v.* 1. fail to hit, find, reach, see, etc. **Ex.** *He threw a stone but missed the bird.* 2. fail to attend, do, etc. **Ex.** *He missed his appointment.* 3. feel or discover the absence of. **Ex.** *The child misses her mother.* —**miss'ing,** *adj.* lost. **Ex.** *My book is missing.*

miss (1) [mis'], *n.* a title of respect for a girl or an unmarried woman. **Ex.** *I want you to meet my friend, Miss Martin.*

missile (4) [mis'əl], *n.* any weapon that can be thrown, hurled, pushed, fired, etc. through the air. **Ex.** *There are missiles that can go thousands of miles into space.*

mission (4) [miš'ən], *n.* 1. a group of people sent by a government, church, etc. for a special purpose. **Ex.** *The trade mission visited six countries.* 2. the special purpose for which the group is sent. **Ex.** *The nurses went on a mission of mercy.* 3. the station or headquarters of the group. **Ex.** *The mission is in that office building.* 4. special purpose in life. **Ex.** *The doctor's mission is to save lives.*

missionary (5) [miš'əne:r`iy], *n.* a person sent on a mission, usually by a church to spread its religion. **Ex.** *He is going abroad as a missionary.*

mist (4) [mist'], *n.* a cloud of very fine drops of water in the air. **Ex.** *It was difficult to see the house through the mist.* —*v.* form a mist; become dim or less clear. **Ex.** *Her eyes misted with tears.*

mistake (2) [misteyk'], *n.* an error; an expression, act, etc. that is wrong. **Ex.** *It was a mistake for us to start our trip in this storm.* —*v.* 1. regard something or somebody as something or somebody else. **Ex.** *He always mistakes my overcoat for his.* 2. fail to understand. **Ex.** *You mistake my meaning.* —**mis·tak'en,** *adj.* wrong; in error; judging wrongly. **Ex.** *He was mistaken about the time of the meeting.* —**mis·tak'en·ly**, *adv.*

mister (1) [mis'tər], *n.* a title of respect for a man, usually written "Mr." **Ex.** *Mr. Jones is here.*

mistress (5) [mis'trəs], *n.* 1. a woman who has authority or control over. **Ex.** *The salesman asked for the mistress of the house.* 2. a woman who lives with a man without being married to him. **Ex.** *The king's mistress had great power.*

mitten (5) [mit'ən], *n.* a kind of glove, with one part for the thumb and another for the four fingers.

mix (2) [miks'], *v.* 1. put or combine together in such a way as to make one. **Ex.** *The painter mixed blue and yellow to make green.* 2. prepare by putting different things together. **Ex.** *The cook mixed a cake.* 3. join in company with. **Ex.** *He likes to mix with people.* —*n.* a group of things mixed together; a mix-

MITTEN

ture. **Ex.** *There are many prepared cake mixes on the market today.* —**mix'ture**, *n.* a product of mixing; a combination. **Ex.** *This mixture is thin.* —**mix up**, confuse. **Ex.** *She was so mixed up by the noise she couldn't think.* —**mixed company**, men and women together in a group. **Ex.** *He acts differently in mixed company.*

moan (4) [mown'], *n.* 1. a long, low sound indicating pain or sorrow. **Ex.** *A moan came from the room of the sick man.* 2. any similar sound. **Ex.** *The wind made a moan as it blew through the trees.* —*v.* make moans. **Ex.** *The girl moaned in pain.* —**moan'ing**, *adj.*

mob (3) [mab'], *n.* a large group of excited people. **Ex.** *The speaker was threatened by an angry mob.* —*v.* crowd about someone to admire or attack. **Ex.** *The spectators mobbed the actor.*

mobile (4) [mow'bəl], *adj.* movable; moving easily; easy to move. **Ex.** *The new, light furniture is very mobile.* —**mo·bil'i·ty**, *n.* the ability to be moved quickly. —**mo'bil·ize**, *v.* organize and make quickly usable, as for war. **Ex.** *Because of the danger of enemy attack, the country was mobilized.* —**mo`bil·i·za'tion**, *n.*

mock (3) [mak'], *v.* 1. treat with scorn. **Ex.** *People once mocked the idea that the earth is round.* 2. make fun of by copying or imitating. **Ex.** *The boy should not have mocked* *his teacher.* —*adj.* not real; imitation. **Ex.** *The soldiers staged a mock battle.* —**mock'ing·ly,** *adv.* scornfully.

mode (4) [mowd'], *n.* manner of being or doing; method. **Ex.** *His mode of living is different from mine.*

model (2) [mad'əl], *n.* 1. a thing or person that is worth copying; an example. **Ex.** *The teacher was his model.* 2. an object or figure, often small, made to show how something looks or will look. **Ex.** *This chair was made as a model by the designer.* 3. design; style. **Ex.** *His car is the latest model.* 4. a person whose work is to wear and display clothing. **Ex.** *The models walked around the room, stopping before each customer.* —*v.* form or make; follow a model. **Ex.** *The boy modeled himself after his father.* —*adj.* 1. suitable as a model; perfect. **Ex.** *He is a model student.* 2. made to show how something looks or will look. **Ex.** *He has a collection of model trains.*

moderate (3) [mad'ərət], *adj.* 1. kept or keeping within reasonable limits; not extreme. **Ex.** *He drinks a moderate amount of coffee.* 2. average in quality, amount, or extent. **Ex.** *The play was a moderate success.* —*n.* a person who takes a position in the middle. **Ex.** *They preferred a moderate for mayor.*

moderate (3) [madəreyt'], *v.* 1. make less strong. **Ex.** *The wind moderated the heat.* 2. act as leader of a discussion or debate. —**mod'er·a'tion,** *n.* state of being moderate. —**mod'er·a'tor,** *n.* one who leads a discussion. **Ex.** *The moderator gave each man five minutes to speak.*

modern (1) [mad'ərn], *adj.* 1. of the present or very recent time. **Ex.** *That pianist plays the music of modern composers.* 2. recent; of the most improved type. **Ex.** *Their house has many modern conveniences.* —**mod'ern·ize,** *v.* make modern.

modest (3) [mad'əst], *adj.* 1. not talking about one's own capabilities, achievements, etc. **Ex.** *He was modest about his heroic action.* 2. not luxurious; simple. **Ex.** *They live in a modest home.* 3. not offending, especially in dress; retiring in manner. **Ex.** *She wore a dress of modest length.* —**mod'est·ly,** *adv.* —**mod'es·ty,** *n.*

modify (4) [mad'əfay'], *v.* 1. change slightly. **Ex.** *He modified his plans.* 2. make less extreme; moderate. **Ex.** *The judge modified the prisoner's sentence.* 3. change the quality of; limit the quantity of; describe. **Ex.** *In the sentence, "She* *wore a green hat," the adjective "green" modifies the noun "hat." —***mod'i·fi'er**, *n.*

moist (2) [moyst'], *adj.* somewhat wet; damp. **Ex.** *Some plants grow best in moist surroundings.* —**moist'en**, *v.* make somewhat wet; dampen. **Ex.** *She moistened his forehead with a wet cloth.* —**mois'ture**, *n.* liquid in the form of small condensed drops.

molasses (5) [məlæs'iz], *n.* the thick, brown, sticky liquid which is a byproduct of manufacturing sugar. **Ex.** *Some people like molasses on bread.*

mold (4) [mowld'], *n.* a hollow form in which something soft or liquid is shaped; the thing shaped. **Ex.** *The dessert had been made in a mold.* —*v.* form into a desired shape or condition. **Ex.** *The artist molded the clay into a figure of a child.* —**mold'ing**, *n.* the act of forming or shaping.

mold (4) [mowld'], *n.* a woolly-looking growth that appears on damp or decaying vegetable or animal substances. **Ex.** *Mold has spoiled the bread.* —*v.* become covered with mold. **Ex.** *The bread has molded.* —**mold'y**, *adj.*

mole (5) [mowl'], *n.* a dark-colored spot or growth, usually brown. **Ex.** *He has a small mole on the side of his nose.*

mole (5) [mowl'], *n.* a small, soft, furry animal that lives mostly underground. **Ex.** *The mole digs its own tunnels.*

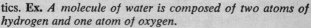

molecule (3) [mal'əkyuwl'], *n.* the smallest fragment of a chemical compound which is a chemical characteris-

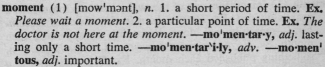

MOLE

tics. **Ex.** *A molecule of water is composed of two atoms of hydrogen and one atom of oxygen.*

moment (1) [mow'mənt], *n.* 1. a short period of time. **Ex.** *Please wait a moment.* 2. a particular point of time. **Ex.** *The doctor is not here at the moment.* —**mo'men·tar·y**, *adj.* lasting only a short time. —**mo'men·tar'i·ly**, *adv.* —**mo·men' tous**, *adj.* important.

monarch (4) [man'ərk, man'ark'], *n.* a sole ruler, such as an emperor, king, queen, etc. **Ex.** *The band played for the visiting monarch.* —**mon'arch·y**, *n.* government by a monarch.

Monday (1) [mən'diy], *n.* the second day of the week.

a, far; æ, am; e, get; ey, late; i, in; iy, see; ɔ, all; ow, go; u, put; uw, too; ə, but, ago; ər, fur; aw, out; ay, life; oy, boy; ŋ, ring; θ, think; ð, that; ž, measure; š, ship; ǰ, edge; č, child.

money (1) [mən'iy], *n.* 1. stamped metal coins and printed paper bills of definite value issued by a government and used for buying and selling. **Ex.** *He is saving money to buy a car.* 2. property; wealth. **Ex.** *He seems to have money.*

monitor (5) [man'ətər], *n.* a person or thing that watches and warns or reminds. **Ex.** *The monitor flashed a red warning signal.* —*v.* listen to or watch over a monitoring device. **Ex.** *They monitored the flight of the spaceship.*

monk (4) [məŋk'], *n.* a member of a religious organization devoting his life to prayer and religious exercises. **Ex.** *He left his successful business and life of luxury to become a monk.*

monkey (4) [məŋ'kiy], *n.* a tree-climbing animal with a long tail and with paws that look like human hands.

MONKEY

monopoly (4) [mənap'əliy], *n.* sole or complete control of the production and/or sale of a product or service. **Ex.** *Railroads are government monopolies in some countries.*

monotony (5) [mənat'əniy], *n.* a lack of change; tiring sameness. **Ex.** *He found the monotony of his factory job difficult to bear.* —**mo·not'o·nous,** *adj.* of a sameness; having little change. **Ex.** *His speech was monotonous.*

monster (4) [man'stər], *n.* 1. any animal or plant that is unnatural or extreme in shape or size or very ugly. **Ex.** *The monster had a head larger than its body.* 2. a very wicked or cruel person. **Ex.** *That monster is head of a crime ring.* —**mon'strous,** *adj.* horrible; shocking.

month (1) [mənθ'], *n.* one of the twelve portions into which a year is divided. **Ex.** *He was born in the month of December.* —**month'ly,** *adj.* done, happening, or appearing each month. **Ex.** *He makes monthly payments on the house.* —*n.* something published each month. **Ex.** *This magazine is a monthly.* —*adv.* one time in each month. **Ex.** *We make our house payments monthly.*

monument (3) [man'yəmənt], *n.* 1. something erected in memory of a person or event. **Ex.** *The statue is a monument to the discoverer of America.* 2. any great literature, art, structure, etc. that endures. **Ex.** *His writings are monuments of the culture of his time.* —**mon'u·men'tal,** *adj.* 1. like a monument. 2. larger than life-size. 3. of great significance.

mood (3) [muwd'], *n.* a state of mind; the way one feels about oneself. **Ex.** *He was usually in a happy mood.* —**mood'y,** *adj.* having frequent changes of mood.

moon (1) [muwn'], *n.* a heavenly body that revolves from west to east around the earth once about every 29 days. **Ex.** *The moon is very bright tonight.*

mop (5) [map'], *n.* materials such as coarse string, rags, cloth, etc. fastened at the end of a stick for cleaning floors. —*v.* clean or wipe with a mop. **Ex.** *He mopped the floor.*

moral (2) [mɔ:r'əl, mar'əl], *adj.* 1. concerned with the principles of right and wrong in modes of conduct and character. **Ex.** *He has high moral standards.* 2. of good character; right or proper in conduct. **Ex.** *A teacher must be a moral person.* —*n.* a lesson about what is right or wrong, shown by a story. **Ex.** *What is the moral of this story?* —**mor'als,** *n.* character; principles in regard to conduct; standards of behavior. **Ex.** *He was a man of high morals.* —**mor'al·ist,** *n.* one who talks about morals. —**mo·ral'i·ty,** *n.* 1. a set of morals by which one is guided. 2. the quality of being moral. —**mor'al·ly,** *adv.* in a moral way.

more (1) [mɔ:r'], *adj.* 1. greater in size, amount, etc. **Ex.** *He does more work than you do.* 2. greater in number. **Ex.** *We will need two more men.* 3. additional; further. **Ex.** *You can get more information tomorrow.* —*n.* a greater number, amount, or degree. **Ex.** *Give him some more.* —*adv.* 1. in or to a greater extent or degree. **Ex.** *A plane travels more rapidly than a train.* 2. in addition; again. **Ex.** *Tell me the story once more.*

moreover (3) [mɔrow'vər], *adv.* also; besides; in addition. **Ex.** *He is a quick worker; moreover, he is careful.*

morning (1) [mɔr'niŋ], *n.* the early part of the day, ending at noon; from midnight to noon. **Ex.** *Where were you yesterday morning?* —*adj.* of or happening in the morning. **Ex.** *Morning classes begin at eight.*

morsel (5) [mɔr'səl,], *n.* a small quantity. **Ex.** *The hungry children did not leave a morsel of food on their plates.*

mortal (3) [mɔr'təl], *adj.* 1. certain to die. **Ex.** *Man is mortal.* 2. causing death. **Ex.** *The soldier received a mortal wound.* —*n.* man; a human being. **Ex.** *We are mortals, not gods.* —**mor·tal'i·ty,** *n.* 1. condition of being mortal. 2. death rate. —**mor'tal·ly,** *adv.* in a way that kills. **Ex.** *He was mortally wounded.*

mortgage (4) [mɔr'giǰ], *n.* a claim to property given as an assurance for the repayment of a cash loan. **Ex.** *The bank holds a $10,000 mortgage on the house.* —*v.* give a lender a claim to one's property in case a debt is not paid when due. **Ex.** *They mortgaged the house in order to obtain a cash loan for hospital bills.* —**mort`ga·gee'**, *n.* person to whom property is mortgaged; the lender of money. —**mort·ga·gor'**, *n.* one who gives a mortgage; the borrower.

mosquito (5) [məskiy'tow], *n.* a small, flying insect, the female of which bites men and animals. **Ex.** *Some mosquitoes cause disease.*

moss (4) [mɔːsʼ], *n.* very small, soft, green plants that grow close together on ground, rocks, trees, etc. **Ex.** *The stones were covered with moss.*

MOSQUITO

most (1) [mowstʼ], *adj.* 1. greatest in number, amount, or degree. **Ex.** *This is the most cake I have ever eaten.* 2. almost all. **Ex.** *Most schools open in September.* —*adj.* in or to the greatest degree or extent; very. **Ex.** *He was most willing to help us.* —*n.* the greatest amount or degree. **Ex.** *We invited the whole class, and most came.* —**most'ly**, *adv.* mainly; chiefly. **Ex.** *The children mostly wanted to play.* —**at most, at the most,** not more than. **Ex.** *At the most, five of us will go.* —**for the most part,** mainly; chiefly. **Ex.** *For the most part, they are happy.* —**make the most of,** use to full advantage. **Ex.** *While we wait, let's make the most of our time by reading.*

moth (5) [mɔːθʼ], *n.* an insect that has large, dull-colored wings and usually flies at night.

MOTH

mother (1) [məð'ər], *n.* 1. a female parent. **Ex.** *The mother was bathing her baby.* 2. the origin, source, or cause of something. **Ex.** *We can learn a great deal from Mother Nature.* —*v.* act as a mother to; care for. **Ex.** *It was strange to see a dog mothering a little cat.* —*adj.* of, like, or as if from a mother. —**moth'er·ly**, *adj.*

mother-in-law [məð'ərənlɔːʼ], *n.* the mother of one's wife or husband.

motion (2) [mow'šən], *n.* movement; change of position or place. **Ex.** *The ship's motion made the passengers feel sea-*

sick. —*v.* make a meaningful movement, as of the hands or the head. **Ex.** *The policeman motioned the car to stop.*

motion picture [mow'šən pik'čər], movie; photographic pictures seen so quickly, one after another, that the things in them appear to move. **Ex.** *That motion picture has been seen at theaters everywhere.*

motive (3) [mow'tiv], *n.* a thought or feeling that makes one act; a reason for acting in a certain manner. **Ex.** *What was his motive for taking them on that trip?* —**mo'tiv·ate,** *v.* give or provide a motive. **Ex.** *I was motivated to go by what I had heard about the place.*

motor (2) [mow'tər], *n.* an engine that makes a machine run. **Ex.** *An electric motor makes the fan turn.* —*adj.* run by a motor. **Ex.** *They made that trip in a motor bus.* —*v.* travel by automobile. **Ex.** *They motored to town.* —**mo'tor·ist,** *n.* a person who drives an automobile or travels by automobile.

motto (4) [mat'ow], *n.* a short saying to guide one's actions. **Ex.** *"Live and let live" is a good motto.*

mound (5) [mawnd'], *n.* a small hill; a raised bank of earth, stones, sand, etc. **Ex.** *They built mounds over their dead.*

mount (2) [mawnt'], *v.* 1. go up; ascend; climb. **Ex.** *He mounted the steps.* 2. get up on. **Ex.** *She mounted her horse.* 3. rise; increase. **Ex.** *Prices are mounting rapidly.* 4. fasten in a proper setting or frame. **Ex.** *The photograph was mounted on white paper.* —*n.* a horse for riding. **Ex.** *She chose a fine mount.* —**mount'a·ble,** *adj.*

mount (2) [mawnt'], *n.* a mountain or hill, used only in poems or as part of a name. **Ex.** *Mount Everest is the highest mountain in the world.*

mountain (1) [mawn'tən], *n.* a part of the earth's surface that rises very high above the area around it. **Ex.** *The mountains were topped with snow.* —*adj.* of mountains. **Ex.** *The mountain air is clear.* —**moun'tain·ous,** *adj.* full of mountains. **Ex.** *He lives in a mountainous area.*

mourn (3) [mɔrn'], *v.* feel or express sorrow or grief. **Ex.** *They mourned the death of their father.* —**mourn'er,** *n.* —**mourn'ful,** *adj.* —**mourn'ing,** *n.* the showing of sorrow over someone's death or a loss. **Ex.** *As a sign of mourning, his wife is wearing black.*

---

a, far; æ, am; e, get; ey, late; i, in; iy, see; ɔ, all; ow, go; u, put; uw, too; ə, but, ago; ər, fur; aw, out; ay, life; oy, boy; ŋ, ring; θ, think; ð, that; ž, measure; š, ship; ǰ, edge; č, child.

mouse (3) [maws'], *n.* a small animal, found in fields or in houses.

MOUSE

mouth (1) [mawθ'], *n.* 1. the opening in the face of a person or animal through which food and drink are taken in and sounds are made; the space containing the tongue and teeth. **Ex.** *He raised the glass to his mouth.* 2. an opening resembling the mouth or acting like a mouth. **Ex.** *There were many fish at the mouth of the river.*

MOUTH 1

—**mouth'ful**, *n.* as much as the mouth will hold or as is usually put into the mouth. **Ex.** *He took a mouthful of food.*

move (1) [muwv'], *v.* 1. change the position or place of. **Ex.** *He moved the chair from one side of the room to the other.* 2. change one's place of living. **Ex.** *They moved to another town.* 3. put or keep in motion. **Ex.** *The wind moved the leaves.* 4. go. **Ex.** *The train moved slowly.* 5. stir or excite the emotions. **Ex.** *She was so moved by the speech that she cried.* —*n.* 1. the act of moving. **Ex.** *He made a sudden move toward the door.* 2. a change of dwelling place. **Ex.** *The move to their new home was made yesterday.*

movement (1) [muwv'mənt], *n.* 1. the act or activity of moving or a way of moving. **Ex.** *The movements of the dancer were very graceful.* 2. a series of acts or efforts for a definite purpose. **Ex.** *A movement was begun to stop the sale of certain drugs.*

movie (2) [muw'viy], *n.* 1. motion picture. **Ex.** *Did you enjoy the movie you saw last night?* 2. the place where motion pictures are shown. **Ex.** *We went to the movie last night.*

Mr. (1) [mis'tər], *n.* the abbreviated form of *mister*, used before a man's last or full name or some titles. **Ex.** *Mr. Jones just arrived.*

Mrs. (1) [mis'iz], *n.* the abbreviated form of *mistress*, used before the last or full name of a married woman. **Ex.** *Mrs. Jones is returning Thursday.*

much (1) [məč'], *adj.* great in amount or degree. **Ex.** *Does he have much work to do?* —*adv.* to a great extent or degree. **Ex.** *He is much taller than his brother.* —*n.* a great part or amount. **Ex.** *Much of this is not true.*

mud (1) [məd'], *n.* soft, sticky, wet earth. **Ex.** *A lot of mud stuck to our shoes.* —**mud'dy**, *adj.* covered with mud.

muffle (5) [məf'əl], *v.* wrap up to make quieter or to cover.

Ex. *She muffled the bell so that it would not awaken the family.* —**muf'fler,** *n.* 1. a device for quieting sound. 2. a scarf worn around the neck.

mug (5) [məg'], *n.* a large, heavy drinking cup with a handle. Ex. *The child drank milk from a mug.*

mule (3) [myuwl'], *n.* animal born from the union of a donkey and a horse.

multi- (3) [məlti, məltə], *prefix.* containing many; consisting of many; having many of. Exs. *Millionaire, multimillionaire; colored, multicolored.*

MULE

multiply (3) [məl'təplay`], *v.* 1. add the same number as many times as stated. Ex. *Five multiplied by four equals twenty. 5 x 4 = 20.* 2. increase in number or amount. Ex. *The population of the city is multiplying rapidly.*

multitude (4) [məl'tətuwd`, məl'tətyuwd`], *n.* 1. a great number. Ex. *There were a multitude of reasons for not going.* 2. a crowd. Ex. *Multitudes came to see the games.*

mumble (5) [məm'bəl], *v.* speak indistinctly, as one does when the lips are partly closed. Ex. *The old man mumbled, and I could not understand him.* —*n.* low, indistinct words.

municipal (4) [myuwnis'əpəl], *adj.* of or concerning the affairs or laws of a city, town, or village. Ex. *The mayor's office is in the municipal building.* —**mu·nic`i·pal'i·ty,** *n.* a town or city with powers of local self-government.

murder (2) [mər'dər], *n.* the crime of killing a person with intent to do so. Ex. *The man was guilty of murder.* —*v.* kill a human being unlawfully and intentionally. Ex. *He murdered his wife.* —**mur'der·er,** *n.* —**mur'der·ous,** *adj.* causing murder or great harm.

murmur (4) [mər'mər], *n.* 1. a soft, low, continuous sound, like voices. Ex. *We heard the murmur of a stream.* 2. complaining word or words spoken in a low voice. Ex. *The child went to bed without a murmur.* —*v.* speak softly and indistinctly; complain in a low voice. Ex. *The children murmured among themselves.*

muscle (2) [məs'əl], *n.* the tissue in the body that tightens or stretches to move a part of the body. Ex. *He injured the muscles of his arm throwing the heavy weight.* —**mus'cu·lar,** *adj.*

museum (3) [myuwziy'əm], *n.* a building where objects of permanent interest in the arts or sciences are preserved and shown. **Ex.** *They took the children to the art museum.*

mushroom (5) [məš'ruwm], *n.* a small, quick-growing plant that has a stalk topped by an umbrella-shaped cap.

MUSHROOM

music (1) [myuw'zik], *n.* 1. the art of inventing, writing, or producing pleasing or meaningful sound patterns for singing or playing on musical instruments. **Ex.** *He is studying music.* 2. such arrangements in written form. **Ex.** *The pianist brought his music with him.* 3. pleasing sounds such as those made by singing voices or musical instruments. **Ex.** *The music of her voice filled the room.* —**mu·si'cian,** *n.* a person skilled at writing or playing music. —**mu'si·cal,** *adj.* like or containing music.

must (1) [məst'], *v.* used with another verb to mean: 1. be necessary or required to. **Ex.** *Man must eat to live.* 2. be certain to, may reasonably be supposed to. **Ex.** *He must have arrived there by now.* —*n.* that which is required or necessary.

mustache (5) [məs'tæš`, məstæš'], *n.* hair that grows on a man's upper lip. **Ex.** *He wears a black mustache.*

mutter (3) [mət'ər], *v.* utter words indistinctly, especially to oneself or in suppressed disapproval. **Ex.** *The boy muttered something we could not hear.* —*n.* the act of muttering; something muttered.

mutton (4) [mət'ən], *n.* the flesh of fully grown sheep used as food. **Ex.** *We prefer lamb to mutton.*

mutual (4) [myuw'čuwəl], *adj.* 1. done or felt by each of two toward the other. **Ex.** *They were mutual friends.* 2. shared together. **Ex.** *We have a mutual friend in our teacher.* —**mu'tu·al·ly,** *adv.* —**mu'tu·al'i·ty,** *n.*

muzzle (5) [məz'əl], *n.* 1. nose, mouth, and jaws of a four-footed animal. **Ex.** *The dog put his muzzle through a hole in the fence.* 2. a cover made of wire or leather to put over an animal's mouth to keep it from biting. **Ex.** *In this town, dogs are required to wear muzzles.* 3. the open front end of a rifle, cannon, etc. **Ex.** *He pointed the muzzle of the gun toward me.*

my (1) [may'], *pron.* of, or belonging to me. **Ex.** *That is my hat.*

myself (2) [mayself', məself'], *pron.* 1. my own self. Ex. *I cut myself on some broken glass.* 2. I, not someone else. Ex. *I, myself, will carry the message.* 3. my usual self. Ex. *I do not feel like myself today.*

mystery (2) [mis'təriy], *n.* 1. something that is not or cannot be explained or understood; something kept secret which arouses interest. Ex. *The disappearance of the ship is a mystery.* 2. a story or play about something unknown. Ex. *He likes to read murder mysteries.* —**mys·te'ri·ous**, *adj.*

mystic (5) [mis'tik], *n.* a person who believes that he learns special truths through experiences of the spirit. Ex. *Their leader is a mystic.* —*adj.* referring to mystics. Ex. *Mystic symbols are used in most religions.* —**mys'ti·cal·ly**, *adv.*

myth (5) [miθ'], *n.* 1. a traditional story used to explain the origin or existence of something. Ex. *There are many myths about how the world began.* 2. an imaginary person or thing. Ex. *The girl's handsome lover was a myth.* —**myth'i·cal**, *adj.* imaginary; not real.

N

N, n [en'], *n.* the fourteenth letter of the English alphabet.

nail (2) [neyl'], *n.* 1. a thin pin of metal, pointed at one end, used for hammering into wood or walls. 2. the hard growth on the ends of fingers and toes. —*v.* fasten with a nail or nails. Ex. *He nailed the two boards together.*

NAIL 1

NAIL 2

naked (2) [ney'kid], *adj.* 1. unclothed; bare. Ex. *Naked boys were swimming in the river.* 2. without usual or natural covering. Ex. *Cold weather caused the leaves to fall and left the trees naked.* —**na'ked·ness**, *n.* the condition of being naked.

name (1) [neym'], *n.* word or words by which a person, animal, place, or thing is known or called. Ex. *The*

a, far; æ, am; e, get; ey, late; i, in; iy, see; ɔ, all; ow, go; u, put; uw, too; ə, but, ago; ər, fur; aw, out; ay, life; oy, boy; ŋ, ring; θ, think; ð, that; ž, measure; š, ship; j, edge; č, child.

man's name is John Henry Brown. —*v.* 1. give a name to. **Ex.** *They have not yet named the baby.* 2. mention by name; tell the name or names of. **Ex.** *He learned to name the months of the year in school.* —**first name, middle name, last name. Ex.** *His first name is John, his middle name is Henry, and his last name is Brown.* —**in the name of,** by the authority of. **Ex.** *Surrender in the name of the law!*

namesake [neym'seyk`], *n.* a person given the same name as another, especially as an honor. **Ex.** *Among his grandchildren, John loved his namesake, John, Jr., best.*

nap (4) [næp'], *n.* a brief sleep. **Ex.** *The children take a nap every afternoon.* —*v.* take a brief sleep. **Ex.** *He often naps in his chair.*

napkin (3) [næp'kin], *n.* a piece of paper or cloth used during meals to keep clothing clean and to wipe the fingers and lips. **Ex.** *Please place a napkin to the left of each fork on the dining table.*

narrate (5) [næreyt', ne:r'eyt], *v.* tell a story; give an account of. **Ex.** *He narrated the events of yesterday.* —**nar'ra·tor,** *n.* one who tells a story or describes an event. —**nar·ra'tion,** *n.* a telling of a story or description of an event.

narrow (2) [nær'ow, ne:r'ow], *adj.* 1. not wide; not broad. **Ex.** *This road is too narrow for two cars to pass each other.* 2. limited in size or amount. **Ex.** *We were offered a narrow choice of foods.* 3. close. **Ex.** *He had a narrow escape from death.* —**nar'row·ly,** *adv.* —**nar'row·ness,** *n.*

narrow-minded [nær`owmayn'dəd], *adj.* not trying to understand the ideas of others; not tolerant. **Ex.** *He is too narrow-minded to listen to what we say.*

nasty (5) [næs'tiy], *adj.* 1. offensive; disgusting; dirty. **Ex.** *The spoiled meat had a nasty smell.* 2. not decent or proper. **Ex.** *The drunken man used nasty language.* 3. unpleasant; mean; disturbing. **Ex.** *The weather was cold and nasty.* —**nas'ti·ly,** *adv.* —**nas'ti·ness,** *n.* meanness.

nation (1) [ney'šən], *n.* a group of people united under one government. **Ex.** *The United States of America is one nation.* —**na'tion·al,** *n.* a citizen of a nation. **Ex.** *He is an American national.* —*adj.* of a nation as a whole. **Ex.** *All schools are closed on national holidays.* —**na'tion·al·ly,** *adv.* in a national way. —**na'tion·al·ism,** *n.* strong feeling of love for or loyalty to one's country's interests. —**na`tion·al'-**

i·ty, *n.* citizenship. **Ex.** *His nationality is American.* —**na'-tion·al·ize,** *v.* place a private business, land, etc. under government ownership.

native (2) [ney'tiv], *adj.* 1. relating to the place where one was born. **Ex.** *America is my native land.* 2. belonging naturally to a particular place or person. **Ex.** *Palm trees are native to warm climates.* —*n.* a person who is born in a particular place. **Ex.** *He is not a native of this city.*

nature (1) [ney'čər], *n.* 1. the world and everything in and on it. 2. the force or forces that seem to control or guide the physical world. **Ex.** *The weather is governed by nature.* 3. that in a thing or animal that is usual or common to its kind. **Ex.** *It is in the nature of mothers to defend their children.* 4. anything not made by man or changed by man. **Ex.** *She loved the wild flowers found in nature.* 5. the special manner of a person; the unlearned ways which direct conduct. **Ex.** *His father's nature was stern.* —**nat'-u·ral,** *adj.* 1. not learned or acquired; common to its kind. **Ex.** *It is natural for parents to love their children.* 2. true to nature; normal; usual. **Ex.** *Although she was angry, she tried to speak in a natural manner.* 3. concerning nature; existing in nature; dealing with the forces of nature. **Ex.** *He teaches the natural sciences.* —**nat'u·ral·ly,** *adv.* in a normal manner. —**nat'u·ral·ist,** *n.* a student of nature. —**nat'u·ral·ize,** *v.* 1. change to agree with nature or its surroundings. 2. make a citizen of someone who is not. **Ex.** *He was born in France and naturalized in this country.*

naughty (4) [nɔ:'tiy], *adj.* 1. not obeying; behaving badly. **Ex.** *The teacher punished the naughty girl.* 2. not nice or proper. **Ex.** *His naughty joke shocked his father.* —**naugh'ti·ly,** *adv.* —**naugh'ti·ness,** *n.*

naval (5) [ney'vəl], *adj.* of or for a navy. **Ex.** *Ships are repaired in a naval yard.*

navigate (5) [næv'əgeyt'], *v.* guide or direct the course a boat, ship, or plane will travel. **Ex.** *He navigated the ship across the ocean.* —**nav'i·ga'tion,** *n.* the act of navigating. —**nav'i·ga'tor,** *n.* one who navigates.

navy (3) [ney'viy], *n.* the sea force of a nation, including all ships, officers, men, and supplies. **Ex.** *The navy defends the country's shores and seas.*

navy blue [ney'viy bluw'], a dark shade of blue. **Ex.** *The color of naval uniforms is navy blue.*

near (1) [ni:r'], *adv.* 1. not far; close in space. **Ex.** *Coming near, we saw flames.* 2. soon; close in time. **Ex.** *Vacation is drawing near.* —*adj.* 1. not distant. **Ex.** *The swimmers will gather on the near side of the beach.* 2. closely related; intimate. **Ex.** *Only near relatives attended the wedding.* —*prep.* close in place or time. **Ex.** *We live near the ocean.* —*v.* draw close; approach. —**near'ness,** *n.*

nearby [nir'bay'], *adj., adv.* near. **Ex.** *He lives nearby.*

nearly (1) [nir'liy], *adv.* almost. **Ex.** *I nearly missed the train.*

nearsighted [nir'say'tid], *adj.* able to see clearly only what is near. **Ex.** *Nearsighted people must wear glasses to drive a car.*

neat (3) [niyt'], *adj.* 1. clean; orderly. **Ex.** *The child was taught to put away her toys and clothes to keep her room neat.* 2. correct in detail. **Ex.** *He kept neat records.* 3. able and willing to keep things neat. **Ex.** *She is a neat child.* 4. pleasing and tasteful in design or appearance. **Ex.** *She wore a neat dress.* —**neat'ly,** *adv.* —**neat'ness,** *n.*

necessary (1) [nes'əse:r'iy], *adj.* needed; required; essential. **Ex.** *Food is necessary to life.* —**nec'es·sar'i·ly,** *adv.* —**ne·ces'si·ty,** *n.* that which is necessary. **Ex.** *They gave him food and other necessities.*

neck (1) [nek'], *n.* the part of the body that connects the head with the shoulders. **Ex.** *She wore a thin gold chain around her neck.*

necktie (3) [nek'tay'], *n.* a narrow strip of cloth worn usually by men around the neck, under the collar, and tied in front.

NECKTIE

need (1) [niyd'], *n.* 1. a condition in which something is necessary; a lack of something; a desire for something; a reason for. **Ex.** *The need for rest made him stop for a few moments.* 2. the thing needed. **Ex.** *Food and clothing are their most important needs.* 3. poverty; a condition of want. **Ex.** *He helped me to find a job when I was in need.* —*v.* 1. require; want. **Ex.** *Babies need milk.* 2. be compelled; be obliged. **Ex.** *We need not go today.* —**need'y,** *adj.* very poor. **Ex.** *The needy family was given food.*

needle (1) [niy'dəl], *n.* 1. a thin sewing tool, sharp at one end and with a hole at the other end through which to pass a thread. 2. the needle-shaped leaf of some trees. **Ex.** *The ground was covered with pine needles.* 3. a thin steel pointer on a compass or instrument. 4. a slender, hollow, pointed doctor's instrument for forcing medicine through the skin. **Ex.** *He hardly felt the doctor's needle.*

NEEDLE 1

negative (3) [neg'ətiv], *adj.* 1. expressing refusal; disagreeing. **Ex.** *His negative reply meant I could not go.* 2. lacking firm or positive qualities. **Ex.** *The unhappy man has a negative attitude toward life.* —*n.* 1. an expression which denies, refuses, or disagrees. **Ex.** *She cried because her request was answered in the negative.* 2. the image, on a film or plate, used for printing a photograph. **Ex.** *The photographer developed the negatives.* —**neg'a·tive·ly**, *adv.*

neglect (3) [nəglekt'], *v.* 1. give too little care to; fail to perform duties. **Ex.** *She was unhappy because he neglected her.* 2. leave undone through carelessness or forgetfulness. **Ex.** *The boy had bad teeth because he neglected to brush them.* —*n.* the act of neglecting or the condition of being neglected. **Ex.** *Their yard was a mess because of their neglect.*

neighbor (1) [ney'bər], *n.* 1. a person who lives nearby. **Ex.** *My nearest neighbor lives across the street.* 2. any person, group, etc. that is near. **Ex.** *Our country has good relations with its neighbors.* —**neigh'bor·ing**, *adj.* close to each other. **Ex.** *The United States and Mexico are neighboring countries.* —**neigh'bor·ly**, *adj.* friendly; acting as a good neighbor should.

neighborhood (3) [ney'bərhud'], *n.* 1. a small section of a city or town; a region near some place or thing. **Ex.** *They live in a neighborhood of small homes.* 2. the people living in a particular locality. **Ex.** *The whole neighborhood attended the dance.*

neither (1) [niy'ðər], *conj.* not either. **Ex.** *He neither drinks nor smokes.* —*adj.* not one or the other of two. **Ex.** *Neither statement is true.* —*pron.* not the one or the other. **Ex.** *Neither of the boys would go.*

nephew (2) [nef'yuw], *n.* the son of one's brother or sister.

nerve (1) [nərv'], *n.* 1. a threadlike structure or bundle of such structures, connecting the brain with other parts of the body, through which actions of the body are controlled. 2. control of one's feelings; courage. **Ex.** *Working on very tall buildings requires nerve.* —*v.* arouse strength and courage. **Ex.** *He nerved himself for the dangerous task.* —**nerv'ous,** *adj.* 1. of or having to do with the nerves. 2. easily excited; restless. **Ex.** *She is a nervous person after a long day of work.* 3. anxious; feeling fear. **Ex.** *Riding in an airplane makes me nervous.* —**nerv'ous·ly,** *adv.* —**nerv'ous·ness,** *n.*

-ness (1) [nis, nəs], *suffix.* quality or state of being. **Exs.** *Good, goodness; kind, kindness; ill, illness.*

nest (2) [nest'], *n.* a home built by birds and other creatures, such as mice, squirrels, and some insects, in which to lay their eggs and raise their young. —*v.* build or have a nest. **Ex.** *Birds are nesting in that tree.*

NEST

net (2) [net'], *adj.* remaining after all necessary expenses are paid. **Ex.** *The net profit of the business was small.* —*v.* earn as profit. **Ex.** *He netted a profit on the sale of his house.*

net (2) [net'], *n.* 1. material made of string, cord, thread, etc. tied, twisted, or woven together. 2. a device made of such material used to catch fish, insects, etc.

NET 2

network (5) [net'wərk'], *n.* any combination of things that cross and join many times like a net. **Ex.** *A network of roads connected the towns and cities.*

neutral (4) [nuw'trəl], *adj.* 1. not on either side in a dispute. **Ex.** *He remained neutral in the argument between his two friends.* 2. of no notable kind, quality, color, etc. **Ex.** *Gray is a neutral color.* —*n.* a person, country, etc. that does not support either side in a dispute. **Ex.** *The judge in a court of law must be a neutral in a trial.* —**neu·tral'i·ty,** *n.*

never (1) [nev'ər], *adv.* not ever; at no time. **Ex.** *He has never been at our house.*

nevertheless (2) [nev`ərðələs`], *adv.* however; in spite of that; yet. **Ex.** *He did not like the man but helped him nevertheless.*

new (1) [nuw`, nyuw`], *adj.* 1. not existing before; not known before. **Ex.** *He discovered a new way to solve the problem.* 2. recently made, built, bought, grown, etc. **Ex.** *He bought a new suit.* 3. another. **Ex.** *After resting, we made a new attempt to lift the stone.*

news (1) [nuwz`, nyuwz`], *n.* 1. information about any recent happenings or events, especially as reported on the radio, in the newspapers, etc. **Ex.** *We watched the news on television.* 2. new or unfamiliar information. **Ex.** *That she had been married before was news to me.*

newspaper [nuwz`pey`pər, nyuwz`pey`pər], *n.* a daily or weekly publication which reports the latest news. **Ex.** *The boy sells newspapers on that corner each day.*

next (1) [nekst`], *adj.* coming immediately before or after; nearest. **Ex.** *This house is number 1; number 3 is next to it.* —*adv.* 1. the first time after this. **Ex.** *I will tell him when I next see him.* 2. in the place, time, or position that is nearest. **Ex.** *His name comes next on the list.* —**next door,** in or at the next house. **Ex.** *That woman lives in the house next door.*

nice (1) [nays`], *adj.* 1. pleasant; agreeable. **Ex.** *We had a nice time at the party.* 2. thoughtful; kind. **Ex.** *Giving her flowers was a nice thing to do.* —**nice`ly,** *adv.*

nickel (5) [nik`əl], *n.* 1. a hard silver-white metal that is used to combine with other metals. **Ex.** *Nickel and copper combine well.* 2. in the United States and Canada, a five-cent coin.

nickname (5) [nik`neym`], *n.* a name other than one's own by which one is called. **Ex.** *Because his hair is red, George's nickname is "Red."*

niece (1) [niys`], *n.* the daughter of one's brother or sister.

night (1) [nayt`], *n.* the time from sunset to sunrise when there is little or no light. **Ex.** *I slept all night.* —*adj.* at, for, or of night. **Ex.** *He goes to night school and works at an office during the day.* —**night`ly,** *adv.* every night.

nightclub [nayt`kləb`], a place where people go at night to dance, eat, drink, etc.

nightfall [nayt'fɔ:l'], *n.* the end of the day, immediately after the sun has set.

nightmare (5) [nayt'me:r'], *n.* 1. a dream which causes fear or dread. Ex. *The child had a nightmare and awoke crying.* 2. any experience which causes great fear or dread. Ex. *The automobile accident was a nightmare for him.*

nine (1) [nayn'], *n., adj.* the number between eight and ten; the number *9.* —**ninth'**, *n., adj.* coming after eight others. —**nine'teen'**, *n., adj.* the number *19.* —**nine'teenth'**, *n., adj.* coming after eighteen others. —**nine'ty**, *n., adj.* the number *90.* —**nine'ti·eth**, *n., adj.* coming after eighty-nine others.

nitrogen (5) [nay'trəjən], *n.* a colorless, odorless, tasteless gas which occurs as a part of all animal and vegetable matter. Ex. *The air is composed of about eighty percent nitrogen.*

no (1) [now'], *adv.* 1. used to express denial or refusal. Ex. *No, you may not go with them.* 2. not so. Ex. *No, I don't agree with you.* 3. not at all. Ex. *She is no better today.* —*adj.* not any; not at all. Ex. *He has no friends and is lonely.* —*n.* a denial; a refusal. Ex. *Your "no" to my request surprises me.*

noble (2) [now'bəl], *adj.* 1. honorable; generous; showing dignity or excellence of character. Ex. *Giving his life to save the child was a noble thing to do.* 2. of high birth or rank. Ex. *The lord is a member of a noble family.* —**no'ble·ness**, *n.* —**no'bly**, *adv.*

nod (2) [nad'], *v.* 1. bend the head forward slightly as a sign of agreement or greeting. Ex. *The teacher nodded her approval.* 2. let the head fall forward in going to sleep. Ex. *The old man nodded in his chair and went to sleep.* —*n.* the act of bending the head forward in agreement or greeting. Ex. *She greeted her neighbor with a nod.*

noise (1) [noyz'], *n.* sound, especially when loud, confused, or unpleasant. Ex. *The children are making too much noise.* —**nois'i·ly**, *adv.* —**nois'y**, *adj.*

nominate (4) [nam'əneyt'], *v.* 1. name as a candidate for an election. Ex. *His party nominated him to run for mayor.* 2. propose or offer for a position. Ex. *The President nominated him to be an ambassador.* —**nom'i·na'tion**, *n.* state of being nominated. —**nom'i·nee'**, *n.* the person nominated.

non- (2) [nan], *prefix.* not. **Exs.** *Member, nonmember; owner, nonowner.* A mark (-) is placed after "non" when it is used with a word beginning with a capital letter. **Exs.** *African, non-African; Swiss, non-Swiss.*

none (1) [nən¹], *pron.* 1. not one; no one. **Ex.** *None would offer his help.* 2. not any; no part. **Ex.** *None of her work is done.* —*adj.* not at all; to no extent. **Ex.** *He came none too soon.*

nonsense (3) [nan¹sens], *n.* 1. words, ideas, or acts not understandable. **Ex.** *The fool is talking nonsense.* 2. foolish conduct. **Ex.** *Strict parents permit no nonsense from their children.* —**non·sen¹si·cal,** *adj.*

noon (1) [nuwn¹], *n.* the middle of the day; twelve o'clock in the daytime. **Ex.** *We always eat lunch at noon.*

nor (1) [nɔːr¹], *conj.* and not; or not; used usually with the word "neither" to show the second of two negatives. **Ex.** *She has neither father nor mother.*

normal (2) [nɔr¹məl], *adj.* regular; usual; standard; in agreement with the rules. **Ex.** *Snow is normal weather for this month.* —*n.* the usual condition, amount, form, or state; the average. **Ex.** *His temperature is above normal.* —**nor¹mal·ly,** *adv.* usually.

north (1) [nɔrθ¹], *n.* 1. the direction to the left of a person facing the rising sun; one of the four points of the compass. **Ex.** *The wind is coming from the north.* 2. the part of any country in or toward the north. **Ex.** *American winters are colder in the north.* —*adj.* 1. of, in, to, at, or toward the north. **Ex.** *They live on the north side of the city.* 2. from the north. **Ex.** *A cold north wind is blowing today.* —**north¹ern,** *adj.* characteristic of the north; in, of, to, or from the north. —**nor¹th·ern·er,** *n.* one from the north.

nose (1) [nowz¹], *n.* the part of the face just above the mouth, through which one breathes and smells.

nostril (4) [nas¹trəl], *n.* either of two openings of the nose. **Ex.** *He put some medicine in each nostril.*

NOSE

not (1) [nat'], *adv.* a word showing that something is denied;
in no way; to no degree. **Ex.** *His story is not true.* **—n't,**
short form which is not used in formal writing. **Exs.** *Does
not, doesn't; has not, hasn't; is not, isn't.*

notable (4) [now'təbəl], *adj.* worthy of notice or attention;
remarkable; distinguished. **Ex.** *His lecture was a notable
success.* **—n.** a person or thing of distinction. **Ex.** *All the
notables of the city came to the opening of the new museum.*

notation (5) [nowtey'šən], *n.* 1. something written to help
one remember. **Ex.** *He made a notation of the appointment.*
2. a system of signs and symbols, used in the sciences and
arts to represent words, quantities, sound, etc. **Ex.** *Music
is written in musical notation.*

note (1) [nowt'], *n.* 1. a word or words
written down to help one's memory. **Ex.**
He took notes on the lecture. 2. notice;
careful attention. **Ex.** *Take note of what
the professor says and remember it for the
examination.* 3. a short letter. **Ex.** *She
wrote a note of thanks for the gift.* 4. a
musical tone or the symbol for a musical
tone. 5. hint; indication; suggestion. **Ex.** *A note of triumph
was in her voice.* **—v.** 1. notice; pay attention to; observe.
Ex. *The policeman noted the footprints in the soft earth.*
2. write down as a thing to remember. **Ex.** *Please note
that address.* **—not'ed,** *adj.* famous. **Ex.** *His father is a
noted violinist.*

NOTE 4

nothing (1) [nəθ'iŋ], *n.* 1. not anything; no thing. **Ex.** *An
empty box contains nothing.* 2. that which is of no importance or value. **Ex.** *I cut my finger, but it is really
nothing.* **—adv.** in no way; not at all. **Ex.** *This suit is nothing like your old suit.*

notice (1) [now'tis], *v.* see; observe; pay attention to. **Ex.** *I
notice that you are wearing a new hat.* **—n.** 1. attention.
Ex. *Bring the letter to his notice.* 2. warning; announcement;
information. **Ex.** *The notice on the wall of the house said:
"For Sale."* 3. a warning that one will end an agreement
with another at a certain time. **Ex.** *You must give a month's
notice before quitting your job.* **—no'tice·a·ble,** *adj.* can be
seen easily. **—no'tice·a·bly,** *adv.* **—serve notice,** give advance
warning. **Ex.** *He served notice that he was leaving.*

notify (3) [now'təfay`], *v.* give notice; inform. **Ex.** *We will notify you when the books arrive.*

notion (3) [now'šən], *n.* 1. an impression; a vague idea. **Ex.** *He had only a notion of the difficulties he was to encounter.* 2. an opinion or belief; a view. **Ex.** *It was her notion that planes were safer than trains.*

notorious (5) [nowtɔ:r'iyəs], *adj.* 1. widely known for something bad. **Ex.** *A notorious criminal was caught yesterday.* 2. generally known. **Ex.** *He was notorious for being late.* —**no·to'ri·ous·ly,** *adv.* —**no·to·ri'e·ty,** *n.* bad reputation.

noun (5) [nawn'], *n.* in grammar a word that is used as the name of a person, place, or thing. **Ex.** *In the sentence, "John has a new ball," the word "John" and "ball" are nouns.* —**common noun,** a name of one kind of thing. **Exs.** *Boy; ball.* —**proper noun,** a name of a specific one of a kind, beginning with a capital letter. **Exs.** *John; America.*

nourish (4) [nə:r'iš], *v.* feed; help to grow; support. **Ex.** *Babies are nourished with milk.* —**nour'ish·ment,** *n.*

novel (2) [nav'əl], *n.* a story of book length that tells of imaginary people and events. **Ex.** *This novel is about a young man's struggle to become a doctor.* —**nov'el·ist,** *n.* one who writes novels.

novel (2) [nav'əl], *adj.* different; new; strange. **Ex.** *The new car had a novel appearance.* —**nov'el·ty,** *n.* 1. something new and strange or unusual. **Ex.** *Snow is a novelty to people from tropical countries.* 2. newness or strangeness. **Ex.** *The novelty of the new car did not last long.*

November (1) [nowvem'bər], *n.* the eleventh month of the year.

now (1) [naw'], *adv.* at the present time; at this moment; immediately. **Ex.** *She is here now.* —*n.* the present; this time. **Ex.** *Now is the time to sell your house.* —*conj.* since. **Ex.** *I need not stay, now that you are here.* —**now and then, now and again,** at one time or another; sometimes. **Ex.** *I see him now and again.*

nowhere [now'hwe:r`], *adv.* not in, to, or at any place. **Ex.** *This road leads nowhere.*

nuisance (4) [nuw'səns, nyuw'səns], *n.* an act, thing, or person that causes trouble, annoys, or offends. **Ex.** *It is a nuisance to have a cold.*

number (1) [nəm'bər], *n.* 1. words or symbols used to show the order or quantity of things in a series. **Ex.** *The number between numbers 1 and 3 is number 2.* 2. a quantity; total. **Ex.** *A large number of books lay on the desk.* —*v.* have a number; give a number to. **Ex.** *The pages were numbered from 1 to 100.*

numerical (2) [nuwme:r'ikəl, nyuwme:r'ikəl], *adj.* having to do with numbers. **Ex.** *Each card has a number, and the cards are placed in numerical order.*

numerous (2) [nuw'mərəs, nyuw'mərəs], *adj.* consisting of many. **Ex.** *He has numerous problems.*

nun (5) [nən'], *n.* one of a group of women who have taken religious vows to live according to the rules of their group. **Ex.** *That nun is a teacher.*

nurse (2) [nərs'], *n.* 1. a person trained to care for the sick and the injured. **Ex.** *Several nurses assisted the doctor.* 2. a woman employed to take care of a child or children. **Ex.** *A nurse took care of the children while their parents worked.* —*v.* take care of; tend a sick person. **Ex.** *She nursed him back to health.*

nursery (5) [nər's(ə)riy, nər'šriy], *n.* 1. a room for the use of small children and babies. **Ex.** *The children had their supper in the nursery.* 2. a school for children too young to be placed in regular school. **Ex.** *The youngest child was taken to a nursery every morning.* 3. a place where trees and plants are grown and sold. **Ex.** *He bought some strong, young trees at the nursery.*

nursery rhyme [nər's(ə)riy raym'], a very short story for children in the form of a poem.

nursery school [nər's(ə)riy skuwl'], a school for very young children, usually less than five years old.

nut (2) [nət'], *n.* 1. a dry fruit in a hard, woodlike shell; the fruit of certain trees. 2. a piece of metal that has a threaded hole which screws on a bolt.

NUT 2

nylon (3) [nay'lan], *n.* a strong manmade material which can be formed into thread, cloth, etc. **Ex.** *Her umbrella is made of nylon.*

O

O, o [ow'], *n.* the fifteenth letter of the English alphabet.

oak (2) [owk'], *n.* 1. a large, hardwood tree that bears bitter nuts. **Ex.** *A great oak tree stood in front of the house.* 2. the wood of this tree, which is used in building, making furniture, etc. **Ex.** *The desk was made of oak.*

oar (3) [ə:r'], *n.* a pole with a broad, flat end, used to row a boat.

oat (4) [owt'], *n.* the grain of a tall cereal grass; the cereal grass. **Ex.** *The horses are eating their oats.*

OAR

oath (4) [owθ'], *n.* 1. a serious promise or pledge, often calling upon a god, person, or thing one honors. **Ex.** *He placed his hand on the Bible as he spoke the oath of office.* 2. a curse; the name of a god or other sacred person or thing spoken in anger or for emphasis. **Ex.** *In his rage he uttered terrible oaths.* —**take an oath,** promise in formal ceremony to do something. **Ex.** *The witness took an oath to tell the truth in court.* —**under oath,** obliged or required by oath. **Ex.** *The judge reminded the witness he was under oath to tell the truth.*

obedience (4) [owbiy'diyəns, əbiy'diyəns], *n.* obeying; submitting to authority or law. **Ex.** *The parents demanded obedience from their children.* —**o·be'di·ent,** *adj.*

obey (2) [owbey', əbey'], *v.* 1. act as one is ordered to act. **Ex.** *The soldier obeyed the order immediately.* 2. be ruled, controlled, or guided by. **Ex.** *He obeyed the laws of the government.*

object (1) [əbǰekt'], *v.* 1. show that one does not like or approve; protest. **Ex.** *He objected to the way she drove the car.* 2. give reasons for being against something. **Ex.** *He objected that our plans were too dangerous.* —**ob·jec'tion,** *n.* a statement of disapproval or protest. **Ex.** *He stated his objection to the new idea at the meeting.* —**ob·jec'tion·able,** *adj.* —**ob·jec'tor,** *n.* one who objects.

a, far; æ, am; e, get; ey, late; i, in; iy, see; ɔ, all; ow, go; u, put; uw, too; ə, but, ago; ər, fur; aw, out; ay, life; oy, boy; ŋ, ring; θ, think; ð, that; ž, measure; š, ship; ǰ, edge; č, child.

object (1) [ab'jikt], *n.* 1. something that can be seen or touched; something that can be perceived by the senses. **Ex.** *He handed me a small, round object.* 2. purpose; aim; goal. **Ex.** *His only object in life was to become rich.* 3. the person or thing which receives the action of the verb or is the noun or pronoun in a prepositional phrase. **Ex.** *In the sentence, "He gave the book to her," "book" is the object of the verb "gave," and "her" is the object of the preposition "to."* —**ob·jec'tive**, *n.* goal or aim of what one does. **Ex.** *His objective was to be rich.* —*adj.* not favorable to one more than another; fair. **Ex.** *Let him decide; he will be objective.*

oblige (2) [əblayĵ'], *v.* 1. compel to do by law, promise, or duty. **Ex.** *Parents are obliged by law to send their children to school.* 2. feel bound or in debt to another because of a favor. **Ex.** *I am very much obliged to you for helping me with my lesson.* —**ob·li·ga'tion**, *n.* that which one is obliged to do. **Ex.** *He has an obligation to feed his children.* —**ob·lig'a·tor·y**, *adj.* required. —**o·blig'ing**, *adj.* helpful; ready to do favors. **Ex.** *He has always been most obliging to everyone.*

obscure (4) [əbskyu:r'], *adj.* 1. not well-known. **Ex.** *He is an obscure poet.* 2. not easily noticed or seen; hidden. **Ex.** *We had difficulty finding the obscure path through the forest.* 3. not understood; not clear. **Ex.** *The true meaning of his lengthy explanation was obscure.* 4. dark; dim. **Ex.** *Heavy curtains made the room obscure.* —*v.* make obscure; dim. **Ex.** *The fog obscured the road.* —**ob·scur'i·ty**, *n.* condition of being obscure.

observe (2) [əbzərv'], *v.* 1. watch; notice; look at carefully. **Ex.** *He observed a man leaving by the rear door.* 2. keep; honor. **Ex.** *We observed the New Year by visiting old friends.* 3. obey or follow. **Ex.** *He was careful to observe the laws.* —**ob·serv'ance**, *n.* keeping; honoring. **Ex.** *The observance of holidays is a general practice.* —**ob·serv·va'tion**, *n.* 1. the act of seeing or being seen; the act of noticing. 2. a remark, a comment, or an opinion. **Ex.** *The critic's observations about the play were not favorable.* —**ob·serv'ant**, *adj.* —**ob·serv'er**, *n.* one who observes.

obstacle (4) [ab'stikəl], *n.* something that blocks or stops progress. **Ex.** *An obstacle in the road prevented the cars from moving.*

obstinate (5) [ab'stənit], *adj.* firmly holding to one's own opinion or purpose. **Ex.** *The obstinate girl refused to go.* —**ob'stin·a·cy**, *n.* —**ob'sti·nate·ly**, *adv.*

obstruct (4) [əbstrəkt'], *v.* prevent passage or progress. **Ex.** *A fallen tree obstructed the road.* —**ob·struc'tion**, *n.* something that stops progress. —**ob·struc'tive**, *adj.*

obtain (2) [əbteyn'], *v.* acquire; get; gain by effort. **Ex.** *He obtained an education by going to school at night.* —**ob·tain'a·ble**, *adj.*

obvious (3) [ab'viyəs], *adj.* clear; evident; easily seen or understood. **Ex.** *It was obvious that he did not hear the warning until it was too late.* —**ob'vi·ous·ly**, *adv.*

occasion (2) [əkey'žən], *n.* 1. a particular time when a certain thing happened. **Ex.** *We last saw her on the occasion of her marriage.* 2. an important event. **Ex.** *The President's reception was quite an occasion.* 3. a favorable time; a good chance; an opportunity. **Ex.** *When the occasion presents itself, I will ask his help.*

occasional (3) [əkey'žənəl], *adj.* not happening, appearing, or used regularly. **Ex.** *He is only an occasional visitor to our home.* —**oc·ca'sion·al·ly**, *adv.*

occupation (2) [ak'yəpey'šən], *n.* 1. one's regular business, trade, profession, or work. **Ex.** *He said his occupation was that of a student.* 2. the act of occupying; the state of being occupied. **Ex.** *Our occupation of the house began the day we moved the furniture into it.* 3. the taking and holding of land by force. **Ex.** *The occupation of the defeated nation by the enemy lasted three years.* —**oc·cu·pa'tion·al**, *adj.*

occupy (2) [ak'yəpay'], *v.* 1. fill space. **Ex.** *The building occupies an entire block.* 2. engage the time or attention of someone. **Ex.** *Her mind was occupied with her own troubles.* 3. take and hold by force or by living in. **Ex.** *The enemy occupied the fort.* 4. live in. **Ex.** *We occupy the house next to yours.* 5. hold or have as an office or job. **Ex.** *What position does he occupy?* —**oc'cu·pan·cy**, *n.* act of occupying. —**oc'cu·pant**, *n.* one who occupies.

occur (2) [əkə:r'], *v.* 1. happen. **Ex.** *The accident occurred on Friday.* 2. found to exist. **Ex.** *Iron occurs in combination with many other elements.* 3. come to mind. **Ex.** *It did not occur to her to be afraid.* —**oc·cur'rence**, *n.* 1. the act of occurring. **Ex.** *The occurrence of so many accidents caused alarm.* 2. a happening; an event. **Ex.** *Sunrise is a daily occurrence.*

ocean (1) [ow'šən], *n.* the body of salt water that covers almost three-fourths of the earth's surface; any of the five main divisions of this water. **Ex.** *We crossed the ocean in five days.* —**o·ce·an'ic,** *adj.*

o'clock (1) [əklak', owklak'], *adv.* of the clock; according to the clock. **Ex.** *He left at ten o'clock.*

October (1) [ak'tow'bər], *n.* the tenth month of the year.

odd (2) [ad'], *adj.* 1. strange; unusual; not normal. **Ex.** *The sounds of a foreign language are odd.* 2. not one of a pair; lacking a mate. **Ex.** *I am going to throw away this odd glove.* 3. having one remaining when divided by two. **Ex.** *Seven is an odd number.* —**odd'ly,** *adv.* —**odd'ness,** *n.* —**odd'i·ty,** *n.*

odds (5) [adz'], *n.* 1. a difference that gives one the advantage over another. **Ex.** *The smaller army struggled against great odds.* 2. the relationship between the chances that something will or will not happen, is or is not true, etc. in gambling. **Ex.** *The odds against the horse winning were 5 to 1.* —**at odds,** disagree. **Ex.** *The two boys were at odds over which had seen it first.* —**odds and ends,** scraps; small pieces of different kinds of things. **Ex.** *The child picked up a small stone and put it in a box containing bottle caps, pieces of glass, and other odds and ends.*

odor (3) [ow'dər], *n.* smell. **Ex.** *There was an odor of roses and of other flowers in the air.* —**o'dor·less,** *adj.* having no smell. **Ex.** *Water is odorless and has no color.*

of (1) [əv', av'], *prep.* 1. made from. **Ex.** *This chair is made of wood.* 2. belonging to. **Ex.** *The cover of this pot is broken.* 3. containing. **Ex.** *She drank a cup of tea.* 4. at a distance from; away from. **Ex.** *Our house is within three miles of the city.* 5. about; concerning. **Ex.** *He likes to tell of his adventures.* 6. by; produced by. **Ex.** *Is this one of that writer's books?* 7. with; having. **Ex.** *He is a man of great strength.* 8. included among. **Ex.** *He is one of my friends.* 9. before. **Ex.** *It is five minutes of ten.*

off (1) [ɔ:f'], *adv.* 1. away; to a distance. **Ex.** *The bird flew off.* 2. away from the top or outside. **Ex.** *She took her hat off.* 3. away in future time. **Ex.** *Our holidays are still a month off.* 4. so that something is no longer in operation, continuing, etc. **Ex.** *He turned the lights off.* 5. away from work. **Ex.** *I took time off this afternoon, but I must work tomorrow.* —**prep.** 1. not on; not attached to; removed from; distant from; away from. **Ex.** *The train is off the tracks.* 2. not doing; not occupied with. **Ex.** *The soldiers are off duty after three o'clock.* —*adj.* 1. not on; removed. **Ex.** *His coat was off.* 2. not on; not connected; not continuing, etc. **Ex.** *The electricity is off.* 3. going; on the way. **Ex.** *They are off to the theater.* —**be off,** leave. **Ex.** *I must be off now.* —**off and on,** occasionally; sometimes. **Ex.** *He is not a regular visitor but comes here off and on.* —**take off,** 1. leave. **Ex.** *I must take off for home.* 2. go into the air. **Ex.** *I watched the planes take off and land.*

offend (3) [əfend¹], *v.* 1. anger; cause displeasure to. **Ex.** *He offended me by the way he spoke.* 2. be unpleasant to the sense of sight, sound, etc. **Ex.** *The sight of the dead dog offended his eyes.* —**of·fen'der,** *n.* one who commits an offense. **Ex.** *The judge sentenced the offender.*

offense (3) [əfens¹], *n.* 1. a wrong; a sin; a breaking of the law. **Ex.** *He was arrested for the offense of stealing.* 2. the act of attacking. **Ex.** *The enemy's offense had been carefully planned.* —**of·fen'sive,** *adj.* 1. having to do with attacking. **Ex.** *Their army has offensive weapons.* 2. unpleasant to the senses. **Ex.** *There was an offensive smell in the air.* —*n.* movement or position of attack. **Ex.** *He took the offensive.*

offer (1) [ɔf'ər], *v.* 1. present for acceptance or refusal. **Ex.** *He offered her his chair.* 2. show willingness to do. **Ex.** *The boy offered to carry my packages.* 3. bid, as a price. **Ex.** *He offered ten dollars for the table.* —*n.* the act of offering; that which is offered. **Ex.** *We were pleased by his offer.*

offhand [ɔːf'hænd¹], *adv.* without having to consult notes or reference books; without considering. **Ex.** *Do you know offhand how many people live in this city?* —*adj.* done without consideration. **Ex.** *His was an offhand remark.*

office (1) [ɔːf'is, af'is], *n.* 1. a place in which business or work is done. **Ex.** *The doctor is in his office.* 2. a public position to which a person is elected. **Ex.** *He was elected to the office of President.*

office boy [ɔːf'is boy¹], a boy who performs errands and other jobs in an office. **Ex.** *The office boy brought us coffee.*

officeholder [ɔːf'ishowl`dər], *n.* one who has a government position.

---

a, far; æ, am; e, get; ey, late; i, in; iy, see; ɔ, all; ow, go; u, put; uw, too; ə, but, ago; ər, fur; aw, out; ay, life; oy, boy; ŋ, ring; θ, think; ð, that; ž, measure; š, ship; j, edge; č, child.

officer (2) [ɔ:f'əsər, af'əsər], *n.* 1. a person in the armed forces who commands men. **Ex.** *A general is an officer in the army.* 2. any policeman. **Ex.** *The officer told him to stop making noise.* 3. a person in an important position. **Ex.** *Which officer of the company do you wish to see?*

official (3) [əfiš'əl], *n.* a person who is in a position of authority. **Ex.** *The President is the most powerful government official.* —*adj.* 1. of or concerning an office. **Ex.** *He came here on official business.* 2. issue with or by authority. **Ex.** *The official report is published by the government.* —**of·fi'cial·ly,** *adv.*

offset [ɔf'set'], *v.* balance; compensate for. **Ex.** *The money he won partly offset his losses.*

offshoot [ɔf'šuwt'], *n.* a branch off from a main stem; a side result. **Exs.** *Offshoots of the tree grew all around us. One offshoot of his study of plants was a new medicine.*

offspring [ɔf'spriŋ'], *n.* children or descendants. **Ex.** *He is the oldest of his father's offspring.*

off-the-record [ɔf'ðərek'ərd], *adj.* not official; not to be published. **Ex.** *The President gave an off-the-record speech.*

often (1) [ɔ:f'ən], *adv.* many times; frequently. **Ex.** *I often see him at the office.*

oh (1) [ow'], *interj.* exclamation of surprise, pain, or any emotion. **Exs.** *Oh, how worried I was! Oh! You are not going?*

oil (1) [oyl'], *n.* 1. fatty liquid that does not mix with water and that burns easily. **Ex.** *Oils found in animal or vegetable substances are used in cooking and in making soap.* 2. petroleum; a yellow or black liquid taken from the ground and used as fuel. —*v.* put oil on or in. **Ex.** *He oiled the machine.* —**oil'y,** *adj.*

O.K., OK, okay (3) [ow'key'], *adj.* correct; all right. **Ex.** *I have checked your work carefully, and it is O.K.* —*v.* approve. **Ex.** *Will you O.K. my request for a loan?* —*n.* approval. **Ex.** *Do I have your O.K. to continue?*

old (1) [owld'], *adj.* 1. not young; having lived for many years. **Ex.** *My parents are old.* 2. of age; in age. **Ex.** *The baby is one year old.* 3. not new; made or built a long time ago. **Ex.** *The old building was built two hundred years ago.* 4. used, worn, or owned for a long time. **Ex.** *My old shoes need to be repaired.* —*n.* a time long past. **Ex.** *They hunted with bows and arrows as in the days of old.*

old-timer [owld'tay'mər], *n.* one who has been a resident, member, etc. for a long time, or whose knowledge extends back many years. **Ex.** *He is an old-timer in our office.*

olive (3) [al'iv], *n.* a tree which bears a small green or black fruit; the fruit itself. **Ex.** *A cooking oil is made from pressed olives.* —*adj.* a greenish-yellow color. **Ex.** *She bought an olive coat.*

omit (3) [owmit'], *v.* leave out; fail to include. **Ex.** *He was not invited because his name was omitted from the list.*

on (1) [an', ɔːn'], *prep.* 1. above and held up by; touching the upper surface of. **Ex.** *The book is on the table.* 2. located in, covering, or touching any surface. **Ex.** *A black mark was on the side of the box.* 3. at the time when; within the period of. **Ex.** *He began his new job on Monday.* 4. in a state of; in the condition of. **Ex.** *The house is on fire.* —*adv.* 1. in or into a position of touching, covering, or being fastened to. **Ex.** *He put his gloves on.* 2. to a working condition; into operation. **Ex.** *She turned the lights on.* —*adj.* in a working condition; in operation. **Ex.** *The machine is on.* —**on time,** at the appointed time. **Ex.** *We were worried when he did not appear on time.* —**on and on,** for a long time; continuously. **Ex.** *He talked on and on, and I fell asleep.*

once (1) [wəns'], *adv.* 1. at a time past; formerly. **Ex.** *I once attended that school.* 2. a single time. **Ex.** *January 1 occurs once a year.* —*conj.* if ever; whenever; as soon as. **Ex.** *Once you have heard the song, you will never forget it.* —*n.* one time; a single time. **Ex.** *Once is enough.* —**all at once,** 1. all at the same moment. **Ex.** *I cannot do the work all at once.* 2. suddenly. **Ex.** *He turned out the lights, and all at once it was dark.* —**at once,** immediately. **Ex.** *They came at once when I called for help.* —**once upon a time,** long ago. **Ex.** *The old man said that once upon a time there was a large tree here.*

oncoming [an'kəm'iŋ], *adj.* moving nearer. **Ex.** *He ran to escape the oncoming train.*

one (1) [wən'], *n.* 1. a single unit; the number *1.* 2. a single person or thing. **Ex.** *The children arrived one at a time.* —*pron.* 1. a certain person or thing. **Ex.** *One of the men smiled.* 2. any person or thing. **Ex.** *One must work to earn one's living.* —*adj.* 1. of a single unit, person, or thing; not two or more. **Ex.** *They have only one child.* 2. united; undivided. **Ex.** *The crowd answered with one voice.*

oneself, one's self (1) [wən'self¹, wənz'self¹], *pron.* one's own self. **Ex.** *One must do the work oneself.*

one-sided [wən'say'did], *adj.* having, happening, or showing one side only; partial. **Ex.** *He told a one-sided story that was not fair to us.*

onion (3) [ən'yən], *n.* a plant with a strong smell and taste; the edible bulb of the plant.

ONION

only (1) [own'liy], *adj.* 1. being the single one or ones. **Ex.** *She is their only daughter.* 2. alone by reason of being the best. **Ex.** *For your purposes this is the only kind to buy.* —*adv.* merely; just. **Ex.** *He bought only three books.*

onrush [an'rəš`, ɔn'rəš], *n.* a rushing forward. **Ex.** *He was caught in the onrush of traffic.*

onset [an'set`, ɔn'set`], *n.* a beginning. **Ex.** *He was here at the onset of the trouble.*

onto (2) [an'tuw, ɔn'tuw], *prep.* to a position on. **Ex.** *He dropped the book onto the floor.*

onward (3) [an'wərd, ɔn'wərd], *adv.* forward; ahead. **Ex.** *The soldiers marched onward.* —*adj.* moving in a forward direction. **Ex.** *The army continued its onward march.*

open (1) [ow'pən], *adj.* 1. not shut; allowing free entry. **Ex.** *He walked through the open door.* 2. not concealed; not hidden; not secret. **Ex.** *He was very open about his feelings.* 3. used by all; entered freely. **Ex.** *The meeting is open to all who wish to attend.* 4. ready for business. **Ex.** *The office is open at nine o'clock.* 5. available; not filled. **Ex.** *We still have one position open for an English teacher.* —*v.* 1. cause to be no longer closed. **Ex.** *Please open the door.* 2. make or become ready for business. **Ex.** *The new store will open today.* 3. spread out. **Ex.** *Open your book to the first page.* 4. begin; start. **Ex.** *The president opened the meeting by asking the secretary to speak.* —**o'pen·er,** *n.* a tool used to open containers. **Ex.** *He removed the caps from the bottles with a bottle opener.*

open-handed [ow'pənhæn'did], *adj.* generous. **Ex.** *The open-handed uncle bought candy for all the children.*

open-minded [ow'pənmayn'did], *adj.* willing to listen to and try to understand different ideas. **Ex.** *He has always been very open-minded.*

opera (3) [ap'(ə)rə], *n.* a play that is sung, usually with accompaniment by an orchestra. **Ex.** *She will sing in the opera.* —**op'er·at'ic**, *adj.* —**op'er·et·ta**, *n.* a short opera, usually humorous.

operate (2) [ap'əreyt`], *v.* 1. do work or run, as a machine does. **Ex.** *This machine operates very well.* 2. control or use. **Ex.** *She can operate a sewing machine.* 3. perform surgery. **Ex.** *The doctor operated on my brother this morning.* —**op·er·a'tion**, *n.* —**op'er·a·tor**, *n.* 1. one who operates a machine. 2. A person who works at a central point in a telephone system and who gives assistance when needed to people making calls. **Ex.** *Operator, please give me the telephone number of the mayor's office.*

opinion (1) [əpin'yən], *n.* 1. a belief based on one's own ideas and thinking and not on certain knowledge. **Ex.** *In my opinion, he will win the race.* 2. impression; judgment. **Ex.** *He has a good opinion of your ability.* 3. expert belief. **Ex.** *They asked for the doctor's opinion of the illness.*

opponent (4) [əpow'nənt], *n.* a person who is on the other side in a fight, discussion, etc. **Ex.** *He could not match the skill of his opponent.*

opportunity (2) [ap'ərtuw'nətiy, ap`ərtyuwn'ətiy], *n.* a favorable time or occasion; a good chance. **Ex.** *The meeting was a good opportunity for them to discuss their problems.*

oppose (2) [əpowz'], *v.* resist; be against; fight against. **Ex.** *He opposed all of my ideas for change.* —**op'po·si'tion**, *n.* that which opposes. **Ex.** *His opposition did not want him to speak.*

opposite (2) [ap'əzit], *adj.* 1. against; exactly at the other extreme; different; contrary. **Ex.** *They held opposite ideas on the subject.* 2. facing each other; on the other side; on the other end. **Ex.** *The two houses are on opposite sides of the street.* —*n.* that which is opposite or very different. **Ex.** *Happy people and sad people are opposites.* —*prep.* facing. **Ex.** *We sat opposite each other across the table.*

oppress (4) [əpres'], *v.* 1. worry; burden the mind. **Ex.** *His troubles oppressed him.* 2. control by the use of unjust and

a, far; æ, am; e, get; ey, late; i, in; iy, see; ɔ, all; ow, go; u, put; uw, too; ə, but, ago; ər, fur; aw, out; ay, life; oy, boy; ŋ, ring; θ, think; ð, that; ž, measure; š, ship; ǰ, edge; č, child.

cruel force or authority. **Ex.** *Bad governments oppress the people.* —**op·pres'sor,** *n.* one who oppresses. —**op·pres'sion,** *n.* the act of oppressing or being oppressed. —**op·pres'sive,** *adj.*

optimism (5) [ap'təmiz'əm], *n.* a feeling that the best will always happen. **Ex.** *The candidate's optimism about his chances of winning encouraged his supporters.* —**op'ti·mist,** *n.* one who usually believes the best will happen. —**op·ti·mis'tic,** *adj.* —**op·ti·mis'tic·al·ly,** *adv.*

or (1) [ɔ:r'], *conj.* 1. introducing the second of two choices. **Ex.** *Do you want to return or stay here?* 2. introducing the last of a series of choices. **Ex.** *You may have tea, coffee, or milk.* 3. introducing the second of two choices with "either" or "whether." **Ex.** *Either you or I must go.*

-or (3) [ər], *suffix.* the person or thing doing something. **Exs.** *Act, actor; distribute, distributor; govern, governor.*

orange (2) [ɔ:r'inǰ, ar'inǰ], *n.* 1. a round, reddish-yellow fruit which is sweet and full of juice. 2. a reddish-yellow color. —*adj.* 1. of the color orange. **Ex.** *She wore an orange dress.* 2. of an orange. **Ex.** *He drank a glass of orange juice.*

ORANGE 1

orator (5) [ɔ:r'ətər, ar'ətər], *n.* a skillful and forceful public speaker. **Ex.** *To become a member of the high school debating team you must be a good orator.* —**o·rate',** *v.* speak too seriously and with too much feeling. —**o·ra'tion,** *n.* a formal speech given on a special occasion such as a holiday, dedication, etc.

orbit (3) [ɔr'bit], *n.* the curved path of a planet or other body moving in space around another heavenly body. **Ex.** *The moon travels in an orbit around the earth.* —*v.* travel in space around the earth, moon, or other heavenly bodies. **Ex.** *The Apollo 11 spaceship orbited the moon before landing.*

orchard (4) [ɔr'čərd], *n.* a large area of ground on which fruit trees are grown; the collection of such trees. **Ex.** *These apples come from an orchard near here.*

orchestra (3) [ɔr'kistrə], *n.* a large group of people who play musical instruments together, including stringed instruments; the instruments they play. **Ex.** *Our city has a famous symphony orchestra.*

order (1) [ɔr'dər], *n.* 1. a command; a direction. **Ex.** *The troops received orders to attack.* 2. a request for goods or services. **Ex.** *He gave the company an order for the books.* 3. the goods requested. **Ex.** *Your order should reach you soon.* 4. the arrangement of people or things one after the other. **Ex.** *Put these in order according to number.* —*v.* 1. give an order, direction, or command to. **Ex.** *The general ordered his men to advance.* 2. ask for something one wants; give an order for. **Ex.** *She ordered food from the store.* —**in order,** a proper, customary arrangement. **Ex.** *A neat room is always in order.* —**out of order,** not in working condition. **Ex.** *No one answered because the front door bell is out of order.* —**in order that,** so that. **Ex.** *They used the loudspeaker system in order that everyone would be able to hear.* —**in order to,** for the purpose of. **Ex.** *He lit the candle in order to see.* —**in short order,** very soon; rapidly. **Ex.** *You will reach home in short order if you go by air.* —**to order,** especially made or fitted. **Ex.** *His clothes fit him because he has them made to order by a tailor.*

orderly (1) [ɔr'dərliy], *adj.* 1. in order; neat. **Ex.** *His books were arranged in an orderly way.* 2. well-behaved. **Ex.** *The crowd was quiet and orderly.* —**or'der·li·ness,** *n.* state of being orderly.

ordinary (2) [ɔr'dəne:r'iy], *adj.* 1. usual; common. **Ex.** *This is not an ordinary day but a holiday.* 2. average; neither good nor bad. **Ex.** *The food at most restaurants is just ordinary.* —**or'di·nar'i·ly,** *adv.*

ore (4) [ɔ:r'], *n.* material taken from the ground for the purpose of obtaining the metal it contains. **Ex.** *This ore will provide a good grade of iron.*

organ (3) [ɔr'gən], *n.* 1. a part of a plant or animal performing certain work. **Ex.** *The heart is the organ that pumps blood throughout the body.* 2. a large instrument that makes musical sounds when air is sent through sets of pipes. **Ex.** *The music of the organ filled the church.* —**or'gan·ic,** *adj.* of or concerning organs of the body.
—**or'gan·ist,** *n.* a musician who plays an organ.

ORGAN 2

organization (3) [ɔr'gənəzey'šən], *n.* 1. a group of people joined together for a common purpose. **Ex.** *The United Nations is a large organization.* 2. the act of coming together into a single body or group for a common purpose. Ex. *Were you here at the time of the organization of this club?*

organize (2) [ɔr'gənayz`], v. 1. bring together into a group to work for a common purpose; start. Ex. *They are trying to organize a new political party.* 2. arrange or place according to a system; put in order. Ex. *This book of poems is organized according to author.* —**or'gan·ized**, *adj.* planned; orderly. Ex. *He is a very organized person.*

origin (2) [ɔːr'əjin, ar'əjin], n. the place where something started; source. Ex. *The origin of this river is a stream in the mountains.*

original (2) [əriĵ'ənəl], adj. 1. first; belonging to the beginning. Ex. *The original settlers came to the island long ago.* 2. new; done for the first time; not copies. Ex. *That is an original approach to the problem.* 3. being the one of which a copy or copies are made. Ex. *She made six copies of the original letter.* —n. a thing which is not a copy. Ex. *Her dress is an original she designed and made herself.* —**o·rig'i·nal·ly**, *adv.* at the beginning. —**o·rig'i·nal'i·ty**, n. the ability to do original work.

originate (2) [əriĵ'əneyt`], v. begin; invent; create. Ex. *The idea for a new book originated in a meeting of teachers.* —**o·rig'i·na`tor**, n.

ornament (3) [ɔr'nəmənt], n. something that decorates and adds beauty. Ex. *There were carved ornaments on the cabinet doors.* —**or'na·men'tal**, *adj.*

orphan (4) [ɔr'fən], n. a child whose parents are dead. Ex. *The orphan went to live with his aunt.* —adj. of or for orphans. Ex. *Eighty children lived in the orphan home.* —v. make an orphan of. Ex. *The child was orphaned at the age of eight.* —**or'phan·age**, n. home for orphans.

other (1) [əδ'ər], adj. 1. additional. Ex. *Some people are already here, and other people will come later.* 2. different. Ex. *Have you any other problems to discuss?* 3. the one of two or more not yet mentioned, seen, found, etc. Ex. *He was looking for his other glove.* —pron. 1. the other one. Ex. *Each blames the other.* 2. an additional person or thing. Ex. *Two children went, and the others stayed home.* —adv. in a different way; otherwise. Ex. *I cannot do other than agree with you.* —**every other**, every second one. Ex. *She always works at our house every other Monday morning.*

—**the other day**, a recent day. **Ex.** *I saw his new bicycle the other day.*

otherwise (2) [əð'ərwayz'], *adv.* 1. in a different way. **Ex.** *He had no choice and could not do otherwise.* 2. in all other ways. **Ex.** *He is slow, but otherwise he is a good worker.* —*adj.* different. **Ex.** *I was there and know that the facts are otherwise.*

ought (1) [ɔ:t'], *v.* used with the simple form of another verb to show: 1. have a duty or obligation. **Ex.** *Children ought to obey their parents.* 2. be advisable or proper. **Ex.** *I wonder if we ought to stay longer.* 3. be very likely; be expected. **Ex.** *It ought to rain soon.*

ounce (3) [awns'], *n.* 1. a unit of weight equal to 1/16 of a pound. **Ex.** *This package contains five ounces.* 2. a unit of measure for fluids. **Ex.** *A measuring cup filled with liquid usually contains eight ounces.* See **Weights and Measures.**

our (1) [awr', ar'], *pron.* used as an *adj.* of or belonging to us. **Ex.** *We left our coats at home.*

ours (2) [awrz', arz'], *pron.* that or those which belong to us. **Ex.** *Their children stay up late, but ours go to bed early.*

ourselves (2) [awrselvz', arselvz'], *pron.* 1. our own selves. **Ex.** *We bought ourselves a new car.* 2. we, not someone else. **Ex.** *We ourselves painted the house.*

-ous (3) [əs], *suffix.* the person or thing has, is full of, or is like. **Exs.** *Ambition, ambitious; anxiety, anxious.*

out (1) [awt'], *adv.* 1. forth from; into the open. **Ex.** *Take the dog out.* 2. away from the inside. **Ex.** *He looked out of the window.* 3. away from the home, office, or other place where one usually is. **Ex.** *He was out when you called.* 4. to the point of not existing. **Ex.** *The fire burned out during the night.* 5. reaching beyond the usual limit. **Ex.** *The shop sign extends out over the sidewalk.* —*adj.* 1. absent; away from work, school, etc. **Ex.** *Several students are out because of illness.* 2. no longer concealed. **Ex.** *The secret is out, and everybody knows it now.* 3. not working; not on. **Ex.** *The lights are out.* —*prep.* away from the inside. **Ex.** *The bird flew out the window.* —**all out,** holding nothing back from the effort. **Ex.** *He went all out to win the race.* —**out to,** trying to. **Ex.** *He is out to win the race.*

---

a, far; æ, am; e, get; ey, late; i, in; iy, see; ɔ, all; ow, go; u, put; uw, too; ɔ, but, ago; ər, fur; aw, out; ay, life; oy, boy; ŋ, ring; θ, think; ð, that; ž, measure; š, ship; j, edge; č, child.

out- (1) [awt], *prefix.* 1. greater or better than in quality or action. **Exs.** *Do, outdo; talk, outtalk.* 2. away from the center; outward in direction. **Exs.** *Bound, outbound; break, outbreak.* 3. located or set near or beyond. **Exs.** *Door, outdoor; side, outside.*

outcome [awt'kəmˇ], *n.* result. **Ex.** *What was the outcome of the race?*

outdoors [awt'dɔrz'], *n.* the area in the open air; not inside a building. **Ex.** *People are healthier if they spend time in the outdoors.* —**outdoor,** *adj.*

outer (1) [awt'ər], *adj.* being at, on, or near the outside. **Ex.** *The fort was protected by an outer wall.*

outer space [awt'ər speys'], the part of space which is beyond the earth's atmosphere.

outfit (4) [awt'fitˇ], *n.* 1. a set of clothing or other things needed for a certain purpose. **Ex.** *She bought him a baseball outfit for his birthday.* 2. a group of people who work together, especially in a military unit. **Ex.** *The soldier returned to his outfit.* —*v.* supply what is necessary; equip. **Ex.** *The men were outfitted for their fishing trip.* —**out'fit·ter,** *n.*

outlaw [awt'lɔ:ˇ], *n.* a person who habitually commits crimes. **Ex.** *The police are seeking that outlaw.*

outlet (4) [awt'letˇ], *n.* 1. the opening by which anything is let out. **Ex.** *The room had four electrical outlets.* 2. a means or way of expressing emotions, energy, etc. **Ex.** *Music is an outlet for the emotions.* 3. a market for goods. **Ex.** *A nearby canning factory was the outlet for the farmer's corn crop.*

outline (4) [awt'laynˇ], *n.* 1. a bordering line showing the shape of an object. **Ex.** *In the dim light I could see only the outline of a man's figure.* 2. a drawing made of such lines. **Ex.** *He drew an outline of the child's head.* 3. a brief report giving the main parts but not the details of a speech, piece of writing, etc. **Ex.** *He showed a publisher the outline of the book he wanted to write.* —*v.* make, give, or draw an outline of. **Ex.** *He outlined his plans to the voters.*

outlook [awt'lukˇ], *n.* the way one looks at or thinks about the world, life, etc. **Ex.** *He has a cheerful outlook about what will happen.*

output (4) [awt'putˇ], *n.* the amount produced in a given time. **Ex.** *The company has not matched last year's output.*

outrage (4) [awt'reyjˇ], *n.* 1. a very wicked or evil act. **Ex.**

Many outrages are committed during a war. 2. an act which shocks or hurts the feelings. **Ex.** *It was an outrage for him to ignore their call for help.* —*v.* shock; greatly disturb. **Ex.** *They were outraged by the violent acts.* —**out·ra'geous,** *adj.* —**out·ra'geous·ly,** *adv.*

outset [awt'set'], *n.* a beginning. **Ex.** *He was here at the outset of the expedition.*

outside (1) [awt'sayd'], *n.* the outer side, surface, or part. **Ex.** *They painted the outside of the house.* —*adv.* on or to the outside. **Ex.** *Go outside and see if the sun is shining.* —*prep.* on, to, or near the outside of. **Ex.** *They stood outside the door.* —*adj.* 1. of, at, or concerning only the outer side, surface, or part. **Ex.** *All the outside doors have locks.* 2. being, acting, or coming from beyond the outer limits of an area, group, etc. **Ex.** *They did not want their children to be affected by outside influences.* —**out·sid'er,** *n.* one who does not belong; a stranger. **Ex.** *The meeting is for members only; outsiders cannot attend.* —**outside of,** except for. **Ex.** *Outside of her, no one is going.*

outstanding (4) [awt'stæn'diŋ], *adj.* 1. well-known; important; excellent. **Ex.** *That is his most outstanding book.* 2. unpaid. **Ex.** *His debt is still outstanding.*

outwit [awtwit'], *v.* be more clever or cunning. **Ex.** *He tried to catch her, but she outwitted him and escaped.*

oval (3) [ow'vəl], *adj.* having a shape like an egg.

oven (3) [əv'ən], *n.* an enclosed space for baking, heating, or drying. **Ex.** *Bread is baking in the oven.*

over (1) [ow'vər], *prep.* 1. above. **Ex.** *They have a light over the door.* 2. on; upon. **Ex.** *She put her coat over her shoulders.* 3. across; on or to the other side. **Ex.** *The boy jumped over the wall.* —*adv.* 1. above. **Ex.** *He heard a plane flying over.* 2. again. **Ex.** *He had to do the work over.* 3. to another side; to a particular place; across. **Ex.** *They sailed over to see the island.* —**all over,** 1. in or on every place. **Ex.** *There are people all over the world.* 2. finished. **Ex.** *We arrived late, after the game was all over.* —**over and above,** in addition to. **Ex.** *His work for me was over and above what was required of him.*

over- (1) [ow'vər], *prefix.* 1. above in place, quality, position, etc. **Exs.** *Look, overlook; see, oversee.* 2. across or beyond. **Exs.** *Seas, overseas; cloud, overcloud.* 3. too much; to a great degree. **Exs.** *Do, overdo; eat, overeat.* 4. become upside down; cause to fall. **Exs.** *Turn, overturn; throw, over-throw.*

overall [ow'vərɔ:l], *adj.* 1. from one end to the other, usually in measurement. **Ex.** *The overall size of the table is six feet.* 2. including everything. **Ex.** *What was the overall cost of the house?*

overboard [ow'vərbɔrd'], *adv.* over the side of a ship. **Ex.** *He fell overboard.*

overcast [ow'vərkæst'], *adj.* cloudy; gloomy. **Ex.** *It is a rainy, overcast day.*

overcome (3) [ow'vərkəm'], *v.* 1. defeat; conquer. **Ex.** *The early settlers had many difficulties to overcome.* 2. make weak or helpless. **Ex.** *He was overcome by the heat.*

overhear (3) [ow'vərhi:r'], *v.* hear something which one is not supposed to hear. **Ex.** *He overheard the quarrel.*

overlook (3) [ow'vərluk'], *v.* 1. fail to see; miss. **Ex.** *In her hurry she overlooked one important item.* 2. ignore; excuse. **Ex.** *Please overlook his rudeness.*

override [ow'vərrayd'], *v.* set aside what others have done or decided; disregard the wishes of others. **Ex.** *Congress may override the President's veto.*

overrule [ow'vərruwl'], *v.* decide opposite to a lesser authority. **Ex.** *The principal overruled the teacher's decision.*

overtake (3) [ow'vərteyk'], *v.* reach. **Ex.** *He ran to overtake his friend.*

overthrow (5) [ow'vərθrow'], *v.* defeat; end by force. **Ex.** *They tried to overthrow the government.* —*n.* the act of overthrowing.

overturn [ow'vərtərn'], *v.* upset; turn so that the bottom side is up. **Ex.** *His car was overturned in the accident.*

overwhelm (5) [ow'vərhwelm'], *v.* 1. defeat or overcome by great force or number; crush. **Ex.** *The attackers over-whelmed the city.* 2. cover completely; bury. **Ex.** *A snowslide overwhelmed the village.* —**o·ver·whelm'ing,** *adj.*

overwrought (5) [ow'vərrɔ:t'], *adj.* very nervous or excited; strained. **Ex.** *His overwrought nerves required rest and quiet.*

owe (2) [ow'], *v.* 1. be in debt for; be obliged to pay. **Ex.** *They still owe a large sum on their house.* 2. feel obliged or want to do, give, etc. **Ex.** *I owe you an explanation.* 3. be indebted for. **Ex.** *He owes his life to his doctor's skill.* —**ow·ing,** *adj.* remaining to be paid; due. **Ex.** *He worked extra hours to pay the money owing on his doctor's bill.*

owl (3) [awl¹], *n.* a night-flying, hunting
bird with a large head and eyes. —**owl¹
ish,** *adj.* like an owl, particularly with
regard to the eyes. Ex. *He gave her an
owlish look.*

own (1) [own¹], *adj.* belonging completely
to oneself. Ex. *Is that his own horse,
or is it borrowed?* —*v.* possess; have
for oneself. Ex. *They own a big house.*
—**own¹er,** *n.* —**hold one's own,** succeed
in resisting difficulties; keep one's position. Ex. *The small group of defenders
held their own against the attacks.*

OWL

ox (2) [aks¹], *n.* a male animal, usually
full-grown, of the cattle family, used
as a work animal. —**ox¹en,** *n. pl.* more
than one ox. Ex. *Two oxen pulled the
plow.*

OX

oxygen (3) [ak¹səɟen], *n.* a gas without
color or taste that is necessary to life
and makes up one-fifth of the air. Ex.
The patient was given oxygen.

oyster (5) [oy¹stər], *n.* a small, boneless
sea animal having a soft body enclosed
in two rough shells.

OYSTER

P

P, p [piy¹], *n.* the sixteenth letter of the English alphabet.

pace (3) [peys¹], *n.* 1. a step; the length of a step in walking,
about two and one half to three feet. Ex. *The winning runner finished several paces ahead of the others.* 2. the rate of
movement, development, etc. Ex. *The man worked at a slow
pace.* —*v.* walk back and forth. Ex. *The anxious mother
paced the floor waiting for the telephone to ring.*

pacify (4) [pæs¹əfay˄], *v.* calm; make peaceful; quiet. Ex. *She
pacified the crying child by giving him milk.* —**pa·cif¹ic,** *adj.*

a, far; æ, am; e, get; ey, late; i, in; iy, see; ɔ, all; ow, go; u, put; uw, too;
ə, but, ago; ər, fur; aw, out; ay, life; oy, boy; ŋ, ring; θ, think; ð, that;
ž, measure; š, ship; ǰ, edge; č, child.

—**pac'i·fi·er,** *n.* one who calms; that which calms. —**pac'i· fism,** *n.* a strong belief that all disputes between nations should be solved peacefully; opposition to military preparations and readiness. —**pac'i·fist,** *n.* one strongly opposed to war.

pack (2) [pæk'], *v.* 1. put things together in a container for carrying or storing. **Ex.** *He packed a suitcase for the trip.* 2. press or crowd closely together. **Ex.** *People packed the room for the meeting.* —*n.* 1. a bundle or large package for carrying on the back. **Ex.** *The camper had cooking equipment in his pack.* 2. a group of animals. **Ex.** *A pack of wolves was seen in the forest.* 3. a set; a package containing a number of items. **Ex.** *He took a pack of cards from his pocket.* —*adj.* used for carrying burdens. **Ex.** *A mule is a pack animal.* —**pack'er,** *n.* one who packs.

package (2) [pæk'ij], *n.* a thing or things packed for storage or carrying. **Ex.** *We mailed the package to him.* —*v.* put into a wrapping or container. **Ex.** *They packaged the rice in two-pound boxes.*

packet (5) [pæk'it], *n.* a small package. **Ex.** *She tied a ribbon around the packet of letters.*

pact (5) [pækt'], *n.* an agreement. **Ex.** *The two countries signed a peace pact.*

pad (3) [pæd'], *n.* 1. a case filled with soft material and used for comfort or protection; a cushion. **Ex.** *An attractive pad was on the seat of the chair.* 2. a number of sheets of paper fastened together at one end. **Ex.** *He wrote the message on a pad.* —*v.* protect or soften with a pad; line or fill with soft material. **Ex.** *The inside of the jewel box was padded with cotton.* —**pad'ding,** *n.* soft material used to pad something.

paddle (4) [pæd'əl], *n.* 1. a short pole with a wide blade at one or both ends, used for moving a canoe through the water. 2. a board shaped like a paddle, used to beat, stir, etc. —*v.* 1. move a boat or canoe with a paddle. **Ex.** *He paddled down the river.* 2. punish by beating as with a paddle. **Ex.** *The mother paddled the bad child.*

PADDLE 1

page (1) [peyj'], *n.* one side of a sheet of paper in a book, magazine, etc., or the printing on the paper. **Ex.** *I have read forty pages of this book.*

page (1) [peyj'], *n.* a person, often a boy, who carries messages and performs other small services in a hotel, an office, etc. Ex. *The pages were dressed in neat uniforms.* —*v.* try to find a person by calling his name. Ex. *A messenger paged the doctor in the hotel dining room.*

paid (1) [peyd'], *v.* past tense and participle of *pay.* Ex. *He paid for the things he bought.*

pail (3) [peyl'], *n.* a round container with a handle, used for carrying liquids.

PAIL

pain (1) [peyn'], *n.* 1. a hurting or suffering somewhere in the body. Ex. *He was in great pain when he was ill.* 2. mental or emotional suffering. Ex. *The news of his death caused them great pain.* —*v.* cause to suffer; hurt. Ex. *The wound pained him.* —**pain'ful,** *adj.* causing pain; unpleasant. Ex. *The painful injury caused her to cry.* —**pain'ful·ly,** *adv.* —**take pains,** take special care. Ex. *He took pains to impress his new employer.*

painstaking [peynz'teyk`iŋ], *adj.* taking or requiring extreme care. Ex. *Repairing watches is painstaking work.*

paint (1) [peynt'], *n.* a liquid coloring substance applied to protect or beautify a surface or to make pictures. Ex. *He put bright paint on the walls with a brush.* —*v.* 1. cover with liquid color. Ex. *They painted the chairs red.* 2. make a picture of something or someone with liquid colors. Ex. *The artist painted several pictures of the girl.* 3. describe clearly. Ex. *The speaker painted an exciting picture of his travels.* —**pain'ter,** *n.* one who paints. —**paint'ing,** *n.* 1. act of covering with liquid color. 2. a picture made with liquid colors.

pair (1) [pe:r'], *n.* 1. two things of a kind used together. Ex. *She bought a pair of gloves.* 2. a single thing with two similar parts. Ex. *He has only one pair of trousers.* 3. two humans or animals that are related, mated, or teamed together. Ex. *The man and his wife are a happy pair.* —*v.* arrange in pairs. Ex. *The two of them were paired at the party.* —**pair off,** form or arrange in a pair.

PAJAMAS

pajamas (3) [pəjæm'əz, pəja'məz], *n.* clothing worn for sleeping, consisting of a loose jacket and trousers.

pal (5) [pæl'], *n.* a close friend. **Ex.** *He went fishing with two of his pals.*

palace (2) [pæl'əs], *n.* official home of a ruler. **Ex.** *They are building a new palace for the emperor.*

pale (2) [peyl'], *adj.* 1. without much color. **Ex.** *The face of the sick girl was very pale.* 2. very weak in color; dim. **Ex.** *I could hardly see in the pale moonlight.* —*v.* make or become pale. **Ex.** *She paled at the sight of the dead body.* —**pale'ness,** *n.*

palm (3) [pam'], *n.* the inside of the hand not including the fingers. **Ex.** *She put a coin in the palm of the beggar's hand.* —**palm'ist,** *n.* a person who tells fortunes by reading the palm.

palm (3) [pam'], *n.* a tall tree with large leaves at the top that grows in warm climates.

PALM

pamphlet (5) [pæm'flit], *n.* a small book, usually with paper covers and few pages. **Ex.** *Several free pamphlets were available at the museum.* —**pam·phlet·eer',** *n.* a person who writes persuasive pamphlets, usually on political subjects.

pan (2) [pæn'], *n.* a broad, shallow cooking dish, usually of metal and sometimes having a handle. —*v.* wash small stones and sand in a pan to find gold. **Ex.** *The men were panning for gold in the creek.*

PAN

pane (4) [peyn'], *n.* a piece of glass in a window or door. **Ex.** *The broken pane in the window was replaced.*

panel (4) [pæn'əl], *n.* 1. a flat piece of wood or other material used in a door, ceiling, or wall, that is framed by the surrounding parts. **Ex.** *The panels of the cabinet door were carved.* 2. a section containing controls or indicators in airplanes, automobiles, and many other machines. **Ex.** *He checked his instrument panel to see if he had enough gas.* 3. a group of people selected for some special purpose such as judging a contest, serving on a jury, or joining in a discussion. **Ex.** *We heard a panel of experts discuss this problem.* —*v.* decorate or cover with panels. **Ex.** *He paneled the walls of his dining room.* —**pan'el·ing,** *n.* the panels on

the wall or the material of which the panels are made.
—**pan·el·ist**, *n.* a person who is a member of a panel.

pang (4) [pæŋ'], *n.* a sudden, sharp feeling of pain or mental suffering. **Ex.** *Pangs of hunger reminded him that it was time to eat.*

panic (4) [pæn'ik], *n.* a sudden, strong, unreasonable fear, often spreading rapidly. **Ex.** *The rapid rise of flood water caused panic among the people.* —*v.* fill with unreasoning fear. **Ex.** *The falling bombs panicked the people in the city.* —**pan'ick·y**, *adj.* —**pan'ic-strick'en**, *adj.* filled with panic.

pant (5) [pænt'], *v.* breathe hard and quickly or in a labored manner. **Ex.** *The runner panted after the race.* —*n.* a gasp; a hard, quick, labored breath. —**pant'ing**, *adj.*

pantry (4) [pæn'triy], *n.* a small room in which food, dishes, and other kitchen supplies are stored. **Ex.** *She brought the cake in from the pantry.*

pants (2) [pænts'], *n.* trousers.

papa (3) [pa'pə], *n.* child's word for father.

paper (1) [pey'pər], *n.* 1. material made from rags or wood, in the form of thin sheets, and used for writing, printing, drawing, wrapping, etc. 2. a newspaper. **Ex.** *The paper is delivered early in the morning.* 3. a written or printed record of proof. **Ex.** *Have you a paper showing you paid your taxes?* 4. an article, report, etc. **Ex.** *The professor read his paper at the meeting.* —*adj.* made of paper. **Ex.** *The children made paper flowers.*

PANTS

paperback [pey'pərbæk'], *n.* a book made with a soft paper cover.

paper boy [pey'per boy'], a boy who delivers or sells newspapers.

parade (4) [pəreyd'], *n.* a march or procession. **Ex.** *Three school bands were among the groups in the parade.* —*v.* march with ceremony. **Ex.** *Soldiers and sailors paraded on the holiday.*

paradise (3) [pær'ədays', pe:r'ədays'], *n.* 1. heaven. **Ex.** *A person as good as he is deserves to go to paradise.* 2. a place

---

a, far; æ, am; e, get; ey, late; i, in; iy, see; ɔ, all; ow, go; u, put; uw, too; ə, but, ago; ər, fur; aw, out; ay, life; oy, boy; ŋ, ring; θ, think; ŏ, that; ž, measure; š, ship; j, edge; č, child.

having an unusual amount of a desired quality such as happiness or beauty. Ex. *The island was a paradise of birds and flowers.*

paragraph (3) [pær'əgræf`, pe:r'əgræf`], *n.* one or more sentences developing one idea and forming a distinct portion of a piece of writing. Ex. *A new paragraph always begins on a new line.*

parallel (4) [pær'əlel`, pe:r'əlel`], *adj.* 1. being the same distance apart at all points and therefore never meeting. Ex. *These two streets are parallel.* 2. similar. Ex. *They have parallel ideas about what to do.*

PARALLEL 1

—*n.* 1. something similar to something else. Ex. *His experiences were parallels to my own.* 2. a comparing of things. Ex. *The critic drew a parallel between the two plays.* —*v.* 1. be parallel to. Ex. *The new highway parallels the old road.* 2. be or find something similar or equal to. Ex. *He could not parallel his father's achievements.*

paralyze (4) [pær'əlayz`, pe:r'əlayz`], *v.* 1. cause loss of ability to move or to feel. Ex. *His arm was paralyzed as the result of the accident.* 2. make inactive or helpless. Ex. *She was paralyzed with fear.* —**pa·ral'y·sis,** *n.* the condition of being paralyzed.

parcel (4) [par'səl], *n.* a package; something that is wrapped. Ex. *She addressed the parcel for mailing.*

pardon (2) [par'dən], *n.* 1. forgiveness. Ex. *I beg your pardon for being late.* 2. a release from punishment. Ex. *The governor reviewed the case and granted the prisoner a pardon.* —*v.* 1. excuse or forgive. Ex. *Please pardon this interruption.* 2. free from punishment. Ex. *The governor of the state pardoned the criminal.*

parent (2) [pær'ənt, pe:r'ənt], *n.* 1. a father or mother. Ex. *Children are dependent upon their parents for food.* 2. a plant or animal that produces another. Ex. *The parents were feeding the young birds.* —**pa·ren'tal,** *adj.*

park (2) [park`], *n.* an area of trees, grass, etc. set apart for the public to enjoy. Ex. *The children were playing in the park.* —*v.* put or leave an automobile, a bicycle, etc. in a particular place for a time. Ex. *You may park your car on this street for two hours.*

parkway [park'wey`], *n.* a road made beautiful with trees and grass. Ex. *They went for a pleasant drive on the parkway.*

parking lot [par'kiŋ lat'], a place to park automobiles. **Ex.** *The parking lots in the city charge a high price.*

parliament (3) [par'ləmənt], *n.* a national lawmaking group. **Ex.** *Parliament is the lawmaking group in Great Britain.* —**par·lia·men'tary**, *adj.* 1. of, about, or like a parliament; having a parliament. **Ex.** *That country has a parliamentary form of government.* 2. in accordance with the rules of a parliament. **Ex.** *The group followed parliamentary procedures in its meetings.*

parlor (3) [par'lər], *n.* a room for receiving or entertaining guests; a living room. **Ex.** *The parlor of their house is nicely furnished.*

parrot (5) [pær'ət, pe:r'ət], *n.* a brightly colored bird with a hooked bill, valued as a pet because it can learn to talk. **Ex.** *She tried to teach the parrot to talk.*

part (1) [part'], *n.* 1. something less than a whole; a piece; a section. **Ex.** *She was not hungry and ate only part of her lunch.* 2. a piece of something. **Ex.** *The automobile needed several new parts.* 3. a share of effort or work. **Ex.** *Each one must do his part.* 4. a character or role in a play. **Ex.** *He played the part of the hero in the play.* —*v.* 1. divide or break into parts; separate. **Ex.** *The crowd parted to let us pass.* 2. go away from; leave. **Ex.** *He was sorry to part from his friends.* 3. comb the hair so there is a line dividing it. **Ex.** *His hair is too short to part.* —*adj.* not entire. **Ex.** *He made a part payment on the car.* —**part'ly**, *adv.* not entirely; to some extent. **Ex.** *It is partly my fault.* —**for the most part,** mostly. **Ex.** *For the most part, what he says is true.* —**in part,** to some extent. **Ex.** *You are right in part.* —**part with,** separate from. **Ex.** *I hate to part with the book, but I will give it to you.* —**take part,** join in. **Ex.** *He took part in the game.*

partial (1) [par'šəl], *adj.* 1. not complete; of a part. **Ex.** *He suffered a partial loss of hearing.* 2. favoring one over the other. **Ex.** *She was partial to her son.* —**par·ti·al'i·ty**, *n.* the act of favoring one over the other. **Ex.** *The teacher showed partiality to the less troublesome students.* —**par·tial·ly**, *adv.* to some extent. **Ex.** *He partially answered the question.*

participate (3) [partis'əpeyt', pərtis'əpeyt'], *v.* be a part of; join with others. **Ex.** *Most of the students participated in the discussion.* —**par·tic'i·pant**, *n.* one who participates. —**par·tic'i·pa'tion**, *n.* the act of participating.

participle (5) [par'tǝsip'ǝl], *n.* a verb form which can be used as an adjective with certain qualities of a verb or as part of a verb phrase with forms of *be* and *have*. Ex. *After we had parted, I watched him through the parted curtains.* The first use of the participle "parted" is as a verb, the second as an adjective. Most present-tense participles end in *-ing*. Exs. *Walk, walking; jump, jumping.* Most past-tense participles end in *-ed, -en, -d, -t,* or *-n.* Exs. *Talk, talked; speak, spoken; say, said; spend, spent; grow, grown.*

particle (4) [par'tikǝl], *n.* a very small part of a whole; a tiny piece or amount. Ex. *A particle of dirt was in his eye.*

particular (2) [pǝrtik'yǝlǝr], *adj.* 1. concerning one single person, thing, etc.; specific. Ex. *That particular chair belonged to my father.* 2. very careful; detailed; special. Ex. *She gave particular attention to her hair.* —*n.* small fact or detail. Ex. *This report agrees with yours in every particular.* —**par·tic'u·lar·ly,** *adv.* especially.

partisan (5) [par'tǝzǝn], *n.* 1. a devoted follower of a cause, person, etc. Ex. *His partisans worked eagerly for his election.* 2. a member of a small band of fighters, not part of a regular army, who fight behind enemy lines. Ex. *The partisans destroyed the supplies of the invaders.* —*adj.* —**par'ti·san·ship,** *n.*

partition (4) [partiš'ǝn, pǝrtiš'ǝn], *n.* 1. division into parts, sections, or shares. Ex. *The partition of the country into two parts caused many problems.* 2. that which divides. Ex. *A partition divided the one room into two.* —*v.* 1. divide into parts, sections, or shares. Ex. *They partitioned the farm among the three sons.* 2. divide by walls. Ex. *They partitioned the room to form two offices.*

partner (3) [part'nǝr], *n.* 1. one who joins another or works in an enterprise. Ex. *This store is owned by two partners.* 2. either one of a couple dancing together. Ex. *When the music stopped, everyone changed partners.* 3. one who plays on the same side in a game. Ex. *They were partners in a card game.* —**part'ner·ship,** *n.* the condition or state of being partners in an enterprise; an association of partners. Ex. *The three friends formed a business partnership.*

part of speech [part' ǝv spiyč'], any of the groups into which words are placed in study of a language. Ex. *Nouns, verbs, and adverbs are all parts of speech.*

party (1) [par'tiy], *n.* 1. a group of people gathered together for enjoyment. **Ex.** *We went to a dinner party last night.* 2. a group of people working together for political reasons. **Ex.** *The Democratic Party and the Republican Party are the leading political parties in the United States.* 3. a group of people working together for some purpose. **Ex.** *A search party hunted for the lost child.*

pass (1) [pæs'], *v.* 1. go by or move past something. **Ex.** *I passed his car on the road.* 2. cause or allow to go, move, proceed, etc. **Ex.** *Please pass the sugar.* 3. successfully meet the requirements of an examination, a trial period, etc. **Ex.** *She passed her history test.* 4. give legal force to; enact. *Congress just passed an education bill.* 5. proceed; move along. **Ex.** *The parade passed down the street.* 6. go away; come to an end. **Ex.** *The storm has passed, and the sun is shining.* 7. change from one form, condition, owner, etc., to another. **Ex.** *The property will pass from father to son.* 8. throw. **Ex.** *He passed the ball to me.* —*n.* a narrow way through which one can go. **Ex.** *The pass is between those mountains.* —**pas'ser,** *n.* one who passes. —**pass'a·ble,** *adj.* 1. capable of being crossed or used. **Ex.** *In spite of the rain, the road was passable.* 2. acceptable; adequate. **Ex.** *Her dancing is not the best, but it is passable.* —**pass'ing,** *adj.* casual; quick. **Ex.** *He made a passing comment I did not hear.* —**in passing,** without serious thought. **Ex.** *He said it only in passing.* —**pass away,** die or end. **Ex.** *The old man passed away and was buried.* —**pass over,** ignore; fail to include. **Ex.** *He was passed over when they chose the team.*

passage (3) [pæs'ij], *n.* 1. a part of a book or other writing, speech, etc. **Ex.** *He read them passages from several books.* 2. the act of passing. **Ex.** *We didn't notice the passage of time.* 3. a way or means of passing. **Ex.** *The passage between the two houses was blocked.* 4. a journey by sea or air; passenger space on such a journey. **Ex.** *He was given passage on a morning plane.*

passenger (2) [pæs'ənjər], *n.* one other than the driver or operator who travels in a car, train, bus, ship, etc. **Ex.** *This ship can carry one hundred passengers.*

passion (2) [pæš'ən], *n.* 1. strong emotion such as love, hate, anger. **Ex.** *The young couple could not hide the passion they felt for each other.* 2. strong liking; enthusiasm. **Ex.**

---

a, far; æ, am; e, get; ey, late; i, in; iy, see; ɔ, all; ow, go; u, put; uw, too; ə, but, ago; ɔr, fur; aw, out; ay, life; oy, boy; ŋ, ring; θ, think; ð, that; ž, measure; š, ship; ǰ, edge; č, child.

He had a passion for sailing. —**pas'sion·ate**, *adj.* —**pas'sion·ate·ly**, *adv.*

passport (5) [pæs'pɔrt'], *n.* a special paper permitting a citizen to travel in other countries and giving him the protection of his government. **Ex.** *Most countries require a visitor to have a passport.*

past (1) [pæst'], *adj.* 1. gone by in time; finished. **Ex.** *He had thought his troubles were past.* 2. recent; immediately before. **Ex.** *He has not been well for the past few days.* 3. former. **Ex.** *The past president of the club welcomed his successor.* —*n.* 1. the time gone by; the time before. **Ex.** *The past seemed more real to her than the present.* 2. one's earlier life or history. **Ex.** *His exciting past made his present job seem dull.* —*adv.* to a point and beyond; by. **Ex.** *The soldiers marched past.* —*prep.* 1. after; later than. **Ex.** *It is past noon.* 2. beyond; farther than. **Ex.** *My house is past the store.*

paste (4) [peyst'], *n.* 1. a mixture of flour and water, or other substances, used to make paper or other thin materials stick together. **Ex.** *She sealed the envelope with paste.* 2. any mixture that is soft, smooth, and moist. **Ex.** *She added tomato paste to the sauce.* —*v.* fasten or stick together with paste. **Ex.** *She pasted the pictures in a little book.* —**pas'ty**, *adj.*

pasteboard [peyst'bɔrd'], *n.* a stiff board made of pieces of paper pasted together; cardboard.

pastry (4) [peys'triy], *n.* 1. pies and other sweet baked goods, made with a shell of flour and oil; all fancy baked goods. **Ex.** *We ate some delicious pastries with our coffee.* 2. the mixture of flour and oil used in making pies, cakes, etc. **Ex.** *She rolled the pastry until it was a large, thin circle.*

pasture (3) [pæs'čər], *n.* 1. ground covered with grass or other plants suitable for the feeding of cows, sheep, etc. **Ex.** *The boy took the cows to the pasture every morning.* 2. the grass or other plants that animals eat. **Ex.** *How many acres of pasture does he own?* —*v.* feed animals on growing grass and plants. **Ex.** *He pastured the sheep on the hill.*

pat (2) [pæt'], *n.* 1. a light, friendly stroke, usually with the hand. **Ex.** *The child gave the dog a pat on the head.* 2. a small piece of something. **Ex.** *She spread a pat of butter on her bread.* —*v.* touch gently; give a pat. **Ex.** *Dogs like to be patted.*

patch (3) [pæč'], *n.* 1. a piece of material used to cover a hole or a weak spot. **Ex.** *She sewed patches on the elbows of his jacket.* 2. a covering put over a wound, sore, or injured eye. **Ex.** *He wore a black patch on his left eye.* 3. a small section of land. **Ex.** *We have a vegetable patch beside our house.* —*v.* put a patch on; mend. **Ex.** *The mother patched the boy's trousers.*

patent (5) [pæt'ənt], *n.* 1. government protection giving an inventor the sole right to make, use, or sell his invention for a certain number of years. **Ex.** *He has applied for a patent on his latest invention.* 2. the official paper granting this right. —*v.* get the sole rights to an invention. **Ex.** *He patented a new process for making fresh water from salt water.*

path (2) [pæθ'], *n.* 1. a narrow way made by the walking of animals or people. **Ex.** *She followed the narrow path up the hill.* 2. course along which something moves. **Ex.** *He jumped out of the path of the approaching car.*

pathetic (5) [pəθet'ik], *adj.* arousing feelings of pity, sorrow, tenderness, or sympathy. **Ex.** *We could not bear to listen to the sick child's pathetic cries.* —**pa·thet'ic·al·ly,** *adv.*

patience (2) [pey'šəns], *n.* the ability to endure pain, troubles, etc. calmly and without complaining. **Ex.** *She endured the long delay with patience.*

patient (2) [pey'šənt], *adj.* 1. showing patience. **Ex.** *He was patient despite the long wait.* 2. showing self-control and tenderness. **Ex.** *He was patient with the children.* 3. continuing to make an effort despite difficulties. **Ex.** *After weeks of patient search, he found an answer to his problem.* —*n.* a person being cared for by a doctor. **Ex.** *The doctor asked the patient to lie down.*

patriot (4) [pey'triyət], *n.* a person who deeply loves and defends his country. **Ex.** *The patriot died while fighting in the war for independence.* —**pa'tri·ot'ic,** *adj.* —**pa'tri·ot·ism,** *n.* a deep love for and willingness to defend one's country. **Ex.** *His patriotism was not questioned.*

patrol (5) [pətrowl'], *v.* make regular, repeated trips around or through an area as a guard or policemen. **Ex.** *Policemen patrol the city day and night.* —*n.* 1. a person or group of persons whose duty it is to guard. **Ex.** *The patrol consisted of three armed men.* 2. the act of patrolling. **Ex.** *They were on patrol.* —**pa·trol'man,** *n.* policeman.

patron (4) [pey'trən], *n.* 1. one who buys regularly at a certain store; a regular customer. **Ex.** *She has been a patron of this store for many years.* 2. a person who gives his approval and support to a person, art, or cause. **Ex.** *The patrons of the museum contributed the money for the new museum building.* —**pa'tron·ize,** *v.* 1. be a regular customer of. **Ex.** *She always patronizes this store.* 2. support; be a patron to. 3. behave toward another as if he were an inferior. —**pa'tron·iz`ing,** *adj.* behaving as if another were an inferior. **Ex.** *She spoke to him in a patronizing manner.* —**pa'tron· age,** *n.* 1. the aid given by a patron. 2. customers; the state of patronizing. **Ex.** *The businessman appreciated their patronage.* 3. authority to appoint government officials or grant political favors. **Ex.** *He received his government job through patronage.*

pattern (2) [pæt'ərn], *n.* 1. a model or plan to be copied in making something. **Ex.** *She bought a pattern for an evening dress.* 2. a design used to decorate. **Ex.** *What is the pattern of your dishes?* —*v.* make, using a pattern or model. **Ex.** *He patterned himself after his father.*

pause (2) [pɔːz'], *n.* a brief stop or hesitation. **Ex.** *During the radio program there were several pauses for advertisements.* —*v.* make a brief stop; hesitate. **Ex.** *He paused, then continued speaking.*

pave (4) [peyv'], *v.* 1. cover a road with a mixture of small stones, concrete, or other materials that harden like stone when they dry. 2. prepare the way. **Ex.** *His research paved the way for the invention of the automobile.* —**pave'ment,** *n.* the covering of a road. **Ex.** *To avoid the mud, he walked on the pavement.*

paw (3) [pɔː'], *n.* the foot of an animal which has claws or nails. **Ex.** *The dog lifted his two front paws.* —*v.* hit, dig, or touch with the paws or feet. **Ex.** *The bull pawed the ground.*

pay (1) [pey'], *v.* 1. give money for something bought or services obtained. **Ex.** *How much did you pay for that suit?* 2. give money to settle a debt or a claim. **Ex.** *He had to pay bills from several stores.* —*n.* wages; salary. **Ex.** *His pay is eighty dollars a week.* —**pay'ment,** *n.* 1. the act of paying. 2. something paid. —**pay'a·ble,** *adj.* due for payment. **Ex.** *The bill is payable today.*

payroll [pey'rowl'], *n.* a list of the people working for an organization and the amount each earns. **Ex.** *Don't do the work until he puts you on the payroll.*

pea (3) [piy¹], *n.* 1. a climbing plant which produces green seeds in cases. 2. the seeds of this plant eaten as a vegetable.

PEA

peace (1) [piys¹], *n.* 1. quiet; freedom from war, fighting, or noise. **Ex.** *The war ended, and the country was at peace.* 2. an agreement to end a war. **Ex.** *They made peace with their enemies.* 3. law and order. **Ex.** *He was arrested for disturbing the peace.* —**peace'ful,** *adj.* quiet. —**peace' a·ble,** *adj.* preferring peace; peaceful.

peach (3) [piyč¹], *n.* 1. a round, juicy, orange-yellow fruit. 2. orange-yellow color.

peak (3) [piyk¹], *n.* 1. a pointed top, as of a cap, roof, etc. **Ex.** *The peak of the roof is the highest part of the house.* 2. highest or greatest point. **Ex.** *The mountain peak was covered with snow.* —**peaked¹,** *adj.* having a peak.

PEACH 1

pear (3) [pe:r¹], *n.* a soft fruit, yellow, green, or brown in color, round at one end and narrowing toward the stem.

pearl (3) [pərl¹], *n.* a smooth, hard, usually white or bluish-gray round stone, formed within some shellfish and used as a gem. —*adj.* made of pearl. —**pearl'y,** *adj.* like pearls.

PEAR

peasant (3) [pez¹ənt], *n.* a farmer or farm laborer, often poor, in Europe and Asia. **Ex.** *The peasants were planting rice.*

pebble (4) [peb¹əl], *n.* a very small, smooth, and rounded piece of rock. **Ex.** *The storm washed many pebbles onto the beach.* —**peb'bly,** *adj.* having many pebbles. **Ex.** *The pebbly road made the cart bounce.*

peck (4) [pek¹], *n.* a dry measure equal to eight quarts. **Ex.** *She bought a peck of potatoes.* See **Weights and Measures.**

peck (4) [pek¹], *v.* strike with the bill or something pointed, as a bird does. **Ex.** *The bird pecked at the bark of the tree.*

peculiar (3) [pikyuwl¹yər], *adj.* 1. unusual; strange; odd. **Ex.** *We heard a peculiar noise.* 2. special; in one person, group, etc. **Ex.** *That problem is peculiar to this area.* —**pe·cul'iar·ly,** *adv.* —**pe·cu'li·ar'i·ty,** *n.*

pedal (5) [ped'əl], *v.* cause to move or work by pushing on a lever, usually with the feet. **Ex.** *He pedaled his bicycle up the hill.* —*n.* a lever pushed by the foot when pedaling. **Ex.** *Bicycles have two pedals.*

peddle (5) [ped'əl], *v.* go from place to place selling, usually small articles. —**ped'dler,** *n.* one who peddles. **Ex.** *The dogs barked at the peddler selling fruit.*

peel (4) [piyl'], *n.* the outer skin of fruit and vegetables. **Ex.** *She used some orange peel to flavor the cake.* —*v.* 1. cut or pull away the outer skin. **Ex.** *She was peeling onions.* 2. come off. **Ex.** *Paint was peeling from the wall.*

peep (4) [piyp'], *v.* make a small, high sound like a young bird or a chicken. **Ex.** *The baby birds peeped in their nest.* —*n.* a peeping sound. **Ex.** *The baby chickens uttered peeps.*

peep (4) [piyp'], *v.* 1. look through a small hole; look without being seen. **Ex.** *The child peeped at the guests through the partly opened door.* 2. appear partly or briefly. **Ex.** *A flower peeped through the grass.* —*n.* a brief or secret look. **Ex.** *She took a peep at the hidden gifts.*

peer (3) [pi:r'], *n.* 1. a person or thing that is equal in some way. **Ex.** *As a lawyer, this man has no peer.* 2. a nobleman. **Ex.** *Her grandfather was a peer.*

peer (3) [pi:r'], *v.* look at closely in an effort to see more clearly. **Ex.** *The old woman peered at the girl.*

peg (5) [peg'], *n.* a short piece of wood or metal used to hold parts together, hang things on, etc. **Ex.** *He hung his hat on a peg.* —*v.* put or drive a peg into; fasten with a peg. **Ex.** *This chair is pegged instead of nailed.*

pen (2) [pen'], *n.* a pointed instrument used with fluid for writing. —*v.* write with a pen. **Ex.** *He penned a letter to his friend.*

pen (2) [pen'], *n.* 1. a small, enclosed space in which animals are kept. **Ex.** *The boy drove the sheep into the pen.* 2. any small, enclosed space. **Ex.** *The baby is in the playpen.* —*v.* put into a pen. **Ex.** *The animals were penned for the night.*

penalty (3) [pen'əltiy], *n.* 1. punishment for committing a crime or breaking the law. **Ex.** *The penalty for his offense was five years in prison.* 2. something paid for breaking an agreement or a rule in a contest. **Ex.** *He had to pay a ten* *percent penalty because his bill was overdue.* —**pe'nal,** *adj.* concerned with punishment. **Ex.** *The penal laws for stealing are severe.* —**pe'nal·ize,** *v.* give a penalty. **Ex.** *He was penalized for cheating.*

pencil (3) [pen'səl], *n.* a round, slender piece of wood containing a strip of black lead and used for writing or drawing. **Ex.** *He wrote a note with a pencil.* —*v.* write, draw, or mark with a pencil. **Ex.** *The artist penciled the outline of the model's face.*

penetrate (4) [pen'ətreyt`], *v.* 1. enter; force a way into or through. **Ex.** *The bullet penetrated the target.* 2. spread through. **Ex.** *The smell of paint penetrated the entire house.* —**pen'e·trat·ing,** *adj.* keen; intelligent. **Ex.** *The teacher had a penetrating mind.* —**pen'e·tra'tion,** *n.*

peninsula (5) [pənin'sələ], *n.* a piece of land surrounded on three sides by water. **Ex.** *Spain is a peninsula.*

penmanship [pen'mənšip`], *n.* art of handwriting. **Ex.** *His penmanship is difficult to read.*

penny (2) [pen'iy], *n.* one cent; a small copper coin worth one hundredth of a dollar in the United States and Canada. —**pen'ni·less,** *adj.* without any money; extremely poor.

pension (4) [pen'šən], *n.* a regular payment of money to one who is retired because of age or bad health. **Ex.** *He will start receiving a pension when he retires at sixty-five.* —*v.* grant a pension. **Ex.** *He was pensioned by the government.* —**pen'sion·er,** *n.* one who receives a pension.

people (1) [piy'pəl], *n.* 1. human beings; any group of persons. **Ex.** *Ten people live in this house.* 2. all the persons of a certain nation, religion, race, etc. **Ex.** *The President spoke to the American people.* 3. the persons living in the same area, having the same interests, doing the same work, etc. **Ex.** *Farming people depend upon the harvest.* 4. ordinary citizens; voters. **Ex.** *The mayor was popular with the people.* —*v.* populate. **Ex.** *The town was peopled with miners.*

pepper (3) [pep'ər], *n.* 1. a black or white, hot-tasting seasoning made by crushing the berries of a certain plant. **Ex.** *This sauce needs more pepper.* 2. a plant that bears sweet or hot, red or green fruits that are eaten as vegetables. **Ex.** *She put a sweet pepper into the salad.* —*v.* put pepper on. **Ex.** *The cook salted and peppered the meat.* —**pep'per·y,** *adj.* hot in taste.

perceive (3) [pərsiyv'], *v.* 1. gain knowledge of or discover through one of the five senses. **Ex.** *He could not perceive any difference between the twins.* 2. understand; comprehend. **Ex.** *He perceived the full meaning of the words.*

percent (2) [pərsent'], *n.* one part of or in every hundred. **Ex.** *Twenty-five percent equals 25/100ths; one hundred percent equals all.* Percent is often written: %. —**per·cent'age,** *n.* a part of a quantity, expressed as a percent. **Ex.** *What percentage of your salary do you spend for rent?*

perception (4) [pərsep'šən], *n.* the capacity for or act of perceiving. **Ex.** *His perception of the problem was good.* —**per·cep'tive,** *adj.*

perch (4) [pərč'], *n.* 1. a place where a bird rests, such as the branch of a tree or the bar in a cage. **Ex.** *The bird flew down from its perch.* 2. any raised seat or position. **Ex.** *The boy looked down from his perch in the tree.* —*v.* rest on or place on, as on a perch. **Ex.** *The bird perched on the woman's shoulder.*

perfect (1) [pər'fikt], *adj.* 1. having no faults or weaknesses. **Ex.** *Each movement of the dancer was perfect.* 2. complete in all respects. **Ex.** *Her accounts were in perfect order.* 3. total; complete. **Ex.** *The man was a perfect stranger.* 4. exact; correct. **Ex.** *The blue of her eyes and of her dress were a perfect match.* —**per·fect',** *v.* complete; improve as much as possible. **Ex.** *He is working to perfect his invention.* —**per·fec'tion,** *n.* —**per'fect·ly,** *adv.*

perform (2) [pərfɔrm'], *v.* 1. do. **Ex.** *He always performs his work with care.* 2. entertain by acting, dancing, singing. **Ex.** *The actors performed their parts well.* —**per·form'ance,** *n.* the act of performing. —**per·form'er,** *n.* one who performs.

perfume (4) [pər'fyuwm, pərfyuwm'], *n.* 1. a sweet smell. **Ex.** *The perfume of roses filled the room.* 2. a liquid used to give a pleasant odor to body or clothing. **Ex.** *She bought a small bottle of perfume.* —**per·fume',** *v.* scent with perfume. **Ex.** *The pine trees perfumed the mountain air.*

perhaps (1) [pərhæps'], *adv.* possibly; maybe. **Ex.** *Perhaps the letter will come today.*

peril (3) [pe:r'əl], *n.* 1. a condition of very great danger. **Ex.** *The ship was in peril.* 2. something dangerous. **Ex.** *The explorer was exposed to many perils.* —**per'il·ous,** *adj.* —**per'il·ous·ly,** *adv.*

period (1) [piːrˈiyəd], *n*. 1. a dot (.) used in writing and printing. **Ex.** *A period is placed at the end of most sentences.* 2. a portion of time marked by certain events, developments, conditions, etc. **Ex.** *During the early period of her life, she lived abroad.* 3. any of the portions of time into which a game, a school day, etc. is divided. **Ex.** *He did his history assignment during a study period.* —**peˈriˑodˈic**, *adj.* —**peˑriˑodˈiˑcal**, *adj.* —**peˑriˑodˈiˑcalˑly**, *adv.* —**peˑriˑodˈiˑcal**, *n.* a magazine or other publication that appears regularly but not daily.

perish (3) [peːrˈiš], *v*. die, especially as a result of violence, lack of food, or fire. **Ex.** *A hundred people perished in the fire.* —**perˈishˑaˑble**, *adj.* likely to spoil quickly. **Ex.** *Perishable foods spoil quickly in hot weather.* —**perˈishˑaˑble**, *n.* something which is likely to spoil quickly, as some food. **Ex.** *On the camping trip, we kept our perishables in an ice chest.*

permanent (3) [pərˈmənənt], *adj.* lasting indefinitely or for a very long time; enduring. **Ex.** *Brick walls are more permanent than wooden fences.* —**perˈmaˑnence**, *n.* the state of being permanent. —**perˈmaˑnentˑly**, *adv.*

permanent wave [pərˈmənənt weyvˈ], a wave in the hair put in by means of heat or a chemical and lasting for several months.

permission (2) [pərmišˈən], *n.* consent; act of permitting. **Ex.** *He asked our permission to enter.* —**perˈmisˈsiˑble**, *adj.* permitted.

permit (2) [pərmitˈ], *v*. 1. allow to do. **Ex.** *Please permit the boy to leave class early.* 2. enable; make it possible. **Ex.** *Windows permit light to enter the house.* —**perˈmit**, *n.* a written order allowing someone to do something. **Ex.** *He must have a permit to learn how to drive.*

perpendicular (5) [pərˌpəndikˈyələr], *adj.* 1. at 90-degree angles. **Ex.** *A square has four 90-degree angles made by its four perpendicular sides.* 2. exactly straight up. **Ex.** *The flag pole was raised to a perpendicular position.* —*n.* a line at a 90-degree angle to another line. **Ex.** *After the storm the flag pole was no longer on a perpendicular.*

perpetual (4) [pərpečˈuwəl], *adj.* 1. continuing forever; for an

a, far; æ, am; e, get; ey, late; i, in; iy, see; ɔ, all; ow, go; u, put; uw, too; ə, but, ago; ər, fur; aw, out; ay, life; oy, boy; ŋ, ring; θ, think; ð, that; ž, measure; š, ship; ǰ, edge; č, child.

unlimited time. **Ex.** *He has a perpetual calendar on his desk.*
2. continuing without interruption. **Ex.** *The perpetual quarreling made her nervous.* —**per·pet'u·al·ly,** *adv.* —**per·pet'u·ate,** *v.* cause to continue or be remembered. **Ex.** *They erected a statue to perpetuate his memory.* —**per'pe·tu'i·ty,** *n.* the state of being perpetual.

perplex (4) [pərpleks'], *v.* make a person uncertain or unsure; confuse. **Ex.** *He was perplexed by her strange behavior.* —**per·plex'i·ty,** *n.*

persecute (5) [pər'səkyuwt'], *v.* 1. cause to suffer constantly, especially for religious or political beliefs. **Ex.** *Some early religious leaders were persecuted by their enemies.* 2. cause distress by constantly bothering. **Ex.** *They were persecuted by unwelcome telephone calls day and night.* —**per·se·cu'tion,** *n.* the act of persecuting. —**per'se·cu·tor,** *n.* one who persecutes.

persist (4) [pərzist', pərsist'], *v.* 1. continue steadily, despite difficulties or resistance. **Ex.** *He persisted in his work until he succeeded.* 2. remain; endure. **Ex.** *In spite of many washings the stains persisted.* —**per·sist'ence,** *n.* —**per·sist'ent,** *adj.* —**per·sist'ent·ly,** *adv.*

person (1) [pər'sən], *n.* 1. a man, woman, or child; a human being. **Ex.** *Four persons saw her leave.* 2. the body or its outward appearance. **Exs.** *There was no money on his person. That actor is appearing in person.* 3. any of three classes of pronouns in grammar: *first person, "I" or "we"; second person, "you"; third person, "he," "she," "it," or "they."* —**per'son·a·ble,** *adj.* of pleasing appearance. **Ex.** *She is a personable young lady.* —**per·son'i·fy,** *v.* 1. represent an idea or thing as a person or having the qualities of a person. **Ex.** *A country is personified when it is referred to as "the Motherland."* 2. think of a person as representing a quality, idea, etc. **Ex.** *To the boy, his mother personified goodness.* —**per'son·age,** *n.* a person, especially an important one.

personal (2) [pər'sənəl], *adj.* 1. private; of a particular person. **Ex.** *His secretary does not open his personal mail.* 2. having to do with the character, habits, conduct, etc. of a person. **Ex.** *His teacher gave him a good personal recommendation.* 3. done by oneself without help. **Ex.** *He made a personal effort to settle the quarrel.* 4. of the body, dress, etc. **Ex.** *He is very careful about his personal appearance.* 5. in grammar, describing the person speaking, the one spoken to, or the person or thing spoken about. Ex. *"You" and "I" are personal pronouns.* —**per'son·al·ly,** *adv.* by, of, or as oneself. Ex. *I answered him personally.* —**per'son·al·ize,** *v.* make personal. Ex. *His shirt was personalized by sewing his initials on the pocket.*

personality (2) [pər'sənæl'ətiy], *n.* 1. the characteristics of a person which make him different from everyone else. Ex. *I can see the writer's personality in what he writes.* 2. personal qualities which attract. Ex. *She was elected class president because of her personality.* 3. a person, especially one who is famous or unusual. Ex. *She invited theater personalities to the party.*

persuade (3) [pərsweyd'], *v.* 1. cause a person to do something, especially by reasoning, urging, advising. Ex. *They persuaded him to stay.* 2. cause to believe. Ex. *He persuaded me that he was right.* —**per·sua'sion,** *n.* —**per·sua'sive,** *adj.* able to persuade. Ex. *He has a persuasive way of talking.*

pest (5) [pest'], *n.* a troublesome person or thing, especially a harmful insect or small animal. Ex. *Garden pests were destroying the roses.*

pet (3) [pet'], *n.* 1. a tame animal kept as a friend. Ex. *The children wanted a rabbit as a pet.* 2. a person treated with special kindness. Ex. *The baby was the pet of the family.* —*adj.* 1. kept or treated as a pet. Ex. *He has a pet dog.* 2. especially liked; favorite. Ex. *Politics is his pet subject.*

petition (4) [pətiš'ən], *n.* a request, carefully prepared, signed by a number of people, and addressed to someone in authority. Ex. *The people signed a petition to stop destruction of the historic buildings.* —*v.* 1. address a petition to. Ex. *The town petitioned the state government for help during the flood.* 2. pray for; request earnestly. Ex. *The prisoner petitioned the governor for mercy.* —**pe·ti'tion·er,** *n.*

petroleum (5) [pətrow'liyəm], *n.* a natural oil found in the earth in certain parts of the world. Ex. *Gasoline and other fuels are made from petroleum.*

petty (4) [pet'iy], *adj.* 1. small; of little worth; not important. Ex. *The children's quarrel concerned a petty problem.* 2. narrow-minded; mean. Ex. *None of us could endure his petty behavior.* —**pet'ti·ness,** *n.*

phase (4) [feyz'], *n.* 1. a stage of development. **Ex.** *Primary school is a phase in a child's education.* 2. one of a number of views presented by something to the eye or the mind; aspect; side. **Ex.** *He consulted an expert on each phase of the problem.*

phenomenon (5) [fənam'ənan'], *n.* 1. any fact or happening which can be observed or can be known through the senses. **Ex.** *Lightning is a phenomenon of nature.* 2. anything or anyone that is extraordinary. **Ex.** *A child who can read at the age of three is a phenomenon.* —phe·nom'en·a, *n. pl.* —phe·nom'en·al, *adj.*

philosophy (3) [filas'əfiy], *n.* 1. the study that attempts to understand the basic principles of man's thoughts about the meaning of life, the relationship of mind to matter, and the problems of right and wrong. **Ex.** *All first-year students at this college are required to take a course in philosophy.* 2. a system of principles derived from such study. **Ex.** *His philosophy was based on the goodness of man.* —phi·los'o·pher, *n.* one who understands or teaches philosophy. —phil·o·soph'i·cal, *adj.* —phil·o·soph'i·cal·ly, *adv.* —phi·los'o·phize, *v.* talk about philosophical ideas. **Ex.** *He philosophized about life and death.*

phone (3) [fown'], *n.* telephone. **Ex.** *We talk on the phone every day.* —*v.* talk to, using a telephone. **Ex.** *She phoned him yesterday.*

photograph (2) [fow'təgræf'], *n.* a picture made with a camera. **Ex.** *He had several photographs of his baby.* —*v.* make a picture of, using a camera. **Ex.** *He photographed the building.* —pho·tog'ra·pher, *n.* one who takes photographs. —pho·to·graph'ic, *adj.* —pho·tog'ra·phy, *n.* the art and practice of taking photographs.

phrase (2) [freyz'], *n.* a group of related words often found within a sentence but that do not form a complete sentence. **Ex.** *In the sentence, "In the park, there was much to do," "In the park" and "to do" are both phrases.* —*v.* express in words. **Ex.** *He carefully phrased his answer to the judge's question.*

physical (2) [fiz'ikəl], *adj.* 1. of the body. **Ex.** *The doctor's examination showed he was in excellent physical condition.* 2. of nature; of matter; material; natural. **Ex.** *They study the physical features of the earth in the science class.* —phys'i·cal·ly, *adv.*

physician (3) [fəziš'ən], *n.* a doctor of medicine.

physics (3) [fiz'iks], *n.* the science of motion, matter, and energy (heat, electricity, mechanics, light, etc.). Ex. *Students learn about gravity in their study of physics.* —**phys'icist**, *n.* a person who specializes in the study of physics.

piano (2) [piyæn'ow], *n.* a large musical instrument that gives out sounds when wire strings are struck by small hammers operated from a keyboard. —**pian'ist**, *n.* one who plays the piano.

PIANO

pick (1) [pik'], *v.* 1. choose, select. Ex. *Pick any book you want.* 2. take up with the finger and thumb. Ex. *He picked a pin from the floor.* 3. gather; harvest. Ex. *They picked all the peaches on the tree.* 4. open a lock with some instrument other than a key. Ex. *She picked the lock with a pin.* 5. empty secretly, as by a thief. Ex. *He had his pocket picked in the crowd.* —*n.* 1. the act of choosing; the thing chosen; a choice. Ex. *They went to the sale early to have first pick of the best items.* 2. the best; those most desired. Ex. *The prize-winning cows are the pick of the herd.* —**pick at,** eat with little appetite. Ex. *Because he was not hungry, he picked at his lunch.* —**pick out,** identify; find. Ex. *She quickly picked out her son in the crowd.* —**pick up,** 1. raise in one's hands. Ex. *Pick up that book on the floor.* 2. learn; discover. Ex. *Where did you pick up that information?* 3. increase. Ex. *The car quickly picked up speed.* 4. clean up. Ex. *He picked up the room before we arrived.*

pick (1) [pik'], *n.* 1. a hand tool with a heavy pointed head used to break up the ground. 2. any tool or instrument used for breaking, removing, etc. Ex. *He broke off a piece of ice with the ice pick.*

PICK 1

pickle (4) [pik'əl], *n.* a vegetable or fruit preserved in salt water or vinegar, flavored with herbs and spices. Exs. *Pickles are most agreeable when eaten with cold meats and salad. She served pickles with the dinner.* —*v.* preserve in spiced salt water or vinegar. Ex. *Mother is pickling peaches in the kitchen.*

picnic (4) [pik'nik], *n.* a meal planned for eating outdoors. **Ex.** *They ate their picnic beside the river.* —*v.* have a picnic. **Ex.** *We picnicked in the woods.* —**pic'nick·er,** *n.* **Ex.** *After lunch, the picnickers made up teams for a game of baseball.*

picture (1) [pik'čər], *n.* 1. a painting, drawing, or photograph. **Ex.** *That picture of the President is seen often in the news-paper.* 2. that which strongly resembles another; an image. **Ex.** *She is the picture of her mother.* 3. a description. **Ex.** *The author gives a lively picture of his life as a sailor.* 4. a motion picture; movie. **Ex.** *The whole family enjoyed the picture we saw last night.* —*v.* describe. **Ex.** *The speaker pictured the scene in colorful words.* —**pic·tor'i·al,** *adj.*

pie (2) [pay'], *n.* a baked dish consisting of a thin shell, and sometimes a cover, made of flour and cooking oil and filled with fruit, meat, etc. **Ex.** *She put the pie in the oven to bake.*

piece (1) [piys'], *n.* 1. an amount or a part considered as an individual unit. **Ex.** *Please give me a piece of writing paper.* 2. a part taken away from something larger. **Ex.** *She cut the pie into six pieces.* 3. a coin. **Ex.** *Can you change this fifty-cent piece?* —*v.* join together; make whole. **Ex.** *She pieced together the broken dish.* —**go to pieces,** become upset or excited. **Ex.** *He goes to pieces when I disagree with him.*

piecemeal [piys'miyl`], *adv.* one part at a time; piece by piece. **Ex.** *He put the machine together piecemeal in his spare time.*

piecework [piys'wərk`], *n.* work paid for by the piece finished instead of by the hour, day, etc. **Ex.** *She does piecework at home.*

pier (3) [pi:r'], *n.* a structure built over the water and used as a landing place for ships and boats. **Ex.** *The ship is at pier seven.*

pierce (4) [pirs'], *v.* 1. break into or through. **Ex.** *The knife had pierced the wall.* 2. make a hole or opening in. **Ex.** *Many girls have their ears pierced for earrings.* 3. force a way through. **Ex.** *They tried to pierce the enemy's defense.* 4. deeply or sharply affect the senses or feelings. **Ex.** *They were pierced by the icy winds.*

pig (2) [pig'], *n.* a farm animal with a broad nose and fat body, raised for its meat.

PIG

pigeon (3) [piĵ'ən], *n.* a bird with a small head, a broad body, and short legs.

pile (2) [payl'], *n.* a number of things or a quantity of something placed or thrown together. **Ex.** *They put all the wood in a pile.* —*v.* 1. make a heap of; put in a pile. **Ex.** *We piled the boxes in the corner.* 2. form a pile or heap; come together. **Ex.** *The snow piled in front of the door.*

PIGEON

pilgrim (5) [pil'grim], *n.* one who travels to a holy place for religious purposes. **Ex.** *The pilgrims entered the church to pray.* —**Pil'grim,** *n.* one of the members of an English religious group that founded a colony in America in 1620. —**pil'grim·age,** the travels of a pilgrim. **Ex.** *The holy men traveled many miles on their pilgrimage to the sacred city.*

pill (4) [pil'], *n.* medicine in a small rounded mass to be swallowed whole. **Ex.** *She took the pills and drank a glass of water.*

pillar (4) [pil'ər], *n.* a slender, upright structure used as a support, decoration, or monument. **Ex.** *The roof of the porch was supported by brick pillars.*

pillow (2) [pil'ow], *n.* a bag filled with feathers, cotton, etc., used to support the head while resting or sleeping.

PILLAR

pilot (3) [pay'lət], *n.* 1. a man who controls an airplane while it is flying. **Ex.** *The pilot landed the airplane safely.* 2. a man who steers a ship into or out of a harbor or through difficult places. —*v.* act as a pilot. **Ex.** *He skillfully piloted the ship into the harbor.* —*adj.* serving as a test or trial. **Ex.** *If the pilot course succeeds, it will be offered to everyone next year.*

pin (2) [pin'], *n.* 1. a short, sharp piece of wire with a round or flat head used for fastening. **Ex.** *She used a pin to fasten the flower to her dress.* 2. an ornament for the clothing fastened with a pointed wire and a clasp. —*v.* 1. fasten with a pin. **Ex.** *She pinned a flower on her dress.* 2. hold firmly in one position. **Ex.** *The fallen tree pinned the man to the ground.* —**pin down,** force to tell what is really planned, wanted, etc. **Ex.** *We must pin him down about how the money was spent.*

pinch (4) [pinč'], *v.* 1. force together between the tips of the finger and thumb; press upon from opposite sides in any way. **Ex.** *He pinched the fruit to see if it was soft.* 2. press upon in a painful manner. **Ex.** *The door pinched his finger.* —*n.* the forcing together between the tips of the finger and thumb; the pressing upon from opposite sides. **Ex.** *She gave her little brother a pinch.*

pine (2) [payn'], *n.* a tree that is green throughout the year and has leaves shaped like needles.

pineapple (5) [payn'æp`əl], *n.* a large, sweet, juicy fruit that grows in warm countries.

PINEAPPLE

pine cone [payn'kown'], *n.* the cone-shaped fruit of the pine.

pink (2) [piŋk'], *n.* pale red. **Ex.** *Her favorite color is pink.* —*adj.* pale red. **Ex.** *She wore a pink dress.* —**pink'ish**, *adj.*

pinpoint [pin'poynt`], *v.* point to the exact place. **Ex.** *He pinpointed on the map where we were going.*

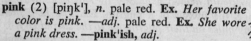

PINE CONE

pint (3) [paynt'], *n.* a measure of volume which equals half a quart; 0.473 liter. **Ex.** *We have only a pint of milk left.* See **Weights and Measures.**

pioneer (3) [pay`əni:r'], *n.* 1. one who leads the way; the first settler in a new region. **Ex.** *The early pioneers encountered many dangers.* 2. one who leads the way in any field or activity. **Ex.** *John Glenn was a pioneer in space travel.* —*v.* open a way for others to follow; act as a pioneer. **Ex.** *Those who pioneer in space travel are greatly admired.*

pious (4) [pay'əs], *adj.* careful in following the rules of one's religion. **Ex.** *He was a pious man who observed every holy day.* —**pi'ous·ly**, *adv.*

pipe (2) [payp'], *n.* 1. a metal tube used to carry liquids and gases from one place to another. **Ex.** *The water froze in the pipes during the cold weather.* 2. a tube, with a small bowl at one end, in which tobacco is smoked. **Ex.** *His father smokes a pipe.* —*v.* send through pipes. **Ex.** *Water and gas are piped into the house.*

pirate (4) [pay'rət], *n.* one who robs at sea. **Ex.** *The pirates attacked the merchant ship.* —*v.* wrongfully copy and publish or use the work of another. **Ex.** *His book was pirated in several countries.* —**pi'ra·cy**, *n.* the act of pirating. —**pi·rat'i·cal**, *adj.*

pistol (4) [pis'təl], *n.* a small gun held and fired with one hand. **Ex.** *The robber had a pistol hidden under his coat.*

pit (3) [pit'], *n*. 1. a hole in the ground. **Ex.** *Men are digging sand from a pit near the road.* 2. any hole or low place in a surface. **Ex.** *The rust made pits in the metal.* —*v*. make a low place in a surface. **Ex.** *The ship's anchor was pitted by rust.*

pit (3) [pit'], *n*. the hard, stony covering containing the seed in the center of peaches, plums, and similar fruits. **Ex.** *This device can be used to remove the pits of cherries or olives.* —*v*. remove the seed with such a covering from fruit.

pitch (3) [pič'], *v*. 1. set up and make ready for occupation. **Ex.** *We pitched our tent under the trees.* 2. throw; toss. **Ex.** *He pitched the hay into the wagon.* 3. throw a ball in a ball game. **Ex.** *The team needs someone who can pitch.* 4. rise and fall by turns; plunge. **Ex.** *The ship pitched violently in the storm.* —*n*. 1. the act of pitching or throwing, as a ball. **Ex.** *The first pitch of the game was very fast.* 2. a rising and falling motion; a plunge. **Ex.** *The sudden pitch of the ship knocked him off his feet.* 3. a point or degree. **Ex.** *Feelings are at a high pitch of excitement.* 4. the degree of slope. **Ex.** *The pitch of the roof was very steep.* —**pitch'er**, *n*. one who throws, or pitches, especially in a ball game. **Ex.** *The pitcher raised his arm to pitch the ball.*

pitcher (5) [pič'ər], *n*. a container, usually with a handle, for holding and pouring liquids.

pitfall [pit'fɔl'], *n*. hidden danger or problem. **Ex.** *There are many pitfalls in his plan.*

pitied [pit'iyd], *v*. past tense and participle of *pity*. **Ex.** *They pitied the crippled man.*

PITCHER

pitiful [pit'ifəl], *adj*. causing pity. **Ex.** *The thin child was pitiful to see.*

pitiless [pit'iləs], *adj*. lacking pity. **Ex.** *The tax collector was pitiless.*

pity (2) [pit'iy], *n*. 1. sorrow or sadness for the suffering of another. **Ex.** *She felt pity for the starving people.* 2. a reason for sorrow or regret. **Ex.** *What a pity it is that you missed him.* —*v*. feel sorrow or sympathy for another. **Ex.** *We pity the sick child.* —**have pity on** or **take pity on,** feel pity for. **Ex.** *Have pity on the poor boy.*

place (1) [pleys¹], *n.* 1. space; region; area. **Ex.** *There are still many places about which we know very little.* 2. location; the portion of space occupied by a person or thing. **Ex.** *The place for those books is on the second shelf.* 3. a country, city, or other particular region. **Ex.** *Write the name of the place where you were born.* 4. a house, apartment, farm, or other dwelling. **Ex.** *They have a pleasant place in the country.* 5. a building or area used for a particular purpose. **Ex.** *There are many nice little eating places near our office.* 6. a position or location given up or previously occupied by another; a space not occupied. **Ex.** *This building will be torn down and another built in its place.* 7. job; rank; position. **Ex.** *People in high places are concerned about this problem.* 8. a particular point or part. **Ex.** *He complained of a sore place on his arm.* —*v.* 1. put in a particular place, position, relation, etc. **Ex.** *She placed her hand on his shoulder.* 2. entrust. **Ex.** *She placed her confidence in him.* —**in place of,** for; instead of. **Ex.** *I went in place of him.* —**take place,** happen; occur.

plague (4) [pleyg¹], *n.* 1. a disease that spreads rapidly and causes much death and sickness. **Ex.** *Hundreds of people died during the plague.* 2. something that causes terrible trouble or suffering. **Ex.** *Floods have been a plague in this region for years.* —*v.* trouble or cause to suffer. **Ex.** *A cough plagued her all winter.*

plain (1) [pleyn¹], *adj.* 1. having little or no decoration. **Ex.** *She wore a plain black dress.* 2. not rich; simple. **Ex.** *The food was plain but good.* 3. not handsome; not pretty. **Ex.** *She was a very plain girl.* 4. ordinary. **Ex.** *He was a plain working man.* 5. easy to do; simple. **Ex.** *She can do plain sewing.* 6. frank; honest. **Ex.** *His plain remarks sometimes offend people.* 7. easy to understand. **Ex.** *His meaning was perfectly plain.* 8. easy to see. **Ex.** *The house was in plain sight.* —*n.* a large, unbroken area of fairly flat land. **Ex.** *Much wheat is grown on these plains.* —**plain'ly,** *adv.* obviously; clearly; simply. —**plain'ness,** *n.* lack of ornament; frankness.

plan (1) [plæn¹], *n.* 1. a previously thought-out method of doing something. **Ex.** *Our plan is to go to the mountains.* 2. a drawing showing the shape or relation between the parts of anything. **Ex.** *The plans for the new building are in my office.* —*v.* 1. consider a method for doing something. **Ex.** *She carefully planned each detail of the party.* 2. make a drawing showing the shape or relation between the parts of anything. **Ex.** *He planned the streets of the new town.* **3**. intend; have as a purpose. **Ex.** *He plans to go on to college after finishing high school.* —**plan'ner,** *n.* one who plans.

plane (3) [pleyn'], *n.* 1. level of development or progress. **Ex.** *Their civilization reached a very high plane.* 2. airplane. **Ex.** *He flies his own plane.* 3. a flat surface. **Ex.** *Each step on the stairs is a different plane.*

planet (3) [plæn'it], *n.* any of the nine large heavenly bodies revolving around the sun. **Ex.** *The earth is a planet.* —**plan'e·tar·y,** *adj.*

plank (4) [plæŋk'], *n.* 1. a long, flat, thick piece of wood. **Ex.** *The bridge was made of rough planks.* 2. a principle of a political party. **Ex.** *The candidate explained each plank in his party's platform.*

plant (1) [plænt'], *n.* 1. a life form that is usually held to the ground by roots, does not have feelings, and makes food from soil, water, and air. **Ex.** *Trees are large plants.* 2. any small form of vegetable life with a stem softer than that of a tree or bush. **Ex.** *She had many kinds of plants in the garden.* 3. the machines, buildings, etc. of a factory, business, or institution. **Ex.** *Automobiles are made in that plant.* —*v.* put into the ground to grow. **Ex.** *He planted vegetables in his garden.* —**plan'ter,** *n.* 1. one who plants. 2. owner of a plantation.

PLANT 2

plantation (5) [plæntey'šən], *n.* a large farm or estate where crops such as bananas, coffee, or rice are raised by workers living on the estate. **Ex.** *He manages a cotton plantation.*

plaster (4) [plæs'tər], *n.* a soft mixture of powdered stone, sand, and water, that becomes hard when dry and is used for coating walls. **Ex.** *The walls cannot be painted until the plaster is dry.* —*v.* cover as with plaster; spread over thickly. **Ex.** *They plastered the walls with announcements of coming shows.* —**plas'ter·er,** *n.* one who plasters.

plastic (3) [plæs'tik], *n.* a material made from chemicals that can be shaped and hardened into many useful things. **Ex.** *The toy car is made of plastic.* —*adj.* 1. made of plastic. **Ex.** *They took plastic dishes on their camping trip.* 2. ca-

plate   392   playmate

pable of being modeled or shaped. **Ex.** *Clay is a plastic material.* 3. having to do with molding or modeling. **Ex.** *This statue is a good example of plastic art.*

plate (2) [pleyt'], *n.* 1. a shallow, usually round, dish from which food is eaten or served. 2. a smooth, flat, thin piece of metal, especially one on which words have been carved. **Ex.** *His name was on a brass plate on the door.* 3. a sheet of metal used to print words from. —*v.* cover with a thin layer of metal. **Ex.** *These cups were plated with gold.*

PLATE 1

plateau (4) [plætow'], *n.* a wide, level stretch of land, higher than the surrounding area. **Ex.** *The airport was built on a plateau.*

platform (3) [plæt'fɔrm'], *n.* 1. a flat, raised surface, usually for speakers, actors, etc. **Ex.** *The President stood on the platform to give his speech.* 2. the statement of policy or plans which a political party presents at elections. **Ex.** *The candidate explained his party's platform.*

play (1) [pley'], *v.* 1. amuse oneself; have fun; engage in sport. **Ex.** *The children were playing outside the school.* 2. take part in a game. **Ex.** *The boys played ball.* 3. act in a show. **Ex.** *She played his sister in that show.* 4. perform on a musical instrument. **Ex.** *He plays the drums.* —*n.* 1. amusement; sport. **Ex.** *Children must have time for play.* 2. a story written in conversation form to be acted on a stage. **Ex.** *The actor's performance in the play was a great success.* —**play'er,** *n.* one who plays. —**play'ful,** *adj.* joking; full of fun. —**play down, play up,** make something appear less or more important. **Ex.** *He played down his role in solving the problem.* —**play into someone's hands,** act in a way that gives someone else an advantage. **Ex.** *Getting angry plays into his hands.* —**play on** or **play upon,** take unfair advantage of another person's weakness or feelings. **Ex.** *He played on their love for the child to get money from them.*

playboy [pley'boy'], *n.* a man with much money who never works and goes to many dances, parties, etc.

playground [pley'grawnd'], *n.* a park; a place specially prepared for children to play in.

playmate [pley'meyt'], *n.* a friend with whom a child plays. **Ex.** *His playmate could not come out today.*

plaything [pley'θiŋ`], *n.* a toy. **Ex.** *They put their playthings away.*

plea (4) [pliy'], *n.* 1. an appeal; an earnest request. **Ex.** *A kind man answered their plea for aid.* 2. something said in defense; an excuse. **Ex.** *Her plea for staying at home was a headache.* 3. answer made in court by an accused person concerning the charge against him. **Ex.** *The murderer's plea was self-defense.*

plead (3) [pliyd'], *v.* 1. ask earnestly; beg. **Ex.** *He pleaded for mercy.* 2. answer in court a charge against one. **Ex.** *The accused man pleaded not guilty.*

pleasant (1) [plez'ənt], *adj.* 1. nice; enjoyable; happy. **Ex.** *We had a pleasant visit with our friends.* 2. having a nice or friendly look, manner, etc. **Ex.** *He was always very pleasant when we met.* —**pleas'ant·ly**, *adv.* —**pleas'ant·ness**, *n.*

please (1) [pliyz'], *v.* 1. give enjoyment to; make one happy. **Ex.** *They did everything they could to please their guests.* 2. desire; wish; choose. **Ex.** *You may do what you please with your own money.* 3. be so good as to; be so kind as to. **Ex.** *Please open the door.* —**pleas'ing**, *adj.*

pleasure (1) [plež'ər], *n.* 1. state of being delighted or satisfied. **Ex.** *He found pleasure in listening to music.* 2. anything that gives delight, enjoyment, or a satisfying feeling. **Ex.** *Going to the theater was one of her many pleasures.* 3. that which satisfies the senses. **Ex.** *He lives only for pleasure.* —**plea'sur·a·ble**, *adj.*

pledge (3) [plej'], *n.* 1. a serious promise or agreement. **Ex.** *I give my pledge that I will help you.* 2. anything given as security or as a sign that something will be done. **Ex.** *He gave his watch as a pledge to the moneylender.* —*v.* 1. promise to give. **Ex.** *Each person pledged a sum of money for the new hospital.* 2. make a serious promise. **Ex.** *He pledged to marry her when he returned.*

plenty (2) [plen'tiy], *n.* all that is needed; a large enough amount. **Ex.** *They had plenty of money for their trip.* —**plen'ti·ful**, *adj.*

plight (5) [playt'], *n.* a difficult or dangerous situation. **Ex.** *The freezing weather made their plight more serious.*

---

a, far; æ, am; e, get; ey, late; i, in; iy, see; ɔ, all; ow, go; u, put; uw, too; ə, but, ago; ər, fur; aw, out; ay, life; oy, boy; ŋ, ring; θ, think; ð, that; ž, measure; š, ship; j, edge; č, child.

plot (3) [plat'], *n.* 1. a secret plan to do something wrong or unlawful. **Ex.** *The police learned of a plot to bomb the courthouse.* 2. the main story in a novel, play, etc. **Ex.** *This mystery story has an exciting plot.* 3. a small piece of ground. **Ex.** *He intends to build a house on this plot.* —*v.* 1. make secret plans. **Ex.** *The men were plotting to rob a bank.* 2. make a plan or map of. **Ex.** *Some of the islands had not been plotted before.*

plow (2) [plaw'], *n.* a farm tool used to loosen and turn up the land for planting. —*v.* 1. turn up the soil with a plow. **Ex.** *Early in the spring the farmer began to plow his fields.* 2. move through anything with difficulty, in the manner of plowing. **Ex.** *The ship plowed through the stormy sea.*

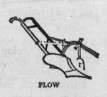

PLOW

plowshare [plaw'šer'], *n.* the blade of a plow.

pluck (3) [plək'], *v.* 1. pull off or out; pick. **Ex.** *She plucked a rose from the bush.* 2. pull the feathers out of. **Ex.** *She was plucking a chicken.* —*n.* 1. courage. **Ex.** *It took pluck for him to express his opinion.* 2. a pull. **Ex.** *He felt a pluck at his sleeve.*

plug (5) [pləg'], *n.* 1. an object used to block or close a hole. **Ex.** *He pulled the plug in the sink to let the water out.* 2. a device used to connect a lamp, iron, etc. to a source of electricity. **Ex.** *That lamp needs a new plug.* 3. an upright and closed pipe on a street from which water can be taken to fight a fire, water the street, etc.; fire plug. —*v.* block or close with something. **Ex.** *They plugged the leak in the boat with a piece of wood.*

PLUG 2

plum (4) [pləm'], *n.* 1. a juicy, smooth-skinned fruit having a small seed. **Ex.** *She bought a pound of blue plums.* 2. the purplish-red color of some plums. **Ex.** *She wore a plum dress.*

plumbing (4) [pləm'iŋ], *n.* the pipes and connections for water and waste in a building. **Ex.** *The plumbing is not working, and we have no water in the house.* —**plumb'er,** *n.* one whose work is fixing plumbing.

plume (4) [pluwm'], *n.* 1. a feather, especially a long or soft full one. **Ex.** *Some birds are hunted for their plumes.* 2. an ornament made of feathers. **Ex.** *She trimmed her hat with plumes.* —*v.* 1. straighten or smooth its feathers. **Ex.** *The bird plumed itself.* 2. feel pride in or be satisfied with oneself. **Ex.** *He plumed himself on his excellent record.* —**plum'age,** *n.* a bird's feathers.

plump (4) [pləmp'], *adj.* rounded in form; somewhat fat. **Ex.** *The girl had a plump figure.* —*v.* make or become rounded or fat. **Ex.** *She plumped the feather pillows.* —**plump'ness,** *n.*

plunder (4) [plən'dər], *v.* rob or take by force. **Ex.** *Enemy troops plundered the town.* —*n.* 1. the act of robbing by force. **Ex.** *Guards were on duty to prevent plunder.* 2. goods taken by force. **Ex.** *The thieves divided the plunder among them.* —**plun'der·er,** *n.*

plunge (2) [plənj'], *v.* 1. thrust or throw into suddenly. **Ex.** *He plunged the red-hot metal into the water.* 2. bring suddenly to some condition. **Ex.** *The news plunged the family into sadness.* 3. leap or throw oneself. **Ex.** *He plunged into the water to rescue his friend.* 4. rush; move recklessly. **Ex.** *He plunged through the door.* —*n.* 1. the act of plunging. **Ex.** *He made a plunge for the door.* 2. a swim. **Ex.** *We like to take a plunge in the ocean before breakfast.* —**plung'er,** *n.* any device that operates with a plunging motion; one who plunges.

plural (5) [plu:r'əl], *adj.* more than one. **Ex.** *The plural form of a word in English often ends in "s" or "es."* —*n.* the form of the word showing that more than one is meant. **Ex.** *The plural of man is men.*

plus (4) [pləs'], *prep.* 1. increased by; added to. **Ex.** *Two plus five equals seven.* 2. in addition. **Ex.** *His intelligence plus his willingness to work will bring him success.* —*adj.* more than zero; showing addition. —*n.* in mathematics, the plus sign: $+$ ($2 + 5 = 7$).

pocket (2) [pak'it], *n.* a small bag sewed into a garment for carrying small articles, money, etc. **Ex.** *He carried a comb in his coat pocket.* —*v.* 1. put into a pocket. **Ex.** *He pocketed his money.* 2. take something not one's own. **Ex.** *He pocketed some of his employer's money.* —*adj.* small enough to be carried in a pocket. **Ex.** *He often carried a pocket dictionary.*

pocketbook [pak'itbuk`], *n.* a woman's handbag or purse. 2. a small paperback book.

poem (2) [pow'əm], *n.* a special arrangement of words and their sounds expressing strong feeling and appealing to the imagination. **Ex.** *He wrote many short poems.*

poet (2) [pow'it], *n.* one who writes poems. **Ex.** *The poet read several of his poems to us.* —**po·et'ic,** *adj.* 1. having the qualities of a poem. 2. referring to a poet or poems.

poetry (2) [pow'itriy], *n.* 1. the art of writing poems. **Ex.** *The teacher praised her efforts at poetry.* 2. poems; verse. **Ex.** *One volume of his poetry has just been published.* 3. something like poetry in quality or feeling. **Ex.** *His painting captured the poetry of the bird's flight.*

point (1) [poynt'], *n.* 1. the sharp tip of anything which becomes smaller toward the end. **Ex.** *His pencil has a sharp point.* 2. exact place or position. **Ex.** *My house is at the point where the road turns.* 3. a particular degree; a limit. **Ex.** *The water was brought to the boiling point.* 4. a unit of counting or scoring. **Ex.** *Our team won with three points to their two.* 5. the most important idea or fact. **Ex.** *I did not understand the point of his story.* 6. a piece of land which extends out into the water. **Ex.** *Many small boats were near the point.* —*v.* 1. direct one's finger toward. **Ex.** *Point to the one you want.* 2. aim. **Ex.** *The boys were told never to point the gun at anyone.* —**poin'ted,** *adj.* 1. having a sharp end. **Ex.** *A pointed stick is dangerous.* 2. directed at. **Ex.** *He made pointed comments to her.* —**point'er,** *n.* 1. one who points. 2. anything, such as a stick, used for pointing. —**beside the point,** not concerned with the subject being discussed. **Ex.** *His remarks were beside the point.* —**make a point of,** treat as important; stress. **Ex.** *He made a point of inviting her.* —**on the point of,** about to do something. **Ex.** *I was on the point of leaving when I saw you.* —**stretch a point,** make an exception to the rule. **Ex.** *Her parents stretched a point and allowed her to stay up beyond her bed time.*

point-blank [poynt'blæŋk'], *adj.* 1. aimed directly at and very close to the target, as with a gun. **Ex.** *The gun was fired point-blank.* 2. stated in very clear, blunt terms. **Ex.** *His answer was a point-blank "no."*

point of view [poynt' əv vyuw'], a way in which or position from which something is looked at or considered. **Ex.** *I liked what she bought, but from her husband's point of view it was expensive.*

poise (4) [poyz'], *n.* 1. assurance; dignity; self-control. **Ex.** *A good public speaker must develop poise.* 2. balance; steadiness. **Ex.** *Poise is required to work high above the ground.* —*v.* 1. balance or be balanced. **Ex.** *The girl poised the basket on her head.* 2. support in a motionless state; seem to be supported. **Ex.** *The eagle hung poised in the sky.*

poison (2) [poy'zən], *n.* 1. a substance which can destroy life or injure health. **Ex.** *They killed all the rats in the house with poison.* 2. anything that harms, damages, or destroys. —*v.* 1. damage or destroy with poison; put poison into. **Ex.** *The man was poisoned.* 2. harm; damage; destroy. **Ex.** *She poisoned her son's mind against his wife.* —**poi'son·ous,** *adj.* able to cause death, etc. —**poi'son·er,** *n.* one who poisons.

poke (4) [powk'], *v.* 1. push or thrust sharply against or into with something. **Ex.** *He poked me in the ribs with his elbow.* 2. cause by pushing or thrusting something. **Ex.** *He accidentally poked a hole in the thin wall.* —*n.* 1. act of poking; thrust. **Ex.** *He gave me a poke in the ribs.* 2. one who moves or acts slowly. **Ex.** *Don't be such a slowpoke!* —**pok'er,** *n.* 1. one who pokes. 2. a metal rod for stirring a fire. 3. a game of cards. —**poke along,** move slowly. **Ex.** *He poked along all day and did not finish his work.* —**poke around,** search in a disorganized way. **Ex.** *He poked around in the bedroom for his shoes.* —**poke fun at,** tease; ridicule. **Ex.** *They poked fun at the way he walked.*

pole (2) [powl'], *n.* 1. a long, slender piece of wood or other material. **Ex.** *We took our fishing poles with us.* 2. either end of an imaginary line that goes through the center of a round body, such as the earth, and around which the body turns. **Ex.** *The earth has a North Pole and a South Pole.* —*v.* push with a pole. **Ex.** *We poled the boat through the shallow water.*

police (2) [pəliys'], *n.* 1. the department of government whose duty it is to guard the public, keep order, make certain that people obey the law, etc. 2. the members of such a department. **Ex.** *The police are looking for the killer.* —*v.* control; protect with police. **Ex.** *The city was well policed.*

policeman [pəliys'mən], *n.* one of the police.

policy (2) [pal'əsiy], *n.* 1. a course of action adopted and followed by a government, a political party, a club, etc. **Ex.** *He is writing a book about the foreign policy of his country.* 2. method or principle of doing things. **Ex.** *The policy of this store is to please the customer.*

policy (2) [pal'əsiy], *n.* a written insurance contract. **Ex.** *If he dies, his children will get ten thousand dollars from his insurance policy.*

polish (3) [pal'iš], *v.* 1. make clean and shiny. **Ex.** *We polished the furniture on the day the guest arrived.* 2. improve. **Ex.** *He polished the story he wrote.* —*n.* 1. a substance used to give smoothness and shine. **Ex.** *I need a can of shoe polish.* 2. smoothness and shine. **Ex.** *His shoes had a fine polish.* 3. correct or elegant manners and speech. **Ex.** *That charming young girl speaks with polish.* —**polish off,** finish. **Ex.** *He polished off the last of the wine.*

polite (2) [pəlayt'], *adj.* 1. showing thoughtfulness for others in manners and speech. **Ex.** *He was polite to everyone he met.* 2. cultured; possessing fine taste. **Ex.** *Music, literature, and art are highly valued in polite society.* —**po·lite'ly,** *adv.* **Ex.** *He politely held the door open for the ladies.* —**po·lite' ness,** *n.*

political science [pəlit'ikəl say'əns], the science of government. **Ex.** *He studied political science at the university.*

politics (2) [pal'ətiks'], *n.* 1. the science dealing with the different forms of government. **Ex.** *He is a student of politics.* 2. the affairs and activities of those who are in public office or seek such an office; the profession of those engaged in government. **Ex.** *The President has spent most of his life in politics.* —**po·lit'i·cal,** *adj.* —**po·lit'i·cal·ly,** *adv.* —**pol'i· ti'cian,** *n.* a person holding or seeking public office whose career is in politics.

poll (4) [powl'], *n.* 1. the voting at an election. **Ex.** *The poll showed him to be the winner.* 2. the number of votes cast. **Ex.** *The poll in this election was the largest ever recorded.* 3. a list of persons, such as voters, taxpayers, etc. **Ex.** *His name was on the poll.* 4. an opinion survey. **Ex.** *A poll was taken to learn which radio program was the most popular.* —*v.* 1. count votes. 2. ask people their opinions. **Ex.** *They polled the neighbors to learn their opinion of the new taxes.* 3. receive a certain number of votes. **Ex.** *The winner polled* *more than two-thirds of the votes.* —**polls'**, *n.* a place where people go to vote.

pollute [pəluwt'], *v.* make dirty or impure; release dangerous or unpleasant waste matter into the air, soil, or water. **Ex.** *Gasoline fumes pollute the city air.* —**pol·lu'tion,** *n.*

pond (2) [pand'], *n.* a pool; a body of water smaller than a lake. **Ex.** *The boys went fishing in the pond.*

ponder (5) [pan'dər], *v.* think about deeply; consider seriously. **Ex.** *They pondered their next move.*

pony (3) [pow'niy], *n.* a kind of horse that is small even when fully grown. **Ex.** *The children like to ride the pony.*

pool (2) [puwl'], *n.* 1. a small amount of any spilled liquid. **Ex.** *A pool of water formed under the leak in the roof.* 2. small body of water, such as a pond. 3. a tank of water for swimming. **Ex.** *The boys went swimming in the pool.*

poor (1) [pu:r'], *adj.* 1. lacking money, goods, or means of support. **Ex.** *The family is poor and needs help.* 2. not of good quality; bad. **Ex.** *The harvest is small because the soil is poor.* 3. unfortunate. **Ex.** *The poor child is tired.* —*n.* people with little or no money. **Ex.** *They gave generously to the poor.* —**poor'ly,** *adv.*

pop (4) [pap'], *v.* 1. make a short, quick sound like a gunshot. **Ex.** *The balloon popped loudly as it burst.* 2. move, come in, or go out suddenly. **Ex.** *He popped in for a moment and then left.* —*n.* 1. a short, quick sound like a gunshot. **Ex.** *We heard a pop as the cork came out of the bottle.* 2. a bubbling drink that is not alcoholic; flavored soda water. **Ex.** *He bought a bottle of orange pop.*

popular (2) [pap'yələr], *adj.* 1. well-liked; having many friends. **Ex.** *He is one of the most popular boys in school.* 2. generally favored among the public. **Ex.** *She enjoys popular music.* 3. of, representing, or engaged in by the mass of people. **Ex.** *His newspaper created popular interest in the need for better schools.* 4. suited to the means of ordinary people. **Ex.** *The tickets were sold at popular prices.* —**pop'u·lar·ly,** *adv.* in a way that is or will be popular. **Ex.** *The tickets are popularly priced.* —**pop·u·lar'i·ty,** *n.* condition of being well-liked. **Ex.** *Her popularity was due to her dancing.* —**pop'u·lar·ize,** *v.* make popular.

population (2) [pap'yəley'şən], *n.* the total number of persons living in a country, place, etc. **Ex.** *The world population is growing very fast.* —**pop'u·late,** *v.* provide with people.

Ex. *Factory workers populated the city.* —**pop'u·lous,** *adj.* having many people. Ex. *China is a very populous country.*

porch (2) [pɔrč'], *n.* 1. a covered approach attached to a house or other building. Ex. *We stood on the porch watching the rain.* 2. a screened or open room attached to the main building. Ex. *They had lunch on the side porch.*

pore (5) [pɔːr'], *v.* study or look at with deep and steady attention. Ex. *He pored over the map for hours.*

pore (5) [pɔːr'], *n.* a very small opening in the skin, in a leaf, etc., through which water or air can pass. Ex. *The hot bath opened his pores and caused him to sweat.*

pork (3) [pɔrk'], *n.* flesh of a pig, used as food. Ex. *They had roast pork for dinner.*

port (2) [pɔrt'], *n.* 1. a city where ships load or unload. Ex. *The sailor had visited many ports.* 2. a harbor; a place along the coast where ships may stop for safety in a storm. Ex. *The storm forced the ship into port.* 3. the side of a ship on one's left when one is facing the front. Ex. *He turned the ship to port.*

portable [pɔr'təbəl], *adj.* small enough to be easily carried. Ex. *He bought a portable radio.*

porter (4) [pɔr'tər], *n.* 1. one employed to carry suitcases. Ex. *The hotel porter carried their bags to their room.* 2. an attendant on a train. Ex. *The porter made the passenger's bed.*

porthole [pɔrt'howl'], *n.* an opening or window in the side of a ship for light and air. Ex. *He could see the stars through his porthole.*

portion (2) [pɔr'šən], *n.* 1. part or share. Ex. *His portion of the family property was the largest.* 2. one serving of food. Ex. *She gave him a large portion of pie.* —*v.* divide into shares; distribute as shares. Ex. *She portioned out the food.*

portly [pɔrt'liy], *adj.* large and dignified. Ex. *A portly senator was the guest of honor.*

portrait (4) [pɔr'treyt', pɔr'trit], *n.* 1. a picture of a person, especially of the face. Ex. *She had her portrait painted by a famous artist.* 2. a description; a picture in words. Ex. *The writer painted a brilliant picture of society life.* —**por'trai·ture,** *n.* 1. art of portraying. 2. a portrait.

portray (5) [pɔrtrey'], *v.* 1. represent by a drawing, statue, etc. Ex. *The artist portrayed liberty in his painting as a* *woman carrying a burning light.* 2. represent in a stage play. **Ex.** *He portrays the hero.* 3. describe in words. **Ex.** *The author portrayed the life of a teacher.* —**por·tray'al,** *n.* act of portraying. —**por·tray'er,** *n.* one who portrays.

pose (4) [powz'], *v.* 1. hold or place in a suitable position for a photographer or artist. **Ex.** *They posed in front of their house.* 2. represent oneself to be what one is not. **Ex.** *He posed as a doctor.* 3. present for consideration. **Ex.** *Their unexpected arrival for dinner posed the problem of what to feed them.* —*n.* 1. attitude or position held for a picture. **Ex.** *The artist told his model to hold the pose.* 2. act of pretending to have a quality which one does not have. **Ex.** *His unfriendly manner is a pose to hide his shyness.*

position (1) [pəziš'ən], *n.* 1. place; location. **Ex.** *The captain checked the ship's position.* 2. the way of holding the body. **Ex.** *He sat in a comfortable position.* 3. the way in which a thing is set or placed. **Ex.** *He placed the books in an upright position.* 4. job; employment. **Ex.** *He hopes to find a teaching position.* 5. social or professional rank. **Ex.** *The judge holds a position of trust in the community.* 6. attitude; point of view. **Ex.** *What is his position concerning the new taxes?*

positive (3) [paz'ətiv], *adj.* 1. expressed with certainty; clear and definite. **Ex.** *The guard has positive instructions not to admit anyone.* 2. very sure; certain. **Ex.** *He is positive that he saw them.* 3. real; practical; worth the time or effort needed. **Ex.** *We hope for some positive results from our work.* —**pos'i·tive·ly,** *adv.*

possess (2) [pəzes'], *v.* 1. have; own. **Ex.** *They no longer possess much land.* 2. have as a part or quality of oneself. **Ex.** *A dog possesses a keen sense of smell.* 3. control or be controlled by; get power over. **Ex.** *Anger possessed him.* —**pos·ses'sor,** *n.* one who possesses. —**pos·ses'sion,** *n.* 1. ownership. 2. that which is possessed. —**pos·ses'sive,** *adj.* desiring to keep or own something; acting like an owner.

possessive case [pəzes'iv keys'], in English grammar, the form of a noun which shows ownership, usually produced by adding "s" to the noun. **Ex.** *In the sentence, "John's clothes are new," "John's" is the possessive case of "John."* Posses-

a, far; æ, am; e, get; ey, late; i, in; iy, see; ɔ, all; ow, go; u, put; uw, too; ə, but, ago; ər, fur; aw, out; ay, life; oy, boy; ŋ, ring; θ, think; ð, that; ž, measure; š, ship; ǰ, edge; č, child.

sive pronouns are: *My, mine, your, yours, his, her, hers, our, ours, their, theirs; whose.*

possible (1) [pas'əbəl], *adj.* 1. capable of being done. Ex. *There are two possible ways of getting here.* 2. capable of being or happening; likely to happen. Ex. *Rain is possible this afternoon.* —**pos'si·bly,** *adv.* —**pos`si·bil'i·ty,** *n.*

post- (2) [powst'], *prefix.* after; following. Exs. *War, postwar; graduate, postgraduate.*

post (2) [powst'], *n.* 1. a long, strong piece of wood or other material used as a support. Ex. *The fence posts were set ten feet apart.* 2. a job, office, or position. Ex. *He holds an important government post.* 3. the place or station of a person on duty. Ex. *The guard cannot leave his post.* 4. a camp; a fort. Ex. *A wall surrounds the army post.* —*v.* 1. place in a mailbox. Ex. *These letters must be posted today.* 2. put a sign or notice on a post or wall. Ex. *Announcements of the show were posted everywhere.* 3. assign as a guard; assign to a particular position. Ex. *A soldier was posted at the door of the President's office.* —**post'al,** *adj.* of mail or the mail service. Ex. *The two countries signed a postal agreement.*

postage (5) [pows'tiĵ], *n.* the charge for mailing a letter or other matter sent by mail. Ex. *How much did the postage cost?*

postage stamp [pows'tiĵ stæmp'], a small paper with a design that one buys and fastens to a letter to pay for mailing.

postman [powst'mən], *n.* a man who delivers mail or works in a post office.

postmark [powst'mark`], *n.* a mark on a letter, covering part of the stamp, that shows the date and place of mailing.

postmaster [powst'mæs`tər], *n.* a person in charge of a post office.

post office [powst' ɔ:f'is], a place where one can mail a letter, buy stamps, etc.

postpaid [powst'peyd'], *adj.* cost of mailing already paid. Ex. *We will mail the package to you postpaid.*

postpone (5) [powstpown'], *v.* delay action until a later time. Ex. *They postponed their trip because of rain.* —**post·pone'ment,** *n.*

pot (1) [pat'], *n.* 1. a deep, round vessel usually made of metal, used for cooking. Ex. *She cooked the soup in a pot on the stove.* 2. any vessel of a similar shape. Ex. *A pot of* *flowers was on the table.* —*v.* put into a pot. **Ex.** *She potted the plants.*

potato (2) [pətey'tow], *n.* one of the thick, rounded parts growing underground on the roots of certain vegetables, usually having light brown skin and a white edible inner part. —**sweet potato,** a yellow root growth similar to a potato, grown in warm climates.

POTATO

potent (5) [pow'tənt], *adj.* 1. powerful; mighty. **Ex.** *He was once a potent ruler in control of a large state.* 2. producing a strong effect. **Ex.** *His potent arguments won support for his proposal.* —**po'ten·cy,** *n.* strength. **Ex.** *What is the potency of that drug?*

potential (5) [pəten'šəl], *adj.* possible, though not yet actually existing or fully in use. **Ex.** *Education often develops potential abilities.* —*n.* something that is capable of being developed. **Ex.** *He seems to have potential as a leader.* —**po·ten'ti·al'i·ty,** *n.*

pouch (5) [pawč'], *n.* 1. a bag; a sack. **Ex.** *He kept his tobacco in a leather pouch.* 2. a fold of skin or flesh shaped like a bag. **Ex.** *The squirrel filled its cheek pouches with nuts.*

poultry (4) [powl'triy], *n.* domestic farm birds raised for food, such as chickens, ducks, and geese. **Ex.** *That market has fresh poultry for sale.*

pound (2) [pawnd'], *n.* a unit of weight equal to 16 ounces. **Ex.** *She bought a pound of butter.* See **Weights and Measures.**

pound (2) [pawnd'], *v.* 1. strike repeatedly with great force. **Ex.** *He pounded a nail into the wall.* 2. break, crush, or soften by beating. **Ex.** *She pounded the meat to make it tender.* 3. beat heavily. **Ex.** *His heart pounded.* —*n.* a heavy blow; the sound of such a blow. **Ex.** *We heard a pound on the door.*

pour (2) [pɔ:r'], *v.* 1. cause to flow continuously. **Ex.** *She poured milk from the bottle into the glasses.* 2. flow as if in a continuous stream. **Ex.** *People poured out of the office building.* 3. rain heavily. **Ex.** *It has been pouring all morning.*

poverty (3) [pa'vərtiy], *n.* 1. the state or condition of being poor and needy. **Ex.** *The poverty of his family made it impossible for him to go to school.* 2. a scarcity or lack of something needed. **Ex.** *The poor crops were due to the poverty of the soil.*

powder (2) [paw'dər], *n.* any dry material in the form of fine, loose pieces. **Ex.** *She bought some face powder.* —*v.* 1. apply powder or something in a powdered form. **Ex.** *She powdered her face.* 2. crush or grind into fine, loose pieces. **Ex.** *She powdered nuts for use in the cake frosting.* —**pow'der·y,** *adj.*

power (1) [paw'ər], *n.* 1. ability to act. **Ex.** *Birds have the power to fly.* 2. force; energy in use. **Ex.** *The power of the hammer blows shaped the hot metal.* 3. authority; influence. **Ex.** *They voted to give the police more power.* 4. force or energy applied or that can be applied to work. **Ex.** *Water power turns the mill wheel.* 5. a person, group, etc. that has authority, strength, or influence. **Ex.** *That nation is a world power.* —*v.* provide power to. **Ex.** *That saw is powered by electricity.* —**pow'er·ful,** *adj.* strong.

practical (2) [præk'tikəl], *adj.* 1. useful. **Ex.** *Her clothes were more practical than elegant.* 2. able to be used; that will work. **Ex.** *His plan was interesting but not practical.* 3. trained by or gained from practice; learned through experience or doing. **Ex.** *He has no practical experience in the business.* —**prac'ti·cal·ly,** *adv.* almost. **Ex.** *The work is practically finished.*

practice (2) [præk'tis], *v.* 1. do again and again in order to learn or become skilled. **Ex.** *He practiced the new words in the vocabulary daily.* 2. do or use often. **Ex.** *Those people practice strange customs.* 3. work at or follow a profession or occupation. **Ex.** *His father practices law.* —*n.* 1. doing repeatedly in order to learn or become skilled. **Ex.** *He spends an hour at music practice daily.* 2. something done regularly or often. **Ex.** *It is our practice to have dinner early.* 3. actual performance. **Ex.** *He wants to put his theory into practice.* 4. the work done in a profession. **Ex.** *The practice of medicine requires many years of training.* —**prac'ticed,** *adj.* skilled.

prairie (5) [pre:r'iy], *n.* an almost treeless piece of even, grassy ground, with good soil. **Ex.** *The prairies were ideal for growing wheat.*

praise (2) [preyz'], *n.* an expression of approval or admiration, in word or song. **Ex.** *Your efforts are worthy of praise.* —*v.* 1. express approval or admiration. **Ex.** *They praised his honesty.* 2. worship. **Ex.** *The people of the tribe praised their god in song.*

pray (2) [prey'], v. make a request to a god or spirit; praise a god or spirit. Ex. *They prayed for rain.*

prayer (2) [pre:r'], n. 1. a request to a god or a spirit. Ex. *She felt that her prayer had been answered.* 2. a set of words used in worship. Ex. *The children learned their prayers from their mother.*

pre- (2) [priy], *prefix.* before in time, position, rank, etc.; ahead of when necessary. Exs. *Dawn, predawn; arrange, prearrange; pay, prepay.*

preach (3) [priyč'], v. 1. give a speech or talk devoted to religion. Ex. *Many people went to church to hear him preach.* 2. advise or urge, especially when the advice is not requested. Ex. *He felt that his teachers preached too much.* —**preach'er,** n.

precaution (5) [prikɔ:'šən], n. something done to avoid future accidents, danger, or trouble. Ex. *They took heavy coats as a precaution against the possibility of cold weather.* —**pre·cau'tion·ar·y,** adj.

precede (4) [priysiyd'], v. be first before another in position, time, or importance, etc. Ex. *January precedes February.* —**pre'ced·ence,** n. that which is before another in position, time, or importance. Ex. *The need for food took precedence over everything else.* —**prec'e·dent,** n. a previous decision, act, etc., which is used as a guide in later actions. Ex. *The precedents all indicated that the judge should send him to jail.* —**pre·ced'ing,** adj. being or going first. Ex. *Look at the preceding page and see what you wrote there.*

precious (2) [preš'əs], adj. 1. of great price or value; expensive. Ex. *The ring was set with precious stones.* 2. loved; dear. Ex. *She had precious memories of her childhood.* —**pre'cious·ly,** adv.

precipice (5) [pres'əpis], n. a very high, steep, almost vertical cliff or ledge. Ex. *He fell over the precipice and was killed.* —**pre·cip'i·tous,** adj. steep; like a precipice.

precise (4) [prisays'], adj. 1. exact; definite. Ex. *He gave a precise account of how much money he had spent.* 2. very careful to follow rules. Ex. *The principal of the school was very precise.* —**pre·cise'ly,** adv. exactly. Ex. *She said pre-*

cisely what she meant. —**pre·cise'ness,** *n.* the quality of being precise. —**pre·ci'sion,** *n.* exactness.

predecessor (5) [pred'əses'ər], *n.* one who preceded another. **Ex.** *His predecessor quit because he was not happy in the job.*

predict (4) [pridikt'], *v.* tell in advance what will happen. **Ex.** *He predicted rain for tomorrow.* —**pre·dic'tion,** *n.* 1. the act of predicting. 2. the thing predicted. —**pre·dict'a·ble,** *adj.* easily predicted. **Ex.** *It was predictable that she would want to go.*

predispose [priy'dispowz'], *v.* establish in advance a favorable feeling toward something. **Ex.** *His childhood predisposed him to like the farm.*

predominate [pridam'əneyt'], *v.* 1. be in control because of strength, numbers, etc. **Ex.** *He predominated over the others because of his size.* 2. exceed in number, size, etc. **Ex.** *Friends predominated at the meeting.* —**pre·dom'i·nant,** *adj.* **Ex.** *Rice is the predominant food of millions of people throughout the world.*

preface (3) [pref'əs], *n.* 1. a statement at the beginning of a book. **Ex.** *In the preface, he explained why he wrote the book.* 2. an introduction to a speech or writing. **Ex.** *As a preface to his speech, he explained his interest in the subject.* —*v.* provide with an introduction. **Ex.** *He prefaced his lecture with a humorous story.* —**pref'a·to·ry,** *adj.*

prefer (2) [prifə:r'], *v.* want one thing more than one wants others; have a higher regard for. **Ex.** *I prefer oranges to bananas.* —**pref'er·a·bly,** *adv.* —**pref'er·ence,** *n.*

prefix (5) [priy'fiks'], *n.* a letter or letters placed before or joined to the beginning of a word that changes the meaning of the word. **Ex.** *Dis-, co-, inter-, and ex- are all prefixes.*

pregnant (5) [preg'nənt], *adj.* bearing a child within the body; expecting to give birth to a baby or babies. **Ex.** *Pregnant women gain weight.* —**preg'nan·cy,** *n.*

prehistoric [priy'(h)istɔ:r'ik], *adj.* concerned with or of ancient times before history was recorded. **Ex.** *Many kinds of prehistoric animals no longer exist.*

prejudice (4) [prej'ədis], *n.* opinion, usually unfavorable, formed without sufficient knowledge, thought, or reason. **Ex.** *He had a prejudice against popular music.* —*v.* 1. cause to have a prejudice. **Ex.** *The judge warned the lawyer not to prejudice the jury.* 2. damage. **Ex.** *His carelessness* *prejudiced his chances for advancement.* —**prej`u·di`cial,** *adj.*

preliminary (5) [prilim'əner`iy], *adj.* coming before or preparing for the main event. **Ex.** *We must make preliminary plans for the party.* —*n.* anything done before or preparing for the main event. **Ex.** *As a preliminary, he assembled the necessary tools.*

premature [priy`mətyu:r', priy`məču:r'], *adj.* happening or being done before the proper time. **Ex.** *It is premature to say now who will win the election next week.*

premier (5) [priy'mir, primi:r'], *n.* the chief official of certain governments. **Ex.** *The people cheered the new premier.*

preoccupy [priyak'yəpay`], *v.* have one's mind concerned with one thing to the exclusion of others. **Ex.** *He was so preoccupied with his troubles that he did not hear her.*

prepare (1) [pripe:r'], *v.* 1. make ready. **Ex.** *The farmer prepared the ground for planting.* 2. complete; put together. **Ex.** *She was preparing dinner.* —**prep'a·ra·tion,** *n.* 1. the act of preparing. 2. the thing prepared. —**pre·par'a·to·ry,** *adj.*

preposition (5) [prep`əziš'ən], *n.* a word with a meaning of relationship, position, direction, time, etc., which is used to join a noun or pronoun with some other word in the sentence. A prepositional phrase is used as an adjective or adverb. **Ex.** *In the sentence, "The man with the suitcase went into the station," "with" and "into" are prepositions.* The prepositional phrase *"with the suitcase"* is used as an adjective to describe the man, while the phrase *"into the station"* is used as an adverb to describe where he went.

prescribe (4) [priskrayb'], *v.* direct the use of as a treatment or cure. **Ex.** *The doctor prescribed some medicine for her cold.* —**pre·scrip'tion,** *n.* that which is prescribed.

present (1) [prez'ənt], *adj.* 1. being at a certain place; being in view. **Ex.** *He was present at the meeting.* 2. now; for now. **Ex.** *My present teacher is a woman.* —*n.* the present time. **Ex.** *He is not here at present but will return next week.* —**pres'ent·ly,** *adv.* 1. soon; in a short period of time from now. **Ex.** *He will be home presently.* 2. now; at present. **Ex.** *He is presently visiting friends.* —**pres'ence,** *n.* 1. the fact of being present; attendence. **Ex.** *Your presence is requested at the dinner.* 2. the area where a person is. **Ex.** *They did not want to argue in the presence of their children.*

present (1) [prizent¹], *v.* 1. offer for consideration. **Ex.** *No new ideas were presented at the meeting.* 2. introduce. **Ex.** *They presented their house guest to their friends.* 3. show; display; exhibit. **Ex.** *The man presented his ticket at the door and was permitted to enter.* —**pres¹ent,** *n.* a gift. **Ex.** *She bought a birthday present for her sister.*

preserve (2) [prizɔrv¹], *v.* 1. keep from injury or harm. **Ex.** *His quick thinking preserved his life.* 2. keep in good condition. **Ex.** *The city decided to preserve the beautiful old building as a museum.* 3. keep; save. **Ex.** *Even though she became poor, she was able to preserve her jewels.* 4. prepare food to resist spoiling by canning, salting, etc. **Ex.** *She preserved many jars of fruit.* —*n.* a place set apart for the protection of animals, trees, etc. **Ex.** *We saw many deer in the preserve.* —**pre·serves¹,** *n.* fruit cooked with sugar to prevent spoiling. **Ex.** *She gave us a jar of orange preserves.*

preside (5) [prizayd¹], *v.* 1. have the place of authority at a meeting; be in charge of a meeting. **Ex.** *The mayor presided over the town meeting.* 2. direct; control. **Ex.** *Her grandmother presided over the family.*

president (1) [prez¹ədənt], *n.* 1. the chief officer of a republic. **Ex.** *He is the President of the United States.* 2. the chief officer of a club, a business firm, etc. **Ex.** *He was elected president of his company.* —**pres¹i·den·cy,** *n.* office or position of president. **Ex.** *George Washington was the first man elected to the Presidency of the United States.* —**pres·i·den¹tial,** *adj.*

press (1) [pres¹], *v.* 1. act upon by weight or force; push. **Ex.** *He pressed the button and waited for the door to open.* 2. take the juice from by using weight or force. **Ex.** *They were pressing grapes to make wine.* 3. embrace; hold close. **Ex.** *The frightened mother pressed the child to her heart.* 4. make clothes smooth and flat by heat and weight. **Ex.** *The tailor pressed the suit.* 5. urge; insist on. **Ex.** *They pressed us to stay.* 6. push against each other in numbers. **Ex.** *Hundreds of people pressed into the theater.* —*n.* 1. the act of pressing or being pressed; pressure. **Ex.** *Because of the press of business, he hired more help.* 2. any machine for pressing. **Ex.** *The apple juice flowed from the press.* 3. a place where printing is done. **Ex.** *There are several commercial presses in this area.* 4. newspapers, magazines, etc. considered as a group or profession. **Ex.** *The press was well represented at the meeting.*

pressure (3) [preš'ər], *n.* 1. the act of pressing or being pressed; force of weight. **Ex.** *The pressure of his shoe became painful.* 2. demands; burden; strain. **Ex.** *The pressure of his work made him neglect many other things.* 3. the force with which air, steam, water, etc. pushes against a certain area. **Ex.** *The air pressure at sea level is nearly 15 pounds for each square inch.* —**pres'sur·ize,** *v.* maintain air pressure at a desired level, as in airplanes at high altitudes.

prestige (5) [prestiyž', pres'tiǰ], *n.* reputation or influence gained from success, rank, character, etc. **Ex.** *The doctor had great prestige among the members of his profession.*

presume (4) [prizuwm', prizyuwm'], *v.* 1. suppose; assume. **Ex.** *I presume you are tired after your long trip.* 2. do something without authority; be too bold; dare. **Ex.** *The stranger presumed to call me by my first name.* —**pre·sump'tion,** *n.* that which is supposed or assumed. **Ex.** *His plans are based on the presumption that it will not rain.* —**pre·sump'tu·ous,** *adj.*

pretend (3) [pritend'], *v.* 1. act as if something not real is real; imagine. **Ex.** *The children pretended they were on a ship.* 2. make a false appearance of; claim falsely. **Ex.** *He pretended to be asleep.* —**pre'tense,** *n.* act of pretending. —**pre·ten'tious,** *adj.* acting, dressing, or spending to appear more important or wealthy.

pretty (1) [prit'iy], *adj.* having delicate and graceful good looks; pleasing in appearance. **Ex.** *The young men watched the pretty young girls.*

prevail (3) [priveyl'], *v.* 1. triumph; succeed. **Ex.** *He believed his cause would prevail against all opposition.* 2. become common; exist generally. **Ex.** *He refuses to work under the conditions that now prevail.* —**pre·vai'ling,** *adj.* current; most frequent. **Ex.** *The prevailing wind is from the south.* —**prevail upon,** persuade. **Ex.** *He prevailed upon his son to stay in school.*

prevalent (4) [prev'ələnt], *adj.* existing in many places; occurring often. **Ex.** *Rainy weather has been prevalent throughout the month.* —**prev'a·lence,** *n.*

prevent (2) [privent'], *v.* 1. keep something from occurring. **Ex.** *A heavy rain prevented the fire from spreading.* 2. keep a person from doing something. **Ex.** *The arrival of unex-pected guests prevented us from leaving.* —**pre·ven'tion,** *n.* —**pre·ven'tive,** *adj.*

preview [priy'vyuw`], *n.* a showing before the time something will be shown generally; that which gives information about what will happen later. **Ex.** *Before the movie was shown to the students, there was a preview for the teachers.*

previous (3) [priy'viyəs], *adj.* coming or occurring before something else. **Ex.** *We had met on a previous occasion.*

prey (5) [prey'], *n.* 1. an animal sought and seized for food by another animal. **Ex.** *The tiger leaped upon its prey.* 2. a person or thing unable to resist someone or something harmful. **Ex.** *The rich widow was an easy prey for fortune hunters.* —*v.* seek for and take by force. **Ex.** *Large animals prey upon smaller ones.*

price (1) [prays'], *n.* 1. the amount of money for which any-thing is bought, sold, or offered for sale. **Ex.** *What is the price of that book?* 2. the amount of effort, feeling, etc. needed to obtain something. **Ex.** *Loneliness was the price of his success.* —*v.* set the amount of money which one wants to receive for something. **Ex.** *The merchant priced the oranges at 50 cents a dozen.* —**price'less,** *adj.* having very great value. **Ex.** *That is a priceless work of art.*

prick (4) [prik'], *v.* 1. pierce with something sharp so as to make a small hole. **Ex.** *She pricked her finger on a thorn.* 2. have or cause a sharp mental pain. **Ex.** *The memory of cheating on his examination pricked his conscience.* —*n.* 1. a small hole made by a needle, pin, or some similar sharp thing. **Ex.** *The pricks in the leather formed a pattern.* 2. the feeling of being stuck with something sharp. **Ex.** *The prick of the needle made her cry out in pain.* —**prick up one's ears,** 1. with animals, to raise the ears to listen. 2. with humans, give full attention to something being said. **Ex.** *The boy pricked up his ears when he heard the word "candy."*

pride (2) [prayd'], *n.* 1. the belief that one's importance or worth is greater than it truly is. **Ex.** *Pride kept him from doing any work with his hands.* 2. self-respect. **Ex.** *I had too much pride to ask for help.* 3. pleasant, rewarding feeling of doing or having something of value. **Ex.** *He takes pride in doing good work.* —*v.* have a feeling of self-respect or take pleasure in doing something well. **Ex.** *They prided them-selves on their reputation for honesty.*

priest (3) [priyst'], *n.* one who devotes his life to the service of a god. **Ex.** *The priest led the church ceremonies.* —**priest'ly,** *adj.* —**priest'hood,** *n.* the occupation of being a priest.

primarily (2) [praymæ:r'əliy, pray'mer'əliy], *adv.* originally; mainly. **Ex.** *The book was written primarily for children.*

primary (3) [pray'mer'iy, pray'məriy], *adj.* 1. chief; principal; most important. **Ex.** *His primary reason for studying was to get a better job.* 2. first in order, position, or time; preparatory for something else. **Ex.** *My younger brother attends primary school.* —**pri'ma·ries,** *n.* an election within a political party to choose candidates for a later election. **Ex.** *He won the nomination in the Democratic primaries but lost to the Republican candidate in the election.*

prime (5) [praym'], *adj.* 1. requiring attention before all else. **Ex.** *Safety is a matter of prime importance.* 2. best in excellence or quality. **Ex.** *Good restaurants serve only prime beef.* —*n.* the period of greatest activity or strength; the age when one is most healthy, strong, etc. **Ex.** *He was in the prime of life.* —*v.* make ready; prepare for. **Ex.** *The student primed for his examination by studying.*

prime minister [praym' min'əstər], the head of government in countries with a parliamentary system.

primer [prim'ər], *n.* a book that gives basic information, in a very simple way, for children or for those who know nothing about the subject. **Ex.** *This book is a primer on how to fix automobiles.*

primitive (5) [prim'ətiv], *adj.* 1. of or concerning the earliest times before recorded history. **Ex.** *Primitive people often lived in caves.* 2. having qualities like those of primitive times; not developed; simple. **Ex.** *He was born in a primitive log cabin.* —**prim'i·tive·ly,** *adv.*

prince (2) [prins'], *n.* 1. the son of a king or queen. **Ex.** *The young prince will someday become king.* 2. a male ruler. **Ex.** *The prince ruled his people fairly.* —**prince'ly,** *adj.* like that of a prince. **Ex.** *The rich man lived in princely style.*

princess (2) [prin'səs], *n.* 1. the daughter of a king or queen. **Ex.** *The princess will become queen if her parents die without having a son.* 2. the wife of a prince.

principal (2) [prin'səpəl], *adj.* first in importance; highest in rank or value; chief. **Ex.** *Our principal needs are food, shelter, and clothing.* —*n.* 1. the head of a school. **Ex.** *The principal asked the teachers to come to a meeting.* 2. a sum of money loaned, saved, or borrowed on which one receives or pays interest. 3. one who is important or most important. **Ex.** *The hero is one of the principals in the play.* —**prin'ci·pal·ly,** *adv.* mostly.

principle (2) [prin'səpəl], *n.* 1. a custom or rule which guides the way one acts. **Ex.** *It was against her principles to smoke.* 2. a truth or ideal upon which a system or method is based. **Ex.** *The students are studying the principles of democracy.* 3. a law of nature or a law by which something operates. **Ex.** *The flow of water in a river is explained by the principle of gravity.*

print (2) [print'], *v.* 1. press a block of metal, wood, etc. on paper so as to make a copy of the marks or letters that are on the block appear on the paper. **Ex.** *This dictionary was printed in the United States.* 2. write in letters that look as if they were printed. **Ex.** *He slowly printed his name.* 3. publish. **Ex.** *The news was printed in the paper.* 4. make photographic pictures. **Ex.** *Will you print this roll of film?* —*n.* 1. letters made by printing. **Ex.** *Can you read the small print?* 2. a copy of a picture or a design made by printing on paper, cloth, etc. **Ex.** *I have prints of that artist's paintings.* 3. a mark made by pressing. **Ex.** *His fingerprints are on the glass.* —**print'ing,** *n.* the making of printed material. —**print'er,** *n.* one whose work or business is printing. —**in print,** 1. published. 2. available for sale. **Ex.** *The book is still in print.* —**out of print,** not available for sale. **Ex.** *That book has been out of print for years.*

printing press [prin'tiŋ pres'], a machine used for printing.

prior (4) [pray'ər], *adj.* earlier than in time, position, rank, etc. **Ex.** *They lived abroad prior to the war.* —**pri·or'i·ty,** *n.* a position of greater importance requiring attention before others or having rights ahead of others. **Ex.** *He gave priority to what he was doing for her.*

prison (2) [priz'ən], *n.* a public place where a person is kept while awaiting trial or to which he is sent as punishment. **Ex.** *The thief was sent to prison for five years.* —**pris'on·er,** *n.* 1. one who is held in prison. **Ex.** *The prisoners were permitted to see visitors once a month.* 2. a soldier captured by the enemy; one held against his will. **Ex.** *The captured soldiers are prisoners of war.*

private (2) [pray'vit], *adj.* 1. belonging to a particular person or group. **Ex.** *My home is private property.* 2. personal. **Ex.**

I discuss private matters only with my wife and close friends. 3. not in public life. Ex. *He has left the government and has become a private citizen.* 4. secret. Ex. *He told no one his private thoughts.* —*n.* a soldier of the lowest rank. Ex. *The general began his military life as a private.* —**pri'vate·ly,** *adv.*

private school [pray'vit skuwl'], any school not owned and controlled by a government. Ex. *Some private schools are expensive.*

privilege (2) [priv'əlij], *n.* special advantage, benefit, or favor enjoyed by an individual or group. Ex. *The oldest son was given the privilege of borrowing the car.* —*v.* grant a privilege or favor to. Ex. *We are privileged to have a distinguished guest with us tonight.*

prize (2) [prayz'], *n.* 1. something offered or won in a contest. Ex. *The boy received a prize for his painting.* 2. anything worth making a great effort to obtain; anything highly desirable. Ex. *That house with its view of the sea is considered a prize.* —*adj.* worthy of a prize; that has received a prize. Ex. *He has written a prize novel.* —*v.* value highly. Ex. *There is one stamp in his collection that he prizes more than the others.*

prize fight [prayz' fayt'], a boxing contest. —**prize'fighter,** one who boxes for pay.

pro- (3) [prow], *prefix.* for; in favor of; in place of. Exs. *American, pro-American; noun, pronoun.*

probable (1) [prab'əbəl], *adj.* likely to be or occur; possible. Ex. *A storm is probable today.* —**prob'a·bly,** *adv.* —**prob'a·bil'i·ty,** *n.*

probe (5) [prowb'], *n.* an examination into the facts concerning something. Ex. *A probe of the moon's surface has begun.* —*v.* examine; question or search thoroughly. Ex. *They probed his former political activities.*

problem (1) [prab'ləm], *n.* 1. a difficult question or situation, the answer or solution to which is not known or not certain. Ex. *The city government discussed the problem of crowded schools.* 2. a question given for solution. Ex. *The teacher gave the children five problems to solve.* —**prob'lem·at·ic** or **prob'lem·at·ic·al,** *adj.*

a, far; æ, am; e, get; ey, late; i, in; iy, see; ɔ, all; ow, go; u, put; uw, too; ə, but, ago; ər, fur; aw, out; ay, life; oy, boy; ŋ, ring; θ, think; ð, that; ž, measure; š, ship; j, edge; č, child.

procedure (3) [prəsiy'jər, prowsiy'jər], *n.* a particular way of acting or doing something. Ex. *The new secretary learned the procedures in the office.* —**pro·ced'ur·al,** *adj.* having to do with procedures.

proceed (2) [prəsiyd', prowsiyd'], *v.* 1. move or go forward again. Ex. *They proceeded on their journey after lunch.* 2. begin and continue an activity. Ex. *They proceeded rapidly with the work.* —**pro·ceed'ing,** *n.* activity or activities. Ex. *The proceeding at the school was a brief one.* —**pro·ceed'ings,** *n.pl.* action taken against someone in a court of law. Ex. *He started proceedings to regain possession of the house.*

process (2) [pras'es, prow'ses], *n.* 1. a method of producing something in a series of operations. Ex. *The process of making rubber was developed many years ago.* 2. a continuous series of changes leading to a particular result. Ex. *Sickness sometimes delays the process of growth.* —*v.* treat or prepare by some process. Ex. *Both butter and cheese are processed at that plant.*

procession (3) [prəseš'ən, prowseš'ən], *n.* persons or things in a group moving forward in an orderly and formal manner. Ex. *We were among those in the wedding procession.*

proclaim (3) [prowkleym'], *v.* announce officially and publicly. Ex. *Many former colonies have proclaimed their independence.* —**proc·la·ma'tion,** *n.* a public statement announcing something officially.

procure (4) [prowkyu:r'], *v.* 1. obtain by care or effort; get. Ex. *They procured the money needed to build the hospital.* 2. cause; bring about. Ex. *The lawyer procured the man's release.*

produce (1) [prəduws', prədyuws'], *v.* 1. bear; bring forth; yield. Ex. *These vines produce good grapes.* 2. make; create; cause. Ex. *Boiling water produces steam.* 3. manufacture. Ex. *Our company produces automobile tires.* 4. show; exhibit. Ex. *She produced a letter to prove her statement.* 5. prepare and bring before the public such as a play, a radio program, etc. Ex. *He produced two movies last year.* —**pro'duce,** *n.* that which is produced; a product. Ex. *The farmers took their produce to market.* —**pro·duc'er,** *n.* person or thing that produces, causes, yields, etc.

product (2) [prad'əkt], *n.* anything produced by growth, labor, study, etc. Ex. *Steel is the product of much work by many people.*

production (2) [prədək'šən], *n.* 1. the act of making or producing something. Ex. *Production at the factory increased when working conditions were improved.* 2. that which is produced, such as a play, movie, etc. Ex. *A new production will open at this theater next week.* —**pro·duc'tive,** *adj.* capable of producing much; producing much. Ex. *The conference was productive of new ideas.* —**pro`duc·tiv'i·ty,** *n.* act or condition of being productive. Ex. *The large amount of food grown this year results from the productivity of the soil.*

profess (5) [prəfes'], *v.* 1. declare openly or freely. Ex. *He professed his love for her.* 2. pretend. Ex. *He professed great admiration for his employer.* 3. declare a belief; be a member, follower of. Ex. *What religion does he profess?* —**professed',** *adj.*

profession (3) [prəfeš'ən], *n.* 1. an occupation, such as law or medicine, requiring special knowledge or training. Ex. *He is preparing for the teaching profession.* 2. all the persons engaged in this work. Ex. *He was known by the profession as a brilliant lawyer.* 3. an open declaration. Ex. *He made a public profession of his faith.* —**pro·fes'sion·al,** *adj.* 1. of, connected with, preparing for, or engaged in a profession. Ex. *A doctor's professional duties are to care for the sick.* 2. engaged for profit in an activity people usually perform for sport or relaxation. Ex. *He is a professional card player.* —*n.* 1. one who belongs to a profession. Ex. *As a professional, he had little patience with untrained workers.* 2. one who earns his living by playing or teaching a sport or some similar activity. Ex. *Everyone enjoyed watching the professionals play ball.* —**pro·fes'sion·al·ly,** *adv.*

professor (2) [prəfes'ər], *n.* a teacher of the highest rank in a university or college. Ex. *He is an excellent history professor.*

profit (2) [praf'it], *n.* 1. the money gained from a business activity after the payment of all expenses. Ex. *That company makes great profits from manufacturing automobiles.* 2. benefit; gain. Ex. *There is no profit in discussing the matter further.* —*v.* 1. gain money. Ex. *He profited from the sale of his house.* 2. benefit; gain. Ex. *You would profit from talking with him.* —**prof'it·able,** *adj.* producing profit, benefit, etc. —**prof'it·ab·ly,** *adv.*

profound (4) [prəfawnd'], *adj.* 1. characterized by great thought or knowledge. Ex. *The professor has written a pro-*

found book. 2. very deep; extreme. **Ex.** *The exhausted man fell into a profound sleep.* 3. intense. **Ex.** *I have a profound admiration for him.* **—pro·found'ly,** *adv.*

program (2) [prow'græm, prow'grəm], *n.* 1. the different events of an entertainment, meeting, etc. **Ex.** *The program included songs sung by the girls and boys.* 2. a paper on which the events of an entertainment or meeting are written. **Ex.** *We read the program while waiting for the show to start.* 3. a plan of action. **Ex.** *The health program for the coming year will lessen the number of sick children.*

progress (2) [prag'res, prow'gres], *n.* 1. development, betterment. **Ex.** *The progress of the students in their reading ability is remarkable.* 2. forward movement. **Ex.** *We made slow progress through the woods.*

progress (2) [prəgres'], *v.* 1. proceed; move forward. **Ex.** *The work progressed rapidly.* 2. develop; advance. **Ex.** *New methods are helping them progress economically.* **—pro·gres'sive,** *adj.* 1. making or showing progress. **Ex.** *He made many progressive changes.* 2. interested in new ideas and reform. **Ex.** *He is a progressive person.* **—pro·gres'sive·ly,** *adv.*

prohibit (4) [prowhib'it, prəhib'it], *v.* 1. forbid, with threat of punishment. **Ex.** *Smoking is prohibited in public buildings.* 2. stop; prevent. **Ex.** *Ill health prohibited him from swimming.*

prohibition (4) [prowəbiš'ən], *n.* 1. a law which forbids the manufacture and sale of alcoholic liquors. **Ex.** *Liquor cannot be sold in states which have prohibition.* 2. the act of forbidding or stopping; an order or law forbidding or stopping anything. **Ex.** *In this city there is a prohibition against constructing buildings more than ten stories high.* **—pro·hi·bi'tion·ist,** *n.* one who favors laws that forbid the sale of liquor.

project (3) [praǰ'ekt, praǰ'ikt], *n.* an activity considered or planned. **Ex.** *The road-building project was discussed at the meeting.*

project (3) [prəjekt'], *v.* 1. plan. **Ex.** *New housing is projected for that area of the city.* 2. throw forward. **Ex.** *The arrow was projected by the bow.* 3. throw an image onto a surface using a beam of light. **Ex.** *The movie was projected on a white wall.* 4. extend out. **Ex.** *The roof of the house projects over the window.* **—pro·jec'tile,** *n.* something made to be projected, such as a rocket, bullet, etc. —**pro·ject'or,** *n.* machine that projects pictures on a screen.

prolong (4) [prəlɔ:ŋ'], *v.* extend the time in which something occurs; make longer in time. **Ex.** *The old woman's life was prolonged by good care.*

prominent (5) [pram'ənent], *adj.* 1. well-known; famous. **Ex.** *Several prominent people were present at the meeting.* 2. especially noticeable; easy to see. **Ex.** *The flower on her hat was quite prominent.* —**prom'i·nent·ly,** *adv.* —**prom'i·nence,** *n.*

promise (1) [pram'is], *n.* 1. an agreement or assurance that one will do or not do something. **Ex.** *He gave us his promise that he would go.* 2. a reason for hoping for or expecting something; an indication of future excellence. **Ex.** *This child shows great promise as a pianist.* —*v.* 1. agree to do or not to do something. **Ex.** *He promised to come again the next day.* 2. give reason to expect. **Ex.** *The dinner promises to be a success.* —**prom'is·ing,** *adj.* —**keep a promise,** do what one has agreed to do. **Ex.** *She kept her promise to visit us on Sunday.*

promote (4) [prəmowt'], *v.* 1. advance in rank or position. **Ex.** *The lieutenant was recently promoted to captain.* 2. encourage or help something to happen. **Ex.** *The salesman tried to promote the sale of his company's products.* —**pro·mot'er,** *n.* one who promotes. —**pro·mo'tion,** *n.* the act of promoting or being promoted.

prompt (3) [prampt'], *adj.* 1. not late; on time. **Ex.** *He was prompt in paying his bills.* 2. ready and quick to act when necessary; done without delay. **Ex.** *His prompt action prevented serious trouble.* —*v.* cause to act. **Ex.** *The clouded sky prompted him to take his umbrella.* —**prompt'ly,** *adv.*

pronoun (5) [prow'nawn], *n.* a word used instead of a noun. **Ex.** *In the sentence, "The student left his hat, but he later returned for it," "he" and "it" are pronouns.*

pronounce (3) [prənawns'], *v.* 1. speak the sounds of; utter. **Ex.** *The teacher pronounced each word slowly and distinctly.* 2. declare seriously or officially. **Ex.** *The judge will pronounce sentence upon the guilty man.* —**pro·nounced',** *adj.*

definite. **Ex.** *Age had made a pronounced change in his appearance.* —**pro·nounce'ment,** *n.* an official or formal statement.

pronunciation (4) [prənən'siyey'šən], *n.* the act or way of saying the sounds of. **Ex.** *His pronunciation of some words is not correct.*

proof (3) [pruwf'], *n.* 1. anything that proves that something is true; evidence. **Ex.** *The man was freed when his lawyer offered proof that he was innocent.* 2. trial; test. **Ex.** *One proof of a diamond is that it will cut glass.* —*adj.* protected against something. **Ex.** *The wall is proof against the wind.*

propaganda (4) [prap'əgæn'də], *n.* a spreading of facts and ideas to inform and change opinions; the ideas or beliefs spread in such a way whether true or false. **Ex.** *The soldiers did not listen to the enemy propaganda.*

proper (2) [prap'ər], *adj.* 1. suitable; right; fit. **Ex.** *She put the book in its proper place on the shelf.* 2. polite; well-mannered. **Ex.** *It would not be proper to arrive late for a dinner party.* —**prop'er·ly,** *adv.*

proper noun [prap'ər nawn'], the name of a particular person, place, or thing, beginning with a capital letter. **Ex.** *"John" is a proper noun.*

property (2) [prap'ərtiy], *n.* 1. anything owned. **Ex.** *These books are the property of a friend.* 2. land. **Ex.** *He bought some property near the river.* 3. a characteristic quality of anything. **Ex.** *One property of steel is its hardness.*

prophet (5) [praf'it], *n.* 1. one who speaks for or delivers messages for a god; a religious leader. **Ex.** *The prophet warned that the world would soon end.* 2. one who tells what is to happen in the future. **Ex.** *He had been the town weather prophet for many years.* —**proph'e·cy,** *n.* the prediction of a happening in the future. **Ex.** *His prophecy was that they would become rich.* —**proph'e·sy,** *v.* tell what will happen; predict. —**pro·phet'ic,** *adj.*

proportion (3) [prəpɔr'šən], *n.* 1. the relation of the size, weight, or number of one kind of thing to the size, weight, or number of another. **Ex.** *The proportion of sunny days to rainy days last month was four to one.* 2. a part; section. **Ex.** *Only a small proportion of that land can be farmed.* —**pro·por'tion·al,** *adj.* —**pro·por'tion·ate,** *adj.* —**pro·por'tion·al·ly,** *adv.* —**pro·por'tion·ate·ly,** *adv.*

propose (2) [prəpowz'], *v.* 1. present to others for consideration. **Ex.** *They proposed a plan for a new school.* 2. plan; intend. **Ex.** *We propose to leave for the city tomorrow.* 3. suggest marriage. **Ex.** *He proposed to her last night.* —**pro·pos'al,** *n.* that which is proposed. —**prop'o·si'tion,** *n.* a proposal.

proprietor (4) [prəpray'ətər], *n.* owner. **Ex.** *I would like to speak to the proprietor of this store.* —**pro·pri'e·tar'y,** *adj.* of, like, or concerned with ownership.

prose (4) [prowz'], *n.* language spoken or written in an ordinary way; writing not in the form of a poem. **Ex.** *The newspaper reporter writes clear, simple prose.*

prosecute (5) [pras'ikyuwt'], *v.* seek punishment of a person in a court by trying to prove a crime. **Ex.** *The men were prosecuted for stealing state funds.* —**pros·e·cu'tion,** *n.* the act of prosecuting. —**pros'e·cu·tor,** *n.* one who prosecutes.

prospect (3) [pras'pekt], *n.* 1. the expectation of something; the thought of something to come. **Ex.** *The prospect of being without water began to worry us.* 2. buyer; candidate. **Ex.** *Have you a prospect for the car you are selling?* —**pros'pects,** *n.* possibility of advancement, success, etc. **Ex.** *His prospects in the company were very good.* —*v.* search for gold, silver, and other valuable metals. **Ex.** *Men are prospecting for gold in those hills.* —**pro·spec'tive,** *adj.* —**pros'pec·tor,** *n.* a person who searches for valuable minerals.

prosper (3) [pras'pər], *v.* be successful; grow in a healthy way; become rich. **Ex.** *His business prospered at its new location.* —**pros·per'i·ty,** *n.* condition of prospering. **Ex.** *In a time of prosperity, most people have good jobs.* —**pros'per·ous,** *adj.*

protect (2) [prətekt'], *v.* defend; guard; shield. **Ex.** *The soldiers protected the city.* —**pro·tec'tion,** *n.* the act of protecting; the condition of being protected; that which protects. —**pro·tec'tor,** *n.* one who protects. —**pro·tec'tive,** *adj.* —**pro·tec'tive·ly,** *adv.*

protest (2) [prow'test], *n.* objection; complaint. **Ex.** *His protests about the noise caused us to end the party.* —**pro·test',** *v.* 1. speak against; object; complain. **Ex.** *They protested against the new tax.* 2. declare strongly. **Ex.** *He protested that he was innocent.* —**under protest,** unwillingly; with spoken objections. **Ex.** *He did what he was told to do, but under protest.*

proud (1) [prawd'], *adj.* 1. well pleased with; feeling pride in.

Ex. *You must be very proud of your son's success.* 2. having self-respect. **Ex.** *He was too proud to ask for a loan.* 3. feeling too much pride; setting too high a value on oneself; vain. **Ex.** *They were too proud to speak to their neighbors.*

prove (1) [pruwv'], *v.* 1. show to be true or real. **Ex.** *Your answers prove that you read the book carefully.* 2. show something is true by experiment. **Ex.** *Scientists can prove that air consists of many tiny bits of solid matter.*

proverb (5) [prav'ərb], *n.* an old, well-known, wise saying. **Ex.** *"Don't put all your eggs in one basket," is a proverb.* —**pro·ver'bi·al,** *adj.* 1. like a proverb. 2. well-known.

provide (2) [prəvayd'], *v.* 1. furnish; supply. **Ex.** *The farm provided them all the food they needed.* 2. prepare for in advance; get before needed. **Ex.** *We must provide for a cold winter by buying coats.* —**pro·vid'ed,** *conj.* on condition that; if. **Ex.** *I shall go, provided the weather is clear.*

province (3) [prav'ins], *n.* 1. a large division of a country having its own local government. **Ex.** *Many countries are divided into provinces.* 2. a field of knowledge or activity. **Ex.** *What you want to know does not come within my province.* —**pro·vin'cial,** *adj.* interested only in local affairs; narrow in thinking.

provision (3) [prəviž'ən], *n.* 1. preparation made for the future. **Ex.** *Provision was made for buying more land when needed.* 2. a part of a written agreement, contract, treaty, or other legal record. **Ex.** *There are provisions in the Constitution concerning fair trials.* —**pro·vi'sions,** *n.* things provided or prepared; food. **Ex.** *We carried our provisions with us.*

provoke (4) [prəvowk'], *v.* 1. cause to feel anger; bother. **Ex.** *Interruptions provoked him.* 2. bring into being; cause. **Ex.** *Her question provoked an interesting discussion.* —**pro·vok'ing,** *adj.* —**prov·o·ca'tion,** *n.* —**pro·voc'a·tive,** *adj.*

prow (5) [praw'], *n.* the front part of a ship.

prowl (5) [prawl'], *v.* wander about quietly and secretly in search of something. **Ex.** *The cat prowled around the cellar looking for mice.* —**prowl'er,** *n.*

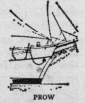
PROW

prudence (5) [pruw'dəns], *n.* carefulness in speaking and acting; practical wisdom. **Ex.** *Ambassadors must act with prudence.* —**pru'dent,** *adj.* —**pru'dent·ly,** *adv.*

prune (4) [pruwn¹], *n.* a dried plum. **Ex.** *We covered the prunes with water and boiled them.*

prune (4) [pruwn¹], *v.* cut off branches, roots, or other parts from a plant, tree, etc. in order to shape it or to make it grow better. **Ex.** *The gardener is pruning the hedges.*

pry (5) [pray¹], *v.* examine closely and curiously. **Ex.** *She was always prying into other people's affairs.*

pry (5) [pray¹], *v.* raise, open, or move by placing one end of a bar under a surface or edge and moving the other end. **Ex.** *The burglar pried open the window.*

psychology (4) [saykal¹əjiy], *n.* 1. the science concerned with the study of the mind and its processes. **Ex.** *Child psychology is a required course in teacher training.* 2. the mental and emotional processes which determine how an individual or group behaves. **Ex.** *Good salesmen understand the psychology of customers.* —**psy·cho·log'i·cal,** *adj.* —**psy·chol'o·gist,** *n.* one who specializes in psychology. —**psy·cho·log'i·cal·ly,** *adv.*

public (1) [pəb'lik], *adj.* 1. of or having to do with the people as a whole. **Ex.** *Public interest in building a new school is very strong.* 2. open to use by all. **Ex.** *He borrowed two books from the public library.* 3. engaged in the service of the people. **Ex.** *The mayor is an honored public servant.* 4. known to most people. **Ex.** *The news was made public.* —*n.* the people as a whole. **Ex.** *He enjoyed singing for the public.* —**pub'lic·ly,** *adv.* —**in public,** in a place where all can see, hear, etc. **Ex.** *He spoke in public.*

public-address system [pəb'likədres' sis'təm], a device for making the voice louder so a person can be heard when giving a speech.

publication (3) [pəb'likey'šən], *n.* 1. a thing that is published, such as a book or magazine. **Ex.** *The publication he wanted was a book on agriculture.* 2. the informing of or giving to the public. **Ex.** *The report received wide publication through the newspapers.*

publicity (4) [pəblis'ətiy], *n.* 1. the attention of the public. **Ex.** *His rescue of the child from the burning house brought him much publicity.* 2. information or activities planned to

bring a person, place, or thing to the attention of the public.
Ex. *Publicity about the play appears in today's newspaper.*

public relations [pəb'lik riley'šənz], actions planned to cause
the public to approve of a business, group, individual, etc.

public school [pəb'lik skuwl'], a government-controlled school
which one does not pay to attend and which is available to
all. **Ex.** *I studied in the public schools.*

public servant [pəb'lik sər'vənt], a person who is appointed
or elected to a government position.

public service [pəb'lik sər'vis], 1. government employment. 2.
a free service for the benefit of the public. **Ex.** *The weather
report was broadcast as a public service.*

public-spirited [pəb'likspi:r'itid], *adj.* interested in the problems of the community; working to improve the community.
Ex. *More public-spirited citizens are needed to make the
cities more livable.*

public utility [pəblik yutilə'tiy], a government-regulated business or industry providing a basic product or service to the
public. **Ex.** *The telephone company is a public utility.*

publish (2) [pəb'liš], *v.* 1. print and offer a newspaper, book,
song, etc. for sale to the public. 2. make known to the public. **Ex.** *The newspapers published an account of the latest
space flight.* —**pub'lish·er,** *n.* a person or company whose
business is printing and distributing newspapers, magazines,
and books.

pudding (3) [pud'iŋ], *n.* a soft, sweet, cooked dessert usually
made with milk, eggs, and flour or other cereal. **Ex.** *They
served rice pudding for dessert.*

puff (5) [pəf'], *n.* a short, quick blast of air, steam, smoke, etc.
Ex. *A sudden puff of wind blew the papers from the desk.*
—*v.* 1. blow short, quick bursts of air. **Ex.** *The wind puffed
about the house.* 2. breathe hard. **Ex.** *The boy was puffing
as he rushed into school.* 3. give out smoke, steam, etc. in
short bursts; move while giving out puffs. **Ex.** *The engine
puffed into the railroad station.* —**puff up,** fill with air in
puffs. **Ex.** *The balloon puffed up as he blew into it.*

pull (1) [pul'], *v.* 1. apply force to cause movement toward
or in the same direction as the person or thing applying
the force. **Ex.** *The horse pulled the wagon along the road.*
2. remove from a fixed place; draw out. **Ex.** *They were pulling weeds in the garden.* 3. tear; cause to come apart. **Ex.**
The dogs pulled the pillow to pieces. —*n.* the applying of

force; the effort of pulling. **Ex.** *It was a hard pull for the horses.* —**pull oneself together,** become calm and self-controlled after being upset. **Ex.** *After crying for an hour, she began to pull herself together.*

pulp (5) [pəlp¹], *n.* 1. the part of a fruit containing the juice. **Ex.** *We ate the pulp of the orange and threw away the skin and seeds.* 2. a mixture of ground wood and rags, softened by liquids and chemicals, which is used to make paper. **Ex.** *The trees were cut down for pulp.*

pulpit (5) [pul¹pit], *n.* raised place in a church from which a minister or other speaker talks to the people. **Ex.** *The minister was standing in the pulpit.*

pulse (4) [pəls¹], *n.* the regular beating of the heart, as it pumps blood through the body. **Ex.** *The doctor felt the patient's pulse.* —*v.* beat regularly as a pulse. **Ex.** *The city was pulsing with life.*

pump (3) [pəmp¹], *n.* a machine that raises or moves water or other liquids, usually by forcing them through a pipe. **Ex.** *The pump supplied water from a deep well.* —*v.* 1. raise or move with a pump. **Ex.** *Water for the fields was pumped from the river.* 2. operate or move as a pump does. **Ex.** *The heart pumps blood through the body.*

punch (4) [pənč¹], *n.* a quick, hard blow with the fist. **Ex.** *In his anger, he gave his brother a punch in the nose.* —*v.* strike or hit with a quick, hard blow of the fist. **Ex.** *During the fight, he was punched in the eye.*

punch (4) [pənč¹], *n.* a tool used to make holes in or to cut a design on materials. **Ex.** *The holes in the belt were made with a punch.* —*v.* cut a design or make holes, as with a punch. **Ex.** *The shoemaker punched a hole in the leather.*

punctual (5) [pəŋk¹čuwəl], *adj.* prompt; on time; not tardy. **Ex.** *He was always punctual in keeping appointments.* —**punc¹tu·al·ly,** *adv.* —**punc˅tu·al¹i·ty,** *n.*

punctuation (3) [pəŋk˅čuwey¹šən], *n.* the system of making writing easier to understand by using periods and other such marks to end sentences or break them into shorter parts. **Ex.** *The punctuation in that sentence is not correct.* —**punc¹tu·ate,** *v.*

punish (2) [pən¹iš], *v.* 1. cause pain, loss, suffering, etc. for doing a bad thing. **Ex.** *The mother will punish the child by not allowing him to eat candy.* 2. set as a penalty for crime.

Ex. *Some states punish murder with death.* —**pun'ish·ment,** *n.* 1. act of punishing. 2. the penalty a person is given for doing wrong.

pup, puppy (5) [pəp', pəp'iy], *n.* the young of a dog. **Ex.** *The puppy was two months old.*

pupil (2) [pyuw'pəl], *n.* one who studies under the direction of a teacher. **Ex.** *Only ten pupils are in my class.*

pupil (2) [pyuw'pəl], *n.* the dark center of the eye which becomes smaller in bright light and larger in dim light. **Ex.** *The pupil of the eye controls the amount of light which enters the eye.*

purchase (2) [pər'čis], *v.* buy with money or with something of equal value. **Ex.** *She purchased a new dress.* —*n.* 1. the act of buying. **Ex.** *They saved their money for the purchase of a house.* 2. something obtained by buying. **Ex.** *Her purchases were delivered to her home.* —**pur'chas·er,** *n.* one who buys.

pure (1) [pyu:r'], *adj.* 1. free from anything which is different or which lessens the value. **Ex.** *Her dress was made of pure silk.* 2. free from anything unclean or unhealthful; clean. **Ex.** *High on the mountain they found pure water to drink.* 3. innocent; not evil. **Ex.** *The saint lived a pure life.*

purple (2) [pər'pəl], *n.* a color made from mixing red and blue together. **Ex.** *That artist likes to use purple in his paintings.* —*adj.* of a bluish-red color. **Ex.** *The grapes were turning purple on the vine.*

purpose (1) [pər'pəs], *n.* 1. what one decides to do; the objective of or reason for one's action; intention. **Ex.** *The purpose of his trip was to visit a new factory.* 2. use; result intended. **Ex.** *What is the purpose of this machine?* —**pur'pose·ly,** *adv.* with a purpose. —**on purpose,** with intent; for a reason. **Ex.** *The bad boy stepped on the other boy's toes on purpose.*

purse (3) [pərs'], *n.* 1. a woman's handbag, used for carrying money, powder, comb, etc.; a small bag for carrying money. **Ex.** *Her brown purse matches her shoes.* 2. a sum of money offered as a prize. **Ex.** *The owner of the winning horse won a large purse.*

pursue (3) [pərsuw', pərsyuw'], *v.* 1. follow someone running with the purpose of catching. **Ex.** *The policeman pursued the thief.* 2. follow with the purpose of reaching or having as a profession. **Ex.** *He is pursuing a career as a pianist.* 3. follow or seek to obtain or accomplish. **Ex.** *He pursues money in everything he does.* —**pur·su'er,** *n.* one who pursues. —**pur·su'ant,** *adj.* following; done in conformance with. **Ex.** *Pursuant to your request that he visit you, I have asked him to come with me to your house.*

pursuit (3) [pərsuwt¹, pərsyuwt¹], *n.* 1. the act of pursuing; a chase. **Ex.** *The hunters joined in the pursuit of the fox.* 2. that which one pursues, follows, or is involved in. **Ex.** *Fishing is his favorite pursuit.*

push (1) [puš¹], *v.* 1. use force against something for the purpose of moving it. **Ex.** *He pushed the cart up the hill.* 2. move oneself by using force against that which stops one from moving. **Ex.** *He pushed his way through the crowd.* 3. seek something actively and with energy. **Ex.** *He pushed the men to sell more.*

push-up [puš¹əpˑ], *n.* an exercise done by lying flat on the floor and, while keeping the body straight, raising the body by pushing up with the arms.

put (1) [put¹], *v.* 1. cause to be in a certain place; set in a position. **Ex.** *He put the money in his pocket.* 2. cause to be in a condition or state. **Ex.** *By singing, she put the baby to sleep.* 3. attach; assign; join to. **Ex.** *He put too high a price on the book.* 4. express; say. **Ex.** *He wanted to go but could not put his wish into words.* —**put aside,** set aside or save for later consideration, use, etc. **Ex.** *They put aside a little money each week.* —**put away,** store in a proper place; save for future use. **Ex.** *She washed the dishes and put them away.* 1. defeat. **Ex.** *The government put down the revolt.* 2. write. **Ex.** *He put his ideas down on a piece of paper.* —**put forth,** extend out; grow out; offer out. **Ex.** *He put forth several good ideas.* —**put off,** cause to wait; delay. **Ex.** *He has put off answering until tomorrow.* —**put on,** 1. dress. **Ex.** *He put on his coat.* 2. produce a performance. **Ex.** *He has put on a new play.* —**put out,** 1. stop a fire or light. **Ex.** *He put out the fire with water.* 2. place outside or in a forward position. **Ex.** *He put out his hand.* —**put through,** 1. cause to be completed, effected, accepted, etc. **Ex.** *He put through a new law.* 2. conduct a demonstration;

subject to. **Ex.** *He put the car through severe tests.* **—put up,**
1. make available; offer. **Ex.** *The land was put up for sale.*
2. build. **Ex.** *He put up a new house.* 3. preserve vegetables,
fruits. **Ex.** *She put up berries.* 4. provide lodgings. **Ex.** *He
put us up for the night.* **—put up with,** suffer without complaining; endure. **Ex.** *He put up with a lot of nonsense.*

puzzle (2) [pəz'əl], *n.* 1. a person or matter difficult to understand; a problem difficult to solve. **Ex.** *She has always been
a puzzle to me.* 2. a game or other device that tests one's
intelligence or skill. **Ex.** *They tried to put the parts of the
puzzle together.* **—v.** 1. be difficult to understand; confuse.
Ex. *Her absence puzzles me.* 2. think deeply about some
difficult problem in order to solve it. **Ex.** *They puzzled over
the question for some time.*

pyramid (5) [pi:r'əmid'], *n.* a structure that
is square at the bottom and has four sides
that come together at the top in a point.

PYRAMID

Q

Q, q [kyuw'], *n.* the seventeenth letter of the English alphabet.

quaint (5) [kweynt'], *adj.* strange or unusual but pleasing
because of past customs, dress, etc. recalled. **Ex.** *She put on
one of her grandmother's quaint dresses.* **—quaint'ly,** *adv.*
—quaint'ness, *n.*

qualify (3) [kwal'əfay'], *v.* 1. make or become fit or able. **Ex.**
He qualified for the job by studying at night. 2. give or obtain legal power or right. **Ex.** *He will be qualified to vote
when he is eighteen.* 3. decrease the strength of; limit. **Ex.**
He qualified his earlier remark. **—qual'i·fi·ca'tion,** *n.* 1. act
of qualifying. 2. that which qualifies. **Ex.** *What are his
qualifications for the job?*

quality (2) [kwal'ətiy], *n.* 1. that which something is known
to have or be; an attribute. **Ex.** *An important quality of steel
is its strength.* 2. excellence; value. **Ex.** *The furniture that
store sells is known for its quality.* 3. degree of excellence.
Ex. *Only materials of the highest quality were accepted.*

quantity (2) [kwan'tətiy], *n.* 1. an amount. **Ex.** *A small quan-*

tity of salt was in the box. 2. a large amount. **Ex.** *She always buys vegetables in quantity.*

quarrel (2) [kwɔːrˈəl, kwarˈəl], *n.* 1. an argument; a dispute. **Ex.** *We have not spoken to each other since our quarrel.* 2. reason for opposing or arguing. **Ex.** *I have no quarrel with what he says.* —*v.* argue or dispute in anger. **Ex.** *The children seldom quarrel.*

quarry (5) [kwɔːrˈiy, kwarˈiy], *n.* a hole in the earth from which marble and other stones are cut or dug. **Ex.** *The men are working in the quarry.* —*v.* obtain stone from a large hole in the ground. **Ex.** *They are quarrying marble.*

quarry (5) [kwɔːrˈiy, kwarˈiy], *n.* an animal being pursued. **Ex.** *The hunter's quarry was a rabbit.*

quart (3) [kwɔrtˈ], *n.* 1. a liquid measure equal to two pints. **Ex.** *Our family drinks a quart of milk a day.* 2. a dry measure equal to two pints. **Ex.** *They picked a quart of berries.* See **Weights and Measures.**

quarter (1) [kwɔrˈtər], *n.* 1. one of the four equal divisions of anything; one fourth (1/4). **Ex.** *We each ate a quarter of the melon.* 2. a silver United States coin worth one fourth of a dollar. **Ex.** *He had two quarters in his pocket.* 3. fifteen minutes; one fourth of an hour. **Ex.** *We went home at a quarter after four.* 4. three months. **Ex.** *We pay our taxes every quarter.* 5. any of the four principal points of the compass; any direction of the compass. **Ex.** *People come to New York from all quarters of the world.* —*v.* 1. divide into four equal parts. **Ex.** *Quarter the orange and give each child a section.* 2. provide a place to live. **Ex.** *The family was quartered in a hotel.* —*adj.* equal to one fourth. —**quarˈter·ly,** *adj.* appearing or happening four times a year. **Ex.** *It was a quarterly meeting.* —*adv.* four times a year. **Ex.** *The meeting occurs quarterly.* —*n.* a magazine published four times a year. **Ex.** *He is reading a quarterly.* —**quarters,** *n.* a place where one lives. **Ex.** *He went to his quarters to change clothes.* —**at close quarters,** very near to each other. **Ex.** *They were fighting at close quarters.*

queen (1) [kwiynˈ], *n.* 1. wife of a king. **Ex.** *The young king did not yet have a queen.* 2. a female ruler. **Ex.** *The queen ordered us to come to the castle.* —**queenˈly,** *adv.* of, like, for, or suited for a queen. **Ex.** *She walks in a queenly way.*

queer (2) [kwiːrˈ], *adj.* not ordinary; unusual. **Ex.** *There was something queer about the way he walked.*

quench (5) [kwenčʲ], *v.* 1. satisfy. **Ex.** *The water quenched his thirst.* 2. stop; put out. **Ex.** *The campers quenched the fire by throwing water on it.*

query (5) [kwiːrʲiy], *n.* question. **Ex.** *In answer to my query, he said that the theater was closed.* —*v.* 1. ask questions. **Ex.** *He queried me about my work.* 2. create a question about; express doubt about. **Ex.** *They queried the need for a new school.*

quest (4) [kwestʲ], *n.* a search; travel in search of something. **Ex.** *He returned from his quest a rich man.*

question (1) [kwesʲčən], *n.* 1. a sentence or word used in asking for information. **Ex.** *He answered my questions with facts.* 2. a problem; a matter to be discussed. **Ex.** *The question at the meeting was whether to build a new road.* 3. a matter of uncertainty. **Ex.** *There is a question about whether or not we need a new roof.* —*v.* 1. ask questions of. **Ex.** *The man was questioned about where he had been.* 2. doubt. **Ex.** *We questioned the wisdom of his actions.* —**beyond question,** without a doubt. **Ex.** *Beyond question, he is the best one for the job.*

quick (1) [kwikʲ], *adj.* 1. rapid; fast. **Ex.** *The soldiers marched at a quick speed.* 2. prompt in action; ready. **Ex.** *His quick reply surprised everyone.* 3. easily angered or excited. **Ex.** *She has a quick temper.* —**quickʲly,** *adv.* —**quickʲness,** *n.*

quiet (1) [kwayʲət], *adj.* 1. making little or no noise; silent. **Ex.** *The children became quiet when the teacher talked.* 2. having little or no movement; calm. **Ex.** *The boat drifted slowly over the quiet water.* 3. not excited; gentle. **Ex.** *He spoke in a quiet voice.* 4. restful; peaceful. **Ex.** *They spent a quiet afternoon together.* —*v.* make or become quiet. **Ex.** *His arrival quieted her fears.* —*n.* a condition of silence, calmness, peacefulness. —**quiʲet·ly,** *adv.*

quilt (5) [kwiltʲ], *n.* a warm covering for a bed made by placing cotton or other soft material between two large pieces of cloth and sewing the whole together in such a way that the threads make a pattern. **Ex.** *In the winter we put three quilts on the bed.* —*v.* make a quilt. **Ex.** *The farmers' wives often quilted at winter parties.*

quit (3) [kwitʲ], *v.* 1. stop doing something; cease. **Ex.** *The doctor told his patient to quit smoking.* 2. leave; depart from. **Ex.** *He had to quit college and get a job.* —**quitʲter,** *n.* one who quits easily.

quite (1) [kwayt'], *adv.* 1. entirely; completely. **Ex.** *She was quite certain of the date.* 2. rather; somewhat. **Ex.** *He was quite tired.*

quiver (3) [kwiv'ər], *v.* shake slightly but rapidly; tremble. **Ex.** *The little dog quivered with fright.* —*n.* the act of quivering; a trembling. **Ex.** *There was a quiver of excitement in the crowd.*

quiver (3) [kwiv'ər], *n.* a container for carrying arrows. **Ex.** *He pulled an arrow from his quiver.*

quote (3) [kwowt'], *v.* repeat exactly the written or spoken words of another. **Ex.** *He quoted from a speech by the President.* —**quo·ta'tion,** *n.*

QUIVER

R

R, r [a:r'], *n.* the eighteenth letter of the English alphabet.

rabbit (2) [ræb'it], *n.* a small animal, with long ears and a short tail.

race (1) [reys'], *n.* 1. a contest to see who or what can move at a faster or the fastest speed. **Ex.** *Which horse won the race?* 2. any contest. **Ex.** *Three candidates have entered the race for mayor.* —*v.* be or cause to be in a contest of speed. **Ex.** *The contestants raced the last hundred feet at very fast speeds.* —**rac'er,** *n.*

RABBIT

race (1) [reys'], *n.* a group of people with common physical characteristics. **Ex.** *People of many races settled in the United States.* —**ra'cial,** *adj.* —**rac'ism,** *n.* the unproved belief that one race of people is better than another.

rack (3) [ræk'], *n.* 1. a framework of shelves or bars on which articles or materials are placed, hung, or carried. **Ex.** *He put the suitcases on the luggage rack.* 2. a framework placed on a car, wagon, etc. for carrying large loads. **Ex.** *The farmer pitched the hay onto the rack.* —*v.* cause to suffer greatly. **Ex.** *His body was racked with pain.*

---

a, far; æ, am; e, get; ey, late; i, in; iy, see; ɔ, all; ow, go; u, put; uw, too; ə, but, ago; ər, fur; aw, out; ay, life; oy, boy; ŋ, ring; θ, think; ð, that; ž, measure; š, ship; j, edge; č, child.

racket (4) [ræk'it], *n.* a loud, confused noise. **Ex.** *The students made a big racket as they left the school.*

racket (4) [ræk'it], *n.* a rounded wooden frame, crossed by strings and having a handle, used to hit a ball in certain games such as tennis.

radiant (4) [rey'diyənt], *adj.* 1. giving forth rays of light; bright; shining. **Ex.** *The radiant moon lighted the path.* 2. bright with joy, health, etc. **Ex.** *The news made her radiant with joy.* —**ra'di·ance,** *n.* —**ra'di·ate,** *v.* —**ra`di·a'tion,** *n.* the rays given out.

RACKET

radiator [rey'diyey`tər], *n.* 1. a device for heating air by means of a series of pipes through which steam or hot water circulates. 2. a cooling device in an engine consisting of a series of pipes through which cool water circulates.

radical (4) [ræd'ikəl], *adj.* 1. fundamental. **Ex.** *There were radical differences between the two systems.* 2. extreme; favoring great changes. **Ex.** *His ideas are too radical to be acceptable to most people.* —*n.* a person who has extreme ideas for change. **Ex.** *In his time, he was called a radical.* —**rad'i·cal·ism,** *n.* —**rad'i·cal·ly,** *adv.*

radio (2) [rey'diyow], *n.* 1. the system of sending and receiving signals or sounds through the air without wires. **Ex.** *The news was sent by radio.* 2. a device for receiving radio broadcasts. **Ex.** *They listened to the radio and heard the President's speech.* —*adj.* used in radio; sent by radio. **Ex.** *What radio program are you listening to?* —*v.* send by radio. **Ex.** *Can we radio for help?*

raft (5) [ræft'], *n.* a platform made of rubber, logs, or boards fastened together and used as a boat. **Ex.** *The children were swimming near the raft.*

rag (3) [ræg'], *n.* a torn piece of cloth without value; any piece of cloth used for washing, cleaning, etc. **Ex.** *He wiped his boots with an old rag.* —**rags',** *n.* old, worn clothing. **Ex.** *The beggar was dressed in rags.* —**rag'ged,** *adj.*

rage (3) [reyj'], *n.* 1. a great anger. **Ex.** *When he found they had gone without him, he flew into a rage.* 2. a popular fashion, usually not lasting. **Ex.** *The new singer quickly became the rage.* —*v.* 1. feel or express great anger. **Ex.** *She raged when she heard the bad news.* 2. act with great violence. **Ex.** *As the storm raged, the waves grew higher and* *higher.* 3. spread at great speed. **Ex.** *The fire raged through the woods.*

raid (4) [reyd'], *n.* 1. a sudden attack made as an act of war or for the purpose of seizing or stealing something. **Ex.** *The radio station was destroyed in the raid.* 2. a forcible entry by the police in order to make arrests, stop something unlawful, or seize goods. **Ex.** *In an early-morning raid, the police found the stolen articles.* —*v.* make a sudden attack. **Ex.** *Thieves raided the store last night.* —**raid'er,** *n.* one who raids.

rail (2) [reyl'], *n.* 1. a piece of wood or metal used as a part of a fence or as a protection at the side of a ship or along a stair. **Ex.** *He leaned over the boat rail to look at the water.* 2. one of the two steel bars on which trains run. **Ex.** *The train stopped because a rail was broken ahead.*

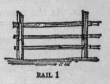

RAIL 1

railing [rey'liŋ], *n.* a fence made of rails. **Ex.** *There is a railing on the porch to make it safe.*

railroad (2) [reyl'rowd'], *n.* 1. a road for trains, with two rails on which the trains travel. **Ex.** *He sat by the railroad and watched the trains go by.* 2. the company which manages such a road, its stations, equipment, managers, etc. **Ex.** *My father worked for the railroad for many years.*

rain (1) [reyn'], *n.* 1. water falling from the sky in drops. **Ex.** *Three inches of rain made the ground soft.* 2. the falling of water; a shower. **Ex.** *Were you out in the rain?* —*v.* fall in drops of water. **Ex.** *It rained all day yesterday.* —**rain'y,** *adj.*

rainbow (4) [reyn'bow'], *n.* a half-circle of colors seen in the sky when the sun shines through raindrops. **Ex.** *After the storm, a rainbow formed in the sky.*

raise (1) [reyz'], *v.* 1. lift up; move to a higher position. **Ex.** *He raised his hand and waved.* 2. excite; awaken. **Ex.** *The good news raised their hopes for success.* 3. cause to grow; grow. **Ex.** *They are raising corn in that field.* 4. increase in amount, rank, etc. **Ex.** *He was raised from clerk to manager.* —*n.* increase in amount, especially of pay. **Ex.** *He received a small raise for his work.*

raisin (2) [rey'zən], *n.* a dried grape. **Ex.** *Mother added raisins to the cake.*

rake (4) [reyk'], *n.* a garden tool with a long
handle and a set of short hooks or teeth, used
for gathering hay, leaves, etc. —*v.* prepare,
gather, or remove with a rake. **Ex.** *He raked
the soil carefully before planting.*

rally (5) [ræl'iy], *v.* 1. bring together or into
order again. **Ex.** *The scattered soldiers were
rallied for the next attack.* 2. gather or call

RAKE

persons together for some united effort; come
in order to help. **Ex.** *After putting out the fire, the neighbors
rallied to provide food.* 3. improve one's health or strength.
Ex. *As the medicine took effect, the patient began to rally.*
—*n.* a meeting or gathering for a special purpose. **Ex.** *We
are going to a political rally tonight.*

ram (4) [ræm'], *n.* 1. a male sheep. **Ex.** *One old ram led the
flock.* 2. any long, heavy object used to break open gates,
doors, etc. **Ex.** *They used a tree trunk as a ram to break
down the wall.* —*v.* strike or push against with great force.
Ex. *The boat rammed into the pier.*

ran (1) [ræn'], *v.* past tense of *run.* **Ex.** *The boy ran to school.*

ranch (4) [rænč'], *n.* a large farm on which animals are
raised. **Ex.** *The children spent the summer on a ranch.*
—**ranch'er,** *n.*

random (5) [ræn'dəm], *adj.* made, done, etc. without definite
aim or purpose. **Ex.** *The rooms were filled with a random
selection of furniture.*

rang (3) [ræŋ'], *v.* past tense of *ring.* **Ex.** *The telephone rang
while you were away.*

range (2) [reynǰ'], *n.* 1. the limit or reach of something; the
greatest distance to which anything, such as sound, a moving
object, etc. can travel. **Ex.** *Everyone within range of his
voice heard the remark and laughed.* 2. the extent of a series
of changes or possibilities. **Ex.** *He spoke on a wide range of
subjects.* 3. a row, line, series, or chain. **Ex.** *A range of
mountains separates the two countries.* 4. a large area of
grassy land where cattle feed. **Ex.** *He rode over the range
looking for some lost cows.* 5. a stove for cooking. **Ex.** *They
have an electric range.* —*v.* 1. vary within certain limits.
Ex. *The children ranged in age from three to ten years old.*
2. place persons or things in order or in rows. **Ex.** *Bottles
and glasses were ranged on the table.* —**rang'er,** *n.* 1. a member of a body of special troops who protect a certain area

of the country. 2. a guard who protects a forest or wild animal and plant life. **Ex.** *Many rangers work in the national parks.*

rank (2) [ræŋk'], *n.* 1. grade in military forces. **Ex.** *He has the rank of major.* 2. relative position in a group of professional or talented people. **Ex.** *He is an artist of the first rank.* —*v.* 1. place in a higher or lower position. **Ex.** *His examination paper was ranked the best in his class.* 2. arrange in a formation. **Ex.** *The men were ranked according to their height.*

ransom (5) [ræn'səm], *n.* 1. money demanded or paid to free a person. **Ex.** *A large ransom was asked for the safe return of the child.* 2. the release of a person in return for payment of money. **Ex.** *The ransom of the child was accomplished during the night.* —*v.* obtain release by paying a price demanded. **Ex.** *The merchant was ransomed by his son.*

rap (4) [ræp'], *n.* a sharp, quick knock or blow. **Ex.** *We heard a rap at the door.* —*v.* strike or tap sharply. **Ex.** *Who is rapping on the table?*

rapid (2) [ræp'id], *adj.* fast; quick; swift. **Ex.** *The rapid growth of the city surprised us.* —**rap'id·ly,** *adv.* —**rap'ids,** *n.* a part of a river which flows swiftly, usually over rocks. —**ra·pid'i·ty,** *n.* swiftness.

rapture (4) [ræp'čər], *n.* a feeling of great joy; delight. **Ex.** *The beauty of the sunset filled everybody with rapture.*

rare (3) [re:r'], *adj.* unusual; uncommon; infrequent. **Ex.** *Horses are rare in cities.* —**rare'ly,** *adv.* —**rare'ness,** *n.* the quality of being rare. —**rar'i·ty,** *n.* something unusual; the condition of being rare.

rare (3) [re:r'], *adj.* only partly cooked. **Ex.** *He likes very rare meat.* —**rare'ness,** *n.*

rascal (4) [ræs'kəl], *n.* 1. a person without principles; a person who is not honest. **Ex.** *Two rascals tricked the old man out of his money.* 2. a lively child who causes trouble in fun. **Ex.** *The boy is a little rascal.*

rash (5) [ræš'], *adj.* acting thoughtlessly and too quickly. **Ex.** *He often makes rash promises.* —**rash'ly,** *adv.* —**rash'ness,** *n.*

a, far; æ, am; e, get; ey, late; i, in; iy, see; ɔ, all; ow, go; u, put; uw, too; ə, but, ago; ər, fur; aw, out; ay, life; oy, boy; ŋ, ring; θ, think; ð, that; ž, measure; š, ship; ǰ, edge; č, child.

rash (5) [ræš¹], *n.* red spots on the skin, sometimes indicating illness. **Ex.** *He has a rash on his arm.*

rat (3) [ræt¹], *n.* a long-tailed animal similar to a mouse but larger. **Ex.** *Many countries have programs to control rats because they spread disease.*

RAT

rate (2) [reyt¹], *n.* 1. amount measured in relation to something else; speed. **Ex.** *She typed our letters at the rate of eighty words a minute.* 2. the price of a unit of any thing or service that is bought or sold. **Ex.** *He is paid at the rate of two dollars an hour.* —*v.* 1. place a price on. **Ex.** *Her jewelry is rated at twice the purchase price.* 2. consider to be in a certain rank or class. **Ex.** *She is rated among the best dancers in the country.* —**at any rate,** anyhow; anyway. **Ex.** *Maybe we should have gone, but at any rate we did not.*

rather (1) [ræð¹ər], *adv.* 1. in or to some degree; somewhat. **Ex.** *It is rather cold today.* 2. more willingly; more gladly; preferably. **Ex.** *I would rather go today than tomorrow.* 3. more accurately. **Ex.** *They had a discussion, or rather, a quarrel.*

ratio (4) [rey¹šow, rey¹šiyow], *n.* relation of one thing to another in number, degree, etc. **Ex.** *The ratio of successful candidates to applicants was one in five.*

ration (5) [ræš¹ən, rey¹šən], *n.* 1. a fixed allowance of food or other supplies allotted a person in times of scarcity. **Ex.** *She used her sugar ration to make jam.* 2. the daily food allowance for a member of the armed forces. **Ex.** *Each soldier was given three rations.* —*v.* divide or distribute as rations. **Ex.** *Water is rationed during the dry season.*

rational (5) [ræš¹ənəl], *adj.* 1. sensible; reasonable. **Ex.** *Does he have a rational explanation for his behavior?* 2. sane; able to reason. **Ex.** *Last night she had a high fever and was not rational.* —**ra¹tion·al·ly,** *adv.* —**ra¹tion·al·ize`,** *v.* give a logical reason without appearing to know that it is not the actual reason. **Ex.** *He rationalized his failure in the examination by saying that the teacher did not like him.*

rattle (5) [ræt¹əl], *v.* 1. make or cause to make short, sharp, rapid sounds. **Ex.** *The windows rattle when the wind blows.* 2. move with a succession of such sounds. **Ex.** *The old car rattled along the road.* —*n.* 1. a series of short, sharp sounds.

Ex. *He was awakened by the rattle of stones against the window.* 2. a baby's toy that rattles.

rave (5) [reyv'], *v.* talk wildly; speak in a confused manner. Ex. *Because of his high fever, the sick man raved and could not be understood.* 2. praise with great enthusiasm. Ex. *The girls raved about the new singer.* —**rav'ing,** *adj.* wild; raging.

raw (2) [rɔ:'], *adj.* 1. uncooked. Ex. *We like to eat raw fruit.* 2. not yet treated or processed. Ex. *The raw cotton is picked and then weighed.* 3. sore, with skin scraped off. Ex. *His hands were raw from working in the garden.* 4. untrained. Ex. *He held off the enemy with a few raw soldiers.*

ray (2) [rey'], *n.* 1. a narrow line of light. Ex. *A ray of light came through a hole in the door.* 2. a slight promise; a small amount. Ex. *The new medicine gave him a ray of hope.* 3. energy coming from some source. Ex. *Rays of heat from the stove soon warmed the room.*

rayon (5) [rey'an], *n.* a manufactured cloth which looks and feels like silk. Ex. *Her dress was made of rayon.*

razor (5) [rey'zər], *n.* an instrument with a sharp edge for shaving hair from the face. Ex. *He put a new blade in his razor.*

re- [riy, ri], *prefix.* 1. again. Exs. *Read, reread; state, restate.* 2. back. Exs. *Pay, repay; act, react.*

reach (1) [riyč], *v.* 1. arrive at; come to. Ex. *The boat reached shore safely.* 2. extend a hand, foot, etc. toward. Ex. *The boy reached for an apple.* 3. touch, strike, or grasp with the hand or with some object. Ex. *The child could not reach the bell.* 4. extend to; stretch out as far as. Ex. *His land does not reach the river.* —*n.* the act of reaching; the power to reach. Ex. *The boy made a quick reach for the ball.*

react (4) [riyækt'], *v.* 1. act as a result of. Ex. *He reacted to my question with surprise.* 2. return to an earlier condition; act in an opposite way. Ex. *When meat prices increased, people reacted by not buying meat.* —**re·ac'tor,** *n.* person or thing that reacts.

reaction (3) [riyæk'šan], *n.* 1. something that is a response or result. Ex. *Did you see his reaction to her arrival?* 2. a return to an earlier thing or state. Ex. *The forces of reaction once again gained political power.* —**re·ac'tion·ar'y,** *adj.* of, showing, or favoring a return to an earlier condition. Ex. *He is a reactionary in his views on education.*

read (1) [riyd'], *v.* 1. look at and understand the meaning of written or printed words, letters, or numbers. **Ex.** *He reads the newspaper every morning.* 2. speak written or printed words. **Ex.** *She likes to read to the children.* —**read'er,** *n.* 1. one who reads. 2. a book for teaching reading.

read (1) [red'], *v.* past tense and participle of *read.* **Ex.** *I read that book last week.*

readable [riyd'əbəl], *adj.* 1. easy to read. **Ex.** *Your writing is very readable.* 2. enjoyable, interesting. **Ex.** *This is a readable book.*

readily (3) [red'əliy], *adv.* 1. quickly; easily; promptly. **Ex.** *One can readily see that he will succeed.* 2. willingly. **Ex.** *We gave him the money readily.*

ready (1) [red'iy], *adj.* 1. prepared; completed; arranged. **Ex.** *Dinner is ready.* 2. willing. **Ex.** *They are always ready to help.* —*v.* prepare. **Ex.** *They readied the house for visitors.* —**read'i·ness,** *n.*

real (1) [riyl'], *adj.* 1. true; actual. **Ex.** *What was his real reason for not coming with us?* 2. not false. **Ex.** *This is a real diamond.* —**real'ism,** *n.* understanding things as they actually are. **Ex.** *Realism tells us that some criminals are incurable.* —**real'ist,** *n.* one who sees things as they actually are. **Ex.** *Realists admit many things cannot be changed overnight.* —**re·al'i·ty,** *n.* state of being real. **Ex.** *In reality, nothing happened.* —**real'ly,** *adv.*

realize (1) [riy'əlayz'], *v.* 1. understand clearly; be aware of. **Ex.** *He did not realize how cold it was until he went outside.* 2. make real; cause to become true. **Ex.** *He realized his dreams when he became a doctor.* —**re·al·i·za'tion,** *n.*

realm (4) [relm'], *n.* a country ruled by a king or queen. **Ex.** *The queen visited every town in her realm.* 2. an area over which some influence or activity extends. **Ex.** *She has read many books about the realm of magic.*

reap (4) [riyp'], *v.* 1. cut and harvest grain. **Ex.** *The farmers reaped their wheat.* 2. receive as the result of effort or behavior. **Ex.** *The man reaped a profit from his invention.* —**reap'er,** *n.* 1. a machine for cutting grain. 2. a person who cuts grain.

rear (2) [ri:r'], *n.* the back part; the farthest end of anything. **Ex.** *The people in the rear of the room could not hear the speaker.* —*adj.* at the back. **Ex.** *The rear window of the car was dirty.*

rear (2) [ri:rˈ], *v.* 1. raise; aid in growing. Ex. *When their parents died, an aunt reared the two boys.* 2. rise up on the back legs, as a four-legged animal; lift up. Ex. *The horse reared at the sight of the snake.*

reason (1) [riyˈzən], *n.* 1. cause for a belief or act; purpose. Ex. *What is the reason for this meeting?* 2. something said that explains; an excuse. Ex. *He could give no reason for being in the building.* 3. the power to think or decide. Ex. *A man of reason can answer the question.* 4. good judgment; sound thinking. Ex. *He was too excited to listen to reason.* —*v.* to think or argue in a way that uses good sense. Ex. *His friends tried to reason with him.* —**reaˈson�·a·ble,** *adj.* having or showing reason. Ex. *He is a reasonable man.*

rebel (3) [rebˈəl], *n.* 1. one who resists or fights the government of his own country. Ex. *The rebels fought because they thought the government was bad.* 2. one who resists any kind of control. Ex. *As a schoolboy, he was considered a rebel.*

rebel (3) [ribelˈ], *v.* 1. rise up against one's government. Ex. *The people rebelled and overthrew the cruel king.* 2. resist authority; refuse to obey. Ex. *The prisoners rebelled against the prison rules.* 3. have a strong feeling of distaste. Ex. *He rebelled at the idea of eating raw meat.* —**re·belˈlion,** *n.* —**re·belˈlious,** *adj.*

rebuke (5) [ribyuwkˈ], *v.* blame sharply. Ex. *The manager rebuked the clerk for his mistake.* —*n.* a sharp criticism of one's actions. Ex. *Her face burned with shame at the rebuke.*

recall (4) [rikɔ:lˈ], *v.* 1. remember. Ex. *He tried to recall where they had met before.* 2. ask to return. Ex. *He was recalled to the hospital for more treatment.* 3. take back; cancel. Ex. *These stamps were recalled because of mistakes in printing.* —*n.* the act of recalling.

receipt (4) [risiytˈ], *n.* 1. the act of receiving. Ex. *Please notify me upon receipt of the package.* 2. a written statement saying that one has received money, a package, etc. Ex. *He signed a receipt for the money.* —*v.* give a written statement of having received. Ex. *Please receipt this bill.* —**reˈceipts,** *n.* the amount of money received in a business. Ex. *She counted the receipts for the day.*

receive (1) [risiyvˈ], *v.* 1. take something that is offered, given,

a, far; æ, am; e, get; ey, late; i, in; iy, see; ɔ, all; ow, go; u, put; uw, too; ə, but, ago; ər, fur; aw, out; ay, life; oy, boy; ŋ, ring; θ, think; ð, that; ž, measure; š, ship; ǰ, edge; č, child.

sent, etc.; get; accept. **Ex.** *I received several books on art for my birthday.* 2. welcome; greet. **Ex.** *They received their guests at the door.* —**re·ceiv'er,** *n.* 1. one who receives. 2. a device for receiving radio waves or similar electrical impulses; a radio set; part of a telephone through which one hears. **Ex.** *She picked up the telephone receiver and listened.*

recent (2) [riy'sənt], *adj.* done or occurring not very long ago. **Ex.** *Recent news confirms last week's reports that he is dead.* —**re'cent·ly,** *adv.*

reception (3) [risep'šən], *n.* 1. an entertainment or party held to greet or honor someone. **Ex.** *After the wedding ceremony, a reception was held in the garden.* 2. the receiving of radio waves and similar electrical impulses. **Ex.** *The quality of radio reception changes with the weather and the time of day.*

recess (4) [rises'], *n.* 1. an open or hollow space in a wall. **Ex.** *There was a statue in a small recess in the wall.* 2. an inner place. **Ex.** *The treasure was found in a recess at the back of the cave.* —*v.* set back into an open or hollow place. **Ex.** *The windows were deeply recessed.*

recess (4) [riy'ses], *n.* a short period of rest from work or study. **Ex.** *During the recess, the children played in the school yard.* —*v.* rest from work or study for a time. **Ex.** *Congress recessed for the holiday.*

recipe (4) [res'əpiy], *n.* a list of the things needed and directions for preparing something to eat or drink. **Ex.** *I would like your recipe for this dessert.*

recipient [risip'iyənt], *n.* one who receives; a receiver. **Ex.** *The recipient of the award was loudly cheered.*

recite (4) [risayt'], *v.* 1. repeat or say aloud from memory. **Ex.** *Several children recited poems.* 2. tell something; give a detailed account of. **Ex.** *She recited all her troubles of the past year.* —**re·cit'al,** *n.* 1. the act of reciting or telling; that which is recited. 2. a musical entertainment. **Ex.** *We went to a piano recital.* —**rec'i·ta'tion,** *n.* 1. the act of reciting. 2. the thing recited.

reckless (3) [rek'lis], *adj.* dangerously thoughtless; rashly careless. **Ex.** *She was arrested for reckless driving.* —**reck'less·ly,** *adv.* —**reck'less·ness,** *n.* a careless act. **Ex.** *His recklessness caused the accident.*

recognize (2) [rek'əgnayz`], *v.* 1. know or recall that someone or something was known or seen before. **Ex.** *I recog-*

nized him as the same man I had seen yesterday. 2. know by knowledge or experience already acquired. **Ex.** *The singing teacher recognized the girl's voice as one worth training.* 3. be aware of; accept as true. **Ex.** *He recognized his inability to do the job.* 4. show appreciation and approval. **Ex.** *They recognized his heroism by giving him a medal.* —rec`og·ni`tion, *n.*

recollect (5) [rek'əlekt'], *v.* remember. **Ex.** *I cannot recollect his name.* —rec`ol·lec`tion, *n.* 1. the act of remembering. **Ex.** *According to my recollection, they were married last year.* 2. something remembered; memory. **Ex.** *They had many happy recollections of their trip.*

recommend (2) [rek`əmend'], *v.* 1. state that someone or something is good for a particular purpose; praise. **Ex.** *His former employer recommended him.* 2. urge as a wise course; advise. **Ex.** *What do you recommend that I read?* 3. make acceptable or pleasing. **Ex.** *That old house has little to recommend it.* —rec`om·men·da`tion, *n.* 1. the act of recommending. 2. a statement, often written, that recommends someone or something. 3. advice. **Ex.** *My recommendation was that he should buy it.*

reconcile (4) [rek'ənsayl`], *v.* 1. cause to be friendly again. **Ex.** *A friend reconciled the couple after their quarrel.* 2. settle. **Ex.** *They reconciled their differences.* 3. bring into agreement. **Ex.** *We could not reconcile his fine conduct with his bad reputation.* 4. cause oneself to accept. **Ex.** *They could not reconcile themselves to the loss of their son.* —rec`on·cil`i·a`tion, *n.*

record (1) [rikɔrd'], *v.* 1. write down something in order to have it for use at a future time, often in official forms or papers. **Ex.** *The teacher recorded the test results.* 2. show by means of a measuring device. **Ex.** *An instrument recorded the amount of electricity used.* 3. put sound in a form that can be kept and heard again. **Ex.** *We recorded the music played by the band.*

record (1) [rek'ərd], *n.* 1. a written account of facts or happenings; writings kept as history. **Ex.** *They kept a record of their expenses.* 2. a round, flat piece of black plastic with markings that reproduce sound. **Ex.** *The young people played records of dance music on the phonograph.* 3. the best performance, amount, rate, etc. **Ex.** *Several swimming records were set this year.* 4. the known facts about and performance of someone or something. **Ex.** *He made a good*

record in school. —**break a record,** do better than the previous best. Ex. *He ran so fast that he broke the record.* —**off
the record,** not to be published or quoted. Ex. *The President
told the press, off the record, what his plans were.*

recover (2) [rikəv'ər], *v.* 1. get again something lost, stolen,
or taken away. Ex. *The police recovered his stolen watch.*
2. return oneself or things to health or to a normal condition. Ex. *She recovered from her cold.* —**re·cov'er·y,** *n.*

recover (2) [rikəv'ər], *v.* cover again. Ex. *She recovered the
chair with striped material.*

recreation (5) [rek`riyey'šən], *n.* 1. a refreshing of one's
strength or spirits by some entertainment or restful activity.
Ex. *They walk for recreation.* 2. any entertainment, game,
etc. which refreshes. Ex. *His favorite recreations were reading and playing ball.* —**rec're·a'tion·al,** *adj.*

recruit (4) [rikruwt'], *n.* a new member, especially of the
armed forces. Ex. *The recruits were issued uniforms.* —*v.*
1. get new men to join the armed forces. Ex. *The navy has
been recruiting here recently.* 2. get new members or helpers
in a business, political group, etc. Ex. *They recruited six
new salesmen.* —**re·cruit'er,** *n.* one who recruits.

red (1) [red'], *adj.* having a bright color like that of blood.
Ex. *She picked a red rose.* —*n.* a bright color like that of
blood. Ex. *Do you like red better than blue?* —**red'den,** *v.*
become red.

Red Cross [red' krɔ:s'], an international organization that cares
for the sick, wounded, etc. in times of trouble.

red-handed [red'hæn'did], *adj.* in the very act of. Ex. *They
caught him red-handed stealing money.*

redeem (5) [ridiym'], *v.* buy back; regain. Ex. *He redeemed
his ring from the moneylender.* 2. make the final payment
on a loan. Ex. *He hopes to redeem his loan next month.* 3.
keep a pledge; fulfill a promise. Ex. *He redeemed his promise to pay half the expenses.* —**re·demp'tion,** *n.*

red tape [red' teyp'], official rules and procedures which cause
delay. Ex. *There is too much red tape when one wants a
license.*

reduce (2) [riduws', ridyuws'], *v.* 1. make smaller in amount,
number, or size. Ex. *His salary was reduced.* 2. lower in
rank or condition. Ex. *The major was reduced to captain.*
3. lose weight by dieting. Ex. *The doctor ordered me to
reduce.* —**re·duc'tion,** *n.*

reed (4) [riyd'], *n.* 1. a slender, hollow-stemmed grass. **Ex.** *Reeds grew along the river.* 2. a thin piece of reed or wood used in the mouthpiece of some musical wind instruments. **Ex.** *The musician carried an extra reed in a small case.*

reel (4) [riyl'], *n.* 1. device on which string, wire, film, etc. is wound and kept. **Ex.** *This movie is on three reels.* 2. the amount of something contained on a full reel. **Ex.** *The movie is three reels in length.* —*v.* 1. put on or take off a reel. **Ex.** *He reeled in his fishing line.* 2. move as if hit or when hit; sway. **Ex.** *He reeled from the blows and fell.*

refer (3) [rifə:r'], *v.* 1. send to for help, information, etc. **Ex.** *She referred me to the library.* 2. go to for information. **Ex.** *He referred to the dictionary for the meaning of the word.* 3. direct attention to; mention. **Ex.** *She often refers to her childhood.*

reference (3) [ref'ərəns], *n.* 1. the act of referring or consulting. **Ex.** *The journalist kept a card file of information on his desk for easy reference.* 2. a source of information. **Ex.** *References such as dictionaries are found in every library.* 3. mention of sources from which information was taken or in which similar information may be found. **Ex.** *His book contains many references to previous books on the subject.* 4. written statements about a person's abilities, character, etc. **Ex.** *The new worker had good references.*

refine (4) [rifayn'], *v.* improve; make less coarse or rough. **Exs.** *He visited a mill where sugar is refined. He refined what he had written.* —**re·fine'ment**, *n.*

reflect (3) [riflekt'], *v.* 1. change the direction in which waves, such as those of light, heat, or sound, are traveling or return these waves to the place they came from. **Ex.** *White walls reflect more light than dark walls.* 2. give back an image. **Ex.** *The mirror reflected the room.* —**re·flec'tion**, *n.* act of reflecting; that which is reflected. **Ex.** *He saw the reflection of his face in the water.*

reflect (3) [riflekt'], *v.* think deeply. **Ex.** *He reflected on his problems.* —**re·flec'tion**, *n.* thought; consideration. **Ex.** *After some reflection, she decided to accept the offer.*

reform (3) [rifɔrm'], *v.* 1. make something better by changing.

Ex. *The new President promised to reform the government.*
2. stop doing bad acts; improve. **Ex.** *The criminal tried to reform.* —*n.* the act of reforming; a change to a better condition. **Ex.** *The President promised many reforms in the tax laws.* —**ref·or·ma'tion,** *n.* act of reforming. —**re·form'a·tor·y,** *n.* a place where minor criminals are sent to be taught to reform.

refrain (4) [rifreyn'], *v.* keep oneself from doing. **Ex.** *In order to lose weight, she refrained from eating candy.*

refrain (4) [rifreyn'], *n.* a phrase, line, or group of lines repeated at intervals in a song or poem. **Ex.** *After each verse, everyone joined in singing the refrain.*

refresh (3) [rifreš'], *v.* make fresh or less tired by rest, food, drink, etc. **Ex.** *A cold drink refreshed the tired travelers.* —**re·fresh'ing,** *adj.* that makes strong or fresh again. **Ex.** *It was a refreshing drink.* —**re·fresh'ments,** *n.* light food and drinks.

refrigerator (4) [rifriǰ'ərey'tər], *n.* a cabinet or room which is kept very cold to prevent food from spoiling. **Ex.** *She put the meat into the refrigerator.* —**re·frig'er·ate,** *v.* cause to become cold or remain cold. **Ex.** *They refrigerated the milk immediately after milking.*

refuge (4) [ref'yuwǰ], *n.* a protected, safe place; shelter from trouble. **Ex.** *The man found a refuge from the rain.* —**ref'u·gee,** *n.* a person who has fled from cruel treatment, danger, etc. to seek refuge. **Ex.** *The flood created thousands of refugees.*

refuse (2) [rifyuwz'], *v.* decline to accept, give, or do something. **Ex.** *He refused to give me the money.* —**re·fus'al,** *n.*

refuse (2) [ref'yuws], *n.* waste; useless material without value. **Ex.** *There was a box for refuse near the door.*

regard (2) [rigard'], *v.* 1. think of; consider. **Ex.** *The children regard him with affection.* 2. give careful attention to; show respect for. **Ex.** *She did not regard the warning.* 3. concern. **Ex.** *My talk with him does not regard you.* —*n.* 1. reference; relation. **Ex.** *I shall speak to him in regard to that matter.* 2. concern; thought; care. **Ex.** *He had no regard for her sufferings.* 3. respect; liking. **Ex.** *We have great regard for that teacher.* —**re·gard'ing,** *prep.* concerning. —**re·gards',** *n.* good wishes; affection. **Ex.** *Please give my best regards to your wife.*

regime (5) [rəžiym', reyžiym'], *n.* a system of governing, ruling, or administering. **Ex.** *The whole country voted for a new regime.*

regiment (4) [rej'əmənt], *n.* a military unit consisting of a number of companies and usually commanded by a colonel. **Ex.** *The camp of the first regiment is beyond that hill.* —*v.* control by a system of strict rules and orders. **Ex.** *His method of teaching regimented the children.*

region (2) [riy'jən], *n.* 1. a large part of the earth. **Ex.** *He came to a region of ice and snow.* 2. a particular area or place. **Ex.** *The wooded region south of the city will become a park.* —**re'gion·al,** *adj.* concerning a particular region.

register (3) [rej'istər], *n.* 1. official list or book where certain information is recorded. **Ex.** *All visitors must sign the hotel guest register.* 2. a device used in business for counting and recording. **Ex.** *She put the money in the cash register.* —*v.* 1. enter or have entered in a register. **Ex.** *You are required to register before an election if you want to vote.* 2. show on a scale. **Ex.** *The thermometer registered a very low temperature last night.* —**reg'is·tra'tion,** *n.* act of registering. **Ex.** *Registration of new students occurs on Monday.*

regret (3) [rigret'], *v.* feel sorry about something that is done or that happens. **Ex.** *We regret that he has to leave.* —*n.* sorrow for something done; distress; a wish that something might be different. **Ex.** *She felt regret for having spoken unkind words.* —**re·grets',** *n.* an expression of being sorry not to attend. **Ex.** *Some of those invited to dinner sent their regrets.*

regular (2) [reg'yələr], *adj.* 1. following some established habit or custom; usual. **Ex.** *He returned home at the regular hour.* 2. steady and uniform; happening at fixed intervals. **Ex.** *I could hear the regular breathing of the sleeping man.* 3. formed according to some rule or principle; balanced. **Ex.** *She chose some material with a regular pattern.* 4. recognized, accepted, or qualified in the usual way. **Ex.** *He is not a regular member.*

regulate (4) [reg'yəleyt'], *v.* 1. govern or control according to rules or laws. **Ex.** *This department regulates commerce.* 2. cause to operate correctly; set at a certain speed, heat, etc. **Ex.** *This clock needs to be regulated.* —**reg'u·la'tion,** *n.* 1. the act of regulating. 2. a law or rule which regulates. **Ex.** *Regulations establish the age at which a young person* *can drive a car.* —**reg'u·la`tor,** *n.* that which or one who regulates. —**reg'u·la·tor`y,** *adj.*

rehearse (5) [rihərs'], *v.* practice a play, music, etc. before presenting it to an audience. **Ex.** *We will rehearse the play this afternoon.* —**re·hears'al,** *n.* the act of rehearsing; practice.

reign (3) [reyn'], *n.* the rule of a king or other person; the time of such rule. **Ex.** *The prince was not in the country during his father's reign.* —*v.* 1. have power as a king. **Ex.** *He reigned for many years.* 2. prevail; exist in a wide area. **Ex.** *After three bad harvests, hunger reigned in the country.*

rein (3) [reyn'], *n.* a strip of leather by which a rider or driver controls a horse. —*v.* guide, control, or stop by reins or by some other means. —**hold the reins,** be in control. **Ex.** *He holds the reins in his business.*

reject (3) [rijekt'], *v.* refuse to accept, use, believe, etc. **Ex.** *He rejected their offer to help.*

reject (3) [riy'ject], *n.* that refused as worthless. **Ex.** *The faulty machine part was sent back to the factory as a reject.*

rejoice (3) [rijoys'], *v.* be or be made happy. **Ex.** *They rejoiced when they heard he was safe.* —**re·joic'ing,** *n., adj.*

relate (3) [rileyt'], *v.* 1. tell; report. **Ex.** *We listened as he related his adventures.* 2. connect; associate. **Ex.** *It was natural to relate his disappearance to the disappearance of the money.* 3. be concerned with; have reference to. **Ex.** *To what does his letter relate?* —**re·lat'ed,** *adj.* of the same family or group. **Ex.** *They are related by marriage.*

relation (2) [riley'šən], *n.* 1. connection. **Ex.** *Weight has a close relation to health.* 2. a person connected by blood or marriage; a member of the same family. **Ex.** *He is staying with his relations.* —**re·la'tions,** the various connections between countries, groups, etc. **Ex.** *Relations between the United States and Canada have been good.* —**re·la'tion·ship,** *n.* state of being related. —**in relation to,** concerning. **Ex.** *What is he doing in relation to that problem?*

relative (3) [rel'ətiv], *n.* a person connected by blood or marriage; a member of the same family. **Ex.** *She has been visiting her relatives.* —*adj.* having meaning only through a comparison with something else; not absolute. **Ex.** *His family lives in relative comfort.* —**rel'a·tive·ly,** *adv.*

relax (4) [rilæks'], *v.* 1. become less firm, stiff, or tight. **Ex.** *His book dropped from his hands as he relaxed into sleep.*

2. rest from work. **Ex.** *They relaxed by going to the movies.*
—**re'lax·a'tion,** *n.* act of relaxing; that which relaxes.

release (3) [riliys'], *v.* 1. free; allow to go. **Ex.** *They released the prisoners.* 2. permit to be known, published, or sold. **Ex.** *The full story has not yet been released.*

reliable (4) [rilay'əbəl], *adj.* worthy of trust; dependable. **Ex.** *I believe what he says because he is very reliable.* —**re·li' ance,** *n.* trust. —**re·li'ant,** *adj.*

relief (2) [riliyf'], *n.* 1. a bringing of comfort or a reduction of pain. **Ex.** *The doctor ordered heat treatments for the relief of the sore arm.* 2. that which gives aid or comfort. **Ex.** *It was a relief to get out of the storm.* 3. a release from work in order to rest. **Ex.** *He worked from noon until dark with no relief.* 4. help given to people in need. **Ex.** *The government provides relief for poor families.*

relieve (3) [riliyv'], *v.* 1. bring comfort or reduce pain and worry. **Ex.** *The medicine relieved her headache.* 2. be released from duty by someone who takes one's place. **Ex.** *The guard at the gate was relieved every four hours.*

religion (2) [rilij'ən], *n.* 1. a belief in or the worship of a god or gods. **Ex.** *They are studying the religions of the world.* 2. a particular system of beliefs or worship centered around a god, a philosophy of life, etc. **Ex.** *What is your religion?* —**re·li'gious,** *adj.* 1. devoted to religion. **Ex.** *He is very religious.* 2. referring to religion. **Ex.** *Religious services are held here every Sunday.* —**re·li'gious·ly,** *adv.*

relish (5) [rel'iš], *n.* 1. enjoyment; satisfaction. **Ex.** *The old man watched the game with relish.* 2. sour, salted, or sweet foods intended to awaken the desire to eat. **Ex.** *Among the relishes she served were olives and tiny onions in vinegar.* —*v.* enjoy. **Ex.** *He relished the idea of a sea voyage.*

reluctant (5) [rilək'tənt], *adj.* unwilling; not inclined. **Ex.** *The mother was reluctant to leave her children alone.* —**re·luc' tant·ly,** *adv.* —**re·luc'tance,** *n.*

rely (4) [rilay'], *v.* depend on; trust. **Ex.** *You can rely on me to help you.*

remain (4) [rimeyn'], *v.* 1. stay in a place after others go away. **Ex.** *One person must remain in the office while we go out.* 2. stay the same. **Ex.** *She has remained as beautiful* *as ever.* 3. continue to exist. **Ex.** *After the fire, nothing remained of the house.* 4. be left after part is removed or lost. **Ex.** *Little remained of the food after the boys had eaten.* —**re·mains¹**, *n.* 1. that which is left. **Ex.** *The remains of a meal were on the table.* 2. a dead body. —**re·main¹der,** *n.* that which remains. **Ex.** *I ate some and gave the remainder to her.*

remark (2) [rimark¹], *v.* say; mention. **Ex.** *He remarked that the weather was fine.* —*n.* an observation; a comment. **Ex.** *I did not like his remark about her.*

remarkable (3) [rimar¹kəbəl], *adj.* unusual; special enough to deserve mention. **Ex.** *He told me a remarkable story.* —**re·mark¹a·bly,** *adv.*

remedy (3) [rem¹ədiy], *n.* 1. a medicine or treatment that cures. **Ex.** *This is a good remedy for a sore foot.* 2. a means of correcting a wrong or an evil. **Ex.** *They built a new school as a remedy for crowded classrooms.* —*v.* cure, improve, or correct. **Ex.** *Being sorry will not remedy the damage you have done.* —**re·me¹di·a·ble,** *adj.* capable of being cured, improved, etc. —**re·me¹di·al,** *adj.* able to remedy. **Ex.** *Remedial lessons were given to the slower students.*

remember (1) [rimem¹bər], *v.* 1. return to the mind. **Ex.** *He could not remember where he put his eyeglasses.* 2. keep in mind. **Ex.** *Remember that you have an appointment with the doctor tomorrow.* —**re·mem¹brance,** *n.* 1. the act of remembering. 2. an object given or kept to remind someone of something.

remind (2) [rimaynd¹], *v.* 1. cause one to remember. **Ex.** *Please remind me to take my medicine.* 2. cause one to think of. **Ex.** *The mountains reminded him of home.* —**re·mind¹er,** *n.* that which helps one to remember.

remit (5) [rimit¹], *v.* 1. send money in payment to a person or place. **Ex.** *Please remit the amount of your bill by check.* 2. forgive or pardon all or a portion of a debt or punishment. **Ex.** *Because of the boy's age, the judge remitted the prison sentence.* —**re·mit¹tance,** *n.* the sending of money; the money sent.

remnant (5) [rem¹nənt], *n.* that part which remains of anything. **Ex.** *Remnants of the meal lay on the table when he had finished eating.*

remodel [riymad¹əl], *v.* rebuild; change the form or design of. **Ex.** *We remodeled our bedroom.*

remote (4) [rimowt'], *adj.* 1. far away. **Ex.** *The accident oc-curred in a remote place.* 2. only slightly related or con-nected. **Ex.** *All members of the family except remote rela-tives were invited.* 3. slight. **Ex.** *There is only a remote possibility that he will be elected.* —**re·mote'ly,** *adv.* —**re·mote'ness,** *n.*

remove (2) [rimuwv'], *v.* 1. take away or off. **Ex.** *She re-moved her hat and coat.* 2. get rid of; put an end to. **Ex.** *She could not remove the spot from the carpet.* 3. put out of a position or office. **Ex.** *He was removed from his job because he was not qualified.* —**re·mov'al,** *n.*

render (4) [ren'dər], *v.* 1. make; cause to be or become. **Ex.** *They were rendered homeless by the fire.* 2. do; perform. **Ex.** *That organization renders great service to the com-munity.* 3. present for payment or consideration. **Ex.** *The lawyer has not yet rendered his bill.* —**ren·di'tion,** *n.* a way of performing music, a play, etc.; a version. **Ex.** *I like her rendition of the song.*

renounce (5) [rinawns'], *v.* 1. give up; abandon. **Ex.** *He re-nounced his citizenship.* 2. refuse to recognize. **Ex.** *Her parents renounced her because of her marriage.* —**re·nun'ci·a'tion,** *n.* act of renouncing.

renown (5) [rinawn'], *n.* fame; high reputation. **Ex.** *He won renown for his courage.*

rent (3) [rent'], *n.* payment regularly made to an owner for the use of land, a building, or other property. **Ex.** *The rent for the house was more than they could afford.* —*v.* use or allow the use of property for which a regular payment is made. **Ex.** *They rented a car for the trip.* —**rent'al,** *n.* the amount paid or received as rent.

repair (2) [ripe:r'], *v.* 1. fix; mend. **Ex.** *He had his shoes repaired.* 2. correct; make right; remedy. **Ex.** *He tried to repair the wrong he had done.* —*n.* 1. the act or process of repairing. **Ex.** *The repair of the car will take a week.* 2. the state of being repaired; the condition of the thing being repaired. **Ex.** *The bicycle is in good repair.*

repeal (4) [ripiyl'], *v.* set aside or end officially. **Ex.** *That law was repealed by Congress.* —*n.* the act of officially setting aside or ending. **Ex.** *Congress is discussing the repeal of that law.*

repeat (2) [ripiyt'], *v.* 1. say again. **Ex.** *She repeated the accu-sation.* 2. say from memory. **Ex.** *He repeated the entire* *poem.* 3. do or make again. **Ex.** *If you repeat that mistake, you will be punished.* —re·peat'ed, *adj.* said, done, or made again. —re·peat'ed·ly, *adv.*

repel (5) [ripel'], *v.* 1. drive or force back. **Ex.** *The enemy was repelled.* 2. push away; refuse. **Ex.** *She repelled his attempts to be friendly.* 3. cause a strong feeling of dislike. **Ex.** *She was repelled by the odor of the spoiled food.* —re·pel'lent, *adj.* —*n.* that which repels.

repent (4) [ripent'], *v.* feel guilt or regret for past conduct. **Ex.** *He repented and confessed his crime.* —re·pent'ant, *adj.* —re·pent'ance, *n.*

repetition (5) [rep'ətiš'ən], *n.* 1. the act of repeating. **Ex.** *Repetition of the word helped him to remember it.* 2. something which is repeated or is a copy. **Ex.** *The builder's last house is a repetition of his first.* —rep·e·ti'tious, *adj.*

reply (1) [riplay'], *v.* answer in words or in writing or by doing something. **Ex.** *She replied to my letter promptly.* —*n.* an answer. **Ex.** *He made no reply to my question.*

report (1) [riport'], *n.* 1. an account of a happening; a statement giving the results of an inquiry or search. **Ex.** *A report of the accident was in the newspapers.* 2. a story or statement told without certainty as to the facts. **Ex.** *I have heard bad reports about him.* —*v.* 1. tell about. **Ex.** *The class reported on its trip to the museum.* 2. tell in a formal statement; give the results of a special study. **Ex.** *The committee reported on housing conditions.* 3. tell officials someone has not acted properly. **Ex.** *She reported him to the police.* 4. appear; arrive at. **Ex.** *Report to my office.* —re·port'er *n.* one who reports, especially for a newspaper.

repose (5) [ripowz'], *n.* 1. rest; sleep. **Ex.** *His brief repose was interrupted by her arrival.* 2. calm; peace. **Ex.** *There was an air of repose in the village.* —*v.* lie at rest. **Ex.** *Many soldiers killed in battle repose in foreign soil.*

represent (2) [rep'rizent'], *v.* 1. express by some symbol or sign; symbolize. **Ex.** *On the map, blue represents water.* 2. show; picture. **Ex.** *This picture represents the artist's boyhood home.* 3. act in the place of or as a substitute for. **Ex.** *Since I cannot go, he will represent me.* 4. serve as an example of. **Ex.** *He represents the modern businessman.* —rep·re·sen·ta'tion, *n.* act of representing or being represented. —rep·re·sent'a·tive, *adj.* one who represents others. —Rep·re·sent'a·tive, *n.* a member of the lower of the two legislative groups that make up the United States Congress or certain other governing groups. This group of the Congress is known as the House of Representatives.

repress (5) [ripres¹], *v.* 1. control. **Ex.** *She repressed her tears in public.* 2. force out of one's awareness. **Ex.** *She repressed her fears of the dark.* —**re·pres¹sion,** *n.* —**re·pres¹sive,** *adj.*

reproach (4) [riprowč¹], *v.* blame; find fault with. **Ex.** *She reproached him for staying out late.* —*n.* 1. the act of blaming; words of blame. **Ex.** *Her mother's reproaches made her unhappy.* 2. the cause for shame or blame. **Ex.** *The poor reading ability of the students was a reproach to the school system.*

reproduce (5) [riy˘prəduws¹, riy˘prədyuws¹], *v.* 1. show or produce again. **Ex.** *He reproduced the letter from memory.* 2. copy or imitate. **Ex.** *I reproduced the letter on the typewriter.* 3. among animals and plants, produce one's kind. **Ex.** *Humans reproduce in nine months.* —**re·pro·duc¹tion,** *n.* 1. the act of reproducing. 2. the thing reproduced.

reprove (5) [ripruwv¹], *v.* blame or find fault with in a gentle way. **Ex.** *She reproved the maid for breaking the dish.* —**re·proof¹,** *n.* act of reproving.

reptile (4) [rep¹til, rep¹tayl], *n.* any cold-blooded animal which creeps or crawls, such as a snake or turtle. **Ex.** *Some reptiles, such as snakes, move very fast.*

republic (3) [ripəb¹lik], *n.* a form of government in which people elect others to represent them and to do the work of the government. **Ex.** *The president of the republic was chosen by the people.* —**re·pub¹li·can,** *adj.* —**Re·pub¹li·can,** *n.* a member of the Republican Party, one of the two main political parties in the United States. **Ex.** *Dwight D. Eisenhower, the 34th President of the United States, was a Republican.*

repulse (5) [ripəls¹], *v.* 1. drive back or force away an attacker. **Ex.** *The enemy was repulsed.* 2. refuse or turn away from in an unfriendly manner. **Ex.** *She repulsed her neighbor's offer of help.* —*n.* 1. the act of driving back. **Ex.** *The quick repulse of his army surprised the general.* 2. refusal. **Ex.** *He was hurt by her repulse of his friendship.* —**re·pul¹sive,**

a, far; æ, am; e, get; ey, late; i, in; iy, see; ɔ, all; ow, go; u, put; uw, too; ə, but, ago; ər, fur; aw, out; ay, life; oy, boy; ŋ, ring; θ, think; ð, that; ž, measure; š, ship; j, edge; č, child.

adj. causing a feeling of strong dislike. —**re·pul'sion,** *n.* act of repulsing or having a strong dislike.

reputation (3) [rep'yutey'šən], *n.* the opinion which people generally have about a person or thing. **Ex.** *That hotel has a reputation for good service.*

request (2) [rikwest'], *n.* 1. the act of asking for. **Ex.** *He would not listen to my request.* 2. the thing asked for. **Ex.** *The old man's dying request was granted.* —*v.* ask for something. **Ex.** *The boy requested permission to go.* 2. ask someone to do something. **Ex.** *He requested me to write a letter of recommendation.*

require (1) [rikwayr'], *v.* 1. need. **Ex.** *The sick man required constant attention.* 2. demand, as by right or authority. **Ex.** *The school required a record of his past studies.*

rescue (3) [res'kyuw], *v.* free from danger, evil, etc. **Ex.** *The passengers were rescued from the sinking ship.* —*n.* the act of saving. **Ex.** *The rescue of the flood victims was accomplished rapidly.* —**res'cu·er,** *n.* one who rescues.

research (3) [risərč', riy'sərč], *n.* careful study to discover correct information. **Ex.** *Scientists are continuing research on peaceful uses of atomic energy.* —*v.* do research. **Ex.** *He has not yet researched that aspect of the subject.* —**research'er,** *n.* one who does research.

resemble (3) [rizem'bəl], *v.* be or look like or similar to. **Ex.** *Her voice resembles her mother's.* —**re·sem'blance,** *n.* similarity. **Ex.** *There is a strong resemblance between the two brothers.*

resent (3) [rizent'], *v.* feel bitterness and anger at. **Ex.** *She resented his remarks about her poor driving.* —**re·sent'ment,** *n.*

reservation [rez'ərvey'šən], *n.* that which has been reserved **Ex.** *We have room reservations at that hotel.*

reserve (3) [rizərv'], *v.* 1. save for future use. **Ex.** *They reserved some of the corn to use as seed.* 2. have set aside for one's use. **Ex.** *We reserved a hotel room for tonight* 3. hold or keep for oneself. **Ex.** *He reserved the right to approve the illustrations for his book.* —*n.* 1. something set aside for future use or a particular purpose. **Ex.** *The city's reserve of water is low.* 2. public land set aside for a particular use. **Ex.** *This park is one of the national forest reserves.*

reservoir (5) [rez'ərvwar', rez'ərvɔ:r'], *n.* 1. a large tank o lake for keeping something, usually liquid, until needed. **Ex.** *Most of the city's water comes from this reservoir.* 2. a supply of anything held back or available for later use. **Ex.** *His reservoir of strength helped him recover.*

reside (3) [rizayd'], *v.* 1. have as one's home; live in a place. **Ex.** *Where do you reside now?* 2. be located in or at. **Ex.** *The power to legislate resides in the legislature.* —**res'i·dence,** *n.* a place where one lives. —**res'i·dent,** *n.* one who resides. —**res'i·den'tial,** *adj.* of or consisting of homes. **Ex.** *He lives in a residential area near the lake.*

resign (3) [rizayn'], *v.* quit one's position, job, etc. **Ex.** *The man resigned from his job because of illness.* —**res`ig·na' tion,** *n.* the act of quitting.

resist (3) [rezist'], *v.* 1. oppose; fight to prevent. **Ex.** *The thief resisted arrest.* 2. prevent oneself from doing. **Ex.** *He could not resist laughing at her mistake.* —**re·sist'ance,** *n.* —**re· sist'ant,** *adj.*

resolute (5) [rez'əluwt`, rez'əlyuwt], *adj.* having an unchanging purpose; constant. **Ex.** *Despite the opposition to his plan, he remained resolute.*

resolution (5) [rez`əluw'šən], *n.* 1. a formal agreement by a group of people. **Ex.** *A resolution to support the government program was voted on by the legislature.* 2. the resolving of something. **Ex.** *The resolution of the problem was a difficult process.* 3. decision on a way of acting. **Ex.** *His resolution was to be kind to people.* 4. condition of being firm and unchanging in purpose. **Ex.** *His resolution to overcome all obstacles made him succeed.* 5. condition of having arrived at an answer to a problem. **Ex.** *Their resolution of the border dispute was praised.*

resolve (3) [rizalv'], *v.* 1. decide or determine to do something. **Ex.** *He resolved to quit smoking.* 2. express a group opinion or decision by voting. **Ex.** *The group resolved to oppose the new highway.* 3. solve. **Ex.** *Most of the problems were resolved at the last meeting.* —*n.* something definitely decided; intention. **Ex.** *His resolve to be a doctor has not changed.*

resort (3) [rizɔrt'], *v.* go to for help. **Ex.** *He resorted to asking his friends for money.* *n.* 1. a place which people visit for a rest or vacation. **Ex.** *They went to a resort in the mountains.* 2. a person, place, or thing from which one seeks help. **Ex.** *He was her last resort.*

resource (4) [risɔrs', riy'sɔrs], *n*. 1. a reserve or source of supply, support, or assistance. **Ex**. *This country has many natural resources.* 2. skill or talent in handling difficulties. **Ex**. *A person of great resource was needed to accomplish the job.* —**re·source'ful**, *adj*. able or skillful in handling difficulties.

respect (2) [rispəkt'], *v*. 1. regard with honor. **Ex**. *We respect him as a great artist.* 2. show consideration or concern for. **Ex**. *They respected his right to differ with them.* —*n*. 1. regard; admiration and honor. **Ex**. *We have great respect for your opinion.* 2. concern or consideration for. **Ex**. *He always shows respect for his elders.* 3. aspect; detail; way. **Ex**. *In many respects, he is more capable than his brother.* —**re·spect'a·ble**, *adj*. highly regarded; correct and acceptable. —**pay one's respects**, show regard formally. **Ex**. *They attended the reception to pay their respects to the new college president.*

respective (5) [rispek'tiv], *adj*. of or for each individual; particular. **Ex**. *Each went his respective way.* —**re·spec'tive·ly**, *adv*. to each in the order mentioned.

respond (4) [rispand'], *v*. 1. reply; answer. **Ex**. *She responded to my question.* 2. act as a result of; show effect. **Ex**. *The sick man responded to the new medicine.*

response (4) [rispans'], *n*. 1. an answer or reply. **Ex**. *I am awaiting your response to my letter.* 2. the reaction produced as a result of. **Ex**. *The doctor was pleased with the patient's response to the medicine.* —**re·spon'sive**, *adj*. being an answer or reaction; willing to respond.

responsible (2) [rispan'səbəl], *adj*. 1. having a duty to do or to take care of; accountable for something that should be done. **Ex**. *Who is responsible for locking the office door?* 2. being the cause or producer. **Ex**. *Which driver was responsible for the accident?* 3. deserving of trust. **Ex**. *You can depend upon him; he is a responsible person.* 4. involving important obligations. **Ex**. *He holds a responsible position in the bank.* —**re·spon'si·bly**, *adv*. —**re·spon'si·bil'i·ty**, *n*. that for which one is responsible. **Ex**. *Locking the doors is his responsibility.*

rest (1) [rest'], *v*. 1. become refreshed by sitting, sleeping, etc. **Ex**. *She rested for half an hour.* 2. lean; lie; be set; be supported. **Ex**. *His arm rested on the table.* —*n*. 1. a period of doing no work and of being inactive or of sleeping, sitting, etc. Ex. *Have a rest and you will not be so tired.* 2. absence of motion. Ex. *The ball came to rest at his feet.* —**rest'ful,** *adj.* quiet; able to give rest. Ex. *The park is a restful place.* —**res'tive,** *adj.* not resting; disturbed. Ex. *The students were restive while he talked.* —**rest'less,** *adj.* without rest; not able to rest. —**rest'less·ly,** *adv.*

rest (1) [rest'], *n.* 1. that which is left; the remainder. Ex. *Eat the rest of your dinner.* 2. those that remain; the others. Ex. *The rest of the students are taking the trip next week.*

restaurant (3) [res't(ə)rənt, res't(ə)rant'], *n.* a public place where meals are served for money. Ex. *They ate dinner at the best restaurant in town.*

restore (4) [ristɔ:r'], *v.* 1. return to an original, usual, or former condition. Ex. *After a long sickness, his health was restored.* 2. return. Ex. *The thief restored the jewels he had stolen.* —**res'to·ra'tion,** *n.* 1. the act of restoring or rebuilding. 2. that which is restored or rebuilt.

restrain (4) [ristreyn'], *v.* hold under control; limit actions. Ex. *She could not restrain the children from running into the street.* —**re·straint',** *n.* 1. the act or means of restraining. 2. reserve; self-control. Ex. *His restraint in not showing his anger was admirable.*

restrict (5) [ristrikt'], *v.* limit; confine. Ex. *The sale of liquor is restricted to people over twenty-one years old.* —**re·stric' tion,** *n.* —**re·stric'tive,** *adj.* limiting. Ex. *The rules are very restrictive.*

restroom [rest'ruwm'], *n.* a room in a public place with toilets, washbowls, etc. Ex. *Where is the restroom, please?*

result (1) [rizəlt'], *n.* that which follows or is produced by a cause; effect. Ex. *I became ill as a result of my long journey.* —*v.* happen or arise from a cause. Ex. *His broken leg resulted from a fall.* —**re·sult'ant,** *adj.*

resume (3) [rizuwm', rizyuwm'], *v.* 1. continue after a stop. Ex. *Classes resumed after vacation.* 2. occupy again. Ex. *After speaking, he resumed his seat.* —**re·sump'tion,** *n.*

résumé (3) [rez'umey', rez'umey'], *n.* a short report of the contents of something longer. Ex. *Give me a five-minute résumé of his talk.*

---

a, far; æ, am; e, get; ey, late; i, in; iy, see; ɔ, all; ow, go; u, put; uw, too; ə, but, ago; ər, fur; aw, out; ay, life; oy, boy; ŋ, ring; θ, think; ð, that; ž, measure; š, ship; ǰ, edge; č, child.

retail (5) [riy'teyl`], *n.* the sale of goods in small quantities to the actual users. **Ex.** *Most people buy meat and groceries at retail.* —*adj.* having to do with selling at retail. **Ex.** *This is a retail store.*

retain (3) [riteyn'], *v.* 1. continue to possess; hold. **Ex.** *They still retain their big house.* 2. remember. **Ex.** *He cannot retain all the facts he has learned.* 3. hire or engage the services of by paying a sum of money. **Ex.** *The prisoner retained a lawyer to defend him.* —**re·tain'er,** *n.* 1. money paid to someone at the time he is hired. 2. that which keeps or holds.

retard (5) [ritard'], *v.* slow progress; delay. **Ex.** *Lack of money retarded the program.* —**re·tard'ed,** *adj.* slow or behind in some way. **Ex.** *Mentally retarded people need special help to learn.*

retire (3) [ritayr'], *v.* 1. leave one's job because of age or poor health. **Ex.** *He retired from his job several years ago.* 2. go to bed. **Ex.** *She did not retire until midnight.* 3. withdraw to be alone or quiet. —**re·tir'ing,** *adj.* shy. **Ex.** *She is very retiring when with people.*

retort (4) [ritort'], *v.* answer quickly in a sharp or clever way. **Ex.** *He retorted that her questions were not worth answering.* —*n.* a sharp or clever reply. **Ex.** *She was not amused by his retort.*

retouch [riytəč'], *v.* change small parts to improve the whole. **Ex.** *He retouched the old painting to eliminate cracks.*

retreat (3) [ritriyt'], *v.* move back and away from action. **Ex.** *The troops retreated from the hill.* —*n.* 1. the act of moving back. **Ex.** *The army's retreat was not expected.* 2. a quiet place in which to be alone. **Ex.** *A shaded corner of the garden was his favorite retreat.*

return (1) [ritərn'], *v.* 1. go or come back to or from. **Ex.** *We returned home by car.* 2. bring, give, send, or put back. **Ex.** *Please return these books to her.* —*n.* 1. the act of going or coming back to or from a place. **Ex.** *We met him on his return from school.* 2. the act of bringing, putting, sending, or paying back; that which is returned. **Ex.** *If you help me, I will help you in return.* —*adj.* of or for a return. **Ex.** *They have tickets for their return trip.*

reveal (2) [riviyl'], *v.* 1. tell or make known something either not known or secret. **Ex.** *The truth was revealed to them by the wise man.* 2. show plainly; display. **Ex.** *He opened the* *door and revealed the garden.* —**rev`e·la`tion,** *n.* act of revealing; something revealed. **Ex.** *That she could cook was a revelation.*

revenge (3) [rivenǰ'], *v.* harm or injure as payment for a harm or injury done. **Ex.** *He revenged the wrongs done to his family.* —*n.* 1. the act of harming or injuring in repayment. **Ex.** *They burned their neighbor's house in revenge.* 2. the desire for revenge. **Ex.** *His mind was filled with revenge.*

revenue (4) [rev'ənuw`, rev'ənyuw`], *n.* money received from any source, such as profit, taxes, income, etc., especially the taxes and other money collected by a government. **Ex.** *The new tax will be an added source of revenue.*

revere (5) [rivi:r'], *v.* feel great honor, respect, and affection toward. **Ex.** *The students revered the old professor.* —**rev'er·ence,** *n.* feeling of great respect. —**rev'er·ent,** *adj.* —**rev'er·ent·ly,** *adv.* —**rev'er·end,** *n.* a title used before the name of a clergyman.

reverse (4) [rivərs'], *adj.* 1. contrary or opposite in direction; backward or upside down. **Ex.** *He read the numbers in reverse order.* 2. of the opposite side to that facing; of the back or rear. **Ex.** *The reverse side is not seen when the dress is worn.* —*n.* 1. that which is the opposite or contrary. **Ex.** *He said he would refuse, but he did the reverse.* 2. the back or rear side of anything. **Ex.** *Some words were written on the reverse of the painting.* —*v.* turn backward; turn inside out; turn upside down. **Ex.** *To reach town they had to reverse their direction.* —**re·vers'ible,** *adj.*

review (3) [rivyuw'], *v.* 1. examine again; study again. **Ex.** *Review all the facts before you decide.* 2. think of again. **Ex.** *He reviewed the events of the day before.* 3. write or make a critical examination and judgment of some art or writing. **Ex.** *This book has been reviewed favorably in several newspapers.* 4. reconsider the findings of a lower court. **Ex.** *Will a higher court review the judge's decision?* —*n.* 1. the process of looking over, discussing, or studying again. **Ex.** *The teacher said that there would be a review of what we had learned.* 2. an article in a magazine or newspaper about a book, painting, etc. **Ex.** *The book received good reviews.* —**re·view'er,** *n.* one who reviews literature and the arts for a newspaper, magazine, etc.

revise (5) [rivayz'], *v.* 1. change or alter. **Ex.** *When you know the facts, you may revise your opinion.* 2. read carefully to correct errors and make more timely. **Ex.** *He has been asked to revise this book.* —**re·vi'sion,** *n.*

revive (4) [rivayv'], *v.* 1. return or be returned to consciousness. **Ex.** *The quick action of the doctor revived the dying man.* 2. return or be returned to health or an active condition. **Ex.** *The wine revived the chilled traveler.* —**re·viv'al,** *n.*

revolt (3) [rivowlt'], *n.* 1. rebellion. **Ex.** *The revolt began at dawn.* 2. a protest; a refusal to follow orders or authority. **Ex.** *The clothes of young people today are a symbol of revolt.* —*v.* 1. rebel against authority. **Ex.** *They revolted against their foreign ruler.* 2. fill with horror or strong feelings of dislike. **Ex.** *He was revolted by the smell and became sick.*

revolution (3) [rev'əluw'šən, rev'əlyuw'šən], *n.* 1. a complete ruin or defeat of an established government or political system and its replacement by another. **Ex.** *The American Revolution occurred in 1776.* 2. any complete or thorough change. **Ex.** *The invention of machines has caused a revolution in the way we live.* 3. the act of revolving one complete turn. **Ex.** *One revolution of the minute hand of a clock takes one hour.* —**rev'o·lu'tion·ar·y,** *adj.* —**rev'o·lu'tion·ize,** *v.* cause a great change. **Ex.** *The airplane revolutionized our lives.*

revolve (3) [rivalv'], *v.* turn around or spin on its own center; move in orbit. **Ex.** *The earth revolves around the sun.*

revolver (5) [rival'vər], *n.* a pistol that can be fired several times without reloading because of a revolving part that holds several bullets.

reward (2) [riword'], *n.* 1. money or honor given for some special service or performance. **Ex.** *As a reward for his bravery, the soldier was given a medal.* 2. money offered for the return of lost or stolen property. **Ex.** *A reward was offered for the return of the dog.* —*v.* give a reward to or for.

rhyme (4) [raym'], *n.* 1. similarity of sounds at the ends of words or lines of poetry. **Ex.** *The poet used the word "flight" as a rhyme for the word "night."* 2. poems in which the sounds at the ends of the lines are similar. **Ex.** *What was your favorite childhood rhyme?* —*v.* 1. sound alike. **Ex.** *"Dear" rhymes with "near."* 2. use a word as a rhyme for another word. **Ex.** *He rhymed "heart" with "part."*

rib (3) [rib'], *n.* 1. any of the arched bones attached to the backbone and enclosing the chest. **Ex.** *The blow he received*

broke a rib. 2. something that looks or feels like a rib. **Ex.**
My umbrella needs a new rib.

ribbon (2) [rib'ən], *n.* 1. a narrow piece of cloth used to form
bows, tie packages as presents, etc. **Ex.** *The girl wore a blue
ribbon in her hair.* 2. something that resembles a ribbon. **Ex.**
A ribbon of smoke curled from the chimney. 3. a narrow,
torn piece of anything. **Ex.** *The sails of the ship were torn to
ribbons by the storm.*

rice (2) [rays'], *n.* the seed or grain from a grass widely grown
in warm climates and used as the main food in many parts
of the world, especially Asia; also the grass itself. **Ex.** *She
served rice with the meat.*

rich (1) [rič'], *adj.* 1. having much money or goods. **Ex.** *He
is a rich man.* 2. yielding or producing much. **Ex.** *The town
is surrounded by rich farmland.* 3. having plenty of. **Ex.** *The
water from this spring is rich in minerals.* 4. valuable, costly.
Ex. *Her gown was made of a rich cloth.* **—rich'ness,** *n.*

rid (3) [rid'], *v.* free or clear of something undesirable; eliminate something from. **Ex.** *He rid the house of rats.* **—get
rid of,** get free or clear of. **Ex.** *He got rid of the smell by
opening a window.* **—rid'dance,** *n.* a getting rid of.

ridden (1) [rid'ən], *v.* past participle of *ride.* **Ex.** *He has ridden
the horse all day.*

riddle (5) [rid'əl], *n.* 1. a puzzle in the form of a question.
Ex. *To the riddle "What walks on four legs in the morning,
two legs at noon, and three legs in the evening?" the answer
is, "Man."* 2. any person or thing that is mysterious or difficult to understand. **Ex.** *That painting has always been a
riddle to me.*

ride (1) [rayd'], *v.* 1. sit on or in and be carried along. **Ex.**
Two people were riding in the car. 2. sit on and cause to
move. **Ex.** *He rides his bicycle to school.* **—n.** a trip in a car,
on a horse, etc. **Ex.** *We are going for a boat ride this evening.* **—rid'er,** *n.* one who rides.

ridge (3) [rij'], *n.* 1. a range of hills or mountains; the upper
part of such a range. **Ex.** *Our camp is just beyond the next
ridge.* 2. any raised, narrow strip or line. **Ex.** *Two birds
were sitting on the ridge of the roof.*

ridiculous (3) [ridik'yələs], *adj.* deserving of or causing scorn;

a, far; æ, am; e, get; ey, late; i, in; iy, see; ɔ, all; ow, go; u, put; uw, too;
ə, but, ago; ər, fur; aw, out; ay, life; oy, boy; ŋ, ring; θ, think; ð, that;
ž, measure; š, ship; j, edge; č, child.

foolish. **Ex.** *That is a ridiculous idea.* **—ri·dic'u·lous·ly,** *adv.*
—rid'i·cule`, *n.* words or actions intended to make a person
or thing seem foolish. **—v.** mock; make fun of. **Ex.** *They
ridiculed his strange clothes.*

rifle (3) [ray'fəl], *n.* a gun with a long barrel,
the inside of which is designed to make a
bullet spin.

RIFLE

right (1) [rayt'], *adj.* 1. agreeing with the
facts; correct. **Ex.** *Most of the student's
answers were right.* 2. of or on the side of
the body on which the hand is usually
stronger and more skillful and quick; on
the side toward the east when facing north.
Ex. *He held the pencil in his right hand.* 3. suitable to the
situation; fit. **Ex.** *Is this dress right to wear to a wedding?*
4. done according to law or according to one's duty or conscience; just; good. **Ex.** *He always did what he believed to be
right.* 5. meant to be seen or placed toward the outside. **Ex.**
Which is the right side of this material? **—n.** 1. that which
is lawful or proper. **Ex.** *He is old enough to know right from
wrong.* 2. something to which a person has a legal and
proper claim. **Ex.** *The rights of the people are protected by
law.* 3. in politics, those most careful and least desirous of
change. **Ex.** *The right does not want a new tax.* 4. the right
hand or side. **Ex.** *An old friend was sitting on my right.*
—adv. 1. according to law, duty, or conscience; correctly.
Ex. *We must try to do it right.* 2. in a straight line; directly.
Ex. *She went right home after school.* 3. exactly. **Ex.** *Put
it right there.* 4. toward the right. **Ex.** *Turn right at the next
corner.* **—v.** correct. **Ex.** *They attempted to right an old
abuse.*

right angle [rayt' æŋ'gəl], an angle of ninety
degrees.

right-hand [rayt'hænd`], *adj.* 1. on or toward
the right. **Ex.** *He made a right-hand turn.*
2. chiefly relied upon. **Ex.** *He is my right-
hand man.*

RIGHT ANGLE

right-handed [rayt'hæn'did], *adj.* tending to prefer the right
hand in use. **Ex.** *Right-handed people usually write with the
right hand.*

right of way [rayt' əv wey'], 1. the right to move, as in driving
a car, before others do. **Ex.** *When the traffic light became
green, he had the right of way.* 2. lawful right to go across

another's property. **Ex.** *We have a right of way through his farm to the highway.*

rigid (4) [rij'id], *adj.* 1. not easily bent; stiff. **Ex.** *The tent was supported by rigid poles.* 2. severe; strict. **Ex.** *Her parents had rigid ideas.* —**rig·id·ly**, *adv.* —**ri·gid'i·ty**, *n.*

rim (4) [rim'], *n.* an edge or border of something rounded or curved. **Ex.** *There was a band of gold around the rim of the cup.*

ring (1) [riŋ'], *n.* 1. a narrow circle of metal, often gold or silver, worn on the finger for ornament. **Ex.** *She is wearing a diamond engagement ring.* 2. any narrow band of material in the shape of a circle used for holding or fastening things. **Ex.** *He carried six keys on his key ring.* 3. any arrangement of things or persons in a circle. **Ex.** *The dancers stood in a ring.* 4. a group of persons working together for some illegal or evil reason. **Ex.** *A ring of thieves stole the money.* —*v.* surround; form a ring around. **Ex.** *The fort was ringed by enemy forces.*

ring (1) [riŋ'], *v.* 1. give or produce a sound, as of a bell. **Ex.** *Did you hear the dinner bell ring?* 2. cause a bell to sound. **Ex.** *Did you ring the bell?* 3. summon or announce with a bell. **Ex.** *Will you please ring for someone to carry my bags?* —*n.* 1. the sound of a bell or something similar to a bell. **Ex.** *I heard a ring of laughter outside.* 2. telephone call. **Ex.** *Give me a ring, and we will talk about the matter.*

ringleader [riŋ'liy'dər], *n.* one who leads or directs a group, usually in illegal activities. **Ex.** *All the members of the ring were caught except the ringleader.*

rinse (3) [rins'], *v.* 1. wash lightly. **Ex.** *She rinsed her hands.* 2. remove the soap from with clean water, as a final step in washing. **Ex.** *She rinsed the dishes.* —*n.* the act of rinsing; the liquid in which something is rinsed. **Ex.** *Do you use a special rinse for your hair?*

riot (4) [ray'ət], *n.* 1. a disturbance created by a large group of people whose behavior is wild and violent. **Ex.** *The police were called to control the riot.* 2. a brilliant and sometimes confusing display. **Ex.** *The flower beds were a riot of color.* —*v.* take part in a riot. **Ex.** *Large crowds were rioting in the streets.* —**ri'ot·ous**, *adj.*

rip (4) [rip'], *v.* cut or tear something roughly. **Ex.** *He ripped his shirt on a nail.* —*n.* a torn place. **Ex.** *She mended the rip in her dress.*

ripe (3) [rayp'], *adj.* 1. ready to be eaten. **Ex.** *This apple is ripe.* 2. having reached full development. **Ex.** *The farmer lived to a ripe old age.* —**rip'en,** *v.* become or make ripe.

ripple (4) [rip'əl], *v.* form small waves or movements like waves. **Ex.** *The breeze began to ripple the surface of the lake.* —*n.* a small wave or movement. **Ex.** *The canvas was stretched over the frame without a ripple.*

rise (1) [rayz'], *v.* 1. go upward; go from a sitting or lying position to a standing position. **Ex.** *She was unable to rise from her seat.* 2. get out of bed; get up after sleeping. **Ex.** *He rises early in the morning.* 3. gain rank, fortune, etc. **Ex.** *Everyone expects him to rise to a top position in the company.* 4. become greater, higher, or stronger. **Ex.** *His voice began to rise as he spoke.* —*n.* 1. the act of rising. **Ex.** *His rise to a position of wealth came suddenly.* 2. increase or advance. **Ex.** *We expect a rise in foods prices this winter.* 3. a hill; a piece of ground higher than that surrounding it. **Ex.** *The city was built on a rise.* —**give rise to,** cause; produce. **Ex.** *His words gave rise to doubts concerning his true intentions.*

risk (3) [risk'], *n.* the possibility of loss, damage, injury; danger. **Ex.** *There are some risks in every adventure.* —*v.* 1. place in a position of danger. **Ex.** *He risked his life to save the child.* 2. take the chance of. **Ex.** *He was not willing to risk losing any more money.* —**risk'y,** *adj.* dangerous.

rival (3) [ray'vəl], *n.* one who tries to equal or do better than another; one who competes for something. **Ex.** *The two boys were rivals for the first prize.* —*adj.* trying for the same thing; competing. **Ex.** *They worked for rival businesses.* —*v.* 1. try to do better. **Ex.** *The two teams rivaled each other for first place.* 2. equal; be as good as. **Ex.** *Nothing can rival the beauty of a sunrise.* —**ri'val·ry,** *n.*

river (1) [riv'ər], *n.* a large body of water that flows into another river, a lake, or an ocean. **Ex.** *After four weeks of rain, the river was swollen to flood level.*

road (1) [rowd'], *n.* 1. a public way or passage for traveling between places by car, bus, etc. **Ex.** *That road takes you to the city quickly.* 2. way; path; course. **Ex.** *He seems to be on the road to fame and fortune.*

roam (4) [rowm'], *v.* wander; go from place to place without plan. **Ex.** *The dog roamed the fields.*

roar (2) [rɔːrˈ], *v.* 1. make a loud, deep cry or sound. **Ex.** *The bull roared in anger.* 2. shout or laugh loudly. **Ex.** *The audience roared at his jokes.* —*n.* a loud, deep sound or noise. **Ex.** *They could hear the roar of the ocean waves.*

roast (3) [rowstˈ], *v.* cook food without water, fat, or oil by placing over fire or in an oven. **Ex.** *Instead of frying, she roasted the meat.* —*n.* a piece of meat cooked or to be cooked in an oven or over a fire. **Ex.** *We had a roast for dinner.* —*adj.* prepared by roasting. **Ex.** *We like roast chicken.*

rob (3) [rabˈ], *v.* take money or property of another by force; steal. **Ex.** *Their house was robbed last night.* —**robˈber,** *n.* —**robˈber·y,** *n.*

robe (3) [rowbˈ], *n.* 1. a long, loose garment worn over other clothes; a gown. **Ex.** *He wore a robe over his pajamas.* 2. a specially shaped, long gown worn by a judge, a priest, etc., showing rank or office.

robin (5) [rabˈin], *n.* a bird with a dark back and a reddish-orange breast.

rock (1) [rakˈ], *n.* 1. a broken piece of stone. **Ex.** *The boy threw a rock through the window.* 2. a large mass of stone, sometimes forming a cliff. **Ex.** *They climbed up on the rock.* —*v.* move back and forth or from side to side; shake strongly. **Ex.** *The chair was rocked by the wind.* —**rockˈy,** *adj.* 1. like rock or having many pieces of stone. 2. moving back and forth; not steady.

rock-bottom [rakˈbatˈəm], *adj.* at the lowest level or limit. **Ex.** *That is the rock-bottom price he will accept.* —**rock bottom,** *n.*

rocket (5) [rakˈət], *n.* a tubelike device moved through the air or into space by burning gases and letting them escape from the rear or bottom. **Ex.** *Rockets placed the spacecraft in orbit around the moon.*

ROCKET

rod (3) [radˈ], *n.* a straight, thin piece of wood, metal, etc. **Ex.** *She hung the curtains on a rod.*

rode (2) [rowdˈ], *v.* past tense of ride. **Ex.** *The boy rode on his bicycle.*

rogue (5) [rowg'], *n.* 1. a person who is not honest and has no principles. **Ex.** *That rogue sold him worthless goods.* 2. a mischievous, fun-loving person. **Ex.** *The little rogue hid my hat.*

role (3) [rowl'], *n.* 1. a part, or character, which an actor takes in a movie or play. **Ex.** *His role in that movie proved his acting ability.* 2. a part or function assumed in life. **Ex.** *His new role as a parent required patience.*

roll (1) [rowl'], *v.* 1. move or be moved like a ball, by turning over and over. **Ex.** *The ball rolled down the hill.* 2. move or be moved on wheels. **Ex.** *The train rolled along rapidly.* 3. wind into a ball or into a rounded shape. **Ex.** *She rolled the string into a ball.* 4. move along regularly and evenly. **Ex.** *Great waves rolled toward the shore.* 5. spread out and make flat by pressing with rollers. **Ex.** *The workers rolled the metal into thin sheets.* —*n.* 1. anything formed into a ball or tube shape. **Ex.** *She bought a roll of paper.* 2. bread baked in a small rounded portion. **Ex.** *He ate two rolls with his lunch.* 3. a list of names of members of a group. —**roll out,** 1. flatten, 2. unwind. —**roll up,** 1. wind into a ball or tube shape. 2. increase. —**roll'er,** *n.* 1. a long rounded object that rolls, smooths, or crushes. 2. small wheel.

roll call [rowl' kɔ:l'], a reading aloud of a roll of names so as to learn who is present. **Ex.** *He was not present at roll call.*

roller skate [row'lər skeyt'], a skate with four wheels for skating on hard surfaces other than ice.

romance (3) [rowmæns', row'mæns], *n.* 1. a love affair. **Ex.** *Their romance began in high school.* 2. a story of heroic deeds and exciting scenes appealing to the imagination; a story of love. **Ex.** *She enjoyed reading romances.* 3. the quality of excitement and love. **Ex.** *They traveled seeking adventure and romance.* —**ro·man'tic,** *adj.* 1. characteristic of or suggesting romance. 2. not practical; tending to dream.

roof (2) [ruwf', ruf'], *n.* 1. the outside top cover of a building. **Ex.** *The roof was beginning to leak.* 2. something which in form or position is like a roof. **Ex.** *He slept in the open; the sky was his roof.* —*v.* cover with a roof. **Ex.** *The house was roofed with tin.*

room (1) [ruwm', rum'], *n.* 1. an area of a building enclosed by walls. **Ex.** *For dinner they went from the living room into the dining room.* 2. space. **Ex.** *There is room in the car* *for one more person.* 3. opportunity. **Ex.** *There is room for advancement in his job.* —**room'er,** *n.* one who rents a room. —**rooming house,** a house in which rooms can be rented. —**room'mate,** *n.* another person with whom one shares a room, house, etc. **Ex.** *She and her roommate work in the same office.*

rooster (3) [ruw'stər], *n.* a male chicken.

root (2) [ruwt¹, rut¹], *n.* 1. the part of a plant that is under the ground and takes food from the soil. **Ex.** *Trees have large roots.* 2. a part of a tooth, hair, nerve, etc. which is under the skin. **Ex.** *The root of the tooth had to be removed.* 3. cause; origin. **Ex.** *Improper food was the root of her trouble.* —*v.* send out roots and begin to grow.

ROOSTER

root (2) [ruwt¹, rut¹], *v.* dig up or search for something. **Ex.** *The pigs rooted in the straw with their noses.*

rope (2) [rowp¹], *n.* a strong cord made of twisted smaller cords. **Ex.** *He led the cow by a rope around its neck.*

rose (2) [rowz¹], *v.* past tense of *rise.* **Ex.** *They rose early in the morning.*

ROPE

rose (2) [rowz¹], *v.* 1. a bush having sweet-smelling flowers on stems with thorns; the flower itself. **Ex.** *Red roses were growing in the garden.* 2. a pinkish-red color. —**ros'y,** *adj.* 1. pink or pinkish-red. 2. fresh; healthy. 3. cheerful; happy. **Ex.** *She has a rosy smile.*

rot (3) [rat¹], *v.* 1. become soft and inedible; spoil. **Ex.** *The apples on the ground rotted.* 2. cause to decay or spoil. **Ex.** *Too much rain rotted the roots of the plants.* —**rot'ten,** *adj.* spoiled; decayed; very bad. **Ex.** *Those eggs smell as if they are rotten.*

rotate (5) [row'teyt], *v.* 1. turn around the center; revolve; spin like a ball. **Ex.** *The earth rotates once in twenty-four hours.* 2. alternate; take turns. **Ex.** *The men rotate at the job so no one gets too tired.* —**ro·ta'tion,** *n.*

rough (2) [rəf¹], *adj.* 1. uneven; unpolished; not smooth. **Ex.** *The wall was made of rough stones.* 2. not gentle in actions. **Ex.** *His rough manner frightened her.* 3. full of wild activity which can hurt. **Ex.** *Several people were hurt in the rough game.* 4. raging with storms and winds. **Ex.** *We had a rough* *sea voyage.* 5. having little comfort or luxury. **Ex.** *The early settlers lived a rough life.* 6. not finished; done in haste and without detail. **Ex.** *He showed me a rough sketch for the painting.* —**rough'en,** *v.* become or cause to become rough. —**rough'ly,** *adv.* not exactly. **Ex.** *I told you roughly what they said.*

round (1) [rawnd'], *adj.* 1. having the shape of a ball, ring, or circle. **Ex.** *Coins are round.* 2. curving; not flat. **Ex.** *We could see the round top of the hill above the trees.* —*adv.* 1. on all sides; in a circle. **Ex.** *They gathered round and listened to him.* 2. in a circle. **Ex.** *The wheel turned round.* —*prep.* 1. enclosing; encircling. **Ex.** *He had a string tied round his finger.* 2. on all sides of. **Ex.** *They gathered round the speaker.* —*n.* a series of events; a routine. **Ex.** *They went to a round of parties during the holidays.* —**rounds,** *n.* a walk, trip, visit, etc. regularly taken in the course of some business or duty. **Ex.** *The doctor is making his rounds.* —**round off** or **out,** 1. make round or curved. **Ex.** *They rounded off the sharp corners.* 2. express a number in the nearest number easy to add, subtract, etc. **Ex.** *He had 147, and we rounded it off to 150.* —**round up,** bring together. **Ex.** *Round up the children.*

roundabout [rawnd'əbawt'], *adj.* not direct. **Ex.** *He was late because he went home by a roundabout way.*

round trip [rawnd' trip'], a trip there and back. **Ex.** *How much is the fare for the round trip?*

rouse (4) [rawz'], *v.* 1. awaken. **Ex.** *The noise roused the baby.* 2. excite. **Ex.** *The incident roused the people to protest.*

rout (5) [rawt'], *n.* a complete defeat, with great confusion and a forced retreat. **Ex.** *The rout of their army ended the war.* —*v.* cause to flee. **Ex.** *The police routed the attacking mob.*

route (2) [ruwt', rawt'], *n.* 1. a way or road for passage or travel. **Ex.** *He had a choice between the shorter or the better route.* 2. a group of customers to whom regular deliveries are made. **Ex.** *The boy has a newspaper route.* —*v.* send by a certain way. **Ex.** *The policeman routed the traffic around the fire.*

routine (4) [ruwtiyn'], *n.* a way of doing things regularly, daily, etc., because of rules or habit. **Ex.** *She quickly became accustomed to the office routine.* —*adj.* done by routine; not requiring much thought. **Ex.** *She is assigned only routine duties.*

row (1) [row¹], *n.* a series of persons or things arranged in a line. **Ex.** *The last two rows of seats were empty.*

row (1) [row¹], *v.* move a boat by using two poles with broad, flat ends. **Ex.** *He rowed the boat across the river.*

row (1) [raw¹], *n.* a noisy quarrel. **Ex.** *We were awakened by a row in the house next door.*

rowboat [row¹bowt¹], *n.* a small boat moved by rowing. **Ex.** *They crossed the river in a rowboat.*

royal (2) [roy¹əl], *adj.* 1. referring to a king, queen, or ruler. **Ex.** *He is a member of the royal family.* 2. part of or belonging to a royal government or its ruler. **Ex.** *This is a ship of the royal navy.* —**roy·al·ly,** *adv.* —**roy·al·ty,** *n.* royal persons. —**Roy·al High·ness,** the king or queen.

rub (2) [rəb¹], *v.* 1. move something over a surface while pressing upon the surface. **Ex.** *He rubbed his sleepy eyes.* 2. move one surface against another with pressure. **Ex.** *Her shoe rubbed her heel.* 3. spread something by rubbing. **Ex.** *He rubbed wax over the wood.* 4. remove by rubbing. **Ex.** *He rubbed the dirt off his shoes.* —**rub·down¹,** *n.* a rubbing of the body for health or relaxation. **Ex.** *The nurse gave him a rubdown with alcohol.*

rubber (2) [rəb¹ər], *n.* a commercially prepared substance which stretches, made from the thick juice of certain plants growing in hot climates. **Ex.** *The tires of my car are made of rubber.* —*adj.* made of rubber. **Ex.** *The doctor wore rubber gloves.*

rubbish (5) [rəb¹iš], *n.* 1. anything useless or without value. **Ex.** *Put the rubbish in the garbage can.* 2. useless or senseless words. **Ex.** *He spoke a lot of rubbish.*

ruby (5) [ruw¹biy], *n.* a red stone, highly valued as a jewel. **Ex.** *Her ring has a ruby in it.* — *adj.* deep red in color. **Ex.** *The wine was ruby red.*

rude (3) [ruwd¹], *adj.* showing intentionally bad manners or lack of respect for others; impolite; crude. **Ex.** *His rude interruptions of the speaker lost him supporters.* —**rude·ly,** *adv.* —**rude·ness,** *n.*

ruffle (4) [rəf¹əl], *v.* 1. gather or draw into tiny folds and sew down as in cloth. **Ex.** *She ruffled the material and used it as edging on the curtains.* 2. disturb the arrangement of slightly.

Ex. *The wind ruffled her hair. —n.* a strip of ruffled material.

rug (2) [rəg'], *n.* a single piece of thick material used on a floor. Ex. *There were several small rugs in the room.*

ruin (2) [ruw'in], *n.* 1. a building that has fallen down; anything which has become worthless through bad use, age, etc. Ex. *We passed the ruin of an old castle.* 2. decay or destruction. Ex. *The church had fallen into ruin.* 3. that which is the cause of destruction or decay. Ex. *His vices were his ruin. —v.* 1. spoil; damage. Ex. *The rain ruined our plans.* 2. destroy financially. Ex. *The loss of his store by fire ruined him. —ru`in·a'tion, n. —ru'in·ous, adj.*

rule (1) [ruwl'], *n.* 1. an order; a guide for conduct which has been established. Ex. *Students must obey the school rules.* 2. the usual way of doing things; one's regular practice; usual behavior. Ex. *It is their rule to eat dinner late.* 3. the government of a king or other person in authority. Ex. *His rule over the country lasted thirty years. —v.* 1. govern; control. Ex. *The queen ruled her country well.* 2. decide officially. Ex. *The court ruled that their activities were punishable. —rul'er, n.* a person who rules a country. Ex. *The country has had only three rulers during this century. —as a rule,* generally; most often. Ex. *As a rule, he will not go to meetings. —rule out,* eliminate from consideration. Ex. *He ruled out going back to school.*

ruler [ruwl'ər], *n.* a flat strip of wood or metal with a straight edge used in drawing lines or for measuring. Ex. *He measured the width of the page with his ruler.*

ruling [ruwl'iŋ], *n.* official decision of a court. Ex. *The court's ruling supported freedom of speech.*

rum (5) [rəm'], *n.* a strong, alcoholic liquor made from the dark liquid remaining when sugar is processed. Ex. *He served his guest a cool drink made with rum.*

rumble (4) [rəm'bəl], *n.* a continuous, low, heavy sound. Ex. *She was awakened during the storm by the rumble of thunder. —v.* make a low, heavy, continuous sound. Ex. *The thunder rumbled in the distance.*

rumor (4) [ruw'mər], *n.* a report or information which may or may not be true. Ex. *There is a rumor that the president will resign. —v.* tell or spread a rumor. Ex. *It is rumored that they will marry.*

run (1) [rən'], *v.* 1. move rapidly by steps faster than those used when walking. **Ex.** *Because he was late, he had to run to catch the train.* 2. take part in a race or contest. **Ex.** *Who is running for mayor?* 3. be in operation. **Ex.** *We could not get the motor to run.* 4. go to and from. **Ex.** *A boat runs between the city and a town across the lake.* 5. lie; stretch; extend. **Ex.** *The road runs through the woods and along the river.* 6. flow; move in a stream. **Ex.** *Sweat was running from his forehead.* —*n.* the act of running. **Ex.** *He was tired after his run.* —**run'ner,** *n.* one who moves rapidly by fast steps.

runaway [rən'əwey'], *n.* a person or thing that flees from a place. **Ex.** *The runaway was returned to his family by friends.*

run-down [rən'dawn'], *adj.* in poor health or in need of fixing. **Ex.** *The run-down house needed a new roof and a new floor.*

rung (3) [rəŋ'], *v.* past participle of *ring.* **Ex.** *The bells were rung last night.* —*n.* the crosspiece of a ladder used as a step.

runner-up [rən'ərəp'], *n.* one who finished a contest behind the winner; number two. **Ex.** *Jones was the winner of the race, and I was the runner-up.*

running mate [rən'iŋ meyt'], one who seeks a lesser elected position by running with one who seeks a greater position. **Ex.** *It is customary for the presidential candidate to choose his running mate.*

run-of-the-mill [rən'əvðəmil'], *adj.* plain; ordinary. **Ex.** *The excellent actors made the run-of-the-mill play interesting.*

runway [rən'wey'], *n.* a path or road from which airplanes take off into the air or on which they land.

rural (4) [ru:r'əl], *adj.* of farming areas; concerning the country. **Ex.** *They lived in a small rural community.*

rush (1) [rəš'], *v.* go, move, or send with unusual speed. **Ex.** *The firemen rushed to the burning building.* —*n.* the hurried movement of people or things. **Ex.** *She feared the rush of cars on the street.*

rush hour [rəš' awr'], a time of much traffic each day, as people go to or return from work. **Ex.** *There are too many cars on the road during the rush hour.*

rust (3) [rəst'], *n.* a rough, reddish-brown covering which forms on iron and steel exposed to air and moisture. **Ex.** *The unpainted metal tools were covered with rust.* —*v.* 1. become covered with rust; cause to rust. **Ex.** *My knife rusted when I left it out in the rain.* 2. spoil or become dull through lack of use. **Ex.** *His talents rusted after he retired.* —**rust'y,** *adj.*

rustle (4) [rəs'əl], *v.* make sounds, as of things rubbing softly together. **Ex.** *Her silk dress rustled as she walked.* —*n.* the soft sounds of things rubbing together or moving. **Ex.** *We heard the rustle of mice in the straw.*

rustle (4) [rəs'əl], *v.* steal cattle. **Ex.** *The cowboy knew who was rustling the cattle.*

rye (5) [ray'], *n.* a grass, the grain of which is used as feed for animals or to make flour; also, the seed or grain from this grass. **Ex.** *Some people prefer the dark bread made from rye to the white bread made from wheat.*

S

S, s (1) [es'], *n.* the nineteenth letter of the English alphabet.

-s (1) [s, z], *suffix.* plural of many nouns. **Exs.** *Book, books; college, colleges; girl, girls.* — **-es,** *suffix.* plural of many other nouns. **Exs.** *Arch, arches; box, boxes; hero, heroes.*

-s (1) [s, z], *suffix.* present tense of some verbs when speaking of a person or thing. **Exs.** *Run: He runs quickly; write: She writes clearly.*

-'s (1) [s, z], *suffix.* 1. showing control or ownership. **Ex.** *That is John's book.* 2. short form of *"is."* **Ex.** *She's late.* 3. short form of *"has."* **Ex.** *He's eaten.* 4. short form of *"us."* **Ex.** *Let's start.*

sack (3) [sæk'], *n.* a bag, usually large and made of heavy, rough cloth. **Ex.** *They put the potatoes in a sack.* —*v.* put into a sack.

sacred (3) [sey'krid], *adj.* concerned with religion; holy. **Ex.** *They played sacred music.*

sacrifice (3) [sæk'rəfays'], *n.* 1. do without something for the benefit of someone else or for the purpose of obtaining something else. **Ex.** *They made great sacrifices to educate their children.* 2. the offering of something to a god; that which is offered. **Ex.** *In most religions, animal sacrifices are no longer offered.* —*v.* 1. do without for the sake of something or someone else. 2. make an offering of.

sad (1) [sæd'], *adj.* 1. unhappy. **Ex.** *Losing friends makes us very sad.* 2. causing unhappiness. **Ex.** *The sad news caused her to cry.* —**sad'den,** *v.* —**sad'ly,** *adv.* —**sad'ness,** *n.*

saddle (2) [sæd'əl], *n.* a seat, usually made of leather and placed on an animal's back, on which people sit.

SADDLE

safe (1) [seyf'], *adj.* 1. out of danger; away from harm. **Ex.** *You will be safe from the storm here.* 2. without risk. **Ex.** *It was a safe trip because of the careful way he had driven.* —*n.* a metal box in which papers, money, and other valuables are locked. **Ex.** *He had an old safe in his office.* —**safe'ly,** *adv.*

safeguard [seyf'gard'], *n.* anything that protects or increases safety. **Ex.** *The brick walls are a safeguard against fires.*

safety (1) [seyf'tiy], *n.* freedom from danger or harm. **Ex.** *They had no accidents on the road and reached home in safety.* —*adj.* intended as or providing protection. **Ex.** *Please fasten your safety belt.*

said (1) [sed'], *v.* past tense and participle of *say.* **Ex.** *He said yesterday that we would go.*

sail (1) [seyl'], *n.* a large piece of cloth raised over a boat so that wind moves the boat. —*v.* 1. travel by boat or ship. **Ex.** *We are sailing to Europe.* 2. start a trip by boat or ship. **Ex.** *The ship sails at midnight.* —**sail'or,** *n.* one who sails.

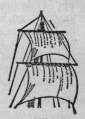

SAIL

saint (3) [seynt'], *n.* 1. a holy person. **Ex.** *They named their child after a saint.* 2. any person of unusual goodness. **Ex.** *He considered his mother a saint.* —**saint'ly,** *adj.* like a saint.

sake (2) [seyk'], *n.* 1. reason for doing. **Ex.** *He fought the war for the sake of his country's freedom.* 2. interest; benefit. **Ex.** *Please do this for my sake.*

salad (3) [sæl'əd], *n.* a dish of cold vegetables, fruit, or meat prepared with oil and vinegar or a similar sauce. **Ex.** *Potato salad is a summer favorite of mine.*

---

a, far; æ, am; e, get; ey, late; i, in; iy, see; ɔ, all; ow, go; u, put; uw, too; ə, but, ago; ər, fur; aw, out; ay, life; oy, boy; ŋ, ring; θ, think; ð, that; ž, measure; š, ship; ǰ, edge; č, child.

salary (2) [sæl'əriy], *n.* a payment at regular periods, such as once each week or month, for work done. Ex. *His salary will be increased next year.*

sale (2) [seyl'], *n.* 1. the act of selling. Ex. *The sale of the house took several months.* 2. a special selling at reduced prices. Ex. *She waited until the sale to buy her coat.* —**sal'a·ble,** *adj.* —**on sale,** 1. offered for sale. 2. offered for sale at a special price. Ex. *Hats are on sale this week.*

salesmanship [seylz'mænšip], *n.* special ability for selling.

salmon (4) [sæm'ən], *n.* a large ocean fish that is reddish-orange in color.

saloon (4) [səluwn'], *n.* a place where beer, wine, etc. is sold and drunk. Ex. *He drank beer in the saloon.*

salt (1) [sɔlt'], *n.* a white substance found in sea water and in the earth, used to season or preserve. Ex. *Salt made the meat taste better.* —*v.* season with salt. Ex. *The cook salted the potatoes.* —**salt'y,** *adj.* tasting of salt.

salt shaker [sɔlt' šey'kər], a container for salt, with holes in the top. Ex. *He used the salt shaker to season his meat.*

salute (4) [səluwt'], *v.* 1. honor by raising the right hand to the forehead. Ex. *The children saluted the flag as they passed it.* 2. greet in a way that shows honor. Ex. *He saluted the ladies with a bow.* —*n.* an act that honors, such as raising the right hand to the forehead. —**sal'u·ta'tion,** *n.* an act of greeting; spoken or written words of greeting. Ex. *"Dear Sir" is a salutation for business letters.*

salvation (5) [sælvey'šən], *n.* the act of saving from danger, difficulty, or evil. Ex. *The gambler was beyond salvation.*

same (1) [seym'], *adj.* 1. not different. Ex. *He wears the same suit every day.* 2. like one another. Ex. *Our hats are almost exactly the same color.* 3. not changed. Ex. *The condition of the sick man is the same as it was yesterday.* —*pron.* the same person, place, thing, etc. Ex. *My friend ordered tea, and I ordered the same.* —*adv.* in the same way. Ex. *She acts the same as she always did.* —**same'ness,** *n.* the quality of being the same.

sample (4) [sæm'pəl], *n.* a small part of something used to show what the whole is like; an example. Ex. *She asked for a sample of the dress material.* —*v.* find out by examining or testing a sample. Ex. *Sample the coffee to see if it is ready to drink.*

sanction (5) [sæŋ(k)'šən], *n.* 1. authority or approval by someone in authority. **Ex.** *The government gave its sanction to the new building.* 2. anything done by one or more nations to force another or others to obey international law. **Ex.** *The sanctions applied against the offending country stopped her trade.* —*v.* give permission; approve. **Ex.** *I cannot sanction such behavior.*

sand (2) [sænd'], *n.* very tiny, hard pieces of crushed rock found in great quantities in deserts and on shores. **Ex.** *The children got sand in their shoes.* —*v.* smooth or polish with sand or sandpaper. **Ex.** *The carpenter carefully sanded the wood.*

sandal (5) [sænd'əl], *n.* a kind of shoe consisting only of a sole held to the foot by narrow strips of leather.

sand bar [sænd' ba:r'], a ridge of sand formed in water by the movement of currents or tides. **Ex.** *Because of a sand bar, large ships could not enter the harbor.*

sandpaper [sænd'pey`pər], *n.* paper with sand attached to it, used for smoothing or polishing when building or making things.

sandwich (3) [sæn(d)'wič], *n.* two or more slices of bread with meat, cheese, or other filling between them. **Ex.** *They ate sandwiches for lunch.* —*v.* put between two other things. **Ex.** *Their house was sandwiched between two tall buildings.*

sane (4) [seyn'], *adj.* 1. in good mental health; having a sound mind. **Ex.** *The court judged the man sane and therefore responsible for his acts.* 2. showing good judgment or wisdom. **Ex.** *You have made a sane decision.* —**sane'ly**, *adv.* —**sane'ness, san'i·ty**, *n.*

sang (2) [sæŋ'], *v.* past tense of *sing.* **Ex.** *We sang the school song.*

sanitary (5) [sæn'əter`iy], *adj.* 1. of or concerned with health. **Ex.** *Sanitary laws are needed to protect the people.* 2. clean; lacking in dirt or anything which brings sickness. **Ex.** *The doctor made sure that the needle was sanitary.* —**san'i·ta'tion**, *n.*

sank (2) [sæŋk'], *v.* past tense of *sink.* **Ex.** *The boat sank beneath the water.*

sap (4) [sæp'], *n.* the juice in a plant or tree that carries food and water to its parts. **Ex.** *Rubber is made from the sap of a tree.*

sap (4) [sæp'], *v.* 1. exhaust gradually; weaken. **Ex.** *The dis-*

ease sapped her strength. 2. weaken by digging away the base; destroy at the base. **Ex.** *The river sapped away the foundation of the house.*

sat (1) [sæt'], *v.* past tense of *sit.* **Ex.** *He sat and read the paper.*

satellite (4) [sæt'əlayt'], *n.* 1. a smaller body in space which moves in a regular path around a larger one. **Ex.** *The moon is a satellite of the earth.* 2. a manmade body which is put into space to revolve around the earth or some other planet. **Ex.** *The American satellite could be seen in the sky.* 3. a nation that is controlled or led by a larger or stronger nation. **Ex.** *Satellites are sometimes forced to pay tribute.*

satin (4) [sæt'ən], *n.* a fine cloth with a smooth, shiny surface. **Ex.** *Her gown was made of satin.*

satisfy (2) [sæt'isfay'], *v.* 1. fulfill the desires, requirements, or demands of. **Ex.** *The water satisfied his thirst.* 2. convince. **Ex.** *Your explanation satisfies me.* 3. pay a debt; meet an obligation. **Ex.** *He could not satisfy the terms of the agreement.* —sat`is·fac'tion, *n.* —sat`is·fac'to·ry, *adj.* —sat`is·fac'to·ri·ly, *adv.*

Saturday (1) [sæt'ərdiy], *n.* the seventh day of the week.

sauce (3) [sɔ:s'], *n.* a soft or liquid preparation put on food to flavor it. **Ex.** *The vegetables were eaten with a cheese sauce.*

saucepan [sɔ:s'pæn'], *n.* a pot with a handle, used for cooking.

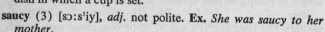

CUP AND
SAUCER

saucer (3) [sɔ:s'ər], *n.* a small, round, shallow dish in which a cup is set.

saucy (3) [sɔ:s'iy], *adj.* not polite. **Ex.** *She was saucy to her mother.*

sausage (4) [sɔ:s'ij], *n.* chopped meat flavored with salt, pepper, etc., and stuffed into an edible casing or tube. **Ex.** *She cooked sausages for dinner.*

savage (3) [sæv'ij], *adj.* 1. uncivilized; untamed. **Ex.** *They needed guns to protect themselves from savage animals.* 2. cruel. **Ex.** *His savage acts quickly turned the people against him.* 3. rough; uncultivated. **Ex.** *The pioneers found the country a savage wilderness.* —*n.* an uncivilized person. **Ex.** *Savages lived in the forest.* —sav'age·ly, *adv.* —sav'age·ness, sav'age·ry, *n.*

save (1) [seyv'], *v.* 1. make safe; remove from harm. **Ex.** *They saved the children from the fire.* 2. set apart for future use. **Ex.** *He was saving money to go to college.* 3. avoid wasting, spoiling, etc. **Ex.** *She saved the remaining meat for another meal.* —**sav'ings,** *n.* money that has been set apart for future use. **Ex.** *Her savings are in the bank.*

saw (1) [sɔ:'], *v.* past tense of *see.* **Ex.** *He saw his aunt yesterday.*

saw (1) [sɔ:'], *n.* a cutting tool that has a thin metal blade with a toothed edge. —*v.* cut with a saw.

say (1) [sey'], *v.* 1. speak. **Ex.** *What did he say?* 2. express in words. **Ex.** *The farmers say that the harvest will be good.* 3. repeat from memory. **Ex.** *Two of the children will say poems.* 4. order. **Ex.** *You must do whatever he says.* —*n.* what one desires to say. **Ex.** *They have had their say.*

SAW

scale (2) [skeyl'], *n.* one of the small, hard skin plates that cover the body of fish and some other animals. —*v.* remove scales from. **Ex.** *He scaled the fish.*

scale (2) [skeyl'], *n.* 1. a measuring instrument consisting of a series of regularly spaced marks upon the surface of a piece of wood, metal, etc., which correspond to the units of some system of measurement. **Ex.** *This ruler has a scale in inches.* 2. a relation between the actual size of an object and its size on a drawing or map. **Ex.** *The scale of this map is one inch to fifty miles.* 3. an arrangement of things in a series from low to high. **Ex.** *The scale of wages at this factory is high.* —**scale',** *v.* climb. **Ex.** *He scaled the mountain.* —**scales',** *n.* an instrument for weighing.

scan (5) [skæn'], *v.* 1. glance at quickly; read hurriedly. **Ex.** *She scanned the newspaper in a few minutes.* 2. examine carefully and closely. **Ex.** *They scanned the mountainside for any sign of the climbers.*

scandal (4) [skæn'dəl], *n.* 1. a shocking act or circumstance; something which brings shame. **Ex.** *His career was marked by many scandals.* 2. shameful talk about others, often not

a, far; æ, am; e, get; ey, late; i, in; iy, see; ɔ, all; ow, go; u, put; uw, too; ə, but, ago; ər, fur; aw, out; ay, life; oy, boy; ŋ, ring; θ, think; ð, that; ž, measure; š, ship; j, edge; č, child.

true. **Ex.** *She will not listen to scandal.* —**scan'dal·ize,** *v.* shock by shameful action or talk. —**scan'dal·ous,** *adj.*

scant (5) [skænt'], *adj.* not enough; scarcely sufficient. **Ex.** *He gave scant attention to the children.* —**scant'i·ly,** *adv.* —**scant'y,** *adj.*

scar (4) [ska:r'], *n.* 1. a mark that remains after a wound, burn, etc. heals. **Ex.** *There was a scar on his right cheek.* 2. the effect on the mind of sorrow or grief. **Ex.** *Her brother's death left a scar on her memory.* —*v.* cause a scar or scars. **Ex.** *Illness scarred his face.*

scarce (2) [skeyrs'], *adj.* 1. not plentiful. **Ex.** *Sugar was scarce during the war.* 2. uncommon. **Ex.** *We lived on a road where travelers were scarce.* —**scarce'ly,** *adv.* 1. hardly. 2. definitely not. —**scar'ci·ty,** *n.* a lack. **Ex.** *There is a scarcity of food.*

scare (3) [ske:r'], *v.* cause fear; become afraid. **Ex.** *The sudden noise scared her.* —*n.* a sudden fright or alarm. **Ex.** *We had a bad scare last night.* —**scar'y,** *adj.*

scarf (3) [skarf'], *n.* 1. a wide strip of material worn about the neck or shoulders or over the head. **Ex.** *The green scarf was the color of her gloves.* 2. a long, narrow strip of material used to cover the top of a table, bureau, etc. **Ex.** *She put a white scarf on the chest of drawers.*

scatter (2) [skæt'ər], *v.* throw or sprinkle loosely in many directions. **Ex.** *The farmer scattered the grass seed.*

scene (1) [siyn'], *n.* 1. the time and place at which an action occurred or is occurring. **Ex.** *The police quickly reached the scene of the crime.* 2. a part of a play. **Ex.** *The hero appears in the first scene.* 3. a picture or view. **Ex.** *She likes to paint winter scenes.* —**scen'er·y,** *n.* 1. the surrounding views. **Ex.** *The scenery in the country is green and fresh.* 2. the background on a stage. —**scen'ic,** *adj.* having much scenery.

scent (3) [sent'], *n.* 1. an odor, especially a pleasant one. **Ex.** *The room was filled with the scent of flowers.* 2. an odor left by an animal. **Ex.** *The hunting dogs followed the scent of the fox.* —*v.* smell; give a smell to. **Ex.** *The flowers scented the room.*

schedule (4) [skej'ul], *n.* 1. a statement of the times at which events are planned to happen. **Ex.** *May I have a bus schedule?* 2. the time when something is planned to happen. **Ex.** *The train arrived on schedule.* —*v.* place in or add to a list

scheme 475 **scoff**

of things to be done; plan a time at which something is to be done. **Ex.** *When is the next meeting scheduled to take place?*

scheme (3) [skiym¹], *n.* 1. a plan of something to be done. **Ex.** *Many schemes for improving the city were offered.* 2. a secret and dishonest plan; a plot. **Ex.** *He had a scheme to get the old man's money.* 3. a manner or system of arrangement. **Ex.** *She planned a new color scheme for the room.* *v.* make secret and dishonest plans. **Ex.** *He schemed to get his brother's share of the family money.*

scholar (4) [skal'ər], *n.* 1. a person famous for his learning; a person of great learning. **Ex.** *He was respected as a great scholar of history.* 2. a student. —**schol'ar·ly,** *n.* 1. of or concerning persons of great learning. 2. showing great learning or careful study. —**schol'ar·ship,** *n.* 1. financial aid given to support and pay the expenses of a student. **Ex.** *He was given a scholarship to attend the university.* 2. great learning obtained through much reading and study.

school (1) [skuwl¹], *n.* 1. a place where people are taught. **Ex.** *The youngest child will go to school this year.* 2. the students and teachers of such a place. **Ex.** *Nearly half of the school stayed home because of bad weather.* 3. a period or course of study during which classes are held. **Ex.** *School begins in September.* 4. a department of a college or university; a place where special subjects are taught or where students are prepared for a particular profession. **Ex.** *He is studying at law school.*

science (2) [say'əns], *n.* 1. knowledge obtained by study and experiments. **Ex.** *In science, we measure carefully.* 2. any branch of such knowledge. **Ex.** *The science of medicine is changing rapidly.*

scientific (2) [say`əntif¹ik], *adj.* of or concerned with science. **Ex.** *He studied the problems in a scientific way.*

scientist (2) [say'əntist], *n.* one who knows and uses a science. **Ex.** *A scientist must always look for facts.*

scissors (3) [siz'ərz], *n.* an instrument with two handles and two blades, used for cutting, often called a pair of scissors. **Ex.** *I need a pair of scissors to cut this paper.*

SCISSORS

scoff (5) [skɔːf¹], *v.* mock; show a lack of respect for by using rude language. **Ex.** *They scoffed at his plan to build an air-*

ship. —*n.* a rude, scornful remark. **Ex.** *We ignored the scoffs of the children.*

scold (4) [skowld¹], *v.* blame sharply and in anger. **Ex.** *His parents scolded him for returning late.* —*n.* a person who often finds fault. **Ex.** *The woman next door was a scold.*

scope (4) [skowp¹], *n.* 1. range of one's freedom to act. **Ex.** *In punishing him, the guard went beyond the scope of his authority.* 2. range of one's understanding. **Ex.** *The ideas of the speaker were beyond the scope of his listeners.* 3. range or extent of material covered. **Ex.** *This book has greater scope than others on the same subject.*

scorch (5) [skɔrč¹], *v.* 1. burn only enough to change the color or taste. **Ex.** *The dress had been scorched.* 2. dry completely. **Ex.** *The sun scorched the grass.*

score (2) [skɔːr¹], *n.* 1. the record of points made by one or both sides in a game. **Ex.** *Our team had the highest score.* 2. a rating in a test or examination. **Ex.** *His score in the English test was 100 percent.* 3. very many. **Ex.** *There are scores of difficulties that must be faced.* 4. twenty of anything. **Ex.** *They have lived here for more than a score of years.* 5. written or printed music showing the parts each musician is to play or sing. **Ex.** *The score for the opera was very good.* —*v.* 1. gain points in a game. **Ex.** *We scored ten points late in the game.* 2. give or receive a rating on a test or examination. **Ex.** *The teacher scored our test papers.*

scorn (3) [skɔrn¹], *n.* 1. a feeling of anger and dislike or low regard. **Ex.** *He felt only scorn for the thief.* 2. the showing of a feeling of anger and dislike or low regard. **Ex.** *She looked at the villagers with scorn.* —*v.* 1. show a feeling of scorn. **Ex.** *In later life, he scorned his school friends.* 2. refuse to do something because of a feeling of scorn. **Ex.** *She would scorn to take anything that was not hers.* —**scorn¹ ful,** *adj.*

scour (5) [skawr¹], *v.* clean or polish by rubbing with soap or a rough material. **Ex.** *She scoured the pots and pans.*

scour (5) [skawr¹], *v.* search thoroughly for something. **Ex.** *He scoured the town looking for the boy.*

scourge (5) [skərǰ¹], *n.* 1. a cause of pain or great difficulty. **Ex.** *Poverty is still the scourge of many cities.* 2. a whip. **Ex.** *The slaves were driven by the scourge.* —*v.* 1. whip. **Ex.** *Sailors were once scourged for many kinds of offenses.* 2. cause pain or great difficulty. **Ex.** *He was scourged by the memory of his past crimes.*

scout (3) [skawt¹], *n.* 1. a soldier, plane, etc. sent out to watch the enemy and get information. Ex. *The scouts went out during the night.* 2. a member of the Boy Scouts or Girl Scouts, groups in which young people develop skills and good character. Ex. *He wants to be a Scout like his older brother.* —*v.* go out to watch and listen. Ex. *We scouted the hills beyond the river.*

scowl (4) [skawl¹], *n.* an expression of anger, doubt, etc. in which the eyebrows and the corners of the mouth point down. Ex. *He always seemed to have a scowl on his face.* —*v.* lower the eyebrows and the corners of the mouth in anger, doubt, etc. Ex. *He scowled at me when I asked for more money.*

scramble (5) [skræm¹bəl], *v.* 1. climb or crawl quickly, using hands and feet. Ex. *The boys scrambled up into the trees.* 2. struggle or compete with others in a way that is not orderly or quiet. Ex. *The children scrambled for the candy.* 3. mix together in a confused way. Ex. *His letters were scrambled together on the desk.* 4. fry eggs which are stirred and mixed. Ex. *She scrambled eggs for breakfast.* —*n.* 1. a quick climb or crawl using hands and feet. Ex. *We were tired from our scramble up the hill.* 2. a disorderly struggle or fight for something. Ex. *The game became a wild scramble for the ball.*

scrap (4) [skræp¹], *n.* 1. a small bit of something; a small part. Ex. *She wrote on a scrap of paper.* 2. old or broken material. Ex. *He buys and sells scrap.* —*adj.* in bits or pieces. Ex. *Scrap metal is often melted and used again.* —*v.* 1. break into pieces; convert into broken metal. Ex. *The owners have decided to scrap the old boat.* 2. throw away something or stop doing something no longer of any value. Ex. *Our carefully prepared plan had to be scrapped.* —**scraps,** *n.* bits of food remaining after eating. Ex. *They fed the scraps to the dog.*

scrape (3) [skreyp¹], *v.* 1. rub with a sharp tool or rough material to make a smooth or clean surface. Ex. *The sailors were scraping the deck of the ship.* 2. remove something by scraping. Ex. *We scraped the old paint from the furniture.* 3. rub something against a rough surface accidentally.

Ex. *She scraped her arm on the rocks.* 4. gather slowly and with difficulty. **Ex.** *He scraped together enough money to buy food.* —*n.* the act or sound of rubbing with something rough. **Ex.** *We heard the scrape of a window opening.*

scratch (3) [skræč'], *v.* 1. tear or mark a surface with something sharp. **Ex.** *The thorns scratched his arms and legs.* 2. rub with the fingernails. **Ex.** *He scratched his head thoughtfully.* 3. make a sharp, unpleasant noise by rubbing against a surface. **Ex.** *His old pen scratched badly as he wrote.* —*n.* 1. a tear, mark, or wound. **Ex.** *There was a deep scratch on the tabletop.* 2. a sharp, unpleasant noise. **Ex.** *We heard only the scratch of his pen.*

scream (2) [skriym'], *v.* cry out loudly and sharply. **Ex.** *We heard someone scream in fright.* —*n.* a loud, sharp cry. **Ex.** *A scream for help came from inside the building.*

screech (5) [skriyč'], *v.* 1. give a sharp, high scream. **Ex.** *The dying bird screeched loudly.* 2. make a high, sharp sound. **Ex.** *The car screeched to a sudden stop.* —*n.* a high, sharp sound or scream. **Ex.** *He heard a screech of anger from the old woman.*

screen (3) [skriyn'], *n.* 1. a net or cloth of fine wire with small openings through which only extremely small objects can pass. **Ex.** *The windows were covered with screens to keep out insects.* 2. a frame or curtain used to protect or conceal. **Ex.** *During the day the bed was hidden by a screen.* 3. a surface on which movies or other pictures are projected. **Ex.** *The screen was covered with silver paint.* —*v.* 1. protect or conceal. **Ex.** *The bushes screened the animals from the hunters.* 2. separate large pieces from small by using a separator. **Ex.** *The broken stone is screened into two sizes.* 3. separate or select people or things by carefully examining. **Ex.** *The workers were screened to determine their mechanical ability.*

screw (3) [skruw'], *n.* a metal fastener that is forced into place by turning. —*v.* fasten or tighten using a screw or screws.

script (5) [skript'], *n.* 1. handwriting. **Ex.** *I recognized my father's careful script.* 2. a written or printed copy of a play used by the actors and directors when preparing for a performance. **Ex.** *She studied the script until she knew her part.*

SCREW

scrub (4) [skrəb'], *v.* wash by rubbing hard with a brush or cloth. **Ex.** *She scrubs the floor every week.*

sculptor (5) [skəlp'tər], *n.* an artist who makes figures or designs by carving, cutting, or molding. **Ex.** *The sculptor made the statue from a block of white stone.*

sculpture (4) [skəlp'čər], *n.* 1. the art of carving, cutting, or modeling figures or designs in various materials, such as wood, stone, and metal. **Ex.** *She studied both painting and sculpture.* 2. the product of such work. **Ex.** *His sculpture of a horse won first prize.* —*v.* form, carve, make a sculpture. **Ex.** *He sculptured a head of the great man.*

sea (1) [siy'], *n.* 1. the salt water that covers the greater part of the earth's surface. **Ex.** *Many ships sail the seas.* 2. any large body of water, smaller than an ocean, and partly or entirely enclosed by land. —**at sea,** on the sea; sailing. **Ex.** *The boat has been at sea for an hour.*

seaboard [siy'bɔrd'], *n.* shore at the edge of a sea. **Ex.** *There are many fishing villages along the seaboard.*

seafood [siy'fuwd'], ocean fish eaten as food. **Ex.** *That restaurant serves good seafood.*

seal (3) [siyl'], *n.* 1. a warm-blooded sea animal living mostly in cold regions. 2. the fur of this animal; sealskin.

SEAL

seal (3) [siyl'], *n.* 1. an impression or design placed on papers, etc. to show that they are official or legal; the device for making such an impression. **Ex.** *The paper had been stamped with the required official seal.* 2. any paper, metal, or other device placed upon a closed door, envelope, etc. in such a way that it cannot be opened without breaking the device. **Ex.** *The seal had been broken on one of the railroad cars.* —*v.* 1. close or fasten tightly. **Ex.** *She sealed the letter.* 2. settle finally; determine definitely. **Ex.** *The decision of the jury sealed the man's fate.*

SEAL 1

sea level [siy' lev'əl], the level of the sea halfway between low and high tides, from which heights are measured. **Ex.** *That hill is 500 feet above sea level.*

seam (4) [siym'], *n.* the line which indicates where two pieces of cloth, leather, etc. have been joined or sewn together. **Ex.** *The sleeve tore at the seam.*

seamanship [siy'mənšip'], *n.* skill in sailing. **Ex.** *Without his seamanship, the ship would have sunk.*

seaplane [siy'pleyn'], *n.* a plane built to land on water.

seashell [siy'šel'], *n.* the hard outer covering of certain forms of sea life. **Ex.** *There were many kinds of seashells on the beach.*

seasick [siy'sik'], *adj.* sick because of the rolling movement of a ship on water. **Ex.** *During the storm, he became seasick.*

search (2) [sərč'], *v.* 1. examine carefully or look through in order to find something. **Ex.** *They searched the house for the lost ring.* 2. examine a person or his personal things in order to find a gun, stolen property, etc. **Ex.** *Both of the men were searched by the police.* —*n.* the act of searching. **Ex.** *He came here in his search for work.*

seaweed [siy'wiyd'], *n.* any plant in the sea. **Ex.** *His foot was caught in the seaweed.*

season (1) [siy'zən], *n.* 1. one of the four parts into which the year is divided. **Ex.** *Winter is the coldest season of the year.* 2. a particular time during the year which is noticeably different from others. **Ex.** *Many people go to the beaches during the holiday season.* —*v.* change or increase the flavor. **Ex.** *She seasoned the meat with salt and pepper.* —**in season,** in the time of year in which something is easily available. **Ex.** *Fresh vegetables are in season during the summer.*

seasoning [siy'zəniŋ], *n.* flavoring that changes the taste of food. **Ex.** *Salt is the most common seasoning.*

seat (1) [siyt'], *n.* 1. the thing on which one sits. **Ex.** *There were four hundred seats in the theater.* 2. the part of the chair on which one places the body. **Ex.** *The seat of the chair was broken.* 3. the part of the body or the part of the clothing on which one sits. **Ex.** *The seat of his trousers was torn.* 4. place to sit or the right to sit there. **Ex.** *He lost his seat in Congress.* 5. the place at which the center of anything is established; the center of government. **Ex.** *This town is the county seat.* —*v.* place on a seat; cause to sit down. **Ex.** *He seated himself beside his friend.* —**be seated, take a seat,** sit. **Exs.** *Please be seated. Please take a seat.*

second (1) [sek'ənd], *adj.* 1. following after one another. **Ex.** *He arrived on the second bus.* 2. the same or about the same as another; another. **Ex.** *A second bathroom is at the end* *of the hall.* —*n.* the one following one other in time, place, importance, etc. Ex. *You are the second to ask that question.* —*adv.* in the place behind or after the first. Ex. *He finished second in the race.* —**sec·ond·ar·y,** *adj.* 1. higher than elementary. Ex. *The older children are in secondary school.* 2. having less power or value. Ex. *The color of the material was a matter of only secondary importance.*

second (1) [sek'ənd], *n.* 1. one of the sixty parts into which a minute is divided. Ex. *This clock is thirty seconds slow.* 2. a moment; a short time. Ex. *For a second he saw a bright light.*

second-class [sek'ənd klæs'], *adj.* not the best or of the best but next to it. Ex. *He stayed at a second-class hotel.*

secondhand [sek'əndhænd'], *adj.* 1. not original or direct. Ex. *He heard the story from an eyewitness, but I heard only a secondhand version.* 2. not new. Ex. *That secondhand car costs only two hundred dollars.* —*adv.*

second nature [sek'ənd ney'čər], habits; actions that seem like but are not part of one's nature. Ex. *He paints so well that painting seems like second nature to him.*

second person [sek'ənd pər'sən], pronoun or verb form referring to the person to whom one is speaking. Ex. *"You" is the second-person pronoun.*

second-rate [sek'ənd reyt'], *adj.* not of the best; poor. Ex. *This is a second-rate hotel.*

secret (2) [siy'krit], *adj.* hidden from others; known only to a few. Ex. *He kept some money in a secret place.* —*n.* 1. something known only to a few and purposely hidden. Ex. *He cannot be trusted to keep a secret.* 2. something not known. Ex. *The old man had learned many of the secrets of nature.* 3. the reason for something; hidden cause. Ex. *What was the secret of his success in business?* —**se'cre·cy,** *n.* the act of keeping something secret.

secretary (2) [sek'rəter'iy], *n.* 1. a person employed to write letters, answer telephones, and manage other details of office business. Ex. *His secretary greeted his visitors.* 2. the man in charge of a government department. Ex. *A new secretary of labor has recently been appointed.*

---

a, far; æ, am; e, get; ey, late; i, in; iy, see; ɔ, all; ow, go; u, put; uw, too; ə, but, ago; ər, fur; aw, out; ay, life; oy, boy; ŋ, ring; θ, think; ð, that; ž, measure; š, ship; j, edge; č, child.

sect (5) [sekt¹], *n.* a group of people, usually religious, who, though they follow the same leader or teacher or hold the same basic beliefs, differ from other similar groups. **Ex.** *That religion has many sects.*

section (2) [sek'šən], *n.* 1. a division; a separate part. **Ex.** *She cut the orange into sections.* 2. a separate or definite part of a town, city, state, or region. **Ex.** *They live in the old section of the city.* —**sec'tion·al,** *adj.* of or concerned with a section.

secure (2) [sikyu:r¹], *adj.* 1. safe from danger; protected against harm. **Ex.** *The fort was secure against any surprise attack.* 2. free from fear or concern. **Ex.** *He was secure in the knowledge that his friends would help him.* 3. fixed firmly; strong. **Ex.** *The house was built upon a secure foundation.* —*v.* 1. fasten firmly in place. **Ex.** *Before the storm, we secured the doors and windows.* 2. get possession of; obtain. **Ex.** *She is hoping to secure a position in a library.* 3. guard; make safe. **Ex.** *A police guard secured the bank against robbery.* —**se·cure'ly,** *adv.*

security (3) [sikyu:r¹ətiy], *n.* 1. a feeling of safety; freedom from danger or harm. **Ex.** *They fled to the security of the mountains.* 2. protection. **Ex.** *They put a new lock on the door as security.* 3. something given or promised as a sign that a debt will be paid. **Ex.** *Their house was their security for the loan.* —**se·cur'i·ties,** *n.* stocks and bonds.

see (1) [siy¹], *v.* 1. come to know or sense by means of the eyes; have the power of sight. **Ex.** *Can you see the bird in that tree?* 2. understand; know the meaning or manner. **Ex.** *He could not see how the money had been spent.* 3. find out; learn. **Ex.** *See whether he has arrived yet.* 4. meet. **Ex.** *I sometimes see him on the street.*

seed (1) [siyd¹], *n.* 1. the part of a plant from which a new plant grows. **Ex.** *This plant grew from a very small seed.* 2. that from which anything grows; a beginning; a source. **Ex.** *The seed of doubt has been planted in his mind.* —*v.* plant with seeds. **Ex.** *Half of the garden has already been seeded.* —**seed'less,** *adj.* without seeds.

seek (2) [siyk¹], *v.* 1. go in search of. **Ex.** *They were seeking a pass through the mountains.* 2. try to obtain; attempt to get. **Ex.** *He is seeking election to the office of mayor.*

seem (1) [siym¹], *v.* appear to be; give the impression of. **Ex.** *She seems tired.*

seen (1) [siyn'], *v.* past participle of *see*. Ex. *I have seen him before*.

seize (2) [siyz'], *v.* 1. take hold of quickly and firmly; grasp. Ex. *She seized the child by the arm*. 2. take control of. Ex. *The army seized the town*.

seldom (2) [sel'dəm], *adv.* rarely; not very often. Ex. *They are seldom at home*.

select (2) [səlekt'], *v.* choose. Ex. *She selected the material carefully.* —*adj.* of fine quality; special; chosen with care. Ex. *That shop sells select fruits.* —se·lec'tion, *n.* 1. the act of selecting. 2. that which is selected. —se·lec'tive, *adj.* specially chosen; tending to select. Ex. *She is selective about the clothes she buys*.

self (1) [self'], *n.* 1. all the qualities that cause one person to be different from others. Ex. *Not many people know his real self*. 2. a part of a person's character. Ex. *We see only his worst self in the early morning*. 3. personal interest or advantage. Ex. *He did his work with no thought of self*.

self- (1) [self], *prefix.* used with nouns and adjectives to show that: 1. the one performing the act is the one affected by it. Exs. *Control, self-control; defense, self-defense*. 2. the action is done only through its own effort or power. Exs. *Starting, self-starting; closing, self-closing*.

selfish (4) [self'iš], *adj.* caring only for oneself; thinking only of one's own comfort or advantage. Ex. *He was too selfish to share his candy*.

selfless [self'ləs], *adj.* not caring or worrying about oneself; unselfish.

self-made [self'meyd'], *adj.* having become successful unaided by others. Ex. *The owner of that business is a self-made man*.

sell (1) [sel'], *v.* 1. give something in exchange for money. Ex. *He is trying to sell his house*. 2. offer to give in exchange for money. Ex. *That store sells shoes*. 3. be offered for sale; be given in exchange for money. Ex. *Fruit sells for a higher price at the beginning of the season*.

semi- (3) [sem'i], *prefix.* 1. half or partly. Ex. *Trained, semi-trained*. 2. happening twice in a period of time. Ex. *Monthly, semi-monthly*.

Senate (2) [sen'it], *n.* the upper and smaller branch of the American Congress and legislative groups of other countries.

Ex. *A new law is being discussed by the Senate.* —**Sen·a·tor,** *n.* a member of a Senate.

send (1) [send'], *v.* 1. cause to go; permit to go. **Ex.** *They hope to send their children to the university.* 2. cause to be carried, taken, or directed to or away from a place. **Ex.** *They will send the food to the island by boat.* 3. request someone to come. **Ex.** *The sick man's wife is going to send for the doctor.*

senior (4) [siyn'yər], *adj.* 1. older. **Ex.** *He was senior to his brother by several years.* 2. more advanced in rank; longer in position or service. **Ex.** *Those who were senior received more pay.* 3. in the final year of study at high school or college. **Ex.** *Their oldest boy is in his senior year.* —*n.* 1. one who is older or holds a higher rank. **Ex.** *He was respectful toward his seniors.* 2. a student in the final year of study at a high school or college. **Ex.** *The seniors are planning a dance.* —**sen·ior'i·ty,** *n.* the position of being older, longer in service, etc. **Ex.** *Because of his seniority, he receives more pay.*

sensation (4) [sensey'šən], *n.* 1. any feeling produced by the operation of the sense of touch, sight, hearing, smelling, or tasting. **Ex.** *Touching the hot stove produced a painful sensation.* 2. that which causes excitement. **Ex.** *The show was a sensation for weeks.* —**sen·sa'tion·al,** *adj.* 1. exciting. 2. intended to shock or cause excitement.

sense (1) [sens'], *n.* 1. any of the powers by which one sees, hears, tastes, smells, or feels. **Ex.** *The old man had lost his sense of hearing.* 2. a feeling produced by one of these powers. **Ex.** *She had a sudden sense of coldness.* 3. understanding; reasoning. **Ex.** *He has a sense of what must be done in time of need.* 4. ability to feel or appreciate. **Ex.** *He has no sense of humor.* —*v.* become aware of; feel. **Ex.** *He sensed that someone was in the room.* —**sense'less,** *adj.* without reason. **Ex.** *That was a senseless thing to do.* —**sen'si·ble,** *adj.* understandable; reasonable. **Ex.** *He made sensible statements.* —**sen'si·bly,** *adv.* —**make sense,** be understandable. **Ex.** *What he says makes sense to me.*

sensitive (4) [sen'sətiv], *adj.* 1. easily or quickly affected by the senses; quick to notice or understand. **Ex.** *A sensitive teacher is aware of a student's difficulties.* 2. too much affected by the senses; easily hurt or offended. **Ex.** *She was so sensitive that she cried when the teacher corrected her.*

3. changing when acted upon by something else. **Ex.** *This chemical is sensitive to light.* —**sen`si·tiv'i·ty,** *n.*

sent (1) [sent'], *v.* past tense and participle of *send.* **Ex.** *I sent a letter to him yesterday.*

sentence (2) [sen'təns], *n.* 1. a group of words, or sometimes a single word, used to state a fact or opinion, to ask a question, or to express a command or request. **Ex.** *This author's paragraphs usually contain from three to six sentences.* 2. the punishment for committing a crime or breaking the law. **Ex.** *He served a prison sentence for his crime.* —*v.* set the punishment of a guilty person. **Ex.** *The judge sentenced him to two years in prison.*

sentiment (3) [sen'təmənt], *n.* 1. words or thoughts based on feeling rather than reason. **Ex.** *There was no time for sentiment.* 2. gentle, loving feelings which are weak or silly. **Ex.** *The young girls preferred stories full of sentiment.* 3. thoughts combined with feelings. **Ex.** *What are your sentiments about electing a new mayor?* —**sen·ti·men'tal,** *adj.* —**sen·ti·men'tal·ly,** *adv.*

separate (1) [sep'əreyt'], *v.* 1. force apart; keep apart. **Ex.** *The policemen separated the fighters.* 2. keep apart by being between. **Ex.** *A wall separates the two gardens.* 3. part; go away from each other. **Ex.** *We said goodnight and separated outside the theater.* 4. divide into parts or groups; set apart. **Ex.** *The farmer's wife separated the cream from the milk.* —**sep·a·ra'tion,** *n.*

separate (1) [sep'(ə)rit], *adj.* 1. not together. **Ex.** *They ate at separate tables.* 2. different; distinct. **Ex.** *Her stories have been printed in thirty separate magazines.* 3. independent; existing alone. **Ex.** *In the United States, the church and state are separate.* —**sep'a·rate·ly,** *adv.*

September (1) [septem'bər], *n.* the ninth month of the year.

sequence (5) [siy'kwəns], *n.* 1. the condition of one thing following after another. **Ex.** *Can you remember the sequence of events yesterday?* 2. the order of things in time or position. **Ex.** *The books were arranged in sequence according to author.*

serene (5) [səriyn'], *adj.* calm; peaceful. **Ex.** *The morning sky was serene.* —**se·rene'ly,** *adv.* —**se·ren'i·ty,** *n.*

---

a, far; æ, am; e, get; ey, late; i, in; iy, see; ɔ, all; ow, go; u, put; uw, too; ʌ, but, ago; ər, fur; aw, out; ay, life; oy, boy; ŋ, ring; θ, think; ð, that; ž, measure; š, ship; ǰ, edge; č, child.

sergeant (4) [sar'jənt], *n.* 1. one of the highest grades of enlisted men. **Ex.** *The sergeant led the troops.* 2. a police officer one rank above an ordinary policeman. **Ex.** *A sergeant and two policemen arrived at the scene of the crime.*

series (2) [si:r'iyz], *n.* a number of similar things or events which follow regularly one after another in time, position, or order. **Ex.** *She attended all the lectures in the series.*

serious (2) [si:r'iyəs], *adj.* 1. thoughtful, earnest, or grave in action and character. **Ex.** *He spoke about the problem in a serious way.* 2. important; needing careful attention. **Ex.** *I am reading a serious book.* 3. dangerous. **Ex.** *He was in a serious automobile accident.* —**se'ri·ous·ly**, *adv.* —**se'ri·ous·ness**, *n.*

sermon (4) [sər'mən], *n.* 1. a talk on a religious subject. **Ex.** *His sermons were always interesting.* 2. a talk on one's morals or manners that bores or angers. **Ex.** *The boy objected to his mother's frequent sermons.*

servant (3) [sər'vənt], *n.* a person employed to do household work in the home of another. **Ex.** *They have two servants, a cook and a maid.* —**civil servant,** a person who works for a government. —**public servant,** a person who is appointed or elected to a government position. **Ex.** *John F. Kennedy was a trusted public servant.*

serve (1) [sərv'], *v.* 1. give food or drink to. **Ex.** *Let me serve you some pie.* 2. assist; help. **Ex.** *Let me know if I can serve you in any way.* 3. work as an official; be employed by the government, especially in the military. **Ex.** *He has served his country in the army for six years.* 4. work as a servant. **Ex.** *The cook had served a wealthy family for many years.*

service (1) [sər'vis], *n.* 1. a helpful act; something done for another. **Ex.** *He did me a great service once.* 2. work done for money. **Ex.** *He needed the services of a lawyer.* 3. the organized supply of something needed. **Ex.** *The bus service in this town is good.* 4. the army, navy, air force, etc. **Ex.** *He spent several years in the service.* 5. a religious ceremony. **Ex.** *He went to the early Sunday morning service.* —**civil service,** the nonmilitary people who work for the government. **Ex.** *He has been in the civil service for many years.* —**serv'ice·a·ble,** *adj.* able to provide good service; long wearing.

session (4) [seš'ən], *n.* 1. the meeting of a group, court, etc. **Ex.** *He missed the first session of the class.* 2. a series of meetings of a class, group, etc. **Ex.** *He went to the spring session at the university.*

set (1) [set¹], *v.* 1. put in a place or position. **Ex.** *She set the lamp on the table.* 2. put in some condition. **Ex.** *He set the house on fire.* 3. put into the right condition; put in order. **Ex.** *She has set the hands of the clock to the correct time.* 4. assign a time, price, or limit to. **Ex.** *We set the time of our meeting for six o'clock.* 5. place a jewel into the metal part of a piece of jewelry. **Ex.** *The diamond was set in a gold ring.* 6. sink below the place where the sky and the earth seem to meet. **Ex.** *The sun sets early in winter.* —*adj.* fixed; established; firm. **Ex.** *School usually begins at a set time.* —*n.* a number of persons, things, activities, etc. that form a group or are related in some way. **Exs.** *She bought a set of dishes. Their meeting resulted from a strange set of circumstances.* —**set'ting,** *n.* 1. the act of putting in place, in order, etc. 2. the metal part in which a jewel is fixed. **Ex.** *The diamond was in a gold setting.* 3. the time and place of a play, story, etc. **Ex.** *New York, 1945, is the setting of the play.* 4. the surrounding scene or view. **Ex.** *The house is located in a beautiful setting.* —**set aside,** 1. keep for a purpose; not in use at the time. **Ex.** *He set some money aside for later use.* 2. dismiss; reject; in law, rule contrary to another court. **Ex.** *The lower court decision was set aside, and he was freed.* —**set back,** slow or reverse progress. **Ex.** *I was set back in my work by illness.* —**set down,** write on paper. **Ex.** *Set down your ideas before you forget them.* —**set forth,** 1. begin a trip. **Ex.** *He set forth for town.* 2. explain; present. **Ex.** *He set forth his ideas in a speech and in a book.* —**set off,** 1. explode. **Ex.** *He set off a firecracker.* 2. begin an action. **Ex.** *He set off for town.* 3. make noticeable by contrast. **Ex.** *The house was set off by two tall trees.* —**set on, set upon,** attack. **Ex.** *He was set on by robbers.* —**set out,** 1. begin an action. **Ex.** *He set out for town.* 2. place where it can be noticed. **Ex.** *He set out the pictures on the table.* —**set to,** begin seriously. **Ex.** *He set to work and finished the job quickly.* —**set up,** build; establish. **Ex.** *He set up a good business.*

settle (1) [set¹əl], *v.* 1. agree upon; decide. **Ex.** *He helped me settle on which car to buy.* 2. put in order; put in place. **Ex.** *He settled his affairs before leaving town.* 3. make a home or homes. **Ex.** *Fearless men settled in the wilderness.* 4. quiet; calm. **Ex.** *His words settled our fears.* 5. sink; move

downward. **Ex.** *The boat settled to the bottom of the river.*
6. pay money that is owed. **Ex.** *He settled his bills monthly.*
—**set'tle·ment,** *n.* 1. the act of settling. 2. a place where
people have recently built homes; a village. **Ex.** *There are
few settlements in the wilderness.* 3. an amount of money
paid according to an agreement. —**sett'ler,** *n.*

seven (1) [sev'ən], *n., adj.* the number between six and eight;
the number 7. —**sev'enth,** *adj., n.* coming after six others.
—**sev`en·teen',** *n., adj.* the number *17.* —**sev`en·teenth',** *adj.,
n.* coming after sixteen others. —**sev'en·ty,** *n., adj.* the number *70.* —**sev'en·ti·eth`,** *adj., n.* coming after sixty-nine
others.

several (1) [sev'(ə)rəl], *adj.* three or more, but not many. **Ex.**
There were several people waiting in the office.

severe (3) [səvi:r'], *adj.* 1. not gentle; cruel; strict. **Ex.** *The
man was given a severe punishment.* 2. causing much pain
or damage. **Ex.** *They were not prepared for the severe storm.*
3. not bright or lively; plain in appearance. **Ex.** *She wore a
severe, dark dress.* —**se·vere'ly,** *adv.* —**se·ver'i·ty,** *n.*

sew (2) [sow'], *v.* 1. mend; join or unite together with needle
and thread. **Ex.** *She sewed the button on his coat.* 2. use
needle and thread. **Ex.** *She likes to sew.* —**sew'ing,** *n.* 1. the
act or work of using needle and thread. 2. something that
has been, or needs to be, sewed. **Ex.** *Her sewing for the day
was on the table.*

sex (3) [seks'], *n.* 1. either the male or female group into
which all living things are divided. **Ex.** *Children of both
sexes attend this school.* 2. the characteristic of being male
or female. **Ex.** *The sex of some birds can be determined by
their feathers.* —**sex'u·al,** *adj.*

shabby (4) [šæb'iy], *adj.* 1. faded and ragged from hard wear.
Ex. *He was wearing a shabby suit.* 2. dressed in faded, ragged clothes. **Ex.** *He looked shabby.* 3. mean; impolite. **Ex.**
They acted in a shabby way. —**shab'bi·ly,** *adv.* —**shab'bi·
ness,** *n.*

shack (5) [šæk'], *n.* a roughly or cheaply built hut. **Ex.** *There
were several shacks along the railroad track.*

shade (1) [šeyd'], *n.* 1. darkness or dimness caused by something which blocks the rays of the sun or of other light. **Ex.**
We sat in the shade of a large tree. 2. something which is
used to cut off the rays of the sun or of a lamp. **Ex.** *The
window shades were made of green cloth.* 3. the amount of

darkness in a color. **Ex.** *She chose a light shade of green paint for the walls.* —*v.* 1. prevent light from reaching; darken. **Ex.** *She shaded her head with an umbrella.* 2. increase the amount of darkness in a color. **Ex.** *The artist shaded part of the house in his picture.* —**shad'y,** *adj.*

shadow (2) [šæd'ow], *n.* 1. a dark image that is made by something that blocks a source of light. **Ex.** *With the light behind him, his shadow could be seen on the wall.* 2. something only slightly present. **Ex.** *The shadow of a smile could be seen on her lips.*

shaft (5) [šæft'], *n.* 1. a long, slender rod or bar, such as the handle of a spear or the long slender parts of tools or machines. **Ex.** *The broken shaft of the car was repaired in the garage.* 2. a narrow opening which goes through the floors of a building or an opening into a mine. **Ex.** *Men go into the mine through that shaft.*

shake (1) [šeyk'], *v.* 1. move or cause to move back and forth or up and down in short, quick movements. **Ex.** *The two men stopped to shake hands.* 2. throw upon or stir by using such movements. **Ex.** *She was shaking salt and pepper on the roast beef.* 3. tremble. **Ex.** *The frightened boy's voice was shaking with terror.* —*n.* the act of shaking. **Ex.** *He gave an angry shake of his head.* —**shak'er,** *n.* a container in or from which something is shaken. —**shake hands,** take the hand of another in greeting, farewell, or agreement.

shall (1) [šæl], *v.* used with another verb to 1. show or ask about action in the future. **Ex.** *I shall see you tomorrow.* 2. request or suggest. **Ex.** *Shall I open the window?*

shallow (3) [šæl'ow], *adj.* 1. not deep. **Ex.** *The lake was too shallow for swimming.* 2. lacking in depth of feeling, understanding, etc. **Ex.** *She is a very shallow person.*

shame (2) [šeym'], *n.* 1. a painful feeling coming from the knowledge of something wrong or not proper, done by oneself or another. **Ex.** *She felt shame at having been so thoughtless.* 2. a loss of regard or honor. **Ex.** *The boy's stealing brought shame upon his parents.* 3. something that brings a loss of regard, honor, etc. **Ex.** *The unjust laws were the shame of the nation.* —*v.* awaken a painful feeling of guilt, loss of honor, etc. **Ex.** *He was shamed by his own*

lack of generosity. —**shame'ful,** *adj.* bringing shame upon.
—**shame'less,** *adj.* showing or feeling no shame.

shape (2) [šeyp'], 1. the form or figure of something, especially in regard to its appearance. **Ex.** *An apple and an
orange have almost the same shape.* 2. something of which
only the general form can be seen. **Ex.** *A dim shape appeared at the window.* —*v.* give form to. **Ex.** *She shaped
the meat into balls.* —**shape'ly,** *adj.* pleasing in form. **Ex.**
She has shapely legs.

share (1) [še:r'], *n.* 1. a part belonging to, given to, or owned
by a single person or a group. **Ex.** *Each son received a share
of the property.* 2. any of the equal interests or rights into
which the ownership of a company is divided. **Ex.** *He owns
two hundred shares of the business.* —*v.* 1. distribute in
portions. **Ex.** *The children shared the cake equally.* 2. use
together. **Ex.** *The two sisters shared a bedroom.* 3. join with
others; have a part of. **Ex.** *The two families shared the expenses of the trip.*

sharp (2) [šarp'], *adj.* 1. having a thin, fine cutting edge or
point. **Ex.** *She cut the meat with a sharp knife.* 2. ending in
a point or edge; somewhat pointed. **Ex.** *She had a small face
with sharp features.* 3. sudden; not gradual. **Ex.** *There is a
sharp curve in the road ahead.* 4. clear; well-defined; distinct. **Ex.** *He saw the sharp outline of a figure in the doorway.* —**sharp'en,** *v.* make or become sharp or sharper.
—**sharp'ly,** *adv.* —**sharp'ness,** *n.*

shatter (4) [šæt'ər], *v.* 1. break or burst into small pieces. **Ex.**
The mirror shattered. 2. damage; destroy completely. **Ex.**
*Their hope of finding him alive was shattered when his body
was found.*

shave (3) [šeyv'], *v.* with a sharp cutting edge remove the hair
or beard close to the skin. **Ex.** *He shaves every day.* —*n.* the
act of cutting off the beard. **Ex.** *He went to the barbershop
for a shave and a haircut.*

shawl (5) [šɔ:l'], *n.* a large scarf or piece of cloth used
around the shoulders or over the head. **Ex.** *Her shawl kept
her warm.*

she (1) [šiy'], *pron.* a female person or animal that has already been mentioned or that has been understood. **Ex.** *My
sister says that she will be late for work.*

shear (5) [ši:r¹], *v.* 1. remove from by cutting. **Ex.** *The farmers sheared the wool from the sheep.* 2. cut with a sharp instrument. **Ex.** *The machine sheared the steel into strips.* —**shears¹**, *n.* large scissors.

shed (3) [šed¹], *n.* a small structure built for the purpose of sheltering or storing, often with an open side. **Ex.** *The garden tools are in that shed.*

shed (3) [šed¹], *v.* 1. pour out; cause to fall or flow; send forth. **Ex.** *The girl shed tears over her loss.* 2. cast off; drop off. **Ex.** *Those trees shed their leaves in the autumn.* 3. keep out rain or moisture. **Ex.** *A roof sheds water.* —**shed light on,** explain; clarify. **Ex.** *His remarks shed new light on the subject.*

sheep (2) [šiyp¹], *n.* a grass-eating animal raised for its flesh and wool. —**sheep'ish,** *adj.* shy; not at ease. —**sheep'ish·ly,** *adv.*

SHEEP

sheer (5) [ši:r¹], *adj.* 1. thin enough to be seen through. **Ex.** *I could see the garden through the sheer curtains of the window.* 2. complete; absolute. **Ex.** *His story was sheer nonsense.* 3. very steep. **Ex.** *From the cliff to the river was a sheer drop of fifty feet.*

sheet (2) [šiyt¹], *n.* 1. a wide piece of cotton cloth used in pairs on a bed next to the body. **Ex.** *She put clean sheets on the guest bed.* 2. a single piece of paper, especially of the sizes used for letters. **Ex.** *He wrote a long letter, covering three sheets.* 3. anything with a broad, long, and thin shape. **Ex.** *A sheet of ice covered the lake.*

shelf (3) [šelf¹], *n.* 1. a thin piece of wood or other material fastened to a wall or forming part of a piece of furniture, that is used to hold things. **Ex.** *That book is on the bottom shelf.* 2. a projection like a shelf. **Ex.** *The wrecked ship rested on a shelf at the bottom of the sea.* —**on the shelf,** no longer being used or worked on.

shell (2) [šel¹], *n.* 1. the hard outer covering of some animals, eggs, nuts, and seeds. **Ex.** *We collected many shells on the beach.* 2. a case for holding the powder and other material that is fired from a gun. **Ex.** *Empty rifle shells were on the ground.* 3. anything similar to a shell. **Ex.** *The house burned until only a shell remained.* —**come out of one's shell,** become less timid. **Ex.** *As she grew older, she came out of her shell.*

shelter (2) [šel'tər], *n.* 1. something that gives protection; a place of safety. **Ex.** *A cave was their shelter for the night.* 2. protection. **Ex.** *They sought shelter from the rain.* —*v.* provide with a shelter; protect. **Ex.** *The closed car sheltered them from the rain.*

shelve (5) [šelv'], *v.* 1. place on a shelf. **Ex.** *The magazines are shelved on the first floor.* 2. put aside until later. **Ex.** *The question was shelved until the next meeting.* —**shelves'**, *n.* plural of *shelf.* —**shel'ving**, *n.* shelves or material of which shelves are made.

shepherd (5) [šep'ərd], *n.* one who herds sheep. **Ex.** *The shepherd guided his sheep down the hill.*

sheriff (3) [še:r'if], *n.* the chief law officer of a county. **Ex.** *The sheriff brought the captured criminal before the judge.*

shield (3) [šiyld'], *n.* 1. a piece of armor usually carried on the left arm and used for defense. **Ex.** *The shield protected him from the blows of his enemy.* 2. anything that defends or protects. **Ex.** *His umbrella is a shield against the rain.* —*v.* protect. **Ex.** *Her wide hat shielded her eyes from the sun.*

shift (3) [šift'], *v.* move, transfer, or change from one place, person, or position to another. **Ex.** *The wind shifted from east to west.* —*n.* 1. a change from one person, thing, or position to another. **Ex.** *A shift in the wind brought rain.* 2. a period or time of work at a place where people work both day and night. **Ex.** *He works the night shift at the factory.* —**shift'less**, *adj.* lazy. —**shift'y**, *adj.* not reliable; tricky.

shine (1) [šayn'], *v.* 1. give out rays of light; glow with light. **Ex.** *The sun is shining.* 2. be bright with reflected light. **Ex.** *A cat's eyes shine in dim light.* 3. cause to give off light; direct a light. **Ex.** *Shine the light into the dark corner.* —*n.* brightness caused by something that gives or reflects light. **Ex.** *The shine of a brass nameplate caught my eye.* —**shin'y**, *adj.*

shingle (5) [šiŋ'gəl], *n.* one of the thin pieces of wood or other material placed on the roof or sides of a house in rows, with each row partly covering another. **Ex.** *The roof was covered with wooden shingles.* —*v.* cover with shingles. **Ex.** *They shingled the roof of the house.*

ship (1) [šip¹], *n.* a large vessel that travels on the ocean. **Ex.** *The ship was loaded with tons of grain.* —*v.* send or carry by ship, railroad, or airplane. **Ex.** *We will ship the goods to you at once.* —**ship¹ment,** *n.* goods shipped at one time. —**ship¹per,** *n.*

-ship (1) [šip], *suffix.* 1. state or quality of. **Ex.** *Friend, friendship.* 2. rank. **Ex.** *Judge, judgeship.* 3. art or skill. **Ex.** *Leader, leadership.*

shipshape [šip¹šeyp`], *adj., adv.* in neat and proper order. **Ex.** *He tries always to keep his office shipshape.*

shirt (1) [šərt], *n.* a garment for the upper part of a man's body, having long or short sleeves and usually a collar. **Ex.** *He wore a white shirt.*

shiver (4) [šiv¹ər], *v.* shake or tremble, especially from cold, excitement, or fear. **Ex.** *The boy shivered in the cold wind.* —*n.* a tremble; the act of shivering. **Ex.** *A shiver ran down her back.*

shock (2) [šak¹], *n.* 1. something that greatly disturbs the mind or emotions; a great disturbance in the mind or emotions. **Ex.** *News of his death was a shock to us.* 2. a blow, a violent shake, or a sudden coming together of two forces. **Ex.** *The shock of the explosion broke the windows.* 3. the effect of electricity on the body. **Ex.** *He received a shock from an electric wire.* —*v.* 1. cause to feel sudden astonishment, horror, etc. **Ex.** *Her appearance shocked us.* 2. give an electric shock to. **Ex.** *He was badly shocked when he touched the electric wire.*

shoe (1) [šuw¹], *n.* a covering for the foot, usually made of leather.

shoestring [šuw¹striŋ`], *n.* a piece of string used to fasten a shoe. **Ex.** *He tied his shoestrings.*

SHOE

shone (2) [šown¹], *v.* past tense and participle of *shine.* **Ex.** *The moon shone on the lake.*

shook (2) [šuk¹], *v.* past tense of *shake.* **Ex.** *He shook with fright.*

shoot (2) [šhuwt'], *v.* 1. cause a gun or other weapon to send out something intended to hit or kill. **Ex.** *As the birds rise, the hunters shoot at them.* 2. hit, wound, or kill with a bullet shot from a gun. **Ex.** *How many rabbits did he shoot?* 3. send or push out. **Ex.** *The plants shot out new leaves.*

shop (1) [šap'], *n.* 1. a store; a place for selling goods. **Ex.** *He bought some chocolates at the candy shop.* 2. a place where a special kind of work is done. **Ex.** *She had the chair repaired at the carpenter's shop.* —*v.* buy; go from shop to shop to look at and buy goods. **Ex.** *The two women liked to shop together.* —**shop'per,** *n.* —**set up shop,** begin a business. **Ex.** *He set up shop as a car dealer.*

shoplifter [šap'lif'tər], *n.* one who steals things from a store. **Ex.** *The store owner watched carefully for shoplifters.*

shore (1) [šɔ:r'], *n.* land alongside an ocean, river, etc. **Ex.** *The boat was near the shore.* —**off shore,** *adj., adv.* in or from the water near the shore. **Ex.** *His boat was just off shore.*

shore line [šɔ:r' layn'], the line where water and shore meet.

short (1) [šɔrt'], *adj.* 1. lasting for only a little while. **Ex.** *I am busy and can stay only for a short time.* 2. having little length. **Ex.** *The string was too short to tie around the package.* 3. having little height. **Ex.** *My younger brother is shorter than I.* 4. rudely brief. **Ex.** *He was very short with me.* 5. not having enough of. **Ex.** *In college, we were always short of money.* —**short'en,** *v.* make shorter. **Ex.** *She shortened her dress.* —**short'ness,** *n.* the state of being short. —**short'age,** *n.* less than the correct or necessary amount. **Ex.** *There is a shortage of food.* —**shorts',** *n.* 1. short trousers for men or women. 2. short trousers used by men as underwear. —**in short,** briefly. **Ex.** *In short, we went home angry.* —**short for,** a briefer way or form. **Ex.** *Tom is short for Thomas.* —**short of,** 1. lacking. **Ex.** *We are short of milk. Will you buy some?* 2. not quite. **Ex.** *We have just short of a quart of milk.* —*adv.*

shortcoming [šɔrt'kəm'iŋ], *n.* weakness. **Ex.** *He is a good man, but he has many shortcomings.*

short cut [šɔrt' kət'], a way of going, doing, etc. that saves time, money, energy, etc. **Ex.** *I know a short cut from here to school.*

shorthand [šɔrt'hænd'], *n.* a fast way of writing, using symbols for words. **Ex.** *The secretary wrote what he said in shorthand and then typed it.*

short-handed [šɔrt'hæn'did], *adj.* lacking enough help. **Ex.** *We are short-handed, so we must all work longer.*

short-sighted [šɔrt'sayt'id], *adj.* seeing only what is near in space or time. **Ex.** *He is too short-sighted to see what the effect will be tomorrow.*

short wave [šɔrt' weyv'], a radio signal or wave of sixty meters or less, used for overseas broadcasts and special broadcasting. **Ex.** *He listened to short wave from America.*

shot (1) [šat'], *v.* past tense and participle of *shoot.* **Ex.** *The hunter shot two rabbits.*

shot (1) [šat'], *n.* 1. a bullet used in a gun. **Ex.** *The deer was killed by one shot.* 2. the act of shooting or the sound made by it. **Ex.** *We heard a shot.* **—long shot,** an effort not likely to succeed. **Ex.** *He has never won before, and it is a long shot that he will now.*

should (1) [šud'], *v.* used with another verb to show: 1. ought to. **Exs.** *She should learn to drive. I should have gone with you.* 2. may happen; likely to happen. **Ex.** *If it should rain, I will close the windows.*

shoulder (1) [šowl'dər], *n.* 1. the part of a human body to which the arms are joined. 2. the part of an animal's body to which the front legs are joined. 3. anything similar to a shoulder. **Ex.** *The car ran onto the shoulder of the road.*

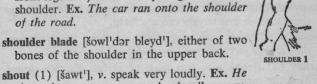

shoulder blade [šowl'dər bleyd'], either of two bones of the shoulder in the upper back.

SHOULDER 1

shout (1) [šawt'], *v.* speak very loudly. **Ex.** *He shouted my name.* **—n.** a loud call or cry. **Ex.** *Shouts of laughter came from the crowd.* **—shout someone down,** silence someone by shouting loudly. **Ex.** *The angry crowd shouted down the speaker.*

shove (4) [šəv'], *v.* 1. push along by applying force. **Ex.** *She shoved the heavy table against the wall.* 2. force aside or away by pushing. **Ex.** *He shoved the people away from the door.* **—n.** a push. **Ex.** *He gave the boy a shove.*

shovel (4) [šəv'əl], *n.* a tool with a long handle used for lifting and moving loose material, such as coal or dirt. —*v.* 1. lift and throw with a shovel. 2. clear or dig with a shovel. **Ex.** *He shoveled the snow out of the road.*

SHOVEL

show (1) [šow'], *v.* 1. allow to be seen; present so as to be seen. **Ex.** *Please show me your new car.* 2. teach; describe; explain. **Ex.** *Please show me how to operate this machine.* 3. guide. **Ex.** *He showed us to our seats.* 4. prove. **Ex.** *Your work shows that you have been careless.* —*n.* 1. act of showing. **Ex.** *He was surprised by her show of grief.* 2. a performance of a movie, play, television program, etc. **Exs.** *They went to the early show. They gave a good show.* 3. an exhibition; a display. **Ex.** *Did you enjoy the flower show?* —**show'y,** *adj.* brightly colored. —**show off,** act in a way to attract attention. **Ex.** *He showed off by dancing.* —**show up,** 1. be easily seen. **Ex.** *The small boy does not show up in the picture.* 2. arrive. **Ex.** *I waited an hour before he showed up for our appointment.*

shower (2) [šaw'ər], *n.* 1. a fall of rain which lasts only a short time. **Ex.** *A sudden shower ended the picnic.* 2. something resembling a rain shower. **Ex.** *He was knocked down by a shower of blows.* 3. a bath in which water falls on the body from above. **Ex.** *He bathed standing up in the shower.* —*v.* 1. give generously. **Ex.** *They showered us with gifts when we left.* 2. fall as rain. **Ex.** *Rain showered on the group.* 3. wash in a spray of water. **Ex.** *He showers every morning.*

showcase [šow'keys'], *n.* a glass case in a store in which things are placed so that buyers can see them.

shown (1) [šown'], *v.* past participle of *show.* **Ex.** *Have you shown your mother your new dress?*

shrank (4) [šrænk'], *v.* past tense of *shrink.* **Ex.** *He shrank from the corpse.*

shred (5) [šred'], *n.* a small piece either cut off or torn off. **Ex.** *Her dress was torn to shreds.* —*v.* cut or tear into small or narrow pieces. **Ex.** *She shredded vegetables for the salad.*

shrewd (4) [šruwd'], *adj.* keen or sharp in business matters. **Ex.** *He is a shrewd businessman.* —**shrewd'ly,** *adv.* —**shrewd'ness,** *n.*

shriek (3) [šriyk'], *v.* utter or make a sharp, high sound or cry; scream. **Ex.** *She shrieked in horror.* —*n.* a sharp, high cry; a scream. **Ex.** *A shriek of pain came from the wounded man.*

shrill (4) [šril¹], *adj.* having or making a high, sharp tone. **Ex.** *She had a shrill voice.* —*v.* make a high, sharp sound. **Ex.** *Insects shrilled in the trees.*

shrine (5) [šrayn¹], *n.* a place that is greatly respected for religious or historic reasons. **Ex.** *Many sacred shrines are in the Orient.*

shrink (4) [šriŋk¹], *v.* 1. make or become smaller. **Ex.** *This shirt will not shrink when it is washed.* 2. draw away from in horror, pain, or fear. **Ex.** *She still shrinks at the sight of blood.* —**shrink'age,** *n.* the amount lost by shrinking.

shroud (5) [šrawd¹], *n.* 1. something that covers or shelters. **Ex.** *They escaped under the shroud of night.* 2. a cloth in which a dead person is wrapped and buried. **Ex.** *The weeping women brought a shroud.* —*v.* cover as with a shroud. **Ex.** *She shrouded her face from curious eyes with a veil.*

shrub (4) [šrəb¹], *n.* a bush; a low, woody plant with many branches. **Ex.** *Many shrubs were planted around the house.* —**shrub'ber·y,** *n.* a group of shrubs.

shrug (4) [šrəg¹], *v.* raise and draw the shoulders together to show lack of interest, knowledge, or concern. **Ex.** *He only shrugged when I questioned him.* —*n.* the act of raising and drawing the shoulders together. **Ex.** *He denied the accusation with a shrug.*

shrunk (4) [šrəŋk¹], *v.* past tense and participle of *shrink.* **Ex.** *The dress had shrunk one inch.*

shudder (4) [šəd¹ər], *v.* tremble suddenly or shake from fear, disgust, etc. **Ex.** *She shuddered with cold.* —*n.* the act of trembling suddenly or shaking from fear, disgust, etc. **Ex.** *A shudder ran through him when he saw the ghost.*

shun (4) [šən¹], *v.* purposely avoid; stay away from. **Ex.** *He shunned his old friends.*

shut (2) [šət], *v.* 1. close an opening, especially to keep something in or out. **Ex.** *Shut the window, please.* 2. close by folding or bringing together the parts of. **Ex.** *The teacher shut her book.* —**shut down,** stop working or operating. **Ex.** *The machines were shut down when the electric power* *failed.* —**shut out,** prevent from entering. **Ex.** *He was shut out of his house when he left the key inside.* —**shut up,** 1. put or keep inside. **Ex.** *They shut up the criminal in a prison cell.* 2. stop talking. **Ex.** *The rude man said we should shut up.*

shutter (5) [šət'ər], *n.* a wooden cover for a window that may be swung closed for protection. **Ex.** *They closed the shutters during the storm.*

SHUTTER

shy (4) [šay'], *adj.* easily frightened; not at ease with others. **Ex.** *She is a shy child.* —*v.* draw back suddenly; start. **Ex.** *The horse shied at the approaching car.* —**shy'ly,** *adv.* —**shy'ness,** *n.*

sick (1) [sik'], *adj.* 1. ill; suffering from disease. **Ex.** *When she became sick, I called the doctor.* 2. filled with regret or grief. **Ex.** *She is sick about failing the test.* —**sick'en,** *v.* cause to become sick; become sick. **Ex.** *He sickened and died.* —**sick'en·ing,** *adj.* causing sickness or disgust. —**sick'ly,** *adj.* in poor health; pale; weak. —**sick'ness,** *n.* —**sick of,** tired of. **Ex.** *He was sick of his job.*

side (1) [sayd'], *n.* 1. any of the lines that form the edges of a surface; any of the surfaces of an object. **Ex.** *A square has four equal sides.* 2. one of the two broad surfaces of something very thin. **Ex.** *He wrote on both sides of the paper.* 3. a surface other than the front, back, top, or bottom. **Ex.** *A railroad passenger car usually has windows on both sides.* 4. a surface or place in relation to something else. **Ex.** *Our house is here; his house is on the other side of the river.* 5. either half of the human body. **Ex.** *He had a pain in his left side.* 6. an aspect or quality of a person, situation, etc. **Ex.** *She shows only her cheerful side to others.* 7. one of two opposing individuals, groups, etc. **Ex.** *Let us choose sides for the game.* —*adj.* being at, on, or of one side. **Ex.** *We entered at a side door.* —*v.* help, favor, etc. one of two sides. **Ex.** *He sided with his brother in the quarrel.* —**side by side,** together. **Ex.** *If we work side by side, we will win.* —**take sides,** support one person or position in an argument. **Ex.** *If you take sides, the others will be angry.*

sideburns [sayd'bərnz'], *n.* the hair in front of the ears on the sides of a man's face. **Ex.** *He preferred to let his sideburns grow long.*

side-step [sayd' step'], *v.* avoid as by stepping aside. **Ex.** *He side-stepped the question by pretending he had not heard it.*

sidewalk [sayd'wɔ:k'], *n.* an area, usually raised and paved, along the side of a street on which people walk. **Ex.** *At lunchtime, the sidewalks are filled with crowds of people.*

sideways [sayd'weyz'], **sidewise** [sayd'wayz], *adv.* viewed from the side or with one side facing the viewer. **Ex.** *When he turned his head sideways, I saw he had a large nose.*

siding [sayd'iŋ], *n.* boards or other material used to cover the side of a wooden building. **Ex.** *They nailed the wood siding to the frame of the house.*

siege (4) [siyǰ'], *n.* 1. the surrounding of a fort or other defended place in order to force its surrender. **Ex.** *During the long siege, food and water became very scarce.* 2. a long, continuing period as of illness, difficulty, etc. **Ex.** *After a siege of three months, the company met union demands.*

sift (4) [sift'], *v.* 1. separate the coarse parts of something from the fine parts by passing it through a screen of fine wire. **Ex.** *She sifted the flour for the cake.* 2. examine closely. **Ex.** *The lawyer sifted the facts before he agreed to take the case.* —**sift'er,** *n.* a device for sifting.

sigh (4) [say'], *v.* 1. draw in one's breath and let it out so that it can be heard, to express sadness, weariness, etc. 2. make a sound like this. **Ex.** *The wind sighed through the trees.* —*n.* the act or sound of sighing. **Ex.** *He breathed a sigh of relief when his bills were paid.*

sight (1) [sayt'], *n.* 1. the power or ability to see. **Ex.** *The old man had lost his sight.* 2. the act of seeing. **Ex.** *Our first sight of the city was at night.* 3. a view; something worth seeing. **Ex.** *The sight of the valley was beautiful.* —*v.* see. **Ex.** *The guard sighted an escaping prisoner.* —**catch sight of,** see briefly; glimpse. **Ex.** *He caught sight of the children running through the forest.* —**not by a long sight,** not likely or not at all. **Ex.** *He will not succeed by a long sight.*

sign (1) [sayn'], *n.* 1. a card, board, or space on which directions, a warning, etc. are written. **Ex.** *The sign says "No Parking."* 2. something that indicates the existence of another thing. **Ex.** *The first robin is a sign of spring.* 3. a motion by which a command is given or a thought expressed. **Ex.** *The traffic policeman made a sign for us to advance.* 4. a symbol representing an idea. **Ex.** *A white flag is the sign of surrender.* —*v.* write one's name. **Ex.** *He signed the letter.* —**sign'er,** *n.* one who signs. —**sign off,** in radio or television, stop broadcasting for the day. —**sign up,** enlist or be hired. Ex. *He signed up in the army.*

signal (2) [sig'nəl], *n.* something that warns, directs, etc. Ex. *The sound of the gun was the signal for the start of the race.* —*adj.* used in signaling. Ex. *The pilot radioed the signal tower for instructions.* —*v.* 1. make a signal to. Ex. *He signaled the man to stop.* 2. send messages by means of signals. Ex. *The ship signaled for help.*

signature (4) [sig'nəčər], *n.* the name of a person as written by his own hand. Ex. *His signature is difficult to read.*

significance (4) [signif'əkəns], *n.* 1. importance. Ex. *He knew the significance of what he said.* 2. meaning. Ex. *What was the significance of his look?* —**sig·nif'i·cant,** *adj.* —**sig·nif'i·cant·ly,** *adv.*

signify (5) [sig'nəfay'], *v.* 1. show by a sign or action. Ex. *If you agree, signify by raising your right hand.* 2. mean. Ex. *The fact that they left signifies nothing.*

silence (2) [say'ləns], *n.* 1. the state of not speaking or of avoiding noise. Ex. *Students are required to maintain silence in the library.* 2. an absence of noise. Ex. *The silence of the falling snow is comforting.* 3. failure or unwillingness to speak out. Ex. *The people were surprised by the President's silence in the case.* —*v.* quiet. Ex. *The speaker silenced the crowd.* —**si'lent,** *adj.* —**si'lent·ly,** *adv.*

silk (2) [silk'], *n.* the fine, bright, threadlike substance produced by a certain kind of worm; also, the thread or cloth made from this substance. Ex. *She selected blue silk for her dress.* —*adj.* made of silk. Ex. *She wore a black silk dress.* —**sil'ken, silk'y,** *adj.* made of silk; smooth, soft, or shiny like silk.

silly (3) [sil'iy], *adj.* without good sense; foolish. Ex. *The children said silly things.* —**sil'li·ness,** *n.*

silver (1) [sil'vər], *n.* 1. a white precious metal that can be easily shaped. Ex. *He wore a ring made of silver.* 2. money; coins made of silver. Ex. *Give me my change in silver, please.* 3. knives, forks, spoons, and other table pieces. Ex. *Please put the silver on the table.* —*adj.* made of silver. Ex. *She poured the tea from a silver pot.* —**sil'ver·y,** *adj.* like silver in color, tone, etc.

silverware (3) [sil'vərwer'], *n.* knives, forks, spoons, and other articles made of silver and used for eating or serving food. Ex. *She put the silverware on the table.*

similar (2) [sim'ələr], *adj.* be like something but not exactly the same. **Ex.** *The two men wore similar suits.* —**sim'i·lar·ly**, *adv.* —**sim\`i·lar'i·ty**, *n.* likeness. **Ex.** *There were similarities in their suits.*

simple (1) [sim'pəl], *adj.* 1. easy to understand; not difficult. **Ex.** *She answered the simple questions without difficulty.* 2. plain. **Ex.** *She wore a simple dress at work.* 3. natural; sincere. **Ex.** *His parents were simple people.* —**sim'pli·fy**, *v.* make simple. —**sim'ply**, *adv.* 1. in a simple way; plainly. **Ex.** *She did the work simply and quickly.* 2. merely; just. **Ex.** *He simply walked away from us.*

simplicity (5) [simplis'ətiy], *n.* 1. the quality of being easy to understand. **Ex.** *The simplicity of his words appealed to the audience.* 2. naturalness. **Ex.** *The child spoke with honesty and simplicity.* 3. plainness; lack of ornament. **Ex.** *The simplicity of her dress was accented by a jeweled pin.*

sin (2) [sin'], *n.* the breaking of a religious law, especially when done purposely; any wrong act. **Ex.** *To be unkind is a sin.* —*v.* break a religious law; commit a fault or sin. **Ex.** *Knowing he had sinned, he felt guilty.* —**sin'ner**, *n.* one who sins.

since (1) [sins'], *prep.* from the time stated until now. **Ex.** *I have known him since childhood.* —*conj.* 1. after the time stated. **Ex.** *Since the factory has shut down, the article cannot be ordered.* 2. because. **Ex.** *You may take this book since I have read it.* —*adv.* 1. from a definite time in the past until now. **Ex.** *He joined the club in 1952 and has been a member ever since.* 2. after a certain time in the past and before the present. **Ex.** *He once wanted to be a doctor but has since changed his mind.*

sincere (4) [sinsi:r'], *adj.* 1. honest; showing good faith. **Ex.** *He was a sincere friend.* 2. real; genuine. **Ex.** *She made a sincere effort to improve.* —**sin·cere'ly**, *adv.* —**sin·cer'i·ty**, *n.* honesty. **Ex.** *She spoke with sincerity.*

sing (1) [siŋ'], *v.* 1. use the human voice to make musical sounds, with or without words. **Ex.** *He is singing a sad song.* 2. make musical sounds. **Ex.** *The birds were singing.* —**sing'er**, *n.*

single (1) [siŋ'gəl], *adj.* 1. one only. **Ex.** *The room was empty*

a, far; æ, am; e, get; ey, late; i, in; iy, see; ɔ, all; ow, go; u, put; uw, too; ə, but, ago; ər, fur; aw, out; ay, life; oy, boy; ŋ, ring; θ, think; ð, that; ž, measure; š, ship; ǰ, edge; č, child.

except for a single chair. 2. unmarried. **Ex.** *Is your sister still single?* 3. for the use of one person. **Ex.** *The traveler asked for a single room.* —**sin'gly,** *adv.* alone; one at a time.

single file [siŋ'gəl fayl'], a line or row of persons or things, one behind the other. **Ex.** *They marched single file.*

single-handed [siŋ'gəlhæn'did], *adj.* with no help. **Ex.** *He fought his attackers single-handed.*

single-minded [siŋ'gəlmayn'did], *adj.* determined and able to work hard for a single objective until it is achieved. **Ex.** *He is a single-minded man who thinks only about the job he is doing.*

singular (5) [siŋ'gyələr], *adj.* 1. remarkable; unusual. **Ex.** *She is a woman of singular beauty.* 2. strange; odd. **Ex.** *We noticed the man's singular behavior.* 3. in grammar, the form referring to a single person or thing. —*n.* the form of a word that refers to only one. **Ex.** *"Leaf" is the singular of "leaves."*

sink (2) [siŋk'], *v.* 1. go down into water or other fluid. **Ex.** *The ship is filling with water and sinking.* 2. go down or seem to go down slowly. **Ex.** *The sun is sinking in the west.* 3. become lower. **Ex.** *Sell now; prices are sinking.* —*n.* a basin or container with a drain and usually having a water supply. **Ex.** *She washed the dishes in the sink.*

sir (2) [sər'], *n.* respectful term used in speaking or writing to a man. **Ex.** *Is this your hat, sir?*

siren (5) [say'rən], *n.* an instrument for making loud, high, easily heard warning signals. **Ex.** *We heard the siren of a police car.*

sister (1) [sis'tər], *n.* a girl or woman with the same parents as another person. **Ex.** *He has two sisters.*

sister-in-law [sis'tərənlɔ:'], *n.* wife of one's brother or sister of one's husband or wife.

sit (1) [sit'], *v.* 1. rest upon the lower part of the body; be seated. **Ex.** *Sit in this chair.* 2. rest. **Ex.** *The birds are sitting in the tree.* 3. occupy a place as a member. **Ex.** *He sits in Congress.* —**sit'ting,** *n.* regular meeting, especially of a court. **Ex.** *The Supreme Court will consider the case at its next sitting.* —**sit in,** join with others, as in a meeting. **Ex.** *He was asked to sit in on committee meetings.* —**sit on,** be a member of a committee or other such group. **Ex.** *He sits on the Selection Committee.* —**sit out,** take a rest from some activity for a period. **Ex.** *She was tired and sat* *out the next dance.* —**sit up,** 1. move the body into a position where one is sitting. **Ex.** *She sat up in the bed.* 2. stay awake and not go to bed. **Ex.** *She sat up all night waiting for her son to come home.*

site (4) [sayt'], *n.* location; position; place. **Ex.** *This is the site of a famous battle.*

situation (2) [sič'uwey'šən], *n.* 1. the general state of affairs. **Ex.** *The political situation is very complicated.* 2. personal condition or state of affairs; position. **Ex.** *He is in a difficult situation.* —**sit'u·ate,** *v.* locate; place. **Ex.** *Their house is situated near the river.*

six (1) [siks'], *n., adj.* the number between five and seven; the number 6. —**sixth',** *n., adj.* coming after five others. —**six'teen',** *n., adj.* the number 16. —**six'teenth',** *n., adj.* coming after fifteen others. —**six'ty,** *n., adj.* the number 60. —**six'ti·eth,** *n., adj.* coming after fifty-nine others.

size (1) [sayz'], *n.* 1. the space occupied by a thing; length, width, and height. **Ex.** *Your house is the same size as ours.* 2. one of a set of measurements accepted as standard. **Ex.** *What is your shoe size?* 3. amount, extent, etc. **Ex.** *The size of his debt is enormous.*

skate (3) [skeyt'], *n.* 1. a blade of metal attached to a shoe, allowing the wearer to glide over ice. 2. a metal frame with rollers attached to a shoe, allowing the wearer to glide over a smooth surface. —*v.* glide on ice or on a smooth surface wearing skates. **Ex.** *The children are skating on the frozen pond.* —**skat'er,** *n.*

skeleton (4) [skel'ətən], *n.* 1. all the bones of a human or other animal body in position, serving as a frame for the flesh. **Ex.** *The explorers discovered a skeleton in the cave.* 2. anything like a skeleton, such as the frame of a building or a ship. **Ex.** *They could see skeletons of ruined buildings.* —**skel'e·tal,** *adj.*

skeleton key [skəl'ətən kiy'], a specially made key that can open many different locks.

sketch (3) [skeč'], *n.* 1. a drawing or painting done simply and quickly. **Ex.** *We liked his sea sketches best.* 2. a rough plan or design. **Ex.** *His sketch included the main points of his plan.* —*v.* draw or paint simply and quickly. **Ex.** *He sketched her as she stood in the doorway.* —**sketch'y,** *adj.* incomplete; lacking detail.

skill (2) [skil'], *n.* 1. the ability which results from training, experience, etc. **Ex.** *He plays the piano with skill.* 2. a particular art or science, especially one that requires the use of the hands. **Ex.** *Making fine furniture is a skill.* —**skilled¹**, *adj.* requiring or having a particular skill. **Ex.** *Making watches is skilled work.* —**skill'ful**, *adj.* having skill. **Ex.** *He is a skillful surgeon.* —**skill'ful·ly**, *adv.*

skim (4) [skim¹], *v.* 1. remove with some instrument that which floats or comes to the top of a liquid. **Ex.** *The cook skimmed the fat from the soup.* 2. read rapidly and not thoroughly. **Ex.** *He skimmed the newspaper.* 3. pass or cause to pass quickly and lightly over. **Ex.** *The motorboat skimmed over the water.*

skim milk [skim¹ milk¹], milk from which the cream has been skimmed.

skin (1) [skin¹], *n.* 1. the outer covering of a human or other animal body. **Ex.** *Her skin was smooth and soft.* 2. the fur of an animal after it is removed from the body. **Ex.** *The collar of her coat was made from a fox skin.* —*v.* remove the skin. **Ex.** *The hunter skinned the deer.* —**skin'less**, *adj.* without skin. —**skin'ny**, *adj.* very thin. **Ex.** *He is a skinny boy.*

skip (4) [skip¹], *v.* 1. move from one point to another without touching what is in between. **Ex.** *She skipped chapter two of the book.* 2. move forward by jumping or hopping from one foot to the other. **Ex.** *The children skipped along on their way to school.*

skirt (2) [skərt¹], *n.* the lower part of a dress or a separate garment for women or girls that hangs from the waist.

skull (4) [skəl¹], *n.* the bone frame of the head that covers and protects the brain. **Ex.** *He was knocked unconscious by a blow on the skull.*

sky (1) [skay¹], *n.* the space above the earth; the upper air; the heavens. **Ex.** *There is not a cloud in the sky.*

SKIRT

skylight [skay¹layt`], *n.* a window in a roof. **Ex.** *He could see stars through the skylight.*

skyline [skay¹layn¹], *n.* the line of sight where the earth or things on it meet the sky; the horizon. **Ex.** *The skyline of a big city is a beautiful sight.*

SKULL

skyscraper [skay'skreyp`er], *n.* a very tall building. **Ex.** *New York is famous for its skyscrapers.*

slain (3) [sleyn'], *v.* past participle of *slay.* **Ex.** *Thousands were slain in the battle.*

slam (4) [slæm'], *v.* 1. shut violently and noisily. **Ex.** *She slammed the door shut.* 2. throw or place violently and noisily. **Ex.** *She slammed the pans into the sink.*

slang (5) [slæŋ'], *n.* 1. language that is not considered part of standard speech or writing. **Ex.** *The city children used interesting slang.* 2. special words used by people in a profession.

slant (3) [slænt'], *v.* be or lie in a direction that is not level or straight up and down but inclines; slope. **Ex.** *Her handwriting slants to the left.* —*n.* a slope; a slanting line or surface. **Ex.** *The slant of the roof is steep.* —**slant'ing,** *adj.*

slap (4) [slæp'], *v.* hit or strike with the open hand or with something flat. **Ex.** *She slapped the child on the cheek.* —*n.* a blow with the open hand or with something flat. **Ex.** *We heard the slap of the waves against the boat.*

slash (5) [slæš'], *v.* 1. make long, quick cuts with something sharp. **Ex.** *He slashed a path through the high grass with a long knife.* 2. reduce or lower very much. **Ex.** *The businessman slashed prices.* —*n.* the cut, or opening, made by slashing. **Ex.** *The slash on his cheek was slow to heal.*

slate (5) [sleyt'], *n.* hard, flat, blue-gray stone, often used as roof tile or as a surface to write upon with chalk.

slaughter (4) [slɔ:'tər], *n.* 1. the killing of animals to be used as food. **Ex.** *The cattle were sent to the city for slaughter.* 2. the violent killing of human beings; the killing of people in large numbers. **Ex.** *The battle became a slaughter.* —*v.* 1. kill animals for food. **Ex.** *The lambs were slaughtered for market.* 2. kill violently or in large numbers. **Ex.** *Hundreds of the enemy were slaughtered.* —**slaugh'ter·er,** *n.*

slave (2) [sleyv'], *n.* 1. a human being controlled by another as property. **Ex.** *The slaves were working in the fields.* 2. one who is controlled by a habit. **Ex.** *He is a slave to alcohol.*

—*v*. work very hard. —**slav'er·y**, *n*. 1. the condition of a slave. 2. the keeping of slaves.

slay (5) [sley'], *v*. kill violently. **Ex.** *He intended to slay his father's murderer.* —**slay'er**, *n*.

sled (5) [sled'], *n*. a flat wooden frame on metal runners, used for carrying people or loads over snow or ice.

SLED

sleep (1) [sliyp'], *n*. a resting of the mind and body with the eyes closed, usually while lying down. **Ex.** *He had a good night's sleep.* —*v*. rest in this way. **Ex.** *Most people sleep during the night.* —**sleep'er**, *n*. 1. one who sleeps. 2. a car of a train which has beds. **Ex.** *He took a sleeper on his trip across the country.* —**sleep'y**, *adj*. feeling a need for sleep.

sleeve (3) [sliyv'], *n*. the part of clothing that covers the arm. **Ex.** *The sleeves of his coat were too long.*

slender (3) [slen'dər], *adj*. small in width as compared to height; pleasingly thin. **Ex.** *She was a tall, slender blonde.*

slept (1) [slept'], *v*. past tense and participle of *sleep*. **Ex.** *He slept until noon today.*

slice (3) [slays'], *n*. a thin, flat piece cut from something. **Ex.** *He ate two slices of bread.* —*v*. make slices by cutting. **Ex.** *Please slice the cake.*

slick (5) [slik'], *adj*. 1. shiny and smooth. **Ex.** *The magazine was printed on slick paper.* 2. slippery. **Ex.** *The roads were slick with ice.*

slide (3) [slayd'], *v*. 1. move smoothly over a surface as if on ice. **Ex.** *This window slides up and down easily.* 2. lose balance; slip. **Ex.** *Did you see him slide on the ice?*

slight (2) [slayt'], *adj*. 1. small in amount or degree; not important. **Ex.** *She stayed home for a day because of a slight illness.* 2. frail; delicate. **Ex.** *The girl was too slight to carry the heavy bundle.* —**slight'ly**, *adv*. in a small degree. —*v*. act toward as unimportant; ignore. **Ex.** *She slighted him by speaking to all of the others first.* —*n*. act of slighting. **Ex.** *His slights made her cry.*

slim (4) [slim'], *adj*. slender in form; slight. **Ex.** *She has a slim figure.* —*v*. make or become slim. **Ex.** *She slimmed her figure by dieting.*

sling (5) [sliŋ'], *n.* 1. a loop of rope or other strong material put under heavy objects so that they can be lifted more easily. 2. a bandage which is folded so that the arm is supported in the fold and two ends are tied in a loop around the neck. —*v.* 1. put in a sling to raise or lower; carry by a sling. 2. throw, using a sling.

SLING 1

slingshot [sliŋ'šat'], *n.* a Y-shaped weapon with an elastic strap attached to the top parts, which throws a stone or other hard object when the elastic strap is released.

slip (2) [slip'], *v.* 1. slide; shift from a position; slide and fall. **Ex.** *She slipped on the ice and hurt her hand.* 2. leave quickly and smoothly, as in escaping. **Ex.** *The child slipped out of the house and ran away.* 3. move easily or cause to move easily. **Ex.** *The boat slipped along the river.* —*n.* 1. the act of slipping. **Ex.** *His slip on the stairway caused a broken leg.* 2. a woman's undergarment, extending from the shoulders to the end of the skirt. **Ex.** *The slip she wore was too long.* —**slip one's mind**, be forgotten. **Ex.** *The entire problem slipped my mind for a while.*

slip (2) [slip'], *n.* a small piece of paper. **Ex.** *The clerk gave me a sales slip with my purchase.*

slip cover [slip' kəv'ər], a removable cover, usually of cloth, put over a chair or sofa to keep it clean.

slipper (4) [slip'ər], *n.* a light shoe that slips on and off easily, usually worn indoors. **Ex.** *He liked to wear slippers in the evening.*

slippery (5) [slip'əriy], *adj.* 1. able to cause slipping. **Ex.** *Spilled oil caused the floor to be slippery.* 2. likely to slip easily. **Ex.** *The slippery dish fell from his hands.*

slit (5) [slit'], *v.* 1. cut open along a line. **Ex.** *She slit the envelope with a knife.* 2. cut into strips. —*n.* a long, narrow cut or opening. **Ex.** *The sunshine entered through a slit between the curtains.*

slogan (5) [slow'gən], *n.* a word used by a group or business to get attention for its ideas or products. **Ex.** *"Votes for Women" was a slogan of the early 1900's.*

slope (3) [slowp'], *v.* incline up or down; have a slant. **Ex.** *The ground slopes down to the water.* —*n.* 1. a surface that has one side higher or lower than the other side; a surface that slants. **Ex.** *We climbed the slope of the hill.* 2. the amount of slant. **Ex.** *The slope of that roof is very steep.*

slow (1) [slow'], *adj.* 1. not fast in moving, talking, etc. **Ex.** *The old man is a slow worker.* 2. using more time than usual. **Ex.** *The trip is two hours longer by the slow train.* 3. not interesting; not lively; not busy. **Ex.** *The ice cream business is slow on cold days.* 4. behind the real time. **Ex.** *My watch is five minutes slow.* —*v.* become, go, or make slow or slower. **Ex.** *The car slowed to a stop.* —**slow'ly**, *adv.* —**slow'ness**, *n.*

slum (5) [slǝm'], *n.* a section of a town or city where many people live crowded together in poor and often dirty conditions. **Ex.** *The government is tearing down the slums and building new housing.*

slumber (5) [slǝm'bǝr], *n.* sleep. **Ex.** *The bell woke him from his slumber.*

slump (5) [slǝmp'], *v.* 1. drop or fall heavily or suddenly. **Ex.** *The wounded man slumped to the ground.* 2. sit, stand, or walk in a drooping manner. **Ex.** *The bored children slumped over their desks.* —*n.* a decline in sales or prices. **Ex.** *There was a slump in the sale of cars.*

sly (4) [slay'], *adj.* cunning and secretive; skillful at tricking. **Ex.** *He is too sly to be trusted.* 2. full of playful tricks. **Ex.** *We enjoyed his sly humor.* —**sly'ly**, *adv.* —**sly'ness**, *n.* —**on the sly**, so as not to be seen. **Ex.** *He took a handful of candy on the sly.*

small (1) [smɔ:l'], *adj.* 1. little in size. **Ex.** *She is small for her age.* 2. little in amount. **Ex.** *He could buy only one with the small sum of money he had.* 3. few in number. **Ex.** *A small crowd gathered.* 4. not important. **Ex.** *This is only a small problem.* —**small'ness**, *n.*

small arms [smɔ:l' armz'], guns small enough to be carried in the hand, such as pistols and rifles.

small hours [smɔ:l' awrz'], the very early hours of the morning after midnight. **Ex.** *The party lasted until the small hours of the morning.*

small letter [smɔ:l' let'ǝr], any letter other than a capital letter. **Ex.** *In "The," "h" and "e" are small letters; "T" is a capital letter.*

small-minded [smɔ:l'mayn'did], *adj.* not generous; mean; intolerant. **Ex.** *Gossips are small-minded people.*

small talk [smɔːl' tɔːk'], unimportant conversation. **Ex.** *He made small talk about the weather.*

smart (3) [smart'], *adj.* 1. quick to learn; showing intelligence; clever. **Ex.** *Both children are very smart.* 2. clean and neat; well-dressed. **Ex.** *They liked his smart appearance.* 3. painful. **Ex.** *She gave him a smart slap.* —*v.* cause or feel stinging pain. **Ex.** *Her eyes smarted from the smoke.* —**smart'ly,** *adv.* —**smart'ness,** *n.*

smash (3) [smæš'], *v.* 1. break or be broken into many pieces by force, often with a crashing sound; crush. **Ex.** *The cup smashed when the girl dropped it.* 2. hit or move with force. **Ex.** *The two cars smashed into each other.* —*n.* a breaking or hitting; the sound of breaking or hitting. **Ex.** *He heard a smash through his window.*

smashup [smæš'əp'], *n.* a bad wreck. **Ex.** *His car was destroyed in a smashup.*

smear (5) [smiːr'], *v.* 1. rub, spread, or cover with oil, fat, etc. **Ex.** *The children's faces were smeared with dirt.* 2. unfairly damage or hurt the reputation of. **Ex.** *Each political party accused the other of smearing its candidate.*

smell (1) [smel'], *v.* 1. sense with the nose; perceive through the nose. **Ex.** *He smelled something burning.* 2. have or give off a characteristic odor which can be sensed by the nose. **Ex.** *The mountain air smelled of pine trees.* —*n.* 1. something sensed by the nose. **Ex.** *The smell of the cooking made them hungry.* 2. the special sense in the nose by which one notices smells. **Ex.** *The dog has a keen sense of smell.* —**smell'y,** *adj.* having an odor.

smile (1) [smayl'], *n.* an expression of the face which shows happiness, pleasure, amusement, etc. **Ex.** *She met her friend with a smile.* —*v.* show by facial expression that one is happy, pleased, or amused. **Ex.** *She smiled at the funny story.* —**smil'ing,** *adj.* —**smil'ing·ly,** *adv.*

smoke (1) [smowk'], *n.* 1. that which can be seen rising into the air from something burning. **Ex.** *Cigarette smoke filled the room.* 2. the act of using a cigarette, cigar, etc., or the period of time taken to use one. **Ex.** *They stopped their work for a smoke.* —*v.* 1. produce smoke. **Ex.** *The wet wood made the fire smoke heavily.* 2. use cigarettes, pipes, etc. **Ex.** *She does not smoke, but her husband does.* 3. preserve meats by placing in a special smoke-filled enclosure. **Ex.** *They cooked some of the fish and smoked the rest.* —**smok'er,** *n.* —**smok'y,** *adj.* —**smoke'less,** *adj.* not producing smoke.

smooth (2) [smuwð'], *adj.* 1. having an even surface. **Ex.** *There was no wind, and the lake was as smooth as glass.* 2. steady in motion. **Ex.** *An airplane trip in good weather is very smooth.* —*v.* 1. cause to have an even surface. **Ex.** *He smoothed his hair.* 2. make easy by help or by removing difficulties. **Ex.** *Letters of introduction smoothed his way into the college of his choice.* —**smooth'ly,** *adv.* —**smooth'-ness,** *n.* —**smooth over,** describe as or try to make appear less serious or bad. **Ex.** *She smoothed over the children's quarrel.*

smother (5) [sməð'ər], *v.* 1. prevent from breathing freely; kill by preventing from breathing. **Ex.** *The dead man had been smothered by smoke.* 2. put out or deaden a fire by keeping out the air. **Ex.** *We smothered the fire with sand.*

smuggle (5) [sməg'əl], *v.* 1. bring into the country or remove from the country in a manner contrary to the law. **Ex.** *They smuggled the diamonds across the border.* 2. bring in or take out secretly. **Ex.** *The boy smuggled a pie out of the house.* —**smug'gler,** *n.*

snack (5) [snæk'], *n.* a small amount of food or drink; a light meal eaten between regular meals. **Ex.** *He enjoyed a bedtime snack.*

snake (3) [sneyk'], *n.* a cold-blooded crawling animal with a long slender body and no legs.

SNAKE

snap (3) [snæp'], *v.* 1. make or cause to make a sharp, sudden sound by breaking, closing, etc. **Ex.** *The lock snapped shut.* 2. bite; attempt to bite or seize sharply and suddenly. **Ex.** *The dog snapped at the child.* 3. speak in a sharp, angry way. **Ex.** *He snapped at the noisy children.* —*n.* 1. a sudden bite or attempt to bite; seizing or grasping. **Ex.** *The fish made a snap at the hook.* 2. a sharp, sudden sound caused by breaking, closing, etc. **Ex.** *He broke the branch with a snap.* 3. any fastening device that closes with a snapping sound. **Ex.** *The snap on the dress was broken.* —*adj.* given, done, etc. carelessly and hurriedly. **Ex.** *He made a snap decision to go with us.*

snapshot [snæp'šat'], *n.* a photograph taken quickly with a small camera held in the hand. Ex. *He showed us snapshots of his wife and children.*

snare (5) [sne:r'], *n.* 1. a device for capturing birds or animals. Ex. *The hunter set snares.* 2. anything by which one is trapped. Ex. *The question was a snare to catch him in a lie.* —*v.* capture with a snare. Ex. *He snared several rabbits.*

snarl (5) [snarl'], *v.* 1. make an angry rolling sound in the throat while showing the teeth. Ex. *The dog snarled at the stranger.* 2. say with an angry voice. Ex. *The angry man snarled his answer.* —*n.* the sound or act of snarling. Ex. *We heard the snarls of the lions.*

snarl (5) [snarl'], *v.* tangle. Ex. *The boy had snarled the string of his kite.* —*n.* a tangle or group of unwanted knots. Ex. *We were caught in a snarl of traffic.*

snatch (3) [snæč'], *v.* seize or try to seize suddenly. Ex. *The thief snatched the money and ran.* —*n.* 1. the act of snatching. Ex. *He made a snatch at the rope and missed.* 2. very small or brief parts. Ex. *He knows snatches of the poem.*

sneak (5) [sniyk'], *v.* move, act, carry, etc. quietly and secretly to avoid being seen. Ex. *The boys sneaked some food out of the house.* —*n.* a person who is not honest. Ex. *A sneak stole the clothes from the line on which they were drying.* —**sneak'y**, *adj.* —**sneak'i·ly**, *adv.*

sneer (5) [sni:r'], *v.* express a scornful feeling, indicate that something or someone is worthless by showing scorn on the face. Ex. *He sneered at their plans.* —*n.* a scornful expression of the face; a scornful remark. Ex. *She answered with a sneer.* —**sneer'ing**, *adj.*

sneeze (5) [sniyz'], *v.* let out the breath from the mouth and nose suddenly with force and noise. Ex. *The dust made me sneeze.* —*n.* the act or sound of sneezing. Ex. *He tried to hold back a sneeze.*

sniff (4) [snif'], *v.* 1. draw air into the nose noisily. Ex. *He sniffed the cold air.* 2. smell in this manner. Ex. *She sniffed the flowers.* —*n.* 1. the act or sound of sniffing. Ex. *The dog took a sniff of the meat.* 2. the odor sniffed. Ex. *There was a sniff of gasoline in the air.*

snore (5) [sno:r'], *v.* breathe noisily while sleeping. Ex. *He snores loudly.* —*n.* the act or sound of snoring. Ex. *His snores often waken her.*

snort (5) [snɔrt'], *v.* 1. force out the breath from the nose suddenly and loudly. **Ex.** *The horse snorted.* 2. express scorn, anger, etc. by such a sound. **Ex.** *The old man snorted in anger.* —*n.* the act or sound of snorting. **Ex.** *He gave a snort of laughter.*

snow (1) [snow'], *n.* 1. soft white pieces of frozen water which fall from the sky. **Ex.** *Several inches of snow covered the ground.* 2. the fall of such pieces. **Ex.** *We had a light snow yesterday.* —*v.* fall as snow. **Ex.** *It snowed all night.* —**snow'y,** *adj.*

snowbank [snow'bæŋk'], *n.* a pile of snow.

snow-blind [snow'blaynd'], *adj.* unable to see for a time as a result of sunlight reflected by the snow. —**snow' blind'ness,** *n.*

snowbound [snow'bawnd'], *adj.* prevented from traveling by deep snow. **Ex.** *We were snowbound at the farm and could not go to town.*

snug (5) [snəg'], *adj.* 1. sheltered and warm. **Ex.** *The children were snug in their beds.* 2. just large enough; small but comfortable. **Ex.** *They live in a snug little house.*

so (1) [sow'], *adv.* 1. in such a way; in the manner described. **Ex.** *He raised his fist and held it so for a moment.* 2. also; too. **Ex.** *She left early, and so did we.* 3. very. **Ex.** *I am so tired.* 4. to such an extent; of such an amount. **Ex.** *I have so much to tell you and so little time.* 5. as a result; therefore. **Ex.** *He was ill and so could not come.* 6. more or less. **Ex.** *I shall be home in an hour or so.* —*conj.* in order that; for the purpose. **Ex.** *Come early so that we can discuss our plans.* —*interj.* an exclamation of surprise, doubt, etc. **Ex.** *So, this is how you spend your evenings!* —**and so on, and so forth,** et cetera. **Ex.** *He gave her cake, pie, candy, and so forth.*

soak (3) [sowk'], *v.* 1. be in or place in water or some other liquid until thoroughly wet. **Ex.** *She soaked the clothes before washing them.* 2. draw in; suck up. **Ex.** *Use this cloth to soak up the spilled milk.* 3. penetrate or be absorbed through. **Ex.** *The oil soaked through the paper bag.* —*n.* the act of soaking. **Ex.** *Give your injured hand a good soak in hot water.*

soap (2) [sowp'], *n.* a substance used with water for washing and cleaning. **Ex.** *The soap slipped from his hand.* —*v.* rub

soap on or over. **Ex.** *She soaped the collar of the shirt.*
—**soap'y,** *adj.*

soar (4) [sɔːr¹], *v.* 1. fly up into the air as a bird or fly at a
great height. **Ex.** *The planes soared above us.* 2. rise above
the usual level. **Ex.** *Because of the shortage, the price of
food soared.*

sob (3) [sab¹], *v.* cry or weep with gasping sounds. **Ex.** *She
sobbed when she heard the bad news.* —*n.* the sound of
sobbing. **Ex.** *She answered with a sob.*

sober (3) [sow¹bər], *adj.* 1. not under the influence of alcohol.
Ex. *The minister was the only sober man at the party.* 2.
moderate, especially in the use of liquor. **Ex.** *He has become
more sober with age.* 3. serious; quiet; plain; etc. **Ex.** *Everyone at the funeral wore sober clothing.* —*v.* make or become sober. **Ex.** *The news sobered him.* —**so'ber·ly,** *adv.*

so-called [sow¹kɔld¹], *adj.* commonly named as; known as, often suggesting doubt as to the correctness of the term. **Ex.**
Our so-called leaders do not lead us.

social (2) [sow¹šəl], *adj.* 1. of or having to do with people as
a group with interests in common. **Ex.** *Better housing is a
serious social problem in this city.* 2. friendly; liking to be
with others. **Ex.** *He is a very social person with many
friends.* 3. of or having to do with society, especially those
persons of wealth and fashion. **Ex.** *That dance was the social event of the season.* 4. of or for companionship. **Ex.** *It
was a social meeting, and no one discussed business.* —**so'
cial·ly,** *adv.*

socialism (5) [sow¹šəlizəm], *n.* a political or economic system
in which means of production are owned by the people in
common or by the government. —**so'cial·ist,** *n.* one who believes in and favors socialism. **Ex.** *Socialists want the government to own the factories.* —**so'cial·ize,** *v.* bring under
government control or ownership.

social science [sow¹šəl say¹əns], any of the areas of study
which are concerned with society, such as history, government, economics, etc.

social security [sow¹šəl sikyur¹ətiy], a government plan which
provides help to those who are old, not able to work, etc.

a, far; æ, am; e, get; ey, late; i, in; iy, see; ɔ, all; ow, go; u, put; uw, too;
ə, but, ago; ər, fur; aw, out; ay, life; oy, boy; ŋ, ring; θ, think; ð, that;
ž, measure; š, ship; ǰ, edge; č, child.

society (2) [səsayʹətiy], *n.* 1. the community of all human beings. **Ex.** *One must obey the rules of society.* 2. a group or organization of persons who meet for a special purpose. **Ex.** *The stamp collectors organized a stamp society.* 3. rich and fashionable people. **Ex.** *He knows many people in high society.*

sock (4) [sakʹ], *n.* a short stocking. **Ex.** *Put on a pair of clean socks.*

sod (5) [sadʹ], *n.* a piece of grass-covered earth held together by the roots of the grass. **Ex.** *He bought some sod to put in the bare spots of his lawn.* —*v.* cover with sod. **Ex.** *He sodded the land around his house.*

soda (3) [sowʹdə], *n.* 1. any of various substances, usually in the form of a white powder, all having a common element, which are used in cooking, medicine, etc. **Ex.** *She added baking soda to the cake mixture.* 2. a drink made of water treated with a gas which causes the water to bubble. **Ex.** *He poured a glass of soda.* 3. a drink containing soda water, flavoring, and ice cream. **Ex.** *The two boys ordered chocolate sodas.*

soda cracker [sowʹdə krækʹər], light crisp cracker containing soda.

soda fountain [sowʹdə fawnʹtən], a counter at which customers sit on stools on one side to drink sodas or eat ice cream prepared on the other side.

sofa (3) [sowʹfə], *n.* a couch stuffed with soft material and having a back and arms. **Ex.** *She and her husband sat on the sofa.*

soft (1) [sɔftʹ], *adj.* 1. easily shaped, formed, etc.; yielding to the touch or pressure. **Ex.** *She likes to sleep on a soft bed.* 2. not strong, bright, sharp, etc. **Ex.** *A soft wind was blowing.* 3. gentle; tender; full of sympathy. **Ex.** *He spoke roughly to conceal his soft heart.* 4. smooth; delicate. **Ex.** *The baby's skin was very soft.* 5. quiet. **Ex.** *He spoke in a soft voice.* —**softʹen**, *v.* make or become soft. —**softʹly**, *adv.* —**softʹness**, *n.*

soft-boiled [sɔf(t)ʹboyldʹ], *adj.* of an egg cooked by boiling in water just enough so that the yellow part is still soft.

soil (1) [soylʹ], *n.* 1. the earth which is loose and in which plants grow. **Ex.** *The farmer tilled the soil.* 2. a country; a region. **Ex.** *He died far from home on foreign soil.*

soil (1) [soyl'], *v.* make dirty or unclean. **Ex.** *She soiled her hands working in the garden.* —*n.* a spot, mark, or stain. **Ex.** *Washing removed the soil from the dress.*

solar (5) [sow'lər], *adj.* from, of, or concerning the sun. **Ex.** *Solar energy makes the plants grow.*

solar system [sow'lər sis'təm], the sun and all the bodies, including the earth, that circle around the sun.

sold (1) [sowld'], *v.* past tense and participle of *sell.* **Ex.** *He sold his house at a profit.*

soldier (1) [sowl'jər], *n.* one serving in the army, especially one not an officer. **Ex.** *The soldier cleaned his gun.*

sole (3) [sowl'], *n.* 1. the under part of the foot. **Ex.** *The stone cut the sole of his foot.* 2. the under part of a shoe, boot, etc., not including the heel. **Ex.** *He had new soles put on his old shoes.*

sole (3) [sowl'], *adj.* being the only one or ones; belonging to one person or group; only. **Ex.** *He is the sole owner of the store.* —**sole'ly,** *adv.*

solemn (3) [sal'əm], *adj.* 1. formal; serious; sober. **Ex.** *He gave his solemn promise to defend his country.* 2. exciting or inspiring respectful fear and wonder. **Ex.** *They watched in awe the solemn ceremony in the church.* —**sol'emn·ly,** *adv.* —**sol·em'ni·ty,** *n.*

solicit (5) [səlis'it], *v.* request or ask for seriously; appeal to or for. **Ex.** *They solicited help for the blind.* —**so·lic'it·or,** *n.* one who solicits. —**so·lic'i·ta'tion,** *n.* act or practice of soliciting.

solid (2) [sal'id], *adj.* 1. having a definite shape and volume; not in the form of a liquid or gas. **Ex.** *The water had frozen into a solid block of ice.* 2. not hollow; having no empty spaces within. **Ex.** *That door is made of a solid piece of wood.* 3. strong; firm; dependable. **Ex.** *The mayor is a man of solid character.* 4. of one material, color, etc. **Ex.** *Her dress was solid black.* —*n.* something that is not a liquid or a gas. **Ex.** *After his liquid diet, the patient began to eat solids again.* —**sol'id·ly,** *adv.* —**so·lid'i·fy,** *v.* form into a solid.

solution (2) [səluw'šən, səlyuw'šən], *n.* 1. the answer to a problem. **Ex.** *The teacher gave them the correct solution to the problem.* 2. a mixture made by dissolving a solid substance in liquid. **Ex.** *He made a solution of salt and water.*

solve (2) [sɔlv'], *v.* find the solution or answer; find an explanation. **Ex.** *Scientists have solved the problem of making drinking water from sea water.*

somber (5) [sam'bər], *adj.* 1. dark; dimly lighted and shadowy. **Ex.** *She was depressed by the somber house.* 2. sad and gloomy. **Ex.** *He was sad, and his thoughts about the future were very somber.* —**som'ber·ly,** *adv.*

some (1) [səm'], *adj.* 1. of an amount, number, or part not stated. **Ex.** *I bought some apples.* 2. of a certain person or thing unknown or unstated. **Ex.** *Some man called you while you were away.* —*pron.* an unstated number or amount but less than all; a portion. **Ex.** *Some of the people had already gone home.*

somebody [səm'bad'iy], *pron.* an unnamed person. **Ex.** *Will somebody please help me?*

somehow [səm'haw'], *adv.* in some way not known. **Ex.** *Don't worry; I will finish the work somehow.*

someone [səm'wən'], *pron.* an unnamed person. **Ex.** *Is someone at the door?*

something [səm'θiŋ'], *pron.* an unnamed thing. **Ex.** *He left something for you.*

sometimes [səm'taymz'], *adv.* at times; occasionally. **Ex.** *I go there sometimes, but not often.*

somewhat (2) [səm'(h)wət, səm'hwat'], *adv.* a little; to an unknown degree. **Ex.** *He is somewhat tired.*

somewhere [səm'hwe:r'], *adv.* in an unnamed place. **Ex.** *I left my gloves somewhere.*

son (1) [sən'], *n.* a male child considered in relation to his father, his mother, or both parents. **Ex.** *Their son is a doctor.*

son-in-law [sən'ənlɔ:'], *n.* the husband of one's daughter.

song (1) [sɔ:ŋ'], *n.* 1. words and music for singing. **Ex.** *She sang three songs.* 2. a musical sound like singing. **Ex.** *We heard the song of the birds in the forest.*

soon (1) [suwn'], *adv.* 1. not long after the present time; in a short time. **Ex.** *We must hurry because our train is leaving soon.* 2. early; not long after an unmentioned time. **Ex.** *How soon can you come?* 3. quickly; rapidly. **Ex.** *They were soon tired of the game.*

soothe (4) [suwð'], *v.* 1. lessen or relieve pain, anxiety, etc.

Ex. *The presence of friends soothed her grief.* 2. calm or quiet. **Ex.** *A cup of tea soothed her.*

sordid (5) [sɔr'did], *adj.* 1. dirty; foul. **Ex.** *Slums are sordid places.* 2. morally bad; base; selfish. **Ex.** *The criminal had a sordid reputation.* —**sor'did·ly,** *adv.*

sore (2) [sɔ:r'], *adj.* 1. physically painful; aching. **Ex.** *His sore leg made walking difficult.* 2. sorrowful; grieving. **Ex.** *She is sore at heart over the loss of her daughter.* 3. causing painful or angry feelings. **Ex.** *The failure of their daughter's marriage is a sore point with them.* —*n.* a spot or place on the body where the flesh is hurt and marked or broken. **Ex.** *The sore on her arm has not yet healed.* —**sore'ly,** *adv.* very much. **Ex.** *The flood victims were sorely in need of food.*

sorrow (2) [sa:r'ow, sɔ:r'ow], *n.* 1. suffering; sadness; grief. **Ex.** *The widow had a look of sorrow on her face.* 2. something that causes suffering, sadness, or grief. **Ex.** *His bad behavior was a great sorrow to his parents.* —*v.* be sad; grieve. **Ex.** *They are still sorrowing for their son who died two years ago.* —**sor'row·ful,** *adj.* —**sor'row·ful·ly,** *adv.*

sorry (1) [sa:r'iy, sɔ:r'iy], *adj.* 1. feeling sorrow. **Ex.** *I am sorry to hear you have been ill.* 2. regretful. **Ex.** *We are sorry we are unable to attend your party.*

sort (1) [sɔrt'], *n.* 1. any class or group of persons or things that are the same or like each other in some way. **Ex.** *What sort of people do you like?* 2. type; character; kind. **Ex.** *We have books of all sorts.* —*v.* separate according to type, kind, or class. **Ex.** *The farmer's wife sorted the large eggs from the small ones.*

sought (3) [sɔ:t'], *v.* past tense and participle of *seek*. **Ex.** *He was not the man they sought.*

soul (3) [sowl'], *n.* 1. in many religions, the center of feeling, thought, and action in man, regarded as separate from the physical body; the spirit. **Ex.** *He earned hardly enough to keep body and soul together.* 2. the spirit of man, in relation to a god, believed to be separate from the body and to continue to live after its death. **Ex.** *They were praying for the souls of the dead.* 3. man's emotional nature, especially as shown in what he writes, paints, etc. **Ex.** *He put his soul*

a, far; æ, am; e, get; ey, late; i, in; iy, see; ɔ, all; ow, go; u, put; uw, too; ə, but, ago; ər, fur; aw, out; ay, life; oy, boy; ŋ, ring; θ, think; ð, that; ž, measure; š, ship; ǰ, edge; č, child.

into his work. 4. a person. **Ex.** *Not a soul offered to help.*
—**soul'ful**, *adj.* showing one's strongest emotions. —**soul'less**, *adj.* lacking feeling.

sound (1) [sawnd'], *n.* 1. rapidly moving waves of energy that affect the ear and result in hearing. **Ex.** *How fast does sound travel?* 2. that which is heard. **Ex.** *They heard the sound of the train whistle.* —*v.* 1. make a noise or sound. **Ex.** *The music sounds too loud.* 2. cause to sound. **Ex.** *He sounded the fire alarm.* 3. appear; seem. **Ex.** *His plan sounds practical.*

sound (1) [sawnd'], *adj.* 1. good; in undamaged or healthy condition. **Ex.** *The doctor said the patient's heart was sound.* 2. safe; secure. **Ex.** *He put his money in a sound business.* 3. showing good judgment. **Ex.** *He has sound plans.* —**sound'ly**, *adv.* —**sound'ness**, *n.*

soundproof [sawnd'pruwf'], *adj.* having the quality of preventing sound from going through. **Ex.** *The room is quiet because of the soundproof walls.* —*v.* make soundproof. **Ex.** *They soundproofed the television studio.*

soup (2) [suwp'], *n.* a liquid food made by cooking meat, fish, vegetables, etc. in water. **Ex.** *We had chicken soup for lunch.*

sour (2) [sawr'], *adj.* 1. having an acid taste, like that of fruit not yet ripened. **Ex.** *Those grapes taste sour.* 2. changed chemically to an acid or spoiled condition. **Ex.** *She made cheese from the sour milk.* 3. unpleasant; unfriendly. **Ex.** *He greeted me with a sour look.*

source (2) [sɔ:rs'], *n.* 1. a person, place, or thing that provides something or from which something comes. **Ex.** *This region is an important source of coal.* 2. the beginning or starting place of a stream of water. **Ex.** *The source of the river was in the mountains.*

south (1) [sawθ'], *n.* the direction to the right when a person faces the morning sun; one of the four points of the compass. **Ex.** *There is a warm breeze blowing from the south.* —*adj.* 1. in, of, or toward the south. **Ex.** *They live on the south side of the city.* 2. from the south. **Ex.** *A warm south wind was blowing.* —*adv.* in, of, or toward the south. **Ex.** *We traveled three miles south.* —**south'ern**, *adj.* characteristic of the south; in, of, or from the south. —**south'ern·er**, *n.* a person from the south.

sovereign (5) [sav'(ə)rin], *n.* a ruler, king, or queen. **Ex.** *The* *sovereign rules the country.* —*adj.* 1. highest in power, authority, or rank; supreme. 2. independent of any other; possessing independent authority. **Ex.** *The members of the United Nations are sovereign states.* —**sov'er·eign·ty,** *n.* state of being independent of others and having independent power.

sow (3) [saw'], *n.* an adult female pig. **Ex.** *The sow had eight little pigs.*

sow (3) [sow'], *v.* 1. plant seed on or in the earth. **Ex.** *The farmer will sow his wheat next week.* 2. plant in the mind. **Ex.** *The enemy agents tried to sow discontent among the people.*

sown (3) [sown'], *v.* past participle of *sow.* **Ex.** *The grain was sown in early spring.*

space (1) [speys'], *n.* 1. the unlimited area in which all things are found or located; the area within which the sun, moon, stars, etc. are. **Ex.** *Men travel through outer space to reach the moon.* 2. the area between or inside things. **Ex.** *As their family increased, they needed a house with more space.* 3. an area used for a particular purpose. **Ex.** *I could not find space to park my car.* —*v.* place in a row with space between. **Ex.** *The trees were spaced ten feet apart.* —**spa'cious,** *adj.* very large; containing much space. **Ex.** *This is a spacious room.*

spacecraft [speys'kræft'], a vehicle which is powered by rockets and is capable of traveling outside the earth's atmosphere.

space suit [speys' suwt'], a special suit worn by an astronaut when leaving a spaceship in outer space and having devices for maintaining air pressure and furnishing oxygen.

spade (3) [speyd'], *n.* a tool, usually with a short handle and a flat blade, used for digging. —*v.* dig or take away with a spade. **Ex.** *He spaded the garden.*

SPADE

spank (5) [spæŋk'], *v.* strike the rounded parts of the lower back with a flat object or with the open hand in punishment. **Ex.** *The father spanked the child.* —*n.* a single blow given in this manner. **Ex.** *The doctor gave the baby a spank to start him breathing.* —**spank'ing,** *n.* a series of spanks. **Ex.** *She gave him a spanking for disobeying her.*

spare (2) [spe:r'], *v.* 1. part with; do without. **Ex.** *He could not spare the time for a vacation.* 2. keep from harming or destroying; show mercy; treat gently. **Ex.** *He tried to spare her feelings.* 3. save; use without wasting and with care. **Ex.** *He did not spare expenses when he built his new house.* —*adj.* 1. not being used; extra. **Ex.** *They have a spare room for guests.* 2. free from required activity. **Ex.** *He likes to read in his spare time.* —*n.* that which is extra or not immediately needed or used. **Ex.** *Take my pen; I have a spare if I need one.*

spark (3) [spark'], *n.* 1. a tiny, glowing piece of material thrown off by something that is burning. **Ex.** *Sparks from the burning house were carried by the wind.* 2. anything like a spark, such as a small flash of electricity. **Ex.** *The broken wire sent out sparks.* 3. a small trace; a suggestion. **Ex.** *A spark of interest showed in his eyes.* —*v.* produce or give out sparks. **Ex.** *The old lamp sparked when she touched it.*

sparkle (3) [spark'əl], *v.* 1. produce sparks or sparklike lights. **Ex.** *The lake sparkled in the sunshine.* 2. be attractive, bright, or lively. **Ex.** *The conversation at the party sparkled.* —*n.* spark; brilliance. **Ex.** *She admired the sparkle of the diamond.*

spark plug [spark' pləg'], one of the parts in an engine that produces sparks that explode the gasoline. **Ex.** *My car has six spark plugs.*

speak (1) [spiyk'], *v.* 1. say words; talk. **Ex.** *The child began to speak at the age of two.* 2. express one's thoughts; converse; talk with. **Ex.** *Let me speak to him.* 3. give a speech or lecture. **Ex.** *He is going to speak about modern art.* 4. use a language. **Ex.** *Does he speak English?* —**speak out,** speak on a subject publicly or openly. **Ex.** *It is time for us to speak out and tell them what we think.* —**speak up,** speak in a louder voice. **Ex.** *Speak up so I can hear you.*

spear (3) [spi:r'], *n.* a weapon with a long handle and a sharp head or blade for throwing or thrusting. —*v.* thrust into as with a spear.

spearhead [spi:r'head'], *n.* 1. the head or point of a spear. 2. a person, group, etc. at the front leading in a fight or other activity. **Ex.** *The police are the spearhead of the effort to control crime.*

SPEAR

special (1) [speš'əl], *adj.* 1. of a particular kind; different; unusual. **Ex.** *She has a special way of making bread.* 2. not for general use; having a particular purpose. **Ex.** *There is a special room for dancing.* 3. an unusual degree of; great. **Ex.** *The seriously wounded man needed special care.* —**spe'cial·ist,** *n.* a person who specializes, especially in medicine. **Ex.** *The patient was advised to see a heart specialist.* —**spe'cial·ize,** *v.* study or practice a special kind of work. **Ex.** *That teacher specializes in reading problems.* —**spe'cial·ty,** *n.* that on or in which one specializes or is unusually good. **Ex.** *The cook's specialty is cakes.*

species (4) [spiy'šiyz], *n.* a group of animals or plants which have one or more characteristics in common. **Ex.** *The wolf and the dog belong to the same species.*

specific (4) [spisif'ik], *adj.* definite; particular; precise. **Ex.** *He had specific instructions to follow.* —**spe·cif'i·cal·ly,** *adv.*

specify (5) [spes'əfay], *v.* 1. state exactly or in detail. **Ex.** *Please specify which color you want.* 2. state that something is required. **Ex.** *The contract specifies that brick, not wood, is to be used.* —**spec'i·fi·ca'tion,** *n.* a detailed statement of what is wanted or required.

specimen (4) [spes'əmən], *n.* a part or one of a group of things intended to show what the rest is like; an example; a sample. **Ex.** *The doctor took a specimen of the boy's blood.*

speck (4) [spek'], *n.* 1. a small spot or piece. **Ex.** *A few specks of dirt got on the paper.* 2. a bit; a little. **Ex.** *There is just a speck of butter left.*

spectator (5) [spek'teytər, spektey'tər], *n.* one who observes. **Ex.** *Many spectators watched the ball game.*

speculate (5) [spek'yəleyt'], *v.* 1. think long and carefully about some subject; theorize; guess. **Ex.** *They speculated about the author's hidden meaning.* 2. engage in any business that is risky but that might bring large profits. **Ex.** *He speculated in land.* —**spec'u·la·tor,** *n.* one who speculates. —**spec'u·la'tion,** *n.* the act of speculating. —**spec'u·la'tive,** *adj.*

sped (3) [sped'], *v.* past tense and participle of *speed*. **Ex.** *He sped through the city.*

speech (2) [spiyč'], *n.* 1. a talk given to an audience. **Ex.** *They cheered him after his speech.* 2. the power of speaking. **Ex.** *The illness caused him to lose his speech.* 3. the manner of speaking. **Ex.** *I know from your speech that you are a stranger here.*

speed (2) [spiyd'], *n.* 1. swiftness; rapidity in moving. **Ex.** *The train gained speed.* 2. rate of motion. **Ex.** *The airplane flew at a speed of 500 miles an hour.* —*v.* drive a car fast or faster than the law allows. **Ex.** *He was speeding when the police stopped him.* —**speed'er,** *n.* one who speeds. —**speed'y,** *adj.* —**speed up,** increase the speed of.

spell (2) [spel'], *v.* 1. say or write the letters of a word in proper order. **Ex.** *Can you spell "cat"?* 2. form a word. **Ex.** *The letters "c" "a" "t" spell "cat."* —**spell'er,** *n.* 1. one who spells. 2. a book from which one learns to spell. —**spell'ing,** *n.* saying or writing the letters of a word in the proper order; the form in which words are spelled. **Ex.** *Give me the spelling of "cat."*

spell (2) [spel'], *v.* do the work of another, usually so he can rest. **Ex.** *Let me spell you for a while; you look tired.* —*n.* a period of time. **Ex.** *We had a long cold spell this winter.*

spell (2) [spel'], *n.* magic words or actions that influence or control someone. **Ex.** *He is under my spell and will do as I say.*

spellbound [spel'bawnd'], *adj.* fascinated; awed. **Ex.** *We were spellbound by his speech.* —**spell'bind·er,** *n.* a speaker who causes his listeners to be spellbound.

spend (1) [spend'], *v.* 1. give out as payment. **Ex.** *How much money do you spend each week for food?* 2. use. **Ex.** *He spends too much time at play.* 3. pass the time of. **Ex.** *We like to spend the holidays at home.*

spent (1) [spent'], *v.* past tense and participle of *spend.* **Ex.** *He had spent his vacation in Europe.*

sphere (4) [sfi:r'], *n.* 1. a round body whose surface at all points is equally distant from the center; a ball; a globe. **Ex.** *The earth is a sphere.* 2. the area within which a person or thing exists, acts, or moves. **Ex.** *His new position as manager has enlarged his sphere of influence.* —**spher'i·cal,** *adj.* round. **Ex.** *A ball is a spherical object.*

spice (5) [spays'], *n.* a vegetable substance used to flavor foods. **Ex.** *She used several spices in cooking the meat.* —*v.*

flavor with spices. **Ex.** *The cook spiced the food with pepper.*
—**spic'y,** *adj.*

spider (3) [spay'dər], *n.* a small creature with
eight legs that spins threads to form a web
and a trap for insects. —**spi'der·y,** *adj.* like a
spider. **Ex.** *The tall man had long, spidery
legs.*

SPIDER

spill (3) [spil'], *v.* 1. cause or allow liquid or
any loose material to run or fall from a container. **Ex.** *The child spilled the milk on the
floor.* 2. fall or run out. **Ex.** *Water spilled from the fountain.*

spilt (3) [spilt'], past tense and participle of *spill*. **Ex.** *Flour
had been spilt on the table.*

spin (3) [spin'], *v.* 1. turn or cause to turn rapidly around a
center point. **Ex.** *The earth spins as it moves around the
sun.* 2. make threads by drawing out and twisting wool or
the threadlike structure of certain plants. **Ex.** *There were
hundreds of machines spinning cotton.* 3. form a thread
from a substance produced by the body. **Ex.** *We watched
the spider spin its web.*

spine (4) [spayn'], *n.* the backbone of a man or animal from
the tail to the head. **Ex.** *His spine was broken in the accident.* —**spin'al,** *adj.* —**spine'less,** *adj.* 1. having no spine. 2.
weak; without determination or courage.

spirit (3) [spir'it], *n.* 1. mood; attitude; general outlook. **Ex.**
She took his advice in the right spirit. 2. the part of man
that is not physical; the soul. **Ex.** *Though he is dead, he is
with us in spirit.* 3. liveliness; character and energy. **Ex.** *He
showed spirit in his answers.* 4. a being that cannot be explained by the laws of nature and that has no physical
reality, such as an angel, fairy, devil, etc. **Ex.** *He believes in
evil spirits.* 5. alcohol. **Ex.** *He likes strong spirits.* —*v.* carry
away secretly and quickly as if by spirits. **Ex.** *Someone
spirited the child away.* —**spir'it·ed,** *adj.* full of energy;
active. —**spir'it·u·al,** *adj.* concerning religion.

spit (3) [spit'], *v.* 1. throw out from the mouth. **Ex.** *He spit
out the seeds of the orange.* 2. throw out as if spitting. **Ex.**
He spit his words at us angrily. —*n.* the act of spitting; also,
the matter forced out. **Ex.** *She wiped the spit from the corner of the baby's mouth.*

splash (4) [splæš'], *v.* cause liquid to scatter in all directions
by striking or throwing it. **Ex.** *The children were splashing*

water on each other in the swimming pool. —*n.* 1. the sound of liquid splashing. **Ex.** *We heard the splash of waves against the boat.* 2. liquid splashed or a spot made by it. **Ex.** *There was a splash of paint on the floor.*

splendid (2) [splen'did], *adj.* 1. magnificent; elegant; brilliant. **Ex.** *The rich man lives in a splendid house.* 2. excellent; distinguished. **Ex.** *The artist did a splendid piece of work.* —**splen'did·ly,** *adv.*

splinter (5) [splin'tər], *n.* a very thin, long piece of wood or other material broken from a larger piece. **Ex.** *The carpenter got a splinter in his finger.* —*v.* split or break into splinters. **Ex.** *A shot splintered the window.*

split (3) [split'], *v.* 1. break or divide lengthwise, from end to end into two or more parts. **Ex.** *He split the wood with an ax.* 2. burst. **Ex.** *The ripe melon split in the sun.* 3. divide into portions or parts. **Ex.** *The boys split the money into four shares.* 4. divide into groups. **Ex.** *Our club was split by the argument.* —*n.* 1. the opening made by splitting. **Ex.** *She mended the split in his coat.* 2. a division. **Ex.** *There was a split in the party on the issue of new taxes.* —**split'ting,** *adj.* sharp or painful. **Ex.** *I have a splitting headache.*

spoil (2) [spoyl'], *v.* 1. damage; cause to become useless; rot. **Exs.** *She spoiled the meat by burning it. Milk spoils quickly if it is not kept in a cold place.* 2. damage or weaken the character by granting every wish. **Ex.** *He was their only son, and they spoiled him.* —**spoil'age,** *n.* act of spoiling or that which is spoiled. —**spoils',** *n.pl.* things taken from another, by force, as from the enemy in war.

spoke (1) [spowk'], *n.* one of the bars or rods that goes from the center of a wheel to the rim and acts as a support for the rim. **Ex.** *One of the spokes is missing.*

spoke (1) [spowk'], *v.* past tense of *speak.* **Ex.** *He spoke to me about that problem yesterday.*

spoken (2) [spow'kən], *v.* past participle of *speak.* **Ex.** *He had spoken to her about the problem before she left.* —*adj.* 1. said aloud; uttered. **Ex.** *He gave a spoken order.* 2. speaking in a certain kind of way. **Ex.** *She is a soft-spoken woman.*

spokesman [spowks'mən], *n.* one who speaks as a representative of another or of a group. **Ex.** *At the meeting, a spokesman for the government gave us the President's views.*

sponge (4) [spənj'], *n.* many tiny animals living together, usually under water, in a mass full of holes; the skeleton of this mass or an absorbent material like this used for cleaning, bathing, etc. Ex. *He cleaned his car with a sponge.* —*v.* clean or soak up as with a sponge. Ex. *She sponged the table clean.* —**spon'gy,** *adj.* soft and absorbent like a sponge.

spontaneous (5) [spantey'niyəs], *adj.* 1. proceeding naturally, without plan, effort, or thought. Ex. *The children's laughter was spontaneous.* 2. caused by a force within; independent of anything outside oneself or itself. Ex. *A spontaneous fire started in the hay.* —**spon·ta'ne·ous·ly,** *adv.* —**spon`ta·ne' i·ty,** *n.*

spool (5) [spuwl'], *n.* a tube of wood or metal on which something is wound. Ex. *Please hand me the spool of thread.*

spoon (2) [spuwn'], *n.* a tool with a handle and a small bowl, used for eating, stirring, and serving food.

SPOON

sport (2) [sport'], *n.* 1. a particular activity performed for amusement, exercise, or relaxation. Ex. *Swimming is her favorite summer sport.* 2. fun; amusement. Ex. *Jumping in the leaves was great sport for the children.* —**sports,** *adj.* suitable for sports. Exs. *He wore a sport shirt. She was wearing a sports dress. He wore sports clothes.*

sporting [sport'iŋ], *adj.* fair; like a sportsman. Ex. *He gave his rival a sporting chance.*

sportsman [sports'mən], *n.* 1. one who participates in sports. 2. one who is courteous and obeys the rules of the game without complaining. Ex. *He was a sportsman about losing the game.*

spot (1) [spat'], *n.* 1. a small mark on or in a surface. Ex. *She has a paint spot on her dress.* 2. a particular place; a location. Ex. *They are building their house in a beautiful spot.* —*v.* mark or become marked with spots. Ex. *The soup spotted his tie.* —**spot'less,** *adj.* without spots. —**spot'ty,** *adj.* having spots; not even or regular.

spotlight [spat'layt`], *n.* 1. a lamp with a strong ray of light used in theaters to shine on an actor or actors to draw attention to them. 2. public attention. Ex. *Her romance with the governor had put her in the spotlight.*

---

a, far; æ, am; e, get; ėy, late; i, in; iy, see; ɔ, all; ow, go; u, put; uw, too; ə, but, ago; ər, fur; aw, out; ay, life; oy, boy; ŋ, ring; θ, think; ð, that; ž, measure; š, ship; ǰ, edge; č, child.

spout (5) [spawt'], *v.* discharge or throw out a liquid with force. **Ex.** *Gasoline spouted from the hole in the tank.* —*n.* a pipe or tube through which liquid is discharged. **Ex.** *Steam was coming from the spout of the kettle.*

sprang (3) [spræŋ'], *v.* past tense of *spring*. **Ex.** *At the sound of the alarm, he sprang out of bed.*

spray (3) [sprey'], *n.* 1. water or other liquid scattered in a large mass of tiny drops. **Ex.** *Spray from the high waves hit our faces.* 2. an instrument for scattering liquid in this manner or the liquid so scattered. **Ex.** *He used a spray to kill the insects.* —*v.* discharge spray upon; let fall as spray. **Ex.** *She sprayed the flowers with water.* —**spray'er,** *n.*

spread (1) [spred'], *v.* 1. extend in length and width; open out. **Ex.** *She spread a cloth on the table.* 2. make or become more widely known; scatter or become scattered widely. **Ex.** *The bad news spread quickly.* 3. cover with. **Ex.** *She spread butter on the bread.* —*n.* the act of spreading. **Ex.** *The spread of learning has been furthered by the radio.* —**spread'er,** *n.* that which spreads.

spring (1) [spriŋ'], *v.* 1. leap; rise suddenly. **Ex.** *The sound of a shot made him spring from his chair.* 2. return to position or shape after being stretched. **Ex.** *He saw the door spring shut.* 3. come into being. **Ex.** *The city seemed to spring up overnight.* —*n.* 1. the season between winter and summer. **Ex.** *The days became warmer when spring came.* 2. the act of springing; a leap. **Ex.** *The sudden spring of the lion surprised him.* 3. a place where water rises from the earth. **Ex.** *Their drinking water comes from a spring.* 4. stiff steel, wire, etc. wound in a series of circles which yield when pressed but return to the original shape when freed. **Ex.** *The spring in the clock is broken.* —*adj.* of or for the spring season. **Ex.** *In April, he bought some spring clothes.* —**spring'y,** *adj.*

sprinkle (3) [spriŋ'kəl], *v.* 1. scatter in drops or very small pieces. **Ex.** *He sprinkled salt and pepper on his food.* 2. rain lightly. **Ex.** *Take your umbrella with you; it is sprinkling.* —*n.* a light rain. **Ex.** *It was only a sprinkle, and I did not get very wet.* —**sprink'ler,** *n.* that which sprinkles. —**sprink'ling,** *n.* not very many; a few. **Ex.** *There was only a sprinkling of people in the theater.*

sprung (3) [sprəŋ'], *v.* past tense and participle of *spring*. **Ex.** *He had sprung from the bed.*

spun (4) [spən¹], *v.* past tense and participle of *spin.* **Ex.** *He spun around to see who was behind him.*

spur (4) [spə:r¹], *n.* 1. a metal device with sharp points put on the heel of a rider's shoe or boot and used to urge a horse to move. **Ex.** *The horse leaped over the fence at the touch of the spur.* 2. anything that resembles or acts as a spur. **Ex.** *The teacher's words were a spur to the girl's imagination.* —*v.* 1. apply spurs to a horse. **Ex.** *He spurred the horse into a gallop.* 2. urge. **Ex.** *Danger spurred him on.*

spy (3) [spay¹], *n.* 1. one who watches others secretly. **Ex.** *The manufacturer sent a spy to learn the methods of a rival company.* 2. one employed by a government to obtain secret information about another country. **Ex.** *The spy reported the development of a new weapon.* —*v.* 1. act as a spy. **Ex.** *His job was to spy on the enemy.* 2. catch sight of; glimpse; see. **Ex.** *She spied her friends walking down the street.*

squad (5) [skwad¹], *n.* 1. a small group of soldiers, usually eight or ten men. **Ex.** *The squad marched on the field.* 2. any small group of persons organized for a particular purpose. **Ex.** *A police squad hurried to the scene of the trouble.*

squad car [skwad¹ kar¹], a car used by police to patrol streets.

squadron (5) [skwad¹rən], *n.* a military organization of airplanes or ships that moves as a unit. **Ex.** *Those two pilots formerly flew in the same squadron.*

square (1) [skwe:r¹], *n.* 1. a flat shape having four equal sides and four right or 90-degree angles. 2. an open area in a town or city with streets on all four sides. **Ex.** *There were many shops around the square.* 3. the number which results from multiplying one number by itself. **Ex.** *The square of 4 is 16, that is,* SQUARE 1

$4 \times 4 = 16.$ —*v.* 1. multiply a number by itself. **Ex.** *If you square 4, the result is 16.* 2. straighten; make square. —*adj.* 1. shaped like a square. **Ex.** *She was carrying a square box.* 2. having the same length and width. **Ex.** *A square yard is one yard long and one yard wide.* —**square¹ly,** *adv.*

square root [skwe:r¹ ruwt¹], a number which, when multiplied by itself, equals a known number. **Ex.** *The square root of 4 is 2.*

squeak (4) [skwiyk¹], *n.* a thin, sharp, high cry or sound. **Ex.**

The squeak of the mouse scared her. —*v.* make this sound.
Ex. *The door squeaked as I opened it.* —**squeak'y,** *adj.*

squeeze (4) [skwiyz'], *v.* 1. apply pressure. **Ex.** *He squeezed
my hand in greeting.* 2. apply pressure in order to get out.
Ex. *She squeezed the juice from several oranges.* 3. push
one's way into or through a small space. **Ex.** *They squeezed
through the crowd.* —*n.* the act of squeezing. **Ex.** *She gave
the child an affectionate squeeze.* —**squeez'er,** *n.* that which
squeezes.

squirrel (3) [skwər'əl], *n.* a small, bushy-tailed
tree-climbing animal. **Ex.** *The squirrel was
busy gathering nuts.*

stab (5) [stæb'], *v.* cut into or through with a
pointed weapon; thrust. **Ex.** *He stabbed the
man with a knife.* —*n.* the thrust or wound
made with a pointed weapon. **Ex.** *He received
a stab in the chest.* —**stab'ber,** *n.*

SQUIRREL

stable (3) [stey'bəl], *adj.* 1. firm; not easily
shaken; solid. **Ex.** *They built the house upon a stable foundation.* 2. remaining the same; unchanging. **Ex.** *Prices have
been stable for the last year.* —**sta·bil'i·ty,** *n.* the condition
of being stable. —**sta'bi·lize,** *v.* make stable. —**sta'bi·liz·er,**
n. that which stabilizes.

stable (3) [stey'bəl], *n.* a building for the housing and feeding
of horses or cattle. **Ex.** *He fed the horses in the stable.* —*v.*
put or keep in a stable. **Ex.** *They stabled the horses for the
night.*

stack (4) [stæk'], *n.* a large rounded pile. **Ex.** *They piled the
straw into a stack.* —*v.* pile up in a stack. **Ex.** *She stacked
the dirty dishes in the sink.*

staff (3) [stæf'], *n.* 1. a group of assistants to a manager, chief,
etc. **Ex.** *He explained the new policy to the editorial staff.*
2. a stick used as a support. **Ex.** *He leaned on his staff.* —*v.*
supply with a staff. **Ex.** *They staffed the school with excellent teachers.*

stage (2) [steyǰ'], *n.* 1. a platform, raised so that it can be
easily seen, on which a play is acted, a speech is given, etc.
Ex. *There were two actors on the stage.* 2. the acting profession. **Ex.** *She wants to go on the stage.* 3. a single step in a
process; a period of development. **Ex.** *The child is at an
interesting stage.* —*v.* put or exhibit on a stage. **Ex.** *They
will stage that play for the first time.*

stage coach [steyǰᶦ kowč'], a passenger carriage pulled by horses.

stage fright [steyǰᶦ frayt'], nervousness felt when going before a group of people to act, speak, etc.

stagehand [steyǰ'hænd`], *n.* one who works in a theater fixing the lights, scenery, etc., but does not act.

stage-struck [steyǰ'strək`], *adj.* full of the desire to be an actor or actress.

stagger (4) [stæg'ər], *v.* 1. sway when standing or walking; walk or stand unsteadily. **Ex.** *The drunken man staggered along the road.* 2. cause to stagger; shock; affect strongly. **Ex.** *The terrible news staggered him.*

stain (3) [steyn'], *n.* 1. a dirty spot; an unwanted spot. **Ex.** *A coffee stain was on his shirt.* 2. a coloring matter used on wood or other materials. **Ex.** *He rubbed the table with a brown stain.* —*v.* 1. discolor; make dirty. **Ex.** *The child stained her dress with berries.* 2. change the color. **Ex.** *The carpenter stained the chair.* —**stain'less**, *adj.* 1. spotless; without stains. 2. able to resist staining or rusting.

staircase (5) [ste:r'keys`], *n.* a series of steps including the railing at the sides. **Ex.** *An outside staircase leads to the garden.*

stairs (2) [ste:rz'], *n.* a series of steps used in going up or down from one level to another. **Ex.** *Those stairs go up to the bedroom.*

stairway [ste:r'wey`], *n.* a series of steps; a staircase.

stake (3) [steyk'], *n.* 1. a pointed post or piece of wood forced into the ground. **Ex.** *Stakes marked his property line.* 2. an interest in something, as money put into a business. **Ex.** *As a partner, he has a stake in that business.* —*v.* mark or identify by stakes. **Ex.** *The settlers staked out their land.* —**stakes'**, *n.* something, such as money, risked in a game or contest. **Ex.** *He left the gambling game when the stakes became too high.*

stale (4) [steyl'], *adj.* 1. dry, flat, etc. in taste because old. **Ex.** *There was only a piece of stale cake left.* 2. of no more interest; having lost strength, energy, or interest in. **Ex.** *She has grown stale in her job and needs a change.*

stalk (3) [stɔ:k'], *v.* 1. follow and approach quietly, in pursuit. **Ex.** *The hunters stalked the lion.* 2. walk stiffly and proudly. **Ex.** *With her head in the air, she stalked from the room.*

stalk (3) [stɔːkˈ], *n.* the main stem of a plant; any part like this.

stall (4) [stɔːlˈ], *n.* 1. a section of a stable or shed for one animal. **Ex.** *The horse was missing from its stall.* 2. a small table or section where business is done. **Ex.** *They sell their vegetables at a stall in the farmer's market.* —*v.* come or bring to a stop without intending to. **Ex.** *The motor stalled because the car was out of gas.*

STALK

stammer (4) [stæmˈər], *v.* speak in a hesitating way by pausing between words or repeating parts of words. **Ex.** *The frightened girl could only stammer a reply.* —*n.* the act of speaking in this way. **Ex.** *He speaks with a stammer.*

stamp (2) [stæmpˈ], *v.* 1. strike or hit noisily and with force. **Ex.** *He stamped his feet to keep warm.* 2. print on or press into with some mark, design, etc. **Ex.** *The name of the manufacturer was stamped on the box.* —*n.* 1. a small paper put on letters and certain products to show that a fee or tax has been paid. **Ex.** *She put an airmail stamp on the letter.* 2. any device which prints on or presses into; the mark made by such a device. **Ex.** *He has a rubber stamp with his name on it.*

stand (1) [stændˈ], *v.* 1. move into or be in an upright or erect position in which only the feet are on a surface. **Ex.** *He always stands when older people come into the room.* 2. be or grow in a position. **Ex.** *A tall tree stands in front of the house.* 3. remain; not run away. **Ex.** *You must stand and fight.* 4. bear; endure. **Ex.** *I cannot stand this cold weather.* —*n.* 1. the act of standing firmly; the act of holding a belief or opinion. **Ex.** *What is your stand on that question?* 2. a small table on which something rests. **Ex.** *She put the two brass figures on a stand.* 3. a table on which something is placed for sale. **Ex.** *She stopped at the baked goods stand to buy a cake.* —**stand a chance,** have a prospect or possibility. **Ex.** *He is a good student and stands a good chance of graduating with honors.* —**stand by,** 1. stay or stand near. 2. support. **Ex.** *I will stand by you when you are in trouble.* —**stand for,** 1. endure. **Ex.** *I will not stand for this treatment.* 2. be a symbol of. **Ex.** *Our flag stands for our coun-*

try. 3. seek to be elected. **Ex.** *He is standing for office this year.* —**stand in,** substitute for someone else. **Ex.** *My brother will stand in for me at work while I am away.* —**stand off,** 1. stand away from. 2. prevent from coming near by force. **Ex.** *He can stand off ten men.* —**stand out,** be noticeable. **Ex.** *She stands out from the other girls because of her dress.* —**stand up,** 1. stand; move into a standing position. 2. last; continue to operate. **Ex.** *A good car will stand up under difficult driving conditions.* —**stand up for,** defend; support. **Ex.** *He stands up for the ideas in which he believes.* —**stand up to,** bravely meet a danger and not run. **Ex.** *He will stand up to anyone who tries to hurt her.*

standard (2) [stæn'dərd], *n.* anything accepted by general agreement as a basis of comparison; a model. **Ex.** *The standards for admission to this school are very high.* —*adj.* not special; usual; agreed or established. **Ex.** *This store sells standard sizes in shoes and stockings.* —**stand'ard·ize,** *v.*

standing army [stæn'diŋ ar'miy], a permanent army. **Ex.** *Our country has a strong standing army.*

standpoint [stænd'poynt'], *n.* position from which things are regarded. **Ex.** *From my standpoint, we should leave early.*

stanza (5) [stæn'zə], *n.* a group of lines of verse which form a part of a poem or song. **Ex.** *That poem has four stanzas.*

staple (5) [stey'pəl], *n.* 1. a principal product of a country or area. **Ex.** *Rice is a staple of Burma.* 2. a frequently used item of food in a household. **Ex.** *We keep a supply of staples, such as flour, sugar, and coffee, in the house at all times.* —*adj.* produced, used, or sold in large quantities; principal. **Ex.** *Bread is a staple food in many countries.*

star (1) [star'], *n.* 1. any of the light-giving heavenly bodies that appear in the night sky. 2. a flat figure having five or more points often used to represent something. **Ex.** *There is one star in our flag for each of the states.* 3. a brilliant person; a famous actor. **Ex.** *She is a movie star.* —*v.* act the most important part in a movie or play. **Ex.** *She starred in that play.* —**star'ry,** *adj.*

STAR 2

starch (5) [starč'], *n.* 1. a white, tasteless substance found in certain foods, such as potatoes and rice. **Ex.** *Eating too much starch will make you fat.* 2. a preparation of this substance mixed with water to stiffen cotton and linen mate-

rials. **Ex.** *He likes to have a little starch in his shirt collars.*
—*v.* stiffen with starch. **Ex.** *She starched the dresses.*
—**starch'y**, *adj.*

stare (2) [ste:r'], *v.* gaze steadily. **Ex.** *He stared at the strange man.* —*n.* a steady gaze. **Ex.** *She turned away from his stare.*

stark (5) [stark'], *adj.* 1. complete; absolute. **Ex.** *Stark fear shone in his eyes.* 2. rough; severe; cheerless. **Ex.** *We walked over the stark, frozen fields.* —*adv.* entirely. **Ex.** *The baby was stark naked.*

start (1) [start'], *v.* 1. begin. **Ex.** *We started on our trip yesterday.* 2. cause to begin. **Ex.** *He started the engine of his car.* —*n.* a beginning. **Ex.** *He made a good start on his work.* —**start'er**, *n.* one who or that which starts. —**start in,** begin some activity. —**start out,** begin a trip. **Ex.** *He started out for his office.*

startle (3) [star'təl], *v.* cause sudden fright; cause to jump in surprise. **Ex.** *Your knock startled me.* —**star'tling**, *adj.*

starve (2) [starv'], *v.* 1. be very hungry for food; suffer from hunger; die from lack of food. **Ex.** *Many animals starved during the snowstorm.* 2. suffer for lack of something needed. **Ex.** *The children without parents were starving for affection.* —**star·va'tion**, *n.*

state (1) [steyt'], *n.* 1. the condition of a person or thing. **Ex.** *He was in an angry state.* 2. a group of people under one government; a nation. **Ex.** *Many foreign states were represented at the meeting.* 3. one of the political divisions of some nations. **Ex.** *The United States consists of fifty states.* —*v.* declare; say. **Ex.** *He stated his views on the subject.* —**state'ment**, *n.* 1. the act of stating. 2. something stated.

stately (4) [steyt'liy], *adj.* majestic; showing great dignity. **Ex.** *We were impressed by her stately appearance.* —**state'li·ness**, *n.*

stateroom [steyt'ruwm'], *n.* cabin or bedroom for passengers on a ship.

statesman (3) [steyts'mən], *n.* a man who shows ability and wisdom in the affairs of government. **Ex.** *They honored him as their leading statesman.* —**states'man·ship**, *n.* the art of diplomacy or governing wisely.

station (1) [stey'šən], *n.* 1. a place of special work or duty. **Ex.** *We called the police station for help.* 2. a place for passengers to get on or get off along a train or bus route; the building at such a place. Ex. *We bought our tickets at the railroad station.* 3. a place equipped for sending out or receiving radio or television broadcasts. Ex. *We could see the tower of the radio station.* —*v.* put in a certain place or position. Ex. *A guard was stationed at the gate.* —**sta'tion·ar`y**, *adj.* fixed; not changing or moving.

statistics (4) [stətis'tiks], *n.* numbers counted and arranged to express facts; the science of gathering and arranging such facts. Ex. *Statistics show that the population of the world is increasing.* —**sta·tis'ti·cal**, *adj.* —**sta·tis'tic·al·ly**, *adv.* —**stat`is·tic'ian**, *n.* a person who works with numbers.

statue (3) [stæč'uw], *n.* a figure of a person or animal, made in metal, carved in wood, etc. Ex. *A marble statue stands in the garden.*

stature (5) [stæč'ər], *n.* 1. height. Ex. *The boy did not reach the stature of his father.* 2. growth; development. Ex. *The professor is a man of great mental stature.*

status (5) [stey'təs, stæt'əs], *n.* 1. state or condition of affairs. Ex. *What is the present status of our foreign relations?* 2. position; rank. Ex. *The status of a doctor is very high in this community.*

statute (5) [stæč'uwt], *n.* a rule; a law, especially one passed by a lawmaking body. Ex. *The new statute increased the taxes we must pay.* —**stat'u·tor·y**, *adj.*

stay (1) [stey'], *v.* 1. remain in a place; not go. Ex. *We stayed there for three hours.* 2. be a guest; live for a time. Ex. *Our friends are staying with us for a month.* 3. continue to be. Ex. *The children stayed clean most of the day.* —*n.* the act of remaining in a place; a visit. Ex. *How long was your stay in the country?*

stead (5) [sted'], *n.* the place of someone or something taken by a substitute. Ex. *While I am away, he will act in my stead.*

steady (2) [sted'iy], *adj.* 1. not changing; not stopping; regular. Ex. *A steady wind was blowing.* 2. serious; dependable. Ex. *His employers know him to be a steady worker.* 3. firm; well-supported. Ex. *The table is steady.* —*v.* make or become steady. Ex. *Please steady the ladder.* —**stead'i·ly**, *adv.* —**stead'i·ness**, *n.*

steak (3) [steyk'], *n.* meat or fish cut in slices for cooking close to a flame or for frying. **Ex.** *They served steak to their guests.*

steal (2) [stiyl'], *v.* take away unlawfully. **Ex.** *The thief tried to steal my watch.*

steam (2) [stiym'], *n.* 1. the gas that forms when water boils. **Ex.** *Steam rose from the pot.* 2. this gas used under pressure as a source of energy. **Ex.** *This engine is run by steam.* —*v.* 1. produce steam. **Ex.** *The food is steaming.* 2. move or run by steam. **Ex.** *The ship steamed up the river.* —*adj.* using or operating by steam. **Ex.** *They have steam heat in their house.* —**steam'y,** *adj.* —**steam'er,** *n.* a ship powered by steam.

steel (2) [stiyl'], *n.* iron made harder and stronger by mixing it with other substances. **Ex.** *His tools were made of steel.* —*adj.* of or like steel in strength.

steep (3) [stiyp'], *adj.* having a slope or slant almost straight up and down. **Ex.** *The hill was too steep for them to climb.* —**steep'ly,** *adv.* —**steep'ness,** *n.*

steer (3) [sti:r'], *n.* any young male cattle raised to be eaten; an ox. **Ex.** *The steers were fattened for market.*

steer (3) [sti:r'], *v.* 1. guide or direct the course of a car, ship, etc. **Ex.** *We steered the boat toward land.* 2. be guided or directed. **Ex.** *The car steers easily.*

steerage [sti:r'ij], *n.* formerly the least expensive and desirable accommodations for passengers on a ship.

stem (3) [stem'], *n.* 1. the part of a plant from which the leaves and flowers grow. **Ex.** *She chose roses with long stems.* 2. any thing or part that looks like a stem. **Ex.** *The tall glass had a slender stem.*

step (1) [step'], *n.* 1. a movement made by lifting one foot and placing it in a new position. **Ex.** *The baby took his first steps today.* 2. a measure of the distance covered in one such movement. **Ex.** *He walked three steps ahead of me.* 3. the manner of walking. **Ex.** *He walked with a firm step.* 4. that on which one places the foot in going up or down. **Ex.** *He walked up the steps to the front door.* 5. an action, phase, degree, or rank in a series. **Ex.** *What steps must I take to obtain a driver's permit?* —*v.* walk; move or go by making a step. **Ex.** *She stepped aside.* —**step down,** 1. go from a higher to lower position. 2. resign from a job. **Ex.** *The previous president stepped down a year ago.* —**step up,** 1. go from a lower to higher position. 2. increase. **Ex.** *The*

new fertilizer has stepped up the amount of rice grown.
—take steps, do something toward an objective. **Ex.** *He took steps to prevent such an accident from happening again.*

stepbrother [step'brə ͡ðˊər], *n.* the son of one's stepparent by a former marriage.

stepchild [step'čayldˊ], *n.* stepson or stepdaughter.

stepdaughter [step'dɔː ͟'tər], *n.* daughter of one's husband or wife by a previous marriage.

stepfather [step'faː ͟'ðˊər], *n.* husband of one's mother after she remarries.

stepmother [step'mə ͡ðˊər], *n.* wife of one's father after he remarries.

stepparent [step'pær ͟'ənt, step'peːr ͟'ənt], *n.* stepfather or stepmother.

steppingstone [step'iŋstownˊ], *n.* 1. a stone on which to step, as in crossing a stream. 2. anything which is a step toward progress in one's career, life, etc. **Ex.** *This job is a steppingstone to success.*

stepsister [step'sis ͟'tər], *n.* the daughter of one's stepparent by a former marriage.

stepson [step'sənˊ], *n.* son of one's husband or wife by a previous marriage.

stern (3) [stərnˊ], *adj.* 1. severe; strict. **Ex.** *The judge's face was stern as he spoke.* 2. firm; unchanging. **Ex.** *He made a stern resolve to do better in the future.* **—sternˊly,** *adv.* **—sternˊness,** *n.*

stern (3) [stərnˊ], *n.* the back part of a ship. **Ex.** *We watched the stern of the ship disappear.*

stew (4) [stuwˊ, styuwˊ], *v.* boil food slowly. **Ex.** *She stewed some fruit for dessert.* **—n.** a dish, somewhat thicker than soup, prepared in this manner. **Ex.** *We had lamb stew for dinner.*

stick (1) [stikˊ], *n.* 1. a branch or part of a tree or bush when broken or cut off. **Ex.** *The men picked up sticks and used them to start a fire.* 2. any long, slender piece of wood. **Ex.** *The children were fighting with sticks.* 3. a long, slender piece. **Ex.** *We bought two sticks of candy.* **—v.** 1. be held or caught and unable to move. **Ex.** *What made the door stick?* 2. push a pointed thing so as to pierce with it. **Ex.** *Be careful or you will stick the needle in your finger.* 3. fasten or be fastened by piercing with a point or by gluing.

Ex. *May I stick this notice on the wall?* 4. push forward; push into. Ex. *Stick this letter in the mailbox, please.* 5. stay with or by; continue doing. Ex. *Stick to your work until you finish it.* —**stick'y,** *adj.* 1. sticking because it has glue or something similar on it. Ex. *The child's hands were sticky with honey.* 2. hot and damp. Ex. *This sticky weather is tiring.* —**stick'i·ness,** *n.* —**stick by,** remain loyal. Ex. *His wife stuck by him after all his friends deserted him.* —**stick out,** be noticeable. Ex. *A smart boy sticks out in a group.*

stiff (2) [stif'], *adj.* 1. not easily bent; hard. Ex. *The paint brush was too stiff to use.* 2. not easily moved. Ex. *My neck is stiff.* 3. formal. Ex. *She was stiff and unfriendly in her greeting.* 4. strong; severe. Ex. *He was given a stiff punishment.* —**stiff'en,** *v.* —**stiff'ly,** *adv.* —**stiff'ness,** *n.*

stifle (5) [stay'fəl], *v.* 1. cause difficulty in breathing. Ex. *We were stifled by the heat.* 2. prevent from doing, happening, etc. Ex. *She stifled a sob.* —**sti'fling,** *adj.* lacking fresh air.

stigma (5) [stig'mə], *n.* a mark or stain on one's name or reputation. Ex. *The stigma of his crime caused him many difficulties.*

still (1) [stil'], *adj.* 1. not moving; motionless. Ex. *The hot summer air was still.* 2. quiet; noiseless; silent. Ex. *He asked the shouting children to be still.* —*adv.* 1. up till the present or a stated time. Ex. *Was he still here when you arrived?* 2. even yet. Ex. *He has a lot of money, but he wants still more.* 3. nevertheless; even so. Ex. *She knew the work was hard, but she still wanted to try it.* —**still'ness,** *n.*

still (1) [stil'], *n.* a device for making strong alcoholic liquors.

stillborn [stil'bɔrn'], *adj.* born dead. Ex. *She was grief-stricken over the birth of her stillborn child.*

still life [stil' layf'], a picture or painting of objects. such as fruit or flowers, pleasingly arranged. Ex. *She bought a still life of oranges and lemons in a blue bowl.*

stimulate (4) [stim'yəleyt'], *v.* cause to become active or more active; excite. Ex. *Reading good books stimulates thought.* —**stim'u·lant,** *n.* something that stimulates. Ex. *Coffee is a stimulant.*

sting (3) [stiŋ'], *v.* 1. cause pain by sticking with something sharp. Ex. *Be careful or the bee will sting you.* 2. cause or suffer a sharp, quick pain. Ex. *His face was still stinging from the blow.* 3. cause or suffer hurt to the feelings. Ex. *His unkind comments sometimes sting.* —*n.* 1. the act of stinging. **Ex.** *The sting of a bee is painful.* 2. the wound or pain caused by stinging. **Ex.** *Put some medicine on the sting.*

stir (2) [stiːrˈ], *v.* 1. mix. **Ex.** *She stirred some sugar into her coffee.* 2. move somewhat. **Ex.** *The sleeping patient had not stirred for an hour.* 3. excite. **Ex.** *The people were deeply stirred by his rousing speech.* —*n.* a state of excitement. **Ex.** *The good news caused a stir.* —**stir′rer**, *n.* one who or that which stirs. —**stir′ring**, *adj.*

stirrup (5) [stəːrˈəp, stiːrˈəp], *n.* a flat-bottomed ring of metal or wood hung from the saddle of a horse to support the rider's foot. **Ex.** *He placed his foot in the stirrup.*

stitch (4) [stičˈ], *n.* in sewing, a single movement of a threaded needle into and out of the material; a loop of the thread made in this way. **Ex.** *She made a neat row of stitches along the edge of the collar.* —*v.* sew; join together by stitches. **Ex.** *She stitched the two lengths of cloth together.*

stock (1) [stakˈ], *n.* 1. a supply of goods available. **Ex.** *That store has a large stock of canned goods for sale.* 2. animals kept on a farm. **Ex.** *He got up early to feed the stock.* 3. shares of ownership in a company. **Ex.** *He owns stock in several companies.* —*v.* store away; have available for sale. **Ex.** *Our store stocks this shoe in both black and brown.* —**take stock,** 1. count, weigh, or measure the amount of each item in stock. 2. consider all aspects of a situation before acting. **Ex.** *The commander took stock of the situation and planned his next move.*

stockbroker [stakˈbrowˋkər], *n.* a person who buys and sells shares of stocks, bonds, etc.

stock exchange [stakˈ iksčeynǰ'], a place where stocks and bonds are bought and sold.

stockholder [stakˈhowlˋdər], *n.* a person who owns shares in a business. **Ex.** *That stockholder owns ten shares.*

stocking (2) [stakˈiŋ], *n.* a close-fitting cloth covering for the legs and foot, usually knitted. **Ex.** *She bought three pairs of black stockings.*

stock market [stakˈ marˋkit], a place where stocks and bonds are bought and sold.

---

stockpile [stak'payl`], *n.* a large amount of some material set aside for later use when the material may be scarce. **Ex.** *The government is creating a stockpile of wool.*

stockyard [stak'yard`], *n.* a place where animals are kept briefly until they are slaughtered or shipped to another place.

stole (2) [stowl'], *v.* past tense of *steal.* **Ex.** *They stole the money.*

stomach (2) [stəm'ək], *n.* 1. the large, pouchlike organ of the body into which food goes after it is eaten. **Ex.** *He has a pain in his stomach.* 2. the part of the body in which this organ is located. **Ex.** *Lie flat on your stomach.*

stone (1) [stown'], *n.* 1. hard earthy or mineral matter which is not metal; rock. **Ex.** *The house was made of stone.* 2. a small piece of rock. **Ex.** *The stone hit the window.* 3. a gem; a jewel. **Ex.** *Her ring is set with precious stones.* —*adj.* made of stone. **Ex.** *The building was surrounded by a stone wall.* *v.* throw stones at. **Ex.** *The boys stoned the strange dog.* —**ston'y**, *adj.* having many stones. **Ex.** *The road was stony.*

stood (1) [stud'], *v.* past tense and participle of *stand.* **Ex.** *My friend stood next to me.*

stool (4) [stuwl'], *n.* a chair without arms or a back.

STOOL

stoop (3) [stuwp'], *v.* 1. bend the body forward and down; stand or walk with the shoulders bent forward. **Ex.** *He stooped to pick up the paper.* 2. act beneath one's dignity or position. **Ex.** *He would not stoop to trickery.* —*n.* the act or position of stooping. **Ex.** *He walked with a stoop.*

stop (1) [stap'], *v.* 1. cease moving or cause to cease moving. **Ex.** *Stop this car so that I can get out.* 2. come or bring to an end; discontinue. **Ex.** *We stopped talking so that we could hear the music.* —*n.* 1. the act of stopping; the halting of any movement or action. **Ex.** *He put a stop to the noise.* 2. a place at which to stop. **Ex.** *He is getting off the bus at the next stop.* —**stop'per**, *n.* something that stops or closes. **Ex.** *Put a stopper on that bottle.* —**stop off, stop over,** stop at one place while traveling to another. **Ex.** *Stop off and see us on your way home.* —**stop up,** prevent the flow or passage of by filling, blocking, etc. **Ex.** *Rust had stopped up the pipes.*

store (1) [stɔ:r'], *n*. 1. any place where goods are available for sale; a shop. **Ex.** *She went to the store to buy bread.* 2. a supply of something for future needs. **Ex.** *They kept a large store of food in their kitchen.* —*v*. 1. set aside something for future needs. **Ex.** *They stored fruit for the cold winter.* 2. put away to keep safe. **Ex.** *She stored the winter clothes in a dry place.* —**stor'age**, *n*. 1. act of storing; condition of being stored. 2. a place for storing.

storm (1) [stɔrm'], *n*. 1. strong winds together with rain or snow; heavy fall of rain or snow. **Ex.** *The boat was lost in the storm.* 2. something like a storm in force. **Ex.** *A storm of shouts greeted the speaker.* —*v*. 1. blow violently with rain, snow, etc. **Ex.** *It stormed last night.* 2. act angrily or violently. **Ex.** *The angry crowd stormed through the streets.*

story (1) [stɔ:r'iy], *n*. 1. the telling or writing of some happening, whether true or imagined. **Ex.** *He told us the story of his life.* 2. a short tale about imagined happenings. **Ex.** *This book contains many interesting stories.*

story (1) [stɔ:r'iy], *n*. one level of a building with the rooms or space on it. **Ex.** *Most of these houses have only one story.*

stout (3) [stawt'], *adj*. 1. heavily built; fat. **Ex.** *He was too stout to fit into his old clothes.* 2. sturdily made; strong. **Ex.** *He tied the package with a stout cord.* —**stout'ly**, *adv*. —**stout'ness**, *n*.

stove (2) [stowv'], *n*. a heating or cooking device, usually in the kitchen. **Ex.** *The pot is boiling on the stove.*

straight (1) [streyt'], *adj*. 1. without a bend, curve, or wave. **Ex.** *She drew a straight line.* 2. in good order. **Ex.** *He could not keep his room straight.* —*adv*. 1. in a straight line; upright. **Ex.** *Sit up straight.* 2. directly. **Ex.** *Go straight home.* —**straight'en**, *v*. 1. make or become straight. 2. put in order. **Ex.** *Straighten your room; it is a mess.* —**straight away**, immediately. **Ex.** *Do the work straight away.*

straight face [streyt' feys'], a face that is without expression. **Ex.** *He told the story with such a straight face that we almost believed him.* —**straight'-faced,** *adj*.

straightforward [streyt'fɔr'wərd], *adj*. in a direct, honest way. **Ex.** *He gave us straightforward answers.*

strain (2) [streyn'], *v*. 1. stretch tight; pull with force. **Ex.** *The dog strained at the rope.* 2. injure by stretching. **Ex.** *He strained his back lifting the heavy package.* 3. try as hard as possible. **Ex.** *She strained herself to get the work*

finished. 4. put or force through a metal netting to separate.
Ex. *She strained the soup to remove the pieces of bone.* —*n.*
1. the act of straining; the condition of being strained. **Ex.**
The strain of his work caused him to become ill. 2. an injury.
Ex. *The doctor said the pain was caused by a back strain.*
—**strain'er**, *n.* any device used to strain for the purpose of
separating. **Ex.** *They used cloth as a strainer to separate the
meat from the soup.*

strait (5) [streyt¹], *n.* 1. a narrow passage of water connecting
two larger bodies of water. **Exs.** *This ship sails through the
Strait of Gibraltar. The water is often rough in these straits.*
2. a condition of trouble or distress. **Ex.** *The family was in
desperate financial straits.*

strange (1) [streynǰ¹], *adj.* 1. odd; unusual. **Ex.** *I saw a strange
sight today.* 2. not known; unfamiliar. **Ex.** *A strange man
knocked at the door.* —**strange'ly**, *adv.* —**strange'ness**, *n.*

stranger (1) [streyn'jər], *n.* 1. somebody from another place.
Ex. *Many strangers visit our city.* 2. an unfamiliar or unknown person. **Ex.** *We warned the children not to talk to
strangers.*

strap (4) [stræp¹], *n.* a narrow strip of material, such as leather,
used for binding, wrapping, or holding things together; any
narrow strip like such a strap. **Ex.** *The strap of her purse
broke.* —*v.* bind with a strap. **Ex.** *He strapped the books
together.*

strategy [stræt'əjiy], *n.* 1. the science of military operations,
especially those intended to trick or surprise the enemy. **Ex.**
The general was famous for his superior strategy. 2. plans
involving tricks and surprises used in politics, business, or
personal affairs. **Ex.** *His strategy helped him win the
election.*

straw (3) [strɔ:¹], *n.* 1. a single dried stem or stalk of grain;
these items or stalks in a mass, especially after being cut and
dried. **Ex.** *The farmer covered the barn floor with straw.*
2. a hollow paper tube used for drinking. **Ex.** *She drank her
soda through a straw.* —*adj.* made of straw. **Ex.** *He was
wearing a straw hat.*

strawberry (5) [strɔ:'berˇiy, strɔ:'bəriy], *n.* a small, sweet, red
fruit which grows on a vine. **Ex.** *We had strawberries and
cream for dessert.*

stray (4) [strey¹] *v.* go away from a usual or proper place,
with no aim in mind; wander. **Ex.** *The child strayed from*

home. —*adj.* 1. having wandered and become lost. **Ex.** *They are hunting for the stray sheep.* 2. occasional. **Ex.** *Except for a stray remark, he said nothing about his business.* —*n.* a person, animal, or thing that has wandered. **Ex.** *This animal shelter is a home for strays.*

streak (4) [striyk¹], *n.* a line or mark differing in color or feel from its background. **Ex.** *He has streaks of gray in his hair.* —*v.* mark; form streaks. **Ex.** *Lightning streaked across the sky.*

stream (1) [striym¹], *n.* 1. a current or flow of water such as a brook, river, etc. **Ex.** *They walked along the bank of the stream.* 2. anything that flows steadily; a continuous movement. **Ex.** *A stream of light came through the open door.* —*v.* flow or pour out in a stream or like a stream. **Ex.** *Blood streamed from the cut.*

street (1) [striyt¹], *n.* road in a city or town, usually with sidewalks and buildings. **Ex.** *Our house is on this street.*

streetcar (3) [striyt¹kar⁒], *n.* a public passenger car that travels on rails along the streets. **Ex.** *He rides on a streetcar to and from work.*

strength (1) [streŋθ¹, streŋkθ¹], *n.* 1. power or force of a body or part of a body. **Ex.** *The sick man was told to eat meat to regain his strength.* 2. mental power; moral power. **Ex.** *Our leader has great strength of character.* 3. force, as measured in size and numbers, as of men, ships, etc. **Ex.** *They did not know the strength of the enemy.* 4. ability to resist breaking, tearing, etc. **Ex.** *They used steel because of its strength.* —**strength¹en**, *v.* make or become stronger.

strenuous (5) [stren¹yuwəs], *adj.* active; full of energy, requiring much energy. **Ex.** *Pioneers led a strenuous life.* —**stren¹u·ous·ly**, *adv.*

stress (4) [stres¹], *v.* emphasize. **Ex.** *He stressed the need for understanding between nations.* —*n.* 1. emphasis; the importance placed on something. **Ex.** *His parents placed stress on honesty.* 2. strain; pressure. **Ex.** *He is able to work well under stress.*

stretch (2) [streč¹], *v.* 1. extend over a distance. **Ex.** *The forest stretched for miles along the road.* 2. extend the body or a part of the body. **Ex.** *She stretched out on the bed to rest.*

3. pull out to a fuller or greater length. **Ex.** *This material stretches easily.* —*n.* 1. the act of stretching; the state of being stretched. **Ex.** *He stopped writing and took a stretch.* 2. a continuous space or time. **Ex.** *We met again after a stretch of three years.* 3. the ability to stretch or be stretched. **Ex.** *This rubber band has lost its stretch.*

stricken (4) [strik'ən], *v.* past participle of *strike.* **Ex.** *He had been stricken by illness.* —*adj.* suffering from serious illness, troubles, wounds, etc. **Ex.** *Neighbors helped the stricken family.*

strict (3) [strikt'], *adj.* 1. requiring that rules be obeyed or followed closely. **Ex.** *The teacher was strict.* 2. exact; complete. **Ex.** *He told me this in strict confidence.* —**strict'ly,** *adv.* 1. exactly. **Ex.** *Is that strictly true?* 2. absolutely. **Ex.** *It is strictly forbidden to smoke here.* —**strict'ness,** *n.*

stride (4) [strayd'], *v.* walk with long steps. **Ex.** *I saw him striding down the street.* —*n.* a long step. **Ex.** *He reached the door in one stride.* —**strides',** *n.* progress. **Ex.** *Great strides have been made in science.* —**hit one's stride,** achieve one's normal speed, efficiency, etc. **Ex.** *After two weeks in his new job, he hit his stride.* —**take in one's stride,** manage without difficulty. **Ex.** *He had done that kind of work before and took it in his stride.*

strife (4) [strayf'], *n.* fighting or quarreling. **Ex.** *There had always been strife between the two families.*

strike (3) [strayk'], *v.* 1. hit with a blow; hit against with force. **Ex.** *We saw the car strike the dog and kill it.* 2. attack. **Ex.** *The enemy may strike at any time.* 3. produce a sound by hitting some part. **Ex.** *The clock is striking seven.* 4. produce a light, flame, etc. by rubbing. **Ex.** *Strike a match so we can see.* 5. enter the mind or imagination; impress. **Ex.** *How did that idea strike you?* 6. stop work to compel an employer to meet certain demands. **Ex.** *The men are striking for more money.* —*n.* 1. the act of hitting. **Ex.** *He was not prepared for the snake's sudden strike.* 2. the act of quitting work until certain demands, such as for more money or better working conditions, have been satisfied. **Ex.** *The men are on strike for more pay.* —**strike dumb,** surprise; make speechless with astonishment. **Ex.** *I was struck dumb by the terrible news.* —**strike up,** start; begin. **Ex.** *When did they strike up a friendship?*

string (2) [striŋ'], *n.* 1. a thin cord used to tie or bind things.

Ex. *She used string to tie the package.* 2. a connected series of things. **Ex.** *He bought her a string of pearls.* 3. wire or cord tightly stretched on a musical instrument to produce a tone. **Ex.** *She tightened the strings of her violin.* —**pull strings**, get what one desirés, such as favor, power, etc., by using influence. **Ex.** *He became managing director by pulling strings.*

strip (2) [strip¹], *v.* 1. remove one's clothing. **Ex.** *He stripped to the skin.* 2. remove a covering. **Ex.** *She stripped the skin from the banana.* 3. remove. **Ex.** *The movers stripped the house of furniture.*

strip (2) [strip¹], *n.* a long, narrow piece. **Ex.** *He cut the paper into strips one inch wide.*

stripe (4) [strayp¹], *n.* a long, narrow strip or band of something different in color, material, etc. from the area on each side of it. **Ex.** *The flag of the United States has seven red stripes and six white ones.*

strive (4) [strayv¹], *v.* 1. work hard; make a great effort. **Ex.** *We must strive to finish the job today.* 2. fight; struggle. **Ex.** *She had to strive against her fears.*

stroke (2) [strowk¹], *n.* 1. the act of hitting a blow. **Ex.** *He broke the lock with one stroke of the hammer.* 2. the sound produced by striking. **Ex.** *The stroke of the church bell awakened him.* 3. a movement with an instrument. **Ex.** *He paints his pictures with broad strokes.* 4. a sudden, unexpected act. **Ex.** *He had a stroke of good luck.* —*v.* move the hand over lightly or lovingly. **Ex.** *The children stroked the cat.*

stroll (4) [strowl¹], *v.* walk slowly or idly. **Ex.** *The couple strolled arm in arm.* —*n.* a slow, easy walk. **Ex.** *They went for a stroll in the park.* —**strol¹ler**, *n.* a person strolling. **Ex.** *The park is full of strollers.*

strong (1) [strɔːŋ¹], *adj.* 1. having great physical or mental strength; forceful. **Ex.** *He has strong arms.* 2. not easily broken or destroyed. **Ex.** *We need a strong chain for the dog.* 3. affecting one of the senses powerfully. **Ex.** *He likes the taste of strong coffee.* —**strong¹ly**, *adv.*

struck (2) [strək¹], *v.* past tense and participle of *strike.* **Ex.** *He struck his head on the table as he fell.*

structure (3) [strək¹čər], *n.* 1. something built or constructed. **Ex.** *The new bridge is a structure made of steel.* 2. manner of building, forming, or organizing. **Ex.** *He is writing a book* *about the structure of modern society.* —**struc'tur·al,** *adj.* of or used in making a structure.

struggle (2) [strəg'əl], *v.* 1. fight with. **Ex.** *The two fighters struggled together.* 2. use great effort. **Ex.** *They are struggling to learn English.* —*n.* 1. a great effort. **Ex.** *It often is a struggle to arrive at work on time.* 2. a contest; a fight. **Ex.** *There was a court struggle for control of the property.*

stubborn (4) [stəb'ərn], *adj.* 1. insisting on having one's own way; unyielding. **Ex.** *The stubborn child refused to eat.* 2. difficult to treat or work with; resistant. **Ex.** *She has a stubborn cold.* —**stub'born·ly,** *adv.* —**stub'born·ness,** *n.*

stuck (3) [stək'], *v.* past tense and participle of *stick.* **Ex.** *The car was stuck in the mud.*

student (1) [stuw'dənt, styuw'dənt], *n.* one who attends a school; one who studies. **Ex.** *She will be a college student next year.*

studio (4) [stuw'diyow, styuw'diyow], *n.* 1. the workroom of an artist. **Ex.** *The studio was filled with paintings.* 2. a place where motion pictures are made. **Ex.** *We visited a studio where a movie was being filmed.* 3. a room or rooms from which radio and television programs are broadcast.

study (1) [stəd'iy], *n.* 1. the act of using the mind for the purpose of gaining knowledge. **Ex.** *My college courses require many hours of study.* 2. close examination for the purpose of learning. **Ex.** *Doctors are making a study of the heart.* —*v.* 1. make an effort to gain knowledge by using the mind. **Ex.** *She studies at the university.* 2. examine carefully. **Ex.** *He studied the picture.* 3. read in order to understand. **Ex.** *Study the next lesson in the book.* —**stu'di·ous,** *adj.*

stuff (2) [stəf'], *n.* 1. any unnamed substance. **Ex.** *The shoes were made of some soft stuff that looked like leather.* 2. a number of different things. **Ex.** *The boy emptied all the stuff from his pockets.* —*v.* fill until very full. **Ex.** *She stuffed the trunk with old clothing.* —**stuf'fing,** *n.* anything used to stuff. —**stuff'y,** *adj.* close; lacking air. **Ex.** *The windows were closed, and the room was stuffy.*

stumble (3) [stəm'bəl], *v.* 1. trip while walking or running. **Ex.** *He stumbled over the stone in the path.* 2. speak or act unsteadily or in an unsure manner. **Ex.** *The young actor stumbled over his words.* —**stumble on** or **upon,** find unexpectedly. **Ex.** *I stumbled on some letters of yours in a trunk.*

stump (3) [stəmp¹], *n.* 1. the part of a tree trunk that remains in the earth after the main part is cut off. **Ex.** *He sat on the tree stump.* 2. the part of anything, such as an arm, leg, etc., that remains after the main part is removed.

stun (5) [stən¹], *v.* 1. cause loss of strength or consciousness by a fall, a blow, or other violence. **Ex.** *The heavy blow stunned him.* 2. shock; astonish. **Ex.** *The bad news stunned us.* —**stun'ning,** *adj.*

stung (3) [stəŋ¹], *v.* past tense and participle of *sting.* **Ex.** *He was stung by a bee.*

stunt (5) [stənt¹], *v.* slow or stop the growth of; keep from normal growth. **Ex.** *The child's growth had been stunted by a poor diet.*

stunt (5) [stənt¹], *n.* a trick or display of strength or skill, especially one done to attract attention. **Ex.** *The skaters did stunts on the ice.*

stupid (3) [stuw¹pid, styuw¹pid], *adj.* 1. not bright mentally; not able to learn much; lacking in understanding. **Ex.** *He was too stupid to learn to read.* 2. foolish. **Ex.** *Playing with matches is a stupid thing to do.* —**stu'pid·ly,** *adv.* **stu·pid'i·ty,** *n.*

sturdy (4) [stər¹diy], *adj.* 1. of a strong build; firmly built. **Ex.** *Pack these books in a sturdy box.* 2. firm; unyielding. **Ex.** *We had to admire their sturdy refusal to surrender.* —**stur'di·ly,** *adv.* —**stur'di·ness,** *n.*

style (2) [stayl¹], *n.* 1. a way or manner of painting, writing, speaking, doing, etc. **Ex.** *That author's style of writing appeals to me.* 2. a way or manner of dressing, living, etc. of a particular time or period. **Ex.** *Clothing styles change rapidly.* 3. a quality of excellence in painting, writing, speaking, etc. **Ex.** *His acting has style.* —*v.* design according to a certain style. **Ex.** *Her hair was styled according to the latest fashion.* —**styl'ish,** *adj.* in the latest fashion.

sub- (3) [səb], *prefix.* 1. almost; nearly; less than. **Exs.** *Human, subhuman; total, subtotal.* 2. below or lower in position, rank, etc. **Exs.** *Soil, subsoil; station, substation.* 3. further divided into smaller parts. **Exs.** *Divide, subdivide; section, subsection.*

subdue (4) [səbduw¹, səbdyuw¹], *v.* 1. conquer. **Ex.** *The at-*

tacking forces quickly subdued the guards. 2. reduce in force or strength; lower. **Ex.** *Voices were subdued in the sickroom.*

subject (1) [səb'jikt], *n.* 1. the person or thing discussed, examined, painted, etc. **Ex.** *She was the subject of our discussion.* 2. a branch of knowledge; a course of study. **Ex.** *He is an expert on the subject of children's diseases.* 3. a person under the control of a government or of another person, especially a monarch. **Ex.** *They were subjects of the king.* 4. the person or thing with which a sentence is concerned. **Ex.** *In the sentence, "The boys went fishing," "boys" is the subject.* —*adj.* 1. under the power of. **Ex.** *The islanders did not want to remain a subject people.* 2. tending to get or have. **Ex.** *The child is subject to colds.* 3. dependent upon. **Ex.** *The sale of the group's land was subject to the members' approval.*

subject (1) [səbjekt'], *v.* 1. bring under control. **Ex.** *The country was subjected to foreign rule.* 2. foolishly expose oneself to. **Ex.** *He went out and subjected himself to the bad weather.* 3. cause to endure. **Ex.** *He was subjected to many tests.* —**sub·jec'tive,** *adj.* showing or affected by personal feelings, background, etc. **Ex.** *His writing is very subjective.*

subject matter [səb'jikt mæt'ər], that with which a piece of writing, talk, etc. is concerned. **Ex.** *Trees are the subject matter of his book.*

sublime (5) [səblaym'], *adj.* noble; high in thought or feeling. **Ex.** *That poet expresses sublime thoughts in simple language.*

submarine (4) [səb'məriyn'], *n.* a ship that travels under water. **Ex.** *The submarine rose to the surface of the water.* —*adj.* being, living, etc. deep in the sea. **Ex.** *Fish are a kind of submarine life.*

submerge (4) [səbmerj'], *v.* sink; go down into or put under water. **Ex.** *She submerged the baby's bottle in boiling water.*

submit (3) [səbmit'], *v.* 1. yield or surrender to the power of another. **Ex.** *They had to submit to the superior force of the enemy.* 2. refer to others for their consideration or judgment. **Ex.** *They submitted their plan to the committee.*

subordinate (5) [səbɔr'dənit], *adj.* in or of a lower rank, position, or importance. **Ex.** *A clerk in a business occupies a subordinate position to that of the owner.* —*n.* a person who is below another in order, rank, or position. **Ex.** *A good leader is concerned about the welfare of his subordinates.*

—*v.* place in a lower order, rank, or position; consider of less importance. **Ex.** *The mother subordinated her wishes to the needs of her family.*

subordinate clause [səbɔr'dənit klɔːz'], a clause which is not a complete sentence. **Ex.** *In the sentence "He read a book which he got from the library," "which he got from the library" is a subordinate clause.*

subscribe (5) [səbskrayb'], *v.* 1. order and pay for the regular delivery of a news̄ ꞏꞏper, magazine, etc. **Ex.** *They subscribed to several mont¹ ɟ magazines.* 2. contribute or give to. **Ex.** *They subscribe̶ to the hospital fund.* —**subꞏscribꞏer**, *n.* one who subscribes. —**subꞏscripꞏtion**, *n.* 1. an agreement to pay for the regular delivery of a newspaper, magazine, etc. for a certain period of time. 2. a contribution or gift to.

subsequent (4) [səb'səkwənt], *adj.* later in time, order, or place; following. **Ex.** *This machine is discussed in a subsequent chapter of the book.* —**subꞏseꞏquentꞏly**, *adj.*

subsist (5) [səbsist'], *v.* manage or continue living. **Ex.** *The sick man subsisted on bread and milk.* —**subꞏsisꞏtence**, *n.* 1. act of continuing to live. 2. a means of support; food. **Ex.** *Their vegetable garden is a source of subsistence in the summer.* —**subꞏsisꞏtent**, *adj.*

substance (2) [səb'stəns], *n.* 1. the actual physical material of which a thing consists. **Ex.** *The tips of matches are covered with a chemical substance.* 2. the nature of a thing; the main or essential part. **Ex.** *He told me the substance of the discussion.*

substantial (3) [səbstæn'šəl], *adj.* 1. large in amount or size. **Ex.** *He received a substantial payment.* 2. strong. **Ex.** *The walls were substantial and did not fall.* 3. wealthy; rich; important. **Ex.** *He has substantial business interests.* 4. of or having substance; not imagined. **Ex.** *He has substantial evidence for his claim.*

substitute (3) [səb'stətuwt', səb'stətyuwt'], *n.* a person or thing put or used in the place of another. **Ex.** *Nylon is one of several substitutes for silk in stockings.* —*v.* put or use in the place of another. **Ex.** *She substituted for our regular teacher.* —**subꞏstiꞏtuꞏtion**, *n.*

subtle (4) [sət'əl], *adj.* 1. able to perceive, understand, or express small differences; mentally keen. **Ex.** *He is a subtle writer.* 2. showing such small differences that it is difficult to perceive or to understand them. **Ex.** *At first the subtle* *meanings in his words were not clear.* 3. mysterious; faint; delicate. **Ex.** *Her subtle smile made him curious.* —**sub'tle·ty,** *n.*

subtract (3) [səbtrækt'], *v.* reduce in size or amount by taking part away. **Ex.** *Subtract 2 from 4, and the remainder is 2 (4 − 2 = 2).* —**sub·trac'tion.** *n.*

suburb (4) [səb'ərb], *n.* an area of many homes on the edge of or close to a large city. **Ex.** *They would rather live in the suburbs than in the city.* —**sub·ur'ban,** *adj.* —**sub·ur'ban·ite,** *n.* one who lives in the suburbs.

subway [səb'wey'], *n.* a train operating underground in a city. **Ex.** *He goes to work on the subway.*

succeed (1) [səksiyd'], *v.* 1. reach one's object or desires; accomplish one's aim. **Ex.** *He succeeded in reaching home before the rain started.* 2. come next after another; follow. **Ex.** *They must elect someone to succeed the mayor.*

success (1) [səkses'], *n.* 1. a favorable or satisfactory ending or result. **Ex.** *He met with great success in his work.* 2. a person or thing that succeeds. **Ex.** *He is a success in business.* —**suc·cess'ful,** *adj.*

succession (4) [səkseš'ən], *n.* 1. a series of things or persons, each following the other. **Ex.** *After a succession of warm days, the weather became cold.* 2. the act of following another in position or office. **Ex.** *His succession to the throne occurred after the death of the king.* —**suc·ces'sive,** *adj.* —**suc·ces'sive·ly,** *adv.* —**suc·ces'sor,** *n.* one who follows another in a position or office. **Ex.** *Has his successor been selected yet?*

such (1) [səč'], *adj.* 1. of this or that sort; of these or those sorts. **Ex.** *Such people are dangerous.* 2. of the same kind as; similar to. **Ex.** *A painting such as this is very expensive.* 3. so great; so much of. **Ex.** *We had such a good time at your party.*

suck (3) [sək'], *v.* 1. draw in with the mouth. **Ex.** *He sucked his soda through a straw.* 2. draw in or from, as with the mouth. **Ex.** *The baby sucked milk from its mother's breast.* 3. eat something in the mouth slowly without chewing it. **Ex.** *She was sucking a piece of candy.* —**suc'tion,** *n.* act of sucking.

sudden (1) [səd'ən], *adj.* 1. not expected; without warning. **Ex.** *There was a sudden change in the weather.* 2. done or occurring quickly or without preparing. **Ex.** *She made a* *sudden turn.* —**sud'den·ly,** *adv.* —**sud'den·ness,** *n.* —**all of a sudden,** suddenly. Ex. *All of a sudden, the wall fell.*

sue (5) [suw'], syuw'], *v.* start a law case against. Ex. *They are suing for the money owed them.*

suffer (1) [səf'ər], *v.* 1. feel pain of body or mind. Ex. *They are suffering from hunger.* 2. receive or experience pain, grief, etc. Ex. *He suffered a broken leg when he fell.* 3. endure; become worse. Ex. *He cannot suffer much more pain.* —**suf'fer·ing,** *n.* condition of one feeling pain of body or mind.

sufficient (2) [səfiš'ənt], *adj.* enough for the need; adequate. Ex. *He bought a sufficient quantity of paint to paint the house.* —**suf·fi'cient·ly,** *adv.* —**suf·fi'cien·cy,** *n.* that which is enough.

suffix (5) [səf'iks], *n.* letters at the end of a word or added to a word which affect or change the meaning or part of speech. Ex. *The letters "-er," "-ly," and "-ment" are very common suffixes.*

sugar (1) [šug'ər], *n.* a sweet substance in crystal form made from the juice of certain plants. Ex. *She added some sugar to his coffee.* —**sug'ar·y,** *adj.* like or containing sugar.

suggest (2) [səgǰest'], *v.* 1. offer or propose as something to think about. Ex. *He suggested they come next week.* 2. cause one to think about something by association or connection of ideas. Ex. *His behavior suggests that he is sick.* —**sug·ges'tion,** *n.* 1. the act of suggesting; that which is suggested. Ex. *They liked his suggestion that we eat in town.* 2. a slight trace or hint. Ex. *There was a suggestion of snow in the air.* —**sug·ges'tive,** *adj.* —**sug·ges'tive·ly,** *adv.*

suicide (4) [suw'isayd`, syuw'isayd`], *n.* 1. the act of ending one's own life intentionally. Ex. *When her husband died, she committed suicide.* 2. a person who intentionally ends his own life. Ex. *The dead man was a suicide.* —**su`i·cid'al,** *adj.*

suit (1) [suwt', syuwt'], *n.* 1. a set of outer clothes to be worn together. Ex. *He tried on his new winter suit.* 2. a case in a court of law. Ex. *She has started a suit to get the money he owes her.* —*v.* meet the wants or needs of; satisfy. Ex. *The house suited their large family.* —**suit'a·ble,** *adj.* fitting; meeting one's needs.

a, far; æ, am; e, get; ey, late; i, in; iy, see; ɔ, all; ow, go; u, put; uw, too; ə, but, ago; ər, fur; aw, out; ay, life; oy, boy; ŋ, ring; θ, think; ð, that; ž, measure; š, ship; ǰ, edge; č, child.

suitcase (3) [suwt'keys`, syuwt'keys`], *n.* a long, flat traveling bag large enough for containing clothing. **Ex.** *He took two suitcases with him on the trip.*

sulfur (5) [səl'fər], *n.* a chemical element of a pale yellow color, used in making gunpowder, matches, medicine, etc. —**sul·fur'ic,** *adj.* containing sulfur. —**sul'fur·ous,** *adj.* of or like sulfur.

sullen (4) [səl'ən], *n.* 1. silent, bitter, and unpleasant. **Ex.** *The angry child gave him a sullen look.* 2. having or giving a feeling of deep sadness. **Ex.** *The sullen weather made her feel depressed.* —**sul'len·ly,** *adv.* —**sul'len·ness,** *n.*

sultry (5) [səl'triy], *adj.* hot and moist with little air movement. **Ex.** *The day was so sultry that they had little energy.* —**sul'tri·ness,** *n.*

sum (2) [səm'], *n.* 1. an amount, usually of money. **Ex.** *He gave me a large sum of money.* 2. the number that results from adding two or more numbers or quantities together. **Ex.** *The sum of 3 and 5 is 8.* —**sum up,** give a summary by mentioning the important points. **Ex.** *He summed up the situation in three short sentences.*

summary (5) [səm'əriy], *n.* a brief statement which gives all the important parts of a longer matter. **Ex.** *He gave a summary of the events that led to the accident.* —*adj.* 1. brief. **Ex.** *He presented a summary account.* 2. done swiftly and without attention to ceremony. **Ex.** *She complained about the summary treatment given her.* —**sum'ma·rize,** *v.*

summer (1) [səm'ər], *n.* the hottest season of the year, occurring between spring and fall. **Ex.** *They have gone to the mountains for the summer.* —*adj.* suitable for or characteristic of summer. **Ex.** *She bought light summer clothes.*

summit (5) [səm'it], *n.* the top; the highest point. **Ex.** *The mountain climbers reached the summit.*

summon (3) [səm'ən], *v.* 1. formally command to come. **Ex.** *He was summoned to appear in court.* 2. request to come; ask to appear. **Ex.** *They were summoned to the bedside of their dying father.* 3. call forth. **Ex.** *He summoned all his courage to meet the danger.* —**sum'mons,** *n.* an order to appear in court; a request to appear.

sun (1) [sən'], *n.* 1. the light- and heat-giving heavenly body around which the earth and the other planets move. **Ex.** *The sun rises in the east.* 2. the heat or light received from the sun. Ex. *Her wide hat protected her from the sun.* —**sun'ny,** *adj.* bright.

sunbathe [sən'beyδ'], *v.* expose one's body to the sun, especially to acquire a tan.

sunbeam [sən'biym'], *n.* a ray of light from the sun. Ex. *Sunbeams came through the open door.*

sunburn [sən'bərn'], *n.* a reddening of the skin caused by exposure to the sun. —*v.*

Sunday (1) [sən'diy], *n.* the first day of the week.

sundry (5) [sən'driy], *adj.* of various kinds. Ex. *Sundry problems were discussed.* —**sun'dries,** *n.* various small and less important articles or items. Ex. *This store sells dress materials and sundries.*

sung (2) [səŋ'], *v.* past participle of *sing.* Ex. *He had sung the song before.*

sunglasses [sən'glæs'əz], *n.* eyeglasses designed to protect the eyes from bright sun.

sunk (2) [seŋk'], *v.* past tense and participle of *sink.* Ex. *The boat had sunk.* —**sunk'en,** *adj.*

sunstroke [sən'strowk'], *n.* an illness caused by too much exposure to the heat of the sun.

super- (3) [suw'pər, syuw'pər], *prefix.* 1. greater in quantity, size, strength, etc. Exs. *Man, superman; market, supermarket.* 2. specially; unusually. Ex. *Careful, supercareful.* 3. above; add on top. Exs. *Impose, superimpose; structure, superstructure.*

superb (5) [suwpərb', syuwpərb'], *adj.* 1. splendid; noble; majestic. Ex. *The city has several superb old buildings.* 2. one of the best of one's kind. Ex. *He is a superb pianist.* —**su·perb'ly,** *adv.*

superintendent (4) [suw'pərinten'dənt, syuw'pərinten'dənt], *n.* one whose duty is to direct or manage. Ex. *He is the superintendent of the hospital.*

superior (2) [səpi:r'iyər, suwpi:r'iyər], *adj.* 1. better or greater in ability, quality, quantity, etc. Ex. *The clothing at that expensive shop is superior.* 2. higher in rank, degree, or grade. Ex. *The soldiers obeyed their superior officer.* 3. showing too much pride; scornful. Ex. *She felt superior to her schoolmates.* —*n.* one in a higher position of authority; a person of greater skill. Ex. *The secretary types letters for her superior.* —**su·per'i·or'i·ty,** *n.*

superstition (4) [suw`pərstiš'ən, syuw`pərstiš'ən], *n.* belief based on fear rather than reason; belief in magic, spells, etc. **Ex.** *She had a superstition that breaking a mirror brings bad luck.* —**su`per·sti'tious,** *adj.* —**su`per·sti'tious·ly,** *adv.*

supervise (5) [suw`pərvayz`, syuw`pərvayz`], *v.* direct work of others. **Ex.** *The architect supervised the building of the house.* —**su`per·vi'sion,** *n.* the act of supervising. **Ex.** *He works well without supervision.* —**su'per·vi'sor,** *n.* one who supervises. —**su`per·vi'so·ry,** *adj.*

supper (2) [səp'ər], *n.* the evening meal. **Ex.** *The children went to bed after supper.*

supplement (5) [səp'ləmənt], *n.* something added, especially an extra section added to a book or newspaper to give further information, provide special articles, etc. **Ex.** *Today's newspaper has a supplement on the new automobile models.* —*v.* add to or supply something lacking. **Ex.** *He supplemented his salary by working at a second job.* —**sup`ple·men'ta·ry,** *adj.* —**sup`ple·men'tal,** *adj.*

supply (1) [səplay'], *v.* give or provide what is needed, asked for, or lacking. **Ex.** *Father supplied us with food and clothing.* —*n.* the quantity or amount of something one has available. **Ex.** *Our supply of flour is very low.*

support (2) [səport'], *v.* 1. bear the weight of; hold up or in position; keep from falling. **Ex.** *That chair will not support a heavy person.* 2. provide the needs of a person or a family. **Ex.** *He supports his parents.* 3. aid a person, group, cause, etc. **Ex.** *I will support you in your efforts.* 4. make more certain; strengthen. **Ex.** *This new evidence supports my theory.* —*n.* 1. the act of supporting; condition of being supported. **Ex.** *We are hoping for your support.* 2. one who or that which supports. **Ex.** *He is the main support of his family.* —**sup·port'er,** *n.* one who or that which supports.

suppose (1) [səpowz'], *v.* 1. believe; think; imagine. **Ex.** *I suppose you are right.* 2. expect. **Ex.** *It is supposed to snow tonight.* 3. assume something is true for the purpose of argument. **Ex.** *Suppose you had the money; would you give it to me?* —**sup·posed',** thought to be true. —**sup·pos'ed·ly,** *adv.* —**sup·po·si'tion,** *n.* that which is supposed or assumed.

suppress (4) [səpres'], *v.* 1. subdue by force or authority; crush. **Ex.** *The army was called to suppress the revolt.* 2. keep back from the public; hide. **Ex.** *He suppressed his anger.* —**sup·pres'sion,** *n.*

supreme (3) [suwpriym', səpriym'], *adj.* 1. highest in authority, rank, or power. **Ex.** *The President is the supreme commander of the armed forces.* 2. highest in quality, character, importance, etc.; greatest. **Ex.** *He showed supreme courage in his decision.* —**su·preme'ly,** *adv.* —**su·prem'a·cy,** *n.*

Supreme Being [suwpriym' biy'iŋ], God.

Supreme Court [suwpriym' kɔrt'], the highest American court.

sure (1) [šu:r'], *adj.* 1. confident; convinced; certain. **Ex.** *I am sure of his honesty.* 2. steady; reliable. **Ex.** *I have known him all my life, and he is a sure friend.* 3. very probable; almost certain to happen. **Ex.** *You are sure to reach town if you follow this road.* —**sure'ly,** *adv.* —**sure'ness,** *n.*

sure-footed [šu:r'fut'id], *adj.* unlikely to fall, slip, or stumble. **Ex.** *Mountain animals are sure-footed.*

surface (3) [sər'fis], *n.* 1. an outer side of a body or thing. **Ex.** *Leaves were floating on the surface of the pond.* 2. the outer appearance. **Ex.** *On the surface, the two men seemed friendly.* —*v.* 1. come from within to a surface. **Ex.** *The fish surfaced from time to time.* 2. provide with a surface. **Ex.** *They surfaced the road with stone.* —*adj.* having little or no depth; of, on, or at the surface. **Ex.** *Surface appearances are often deceiving.*

surge (5) [sərj'], *n.* 1. a large, rolling movement of water; a large wave. **Ex.** *He watched the surge of the ocean.* 2. a strong, rushing movement or feeling. **Ex.** *He felt a surge of anger at the sight of his rival.* —*v.* rise and swell to great volume. **Ex.** *The waves surged over the deck.*

surgeon (3) [sər'jən], *n.* a doctor who specializes in surgery.

surgery (3) [sər'jəriy], *n.* 1. the science of treating diseases and injuries by cutting, either to remove the diseased parts of the body or to repair injuries. **Ex.** *The young doctor is studying surgery.* 2. the room where such treatment is performed. **Ex.** *The doctor is in surgery.* —**sur'gi·cal,** *adj.* of or concerned with surgery.

surmise (5) [sərmayz'], *v.* form an idea or opinion with few supporting facts; guess. **Ex.** *We surmise that he left early this morning.* —*n.* an idea or opinion with few supporting facts. **Ex.** *It is my surmise that he will resign.*

surname (5) [sər'neym`], *n.* the name of one's family; one's last name. **Ex.** *The surname of John Smith is Smith.*

surpass (5) [sərpæs'], *v.* 1. be greater than in amount, extent, or degree; be better than. **Ex.** *She surpasses her sister in intelligence.* 2. go beyond; exceed. **Ex.** *He surpassed the speed limit.*

surplus (4) [sər'pləs], *n.* an amount which exceeds that which is needed. **Ex.** *He kept enough corn to feed his cattle and sold the surplus.* —*adj.* being extra; remaining. **Ex.** *She used the surplus material to make a jacket.*

surprise (1) [sərprayz'], *v.* 1. cause a feeling of wonder because something is not expected. **Ex.** *His sudden appearance surprised us.* 2. discover a person, a thing, or an act suddenly or unexpectedly. **Ex.** *The police surprised the man in the act of taking the money.* 3. attack unexpectedly. **Ex.** *They surprised the enemy and won the battle.* —*n.* 1. something unexpected. **Ex.** *Their visit was a surprise.* 2. the feeling caused by something unexpected. **Ex.** *We felt some surprise at his strange question.* —**sur·pris'ing,** *adj.* —**sur·pris'ing·ly,** *adv.*

surrender (3) [səren'dər], *v.* 1. yield something to another; abandon. **Ex.** *He surrendered his rights to the property.* 2. deliver oneself to the control of another. **Ex.** *The hunted man surrendered to the police.* —*n.* the act of surrendering. **Ex.** *They expect the enemy's surrender soon.*

surround (2) [sərawnd'], *v.* form a circle around. **Ex.** *Troops surrounded the city.* —**sur·round'ings,** *n.* the things and conditions that surround a person or place. **Ex.** *She works in pleasant surroundings.*

survey (3) [sərvey'], *v.* 1. examine; look carefully at the whole of something. **Ex.** *He stood on the hill and surveyed the surrounding country.* 2. determine the exact location, size, and shape of a piece of land by measuring. **Ex.** *He had the land surveyed before buying it.* —**sur'vey,** *n.* 1. the act of surveying a piece of land. **Ex.** *A survey of the property is being made.* 2. a study giving a general view of the whole of a subject. **Ex.** *The survey shows a need for more houses.* —**sur·vey'or,** *n.* one who surveys.

survive (4) [sərvayv'], *v.* 1. remain alive despite something. **Ex.** *A few people survived the flood.* 2. continue to live or exist longer than. **Ex.** *Few of the old customs survived the* *war.* —**sur·vi'vor,** *n.* one who survives. —**sur·vi'val,** *n.* that which survives; the act of surviving.

suspect (2) [səspekt'], *v.* 1. imagine a person to be guilty, bad, undesirable, etc. without much proof. **Ex.** *The police suspected him of the crime.* 2. have doubts about. **Ex.** *They suspect his motives.* 3. imagine to be true or probable; have an uncertain or indefinite idea. **Ex.** *I suspect we will see him again.* —**sus'pect,** *n.* one who is suspected. **Ex.** *Who are the suspects in the case?*

suspend (4) [səspend'], *v.* 1. hang free except for a support from above. **Ex.** *The swing was suspended from a branch of the tree.* 2. cause to stop for a time. **Ex.** *The train schedule was suspended until the railroad tracks were repaired.* 3. stop a person from attending or being a part of for a time. **Ex.** *The boy was suspended from school for a week.* —**sus·pen'sion,** *n.* the act or condition of being suspended. —**sus·pense',** *n.* a state of doubt or uncertainty; the anxiety resulting from such a state. **Ex.** *She could hardly bear the suspense of waiting for a decision.*

suspicion (3) [səspiš'ən], *n.* the act of suspecting or the state of being suspected. **Ex.** *He is under suspicion of murder.* —**sus·pic'ious,** *adj.* 1. causing suspicion. **Ex.** *The broken lock was suspicious.* 2. feeling or showing distrust. **Ex.** *Wild animals are suspicious of people.* —**sus·pi'cious·ly,** *adv.*

sustain (4) [səsteyn'], *v.* 1. support the weight of; hold up. **Ex.** *Large columns sustained the roof.* 2. support; maintain; give strength to. **Ex.** *Thoughts of home sustained their spirits.* 3. undergo; endure. **Ex.** *He sustained a broken arm.*

swallow (3) [swal'ow], *v.* 1. take into the stomach through the mouth and throat. **Ex.** *He swallowed the hot coffee.* 2. make swallowing movements with the muscles of the throat. **Ex.** *He swallowed before starting to speak.*

swallow (3) [swal'ow], *n.* a small, swift bird with long wings. **Ex.** *In the early evening, the air was filled with graceful swallows.*

swam (3) [swæm'], *v.* past tense of *swim.* **Ex.** *He swam across the lake.*

swamp (4) [swamp'], *n.* soft land that is almost always wet but not entirely covered with water. **Ex.** *The hunter was lost in the swamp.* —*v.* flood or cover, as with water. **Ex.** *The roads were swamped after the heavy rain.* —**swamp'y,** *adj.*

swarm (4) [swɔrm¹], *n.* 1. a group of bees traveling with a queen bee. **Ex.** *The swarm of bees entered the hollow tree.* 2. a large, active group of insects, things, people, etc. **Ex.** *A swarm of people surrounded the car.* —*v.* move or come together in large numbers. **Ex.** *The children swarmed into the park.*

sway (3) [swey¹], *v.* 1. move the body back and forth without moving the feet. **Ex.** *The dancers swayed to the music.* 2. move or lean as to one side. **Ex.** *The car swayed to the left as it rounded the corner.* 3. cause to change one's thinking; influence. **Ex.** *We were not able to sway her opinion.*

swear (4) [swe:r¹], *v.* 1. declare or promise earnestly, asking a god to be witness to the truth. **Ex.** *He is willing to swear to the truth of this statement.* 2. use bad language; curse. **Ex.** *He often swears when he is angry.*

sweat (3) [swet¹], *v.* give out moisture through the skin. **Ex.** *Unloading the truck made him sweat.* —*n.* the moisture given out through the skin. **Ex.** *Sweat dripped from the runner's forehead.*

sweater (3) [swet¹ər], *n.* a knitted jacket, usually of wool. *She was wearing a sweater and skirt.*

sweatshop [swet¹šap¹], *n.* a factory or other place in which people work many hours each day for little money under poor conditions. **Ex.** *Unions oppose sweatshops.*

sweep (2) [swiyp¹], *v.* 1. clean or remove dirt from a floor, rug, etc. by using a broom. **Ex.** *She is sweeping the floor.* 2. move or push away by force; destroy. **Ex.** *The storm was sweeping everything before it.* 3. move swiftly and steadily. **Ex.** *She swept into the room in a long, flowing dress.* —*n.* the act of sweeping; a sweeping movement. **Ex.** *A sweep of his hand meant they should go.* —**sweep¹ing,** *adj.* 1. that sweeps. 2. general but including very much; of wide range. **Ex.** *The new President made sweeping changes in the government.*

sweet (1) [swiyt¹], *adj.* 1. having the taste of sugar or honey; not salted or bitter; not spoiled. **Ex.** *This cake is very sweet.* 2. pleasant to feel, hear, see, etc. **Ex.** *She has a sweet voice.* 3. pleasing; agreeable; dear. **Ex.** *She is a sweet young lady.* —*n.* something sweet. **Ex.** *Most children like sweets.* —**sweet¹en,** *v.* —**sweet¹en·er, sweet¹en·ing,** *n.* that which is used to sweeten. —**sweet¹ly,** *adv.* —**sweet¹ness,** *n.*

sweetheart [swiyt'hart`], *n.* a person much loved by another. **Ex.** *She was his sweetheart.*

sweet potato [swiyt' pətey'tow], a thick, yellow root which is used as a vegetable. **Ex.** *She boiled the sweet potatoes.*

swell (2) [swel'], *v.* grow or increase in size, amount, degree, bulk, etc. **Ex.** *His injured arm began to swell.* —**swel'ling,** *n.* 1. a growth in size. 2. a part on the body that has swelled. **Ex.** *There was a swelling on her arm.*

swept (2) [swept'], *v.* past tense and participle of *sweep.* **Ex.** *She was swept along by the crowd.*

swift (3) [swift'], *adj.* 1. moving or able to move with great speed; very fast. **Ex.** *The current of the river is swift.* 2. happening, coming, or done in a very short time. **Ex.** *He was swift to act in the emergency.* —**swift'ly,** *adv.* —**swift' ness,** *n.*

swim (2) [swim'], *v.* 1. go forward or backward in water by moving the hands and feet or the tail and body. **Ex.** *Fish were swimming in the pond.* 2. move over or across as by swimming. **Ex.** *He can swim the river in half an hour.* 3. seem to be spinning. **Ex.** *His head was swimming.* —*n.* the act of swimming; a period of swimming. **Ex.** *They went for a long swim.* —**swim'mer,** *n.*

swing (2) [swiŋ'], *v.* 1. cause to move back and forth, as something supported from above. **Ex.** *She was swinging the basket, holding it by its handle.* 2. move or cause to move back and forth around a fixed point; turn. **Ex.** *The gate swings open easily.* 3. move with a long, continuous motion. **Ex.** *He tried to swing the bag over his shoulder.* —*n.* a seat hanging from ropes or chains fastened to a strong overhead support on which one swings for pleasure. **Ex.** *The children were playing on the swings.*

switch (4) [swič'], *n.* 1. the act of turning, shifting, or changing. **Ex.** *The city plans a switch from streetcars to buses.* 2. a device for turning electric current on and off. **Ex.** *He reached for the light switch.* 3. a slender, easily bent stick or branch used for whipping. **Ex.** *The father whipped the boy with a switch.* —*v.* 1. turn, shift, change, or exchange. **Ex.** *The two girls switched hats.* 2. connect or disconnect an electric current by a switch. **Ex.** *He switched on the*

---

lights. 3. swing suddenly or sharply. **Ex.** *The horse switched its tail to chase the flies.*

swollen (2) [swowl'en], *v.* past participle of *swell.* **Ex.** *His ankle is swollen.*

sword (2) [sɔrd'], *n.* a heavy weapon con- sisting of a long, sharp blade and a handle.

swore [swɔ:r'], past tense of *swear.* **Ex.** *He swore he would not go.*

sworn [swɔ:rn'], *v.* past participle of *swear.* **Ex.** *He had sworn before that he would not go.*

SWORD

swum (3) [swəm'], *v.* past participle of *swim.* **Ex.** *He has swum in this river often.*

swung (2) [swəŋ'], *v.* past tense and participle of *swing.* **Ex.** *The door swung open.*

syllable (4) [sil'əbəl], *n.* a word or part of a word which is spoken as one sound. **Ex.** *The word "girl" has one syllable; the word "happiness" has three syllables.* —**syl·lab'ic,** *adj.*

symbol (3) [sim'bəl], *n.* 1. that which stands for or represents something else. **Ex.** *The color red is a symbol for danger in many countries.* 2. in writing or printing, a sign, letter, mark, etc. used to represent something. **Ex.** *The symbol for cent is "¢."* —**sym·bol'ic,** *adj.* —**sym'bol·ize,** *v.* be a symbol of; represent. —**sym'bol·ism`,** *n.* a set of symbols.

sympathy (2) [sim'pɑθiy], *n.* 1. a sharing in the feeling of an- other, particularly one who is sad or in trouble. **Ex.** *They expressed their sympathy by sending flowers to her hus- band's funeral.* 2. approval; support. **Ex.** *He was in sym- pathy with their aims.* —**sym'pa·thize,** *v.* —**sym`pa·thet'ic,** *adj.*

symphony (3) [sim'fəniy], *n.* a long musical composition, usu- ally in four parts, written for a large orchestra. **Ex.** *His symphony was performed for the first time today.* —**sym· phon'ic,** *adj.*

symptom (4) [simp'təm], *n.* that which is evidence or a sign of the existence of something else. **Ex.** *A cough is sometimes a symptom of a serious disease.* —**symp`to·mat'ic,** *adj.* indi- cating or showing. **Ex.** *A fever is symptomatic of a cold.*

syrup (5) [sə:r'əp, si:r'əp], *n.* a thick, sweet liquid made by boiling juice, sap, or water containing sugar until it becomes thick. **Ex.** *He liked maple syrup on his biscuits.*

system (1) [sis'təm], *n.* 1. a group of related things combined into or working as an organized whole. **Ex.** *A system of railroads joins the country's larger cities.* 2. an arranged body of facts, ideas, procedures, etc. **Ex.** *What is their system of government?* 3. arrangement; order; method. **Ex.** *He has developed a better system for doing his work.*

systematic (5) [sis`təmæt'ik], *adj.* 1. using a method or system. **Ex.** *They made a systematic search for the lost ring.* 2. well organized; planned. **Ex.** *She was systematic in her housework.* —**sys'tem·at'ic·al·ly,** *adv.* —**sys'tem·a·tize,** *v.* organize; make a planned way of doing.

T

T, t [tiy'], *n.* the twentieth letter of the English alphabet.

table (1) [tey'bəl], *n.* 1. a flat surface supported by one or more legs, used as a piece of furniture. **Ex.** *Put the books on the table.* 2. a list of figures, facts, or information arranged according to a system. **Ex.** *The titles of the chapters are listed in the book's table of contents.*

TABLE 1

tablespoon (4) [tey'bəlspuwn`], *n.* a large spoon used for measuring and serving food; the amount that this spoon will hold. **Ex.** *She mixed two tablespoons of flour with two tablespoons of butter.*

tablet (5) [tæb'lit], *n.* 1. a pad of writing paper consisting of many sheets glued together at the top. **Ex.** *She tore a sheet of paper from her tablet.* 2. a small portion of medicine pressed into a flat, round cake. **Ex.** *The doctor told her to take three tablets a day.*

table tennis [tey'bəl ten'is], a game similar to tennis, played on a table.

tack (5) [tæk'], *n.* a short, sharp-pointed nail with a large, flat, or rounded head, used to fasten something. **Ex.** *The carpet was fastened to the floor with tacks.* —*v.* fasten or attach with tacks. **Ex.** *They tacked the notice to the door.*

tackle (4) [tæk'əl], *n.* 1. equipment used for a particular sport or activity. **Ex.** *He bought some fishing tackle.* 2. a special arrangement of wheels and ropes for raising and lowering heavy loads. **Ex.** *The tackle broke as they lifted the piano.* 3. the act of seizing or grasping in order to stop, often by forcing or pushing to the ground. **Ex.** *His tackle stopped the man from escaping.* —*v.* 1. seize or grasp and stop. **Ex.** *The policeman tackled the thief.* 2. agree to do; try to do. **Ex.** *He was eager to tackle the job.*

tact (5) [tækt'], *n.* the ability to say and do the right thing without annoying people or making them feel hurt; diplomacy. **Ex.** *Your answer showed tact.* —**tact'ful,** *adj.* having or using tact. **Ex.** *The way he corrected her was very tactful.* —**tact'ful·ly,** *adv.*

tactics (5) [tæk'tiks], *n.pl.* 1. the science of organizing and using military forces in war. **Ex.** *The captain's tactics won the battle.* 2. any method of accomplishing an end. **Ex.** *His tactics brought results.* —**tac'ti·cal,** *adj.*

tag (5) [tæg'], *n.* any small piece of paper, metal, etc. attached to something, usually with markings to show what it is, who owns it, etc. **Ex.** *Each dress in the store had a tag on it showing the price.* —*v.* attach a tag to. **Ex.** *All dogs in this town are required to be tagged.*

tail (1) [teyl'], *n.* 1. the long, thin, rear part of an animal's body that extends beyond the rest. **Ex.** *The cat's tail stood straight up in the air.* 2. anything like a tail in location or shape; the last part; the back end. **Ex.** *Ice formed on the tail of the airplane.*

TAIL 1

taillight [teyl'layt'], *n.* a light on the rear of a car or truck. **Ex.** *In the dark, he could see two red taillights on the car ahead of him.*

tailor (3) [tey'lər], *n.* a person whose work is making or repairing suits, coats, etc. **Ex.** *The tailor repaired a hole in my trousers.* —*v.* make, repair, or fit as a tailor. **Ex.** *He tailored the coat to fit me.* 2. alter, change, form, etc. to meet certain requirements. **Ex.** *The program was tailored for young children.*

take (1) [teyk'], *v.* 1. grasp; hold. **Ex.** *He wanted to take her in his arms.* 2. seize; capture; win. **Ex.** *Did the soldiers take the city?* 3. bring; carry; guide. **Ex.** *They take the children* *to school.* 4. come to possess; get as one's own; assume. **Ex.** *He is taking a job in the city.* 5. occupy. **Ex.** *Please take this chair; it's very comfortable.* 6. use. **Ex.** *He could not take the time to see us.* 7. select; choose. **Ex.** *Take the one you like best.* 8. remove. **Ex.** *Who took the book?* 9. do; perform. **Exs.** *Shall we take a walk? I will take the child's picture.* 10. need; require. **Ex.** *How long will the trip take?* 11. breathe in; eat; drink; etc. **Ex.** *He took a drink of water.* 12. board and ride in a car, plane, ship, etc. **Ex.** *She will take the train to the city.* 13. study. **Ex.** *What courses are you taking?* 14. order and pay for the regular delivery of a magazine, newspaper, etc. **Ex.** *We take three daily newspapers.* 15. photograph. **Ex.** *Will you take my picture?* —**take after,** look like; resemble. **Ex.** *The boy takes after his father.* —**take down,** 1. reduce in position or rank; lower. **Ex.** *They took down the flag.* 2. write. **Ex.** *Take down what he says.* —**take for,** think to be, sometimes mistakenly. **Ex.** *I take him for a rich man.* —**take in,** 1. receive; admit. **Ex.** *That house takes in boarders.* 2. make smaller. **Ex.** *The tailor took in my coat so it would fit better.* 3. include. **Ex.** *His speech took in many subjects.* —**take it,** accept; assume. **Ex.** *I take it you do not want to go.* —**take off,** 1. remove. **Ex.** *Take off your clothes.* 2. rise from the ground or a level. **Ex.** *The plane took off quickly.* —**take on,** 1. employ. **Ex.** *We took on extra workers.* 2. begin to do or try. **Ex.** *We took on the problem.* 3. assume a look, quality, etc. **Ex.** *He took on the appearance of a sick man.* —**take one's time,** go or do slowly. **Ex.** *He took his time coming to my house.* —**take over,** assume control of. **Ex.** *The soldiers took over the government.* —**take the floor,** become the center of attention for the purpose of speaking. **Ex.** *He took the floor at the meeting to give a speech.*

taken (1) [tey'kən], *v.* past participle of *take.* **Ex.** *He was taken to school.*

tale (2) [teyl¹], *n.* a story about either imaginary or real events. **Ex.** *The children listened to the old soldier's tales.*

talent (3) [tæl'ənt], *n.* 1. a special and unusual ability or skill. **Ex.** *He is a pianist of great talent.* 2. people of special and unusual ability or skill, considered as a group. **Ex.** *The di-*

rector of the play engaged the best talent he could find.
—**tal'ent·ed,** *adj.*

talk (1) [tɔːkˈ], *n.* 1. the act of expressing thoughts in spoken words; conversation. **Ex.** *I had a long talk with my friend.* 2. a speech. **Ex.** *She gave a talk on gardening.* 3. a meeting for discussion. **Ex.** *Talks were held to resolve the labor dispute.* —*v.* speak; express thoughts in spoken words; discuss. **Ex.** *The student talked with his teacher about his problems.* —**talk'a·tive,** *adj.* talking very much; liking to talk very much. —**talk back,** answer impolitely. **Ex.** *A child should not talk back to his mother.* —**talk down to,** talk simply as if to show that the other person has little understanding. **Ex.** *The manager talks down to the clerks.*

tall (1) [tɔːlˈ], *adj.* 1. higher than the average of its kind; not short. **Ex.** *The city has many tall buildings.* 2. having a stated height. **Ex.** *She is five feet tall.*

tame (3) [teymˈ], *adj.* 1. not wild; taught to be useful or friendly to man. **Ex.** *He has a tame rabbit.* 2. easy to handle; gentle. **Ex.** *She rode the tame horse.* 3. dull. **Ex.** *Life in the country was too tame for him.* —*v.* 1. teach to obey; train. **Ex.** *They tamed the elephant.* 2. control; make manageable. **Ex.** *She tried to tame her temper.* —**tame'ly,** *adv.*

tan (4) [tænˈ], *n.* 1. a light brown color. **Ex.** *She likes tan better than red.* 2. a brown color of the skin from exposure to the sun. **Ex.** *He has a good tan from working in the sun.* —*adj.* light brown. **Ex.** *He wore tan shoes.* —*v.* 1. make leather from the skins of animals by using an acid. **Ex.** *The goat skins were tanned to make coats.* 2. become brown in the sun. **Ex.** *I tan easily.*

tangible (5) [tænˈjəbəl], *adj.* 1. able to be touched. **Ex.** *A collection of stamps was his only property of any tangible value.* 2. able to be understood by the mind or given mental form; real; actual. **Ex.** *He found tangible benefits in their plan.*

tangle (4) [tænˈgəl], *v.* 1. twist or knot together; become twisted or knotted. **Ex.** *His fishing line tangled in the weeds.* 2. involve and hold. **Ex.** *His feet became tangled in the grass, and he fell.* —*n.* 1. a tangled mass. **Ex.** *She combed the tangles from her hair.* 2. a complicated state or condition. **Ex.** *His business affairs were in a tangle.*

tank (3) [tæŋkˈ], *n.* 1. a large basin or other container for liquids. **Ex.** *The garage put gas in the tank of the car.* 2. a large, heavy military car with armor and heavy guns that travels on belts instead of wheels. **Ex.** *The tanks moved easily over the rough road.*

tanker [tæŋk'ər], *n.* a ship with large tanks used to carry liquids. **Ex.** *The tanker carried a load of oil.*

tap (3) [tæp'], *v.* strike or hit lightly or gently. **Ex.** *He tapped me on the shoulder.* —*n.* a light or gentle blow; the sound of such a blow. **Ex.** *I heard a tap on the door.*

tap (3) [tæp'], *n.* a device to start or stop the flow of water or other liquid in a pipe. **Ex.** *Hot water flowed from the tap.* —*v.* make a hole or connection through which a liquid, gas, current, etc. can flow. **Ex.** *The rubber trees were ready to tap.*

TAP

tape (5) [teyp'], *n.* 1. a narrow strip of paper, cloth, or other material used for binding. **Ex.** *He sealed the package with tape and mailed it.* 2. a strip of cloth, etc. marked with inches, feet, etc. for measuring. **Ex.** *He measured the height of the door with his tape.* 3. a strip of material on which sounds are recorded. **Ex.** *They taped his injured ankle.* 2. record on tape. **Ex.** *He taped his speech, and we listened to it later.*

taper (5) [tey'pər], *n.* a long, thin candle. **Ex.** *Lighted tapers were on the dining-room table.* —*v.* 1. narrow to a point; gradually become thin at one end. **Ex.** *The shoe tapered to a pointed toe.* 2. gradually become less and less. **Ex.** *His interest tapered after their first meeting.*

tape recorder [teyp' rikɔr'dər], a device which uses tape to record and reproduce sound.

tar (5) [tar'], *n.* a thick, black, sticky substance made from coal, wood, etc. **Ex.** *The roof was covered with tar.* —*v.* cover or spread with tar. **Ex.** *They tarred the road.*

tardy (5) [tar'diy], *adj.* late; slow. **Ex.** *She was often tardy for work.* —**tar'di·ly**, *adv.* —**tar'di·ness**, *n.*

target (5) [tar'git], *n.* 1. any object, often one marked with circles one around the other, to be aimed at as in shooting. **Ex.** *He hit the target with his first shot.* 2. that which is aimed at, as in an attack, criticism, etc. **Ex.** *His play was a target of the critics.*

tariff (4) [tæːr'if, teːr'if], *n.* 1. a system of taxes placed by a government on imports or exports. **Ex.** *The purpose of this tariff is to protect the market for locally built cars.* 2. the rate of tax placed on an imported or exported article. **Ex.** *What is the tariff on watches?*

tart (5) [tart'], *adj.* 1. sharp and biting to the taste; sour. **Ex.** *She used tart apples to make the pie.* 2. biting; cutting. **Ex.** *She made a tart reply.* —**tart'ly,** *adv.* —**tart'ness,** *n.*

task (2) [tæsk'], *n.* any work or piece of work that it is one's duty to do; burden. **Ex.** *The President has to perform many tasks.*

taste (1) [teyst'], *v.* 1. notice or try the flavor of food or drink by putting it in the mouth. **Ex.** *She tasted the soup to see if it needed salt.* 2. have a certain flavor. **Ex.** *The bread tasted good.* —*n.* 1. the sense by which one learns the flavor of food, drink, etc. **Ex.** *Cigarettes have dulled his taste.* 2. a quality that is perceived or noticed by the tongue; flavor. **Ex.** *The fruit had a sweet taste.* 3. appreciation. **Ex.** *He has a taste for music.* 4. a feeling for what is proper, beautiful, etc. **Ex.** *She shows good taste in her clothing.* —**tast'y,** *adj.* —**in good or bad taste,** proper or improper. **Ex.** *Her clothes are in bad taste.*

taste buds [teyst'bədz'], the cells on the tongue by which one tastes.

taught (2) [tɔːt'], *v.* past tense and participle of *teach.* **Ex.** *How long had he taught?*

taunt (5) [tɔnt'], *v.* bother or annoy by mocking talk; blame bitterly or scornfully. **Ex.** *They taunted him for losing the race.* —*n.* a bitter or mocking remark. **Ex.** *The taunts angered him.*

tavern (4) [tæv'ərn], *n.* 1. a place where people buy and drink liquor; a bar. **Ex.** *They met at the tavern for a drink.* 2. a small hotel. **Ex.** *He found a room for the night at a tavern.*

tax (2) [tæks'], *n.* 1. an amount of money that one is required to pay to meet the cost of government, usually a fixed percent of income, property, etc. **Ex.** *The government has increased the tax one must pay when buying cigarettes.* 2. a heavy strain. **Ex.** *His many duties were a tax on his strength.* —*v.* 1. require the payment of money to help support the government. **Ex.** *The government will tax your income.* 2. place a heavy strain upon. **Ex.** *The heavy work taxed his heart.*

taxi (3) [tæk'si], *n.* an automobile which carries passengers for money. **Ex.** *He went to his office by taxi.* —*v.* travel by taxi. **Ex.** *We taxied to the railroad station.*

tea (3) [tiy'], *n.* 1. a plant grown in Ceylon, China, Japan, etc. for its leaves; the dried leaves of this plant. **Ex.** *Tea is grown on those hills.* 2. a drink made by pouring boiling water over the leaves of this plant. **Ex.** *May I please have a cup of tea?* 3. a party in the afternoon at which tea, coffee, cake, etc. are served. **Ex.** *She gave a tea for the members of her club.*

teach (1) [tiyč'], *v.* 1. show how to do; train. **Ex.** *My father is teaching me to hunt.* 2. give lessons in; give instructions to. **Ex.** *She teaches music.* 3. supply with knowledge; cause to understand. **Ex.** *His illness may teach him the danger of smoking.* 4. work as a teacher. **Ex.** *He teaches at our school.* —**teach'er,** *n.* one who teaches. —**teach'ing,** *n.* the act of training, instructing, etc.

team (2) [tiym'], *n.* 1. persons working, playing, or acting together as a group. **Ex.** *The company employed a team of experts to improve manufacturing methods.* 2. two or more animals harnessed together for work. **Ex.** *A team of horses pulled the plow.* —*v.* join together for some purpose. **Ex.** *Each new man teamed with an experienced one to learn the job.*

teamwork [tiym'wərk'], *n.* effort in which everyone cooperates to accomplish a particular thing. **Ex.** *Excellent teamwork finished the job quickly.*

tear (1) [te:r'], *v.* 1. pull apart; rip; split. **Ex.** *Be careful or you will tear your coat on that branch.* 2. cause by pulling apart. **Ex.** *How did you tear the hole in your coat?* 3. pull off, out, etc.; remove by force. **Ex.** *Please tear the top from this box.* 4. move or act with violence or haste. **Ex.** *He tore out of the house.* —*n.* a place where something has been pulled apart. **Ex.** *There is a tear in his shirt.*

tear (1) [ti:r'], *n.* a drop of the salty fluid which keeps the eyes moist and which flows from the eyes when crying. **Ex.** *Her eyes filled with tears.*

tear gas [ti:r' gæs'], a gas which, when released into the air, pains the eyes and causes tears to flow.

a, far; æ, am; e, get; ey, late; i, in; iy, see; ɔ, all; ow, go; u, put; uw, too; ə, but, ago; ər, fur; aw, out; ay, life; oy, boy; ŋ, ring; θ, think; ð, that; ž, measure; š, ship; j, edge; č, child.

tease (4) [tiyz'], *v.* 1. mock or joke for the purpose of causing someone to be upset or bothered. **Ex.** *His sister teased him about his sweetheart.* 2. beg in a way that bothers for the purpose of obtaining. **Ex.** *The boy teased his mother for some cookies.*

teaspoon (4) [tiy'spuwnˋ], *n.* a small spoon for measuring and for eating food; the amount that this spoon will hold. **Ex.** *He stirred two teaspoons of sugar into his coffee.*

technical (4) [tek'nikəl], *adj.* 1. concerning the mechanical or practical arts or skills. **Ex.** *He is studying automobile repairs at a technical school.* 2. used in a trade, profession, science, etc.; specialized. **Ex.** *He read many technical books while studying to become an engineer.* —**tech'ni·cal·ly,** *adv.*

technician [tekniš'ən], *n.* one who is skilled in the performance of any specialized technical task.

technique (5) [tekniyk'], *n.* the method and skill used in performing artistic work, scientific operations, etc. **Ex.** *We admired the technique of the pianist.*

technology (5) [teknal'əjiy], *n.* the science of industry and mechanical or practical arts. **Ex.** *Space flights require an advanced technology.* —**tech'no·log'i·cal,** *adj.*

tedious (5) [tiy'diyəs, tiy'jˋəs], *adj.* tiring; boring. **Ex.** *The long wait at the airport was tedious.*

teem (5) [tiym'], *v.* be full; overflow. **Ex.** *His mind teemed with ideas.*

-teen (1) [tiyn], *suffix.* added to ten. **Exs.** *Three, thirteen (3, 13); four, fourteen (4, 14); five, fifteen (5, 15).* —**teens',** *n.* the years when one is 13 through 19 years of age. **Ex.** *The girl was in her teens.* —**teen'-age,** *adj.* in, of, or for the teens. **Ex.** *We watched the teen-age dancers.* —**teen'-ag·er,** *n.* a person in his or her teens.

teeth (2) [tiyθ'], *n.* plural of *tooth.* **Ex.** *He brushes his teeth morning and night.* —**teethe',** *v.* grow teeth.

telegram (3) [tel'əgræmˋ], *n.* a message sent by means of electric signals. **Ex.** *The telegram told him of his mother's death.*

telegraph (4) [tel'əgræf'], *n.* a device or system for sending messages by electric signals. —*v.* send a message by electric signals. **Ex.** *We telegraphed him to come home immediately.*

telephone (2) [tel'əfownˋ], *n.* electric device or system for sending sounds, especially the voice, over distances by wire.

Ex. *There is a telephone in the hall.* —*v.* communicate or speak with by telephone. **Ex.** *She telephoned his office.*

telescope (4) [tel'əskowp`], *n.* an instrument for making distant objects seem closer and larger through the use of pieces of curved glass and mirrors. **Ex.** *He was studying the stars through a telescope.*

television (3) [tel'əviž`ən], *n.* 1. a system of sending and reproducing a view or scene, using a device which changes light rays into electrical waves and then changes these back into light rays which are seen as a picture. **Ex.** *The schools in this city use television in teaching.* 2. a device for receiving television broadcasts. **Ex.** *We will be watching television this evening.* —**tel'e·vise**, *v.* send pictures by television.

tell (1) [tel'], *v.* 1. make known by speech or writing; inform. **Ex.** *Can you tell me where he lives?* 2. relate; give an account of. **Ex.** *She was telling the children a story.* 3. express; reveal; show. **Ex.** *Her smile tells me she is happy.* 4. order; command. **Ex.** *Tell him to come back later.* 5. understand; decide; determine. **Ex.** *No one can tell what will happen.* —**tell'er**, *n.* one who tells.

teller [tel'ər], *n.* a bank clerk.

telltale [tel'teyl`], *adj.* revealing what is not meant to be known. **Ex.** *From the telltale blood on the floor, we knew there had been a fight.*

temper (2) [tem'pər], *n.* 1. anger or the inclination to anger. **Ex.** *The child displayed a mean temper.* 2. state or frame of mind; mood. **Ex.** *She was in a good temper yesterday and smiled all day.* 3. self-control; calm disposition. **Ex.** *He loses his temper easily and starts shouting.* —*v.* 1. soften; make less strong. **Ex.** *The judge tempered justice with mercy.* 2. condition to a proper degree of hardness. **Ex.** *The metal was plunged into cold water to temper it.* —**tem'pered**, *adj.*

temperament (5) [tem'p(ə)rəmənt], *n.* 1. the individual nature of a person determined by his mental and physical characteristics. **Ex.** *He has the quiet, serious temperament of a scholar.* 2. easily excited nature. **Ex.** *The painter showed his temperament by shouting at the least criticism.* —**tem`per·a·men'tal**, *adj.* easily disturbed.

temperate (4) [tem'p(ə)rit], *adj.* 1. keeping proper control of one's actions, emotions, appetite, etc.; self-controlled. **Ex.** *He is a man of temperate habits.* 2. neither too hot nor too cold. **Ex.** *The country has a temperate climate.* —**tem¹ per·ate·ly,** *adv.*

temperature (2) [tem'p(ə)rəčər], *n.* 1. the degree of heat or cold, measured on a scale. **Ex.** *What is the temperature of this room?* 2. the degree of heat above normal of a person's body; fever. **Ex.** *The patient had a high temperature.*

tempest (4) [tem'pəst], *n.* 1. a violent windstorm usually accompanied by rain. **Ex.** *The tempest forced the ship onto the rocks.* 2. a violent disturbance. **Ex.** *His speech caused a political tempest.*

temple (2) [tem'pəl], *n.* a building used for worship. **Ex.** *The people went to the temple to pray.*

temple (2) [tem'pəl], *n.* the flat part of the head on either side of the forehead. **Ex.** *He had a cut on his right temple.*

temporary (4) [tem'pəre:r'iy], *adj.* limited; for only a short time; not permanent. **Ex.** *He has a temporary job which ends in two weeks.* —**tem'po·rar'i·ly,** *adv.*

tempt (4) [tempt'], *v.* 1. try to get one to do something wrong by making it attractive. **Ex.** *The boys tempted him to smoke.* 2. attract one to want something or do something; be attractive or desirable to. **Ex.** *They were tempted by the chocolate cake.* —**temp·ta'tion,** *n.*

ten (1) [ten'], *n., adj.* the number between nine and eleven; the number *10.* —**tenth¹,** *adj.* coming after nine others. —*n.* one of ten equal parts of something; 1/10. **Ex.** *One tenth of the property belongs to me.*

tenant (4) [ten'ənt], *n.* one who occupies or uses land or buildings he does not own, usually for periodic payments. **Ex.** *The former tenants of that house have just moved away.* —**ten'an·cy,** *n.* period of time during which one occupies as a tenant. **Ex.** *His tenancy of the house is one year.*

tend (2) [tend'], *v.* be likely to; lean toward; go or move in the direction of. **Ex.** *He tends to be lazy.*

tend (2) [tend'], *v.* take care of; guard. **Ex.** *She tended the baby.*

tendency (3) [ten'dənsiy], *n.* an inclination to act, go, or move in a certain way or direction. **Ex.** *She has a tendency to talk too much.*

tender (2) [ten'dər], *v.* offer for someone to accept. **Ex.** *He tendered us money as payment for the book he had lost.*

tender (2) [ten'dər], *adj.* 1. gentle; loving. **Ex.** *She has a tender heart.* 2. easily harmed or hurt. **Ex.** *The rough material hurt the child's tender skin.* 3. soft; easily cut or chewed; not tough. **Ex.** *They enjoyed the tender steak.* —**ten'der·ly,** *adv.* —**ten'der·ness,** *n.* —**ten'der·ize,** *v.* make tender. **Ex.** *He tenderized the steak.*

tenderfoot [ten'dərfut`], *n.* a beginner. **Ex.** *The tenderfoot had much to learn.*

tenderhearted [ten'dərhar'tid], *adj.* easily moved by suffering; quick to sympathize. **Ex.** *The tenderhearted child wept over the dead bird.*

tennis (4) [ten'is], *n.* a game in which rackets are used to hit a ball back and forth over a net. **Ex.** *The children are learning to play tennis.*

tense (5) [tens'], *adj.* stretched tightly; strained. **Ex.** *Her nerves were tense from waiting.* —*v.* stretch; make tight; strain. **Ex.** *The runner tensed his muscles.* —**tense'ly,** *adv.* —**tense'ness,** *n.*

tense (5) [tens'], *n.* a form of a verb showing when the action or being occurs. **Ex.** *"Will study" is the future tense of the verb "study."*

tension (5) [ten'šən], *n.* 1. the condition caused by stretching, tensing, or straining. **Ex.** *Too much tension caused the steel cable to break.* 2. mental strain; a feeling of anxiety. **Ex.** *He was under great tension during the examination.* 3. a strained relationship between people, governments, etc. **Ex.** *Talk relieved the tension between the two countries.*

tent (2) [tent'], *n.* 1. a light shelter of cloth supported by poles and fastened to the ground. **Ex.** *The campers lived in a tent.* 2. something resembling this. **Ex.** *An oxygen tent was placed over the patient.* —*v.* live in a tent. **Ex.** *They tented on the old campground.*

term (2) [tərm'], *n.* 1. a fixed period or length of time. **Ex.** *This is his third term in office.* 2. a word or expression used in a special sense. **Ex.** *The author uses many medical terms.* —**terms',** *n.pl.* special conditions of a sale, agreement, etc. **Ex.** *The terms of the contract are fair.* —*n.* relations between people. **Ex.** *They are on friendly terms.*

terminate (5) [tər'məneyt'], v. end; stop; bring to a close.
Ex. *They terminated the agreements.* —**ter'mi·nal**, *adj.*
leading to an ending, as death. **Ex.** *He has a terminal illness.*
—**ter·mi·na'tion**, *n.* ending.

terrace (4) [te:r'is], *n.* a flat, raised piece of land, often in a
series one above the other, on a slope or hillside. **Ex.** *The
terrace behind the house was covered with brick.* —*v.* form
into a terrace. **Ex.** *The hills were terraced for growing rice.*

terrible (3) [te:r'əbəl], *adj.* 1. causing terror or horror. **Ex.**
A terrible fire filled the sky with flames. 2. severe; very bad.
Ex. *I have a terrible cold.* —**ter'ri·bly**, *adv.*

terrify (4) [te:r'əfay'], v. cause terror or great fear. **Ex.** *The
armed man terrified the crowd.* —**ter·rif'ic**, *adj.*

territory (2) [te:r'ətər'iy], *n.* 1. a large area of land. **Ex.** *In
this state much territory has been set aside as state parks.*
2. the land under the rule and control of. **Ex.** *The territory
of this nation extends from one ocean to another.* 3. an area
in which a person travels or works. **Ex.** *Each salesman has
his own territory.* 4. that part of a country or empire which
does not have a fully independent government. **Ex.** *Those
two states were territories until recently.* —**ter'ri·to'ri·al**,
adj.

terror (2) [te:r'ər], *n.* 1. extreme fear; great fright. **Ex.** *The
sight of the knife filled him with terror.* 2. that which causes
great fear. **Ex.** *Poverty was a terror that never left him.*
—**ter'ror·ize**, *v.* —**ter'ror·ism**, *n.* act of causing fear, sometimes used as a way of governing or as a way to try to
destroy a government.

test (2) [test'], *n.* 1. a set of questions, problems, etc., to
determine one's knowledge, fitness, or ability; an examination. **Ex.** *She passed her foreign language test.* 2. an attempt
to learn or prove what something is like, why something
happens, etc. by examining, watching, etc. **Ex.** *They are
making a test of the new engine today.* —*v.* measure how
something will perform, act, etc. by watching, examining,
doing, etc. **Ex.** *The automobile tires were tested by driving
on a rocky road.* —**test'er**, *n.*

testify (4) [tes'təfay'], v. give evidence, especially in court.
Ex. *He testified that he had seen the accident.*

testimony (5) [tes'təmow'niy], *n.* 1. the statement of a witness, especially in court. **Ex.** *His testimony helped to prove the guilt of the accused.* 2. serious declaration. **Ex.** *Her testimony at the club meeting made a strong impression.*

test tube [test' tuwb', test' tyuwb'], a tall, thin tube used in making medical or chemical tests. **Ex.** *The scientist filled the test tube with chemicals.*

text (4) [tekst'], *n.* 1. the printed matter of a book or magazine, not including notes, pictures, etc. **Ex.** *The text is printed in large type.* 2. the original words of an author. **Ex.** *He quoted the text and then explained it in his own words.*

textbook [tekst'buk`], *n.* a book of instruction, especially one used in schools.

textile (5) [teks'təl], *n.* cloth made by weaving. **Ex.** *Cotton, wool, and silk are textiles.* —*adj.* having to do with cloth made by weaving. **Ex.** *Rayon fabrics are made at that textile factory.*

texture (5) [teks'čər], *n.* the way a surface or material appears or the way it feels when touched. **Ex.** *The wall has a rough texture.*

-th (1) [θ], *suffix.* 1. a state or quality of being or having. **Exs.** *True, truth; warm, warmth; wide, width.* 2. an order or place of a number in a series. **Exs.** *Six, sixth; four, fourth.*

than (1) [ðæn'], *conj.* 1. in comparison with. **Ex.** *He is younger than his brother.* 2. but; except; besides. **Ex.** *No one called, other than your sister.*

thank (1) [θæŋk'], *v.* say that one has warm feeling toward another because of some act, kindness, etc. **Ex.** *Thank you for your help.* —**thanks'**, *n.pl.* an expression of gratefulness. **Ex.** *They accepted the gift with thanks.* —*interj.* I thank you. **Ex.** *Thanks for the ride.*

that (1) [ðæt'], *adj.* indicating a particular person, place, or thing, usually further from the speaker than would be indicated by the word "this." **Ex.** *That woman is his wife, not this one.* —*pron.* 1. the particular person, place, or thing indicated, usually further from the speaker than would be indicated by the word "this." **Ex.** *That is my friend.* 2. a previously stated fact, idea, or thing. **Ex.** *That is what he said.* 3. who; whom; which. **Ex.** *The man that I saw wore a brown suit.* —*conj.* introducing a dependent clause used as: 1. the subject or object of a sentence. **Exs.** *That he* *denies the story surprises me. I know that he is here.* 2. introducing a dependent clause and showing cause, purpose, or result. Ex. *He worked so hard that he became ill.* —*adv.* to the degree indicated. Ex. *I cannot walk that fast.*

thaw (5) [θɔːˈ], *v.* 1. melt; become liquid. Ex. *The ice in the river will thaw in the spring.* 2. reach a temperature that causes the melting of ice and snow. Ex. *It will probably thaw tomorrow.* 3. become less cold in manner. Ex. *He began to thaw under the warmth of her personality.* —*n.* 1. the act of thawing. Ex. *There has been a thaw in the relations between the two countries.* 2. weather sufficiently warm to melt ice and snow. Ex. *The spring thaw came early this year.*

the (1) [ðiyˈ, ðəˈ], *adj.* 1. referring to one particular person or thing. Ex. *I know the man who wrote that book.* 2. referring to a well-known person or thing. Ex. *Men have now traveled to the moon.* 3. referring in a general way to every person or thing of a class or group. Ex. *The horse is a useful animal.* 4. giving emphasis to; indicating the best one. Ex. *She is the person to ask.* —*adv.* that much. Ex. *She likes him the better for his frankness.*

theater (2) [θiyˈətər], *n.* 1. a public place where movies or plays are shown. Ex. *What is the movie at the theater tonight?* 2. the art of acting in or producing plays; all the people connected with this art. Ex. *She has many friends in the world of the theater.* 3. the scene of action or events. Ex. *The general visited the theater of war.*

theft (5) [θeftˈ], *n.* the act of robbing or stealing. Ex. *They reported the theft to the police.*

their (1) [ðeːrˈ], *adj.* of them; owned by or belonging to them. Ex. *They left their coats in the car.* —**theirs**ˈ, *pron.* the one or ones belonging to them. Ex. *Our children stay up late, but theirs do not.*

them (1) [ðemˈ], *pron.* form of the pronoun *they* used as the object of a verb or preposition. Ex. *I will see them tomorrow.*

theme (4) [θiymˈ], *n.* 1. the main subject or topic of a composition, lecture, etc. Ex. *The theme of his talk was the need for education.* 2. a written composition on a given subject. Ex. *The teacher had the children write themes about their vacations.*

themselves [ðəmselvzˈ], *pron.* 1. their own selves. Ex. *They* *saw the accident themselves.* 2. their usual selves. **Ex.** *They are not acting like themselves.*

then (1) [ðen'], *adv.* 1. at that time. **Ex.** *They were only girls then.* 2. next in order of occurrence. **Ex.** *He had dinner first and then read the newspaper.* 3. in that case; therefore. **Ex.** *If you like it, then you may have it.* —*adj.* existing or being at the time. **Ex.** *My brother, then a soldier, told me the story.* —*n.* that time. **Ex.** *We had not seen him until then.*

theory (2) [θiy'əriy], *n.* 1. a reasonable explanation of why something exists or how something happens, based on experiments or ideas, but not yet proven. **Ex.** *People were slow to accept the theory that the earth revolves around the sun.* 2. the general principles or methods of a science or art as distinguished from its practice. **Ex.** *He is studying the theory of music.* 3. a guess; an idea. **Ex.** *It is my theory that the money was lost.* —**the'o·rize,** *v.*

there (1) [ðe:r'], *adv.* 1. in that place or position. **Ex.** *Who was there yesterday?* 2. to or toward that place. **Ex.** *He is going there now.* 3. on that point; in that matter. **Ex.** *I agree with you there.* 4. used in place of a subject at the beginning of a sentence in which the subject follows the verb. **Ex.** *There are three books on the table.* —*interj.* an exclamation used to show pleasure, sympathy, relief, etc. **Ex.** *There, there. You will be all right.* —*n.* that place. **Ex.** *We left there on Sunday.*

thereafter [ðeræf'tər], *adv.* from that time forward; after that. **Ex.** *He went abroad, and thereafter we did not hear from him.*

thereby [ðerbay'], *adv.* by that means. **Ex.** *He walked through the door first, and thereby we knew he was the king.*

therefore (1) [ðe:r'fɔr'], *adv.* as a result; consequently; for this reason or purpose. **Ex.** *She left home late and therefore missed the bus.*

therein [ðerin'], *adv.* 1. in or into that place. **Ex.** *He was willed the house and all the furniture therein.* 2. in that matter or respect. **Ex.** *He answered her letter, and therein he made his mistake.*

thereupon [ðerəpɔn'], *adv.* immediately afterward. **Ex.** *He told us good-by and thereupon walked away.*

---

a, far; æ, am; e, get; ey, late; i, in; iy, see; ɔ, all; ow, go; u, put; uw, too; ə, but, ago; ər, fur; aw, out; ay, life; oy, boy; ŋ, ring; θ, think; ð, that; ž, measure; š, ship; ǰ, edge; č, child.

thermometer (4) [θərmam'ətər], *n.* an instrument for measuring temperature. **Ex.** *The thermometer shows that it is very cold.*

these (1) [ðiyz'], *pron.* plural of *this.* **Ex.** *These are the books I want.* —*adj.* plural of *this.* **Ex.** *These books are the ones I want.*

they (1) [ðey'], *pron.* 1. plural of *he, she,* or *it.* **Ex.** *Our friends said they would visit us next month.* 2. people in general. **Ex.** *They say it will be a cold winter.*

THERMOMETER

thick (1) [θik'], *adj.* 1. relatively large in extent from one surface to the opposite surface. **Ex.** *He ate a thick slice of bread.* 2. measured between opposite surfaces. **Ex.** *The board is two inches thick.* 3. having its parts close together; crowded. **Ex.** *He has thick hair.* 4. not thin; heavy. **Ex.** *The thick smoke made it difficult to breathe.* —*adv.* in a manner to produce something thick; close together. **Ex.** *The blows came thick and fast.* —**thick'ness,** *n.* —**thick'en,** *v.*

thick-skinned [θik'skind'], *adj.* not easily bothered by criticism or unkindness. **Ex.** *He was so thick-skinned that he laughed at what they said about him.*

thief (3) [θiyf'], *n.* one who steals; a robber. **Ex.** *A thief was climbing through the window.* —**thieves',** *n. pl.*

thigh (5) [θay'], *n.* the upper part of the leg above the knee. **Ex.** *The fisherman's rubber boots came up to his thighs.*

thin (1) [θin'], *adj.* 1. small in extent from one surface to the opposite surface. **Ex.** *This is not a thin book.* 2. not fat; lean. **Ex.** *He is a thin man.* 3. watery; of little substance. **Ex.** *The sick man took only some thin soup.* 4. not close together; not heavy. **Ex.** *The old man's hair is thin.* 5. high and weak; not deep and full. **Ex.** *Her thin voice could not be heard above the music.* —*v.* 1. make or become less thick. **Ex.** *Water will thin the milk.* 2. make or become less crowded; reduce in number. **Ex.** *The crowd thinned until only we were left.* —**thin'ly,** *adv.* —**thin'ness,** *n.*

thin-skinned [θin'skind'], *adj.* very easily bothered by criticism or unkindness. **Ex.** *The thin-skinned author smarted from the critic's unfavorable comments.*

thing (1) [θiŋ'], *n.* 1. any physical object. **Ex.** *A book is just the thing to give her.* 2. any idea, proposal, project, etc.

Ex. *That is the thing to decide.* 3. any act, deed, event, etc. **Ex.** *The thing to do is ask your parents' advice.* —**things'**, *n.pl.* goods, clothing, tools, toys, etc. **Ex.** *Pick up your things.*

think (1) [θiŋk'], *v.* 1. produce thoughts; form in the mind. **Ex.** *I often think of home.* 2. reason; consider. **Ex.** *He is thinking about the problem.* 3. believe; have faith in something. **Ex.** *He thinks he can do it.* 4. judge; conclude. **Ex.** *I think that is a good book.* —**think better of,** 1. consider or regard more favorably than before. **Ex.** *Now that I know his work, I think better of him.* 2. change one's intentions. **Ex.** *Realizing the expense of the trip, I thought better of going.* —**think nothing of,** consider to be unimportant or easy to do. **Ex.** *He thought nothing of walking ten miles.* —**think over,** consider. **Ex.** *Think over my offer before you decide.*

third (1) [θərd'], *adj.* coming after two others. —*n.* 1. the third person or thing. **Ex.** *He is the third in line.* 2. one of three equal parts of anything; ⅓. **Ex.** *He received one third of the money.*

third person [θərd' pər'sən], the form of a pronoun or verb used to indicate the person or thing spoken about. **Ex.** *He, him, she, her, it, they, them, this, these, that, and those are third-person pronouns.*

thirst (3) [θərst'], *n.* 1. the need of the body for liquids; the dry feeling in the mouth and throat caused by such a need. **Ex.** *He died of thirst.* 2. any great longing for anything. **Ex.** *He had a great thirst for knowledge.* —*v.* 1. feel the need to drink. **Ex.** *They thirsted for water.* 2. have a longing for. **Ex.** *He thirsted for revenge.* —**thirst'i·ly,** *adv.* —**thirst'y,** *adj.*

thirteen (1) [θər'tiyn'], *n., adj.* the number between twelve and fourteen; the number *13.* —**thir'teenth',** *n., adj.* coming after twelve others.

thirty (1) [θər'tiy], *n., adj.* the number between twenty-nine and thirty-one; the number *30;* —**thir'ti·eth,** *n., adj.* coming after twenty-nine others.

this (1) [ðis'], *adj.* indicating a particular person, place, or thing, usually nearer the speaker than would be indicated by the word "that." **Ex.** *This boy is my brother.* —*pron.* 1. a particular person, place, or thing, usually nearer the speaker than would be indicated by the word "that." **Ex.** *I like this* *better than that.* 2. a fact, idea, statement, etc. that is to be presented or explained. **Ex.** *Listen to this.*

thorn (3) [θɔːrnʲ], *n.* 1. a needlelike point on a plant. **Ex.** *The stems of roses have many thorns.* 2. a plant or tree with many needlelike points. 3. something that worries or causes discomfort or problems. **Ex.** *His laziness was a thorn in her side.* —**thorn'y,** *adj.*

thorough (3) [θəːrˈow, θəːrˈə], *adj.* 1. having done all that ought to be done; complete and careful in every detail. **Ex.** *She did a thorough job of cleaning.* 2. complete; absolute. **Ex.** *He is a thorough fool.* —**thor'ough·ly,** *adv.* —**thor'ough·ness,** *n.*

thoroughfare [θəːrˈəfeːrʲ], *n.* a main street open at both ends. **Ex.** *His store is on a main thoroughfare.*

those (1) [ðowzʲ], *pron.* plural of *that.* **Ex.** *Those are difficult problems.* —*adj.* plural of *that.* **Ex.** *Those apples are harder to reach than these.*

though (1) [ðowʲ], *conj.* 1. granting the fact that; although. **Ex.** *Though they started early, they arrived late.* 2. still; yet. **Ex.** *They were late, though not too late for dinner.* —*adv.* however. **Ex.** *We did not buy the car; we liked it, though.*

thought (1) [θɔːtʲ], *n.* 1. a single product of the act of thinking; an idea. **Ex.** *The thought of her visit made him happy.* 2. the act or process of thinking. **Ex.** *He seemed to be in deep thought.* 3. consideration; attention. **Ex.** *A lot of thought should be given to that problem.* 4. a way of thinking; the ideas of a certain group, period, etc. **Ex.** *Science is one of the concerns of modern thought.*

thought (1) [θɔːtʲ], *v.* past tense and participle of *think.* **Ex.** *He thought he heard a noise.*

thousand (1) [θawˈzənd], *n.* ten 100's; the number *1,000.* —**thou'sands,** *n. pl.* a great many. **Ex.** *There were thousands of people at the game.* —*adj.* amounting to a thousand in number. **Ex.** *He had saved more than a thousand dollars.*

thrash (4) [θræšʲ], *v.* 1. beat or whip in punishment. **Ex.** *The father thrashed the boy for running away.* 2. move the body in a restless, unplanned way. **Ex.** *He thrashed about in the bed all night.*

thread (2) [θredʲ], *n.* 1. a fine string made by spinning slender bits of cotton, wool, etc. **Ex.** *She used silk thread in sewing her dress.* 2. the principal thought that connects the parts of a story, speech, etc. **Ex.** *The interruption made her lose the thread of the conversation.* 3. the threadlike ridge around a bolt or screw. —*v.* 1. prepare for sewing by putting a thread through a needle. **Ex.** *Please thread this needle.* 2. pass or make one's way through something with difficulty. **Ex.** *He threaded his way through the crowd.*

threat (2) [θret'], *n.* 1. a promise or warning that one will do harm, depending upon certain conditions. **Ex.** *Your threats will not stop me from going.* 2. an indication that something harmful or not desired probably will happen. **Ex.** *The threat of rain drove us inside.* —**threat'en,** *v.* 1. warn that one will do harm, depending on certain conditions. **Ex.** *They threatened to kill him if he did not go with them.* 2. indicate that something harmful will probably happen; be a possible danger or threat. **Ex.** *The rising flood waters threatened the town.*

three (1) [θriy'], *n., adj.* the number between two and four; the number *3.*

threshold (4) [θreš'(h)owld], *n.* 1. the entering or beginning point of something. **Ex.** *He was on the threshold of a new career.* 2. the piece of wood, stone, etc., which extends from one side of the doorframe to the other beneath the door. **Ex.** *He carried his bride over the threshold.*

threw (1) [θruw'], *v.* past tense of *throw.* **Ex.** *They threw their hats into the air.*

thrift (5) [θrift'], *n.* economy; careful use of resources to avoid waste. **Ex.** *Her thrift saved them enough money to buy a house.* —**thrift'y,** *adj.*

thrill (3) [θril'], *v.* 1. feel or cause to feel sudden emotion or excitement. **Ex.** *The music thrilled them.* 2. shake or shiver because of excitement. **Ex.** *Her voice thrilled with delight.* —*n.* 1. a shiver caused by emotion. **Ex.** *Meeting the President gave him a thrill.* 2. something that causes a shiver of excitement. **Ex.** *Piloting a plane was a new thrill.* —**thrill'er,** *n.* something thrilling, especially a sensational novel, play, etc.

thrive (5) [θrayv'], *v.* 1. prosper; grow rich; succeed. **Ex.** *His new business is thriving.* 2. grow with vigor and strength. **Ex.** *That plant will thrive with daily watering.*

a, far; æ, am; e, get; ey, late; i, in; iy, see; ɔ, all; ow, go; u, put; uw, too; ə, but, ago; ər, fur; aw, out; ay, life; oy, boy; ŋ, ring; θ, think; ð, that; ž, measure; š, ship; ǰ, edge; č, child.

throat (2) [θrowt'], *n.* the passage leading from the mouth to the stomach through which food and air go. **Ex.** *The dry bread was stuck in my throat.*

throb (5) [θrab'], *v.* beat or pound with unusual force or speed, as the heart does when one has been running. **Ex.** *His injured leg throbbed with pain.* —*n.* a throbbing or pounding. **Ex.** *They could feel the throb of the engines as the plane started.*

throne (3) [θrown'], *n.* 1. the special chair on which a ruler or high official sits during certain ceremonies. **Ex.** *The throne had been used by kings for hundreds of years.* 2. the authority that a ruler has; also, the ruler himself. **Ex.** *The throne ruled wisely.*

throng (4) [θrɔ:ŋ'], *n.* a large gathering of people; a crowd. **Ex.** *A throng of people awaited him.* —*v.* move into, around, etc. in large numbers. **Ex.** *People thronged into the park to hear the President.*

through (1) [θruw'], *prep.* 1. in at one end and out at the other; from front to back; from top to bottom. **Ex.** *The dog ran through the fields.* 2. by means of; with the help of. **Ex.** *He got his job through a friend.* 3. during. **Ex.** *We talked all through dinner.* 4. by way of. **Ex.** *He went through the hall into the bedroom.* —*adv.* 1. from beginning to end. **Ex.** *He read the letter through.* 2. entirely; completely. **Ex.** *Her clothes were wet through by the rain.* —*adj.* finished. **Ex.** *Are you through with your work?*

throughout (3) [θruwawt'], *prep.* entirely through; everywhere. **Ex.** *They traveled throughout the country.* —*adv.* entirely. **Ex.** *The bowl is silver throughout.*

throw (1) [θrow'], *v.* 1. cause to go through the air by a movement of the arm. **Ex.** *The boys were throwing the ball to one another.* 2. place in a certain position or situation, often suddenly and with force; hurl. **Exs.** *They decided to throw more soldiers into action. The storm threw the ship against the rocks.* 3. put on carelessly or hastily. **Ex.** *As soon as he could throw his coat on, he rushed out.* 4. send; direct. **Ex.** *Throw the light over here.* —*n.* the act of throwing. **Ex.** *His first throw was too high.* —**throw away, throw out,** dispose of. **Ex.** *He threw away the empty cans.* —**throw off,** 1. free oneself from. **Ex.** *He threw off the heavy coat.* 2. send out. **Ex.** *The fire threw off smoke.* —**throw up,**

become sick and expel food in the stomach up through the mouth. **Ex.** *He threw up his dinner.*

throwback [θrow'bæk'], *n.* return to an earlier type or stage of civilization. **Ex.** *This fierce dog is a throwback to the wolves.*

thrown (1) [θrown'], *v.* past participle of *throw*. **Ex.** *He was thrown from his horse.*

thru [θruw'], *prep., adj., and adv.* through.

thrust (3) [θrəst'], *v.* 1. push with force. **Ex.** *She thrust the door open.* 2. cause to pass into or through. **Ex.** *He thrust the oar into the water.* —*n.* 1. a quick, hard push. **Ex.** *He knocked the man down with a thrust of his elbow.* 2. the act of causing something to pass into or through. **Ex.** *The hunter killed the animal with one thrust of the knife.*

thumb (3) [θəm'], *n.* 1. the short, thick finger opposite the other four. **Ex.** *He accidentally hit his thumb with the hammer.* 2. the part of the glove that covers the thumb. **Ex.** *Your glove has a hole in the thumb.*

thumbtack [θəm'tæk'], *n.* a short tack with a large flat head, which can be used to fasten things by pressing on it with the thumb.

thump (4) [θəmp'], *n.* the sound of a blow made by a heavy or thick object. **Ex.** *I heard a thump as he fell.* —*v.* fall or hit as with a heavy, thick object. **Ex.** *The dog thumped his tail on the floor.*

thunder (2) [θən'dər], *n.* 1. a loud, heavy rolling sound that usually follows a flash of lightning. **Ex.** *The thunder woke the children.* 2. any loud, heavy rolling sound. **Ex.** *We heard the distant thunder of guns.* —*v.* produce a loud, heavy rolling sound. **Ex.** *The trucks thundered over the road.*

thunderbolt [θən'dərbowlt'], *n.* a flash of lightning accompanied by thunder.

thundershower [θən'dəršaw'ər], *n.* a sudden, heavy shower with lightning and thunder.

Thursday (1) [θərz'diy], *n.* the fifth day of the week.

thus (2) [ðəs'], *adv.* 1. in this or that way; in the following way. **Ex.** *The money thus obtained was spent for food.* 2. therefore; consequently. **Ex.** *The bus broke down; thus, I was late for work.* 3. to this or that degree, point, or time. **Ex.** *Thus far he has done the work alone.*

tick (4) [tik'], *n.* a light, sharp, repeated sound as of a clock.

Ex. *The silence was broken only by the tick of the clock.*
—*v.* make a ticking sound. **Ex.** *The watch ticked loudly.*

ticket (2) [tikˈit], *n.* 1. a piece of paper, cardboard, etc.
that shows the holder has the right to a seat in a theater, on
a train, etc., usually because he has paid. **Ex.** *He had just
enough money for the price of his train ticket.* 2. a small
piece of paper or cardboard attached to an article for sale
showing its price, size, etc. **Ex.** *According to the ticket,
the price of the dress had been reduced.* 3. a list of candidates chosen by a political party to run for election. **Ex.**
He voted for all the candidates on his party's ticket. —*v.*
issue or attach a ticket to. **Ex.** *The clerk ticketed the coats.*

tickle (4) [tikˈəl], *v.* 1. touch lightly on the body with the
finger, a feather, etc. so as to cause a pleasant sensation;
feel this sensation. **Ex.** *She tickled the baby.* 2. excite agreeably; delight. **Ex.** *The dog's tricks tickled the children and
made them laugh.* —*n.* a light, tickling sensation. **Ex.** *He
felt a tickle in his throat.* —**tickˈlish**, *adj.*

tide (2) [taydˈ], *n.* 1. the daily rising and falling of the surface
of the oceans and the bodies of water connected with them,
caused by the attraction of the moon and the sun and occurring about every twelve hours. **Ex.** *They liked to walk
along the beach at low tide.* 2. any such current or movement of water. **Ex.** *The tide carried the boat out to sea.*
3. a tendency, flow, etc. **Ex.** *The tide of public opinion
favors a new road.* —*v.* help until a time of difficulty has
passed. **Ex.** *Here is some money to tide you over until payday.* —**tidˈal**, *adj.*

tidings (5) [tayˈdiŋz], *n.* a message; information. **Ex.** *He
brought sad tidings.*

tie (1) [tayˈ], *v.* 1. secure, bind, or fasten, as with a string.
Ex. *Please tie this package.* 2. form a knot in order to fasten.
Ex. *She tied the ribbon into a pretty bow.* 3. limit; restrict.
Ex. *Caring for the children ties her down.* 4. even or equal
the score of a game. **Ex.** *Our team tied the score.* —*n.* 1.
anything which unites, binds, or joins. **Ex.** *Business ties
brought them together.* 2. a narrow cloth worn around the
neck by men. **Ex.** *He was wearing a blue and white tie.*
3. a contest in which the score is equal at some point or
remains equal. **Ex.** *The game ended in a tie.* —**tie up**, 1. tie.
Ex. *He tied up the package.* 2. hinder or keep from action.
Ex. *The traffic jam tied us up for hours.*

tiger (3) [tay'gər], *n.* a large, strong cat with fur of dark yellow marked with narrow black bands. **Ex.** *The tiger is a fierce animal.*

TIGER

tight (2) [tayt'], *adj.* 1. firmly and closely fixed in place; not easily moved; secure. **Ex.** *Each joint of the chair was tight and strong.* 2. too closely fitting. **Ex.** *The left shoe is tight.* 3. built so that water or air cannot pass through. **Ex.** *They put a tight roof on the house.* —*adv.* firmly; securely. **Ex.** *Hold tight to the rope!* —**tight'en**, *v.* —**tight'ness**, *n.* —**tight'ly**, *adv.* —**tights'**, *n.pl.* tight-fitting clothing worn on the legs and hips by certain athletes, dancers, etc.

tightfisted [tayt'fis'tid], *adj.* not willing to give or spend; miserly. **Ex.** *He is very tightfisted with his money.*

tight-lipped [tayt'lipt'], *adj.* not willing to say very much. **Ex.** *He is a tight-lipped person.*

tile (4) [tayl'], *n.* a thin piece of stone or baked clay used for roofs, floors, etc.; pipes and hollow blocks of such materials. **Ex.** *Some of the roof tiles were broken.* —*v.* place tiles on. **Ex.** *They tiled the bathroom floor.*

till (1) [til'], *prep.* 1. up to the time of; until. **Ex.** *Wait till tomorrow.* 2. before. **Ex.** *I cannot leave till five o'clock.* —*conj.* up to the time that; until. **Ex.** *He waited till she arrived.*

till (1) [til'], *v.* work land in order to produce crops by plowing, seeding, etc. **Ex.** *He has tilled the soil all his life.* —**till'er**, *n.*

tilt (4) [tilt'], *v.* incline; slope; slant. **Ex.** *He tilted the chair back too far and fell.* —*n.* any slanting, sloping, or leaning to one side. **Ex.** *The floor of the old house has a noticeable tilt.*

timber (3) [tim'bər], *n.* 1. wood suitable for building houses, ships, etc.; lumber. **Ex.** *What kind of timber was used for the frame of the house?* 2. growing trees; wooded land. **Ex.** *There were several acres of fine timber on the farm.* 3. a heavy, single piece of wood forming part of a structure. **Ex.** *Heavy timbers supported the roof.* —**tim'bered**, *adj.*

---

a, far; æ, am; e, get; ey, late; i, in; iy, see; ɔ, all; ow, go; u, put; uw, too; ə, but, ago; ər, fur; aw, out; ay, life; oy, boy; ŋ, ring; θ, think; ð, that; ž, measure; š, ship; ĵ, edge; č, child.

time (1) [taym'], *n.* 1. the particular or exact moment, hour, day, etc. **Ex.** *What time shall I come?* 2. a particular period. **Ex.** *I was away at the time he was sick.* 3. the number of minutes, hours, days, etc. that something continues or endures. **Ex.** *We will be gone only a short time.* 4. the number of occasions on which something is repeated; frequency. **Ex.** *She visited us several times.* 5. opportunity. **Ex.** *Can you find time to help me?* —*v.* 1. measure or record the length of time, the rate of speed, etc. **Ex.** *She timed his speech.* 2. choose or arrange a suitable moment or occasion. **Ex.** *He timed his visit to suit her convenience.* 3. multiplied by. **Ex.** *Two times five is ten.* —**time'ly,** *adj.* occurring at the proper or needed time. **Ex.** *He gave us timely advice.* —**at one time,** 1. together. **Ex.** *They all arrived at one time.* 2. at a time in the past. **Ex.** *At one time, there was a house on this spot.* —**at the same time,** nevertheless; however. **Ex.** *We want to go, but at the same time we do not want to fly.* —**behind the times,** old-fashioned. **Ex.** *Your ideas of dress are behind the times.* —**from time to time,** occasionally. **Ex.** *We see her from time to time.* —**in time,** 1. early enough. **Ex.** *We rushed the child to a doctor in time to save her life.* 2. eventually. **Ex.** *In time, you will learn.* —**on time,** 1. at the right time. **Ex.** *He arrived at work on time.* 2. with payments to be made at periods of a month, week, etc. **Ex.** *He bought the car on time.*

time-honored [taym'an'ərd], *adj.* honored because of age or length of time in use. **Ex.** *We do not like to change the time-honored customs of our ancestors.*

timekeeper [taym'kiyp'ər], *n.* one who measures or controls the time. **Ex.** *The timekeeper said that I was the fastest runner in the race.*

timetable [taym'tey'bəl], *n.* a schedule of arrival and departure times for trains, buses, etc. **Ex.** *Look at the timetable and see when the train arrives.*

timid (4) [tim'id], *adj.* lacking confidence; cautious; fearful. **Ex.** *The timid child would not greet the guest.* —**tim'id·ly,** *adv.* —**ti·mid'i·ty,** *n.*

tin (2) [tin'], *n.* 1. a soft, silver-colored metal that is easily shaped. **Ex.** *A tin can is made of steel protected by a coating of tin.* 2. a container for baking sometimes made of this metal. **Ex.** *She washed the bread tins.* —*adj.* of tin. **Ex.** *The house has a tin roof.*

tinge (5) [tinǰ'], *v.* 1. color slightly. **Ex.** *The sky at sunset was tinged with pink.* 2. give a slight trace of color, odor, taste, etc. to. **Ex.** *Her happiness was tinged with doubt.* —*n.* a slight trace. **Ex.** *There was a tinge of gray in her hair.*

tingle (5) [tiŋ'gəl], *v.* cause or have a stinging feeling as from excitement, noise, cold, etc. **Ex.** *Her ears tingled at the sound of the whistle.*

tinkle (5) [tiŋ'kəl], *v.* make or cause to make a series of short, light, ringing sounds. **Ex.** *The little bells tinkled.* —*n.* a short, light, ringing sound. **Ex.** *We heard the tinkle of ice in their glasses.*

tint (4) [tint'], *n.* a light shade of a color; a pale, delicate color. **Ex.** *There was a tint of pink in the sky.* —*v.* color slightly. **Ex.** *She tints her hair.*

tiny (2) [tay'niy], *adj.* very small. **Ex.** *The baby put his tiny hand in mine.*

-tion (1) [šən], *suffix.* 1. act of doing. **Exs.** *Accuse, accusation; register, registration.* 2. state of being. **Exs.** *Relate, relation; starve, starvation.* 3. the result of. **Exs.** *Perfect, perfection; connect, connection.*

tip (2) [tip'], *n.* 1. the pointed or rounded end of something. **Ex.** *The tip of his nose was sunburned.* 2. a cap or small part of metal, rubber, etc., placed on the end of something. **Ex.** *Shoelaces have metal tips.* —*v.* cover the end of. **Ex.** *The chair legs are tipped with rubber.*

tip (2) [tip'], *v.* 1. incline something so that it falls over; upset. **Ex.** *The child tipped over the glass of milk.* 2. place on an incline; slant. **Ex.** *He tipped his hat as he passed me.*

tip (2) [tip'], *v.* give a small sum of money to for special services provided. **Ex.** *He tipped the waiter generously.* —*n.* a small gift of money for services provided. **Ex.** *She gave a tip to the taxi driver.* —**tip'per**, *n.*

tiptoe [tip'tow'], *v.* walk quietly by rising on one's toes. **Ex.** *He tiptoed up the stairs.*

tire (2) [tayr'], *v.* 1. lessen the strength of by work, exercise, etc.; become weary or exhausted. **Ex.** *She tires easily.* 2. bore. **Ex.** *Hearing the same story again and again tires me.* —**tired'**, *adj.* —**tire'some**, *adj.* causing weariness or boredom. —**tire'less**, *adj.* without becoming tired.

tire (2) [tayr'], *n.* a rubber tube filled with air, placed on the wheel of a bicycle, car, truck, etc.; a band of rubber or metal on a wheel. **Ex.** *A bicycle has two tires; a car has four.*

tissue (4) [tiš'uw], *n.* 1. a group of cells forming a particular kind of structural material in a plant or animal. **Ex.** *Nerve tissue in his arm was damaged as a result of the accident.* 2. a thin, light paper or cloth. **Ex.** *She wrapped the gift in pink tissue with a green bow.*

title (2) [tay'təl], *n.* 1. the name given to a book, picture, movie, etc. **Ex.** *Have you chosen a title for your story?* 2. a word describing the rank, occupation, etc. of a person, used with his name. **Ex.** *We always address him by his title of "Doctor."* 3. a legal right to the possession of property; evidence of ownership. **Ex.** *We have the title to this house.* —**ti'tled**, *adj.* having a title, especially a title of nobility such as "king," "queen," etc.

to (1) [tuw'], *prep.* 1. showing the direction of an action; showing the place toward which an action is directed. **Ex.** *He ran to the door.* 2. showing the ending in time of an action; until. **Ex.** *He works from nine to six.* 3. pointing to the result of an action. **Ex.** *To her surprise, they arrived early.* 4. belonging with; involved with. **Ex.** *I want this room to myself.* 5. when compared with. **Ex.** *His income is equal to mine.* 6. showing the person or thing for whom or which an action is performed. **Ex.** *Give the book to him.* —, used before the simple, or infinitive, form of a verb. **Ex.** *I have to leave now.*

toad (4) [towd'], *n.* a small animal which looks like a frog but lives most of its life on land. **Ex.** *A greenish-brown toad lived in the corner of our garden.*

toadstool [towd'stuwl'], *n.* a mushroom, particularly a poisonous one.

toast (3) [towst'], *v.* brown by placing over or before a fire or hot surface. **Ex.** *She toasted some bread for breakfast.* —*n.* bread browned over or before a fire. **Ex.** *How many slices of toast do you want?* —**toast'er**, *n.* a device for toasting bread.

toast (3) [towst'], *n.* raising glasses and drinking as an expression of honor toward a person, idea, or thing. **Ex.** *At the banquet they drank a toast to the President.* —*v.* drink to the honor of someone or something. **Ex.** *They toasted the newly married couple.* —**toast'mas'ter**, *n.* one who proposes toasts and introduces speakers at dinners or banquets.

tobacco (2) [təbækˈow], *n.* a plant, the leaves of which are dried for smoking in cigarettes, cigars, etc.; the dried, prepared leaves of this plant. **Ex.** *He put some tobacco in his pipe and lighted it.*

today (1) [tədeyˈ], *adv.* 1. on this present day. **Ex.** *Write the letter today.* 2. at or in the present time or period. **Ex.** *Today some airplanes travel faster than sound.* —*n.* 1. the present day. **Ex.** *The lesson for today is easy.* 2. this present time or period. **Ex.** *The women of today have more freedom than those of yesterday.*

toe [towˈ], *n.* 1. one of the five end parts of the foot. **Ex.** *Someone stepped on my toe in the crowded bus.* 2. the portion of a stocking or shoe that covers this part of the foot. **Ex.** *She has a hole in the toe of her stocking.*

together (1) [təgeðˈər], *adv.* 1. in or into one group or place. **Ex.** *The boys were brought together for a meeting.* 2. at the same time; at one time. **Ex.** *They all left the building together.* 3. in or into contact with each other. **Ex.** *The swift current smashed the two boats together.* 4. by combined action; in cooperation. **Ex.** *They worked together to make the plan a success.*

toil (3) [toylˈ], *v.* 1. do difficult, tiring work. **Ex.** *They toiled in the fields.* 2. move with difficulty. **Ex.** *They toiled up the mountain.* —*n.* tiring work. **Ex.** *His back was bent by toil.* —**toilˈer,** *n.*

toilet (4) [toyˈlit], *n.* a bowl with a seat and lid for the disposal of body waste. **Ex.** *The youngest child has not learned how to use the toilet.*

token (4) [towˈkən], *n.* 1. a sign; something kept for memory's sake. **Ex.** *This gift is a token of our respect for you.* 2. a piece of stamped metal used in place of money, especially for bus fare. **Ex.** *The price of bus tokens has increased again.*

told (1) [towldˈ], *v.* past tense and participle of *tell.* **Ex.** *She told him to leave.*

tolerant (5) [talˈərənt], *adj.* having a fair and liberal attitude toward those who differ in opinion, race, religion, politics, etc. **Ex.** *His travels in foreign countries had helped to make him tolerant.* —**tolˈer·antˈly,** *adv.* —**tolˈer·ance,** *n.*

tolerate (5) [tal'əreyt`], *v.* 1. allow; permit. **Ex.** *The principal would not tolerate smoking in the school building.* 2. endure; bear. **Ex.** *She tolerates him only for the gifts he brings.* —**tol`er·a`tion,** *n.*

toll (4) [towl'], *v.* 1. ring a large, heavy bell with single strokes, slowly and evenly, especially to announce a death. **Ex.** *He tolled the church bell.* 2. sound or announce by tolling. **Ex.** *The bell tolled midnight.* —*n.* the sound of a bell. **Ex.** *We heard the mournful toll of the bell.*

toll (4) [towl'], *n.* 1. a payment for some privilege given, such as passage over a road or for some service performed, such as a long-distance telephone call. **Ex.** *Cars have to pay a toll to cross that bridge.* 2. the amount of loss resulting from an accident, fire, flood, etc. **Ex.** *The toll from the fire was in the thousands of dollars.*

tomato (3) [təmey'tow, təma'tow], *n.* a plant bearing a red or yellow fruit which is used as a vegetable; the fruit itself. **Ex.** *She served sliced tomatoes with the meal.*

tomb (4) [tuwm'], *n.* a hole dug in the earth, an opening made in a rock, or a building constructed to receive a dead body; a grave. **Ex.** *When their leader died, the people placed his body in a large tomb.*

tomorrow (1) [təma:r'ow, təmɔ:r'ow], *n.* the day after this present day. **Ex.** *Today is Sunday; tomorrow will be Monday.* —*adv.* on the day following this present day. **Ex.** *This work must be completed tomorrow.*

ton (3) [tən'], *n.* a unit of weight equal to 2,000 pounds. **Ex.** *How many tons of coal does this mine produce yearly?* See **Weights and Measures.**

tone (2) [town'], *n.* 1. a sound or the quality of a sound. **Ex.** *I like the tone of this piano.* 2. a manner of speaking or writing that expresses feeling. **Ex.** *She spoke to him in an angry tone.* 3. that condition of the body and its parts which is healthy. **Ex.** *Swimming will improve your muscle tone.* 4. a quality of color. **Ex.** *I like that tone of red.* —*v.* provide with tone. **Ex.** *He toned his body by exercise.* —**tone down,** make less noisy, colorful, harsh, etc. **Ex.** *I toned down the angry language of the letter.*

tongue (2) [tən'], *n.* 1. the movable organ in the mouth with which one speaks or tastes. **Ex.** *The hot soup burned his tongue.* 2. a language. **Ex.** *He speaks the English tongue.* 3. the manner or tone of speech. **Ex.** *She has a sharp tongue.*

—**hold one's tongue,** avoid or refrain from speaking. Ex. *I asked her to hold her tongue.* —**lose one's tongue,** not be able to speak. Ex. *She was so frightened she lost her tongue.*

tongue-tied [tən'tayd`], *adj.* not able to speak because of a physical defect or because of embarrassment, shyness, etc. Ex. *When asked to speak, he was tongue-tied.*

tonight (2) [tənayt'], *n.* the night of this present day. Ex. *Tonight is the only night they will be here.* —*adv.* on this present or coming night. Ex. *Sleep well tonight.*

too (1) [tuw'], *adv.* 1. also; in addition to. Ex. *I, too, have heard from him.* 2. extremely. Ex. *It is too bad you cannot come with us.* 3. more than enough. Ex. *He ate too much.*

took (1) [tuk'], *v.* past tense of *take.* Ex. *The trip took two hours.*

tool (2) [tuwl'], *n.* 1. anything such as hammers, saws, or mechanical devices, made of metal, wood, etc., and used to do one's work. Ex. *He owns several electric tools.* 2. anything or anyone used to accomplish work. Ex. *Words are a writer's most important tools.*

tooth (2) [tuwθ'], *n.* 1. one of the hard, bony parts growing in the mouth that is used for biting. Ex. *His aching tooth kept him awake all night.* 2. anything which suggests a tooth in shape. Ex. *A tooth of the saw is broken.*

tooth paste [tuwθ' peyst'], a paste for cleaning the teeth.

toothpick [tuwθ'pik`], *n.* a thin, short piece of wood used for removing food stuck between the teeth.

top [tap'], *n.* 1. the upper part, edge, or surface; the highest point. Ex. *They walked up to the top of the hill.* 2. that which serves as a covering, a lid, etc. Ex. *Where did you put the bottle top?* 3. the stem and green parts of a plant above the ground. Ex. *The top of that plant is edible; the roots are not.* 4. the highest rank or degree attained. Ex. *This brilliant student is at the top of his class.* —*adj.* at or concerning the highest. Ex. *Eggs are selling for top prices now.* —*v.* 1. cover or be covered at the top; crown. Ex. *Snow topped the hills.* 2. be more than or exceed in height, weight, amount of, etc. Ex. *He topped his brother's height by three inches.* 3. be the highest in rank, grade, etc.; lead. Ex. *He topped his class in reading.*

topic (4) [tap'ik], *n.* the subject matter of a conversation, a piece of writing, etc. Ex. *We discussed several topics at the meeting.* —**top'i·cal,** *adj.* concerned with topics in the news, being discussed, etc. Ex. *Coming at this time, his talk on guns was topical.*

torch (4) [tɔrč'], *n.* a hand-carried, burning light, such as a piece of wood soaked with some substance that burns easily.

tore (1) [tɔ:r'], *v.* past tense of *tear.* Ex. *She tore her dress when she fell.*

torment (4) [tɔr'ment], *v.* 1. cause great physical or mental suffering. Ex. *She was tormented by fears.* 2. bother greatly. Ex. *The child tormented his mother with questions.* —**tor'ment,** *n.* 1. great physical or mental suffering. Ex. *He was in torment from his wound.* 2. that which causes suffering, concern, or trouble. Ex. *Unpaid bills were a torment to him.*

torn (2) [tɔrn'], *v.* past participle of *tear.* Ex. *His coat was torn at the shoulder.*

torrent (5) [tɔ:r'ənt], *n.* 1. a violent, rapidly flowing stream of water. Ex. *The heavy rains turned the stream into a torrent.* 2. any similar violent, rapid flow or fall. Ex. *The rain came down in torrents.* —**tor·ren'tial,** *adj.*

torture (3) [tɔr'čər], *n.* 1. the act of causing severe pain in order to punish, be cruel to, or acquire information from. Ex. *The torture made him confess.* 2. severe pain. Ex. *It was torture for the sick man to be moved.* —*v.* cause severe pain. Ex. *The prisoners were tortured.*

toss (3) [tɔ:s'], *v.* 1. throw something lightly, without much force. Ex. *He tossed his hat on the chair.* 2. throw or be thrown from side to side or back and forth. Ex. *The ship was tossed by the waves.* 3. raise with a sudden, sharp motion. Ex. *She tossed her head angrily.* —*n.* the act of tossing. Ex. *The running player caught the ball on a long toss.*

total (2) [tow'təl], *adj.* 1. entire. Ex. *What is the total amount of the bill?* 2. complete. Ex. *As a result of the fire, the building was a total loss.* —*n.* the result of adding; the entire amount. Ex. *Add these numbers and tell me the total.* —*v.* add; learn the whole amount by adding the parts together. Ex. *The clerk totaled the bill.* —**to'tal·ly,** *adv.* entirely.

totalitarian (4) [towtæl'əte:r'iyən], *adj.* concerning a government in which the ruling party has complete control and allows no other parties. Ex. *The country is ruled by a totalitarian government.* —*n.* one who supports such a government. —**to·tal·i·tar'i·an·ism',** *n.* belief in such a government.

totter (5) [tat'ər], *v.* sway in an unsteady way. Ex. *The build-*

ing tottered and fell. 2. move with unsteady steps. **Ex.** *The old man tottered to his chair.*

touch (1) [tə̆č¹], *v.* 1. place the finger, hand, etc. on or in something to feel it; come or bring into physical contact with something. **Ex.** *She burned her finger when she touched the hot stove.* 2. affect so as to influence or impress. **Ex.** *The child's suffering touched my heart.* 3. refer to slightly; mention briefly; concern. **Ex.** *We only touched on the subject of money in our talk.* 4. handle or use. **Ex.** *The children were not allowed to touch those dishes.* —*n.* 1. state of touching or being touched. **Ex.** *I felt the touch of a hand on my shoulder.* 2. the sense through which the body perceives or becomes aware of something by contact with it. **Ex.** *One touch told her he had a high fever.* 3. the sensation one gets from feeling something. **Ex.** *The baby's skin had a soft touch.* 4. small amount. **Ex.** *The meat needs a touch of salt.* —**touch'ing,** *adj.* having an effect on one's feelings. **Ex.** *The ragged boy was a touching sight.* —**touch'y,** *adj.* quick to become angry, annoyed, etc. **Ex.** *He is very touchy early in the morning.* —**touch off,** cause; start. **Ex.** *He touched off the explosion by lighting the fuse.* —**touch up,** improve or repair something by making small changes. **Ex.** *The photograph was much clearer after it had been touched up.*

tough (3) [təf¹], *adj.* 1. strong and long lasting; not easily torn. **Ex.** *His shoes are made of tough leather.* 2. not easily cut or chewed. **Ex.** *This meat is tough.* 3. able to endure much without becoming sick or quitting. **Ex.** *Soldiers have to be tough.* —**tough'en,** *v.* make or become tough. —**tough'ness,** *n.*

tour (4) [tuwr¹], *n.* a long trip from place to place within a city, country, etc. **Ex.** *They went on a world tour last year.* —*v.* travel from place to place; go on a tour of. **Ex.** *They are touring several countries.* —**tour'ist,** *n.* one who travels for pleasure or education rather than business.

tournament (5) [tər¹nəmənt], *n.* games or contests among individuals or teams for the purpose of winning a championship. **Ex.** *Are you entering the tennis tournament?*

tow (5) [tow¹], *v.* draw along, as by a rope or chain. **Ex.** *They towed the wrecked car to the garage.* —*n.* a towing; that

a, far; æ, am; e, get; ey, late; i, in; iy, see; ɔ, all; ow, go; u, put; uw, too; ə, but, ago; ər, fur; aw, out; ay, life; oy, boy; ŋ, ring; θ, think; ð, that; ž, measure; š, ship; ǰ, edge; č, child.

which is towed. **Ex.** *The car would not start and needed a tow.*

toward (1) [tɔrd', tow'ərd], *prep.* 1. in the direction of. **Ex.** *They walked toward the lake.* 2. with respect to; about. **Ex.** *How do you feel toward this plan?* 3. leading to; for. **Ex.** *They are working toward a better understanding.* 4. shortly before. **Ex.** *It happened toward the end of the day.*

towards [tɔrdz', tow'ərdz], *prep.* toward.

towel (4) [taw'əl], *n.* a cloth or paper used to make things dry by wiping. **Ex.** *May I have a clean towel to dry the dishes?* —**tow'el·ing, tow'el·ling,** *n.* material from which towels are made.

tower (2) [taw'ər], *n.* a structure which is very much taller than it is wide and usually is part of a building. **Ex.** *The bell in the church tower was ringing.* —*v.* be much taller than; rise far above other objects. **Ex.** *The tall building towered above its neighbors.* —**tow'er·ing,** *adj.* very tall; very great.

town (1) [tawn'], *n.* 1. a center where many people live, larger than a village but not as large as a city. **Ex.** *He lived in the middle of town.* 2. the people of a town. **Ex.** *The whole town came to hear him.* 3. a city. **Ex.** *Where is your home town?* 4. the center or shopping district of a town or city. **Ex.** *We are going to town this afternoon.*

town hall [tawn' hɔ:l'], the building in which a town government is located, where licenses are obtained, etc. —**town'ship,** *n.* the area governed by a city or town government.

toy (2) [toy'], *n.* something for play rather than work, usually a child's game, doll, etc. **Ex.** *The children put their toys away before going to bed.* —*adj.* like a toy; made for play. **Ex.** *The children were playing with toy cars.* —*v.* treat or consider lightly, without serious thought or intent. **Ex.** *The sick man toyed with his food.*

trace (2) [treys'], *n.* 1. a mark or other evidence left behind that shows someone or something has passed. **Ex.** *Sorrow had left its traces on his face.* 2. an almost unnoticeable quantity of something. **Ex.** *There were traces of poison in the cup.* —*v.* 1. follow by finding the trail of marks or other evidence left behind. **Ex.** *The police traced the thief to his hiding place.* 2. follow the course, development, etc. of. **Ex.** *That book traces the history of the Democratic Party.* 3. go back from a particular time, place, etc. to find the origins of. **Ex.** *He traced his family to Ireland.* 4. copy a painting or picture by placing a thin piece of paper over it and marking the lines seen through the paper. **Ex.** *The children traced the pictures in the book.*

track (2) [træk¹], *n.* 1. a mark left behind by anything that has passed. **Ex.** *The hunters saw the tracks of a bear.* 2. a path or trail made by the feet of men or animals. **Ex.** *That track leads to a stream.* 3. the steel lines of rails on which railroad trains move. **Ex.** *The children crossed the railroad track on their way to school.* 4. a course laid out for some particular purpose, as for sports. **Ex.** *They spent the day at the race track.* —*adj.* having to do with sports performed on a track. **Ex.** *The runner was wearing his track shoes.* —*v.* 1. follow the tracks of. **Ex.** *The dogs tracked the fox to its hole.* 2. leave as marks something such as dirt, snow, etc. carried on the feet. **Ex.** *The children tracked mud into the house.* —**keep track of,** continue to have current knowledge of some person or thing. **Ex.** *I kept track of my schoolmates after I left school.* —**lose track of,** not continue to have current knowledge of some person or thing. —**Ex.** *I lost track of him after he moved away.*

tract (4) [trækt¹], *n.* an area of land; a region. **Ex.** *During the floods a large tract of farmland was under water.*

tractor (4) [træk¹tər], *n.* a motor-driven piece of farm equipment used to do the work formerly done by horses or oxen, such as plowing or pulling heavy loads. **Ex.** *The farmer attached the plow to the tractor.*

trade (1) [treyd¹], *n.* 1. the act or business of buying and selling; commerce. **Ex.** *Trade between the two countries has increased this year.* 2. the exchange of one thing for another; barter. **Ex.** *I gave him a piece of candy in trade for a piece of gum.* 3. those engaged in the same business considered as a group. **Ex.** *That news was of interest to the automobile trade.* 4. an occupation using the hands that requires special training and ability. **Ex.** *The young man is learning the shoemaker's trade.* —*v.* 1. buy and sell; be engaged in commerce. **Ex.** *This country trades with most of the countries of the world.* 2. exchange. **Ex.** *Please trade seats with me.* —**trad¹er,** *n.* one who buys, sells, and trades goods.

trademark [treyd¹mark¹], *n.* a mark, design, or word put on a product to identify the maker. **Ex.** *"JS" is the trademark* *that appears on all medicines the Jones-Smith Company makes.*

trade school [treyd¹ skuwl¹], a school at which one specializes in learning a trade rather than the usual school courses. **Ex.** *He is learning to be a carpenter at trade school.*

trade union [treyd¹ yuwn¹yən], a union of workers, particularly in a certain trade, for the purpose of bettering their wages and working conditions; labor union.

trading post [trey¹diŋ powst¹], a store in a place where few people live which exchanges or trades goods in addition to buying and selling.

tradition (3) [trədiš¹ən], *n.* customs and beliefs which have been followed for generations and which are passed from elders to the young, usually by speech or example. **Ex.** *It is a tradition in that family for the sons to study medicine.* —**tra·di·tion·al**, *adj.* —**tra·di·tion·al·ly**, *adv.*

traffic (3) [træf¹ik], *n.* 1. the flow of persons, cars, ships, etc. along a street, river, etc. **Ex.** *There is heavy traffic on this street.* 2. the business of transportation or of communications. **Ex.** *That shipping company has doubled its passenger traffic in the past year.* 3. the business of buying, selling, and trading, often of an illegal kind. **Ex.** *The traffic in liquor is heavily taxed.* —*adj.* concerned with traffic. **Ex.** *He stopped the car when the traffic light was red.*

tragedy (3) [træj¹ədiy], *n.* 1. a serious play which is concerned with extremely sad events, such as the death of a hero. **Ex.** *The audience wept at the tragedy.* 2. an extremely sad event. **Ex.** *His sudden death was a tragedy.*

tragic (3) [træj¹ik], *adj.* 1. concerned with tragedy. **Ex.** *He was a famous tragic actor.* 2. involving much suffering or death; terrible. **Ex.** *There was a tragic accident on the highway yesterday.* —**trag·i·cal·ly**, *adv.*

trail (2) [treyl¹], *v.* 1. drag or allow to drag behind; flow behind. **Ex.** *Her long evening dress trailed on the floor.* 2. follow the marks or path left behind by someone or something. **Ex.** *The hunters trailed the animal to its den.* 3. be or follow behind. **Ex.** *Dogs trailed the children.* 4. weaken; fade. **Ex.** *Her voice trailed off into silence.* —*n.* 1. that which follows behind. **Ex.** *The departing train left a trail of smoke.* 2. a path. **Ex.** *They followed the trail back to camp.* 3. marks or other evidence of passage left behind. **Ex.** *The wounded* *animal left a trail of blood.* —**trail'er,** *n.* a vehicle with no motor which is pulled by a car or truck.

train (1) [treyn'], *n.* 1. an engine and the series of connected cars which it pulls over a railroad track. **Ex.** *He likes to travel by train.* 2. a line of persons, animals, etc. moving along together. **Ex.** *Early settlers often traveled together in wagon trains.* —*v.* 1. teach ways of living, acting, etc. **Ex.** *They trained their children to use good manners.* 2. prepare for a particular kind of work. **Ex.** *The men were trained to fly.* —**train'er,** *n.* one who gives training.

training (1) [treyn'iŋ], *n.* the act of preparing someone for something; the practice and teaching provided by a trainer or received by one being trained. **Ex.** *He is in training to become a teacher.*

trait (5) [treyt'], *n.* a feature or quality which distinguishes one from another; a characteristic. **Ex.** *The boy has many of his father's traits.*

traitor (4) [trey'tər], *n.* one who helps the enemies of his country; one who betrays a confidence or a trust. **Ex.** *The traitor sold secrets to the enemy.* —**trai'tor·ous,** *adj.*

tramp (3) [træmp'], *v.* 1. walk or march with a firm, heavy step. **Ex.** *The soldiers tramped along the street.* 2. bring one's foot down heavily and noisily. **Ex.** *He tramped on my foot.* 3. walk; wander for fun or exercise. **Ex.** *The boys tramped through the forest.* —*n.* 1. a firm, heavy step. **Ex.** *We heard the tramp of his feet on the stairs.* 2. a long, wandering walk. **Ex.** *He went for a tramp on the beach.* 3. a homeless wanderer who begs for food or a little money. **Ex.** *The tramp had slept in the barn.*

trample (4) [træm'pəl], *v.* step heavily and roughly upon in a way that breaks, crushes, etc. **Ex.** *The cows trampled the garden.*

tranquil (5) [træŋ'kwil], *adj.* peaceful; undisturbed. **Ex.** *She enjoyed the tranquil country life.* —**tran·quil'i·ty,** *n.* —**tran' quil·ly,** *adv.*

trans- (3) [træns, trænz], *prefix.* over; across; through. **Exs.** *Arctic, transarctic; oceanic, transoceanic.*

transaction (5) [trænsæk'šən, trænzæk'šən], *n.* the act of doing

a, far; æ, am; e, get; ey, late; i, in; iy, see; ɔ, all; ow, go; u, put; uw, too; ə, but, ago; ər, fur; aw, out; ay, life; oy, boy; ŋ, ring; θ, think; ð, that; ž, measure; š, ship; ǰ, edge; č, child.

and completing business. **Ex.** *Buying a car was an important transaction for them.* —**trans·act'**, *v.* accomplish business.

transfer (3) [trænsfər', træns'fər], *v.* 1. move or be moved from one location, position, etc. to another. **Ex.** *He has been transferred to another job.* 2. change from one bus, car, etc. to another. **Ex.** *He was able to ride all the way home on the bus without having to transfer.* —*n.* the act of transferring or being transferred. **Ex.** *He has asked for a transfer to another job.* —**trans·fer'a·ble,** *adj.* capable of being transferred.

transform (4) [trænsfɔrm'], *v.* change the shape, appearance, or nature of. **Ex.** *The dress transformed the girl into a young lady.* —**trans'for·ma'tion,** *n.*

transit (5) [træn'sit, træn'zit], *n.* 1. the passage from one place to another over or through. **Ex.** *The points of transit from one country to the other are carefully guarded.* 2. the process of carrying things or persons or of being carried. **Ex.** *That city has several systems of transit.*

translate (3) [trænsleyt', trænz'leyt], *v.* express the meaning of the words of one language in those of another. **Ex.** *He translated the poem into English.* —**trans·la'tion,** *n.* the act of translating; the result of translating. **Ex.** *I have read an excellent translation of his book.* —**trans'la·tor,** *n.* one who translates.

transmit (5) [trænsmit', trænzmit'], *v.* 1. pass from one person or place to another. **Ex.** *Her illness was transmitted to other members of the family.* 2. allow to pass through. **Ex.** *These walls are too thick to transmit sound.* 3. send out a signal by means of radio waves. **Ex.** *His message was transmitted by radio.* —**trans·mit'ter,** *n.* the equipment which actually sends signals. **Ex.** *The radio station's transmitter is located on top of that mountain.* —**trans·mis'sion,** *n.* the transmitting process.

transparent (4) [trænspær'ənt, trænspe:r'ənt], *adj.* admitting the passage of light because of thinness, clearness, etc., so that what is on the other side, or beyond, may be seen. **Ex.** *Window glass is transparent.*

transplant [trænsplænt'], *v.* move a plant from one location to another and put into the soil again. **Ex.** *We transplanted flowers from one side of the garden to the other.*

transport (3) [trænspɔrt'], *v.* carry from one place to another

Ex. *Were the goods transported by rail or by ship?* —**trans`por·ta'tion,** *n.* the means or business of transporting. **Ex.** *We have both bus and subway transportation in this area.*

trap (3) [træp'], *n.* 1. a device used for catching animals, especially by hunters. **Ex.** *He put meat in the trap to attract the lion.* 2. a device, trick, or situation prepared for attracting and catching or deceiving someone. **Ex.** *The police set a trap to catch the escaped prisoner.* —*v.* catch or deceive by a trap. **Ex.** *She was trapped by the lawyer's clever question.*

travel (1) [træv'əl], *v.* 1. go on a journey; move about on a trip. **Ex.** *He travels a great deal in his work.* 2. pass through or over. **Ex.** *We travel this road often.* 3. move. **Ex.** *Bad news travels fast.* —*n.* the act of traveling. **Ex.** *She enjoys travel.* —**trav'els,** *n.pl.* journeys. **Ex.** *The explorer told us about his travels.* —**trav'el·er,** *n.* one who travels.

tray (4) [trey'], *n.* a flat surface of wood, metal, etc. with slightly raised edges, used for carrying or holding something. **Ex.** *She brought the cups and saucers on a tray.*

treachery (4) [treč'əriy], *n.* disloyalty; betrayal. **Ex.** *Selling military secrets to the enemy is an act of treachery.* —**treach'er·ous,** *adj.* 1. not faithful; not to be trusted. 2. dangerous because of incorrect appearances of safety. **Ex.** *The rocks just beneath the surface of this river make it treacherous.*

tread (5) [tred'], *v.* walk or step on; trample. **Ex.** *She was afraid he would tread on her feet.* —*n.* a stepping or walking; the manner of doing this. **Ex.** *We heard the tread of marching feet.*

treason (4) [triy'zən], *n.* the act of fighting against one's own country or of helping its enemies. **Ex.** *The traitor was found guilty of treason.* —**trea'son·a·ble, trea'son·ous,** *adj.*

treasure (2) [trež'ər], *n.* 1. a large collection of money, jewels, or other things of great value. **Ex.** *They were diving for sunken treasure.* 2. something or someone greatly loved or appreciated. **Ex.** *Her children were her treasures.* —*v.* guard, care for, or regard as if a treasure. **Ex.** *She treasured his letters.* —**treas'ur·er,** *n.* one who takes care of the money of a government, group, etc. —**treas'ur·y,** *n.* where money is kept. —**Treasury,** *n.* the department of government which issues money.

treat (2) [triyt'], *v.* 1. handle, regard, or act toward in a certain way. **Ex.** *He treated the old man with respect.* 2. attempt to cure, heal, or relieve a disease or illness by means of medicine, surgery, etc. **Ex.** *The doctor is treating my fever.* 3. discuss a subject in writing or speaking. **Ex.** *The author treats that matter very thoroughly.* 4. subject to some physical or chemical action. **Ex.** *This material has been treated to prevent its shrinking.* 5. give or provide without cost something that pleases such as drink, entertainment, etc. **Ex.** *She treated the children to ice cream.* —*n.* 1. the act of providing and paying for another's food, drink, etc.; the things so provided. **Ex.** *We bought her the theater tickets as a treat.* 2. that which gives great pleasure. **Ex.** *It was a treat to eat ice cream.* —**treat'ment,** *n.* 1. the act or manner of treating. 2. the use of medical means to try to heal or cure. **Ex.** *The doctor's treatment made her feel better.*

treaty (3) [triy'tiy], *n.* an agreement or contract between two or more nations. **Ex.** *That trade treaty was signed by five countries.*

tree (1) [triy'], *n.* a tall, woody plant with a single main stem and with branches growing from the stem, usually at some height above the ground. **Ex.** *A large tree shaded the house.*

tremble (2) [trem'bəl], *v.* shake because of fear, excitement, cold, wind, etc. **Ex.** *She trembled when she heard the good news.*

TREE

tremendous (3) [trimen'dəs], *adj.* causing awe because of greatness, size, etc. **Ex.** *The President has tremendous responsibilities.* —**tre·men'dous·ly,** *adv.* greatly. **Ex.** *She helped me tremendously.*

trench (4) [trenč'], *n.* a long, deep ditch. **Ex.** *The farmer dug trenches to drain the fields.*

trend (5) [trend'], *n.* general course, direction, or tendency. **Ex.** *The trend in medicine is for doctors to specialize.*

tri- (3) [tray, tri], *prefix.* 1. having three. **Ex.** *Angle, triangle.* 2. happening every third time. **Ex.** *Weekly, tri-weekly.*

trial (2) [tray'əl], *n.* 1. an examination of a matter in a law court to determine whether a charge or claim is true. **Ex.** *The trial proved him guilty.* 2. the act of testing or attempting. **Ex.** *After a series of trials, the design of the car was changed.* —*adj.* for or used in a test or trial. **Ex.** *He was the pilot during the trial flight.*

triangle (5) [tray'æŋ'əl], *n.* a figure consisting of three straight lines which meet to form three angles; anything shaped like this. **Ex.** *She cut the sandwiches into triangles.* —**tri·an'gu·lar,** *adj.*

TRIANGLE

tribe (3) [trayb'], *n.* a group of families living under and being ruled by a common chief or leader. **Ex.** *Members of that tribe settled along the river.* —**trib'al,** *adj.*

tributary (5) [trib'yəter'iy], *n.* 1. a flow of water, such as a stream, river, etc., which contributes water to a larger body of water. **Ex.** *The Mississippi River has many tributaries.* 2. a nation that is forced to contribute money or other wealth to a more powerful nation. **Ex.** *The Roman Empire had many tributaries.* —*adj.* 1. flowing into a larger body of water. **Ex.** *That lake is fed by a tributary river.* 2. under another nation's power and required to contribute to it. **Ex.** *After its defeat in the war, it had become a tributary nation.*

tribute (4) [trib'yuwt], *n.* 1. a statement of praise, a gift, etc. given to show respect or appreciation. **Ex.** *The statue was a tribute to the explorer's courage.* 2. that which one nation is forced to contribute to a more powerful nation. **Ex.** *Each year a larger tribute was demanded.*

trick (2) [trik'], *n.* 1. an action or practice done to mislead, cheat, etc. **Ex.** *His call to the guard for help was a trick.* 2. a clever performance or act of skill that puzzles. **Ex.** *The tricks of the magician delighted the children.* —*v.* cheat; mislead. **Ex.** *They tricked the old woman into giving them her money.* —**trick'er·y,** *n.* the act of using tricks or cheating. —**trick'ster,** *n.* one who tricks. —**trick'y,** *adj.* —**play a trick,** fool. **Ex.** *They played a trick on her.*

trickle (5) [trik'əl], *v.* flow in a small, thin stream; flow in drops. **Ex.** *The water trickled from the tap.* —*n.* a small, thin flow. **Ex.** *The stream was reduced to a mere trickle.*

tried (1) [trayd'], *v.* past tense and participle of *try.* **Ex.** *He tried to be good.*

tries (1) [trayz'], *v.* present tense of *try,* used with he, she, and it. **Ex.** *She tries to be good.*

trifle (4) [tray'fəl], *n.* 1. something of small importance or value. Ex. *He had no time for trifles.* 2. a small amount or sum. Ex. *The soup needs a trifle more salt.* —*v.* treat lightly; treat without respect. Ex. *It is dangerous to trifle with a man in his position.* —**trif'ling,** *adj.* not of much value or importance.

trigger (5) [trig'ər], *n.* a device which, when pressed, starts an action. Ex. *He pressed the trigger to shoot the gun.* —*v.* start or be the immediate cause of an action. Ex. *The young man's death triggered the riot.*

trim (3) [trim'], *v.* 1. make neat by cutting, clipping, etc. Ex. *The gardener trimmed the dead branches from the trees.* 2. remove something not needed, wanted, etc. by cutting. Ex. *She trimmed her nails.* 3. decorate. Ex. *The hat was trimmed with ribbon.* —*n.* 1. good shape, health, or condition. Ex. *The fighter kept in trim by exercise and diet.* 2. the act of trimming, especially by cutting. Ex. *The barber gave him a good trim.* 3. decorative edging. Ex. *The trim of the house is dark black.* —*adj.* in good condition; neat; well designed. Ex. *The new house has a trim appearance.* —**trim'ly,** *adv.* —**trim'ming,** *n.* materials used to decorate. —**trim'mings,** *n.pl.* all the other dishes, gravy, etc. that go with the main course of a dinner. Ex. *They celebrated with a chicken dinner and all the trimmings.*

trip (1) [trip'], *v.* 1. strike the foot against something while walking and fall or nearly fall. Ex. *I tripped on the step and fell.* 2. make a mistake. Ex. *He tripped on the last question.*

trip (1) [trip'], *n.* a movement from one place to another, usually some distance away; journey. Ex. *We took a trip to the mountains.*

triple (5) [trip'əl], *adj.* 1. made up of three parts. Ex. *She could see the sides of her face in the triple mirror.* 2. three times as many or as much. Ex. *There were triple locks on the front door.* —*n.* an amount and two more equal amounts. Ex. *He sold the land for triple the price he had paid.* —*v.* increase to three times the given amount. Ex. *His business has tripled in a short time.* —**trip'ly,** *adv.*

triumph (3) [tray'əmf], *n.* 1. the act or condition of winning or being successful. Ex. *His triumph over poverty was an example to others.* 2. a state of happiness and rejoicing over success. Ex. *The returned heroes paraded in triumph* *through the streets.* —*v.* be successful; win. **Ex.** *They triumphed over their opponents.* —**tri·um'phal,** *adj.* marking a victory. —**tri·um'phant,** *adj.* having won or rejoicing in a victory.

trivial (5) [triv'iyəl], *adj.* of little importance. **Ex.** *People at parties often speak only of trivial matters.* —**triv`i·al'i·ty,** *n.* anything not important; a small matter.

trod (5) [trad'], *v.* past tense and participle of *tread.* **Ex.** *He trod on her foot while they were dancing.*

troop (2) [truwp'], *n.* a crowd or company of persons. **Ex.** *A troop of soldiers ran along the path.* —**troops',** *n.pl.* soldiers or police. —*v.* gather or move in great numbers. **Ex.** *People trooped in and out of the building all day.* —**troop'er,** *n.* 1. a soldier or policeman on horseback. 2. a state policeman.

trophy (5) [trow'fiy], *n.* something taken in war or hunting, especially when kept as a remembrance; something awarded or kept as a symbol or evidence of victory or success. **Ex.** *The hunter's room was decorated with animal heads, silver cups, and other trophies.*

tropical (4) [trap'ikəl], *adj.* of, in, or like the tropics. **Ex.** *Bright-colored birds fed on the tropical fruit.*

tropics (4) [trap'iks], *n.pl.* the area bordered by two imaginary lines running east and west around the earth, one about 23½ degrees north of the equator and the other about 23½ degrees south. **Ex.** *The tropics have a very warm climate.*

trot (4) [trat'], *n.* 1. the manner, general speed, or movement of a horse which is going forward by moving a front leg and the opposite hind leg at the same time. **Ex.** *The horse was running at a trot.* 2. a slow, even way of running. **Ex.** *At the corner, the boys broke into a trot.* —*v.* move in a slow, running way. **Ex.** *The dog trotted along beside its master.* —**trot'ter,** *n.* a horse which trots.

trouble (1) [trəb'əl], *v.* 1. worry; concern; disturb. **Ex.** *He was troubled by the bad news.* 2. cause inconvenience to; annoy; bother. **Ex.** *He did not trouble himself to write.* —*n.* 1. misfortune; difficulty. **Ex.** *She has lost her job and is in great trouble.* 2. that which causes worry, bother, or inconvenience. **Ex.** *Your visit will be no trouble to us.* —**trou'ble·some,** *adj.* giving trouble. —**take the trouble,** try; make an effort. **Ex.** *He took the trouble to call me.*

trousers (2) [traw'zərz], *n.* an outer garment extending from the waist to the ankles and covering each leg separately. **Ex.** *These trousers need to be pressed.*

truce (5) [truws'], *n.* a time during a war, quarrel, etc. when the fighting stops for a limited time by agreement of all parties. **Ex.** *A five-day truce was declared at the New Year.*

truck (3) [trək'], *n.* 1. a heavy, motor-powered vehicle with space for carrying loads, used especially on highways. **Ex.** *The truck carrying their furniture arrived at their new house.* 2. a wheeled frame pushed by a person and used for moving small, heavy objects. **Ex.** *The porter took her suitcases to the train on a truck.* —*v.* 1. move things by truck. **Ex.** *The farmer trucked the cows to market.* 2. drive a truck. **Ex.** *Those drivers have been trucking for years.* —**truck'ing,** *n.* the business of moving things by truck for payment. —*adj.* concerned with this business.

TROUSERS

trudge (5) [trəj'], *v.* walk wearily or with effort. **Ex.** *The children trudged through the snow to school.*

true (1) [truw'], *adj.* 1. correct; not false. **Ex.** *The teacher says his statement is true.* 2. according to rule or law; real. **Ex.** *I can prove I am the true owner of this land.* 3. faithful. **Ex.** *He has been a true friend for many years.* —**tru'ly,** *adv.* —**truth',** *n.* that which is true; not a lie. **Ex.** *He told us the truth.*

trumpet (4) [trəm'pit], *n.* a small brass horn played by blowing into it while operating its valves with fingers to produce powerful tones. **Ex.** *The sound of trumpets announced his arrival.* —*v.* blow on a trumpet; make a sound like a trumpet. **Ex.** *Suddenly, the elephant trumpeted.* —**trum'pet-er,** *n.* one who plays the trumpet.

trunk (2) [trəŋk'], *n.* 1. the main stem of a tree from the ground up, without the branches and roots. **Ex.** *They sawed the trunk of the tree into boards.* 2. the body of a human being or an animal, except for the head, arms, and legs. **Ex.** *They found the trunk of an ancient statue of a man.* 3. the long, tubelike nose of the elephant. **Ex.** *The elephant raised its trunk.* 4. a box, larger than a suitcase, which will hold many clothes or other articles and is used especially for long journeys. **Ex.** *She packed the trunks for the trip.*

trust (1) [trəst'], *n.* 1. a sure feeling about another that he will do what is needed or what he is able. **Ex.** *We have complete* *trust in our doctor.* 2. duty; responsibility; care. **Ex.** *The child was put in his trust.* 3. property arrangement managed by a lawyer, bank, etc. for the benefit of another. **Ex.** *The wealthy man created a trust for his family.* —*v.* 1. have confidence in. **Ex.** *He trusted his brother with the money.* 2. believe. **Ex.** *I trust what he says.* —**trust'ful,** *adj.* —**trust'y,** *adj.*

try (1) [tray'], *v.* 1. attempt; seek to do. **Ex.** *She is trying to find him.* 2. test; seek to learn or prove something by testing, using, or doing. **Ex.** *We like to try different kinds of food.* 3. conduct the trial of a person or case in a law court. **Ex.** *The judge is going to try that case tomorrow.* —*n.* attempt; effort, endeavor. **Ex.** *He made a good try.* —**try'ing,** *adj.* difficult; annoying.

tub (4) [təb'], *n.* 1. a wide, round container, usually low and lacking a lid. **Exs.** *The butter was packed in wooden tubs. She washed the clothes in a tub.* 2. a tub in the bathroom in which people sit in water and bathe. **Ex.** *Please drain the water from the tub.*

tube (3) [tuwb'], *n.* 1. any long, cylinderlike piece of glass, rubber, metal, etc. in which fluids or gases can flow or be kept. **Ex.** *He used many kinds of glass tubes in his chemistry experiments.* 2. a container of soft metal from which liquids or soft substances are squeezed. **Ex.** *The artist had several tubes of red paint.*

tuck (4) [tək'], *v.* 1. pull together in folds to make shorter or narrower. **Ex.** *She tucked up her skirt and climbed over the fence.* 2. place the edges of something in or under; cover closely or tightly. **Ex.** *She tucked the child into bed.* —*n.* a sewed fold made in cloth for decoration or for shortening, narrowing, etc. **Ex.** *She put a tuck in the dress to make it smaller.*

TUBE 1

Tuesday (1) [tuwz'diy, tyuwz'diy], *n.* the third day of the week.

tuft (5) [təft'], *n.* a small bunch of feathers, hair, etc., loose at one end and close together at the other. **Ex.** *The bird had a tuft of feathers on its head.*

tug (4) [təg'], *v.* pull at hard and with much effort; haul. **Ex.** *The horse tugged the wagon up the hill.* —*n.* 1. a hard pull.

Ex. *He gave several tugs, and the trunk opened.* 2. a small boat that pulls another, usually larger boat; tugboat. **Ex.** *The tug pulled the steamship into the harbor.*

tumble (3) [təmˈbəl], *v.* 1. fall hard in an uncontrolled way. **Ex.** *She tumbled from the ladder.* 2. roll over and over; roll and toss. **Ex.** *The children tumbled about on the grass.* —*n.* fall. **Ex.** *He had a bad tumble down the steps.*

tumbledown [təmˈbəldawnˈ], *adj.* old and broken-down; ready to fall into pieces. **Ex.** *He lived in an old, tumbledown house.*

tumult (5) [tuwˈməlt, tyuwˈməlt], *n.* 1. a loud confusion of cries, yells, and noise created by a crowd; any similar condition. **Ex.** *He was greeted by a tumult of angry voices.* 2. a disturbed condition of the mind. **Ex.** *Her mind was in a tumult.*

tune (3) [tuwnˈ, tyuwnˈ], *n.* 1. musical tones arranged into a pleasing melody. **Ex.** *He whistled a tune as he walked.* 2. the state of producing a proper musical sound. **Ex.** *All the instruments were in tune with the piano.* 3. agreement. **Ex.** *His ideas were in tune with those of the group.* —*v.* fix an instrument so as to produce the proper musical sound. **Ex.** *He tuned the piano.* —**tune**ˈ**ful,** *adj.* having a pleasing melody. —**tune up,** adjust and put in good working order. **Ex.** *The motor of my car is not running smoothly and needs to be tuned up.*

tunnel (4) [tənˈəl], *n.* 1. a passage dug under the ground. **Ex.** *They drove through a long tunnel under the river.* 2. a hole that looks like this dug by an animal as its home. —*v.* make or dig a tunnel. **Ex.** *They tunneled under the wall.*

-ture (1) [čər, čur], *suffix.* act or process; result. **Exs.** *Mix, mixture; fix, fixture.*

turf (5) [tərfˈ], *n.* the upper layer of earth at the surface, held together by grass and roots. **Ex.** *His golf club dug into the turf as he tried to hit the ball.*

turkey [tərˈkiy], *n.* a large American farm bird with a small bare head and a fan-shaped tail. **Ex.** *Mother roasted a turkey for our holiday dinner.*

turn (1) [tərnˈ], *v.* 1. change the direction in which one looks, goes, etc. **Ex.** *We saw her turn the corner.* 2. change the position or part in view. **Ex.** *Turn to the next page.* 3. revolve; move in a circle; spin slowly. **Ex.** *The mill wheel was being turned by water power.* 4. direct one's attention to. **Ex.** *He turned to her for help.* 5. change color, form, shape, etc. **Ex.** *The leaves turned brown.* —*n.* 1. a regular chance or time to do something. **Ex.** *It was his turn to play.* 2. a change of direction, condition, etc. **Ex.** *The car made a sudden turn.* 3. a revolving; a moving around a center point. **Ex.** *The minute hand of the clock makes a complete turn in an hour.* —**turn down,** refuse. **Ex.** *The boss turned down my request for more money.* —**turn in,** 1. change direction to go into or enter. **Ex.** *He turned in at the last house.* —**turn off,** 1. close; stop the flow, operation, etc. **Ex.** *Turn off the radio.* 2. change direction. **Ex.** *Turn off at the next corner.* —**turn on,** open; start the flow, operation, etc. **Ex.** *Turn on the lights.* —**turn out,** 1. close; stop. **Ex.** *Turn out the lights.* 2. produce. **Ex.** *He turns out a lot of work.* 3. appear; come out. **Ex.** *They turned out to see the President.* 4. force out. **Ex.** *They turned the cat out of the house.* 5. become. **Ex.** *Everything turned out well.* —**turn up,** 1. appear or arrive. **Ex.** *He turned up at noon.* 2. find. **Ex.** *He turned up two new books.* 3. increase sound. **Ex.** *Turn up the radio so I can hear it.*

turncoat [tərn'kowt`], *n.* traitor; one who joins the opposition. **Ex.** *Turncoats from our country were helping the enemy.*

turnpike [tərn'payk`], *n.* a road for fast driving which one usually must pay to drive on. **Ex.** *He sped along the turnpike.*

turntable [tərn'tey`bəl], *n.* the revolving part of a phonograph on which one places records.

turtle (4) [tər'təl], *n.* an animal, covered by a hard shell, which can live in water or on land.

TURTLE

tutor (5) [tuw'tər, tyuw'tər], *n.* a teacher who gives private lessons. **Ex.** *His father employed a tutor for him.* —*v.* give private lessons; teach individually. **Ex.** *He tutors during the summer.*

tweed (5) [twiyd`], *n.* a coarse wool cloth, usually made of threads of two or more colors. **Ex.** *The tweed in his jacket was made by hand.*

twelve (1) [twelv`], *n.,* *adj.* number between eleven and thirteen; the number *12.* **Twelfth`,** —*n.,* *adj.* coming after eleven others.

twenty (1) [twen'tiy], *n.,* *adj.* the number between nineteen and twenty-one; the number *20.* —**twen'ti·eth,** *n.,* *adj.* coming after nineteen others.

twice (2) [tways¹], *adv.* two times. **Ex.** *Your friend telephoned you twice.*

twig (4) [twig¹], *n.* a small branch from a tree or bush. **Ex.** *We used some dry twigs to start the fire.*

twilight (5) [tway¹layt¹], *n.* 1. the faint light of the sun remaining after the sun sets just before darkness. **Ex.** *It was difficult to see him in the twilight.* 2. the time or period this light lasts. **Ex.** *She came home just at twilight.*

twin (3) [twin¹], *n.* 1. one of two persons or animals born to a mother during the same birth. **Ex.** *I cannot tell one twin from the other.* 2. one of two very similar things. **Ex.** *The two beds were twins.* —*adj.* 1. born at the same birth. **Ex.** *They are twin sisters.* 2. being one of a pair. **Ex.** *She bought twin beds.*

twine (5) [twayn¹], *n.* a cord made of tough threads braided together. **Ex.** *She used twine to tie the package.* —*v.* twist together; wind around; encircle. **Ex.** *The vine twined around the tree.*

twinkle (4) [twiŋ¹kəl], *v.* 1. give off light in small flashes that come and go; sparkle. **Ex.** *The stars twinkled in the sky.* 2. brighten; become sparkling. **Ex.** *Her eyes twinkled when she smiled.* —*n.* 1. a sparkling light. **Ex.** *She could see a twinkle of light in the distance.* 2. a sparkle in the eye. **Ex.** *She spoke with a twinkle in her eye.*

twirl (5) [twirl¹], *v.* spin rapidly; revolve. **Ex.** *The dancers twisted and twirled.*

twist (3) [twist¹], *v.* 1. wind together or around something. **Ex.** *She twisted her hair into a roll.* 2. bend or force something around out of its usual shape. **Ex.** *He twisted the paper and threw it away.* 3. turn or bend in curves. **Ex.** *The road twisted around the mountain.* 4. purposely give the wrong meaning to. **Ex.** *The reporter twisted my statement.* —*n.* 1. a twisting; something made by twisting. **Ex.** *Put a twist of lemon in my drink.* 2. a sudden, sharp pull or turn. **Ex.** *With a twist of the wheel, he avoided the other car.*

twitch (5) [twič¹], *v.* pull or move suddenly. **Ex.** *The horse twitched its tail at the flies.* —*n.* a sudden pull or movement, often uncontrollable. **Ex.** *The old man had a twitch in his cheek.*

two (1) [tuw¹], *n., adj.* the number between one and three; the number 2.

two-way [tuw¹wey¹], *adj.* having movement, communication, etc. in two directions. **Exs.** *This is a two-way street. Many taxis have two-way radios.*

-ty (2) [tiy], *suffix.* 1. quality or condition of. **Exs.** *Cruel, cruelty; safe, safety.* 2. tens; ten times. **Exs.** *Four, forty; eight, eighty.*

type (2) [tayp¹], *n.* 1. a group having some characteristics in common; kind. **Ex.** *What type of house do you want?* 2. a person, animal, or thing representing a class or group having some characteristics in common. **Ex.** *This is the type of apple I like.* 3. a wooden or metal block bearing a raised letter, figure, etc., an impression of which is transferred, after being inked, to paper; a set of such blocks; the impressions made by them. **Ex.** *This book has clear, easy-to-read type.* —*v.* use a typewriter. **Ex.** *She types quickly.*

typewriter [tayp¹rayt`ər], *n.* a machine with keys for the letters of the alphabet, numbers, and other symbols such as a period, question mark, etc., which makes printed letters on paper when the key for the symbol desired is pressed down. **Ex.** *She wrote a letter to her sister on the typewriter.*

typical (3) [tip¹ikəl], *adj.* representative of a class, group, person, thing, etc.; characteristic. **Ex.** *This is typical July weather.* —**typ·i·cal·ly,** *adv.*

typist [tayp¹ist], *n.* one who writes using a typewriter. **Ex.** *She got a job in the office as a typist.*

tyrant (5) [tay¹rənt], *n.* 1. a ruler who has absolute power or uses his power cruelly and unjustly. **Ex.** *Everyone hated the tyrant.* 2. a person in authority who is cruel. **Ex.** *The clerk complained that the office manager was a tyrant.* —**tyr¹-an·ny,** *n.* the government of a tyrant. —**ty·ran¹ni·cal,** *adj.*

U

U, u [yuw¹], *n.* the twenty-first letter of the English alphabet.

ugly (2) [əg¹liy], *adj.* 1. not pleasant in appearance. **Ex.** *That is an ugly house.* 2. dangerous; promising unhappy events. **Ex.** *Ugly clouds filled the sky.*

---

a, far; æ, am; e, get; ey, late; i, in; iy, see; ɔ, all; ow, go; u, put; uw, too; ə, but, ago; ər, fur; aw, out; ay, life; oy, boy; ŋ, ring; θ, think; ð, that; ž, measure; š, ship; j, edge; č, child.

ulterior (5) [əlti:r'iyər], *adj.* beyond what is stated; purposely concealed. **Ex.** *He was suspected of having ulterior motives for making his generous offer.*

ultimate (4) [əl'təmit], *adj.* 1. final; last. **Ex.** *What was his ultimate goal?* 2. greatest; farthest; highest. **Ex.** *The plane reached its ultimate speed during the test flight.* —*n.* something that is the best possible. **Ex.** *The car was the ultimate in comfort.* —**ul'ti·mate·ly,** *adv.*

umbrella (3) [əmbrel'ə], *n.* a round shelter, usually of cloth, on a folding frame carried over the head to keep one dry in a rain.

un- (1) [ən], *prefix.* 1. not; opposite of. **Exs.** *Able, unable; cut, uncut; sure, unsure.* 2. change the action to the opposite of. **Exs.** *Fold, unfold; tie, untie; lock, unlock.*

unanimous (5) [yunæn'əməs], *adj.* completely agreed; with no opposition. **Ex.** *She was elected secretary of the club by unanimous vote.* —**u·nan'i·mous·ly,** *adv.* —**u·na·nim'i·ty,** *n.*

UMBRELLA

uncle (1) [əŋ'kəl], *n.* the brother of one's father or mother; the husband of one's aunt.

under (1) [ən'dər], *prep.* 1. below; below the surface of; beneath. **Ex.** *He carried the book under his arm.* 2. protected, directed, or taught by. **Ex.** *We studied under a good teacher.* 3. less than. **Ex.** *The price is under five dollars.* 4. subject to; bound by; limited by. **Ex.** *He is under the doctor's care.* 5. in the group or class of; within. **Ex.** *You will find the word "blue" listed under "B."* —*adj.* in a lower place; beneath. **Ex.** *He examined the under part of the car.* —*adv.* in or to a position below something else. **Ex.** *The drowning man went under for the third time.*

under- (1) [ən'dər], *prefix.* 1. below in position; inside. **Exs.** *Ground, underground; shirt, undershirt.* 2. below in rank. **Ex.** *Secretary, undersecretary.* 3. less in quality; not enough. **Exs.** *Paid, underpaid; state, understate.*

undercover [ən'dərkəv'ər], *adj.* hidden; secret. **Ex.** *The undercover agent made a surprise arrest.*

underdog [ən'dərdɔ:g'], *n.* one who is likely to lose in a fight or a contest. **Ex.** *The lawyer was known as a champion of the underdog.*

undergo (4) [ən'dərgow'], *v.* experience; pass through; suffer. **Ex.** *She must undergo a serious operation.*

undergone [ənˈdərgɔːnˈ], *v.* past participle of *undergo.* **Ex.** *He has undergone much suffering.*

undergraduate [ənˈdərgræjˈuwit], *n.* a student at a college or university who is in his first years of study and has not yet received a degree. **Ex.** *This is a course for undergraduates.*

underground [ənˈdərgrawndˈ], *adj.* 1. done below the surface of the earth. **Ex.** *This city has an underground transit system.* 2. done in secret. **Ex.** *He sent an underground message.* —*n.* a political group forced to hide and act in secret because a government is opposed to it. **Ex.** *During the war, the underground fought the enemy at night.*

underhanded [ənˈdərhænˈdid], *adj.* secretive and unfair. **Ex.** *He used underhanded methods to win the election.*

underline [ənˈdərlaynˈ], *v.* draw a line under; emphasize. **Ex.** *He underlined the important sentences with his pencil.*

undermine [ənˈdərmaynˈ], *v.* 1. dig a tunnel or mine under. **Ex.** *Water had undermined the foundations of the building.* 2. weaken by secret efforts. **Ex.** *They undermined his business by telling people his merchandise was bad.*

underneath (4) [ənˈdərniyθˈ], *prep.* below; under. **Ex.** *The ball is underneath the chair.* —*adv.* beneath; on the under surface. **Ex.** *The rock was dry underneath.*

understand (1) [ənˈdərstændˈ], *v.* 1. know what is meant; grasp the meaning of. **Ex.** *Do you understand the question?* 2. be familiar with; have a knowledge of. **Ex.** *She understands English.* 3. accept as being a fact or settled. **Ex.** *He understands he must come tomorrow.* 4. have sympathy with. **Ex.** *She is a person who understands children.* —**unˈderˈstandˈing,** *n.* 1. knowing about something. **Ex.** *He has a very good understanding of banking.* 2. the power to understand; intelligence. **Ex.** *He showed a quick understanding.* 3. agreement. **Ex.** *They have reached an understanding about sharing the costs.* —*adj.* having interest or sympathy.

understood (1) [ənˈdərstudˈ], *v.* past tense and participle of *understand.* **Ex.** *She has not understood the problem.*

undertake (4) [ənˈdərteykˈ], *v.* 1. try; attempt. **Ex.** *He always undertakes more than he can do.* 2. agree to do; promise; pledge. **Ex.** *He said he will undertake to write the letter.* —**unˈderˈtakˈing,** *n.* 1. something undertaken. 2. a promise.

underworld (5) [ənˈdərwərldˈ], *n.* 1. the criminal class of society. **Ex.** *The two murdered men were members of the* *underworld.* 2. hell. **Ex.** *The poem describes the poet's journey through the underworld.*

unforeseen (5) [ən'fɔrsiyn'], *adj.* not seen or known at an earlier time. **Ex.** *Unforeseen difficulties delayed us.*

uni- (3) [yuw'nə, yuw'ni], *prefix.* characterized by or consisting of only one. **Ex.** *Form, uniform.*

uniform (2) [yuw'nəfɔrm'], *adj.* 1. not varying; always the same. **Ex.** *The room was kept at a uniform temperature.* 2. each being the same as another. **Ex.** *The price of this book is not uniform in all stores.* —*n.* a special style of dress worn by members of a particular group. **Ex.** *The nurse was proud of her uniform.* **—u'ni·form·ly,** *adv.* **—u·ni·form'i·ty,** *n.*

unify (5) [yuw'nəfay'], *v.* form into one or one group; unite. **Ex.** *Their common language helped to unify the settlers.*

union (3) [yuwn'yən], *n.* 1. the act of uniting two or more things into one. **Ex.** *He urged a union of the two groups opposing the tax.* 2. a number of states or countries joined together in a larger unit for a common purpose. **Ex.** *The United States is a federal union of fifty states.* 3. an organization of workmen who have joined together to protect and further their interests. **Ex.** *He is a member of a labor union.* **—un'ion·ize,** *v.* organize into a labor union. **Ex.** *He is trying to unionize the employees of the company.*

unique (4) [yuwniyk'], *adj.* single in kind; lacking anything with which to compare. **Ex.** *This ancient jewel is unique.*

unit (3) [yuw'nit], *n.* 1. one thing or a group of things considered as one part of a larger whole or group. **Exs.** *The family is the unit of society. A word is a unit of speech.* 2. a standard of measurement. **Ex.** *An hour is a unit of time.*

unite (2) [yunayt'], *v.* 1. combine into one; join together. **Ex.** *The two groups united to form a club.* 2. join together for a purpose. **Ex.** *The nations united for common protection.* **—u'ni·ty,** *n.* state of being united. **Ex.** *In unity, we have strength.*

universal (3) [yuw'nəvə:r'səl], *adj.* present in all; characteristic of all; intended for all. **Ex.** *The need for understanding and love is universal.* **—u·ni·ver'sal·ly,** *adv.* everywhere.

universe (5) [yuw'nəvərs'], *n.* all of space, including the earth, sun, stars, etc. **Ex.** *Space flights have brought us new knowledge of the universe.*

university (2) [yuw'nəve:r'sətiy], *n.* an institution of higher learning with one or more colleges and usually some professional schools. **Ex.** *That university has a fine school of medicine.*

unless (2) [ənles'], *conj.* except if it happens that. **Ex.** *He will go unless it rains.*

unparalleled [ənpær'əleld`, ənpe:r'əleld`], *adj.* without parallel; without anything equal or similar. **Ex.** *The movie was an unparalleled success.*

unprecedented (5) [ənpres'əden`tid], *adj.* never known before; without a previous example on which to authorize, explain, or base. **Ex.** *The judge made an unprecedented decision.*

unrest [ənrest'], *n.* disturbance; unsettled state. **Ex.** *Food shortages caused unrest among the people.*

unseat [ənsiyt'], *v.* 1. remove from a seat. **Ex.** *The rider was unseated when his horse jumped the fence.* 2. cause a political person to lose his position, by vote. **Ex.** *The Senator was unseated in the election and replaced by a new man.*

unsightly [ənsayt'liy], *adj.* not pleasing to the sight. **Ex.** *Because she did not clean her house, it was unsightly.*

unsung [ənsəŋ'], *adj.* not praised; unknown. **Ex.** *There were many unsung heroes during the war.*

until (1) [əntil'], *conj.* 1. up to the time or point that. **Ex.** *Cook the meat until it is well done.* 2. before. **Ex.** *Do not come until I call you.* —*prep.* 1. up to the time of. **Ex.** *He studied until dinner time.* 2. before. **Ex.** *We cannot leave until tomorrow.*

untold [əntowld'], *adj.* not easily counted, described, expressed, etc. **Ex.** *I have been there untold times.*

up (1) [əp'], *adv.* 1. to, in, or at a higher position. **Ex.** *The sun came up.* 2. to or in an erect position. **Ex.** *Sit up straight.* 3. out of bed. **Ex.** *She is not up yet.* 4. so as to approach, arrive at, or equal. **Ex.** *He ran to catch up with his friend.* 5. into discussion; to notice or attention. **Ex.** *Who brought up that question?* 6. from an earlier time. **Ex.** *This book brings us up to date on the problem.* 7. in or into a certain condition. **Ex.** *He added up the figures.* 8. completely. **Ex.** *She used up the sugar.* —*adj.* going or directed up. **Ex.** *The moon is up.* —*prep.* along; in; into; through; to a higher place; toward a point higher or farther along. **Ex.** *He climbed up the stairs.* —**up for,** be a candidate for election. **Ex.** *He is up for reelection.* —**ups and downs,** changes in luck, fortune, or condition. **Ex.** *He has had his ups and downs in life.*

upbringing [əp'brin'iŋ], *n.* the training a person receives as a child. **Ex.** *That boy shows his good upbringing by his politeness.*

uphold (5) [əphowld'], *v.* support; agree with; aid. **Ex.** *He promised to uphold the law.*

upkeep [əp'kiyp'], *n.* the act or cost of maintaining. **Ex.** *The upkeep of a big house requires a lot of money.*

upon (1) [əpan', əpɔ:n'], *prep.* on; up to a position on. **Ex.** *The child climbed upon the bed.*

upper (2) [əp'ər], *adj.* 1. being farther up or above; higher. **Ex.** *That wall is the upper limit of the property.* 2. superior; of more importance. **Ex.** *He is a member of the upper house of the legislature.*

upper hand [əp'ər hænd'], an advantage; a superior position. **Ex.** *Because he knew more, he had the upper hand in the discussion.*

upright (3) [əp'rayt], *adj.* 1. straight up; erect. **Ex.** *He stood in an upright position.* 2. honest. **Ex.** *He is upright in all his business affairs.*

uproar [əp'rɔ:r'], *n.* a great disturbance or noise. **Ex.** *There was an uproar when they heard he was leaving.*

upset (4) [əpset'], *v.* 1. cause to turn over. **Ex.** *The boys upset the table while playing.* 2. disturb; put in a state of disorder. **Ex.** *The rain upset our plans.* —*adj.* 1. overturned. **Ex.** *He was saved from the upset boat.* 2. in a state of disorder; disturbed. **Ex.** *He has an upset stomach.*

upstanding [əpstæn'diŋ], *adj.* 1. erect. 2. honest; honorable. **Ex.** *He is one of our upstanding citizens.*

up-to-date (3) [əp'tədeyt'], *adj.* current; in fashion. **Ex.** *This is an up-to-date book.*

uptown [əp'tawn'], *adv.* in or toward the part of a town away from the business section. **Ex.** *He lives uptown.*

upward (3) [əp'wərd], *adv.* from a lower to a higher place, position, condition, etc. **Ex.** *They climbed upward.* —*adj.* directed upward. **Ex.** *The conductor made an upward movement of his hand.*

urban (5) [ər'bən], *adj.* 1. concerning, typical of, or forming a city. **Ex.** *Traffic is a major urban problem.* 2. living or located in a city. **Ex.** *American urban populations have greatly increased during the last ten years.*

-ure (1) [ər], *suffix.* act or process; result. **Exs.** *Press, pressure; fail, failure; seize, seizure.*

urge (2) [ərjʹ], *v.* 1. force onward. **Ex.** *The rider urged the horse to greater speed.* 2. beg earnestly; plead. **Ex.** *She urged her children to study.* 3. advise; recommend. **Ex.** *The doctor urged his patient to rest more.* —*n.* a sudden desire; an impulse. **Ex.** *He had a sudden urge to speak.*

urgent (5) [əːrʹjənt], *adj.* 1. requiring immediate attention; pressing. **Ex.** *He was called home on urgent business.* 2. insistent; demanding. **Ex.** *He answered an urgent call for help.* —**urʹgent·ly,** *adv.* —**urʹgen·cy,** *n.*

urn (5) [ərnʹ], *n.* 1. a vase with a large flat base or foot. **Ex.** *There was a pair of stone urns beside the gate.* 2. a container with a spout used for making and serving tea or coffee. **Ex.** *This urn holds 20 cups of coffee.*

URN 2

us (1) [əsʹ], *pron.* the form of *we* used after a preposition or as an object of a verb. **Exs.** *They saw us yesterday. He said he would write to us.*

usage (5) [yuwʹsij], *n.* 1. the manner of using; treatment. **Ex.** *Rough usage had damaged the car.* 2. the customary way of using words, phrases, or language in general. **Ex.** *Usage often changes the meaning of a word.*

use (1) [yuwzʹ], *v.* 1. employ for a purpose; put into action. **Ex.** *He used the car to drive to work.* 2. spend; exhaust. **Ex.** *She had used all her strength to clean the house.* —**usedʹ,** *adj.* that has been used; not new. —**used to,** did at one time in the past. **Ex.** *He used to work but does not now.* —*adj.* accustomed. **Ex.** *He became used to seeing the flowers every day.* —**use up,** use until there is no more. **Ex.** *I used up the soap and bought more.*

use (1) [yuwsʹ], *n.* 1. the act of using or being used. **Ex.** *The car is in use at present.* 2. a particular purpose, need, etc. **Ex.** *This suit is for everyday use.* 3. benefit; advantage. **Ex.** *There is no use in crying.* 4. ability to use; power. **Ex.** *She lost the use of her right leg.*

usher (4) [əšʹər], *n.* one who leads persons to seats in a theater, church, etc. **Ex.** *The usher found seats for us.* —*v.* act as an usher; bring to. **Ex.** *He ushered us to our seats.*

usual (1) [yuwʹžuwəl, yuwʹžul], *adj.* such as is most often encountered, heard, seen, etc.; ordinary; normal. **Ex.** *She took her usual seat at the table.* —**uʹsu·al·ly,** *adv.* most of the time. —**as usual,** as most of the time. **Ex.** *As usual, we began work at nine o'clock.*

utensil (5) [yutenʹsəl, yuwʹtenʹsəl], *n.* container; instrument; etc., especially one used in a kitchen or on a fire. **Ex.** *She washed the baking utensils.*

utility (4) [yutilʹətiy], *n.* 1. usefulness; the ability to be used. **Ex.** *Their furniture was chosen for utility rather than elegance.* 2. water, gas, electricity, etc. provided to the public; the company which provides any of these. **Ex.** *The cost of all utilities except the telephone was paid by the landlord.*

utilize (5) [yuwʹtəlayzʹ], *v.* use; make use of. **Ex.** *He utilizes all his spare time for study.*

utmost (4) [ətʹmowstʹ], *adj.* of the greatest degree, quantity, or number. **Ex.** *I have the utmost respect for him.* —*n.* the most possible. **Ex.** *He tried his utmost to succeed.*

utter (2) [ətʹər], *v.* speak; produce sounds. **Ex.** *He was gone before she could utter a word.* —**utʹter·ance,** *n.* that which is said.

utter (2) [ətʹər], *adj.* complete; absolute. **Ex.** *He was in utter despair.* —**utʹter·ly,** *adv.* completely.

V

V, v [viyʹ], *n.* the twenty-second letter of the English alphabet.

vacancy (5) [veyʹkənsiy], *n.* 1. a job or position which no one is occupying. **Ex.** *There is a vacancy in our office.* 2. a room, apartment, etc. that is for rent. **Ex.** *There are still some vacancies in that hotel.*

vacant (4) [veyʹkənt], *adj.* 1. unoccupied; empty. **Ex.** *The house on the corner is vacant.* 2. without work to do. **Ex.** *She had a few vacant hours.*

vacation (2) [veykey'šən, vəkey'šən], *n.* a period of freedom from work or regular activity; a period for rest; a holiday. **Ex.** *The children are on vacation from school.* —*v.* go away for a rest. **Ex.** *They plan to vacation in the mountains.*

vaccinate (3) [væk'səneyt'], *v.* with a needle introduce into the body some substance that will protect a person from a disease. **Ex.** *He was vaccinated against several diseases at one time.* —**vac`ci·na'tion,** *n.* 1. the act of vaccinating. 2. the mark on the body where a person was vaccinated.

vacuum (5) [væk'yum`, væk'yuəm], *n.* an enclosed space from which most of the air or gas has been removed; a space in which there is no matter. **Ex.** *For that experiment they needed a complete vacuum.*

vague (4) [veyg'], *adj.* not certain or definite. **Ex.** *She was vague about the date of her return.* —**vague'ly,** *adv.* —**vague'ness,** *n.*

vain (2) [veyn'], *adj.* 1. useless, worthless; without real value. **Ex.** *The boy made vain efforts to reach the shore.* 2. too proud. **Ex.** *She is vain about her appearance.* —**vain'ly,** *adv.* without success.

valiant (5) [væl'yənt], *adj.* brave; courageous; heroic. **Ex.** *They made a valiant effort to rescue the children.* —**val'iant·ly,** *adv.*

valid (5) [væl'id], *adj.* 1. that can be logically or factually supported or defended; sound. **Ex.** *Do you have a valid reason for your absences?* 2. legally sound; legally binding. **Ex.** *They had a valid claim to the property.* —**va·lid'i·ty,** *n.*

valley (1) [væl'iy], *n.* a long, low piece of land between ranges of hills or mountains. **Ex.** *Many of the early families settled in the valley.*

valor (5) [væl'ər], *n.* personal bravery or courage, especially in battle. **Ex.** *The men showed great valor in action.*

value (1) [væl'yuw], *n.* 1. the quality of being useful or desirable; worth; importance. **Ex.** *His work was of great value to the business.* 2. the money a thing will bring if sold. **Ex.** *What is the value of this house?* —*v.* 1. place a value or worth on. **Ex.** *She values her diamond ring.* 2. respect greatly; prize. **Ex.** *I value your friendship.* —**val'ues,** *n.* the principles, aims, etc. which people consider to be important.

Ex. *His desire for money has changed his values.* —**val·u·a·ble**, *adj.* —**val·u·a'tion**, *n.* the worth in money.

valve (5) [vælv'], *n.* device by which the flow of a liquid or gas in a pipe can be started or stopped by opening or closing. **Ex.** *He shut the valve before repairing the pipe.*

VALVE

vandal (5) [væn'dəl], *n.* one who destroys or damages things of beauty or property in general. **Ex.** *A vandal had cut the painting.* —**van'dal·ism**, *n.* the act of a vandal. —**van'dal·ize**, *v.*

vanish (3) [væn'iš], *v.* 1. disappear; fade quickly. **Ex.** *The speeding car passed and vanished.* 2. cease to exist. **Ex.** *Their fears vanished when the storm ended.*

vanity (4) [væn'ətiy], *n.* too much pride in one's appearance, possessions, etc. **Ex.** *Her vanity caused her to spend more for clothes than she could afford.*

vanquish (5) [væŋ'kwiš], *v.* conquer; overcome. **Ex.** *She vanquished her fears.*

vapor (3) [vey'pər], *n.* 1. a visible mist, as fog or steam. **Ex.** *Clouds of smoke and vapor floated behind the train.* 2. anything in a gaseous state which is usually in a solid or liquid form. **Ex.** *The vapor from gasoline burns easily.* —**va'por·ous**, *adj.* —**va'por·ize**, *v.* cause to become vapor.

variable (5) [ve:r'iyəbəl], *adj.* 1. able to vary; changeable. **Ex.** *The weather bureau has announced variable winds for tomorrow.* 2. not constant. **Ex.** *Prices in this store are variable.*

variety (2) [vəray'ətiy], *n.* 1. the state of being varied; difference; change. **Ex.** *Lack of variety made him bored with his job.* 2. a number of things different from each other. **Ex.** *That store sells a variety of magazines.* 3. a different form or kind. **Ex.** *She has a new variety of rose in her garden.*

various (1) [ve:r'iyəs], *adj.* 1. different; of many kinds. **Ex.** *She tried on various dresses before selecting one.* 2. several; many. **Ex.** *Various people asked for you at the meeting.* —**var'i·ous·ly**, *adv.*

varnish (5) [var'niš], *n.* a preparation which is dissolved in oil or alcohol and which, when applied to the surface of wood, metal, etc., dries and leaves a hard and rather shiny finish. **Ex.** *He put varnish on the tabletop to protect it.* —*v.* put varnish on. **Ex.** *He varnished the floor.*

vary (2) [veːrˈiy], v. 1. change; alter. Ex. *Methods of teaching have varied over the years.* 2. make different or free from sameness. Ex. *She likes to vary the dishes she cooks.* 3. be different; change. Ex. *The prices of certain foods vary from week to week.*

vase (4) [veysˈ, veyzˈ], n. a container usually used to hold flowers. Ex. *She filled the vase with water.*

vast (2) [væstˈ], adj. very great in size or extent. Ex. *His family has vast wealth.* —**vastˈness**, n. —**vastˈly**, adv.

vault (4) [vɔltˈ], n. 1. an arched ceiling or roof of stone, brick, etc. Ex. *The vault of the church is decorated with paintings.* 2. a room covered by a vault, especially one underground. Ex. *The wine was stored in a vault.*

vault (4) [vɔltˈ], v. jump over by supporting the hands on something. Ex. *He vaulted over the fence.*

vegetable (2) [vcjˈ(ə)təbəl], n. a plant grown for food; the edible parts of plants. Ex. *His favorite vegetables are beans and potatoes.*

vehicle (4) [viyˈəkəl, viyˈhikəl], n. anything upon or in which a person or thing may travel or be carried, especially anything on wheels. Ex. *The road was crowded with vehicles.*

veil (3) [veylˈ], n. 1. a cloth, net, etc. placed to hide something. Ex. *The bride wore a lace veil over her face.* 2. anything which covers or conceals like a veil. Ex. *A veil of clouds hid the mountaintop.* —v. cover as with a veil. Ex. *Fog veiled the city.*

vein (3) [veynˈ], n. 1. any of the tubelike vessels which carry blood to the heart. Ex. *Blood poured from the cut vein.* 2. a body or layer of mineral in rock or in the earth clearly separated from the matter around it. Ex. *He discovered a rich vein of gold.* 3. spirit; mood. Ex. *There was always a vein of sadness in his writings.*

velvet (3) [velˈvit], n. a cloth of silk, nylon, cotton, etc., the threads of which are made to stand up from the base to form a soft surface. Ex. *The sofa is covered with velvet.* —adj. 1. made of or covered with velvet. 2. smooth or soft like velvet. Ex. *She has velvet skin.*

vengeance (4) [venˈjəns], n. the act of harming, troubling, etc. in return for a wrong or an injury. Ex. *He vowed vengeance on his father's murderer.* —**with a vengeance**, with great anger or force.

venture (3) [ven'čər], *n.* an activity with risk or danger. **Ex.** *If his business venture succeeds, he will be wealthy.* —*v.* 1. go into a position of danger; risk. **Ex.** *The boys ventured into the cave.* 2. dare to say, do, etc. **Ex.** *He ventured to say that he disagreed.* —**ven'tur·ous,** *adj.* daring.

verb (5) [vərb'], *n.* 1. a word which expresses action. **Ex.** *In the sentence "The children ran to their mother," "ran" is the verb.* 2. a word which shows existence or state of being. **Ex.** *In the sentence "She looks happy," "looks" is the verb.* —**ver'bal,** *adj.* spoken; not written. **Ex.** *They made a verbal agreement.* —**ver'bal·ly,** *adv.*

verdict (4) [vər'dikt], *n.* 1. the decision of a jury in a trial. **Ex.** *The verdict of the jury was "not guilty."* 2. any decision. **Ex.** *His father's verdict was that he could not buy a car.*

verge (5) [vərj'], *n.* the edge; the rim; the point where something is about to begin. **Ex.** *She was on the verge of tears.* —*v.* incline toward; approach. **Ex.** *Her reply verged on rudeness.*

verify (5) [ve:r'əfay`], *v.* 1. confirm; prove the truth of. **Ex.** *We verified his story.* 2. check the accuracy of. **Ex.** *Please verify the spelling of these names.*

verse (3) [vərs'], *n.* 1. a poem; poetic writing. **Ex.** *A collection of her verse has just been published.* 2. a section of a poem. **Ex.** *This poem has eight verses.*

version (4) [vər'žən], *n.* 1. translation. **Ex.** *Do you have the English version of this book?* 2. one of several accounts or descriptions. **Ex.** *Your version of the accident differs from that of the other witness.*

vertical (4) [vər'tikəl], *adj.* exactly upright; straight up and down. **Ex.** *The old tree is no longer vertical.* —**ver'ti·cal·ly,** *adv.*

very (1) [ve:r'iy], *adv.* 1. extremely; in a high degree. **Exs.** *He was very late. She walked very slowly.* 2. exactly; really; truly. **Ex.** *That was the very first time they met.*

vessel (2) [ves'əl], *n.* 1. a ship or boat. **Ex.** *The vessel sailed at midnight.* 2. anything that is used for containing or holding. **Ex.** *Bowls, cups, and bottles were among the ancient vessels they found.* 3. a tube in the body in which fluids are contained or move. **Ex.** *The mark on her skin was caused by broken blood vessels.*

vest (4) [vest¹], *n.* a short, tight-fitting, sleeve-less garment, worn mostly by men under the coat of a suit. Ex. *He was wearing a red vest.* —*v.* give some authority or right to a person, organization, etc. Ex. *By the power which was vested in him, the president of the university awarded degrees to the graduates.* —**vest'ed,** *adj.* given by authority or right and not removable by others. Ex. *I have a vested interest in the house.* —**vest'ment,** *n.* official clothing worn at ceremonies.

VEST

veteran (4) [vet'(ə)rən], *n.* one who has given a long time to a profession, service, industry, etc., especially to the military service. Ex. *He is a veteran of the stage.* —*adj.* having given long service to some profession, industry, etc. Ex. *He is a veteran politician.*

veto (5) [viy'tow], *n.* 1. the power or right which one branch of a government has to prevent an action or decision of another branch from being effected. Ex. *The President's veto of the new law stopped Congress from increasing taxes.* 2. the power or right to prevent an action. Ex. *The plan was abandoned because of our veto.* —*v.* refuse to approve; reject. Ex. *He always vetoes my suggestions.*

vex (4) [veks¹], *v.* make angry; bother; annoy. Ex. *The neighbors were vexed by the barking dog.*

via (5) [vay'ə, viy'ə], *prep.* by way of. Ex. *We crossed the river via the new bridge.*

vibrant (5) [vay'brənt], *adj.* 1. moving back and forth rapidly; full of energy. Ex. *The city was vibrant with life.* 2. strong and lively; exciting. Ex. *The picture was painted in vibrant colors.*

vibrate (4) [vay'breyt], *v.* 1. move back and forth rapidly; quiver. Ex. *The strings of the instrument vibrated when he touched them.* 2. shake; tremble. Ex. *She vibrated with emotion.* —**vi·bra'tion,** *n.*

vice (3) [vays¹], *n.* 1. a bad habit. Ex. *Use of tobacco is his only vice.* 2. evil; wickedness. Ex. *He led a life of vice.*

vice- (3) [vays], *prefix.* one who takes the place of. Ex. *President, vice-president.*

---

a, far; æ, am; e, get; ey, late; i, in; iy, see; ɔ, all; ow, go; u, put; uw, too; ə, but, ago; ər, fur; aw, out; ay, life; oy, boy; ŋ, ring; θ, think; ð, that; ž, measure; š, ship; j, edge; č, child.

vicinity (4) [vəsin'ətiy], *n.* 1. a region near or next to; neighborhood. **Ex.** *We live in the vicinity of the school.* 2. nearness. **Ex.** *Our two favorite shops are in close vicinity.*

vicious (5) [viš'əs], *adj.* 1. bad or wicked; cruel; harmful. **Ex.** *She told vicious lies about him.* 2. savage; dangerous; fierce. **Ex.** *That is a vicious dog.* —**vi'cious·ly,** *adv.* —**vi'cious·ness,** *n.*

victim (3) [vik'tim], *n.* 1. something alive that is injured, killed, or made to suffer. **Ex.** *Help was sent to the victims of the flood.* 2. one whose money, property, etc. is taken by a trick. **Ex.** *They were the victims of a dishonest merchant.*

victor (5) [vik'tər], *n.* the winner. **Ex.** *Our team was the victor.*

victory (2) [vik't(ə)riy], *n.* success in a fight, contest, or game. **Ex.** *We won the victory.* —**vic·tor'i·ous,** *adj.*

view (1) [vyuw'], *n.* 1. sight; vision. **Ex.** *We watched the ship until it was no longer in view.* 2. that which one sees or a picture of it. **Ex.** *We have a view of the lake from this window.* 3. thought; opinion. **Ex.** *What are your views on this question?* 4. act of looking, seeing, examining, or considering. **Ex.** *On closer view, he saw the driver was a woman.* —*v.* see; look; examine. **Ex.** *They viewed the results of the storm.* —**in view of,** in light of; considering. **Ex.** *In view of what he said, I do not think we shall go.*

vigil (5) [vij'əl], *n.* the act of keeping awake to watch or protect; a period of watching. **Ex.** *She kept an all-night vigil at the bedside of the sick child.* —**vig'i·lance,** *n.* watchfulness. —**vig'i·lant,** *adj.* —**vig'i·lant·ly,** *adv.*

vigor (4) [vig'ər], *n.* strength and force; energy. **Ex.** *He was a man of great mental vigor.* —**vig'or·ous,** *adj.*

vile (4) [vayl'], *adj.* 1. wicked; sinful. **Ex.** *His vile behavior made him a hated man.* 2. highly unpleasant; offensive. **Ex.** *They could not eat the vile food.*

village (3) [vil'ij], *n.* 1. a very small town. **Ex.** *There are fewer than fifty houses in the village.* 2. those who live in such a place. **Ex.** *The village gathered to hear the news.* —**vil'lag·er,** *n.* a person living in a village.

villain (5) [vil'ən], *n.* someone who is bad or evil. **Ex.** *The villain slowly revealed his evil nature.*

vine (3) [vayn'], *n.* 1. any plant with a long, slender stem which extends along the ground or climbs a tree or other support. **Ex.** *The garden wall was covered with vines.* 2. a grapevine. **Ex.** *They picked the grapes from the vine.*

vinegar (3) [vin'igər], *n.* a sour liquid formed by a chemical change in the juice of apples, wine, etc. and used to flavor or preserve foods. **Ex.** *She mixed oil and vinegar for the salad.*

violate (4) [vay'əleyt'], *v.* break; fail to obey. **Ex.** *He violated the rules of the club.* —**vi'o·la'tion,** *n.* the act of breaking a law or promise.

violence (3) [vay'ələns], *n.* 1. great strength or force. **Ex.** *The violence of the wind tore the roof from the house.* 2. rough force which causes injury or damage. **Ex.** *The man died by violence.* —**vi'o·lent,** *adj.* —**vi'o·lent·ly,** *adv.*

violet (3) [vay'ələt], *n.* 1. a small, low plant with purple, bluish-purple, white, or yellow flowers. **Ex.** *The children were picking violets in the woods.* 2. a bluish-purple color. **Ex.** *She found some material to match the violet in her dress.* —*adj.* bluish-purple. **Ex.** *She has violet eyes.*

violin (4) [vay'əlin'], *n.* a musical instrument with four strings and played with a bow. **Ex.** *His sister plays the piano, while he plays the violin.* —**vi·o·lin'ist,** *n.* a violin player.

VIOLIN

virgin (4) [və:r'jin], *adj.* untouched; un-used; pure. **Ex.** *The land was still covered with virgin forest.* —*n.* a person who has not had sexual relations. —**vir·gin'i·ty,** *n.* state of being a virgin.

virtual (5) [vər'čuwəl], *adj.* in effect, although not in form. **Ex.** *Their many paintings made their home a virtual art museum.* —**vir'tu·al·ly,** *adv.* almost.

virtue (2) [vər'čuw], *n.* 1. moral behavior; a morally good quality. **Ex.** *Patience is one of her many virtues.* 2. merit; good quality. **Ex.** *Your plan has the virtue of being practical.* —**vir'tu·ous,** *adj.*

visible (3) [viz'əbəl], *adj.* capable of being seen; in sight. **Ex.** *The house was visible from the road.* —**vis'i·bly,** *adv.* —**vis·i·bil'i·ty,** *n.*

vision (3) [viž'ən], *n.* 1. the sense or power of sight. **Ex.** *Glasses will improve her vision.* 2. something seen in the imagination, a dream, etc. **Ex.** *She had a vision of her son returning home.* 3. the ability to foresee that which does not exist or has not yet been done. **Ex.** *Cities should be planned* *by men of vision.* 4. an unusually beautiful person or thing. **Ex.** *The bride was a vision of loveliness.*

visit (1) [viz'it], *v.* 1. go or come to see for friendly, business, or professional reasons. **Ex.** *The doctor visited the patient this morning.* 2. stay as a guest. **Ex.** *They visited us for a week.* —*n.* the act of visiting. **Ex.** *We look forward to your visit.* —**vis'i·tor,** *n.* one who visits.

visual (5) [viz'uwəl], *adj.* 1. of or having to do with sight. **Ex.** *The contrasting colors created an interesting visual effect.* 2. visible; capable of being seen. **Ex.** *There were still no visual signs of spring.*

vital (4) [vay'təl], *adj.* 1. important to or necessary for life. **Ex.** *The heart is one of the vital organs of the body.* 2. very important or necessary. **Ex.** *The operation of the factory is vital to the community.* 3. full of life and energy. **Ex.** *He has a vital personality.* —**vi·tal'i·ty,** *n.* vigor; health and energy. —**vi'tal·ize,** *v.* make lively; give life or energy to.

vivid (4) [viv'id], *adj.* 1. brightly or intensely colored; sharp and clear; strong. **Ex.** *The accident is still vivid in his mind.* 2. full of life. **Ex.** *He has a vivid personality.* —**viv'id·ly,** *adv.* —**viv'id·ness,** *n.*

vocabulary (2) [vowkæb'yəle:r'iy, vəkæb'yəle:r'iy], *n.* 1. all the words of a language used by a group of people, an individual, etc. **Ex.** *The teacher has a large English vocabulary.* 2. a list of words, usually in alphabetical order and explained. **Ex.** *This dictionary contains a vocabulary of about 5,000 essential words.*

vocal (5) [vow'kəl], *adj.* 1. spoken; said; made by the voice. **Ex.** *She prefers silent to vocal prayer.* 2. expressing one's opinions often and freely. **Ex.** *The students have become more vocal in their demands.* —**vo'cal·ist,** *n.* a singer. —**vo'cal·ly,** *adv.*

vocation (5) [vowkey'šən], *n.* career; a profession for which one is best suited by talent and interest. **Ex.** *He has not yet discovered a vocation.*

voice (1) [voys'], *n.* 1. the sound made by living creatures, especially by human beings, in speaking, etc. **Ex.** *We heard voices in the next room.* 2. the quality of such sounds. **Ex.** *She has a good voice for talking to groups.* 3. the ability or power to speak. **Ex.** *He lost his voice during his illness.* 4. the right to speak; the act of expressing oneself. **Ex.** *He* *had no voice in deciding the matter.* —*v.* say; express in sounds; declare. **Ex.** *They voiced their thoughts about the law.*

void (4) [voyd'], *adj.* 1. empty; containing nothing; vacant. **Ex.** *Their words were void of meaning.* 2. without legal force or effect. **Ex.** *His will is void because he did not sign it.* —*n.* an empty space; a feeling of emptiness. **Ex.** *His death left a void in his political party.* —*v.* 1. cause to no longer have legal effect. **Ex.** *They voided the contract by proving it was not properly written.* 2. empty. **Ex.** *The medicine caused his stomach to void the poison.*

volcano (4) [valkey'now], *n.* an opening in the earth from which hot, melted rock and ash are thrown; a hill or mountain formed around such an opening by these materials. **Ex.** *That volcano has not been active for many years.* —**vol·can'ic,** *adj.*

volume (2) [val'yəm], *n.* 1. a book; one of the books of a set. **Ex.** *The third volume of this set is missing.* 2. a measure of the space something contains. **Ex.** *The volume of the tank was not large enough for their needs.* 3. quantity; amount. **Ex.** *The volume of sales doubled last month.* 4. the loudness or softness of sound. **Ex.** *He raised the volume of his radio.*

voluntary (5) [val'ənte:r'iy], *adj.* given or done freely and by choice, without being forced or required. **Ex.** *The offer was entirely voluntary.* —**vol'un·tar'i·ly,** *adv.*

volunteer (4) [val'ənti:r'], *n.* one who offers himself for service without being forced or required, especially military service. **Ex.** *He is a volunteer in the army.* —*adj.* of or done by volunteers. **Ex.** *The office was staffed by volunteer workers.* —*v.* offer oneself to do without being asked. **Ex.** *She volunteered to help her friend clean house.*

vote (2) [vowt'], *n.* 1. a choice or decision expressed by the voice, raised hand, written means, etc.; the means by which one expresses his choice or decision. **Ex.** *The committee counted the votes.* 2. the total number of expressed choices. **Ex.** *A heavy vote is expected.* 3. the right to such expression. **Ex.** *Women in the United States did not always have the vote.* 4. the act of choosing by such an expression. **Ex.** *He asked to have the matter brought to a vote.* —*v.* 1. express a choice or decision by vote. **Ex.** *They voted for the best man.* 2. bring about by a vote; elect. **Ex.** *They voted him president of the club.* —**vot'er,** *n.* one who votes.

vow (3) [vaw'], *n.* a solemn promise. **Ex.** *He made a vow to return.* —*v.* promise solemnly; bind oneself to do something. **Ex.** *He vowed revenge.*

vowel (5) [vaw'əl], *n.* a speech sound in which the breath is not stopped by the tongue, teeth, or lips; the letters *a, e, i, o, u* and sometimes *y* made in this way. **Ex.** *In the word "why," the letter "y" is a vowel.*

voyage (2) [voy'ij], *n.* journey across water or through air or space. **Ex.** *He expects to take an ocean voyage this summer.* —*v.* travel across water or through the air. **Ex.** *The ship voyaged to distant ports.* —**voy'ag·er,** *n.* one who takes a voyage.

vulgar (4) [vəl'gər], *adj.* bad-mannered; crude; lacking refinement and taste. **Ex.** *He made a vulgar display of his wealth.*

W

W, w [dəb'əlyuw], *n.* the twenty-third letter of the English alphabet.

wade (4) [weyd'], *v.* 1. move on foot through any substance that offers resistance, such as water, snow, etc. **Ex.** *The children were wading in the shallow water.* 2. go through with great effort. **Ex.** *He waded through the uninteresting book.*

wag (4) [wæg'], *v.* move or swing back and forth rapidly. **Ex.** *The dog wagged its tail.*

wage (2) [weyj'], *v.* engage in; carry on. **Ex.** *They waged war against disease.* —**wag'es,** *n.* that which is paid for services or work; pay. **Ex.** *His wages are paid weekly.* —**wag'er,** *n., v.* bet. **Ex.** *I wager he will not win.*

wagon (1) [wæg'ən], *n.* a four-wheeled cart, especially one designed for carrying heavy loads and pulled by a horse or other large animal. **Ex.** *The wagon was filled with stones.*

wail (4) [weyl'], *v.* 1. utter a long, loud cry to show that one is unhappy. **Ex.** *The baby wailed until his mother returned.* 2. make a mournful, crying sound. **Ex.** *The wind wailed through the trees.* —*n.* a mournful, crying sound. **Ex.** *The wails of the children woke us.*

waist (3) [weyst'], *n.* 1. the part of the body just below the ribs; an imaginary line around this part of the body. **Ex.** *She wore a leather belt around her waist.* 2. the narrow part of a woman's dress at this part of the body. **Ex.** *The waist was too large.*

wait (1) [weyt'], *v.* 1. remain inactive until something expected happens. **Ex.** *I am waiting for him to call.* 2. cause to wait; delay. **Ex.** *We can let the shopping wait until tomorrow.* 3. serve food in a restaurant for pay. **Ex.** *She waits tables in that café.* —*n.* the act of waiting; the time waited. **Ex.** *There will be a short wait before the train starts.* —**wait'ing,** *n.* a time during which one waits. **Ex.** *The waiting for news made us nervous.* —**wait on,** act as a servant, a seller in a store, or a waiter in a restaurant. **Ex.** *The clerk will wait on you next.*

waiter (3) [weyt'ər], *n.* a man who serves food at a table, especially at an eating place. **Ex.** *The waiter brought us our dinner quickly.* —**wait'ress,** *n.* a girl or woman who acts as a waiter.

wake (2) [weyk'], *v.* stop sleeping; open the eyes from sleep. **Ex.** *I usually wake very early.* —**wake'ful,** *adj.* not sleeping; alert. —**wake'ful·ness,** *n.* —**wake'ful·ly,** *adv.*

wake (2) [weyk'], *n.* the path made behind by a ship moving in the water; any trail or track left behind. **Ex.** *The flood left destruction in its wake.*

waken (2) [weyk'ən], *v.* 1. stop sleeping. **Ex.** *Please waken me in an hour.* 2. excite; cause to become active. **Ex.** *The book wakened his interest in history.*

walk (1) [wɔ:k'], *v.* 1. move along step by step on foot. **Ex.** *He walks to work.* 2. move through or over on foot. **Ex.** *I walk this street every day.* 3. move with on foot; cause to walk. **Ex.** *She walks the dog every evening.* —*n.* 1. the act of going on foot. **Ex.** *We went for a walk.* 2. the distance walked. **Ex.** *The house is a short walk from here.*

3. the manner of walking. **Ex.** *I recognize his walk.* 4. a path intended for walking. **Ex.** *I saw him coming down the walk.* 5. the direction walked; the way one goes, as in life. **Ex.** *People in every walk of life were her friends.* —**walk out**, go away from; quit; refuse to be a part of. **Ex.** *He walked out on a good job.*

wall (1) [wɔːl'], *n.* 1. stone, wood, etc. made to form one of the sides of a room or building or to enclose a space. **Ex.** *The walls of the room were painted white.* 2. something like a wall. **Ex.** *A wall of fire made them turn back.* —*v.* enclose; separate. **Ex.** *They walled off the large room into two smaller ones.*

wallpaper [wɔːl'peyˌpər], *n.* paper with decorations used to cover walls.

Wall Street [wɔːl' striyt'], a street in New York City which is a principal center for American financial affairs; large American businesses as a group.

walnut (5) [wɔːl'nətˌ], *n.* 1. a large, almost round nut, the seed of which is edible. **Ex.** *She put walnuts in the cake.* 2. the tree on which this nut grows; the wood of this tree. **Ex.** *The chairs were made of walnut.*

wander (2) [wan'dər], *v.* 1. move about without definite purpose or objective. **Ex.** *The children wandered through the woods.* 2. move from a planned route, course, or path by mistake. **Ex.** *The speaker wandered from the subject of his speech.* —**wand'er·er**, *n.* one who wanders.

want (1) [want'], *v.* 1. have a wish or desire for. **Ex.** *He wants a drink of water.* 2. need. **Ex.** *He was hungry and wanted food.* 3. desire that one come, go, or do something. **Ex.** *Someone wants you at the door.* 4. desire for purpose of arrest. **Ex.** *The police want him.* —*n.* 1. lack; shortage. **Ex.** *He died from want of food.* 2. need. **Ex.** *His wants are few.* 3. a wish or desire for something. **Ex.** *We can supply all your wants.* —**want'ing**, *adj.* lacking; needing.

war (1) [wɔːr'], *n.* 1. a fight with arms against another nation or between parts of a nation; an armed struggle. **Ex.** *They declared war on their enemy.* 2. a common effort or struggle. **Ex.** *The doctors are working together in the war against disease.* —*v.* fight a war. **Ex.** *They are warring with a neighboring country.*

ward (5) [wɔrd'], *n.* 1. a division of a hospital. **Ex.** *The doctor is visiting the children's ward.* 2. a division of a city or town for the purpose of administration. 3. a person who is under legal protection. **Ex.** *After his parents' death, the court made him a ward of his aunt.*

-ward, -wards (3) [wərd, wərdz], *suffix.* in the direction of. **Exs.** *Up, upward; back, backward; north, northward.*

warden (5) [wɔr'dən], *n.* 1. an officer who watches over things; a special guard. **Ex.** *The fire warden told us not to light matches in the building.* 2. the chief guard or officer in a prison. **Ex.** *The warden knew most of the prisoners by name.*

wardrobe (5) [wɔrd'rowb'], *n.* 1. clothing in general. **Ex.** *She had a large wardrobe.* 2. a piece of furniture in which clothing is hung. **Ex.** *Two men carried the wardrobe upstairs.*

ware (4) [we:r'], *n.* articles or manufactured products for sale. **Ex.** *The store displayed its wares in the window.*

-ware (4) [we:r], *suffix.* manufactured products made of or from. **Exs.** *Silver, silverware; glass, glassware.*

warehouse (5) [we:r'haws'], *n.* a place for storing goods. **Ex.** *Their furniture will stay in the warehouse until they pay the storage cost.*

warm (1) [wɔrm'], *adj.* 1. having or feeling a small amount of heat. **Ex.** *He is warm today.* 2. giving heat. **Ex.** *The sun is warm.* 3. stopping the loss of, saving, or keeping body heat. **Ex.** *The children wore warm clothing.* 4. eager; showing much good feeling. **Ex.** *They received a warm welcome.* —*v.* 1. give heat to; receive warmth from; become warm. **Ex.** *He warmed himself before the fire.* 2. make or become interested or eager; fill with good feelings. **Ex.** *The news warmed my heart.* —**warm'ly,** *adv.* —**warmth',** *n.* state of being warm; heat.

warm-blooded [wɔrm'bləd'id], *adj.* having warm blood like that of animals and a body temperature that stays the same. **Ex.** *A snake is not a warm-blooded animal.*

warmhearted [wɔrm'har'tid], *adj.* kind; loving; friendly. **Ex.** *His mother is a warmhearted person.*

a, far; æ, am; e, get; ey, late; i, in; iy, see; ɔ, all; ow, go; u, put; uw, too; ə, but, ago; ər, fur; aw, out; ay, life; oy, boy; ŋ, ring; θ, think; ð, that; ž, measure; š, ship; j, edge; č, child.

warn (2) [wɔrn'], v. 1. give notice to; caution. **Ex.** *I warned her of the danger.* 2. let know in advance; advise; inform. **Ex.** *The signal warned us of the approaching train.* —**warn'ing,** n. something that warns.

warp (4) [wɔrp'], v. 1. turn or twist out of shape. **Ex.** *A piece of wood warps when it is not dried properly.* 2. turn or twist away from what is normal, natural, etc. **Ex.** *The boy's mind was warped by his cruel father.* —n. a bend or twist. **Ex.** *The carpenter immediately saw the warp in the floor.*

warrant (4) [wɔ:r'ənt], n. 1. a written order which gives the right or authorization to do something. **Ex.** *The police have a warrant for his arrest.* 2. that which guarantees. **Ex.** *There is no warrant you will be happy.* —v. be a cause for; show to be right. **Ex.** *His work warrants a raise in pay.* —**war'ran·ty,** n. guarantee.

warrant officer [wɔ:r'ənt ɔ:f'əsər], an officer in the military forces of the United States who ranks above enlisted personnel but below a commissioned officer.

warrior (3) [wɔ:r'iyər], n. a man engaged in war or military life; a fighter. **Ex.** *He was a brave warrior.*

was (1) [wəz', waz'], v. past tense of *be* used with *he, she, it,* and singular nouns. **Ex.** *He was happy for many years.*

wash (1) [wɔ:š', waš'], v. 1. clean by dipping, wetting, or rubbing as with water and often soap. **Ex.** *Wash your hands before dinner.* 2. clean clothes by wetting and rubbing with soap and water. **Ex.** *She washes twice a week.* 3. flow against or over. **Ex.** *The waves washed against the boat.* 4. push or carry by means of water or other liquid. **Ex.** *The box was washed on shore.* —n. 1. the act of washing. 2. things such as clothes washed or to be washed at one time. **Ex.** *We have a big wash this week.* 3. a flow or rush, as of water; the sound of a flow or rush. **Ex.** *The wash of the waves put me to sleep.* 4. that with which one washes. **Ex.** *He uses a mouth wash each morning.* —**wash'er,** n. a machine for washing. —**wash'ing,** n. wash. —**wash down,** drink liquid to move food to the stomach. **Ex.** *He washed down his bread with water.* —**wash one's hands of,** stop being involved or responsible. **Ex.** *If he will not do as I ask, I wash my hands of the problem.* —**wash up,** wash oneself. **Ex.** *Would you like to wash up before dinner?*

washed-out [wɔšt'awt'], adj. faded in color. **Ex.** *He wore a washed-out shirt.*

wasp (5) [wasp¹], *n.* a slender flying insect which stings. Ex. *The wasp built a nest at the corner of the roof.*

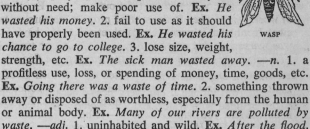

WASP

waste (2) [weyst¹], *v.* 1. spend uselessly or without need; make poor use of. Ex. *He wasted his money.* 2. fail to use as it should have properly been used. Ex. *He wasted his chance to go to college.* 3. lose size, weight, strength, etc. Ex. *The sick man wasted away.* —*n.* 1. a profitless use, loss, or spending of money, time, goods, etc. Ex. *Going there was a waste of time.* 2. something thrown away or disposed of as worthless, especially from the human or animal body. Ex. *Many of our rivers are polluted by waste.* —*adj.* 1. uninhabited and wild. Ex. *After the flood, the valley lay waste.* 2. unused; useless. Ex. *The basket was filled with waste paper.* —**waste¹ful**, *adj.*

watch (1) [wɔ:č¹, wač¹], *v.* 1. look at; observe closely. Ex. *We watched the dancers.* 2. look or wait for; expect. Ex. *Watch for your father to come home.* 3. act as a guard; take care of. Ex. *Please watch the baby for me.* 4. be careful. Ex. *Watch where you walk* —*n.* 1. a device that shows time, carried in the pocket or worn on the arm. Ex. *His watch had stopped.* 2. the act of watching or guarding. Ex. *A guard kept watch at the bank.* 3. the period of time during which a guard is on duty. Ex. *His watch ended at noon.* —**watch¹ful**, *adj.*

water (1) [wɔ:¹tər, wat¹ər], *n.* the liquid that falls from the sky as rain or is found in wells, lakes, rivers, etc. Ex. *I was warm and asked for a glass of cold water.* —*v.* 1. wet with water; supply with water. Ex. *They water the garden every day.* 2. fill with or give off liquid. Ex. *The cold made her eyes water.* 3. make weaker by adding water. Ex. *The sealed containers made it impossible for the storekeeper to water the milk.* —*adj.* 1. referring to water; for water. Ex. *The water pipes are frozen.* 2. done or used in, on, or with water. Ex. *He enjoys water sports.* —**wa¹ter·y**, *adj.* like or containing water. Ex. *This drink is too watery.*

watercolor [wɔ:¹tərkəl·ər], *n.* 1. a paint made with coloring matter and water. Ex. *He paints with watercolors.* 2. a painting made using watercolors. Ex. *I prefer his watercolors to his oil paintings.*

waterfall [wɔːˈtərfɔːlˈ], *n.* a steep fall of water from a dam, cliff, etc. **Ex.** *That is a beautiful waterfall.*

waterfront [wɔːˈtərfrəntˈ], *n.* the land and buildings or the part of a city which is by a river, lake, etc. **Ex.** *Many large ships were at the waterfront unloading goods.*

water level [wɔːˈtər levˈəl], the surface of quiet water; the level or height which a lake, sea, etc. is measured to be.

water line [wɔːˈtər laynˈ], a line on the side of a ship which the water level reaches. **Ex.** *The water line on that ship is very low when the ship is empty.*

waterlogged [wɔːˈtərlɔgdˈ], *adj.* very heavy because of being soaked or filled with water. **Ex.** *The waterlogged boat sank to the bottom of the lake.*

water main [wɔːˈtər meynˈ], one of the largest pipes in a system, usually underground, for bringing water to houses, stores, etc. **Ex.** *Until the broken water main is fixed, we will not have water.*

waterproof [wɔːˈtərpruwfˈ], *adj.* covered with a material or chemicals so as to prevent water from soaking in. **Ex.** *His waterproof coat kept him dry during the rain.*

watertight [wɔːˈtərtaytˈ], *adj.* 1. so tight as to prevent water from entering. **Ex.** *The sides of the ship are watertight.* 2. having no faults or weak points. **Ex.** *His claim that he is the real owner of the house seems watertight.*

waterway [wɔːˈtərweyˈ], *n.* a river, stream, etc. that is used by boats to carry goods or passengers.

waterworks [wɔːˈtərwərksˈ], *n.pl.* a system of pipes, machines, tanks, etc. by which water is furnished to a city or area. **Ex.** *The city's waterworks are very large.*

wave (1) [weyvˈ], *v.* 1. move or cause to move one way and the other, as a flag; flutter. **Ex.** *The branches waved in the wind.* 2. signal by moving the hand one way and the other. **Ex.** *She waved good-by as we left.* 3. seem to flow in curves; be arranged in curves. **Ex.** *Her hair waved softly about her face.* —*n.* 1. a swell which forms in a moving ridge on the surface of water. **Ex.** *The waves carried him to shore.* 2. something that swells, rises, and falls like this. **Ex.** *A wave of anger rose in him.* 3. a curved line or group of curved lines. **Ex.** *Is the wave in her hair natural?*

waver (4) [weyˈvər], *v.* 1. sway one way and then the other; quiver; flicker. **Ex.** *The light wavered and went out.* 2. show doubt or indecision; be hesitant. Ex. *Once he had decided to go, he never wavered.*

wax (4) [wæks'], *n.* 1. a yellowish-white substance that bees make; beeswax. Ex. *Bees use the wax they make to build cells in which to store their honey.* 2. a similar substance. Ex. *Wax from the candles fell on the table.* —*v.* treat, rub, or polish with wax. Ex. *She waxed the furniture.* —**wax'en**, *adj.* made of or like wax.

way (1) [wey'], *n.* 1. method; manner; style. Ex. *That is the wrong way to do it.* 2. direction of travel, motion, etc. Ex. *Which way do we go?* 3. a road; a passage or opening. Ex. *He lives across the way.* 4. distance. Ex. *It is a long way from here.* 5. opportunity or space in which to pass. Ex. *It was difficult to make our way through the crowd.* —**by the way**, incidentally; not directly related but of interest. Ex. *He brought me the book and, by the way, he had read it.* —**by way of**, through. Ex. *He went from Chicago to New York by way of Washington.* —**give way**, break; yield. Ex. *The crowd gave way and let him pass.* —**make one's way**, move through or ahead. Ex. *He made his way in the business world.* —**out of the way**, 1. far from the usual path; remote. Ex. *He visited several out-of-the-way places.* 2. not in a position to hinder or obstruct. Ex. *He put the box out of the way.* —**under way**, going forward; moving ahead. Ex. *The meeting had been under way for an hour when we arrived.*

waylay [wey'ley'], *v.* wait for and meet, stop, or delay, often for the purpose of harming, robbing, etc. Ex. *Reporters waylaid the senator after his speech.*

-ways (1) [weyz], *suffix.* manner; direction. Exs. *Side, sideways; folk, folkways.*

wayside [wey'sayd'], *n.* the side of a road. —*adj.* at or near the side of a road. Ex. *We stopped at a wayside farm.*

wayward (5) [wey'wərd], *adj.* refusing to recognize authority and insisting on following one's own way. Ex. *She is a wayward child.*

we (1) [wiy'], *pron.* plural of *I;* two or more persons, including the speaker or writer. Ex. *He and I will go together, and we shall return together.*

weak (1) [wiyk'], *adj.* 1. not strong bodily or morally. Ex. *He*

a, far; æ, am; e, get; ey, late; i, in; iy, see; ɔ, all; ow, go; u, put; uw, too;
ə, but, ago; ər, fur; aw, out; ay, life; oy, boy; ŋ, ring; θ, think; ð, that;
ž, measure; š, ship; ǰ, edge; č, child.

has a weak character. 2. having lost strength; yielding to ill-ness. Ex. *The sick man is very weak.* 3. lacking skill or mental power; not effective. Ex. *Her English is weak.* —**weak'en,** *v.* —**weak'ling,** *n.* one who is weak. —**weak'ly,** *adv.* —**weak'ness,** *n.* lack of strength.

wealth (2) [welθ'], *n.* 1. a large quantity of possessions, money, or other desired things; riches. Ex. *He was a man of great wealth.* 2. a large quantity. Ex. *She found a wealth of information on that subject in the library.* —**wealth'y,** *adj.*

weapon (3) [wep'ən], *n.* 1. anything used for fighting. Ex. *The soldiers were cleaning their weapons.* 2. any means by which one seeks to win in opposition to another. Ex. *Tears were her favorite weapon.*

wear (1) [we:r'], *v.* 1. use as clothing for the body. Ex. *He seldom wears a coat.* 2. change by use; damage gradually by use; make a hole in by rubbing. Ex. *He wore a hole in his shoe.* 3. remain in good condition when used. Ex. *This heavy material will wear well.* —*n.* 1. the act of wearing; use. Ex. *She needed clothes for school wear.* 2. things worn; clothing. Ex. *Men's wear is sold in this store.* 3. the gradual lessening in value, beauty, etc. caused by use. Ex. *This chair is showing wear.* 4. the quality of remaining in good condition when used. Ex. *There's much wear left in these shoes.* —**wear down,** 1. decrease in size because of use. Ex. *He wore down the heel of his shoe.* 2. decrease opposition by persisting. Ex. *He wore me down by begging, and I loaned him my car.* —**wear out,** 1. gradually destroy or make useless by wearing. Ex. *She has worn out that dress.* 2. gradually become tired. Ex. *I am worn out from working all day.*

weary (3) [wi:r'iy], *adj.* 1. tired; exhausted; lacking strength. Ex. *My feet are weary.* 2. not contented; bored. Ex. *She was weary of cooking.* —*v.* become or cause to become tired, unhappy, or bored. Ex. *He wearies easily.* —**wea'ri·ly,** *adv.* —**wea'ri·ness,** *n.*

weather (1) [weð'ər], *n.* the condition of the air outside with respect to warmth, wetness, wind, etc. Ex. *The sun was shining, and we had good weather for our trip.* —*v.* 1. come safely through. Ex. *The ship weathered the storm.* 2. change or cause to be changed by weather conditions. Ex. *The sun weathered the wood until it was hard and dry.*

weave (4) [wiyv'], *v.* 1. shape into a material or into some article by passing threads, strips of cloth, etc. over and

under each other. Ex. *They are weaving baskets.* 2. move in
and out, from side to side, etc. Ex. *The car was weaving
through traffic.* —*n.* a particular manner of weaving. Ex.
I like the weave of this carpet. —weav'er, *n.* one who
weaves.

web (4) [web'], *n.* 1. the net of threads which a spider makes.
2. anything like a web or that traps like a web. Ex. *He was
caught in a web of lies.*

wedding (2) [wed'iŋ], *n.* the act of marrying; the marriage
ceremony. Ex. *We are going to their wedding.* —wed', *v.*
—wed'ded, *adj.*

wedge (1) [wej'], *n.* 1. a solid, three-cornered piece of metal
with one thin edge used to split a log or something similar;
anything shaped like this. Ex. *She cut him a wedge of cake.*
2. something which gradually divides, splits, or prepares the
way for change. Ex. *His refusal to help was the wedge that
ended their friendship.* —*v.* 1. hold open; hold in place with
a wedge. Ex. *Wedge the door open.* 2. force, crowd, push as
if a wedge. Ex. *The child's foot was wedged between two
rocks.*

Wednesday (1) [wenz'diy], *n.* the fourth day of the week.

weed (3) [wiyd'], *n.* any useless or unwanted plant. Ex. *Many
weeds were growing among the flowers.* —*v.* 1. remove unwanted plants. Ex. *He weeded the garden.* 2. select and remove something or someone not wanted, not useful, etc. Ex.
*They weeded out the club members who did not attend
meetings.*

week (1) [wiyk'], *n.* 1. a period of seven days. Ex. *He will be
gone a week.* 2. a series of working hours or days within a
seven-day period. Ex. *She works a 40-hour week.* —week'ly,
adj. happening, appearing, or done once a week. Ex. *She
made weekly visits to them.* —*adv.* once in each week. Ex.
I write to her weekly. —*n.* a newspaper or magazine that
appears once a week. Ex. *What weeklies do you read?*

weekday [wiyk'dey'], *n.* any day of the week except Sunday.

weekend (3) [wiyk'end'], *n.* the part of the week from Friday
night to Monday morning. Ex. *We are spending the weekend in the country.* —*v.* spend Saturday and Sunday. Ex.
We will weekend in town.

weep (2) [wiyp'], *v.* 1. cry from grief or any strong emotion.
Ex. *She was weeping for joy at the news.* 2. mourn. Ex. *He
wept for his child.*

weigh (2) [wey'], *v.* 1. be of a certain heaviness. **Ex.** *The meat weighs four pounds.* 2. learn the heaviness of an object or person by means of a measure. **Ex.** *He weighed himself on the scale.* 3. measure a quantity as on scales. **Ex.** *He weighed out ten pounds of potatoes.* 4. consider carefully. **Ex.** *The judge weighed all the facts before making a decision.* 5. burden or be burdened by something heavy, serious, or troublesome. **Ex.** *He was weighed down with problems.*

weight (1) [weyt'], *n.* 1. the heaviness of something or someone. **Ex.** *What is the weight of this box?* 2. the pressure or burden of sorrow, responsibility, etc. **Ex.** *The weight of his worries caused him to lose sleep.* 3. a piece of metal or other heavy material used in weighing, for holding something in place, etc. **Ex.** *There was a glass paperweight on his desk.* 4. a system for expressing heaviness; a unit of such a system. **Ex.** *Sixteen ounces equals one pound in weight.* See **Weights and Measures.** —*v.* burden with weight. **Ex.** *She was so weighted with books that she could hardly walk.* —**weight'y,** *adj.* heavy; important. —**carry one's own weight,** do one's share. **Ex.** *Everyone must carry his own weight, if we are to finish.* —**carry weight,** have importance. **Ex.** *His ideas carry weight with me.*

weird (5) [wird'], *adj.* strange; unnatural; ghostly. **Ex.** *We heard a weird cry.* —**weird'ly,** *adv.*

welcome (1) [wel'kəm], *adj.* 1. received gladly. **Ex.** *He was a welcome guest.* 2. permitted or invited willingly. **Ex.** *You are welcome to use our telephone.* 3. without obligation. **Ex.** *He thanked me, and I said, "You are welcome."* —*n.* a friendly greeting. **Ex.** *They extended us a warm welcome.* —*interj.* a greeting given to a person or persons whom one is glad to see. **Ex.** *Welcome!* —*v.* greet or accept with pleasure. **Ex.** *He welcomed us upon our arrival.*

welfare (3) [wel'fe:r'], *n.* the condition of being well in regard to health, comfort, and happiness. **Ex.** *They did everything for the welfare of their children.*

well (1) [wel'], *n.* 1. a hole dug into the earth to get water, oil, etc. **Ex.** *His oil wells made him rich.* 2. a natural spring of water. **Ex.** *He brought some water from the well.* —*v.* pour or flow. **Ex.** *Water welled from the hole.*

well (1) [wel'], *adv.* 1. in a manner that is good, pleasing, favorable, etc. **Ex.** *He does his work well.* 2. fully; completely; thoroughly. **Ex.** *He knows me well.* 3. greatly;

much. **Ex.** *He is well advanced in years.* 4. surely; certainly. **Ex.** *They well know what the trouble is.* —*adj.* 1. in good health; not sick. **Ex.** *She is very well.* 2. satisfactory. **Ex.** *I hope that all is well with you.* —*interj.* used to express surprise, agreement, doubt, etc. **Ex.** *Well, I guess I can go.* —**as well,** 1. also. **Ex.** *He wants to go as well.* 2. as good. **Ex.** *He does the work as well as she.*

well-being [wel'biy'iŋ], *n.* condition of being healthy, happy, etc. **Ex.** *Rest is good for one's well-being.*

well-founded [wel'fawn'did], *adj.* based on sound thought and information. **Ex.** *He has some well-founded ideas on teaching methods.*

well-off [wel'ɔ:f'], *adj.* fortunate; wealthy. **Ex.** *He is well-off and can afford a vacation abroad.*

well-read [wel'red'], *adj.* having much knowledge, because of considerable reading. **Ex.** *His conversation revealed that he was a well-read man.*

well-spoken [wel'spow'kən], *adj.* 1. having the ability to speak well. **Ex.** *He is a well-spoken man.* 2. polite or correct in speech. **Ex.** *His words were well-spoken.*

well-to-do [wel'təduw'], *adj.* rich. **Ex.** *My mother worked for a well-to-do family.*

went (1) [went'], *v.* past tense of *go.* **Ex.** *He went there yesterday.*

wept (3) [wept'], *v.* past tense and participle of *weep.* **Ex.** *She wept at the news.*

were (1) [wə:r'], *v.* past tense of *be* used with we, you, they, and plural nouns. **Ex.** *Where were you this morning?*

west (1) [west'], *n.* 1. the direction in which the sun goes down at night; the direction to the left of one facing north; one of the four points of the compass. **Ex.** *The sun sets in the west.* 2. regions or countries lying west of to the west. —**the West,** that part of the United States west of the Mississippi. **Ex.** *He comes from a large city in the West.* —*adv.* toward the west. **Ex.** *My room faces west.* —*adj.* toward or at the west; from the west. **Ex.** *A west wind is blowing.* —**west'ern,** *adj.* characteristic of the west; in, of, to, or from the west or West. **Ex.** *He likes only western food.* —*n.* a movie or story

about the American West. **Ex.** *He likes to see westerns.*
—**west'ern·er,** *n.* one from the west.

wet (1) [wet'], *adj.* 1. covered or soaked with water or some other liquid. **Ex.** *She removed her wet clothes.* 2. rainy. **Ex.** *We have had several days of wet weather.* 3. damp; not yet dry. **Ex.** *The paint on the wall is still wet.* —*n.* water; rain. **Ex.** *The children were playing in the wet.* —*v.* cover or soak with liquid. **Ex.** *Wet the cloth and wash your face.*

wharf (4) [wɔrf', hwɔrf'], *n.* a structure like a platform, sometimes with a roof, extending over the water or along the shore so that vessels may stay beside it to load and unload; a pier. **Ex.** *Passengers were waiting on the wharf to board the ship.*

what (1) [hwɔt', hwat'], *pron.* 1. the nature of the thing or the particular thing asked about; which particular thing, action, etc. **Exs.** *What is it? What did you say?* 2. that or those which in kind, amount, etc. **Ex.** *Take what you want.* —*adj.* 1. which or which kind. **Ex.** *What ship is that?* 2. as much as; as many as. **Ex.** *Take what money you need.* 3. how great, surprising, etc. **Ex.** *What a sight that was!* —*interj.* an exclamation of surprise, excitement, anger, etc. **Ex.** *What! No bus for another hour!*

whatever [hwətev'ər], *pron.* 1. any thing or amount that. **Ex.** *Take whatever you want of the cake.* 2. no matter what. **Ex.** *He loves her whatever she does.* —*adj.* 1. no matter what. **Ex.** *I can eat whatever food you have.* 2. of any kind. **Ex.** *I have no books whatever.*

wheat (1) [hwiyt'], *n.* a grain which when ground becomes flour and is used in breads, cakes, etc.; the grass bearing this grain. **Ex.** *The fields of wheat were ready to cut.*

WHEEL 1

wheel (1) [hwiyl'], *n.* 1. a round frame which turns on a central point. **Ex.** *A bicycle has two wheels.* 2. anything like a wheel in shape, purpose, or action. **Ex.** *The driver was behind the wheel.* —*v.* 1. roll or move on wheels. **Ex.** *She was wheeling the baby down the street in a carriage.* 2. turn or cause to turn around. **Ex.** *She wheeled around and faced the man who had been behind her.*

when (1) [hwen'], *adv.* at what time. **Ex.** *When are you planning to leave?* —*conj.* 1. at what time. **Ex.** *He does not know when he can come.* 2. at any time. **Ex.** *She gets sick* *when she rides in a car.* 3. after which; and then. Ex. *I had just arrived when you called.* 4. during the time; at the time. Ex. *We liked that game when we were children.* 5. although. Ex. *The boy kept on playing when he knew it was time for bed.* —*pron.* what certain time? Ex. *Till when do we work?*

whenever [hwenev'ər], *conj.* at whatever time. Ex. *Go when-ever you wish.*

where (1) [hwe:r'], *adv.* 1. at or in what place. Ex. *Where is my coat?* 2. to what place. Ex. *Where did you go last night?* 3. from what source, person, or place. Ex. *Where did you get that idea?* —*conj.* 1. at or in what place. Ex. *I know where she is.* 2. at or in the place in or at which. Ex. *This is the house where he lives.* 3. to the place to which. Ex. *The dog goes where she goes.* —*pron.* 1. what or which place. Ex. *Where do you come from?* 2. the place at or in which. Ex. *The store is near where I work.*

whereabouts [hwe:r'əbawts'], *n.* location of a person or thing. Ex. *I do not know his whereabouts.*

whereby [hwe:rbay'], *adv.* by which; through which. Ex. *I have a plan whereby we can become rich.*

wherein [hwe:rin'], *adv.* in what or which respect. Ex. *Wherein did I fail?*

whereof [hwe:rəv'], *adv.* of what, which, or when. Ex. *I know whereof he speaks.*

whereupon [hwe:r'əpan'], *conj.* at which point in time. Ex. *I spoke angrily, whereupon she ran from the room.*

wherever [hwe:rev'ər], *conj.* at, in, or to whatever place. Ex. *I go wherever she goes.*

wherewithal [hwe:r'wiðɔl'], *n.* the means with which to do something. Ex. *We want to go on a trip, but we do not have the wherewithal.*

whether (1) [hweð'ər], *conj.* pointing to two or more choices or possibilities and meanings: 1. if it is true. Ex. *She is call-ing to find out whether or not you are feeling better.* 2. either; one or the other. Ex. *He could not decide whether to go or stay.*

which (1) [hwič'], *pron.* 1. what one or ones of a particular group of persons or things. Exs. *Which do you want? Which are ours?* 2. that. Ex. *The book which I am reading is inter-esting.* —*adj.* what one or ones? Ex. *Which hat do you want?*

whichever [hwičev'ər], *pron.* any one that. **Ex.** *Take whichever you want.*

while (1) [hwayl'], *n.* a space of time. **Ex.** *I will see you in a little while.* —*conj.* 1. at or during the same time that. **Ex.** *The child fell while running.* 2. although. **Ex.** *While the work was difficult, it was interesting.* —*v.* use time pleasantly. **Ex.** *We whiled away the summer afternoon reading and talking.* —**worth'while'**, *adj.* worth the time required. **Ex.** *Her smile made the work worthwhile.*

whine (5) [hwayn'], *v.* 1. utter a low cry or sound in complaint, discontent, etc. **Ex.** *The baby whined.* 2. utter or beg with a whine. **Ex.** *The child whined for ice cream.* —*n.* a low sound of distress. **Ex.** *We heard the whine of a hungry child.*

whip (2) [hwip'], *n.* 1. an instrument, usually consisting of a stiff handle with a piece of leather or cord at one end, used for striking animals or people. **Ex.** *He urged the horse on with a whip.* 2. a stroke or blow, with or as with a whip. **Ex.** *The whip of the wind snapped the sail.* —*v.* 1. strike with or as with a whip. **Ex.** *The boy was whipped for telling a lie.* 2. move, pull, etc. with a sudden motion. **Ex.** *He whipped out a handkerchief and wiped his face.* 3. beat eggs, cream, etc. into a light mass with a fork.

whirl (3) [hwərl'], *v.* 1. spin fast; turn around and around quickly. **Ex.** *The dancer whirled on her toes.* 2. move or be carried along rapidly. **Ex.** *He whirled around the corner on his bicycle.* 3. have the sensation of whirling. **Ex.** *My head is whirling.* —*n.* 1. a rapid turning motion. **Ex.** *He gave the steering wheel a whirl.* 2. something that whirls. **Ex.** *He was lost from sight in a whirl of snow.* 3. a mental state of confusion. **Ex.** *My thoughts are in a whirl.*

whiskey (5) [hwis'kiy], *n.* an alcoholic liquor made from various grains. **Ex.** *He liked a drink of rye whiskey before dinner.*

whisper (2) [hwis'pər], *v.* 1. speak softly and low so as to be heard only by the one or ones talked to. **Ex.** *He whispered that he loved her.* 2. tell privately, as a secret. **Ex.** *People are whispering about their romance.* 3. make a low, hushed sound like a whisper. **Ex.** *The wind whispered through the trees.* —*n.* 1. a soft, low way of speaking. **Ex.** *She spoke in a whisper.* 2. a secret or private utterance. **Ex.** *There were whispers about his past.* 3. a low, hushed sound. **Ex.** *He heard only the whisper of the wind in the grass.*

whistle (2) [hwisʹəl], *v.* 1. make a high, sharp sound by forcing the breath through the teeth or closed lips. Ex. *He whistled for his dog.* 2. make a similar sound by using some mechanical device. Ex. *The policeman whistled for traffic to stop.* 3. move or pass with a high, sharp sound. Ex. *The winter wind whistled around the house.* —*n.* 1. a device for producing a high, sharp sound. Ex. *The brass whistle of the locomotive was brightly polished.* 2. a sound produced by whistling. Ex. *He gave a whistle of surprise.*

white (1) [hwaytʹ], *adj.* 1. of the color of milk or snow. Ex. *She wore a white dress.* 2. relatively light or pale in color. Ex. *Her mother's hair is white.* —*n.* 1. a white color. Ex. *They painted the house white.* 2. clothing of this color. Ex. *She likes to wear white in the summer.* 3. that which is white. Ex. *She used three egg whites in the cake.* —**whitʹen,** *v.*

whitecap [hwaytʹkæpʹ], *n.* a rough wave with white on the top.

white flag [hwaytʹ flægʹ], a white cloth raised when one wants to stop fighting or to surrender.

White House [hwaytʹ hawsʹ], official home of the President of the United States in Washington, D.C.

white lie [hwaytʹ layʹ], an easily forgiven lie about something unimportant, often told to prevent embarrassment. Ex. *She told a white lie to avoid going with him.*

who (1) [huwʹ], *pron.* 1. what person or persons. Ex. *Who was at the door?* 2. which person or persons. Ex. *I do not know who they are.* 3. the person or persons that. Ex. *The man who came left a letter.*

whoever [huwevʹər], *pron.* 1. whatever person or persons. Ex. *Whoever comes should be given the money.* 2. no matter who. Ex. *Whoever it is, I don't want to see him.*

whole (1) [howlʹ], *adj.* 1. the complete amount or extent. Ex. *Tell me the whole story.* 2. not divided; not cut into pieces. Ex. *She served the fish whole.* 3. containing all its parts. Ex. *She bought a whole set of dishes.* 4. not broken, damaged, etc. Ex. *After the storm, not one window was whole.* —*n.* the entire amount or extent; something complete. Ex. *The whole of his experience had not prepared him for this trouble.* —**wholʹly,** *adv.*

a, far; æ, am; e, get; ey, late; i, in; iy, see; ɔ, all; ow, go; u, put; uw, too; ə, but, ago; ər, fur; aw, out; ay, life; oy, boy; ŋ, ring; θ, think; ð, that; ž, measure; š, ship; j, edge; č, child.

wholehearted [howl'har'tid], *adj.* completely enthusiastic, sincere, energetic, etc. Ex. *He made a wholehearted effort to win.*

wholesale (4) [howl'seyl'], *n.* the selling or buying of goods in large quantities by merchants for resale to users. Ex. *He sold goods at wholesale.* —*adj.* 1. of or about the selling of goods in large quantities. Ex. *He bought the medicine at wholesale prices.* 2. extensive; done on a broad scale; general. Ex. *The gang had committed wholesale murder.* —**whole'sal·er**, *n.* one who sells in large quantities.

wholesome (4) [howl'səm], *adj.* healthful; of benefit to the mind or body. Ex. *She prepares wholesome meals for her family.* —**whole'some·ness**, *n.*

whom (1) [huwm'], *pron.* a form of *who* used as the object of a preposition or verb. Exs. *To whom did you speak? That is the man whom I saw.*

whose (1) [huwz'], *pron.* a form of *who* that shows ownership or possession. Exs. *Whose hat is this? We met the man whose son won the race.*

why (1) [hway'], *adv.* 1. for what cause or reason? Ex. *Why did you come?* 2. for which; because of which. Ex. *There is no reason why he cannot go.* 3. the reason for which. Ex. *I do not know why he did it.* —*interj.* an exclamation of surprise, hesitation, etc. Ex. *Why, it's past noon!*

wicked (3) [wik'id], *adj.* sinful; morally wrong. Ex. *The wicked man was punished.* —**wick'ed·ly**, *adv.* —**wick'ed·ness**, *n.*

wide (1) [wayd'], *adj.* 1. having great extent from one side to the other; broad. Ex. *The travelers crossed a wide plain.* 2. measured from side to side. Ex. *The table is too wide for this room.* 3. extensive; not limited; including much. Ex. *He is a man of wide experience.* 4. opened very much. Ex. *Her eyes were wide with surprise.* —*adv.* 1. over a great extent; to a great distance. Ex. *The news spread far and wide.* 2. fully open. Ex. *Open the door wide.* —**wide'ly**, *adv.* —**wid'en**, *v.* —**width'**, *n.* the extent from side to side. Ex. *What is the width of the table?*

wide-awake [wayd'əweyk'], *adj.* fully awake; alert. Ex. *You must stay wide-awake while you work.*

widespread [wayd'spred'], *adj.* extending or occurring over a large area or among many people. Ex. *The flood damage was widespread.*

widow (2) [wid'ow], *n.* a woman who has not remarried after the death of her husband. Ex. *The widow has two children.* —*v.* cause to be a widow. Ex. *She was widowed at the age of forty.* —**wid'ow·er,** *n.* a man who has not remarried after the death of his wife.

wield (5) [wiyld'], *v.* 1. use or handle effectively or skillfully. Ex. *His father taught him to wield an ax.* 2. exercise or use. Ex. *The President wields great power.*

wife (1) [wayf'], *n.* a woman united to a man in marriage. Ex. *I have not met his wife.*

wig (5) [wig'], *n.* a covering made of hair or material which looks like hair, worn on the head, usually to conceal the lack of natural hair or to change one's appearance. Ex. *He has worn a wig for several years.*

wild (1) [wayld'], *adj.* 1. living in a natural state; not culti- vated. Ex. *There were wild animals in the forest.* 2. without inhabitants or cultivation. Ex. *The land along the river is wild.* 3. not civilized. Ex. *The people of that area are still wild.* 4. excited; angry; uncontrolled; etc. Ex. *The ship was driven on the rocks by a wild sea.* 5. unreasonable; crazy. Ex. *People laughed at his wild ideas.* —*adv.* wildly; without control. Ex. *They let their children run wild.* —**wild'ly,** *adv.* —**wild'ness,** *n.*

wilderness (3) [wil'dərnəs], *n.* a region of wild, rough land where no people live. Ex. *They were lost in the wilderness.*

will (1) [wil'], *n.* 1. desire; wish. Ex. *He was forced to sign the paper against his will.* 2. strong intention. Ex. *The sick woman has lost her will to live.* 3. the power of making choices and controlling actions. Ex. *He has a strong will.* 4. feelings toward another. Ex. *There is ill will between them.* 5. a declaration of a person's wishes for disposing of his property after death, usually written. Ex. *The dying man prepared a will.* —*v.* 1. desire; decide. Ex. *Which will you have?* 2. leave property to someone in a will. Ex. *He willed her the house. Will* is used with other verbs to indicate: 1. future action. Ex. *I will go soon.* 2. agreement; willingness. Ex. *Will you help me?* 3. ability. Ex. *This box will hold all your books.* 4. intention. Ex. *I will go to school.* 5. custom or habit. Ex. *She will talk for hours.* —**will'ful, wil'ful,** *adj.* 1. determined in a headstrong way to do something. 2. intentional. Ex. *It was willful murder.*

willing (2) [wil'iŋ], *adj.* 1. consenting; agreeable to doing. **Ex.** *He is willing to pay now.* 2. acting, doing, giving, etc. cheerfully. **Ex.** *They are willing workers.* —**will'ing·ly**, *adv.* —**will'ing·ness**, *n.*

willow (5) [wil'ow], *n.* a tree with long, hanging branches which are tough but so easily bent that they are used for making baskets and woven furniture; the wood of this tree. **Ex.** *Willows grew beside the stream.* —**wil'low·y**, *adj.* slender and graceful.

wilt (5) [wilt'], *v.* 1. droop; lose firmness and freshness. **Ex.** *Give the flowers some water, or they will wilt.* 2. become weak; lose courage. **Ex.** *She seemed to wilt when her request was refused.*

win (1) [win'], *v.* 1. gain or get or arrive at by effort, work, etc. **Ex.** *His work won him many friends.* 2. gain a victory; defeat others in a contest. **Ex.** *Our team is winning the game.* —**win'ner**, *n.* one who wins. —**win'ning**, *adj.*

wind (1) [wind'], *n.* 1. movement of air. **Ex.** *The wind was blowing from the south.* 2. a strong, often damaging movement of air. **Ex.** *The wind blew his hat off.* 3. breath. **Ex.** *He lost his wind during the race.* 4. hint. **Ex.** *He caught wind of their plans.* —*v.* cause to breathe with difficulty. **Ex.** *The walk up the hill winded me.* —**wind'y**, *adj.*

wind (1) [waynd'], *v.* 1. wrap or roll something around something, especially to form a ball. **Ex.** *She is winding the string into a ball.* 2. cover or surround by turning or twisting; grow around. **Ex.** *The vine winds around the house.* 3. cause to operate by turning. **Ex.** *Remember to wind your watch.* 4. move in or follow a curving, turning, and twisting way. **Ex.** *The road winds through our farm.* —**wind'ing**, *adj.* —**wind up**, 1. turn a mechanical device so as to cause to operate. **Ex.** *He wound up the toy car.* 2. finish. **Ex.** *We will wind up this work today.*

windbreak [win(d)'breyk'], *n.* anything that slows or stops the force of the wind. **Ex.** *The trees were a windbreak for the house.*

windfall [wind'fɔl'], *n.* unexpected gain. **Ex.** *The money from his uncle was a windfall.*

windmill [wind'mil'], *n.* a mill that obtains the power for its operation from the wind.

window (1) [win'dow], *n.* 1. an opening in a wall to admit light and air, usually with a movable frame containing glass. **Ex.** *He opened the window.* 2. a piece of glass in a window opening. **Ex.** *He broke the window.*

window-shop [win'dowšap'], *v.* look at goods through a store window without buying. **Ex.** *They window-shopped all afternoon.*

windpipe [wind'payp'], *n.* the passage located at the back of the mouth by which air reaches the chest. **Ex.** *A piece of food lodged in his windpipe.*

windshield [wind'šiyld'], *n.* the window across the front of an automobile. **Ex.** *The windshield was broken in the accident.*

wine (2) [wayn'], *n.* the juice of grapes or of some other fruits or plants changed chemically so that it has an alcoholic content. **Ex.** *She served wine with dinner.* —**win'er·y**, *n.* a place where wine is made.

wing (1) [wiŋ'], *n.* 1. one of the paired parts of a bird or other animal which, when spread and moved, carry it into the air. **Exs.** *The bird's wing was broken. The fly spread its wings and flew away.* 2. any part with the appearance of a wing used for flying. **Ex.** *The wing of the plane is being fixed.* 3. any part which extends from the main part. **Ex.** *They are adding a wing to their house.* 4. a section of a larger political group; a political group with rightist or leftist ideas in politics. **Ex.** *The right wing of his party voted for him.* —**on the wing,** 1. flying. **Ex.** *Birds on the wing are beautiful to watch.* 2. moving about from place to place. **Ex.** *He is on the wing again.* —**under the wing,** under the protection or care. **Ex.** *He took the new boy under his wing.*

wink (4) [wiŋk'], *v.* 1. close and open one of the eyes quickly, usually as a sign. **Ex.** *He winked at the pretty girl.* 2. send out short, rapid sparkles of light. **Ex.** *She saw the winking lights of the city.* —*n.* the act of winking. **Ex.** *She returned his wink.*

winter (1) [win'tər], *n.* the cold season when few plants grow; in northern countries, December to March. **Ex.** *Yesterday we had the first snow of winter.* —*adj.* characteristic of winter; used in winter. **Ex.** *She bought some winter clothes.*

—*v.* pass the winter. **Ex.** *They always winter in the south.*
—**win'try,** *adj.* like winter.

wipe (2) [wayp'], *v.* 1. rub with something soft in order to dry or clean. **Ex.** *He wiped the dishes.* 2. remove, as by rubbing; eliminate. **Exs.** *The mother wiped the child's tears. He wiped out his debt.* —**wip'er,** *n.*

wire (2) [wayr'], *n.* a piece of metal in a long, threadlike form. **Ex.** *Those men are putting up telephone wire.* —*v.* provide with wire; use wire for any purpose. **Ex.** *They are now wiring the building for electricity.* —*adj.* made of wire. **Ex.** *They put a wire fence around their yard.* —**wir'y,** *adj.* like wire.

wise (1) [wayz'], *adj.* 1. judging properly what is true or false, correct, best, etc.; showing sound judgment. **Ex.** *She made a wise choice.* 2. having great learning; knowing much. **Ex.** *The teacher was a wise man.* —**wis'dom,** *n.* —**wise'ly,** *adv.*

-wise (1) [wayz], *suffix.* direction or manner of. **Exs.** *Clock, clockwise; like, likewise.*

wish (1) [wiš'], *v.* 1. want; long for; express a desire or longing. **Exs.** *She wishes to see the house. We wish the work were finished. I wish him well.* 2. express a greeting. **Ex.** *He wished me good morning.* 3. order; request. **Ex.** *He wishes to see you at nine o'clock.* —*n.* 1. a desire; longing. **Ex.** *He had no wish to go.* 2. that which is desired or hoped for. **Ex.** *She got her wish.* 3. a command. **Ex.** *She followed her mother's wishes.* —**wish'es',** *n.pl.* greetings. **Ex.** *We send you our best wishes.*

wit (2) [wit'], *n.* 1. the ability to understand and to express ideas in a clever and amusing way. **Ex.** *He entertained us with his wit.* 2. a clever and amusing person. **Ex.** *The writer was a well-known wit.* —**wits',** *n.pl.* the power to sense and judge. **Ex.** *He kept his wits during the emergency.* —**wit'ty,** *adj.* clever; showing wit. —**at one's wit's end,** no longer able to think and judge; not knowing what to do; completely at a loss. **Ex.** *We have looked everywhere for her, and I am at my wit's end.*

witch (3) [wič'], *n.* 1. a woman believed to practice evil magic. **Ex.** *The villagers thought a witch caused their trouble.* 2. an ugly old woman. **Ex.** *The old witch shouted at the children.*

with (1) [wið', wiθ'], *prep.* 1. accompanied by; along or by the side of. **Ex.** *His family was with him.* 2. showing a general relationship; because of. **Ex.** *We are pleased with your work.* 3. by means of. **Ex.** *She covered the table with a cloth.* 4. using or showing. **Ex.** *We watched them with interest.* 5. having. **Ex.** *He lives in the house with the red door.* 6. being in agreement or disagreement. **Ex.** *He was angry with his friend.* 7. as a result of. **Ex.** *She is ill with a cold.* 8. at the same time. **Ex.** *With these words, she left.*

withdraw (4) [wiðdrɔ:ʹ], *v.* 1. take out, away, or back; remove. **Ex.** *They are withdrawing their son from the school.* 2. go apart or away from others. **Ex.** *She often withdraws into silence.* —**with·draw'al**, *n.* the act of going or taking away; that which one withdraws. **Ex.** *He made a withdrawal from the bank.* —**with·drawn'**, *adj.*

wither (4) [wiðʹər], *v.* 1. become dry and faded. **Ex.** *The grass withered and died for lack of water.* 2. lose or cause to lose freshness and strength. **Ex.** *Age had withered her.*

withhold [wiðhowldʹ], *v.* hold back; not give; not express. **Ex.** *She is withholding information that we need.*

within (1) [wiðinʹ], *prep.* 1. inside a limit of space, time, etc. **Ex.** *We live within sight of the ocean.* 2. inside fixed or required limits. **Ex.** *He kept within the law.* —*adv.* in, into, or on the inner side. **Ex.** *He heard noises within.*

without (1) [wiðawtʹ], *prep.* 1. with no; not having or using; free from. **Ex.** *He was without fear.* 2. avoiding; not doing, giving, etc. **Ex.** *He left without saying good-by.* 3. outside. **Ex.** *Everything within and without the house was in order.*

withstand (5) [wiðstændʹ], *v.* continue to stand despite strong force; endure; resist. **Ex.** *That ship can withstand any storm.*

witness (2) [witʹnis], *n.* 1. one who personally sees or knows about a thing. **Ex.** *He was a witness to the accident.* 2. one who gives evidence of what he has seen. **Ex.** *The lawyer asked him to be in court as a witness.* —*v.* see personally; observe. **Ex.** *He witnessed the fight.*

wizard (5) [wizʹərd], *n.* a person of great, almost magical skill. **Ex.** *He is a wizard at mathematics.*

woe (5) [wowʹ], *n.* 1. grief; great sadness. **Ex.** *Her son's death added to her woe.* 2. misery; suffering. **Ex.** *The flood was the cause of much woe.*

woke (4) [wowkʹ], *v.* past tense of *wake.* **Ex.** *I woke at ten o'clock this morning.*

wolf (2) [wulf'], *n.* a wild, meat-eating, dog-like animal. **Ex.** *The wolf killed many sheep.* —*v.* eat rapidly and greedily. **Ex.** *The starving man wolfed the food.*

WOLF

woman (1) [wum'ən], *n.* 1. an adult female person. **Ex.** *She is a lovely woman.* 2. adult female humans in general. **Ex.** *Some people think a woman's place is in the home.* 3. a female worker. **Ex.** *We have a cleaning woman once a week.*

women (1) [wim'in], *n.* plural of *woman.* **Ex.** *How many women were there?*

won (1) [wən'], *v.* past tense and participle of *win.* **Ex.** *Who won the game?*

wonder (1) [wən'dər], *v.* 1. feel doubt or curiosity about; ask oneself. **Ex.** *They wondered if it would snow.* 2. feel surprised or astonished. **Ex.** *We wondered at the size of the building.* —*n.* 1. a feeling of surprise or astonishment. **Ex.** *They were filled with wonder at the sight.* 2. something surprising or marvelous. **Ex.** *It is a wonder that he lived so long.* —**won'der·ful,** *adj.* marvelous; remarkable. **Ex.** *He showed wonderful courage.* —**won'der·ful·ly,** *adv.*

won't (1) [wownt'], *v.* the shortened form of *will not.* **Ex.** *He won't go.*

woo (4) [wuw'], *v.* seek the love, affection, or support of, usually for the purpose of marrying. **Ex.** *He wooed and won the girl.* —**woo'er,** *n.*

wood (1) [wud'], *n.* the hard substance which makes up most of a tree or bush; this substance prepared for use as building material, firewood, etc. **Ex.** *This kind of wood is often used for making chairs.* —*adj.* made of wood. **Ex.** *That is a heavy wood door.* —**wood'en,** *adj.* made of wood. **Ex.** *There was a wooden dish on the table.* —**wood'ed,** *adj.* covered with trees. **Ex.** *Part of their land was heavily wooded.* —**woods',** *n.* a small forest. **Ex.** *I went for a walk in the woods.*

wool (2) [wul'], *n.* 1. the soft, hairy covering of sheep and some other animals. **Ex.** *The wool was shipped to a factory.* 2. thread, cloth, or clothing made from sheep's hair. **Ex.** *She bought some wool for a dress.* —*adj.* made of wool. **Ex.** *He was wearing a wool sweater.* —**wool'en,** *adj.* made of wool. —**wool'ly,** *adj.* of or like wool.

word (1) [wərd'], *n.* 1. a unit of one or more sounds which has meaning; the written form of this unit. Ex. *How many English words do you know?* 2. a short talk. Ex. *May I have a word with you?* 3. argument. Ex. *She was late, and we had words.* 4. a promise; a pledge. Ex. *She gave me her word that she would write.* 5. a message; news. Ex. *Word came that you were ill.* —*v.* express in words. Ex. *She worded her letter of thanks very well.* —**by word of mouth,** orally. Ex. *The story spread by word of mouth.* —**word for word,** using the same words. Ex. *I told her what you said, word for word.*

wore (1) [wɔːr'], *v.* past tense of *wear.* Ex. *She wore a hat.*

work (1) [wərk'], *n.* 1. effort used to do something; labor. Ex. *Gardening is pleasant work.* 2. that which needs effort; a project. Ex. *There is much work to be done on a farm.* 3. that which is created by effort, such as a book, painting, opera, etc. Ex. *That is a work of art.* 4. the job one does for pay; employment. Ex. *He is trying to find work.* —*v.* 1. use mental or physical effort to make or do something; labor. Ex. *He works very hard at everything.* 2. operate; run; function as it should. Ex. *His car works well.* 3. be employed at or by. Ex. *He works for the government.* 4. cause to labor. Ex. *He works his men too hard.* 5. move slowly and with difficulty. Ex. *They worked their way up the mountain.* —**work'er,** *n.* one who works. —**work'ing,** *adj.* —**works',** *n.* 1. a factory. Ex. *This iron is being sent to the steel works.* 2. the parts of a machine that operate or move. Ex. *The works of this clock are broken.* —**out of work,** lacking a job. Ex. *He is out of work but looking for a job.* —**work out,** 1. end. Ex. *Everything worked out well.* 2. get out by effort. Ex. *He worked his way out of the crowd.* 3. solve. Ex. *He worked out the answer.* —**work up,** 1. progress; advance. Ex. *He has worked up to manager.* 2. plan; develop. Ex. *He worked up a way of doing it.* 3. become excited. Ex. *He was worked up about the problem.*

workday [wərk'dey'], *n.* 1. a day on which one works. Ex. *Sunday is not a workday for me.* 2. the length of time one works in a day. Ex. *He has an 8-hour workday.*

workingman [wɜrk'iŋmæn'], a man who works for pay, usually at physical labor.

workman [wɜrk'mən], *n.* a man who works, often at work requiring skill. —**work'man·like,** *adj.* skillful; well done. **Ex.**
He did a workmanlike job.

world (1) [wɜrld'], *n.* 1. the earth; the globe. **Ex.** *She took a
trip around the world.* 2. the people who live on the earth.
Ex. *He had to work hard in the world to succeed.* 3. the
society and activities of men. **Ex.** *The whole world hopes
for peace.* 4. a special group of people, things, etc. **Ex.** *He
is studying the animal world.* —**world'ly,** *adj.* wise in matters of the world.

worm (3) [wɜrm'], *n.* a small, slender, soft-
bodied animal without legs. **Ex.** *The bird
was looking for worms.* —*v.* move or
act in a slow, twisting way. **Ex.** *The
boy wormed his way under the fence.*
—**worm'y,** *adj.* 1. full of worms. 2. like
a worm.

WORM

worn (1) [wɔrn'], *v.* past participle of *wear.* **Ex.** *She had worn
that dress very often.* —*adj.* 1. damaged by use. **Ex.** *His
clothes looked worn.* 2. tired. **Ex.** *He looked worn at the
end of the day.*

worn-out [wɔrn'awt'], *adj.* 1. worn until no longer usable. **Ex.**
His clothes were worn-out. 2. exhausted. **Ex.** *He looked
worn-out at the end of the week.*

worry (2) [wə:r'iy], *v.* 1. be anxious; be concerned. **Ex.** *They
worry about their son's health.* 2. trouble; bother. **Ex.** *Don't
worry me with your problems.* —*n.* 1. anxiety; concern. **Ex.**
Worry is bad for the health. 2. that which causes anxiety or
concern. **Ex.** *They have financial worries.*

worse (2) [wərs'], *adj.* bad, sick, unpleasant, harmful, etc.
in a greater degree. **Ex.** *He is feeling worse now than before
he drank the medicine.* —*n.* that which is worse. **Ex.** *She
was none the worse for her fall.* —**wors'en,** *n.* become or
make worse.

worship (3) [wər'šip], *v.* show deep religious respect for. **Ex.**
Each worshiped in his own way. —*n.* the act of showing
deep religious respect; a religious service. **Ex.** *They attended morning worship.* —**wor'ship·er,** *n.* one who wor-
ships.

worst (2) [wərst'], *adj.* bad, sick, unpleasant, harmful, etc. in the highest degree. **Ex.** *He is the worst boy in the class.* —*n.* that which is most bad, unpleasant, or harmful. **Ex.** *We have not yet heard the worst.*

worth (1) [wərθ'], *n.* 1. value measured in money. **Ex.** *What is this house worth?* 2. the amount that a sum of money will buy. **Ex.** *Please give me ten cents' worth of candy.* 3. the quality or qualities that make a thing useful, valuable, or desirable; excellence. **Ex.** *Everyone knew the worth of his work.* —*adj.* 1. of value in terms of money. **Ex.** *This car is still worth a lot.* 2. deserving of. **Ex.** *It is not worth my time.* —**wor'thy,** *adj.* deserving of attention, respect, etc.

worthwhile [wərθ'hwayl'], *adj.* worth the time or effort. **Ex.** *Helping children is a worthwhile activity.*

would (1) [wud'], *v.* past tense of *will.* **Ex.** *He would often stop there on his way home.*

wound (2) [wawnd'], *v.* past tense and participle of *wind.* **Ex.** *He wound his watch.*

wound (2) [wuwnd'], *n.* 1. an injury to the body of a man or animal in which the skin is usually cut or broken. **Ex.** *Blood is pouring from the wound.* 2. an injury or hurt to the feelings, reputation, etc. **Ex.** *The experience left a wound upon her memory.* —*v.* injure; hurt. **Ex.** *He was wounded in the leg.*

wove (4) [wowv'], *v.* past tense and participle of *weave.* **Ex.** *They wove baskets of grass.* —**wo'ven,** *v.* past participle of *weave.*

wrap (2) [ræp'], *v.* 1. fold or wind around so as to cover. **Ex.** *She wrapped a scarf around her shoulders.* 2. cover or enclose in paper and string or something similar. **Ex.** *She wrapped the package.* —*n.* an outer garment. **Ex.** *Please remove your wrap.* —**wrap'ping,** *n.* covering or paper used to enclose. —**wrap'per,** *n.* 1. covering or paper used to enclose. 2. one who wraps. 3. a woman's robe.

wrath (4) [ræθ'], *n.* fierce anger; rage. **Ex.** *The wrath of the storm lessened.*

wreath (4) [riyθ'], *n.* a circle made by twisting together flowers, leaves, etc. **Ex.** *The bride wore a wreath of white flowers.* —**wreathe',** *v.* encircle or wind around; decorate with a wreath or something resembling a wreath in shape. **Ex.** *Her face was wreathed in smiles.*

wreck (3) [rek'], *v.* 1. damage greatly; ruin. **Ex.** *His hopes were wrecked when he failed the examination.* 2. tear down; demolish. **Ex.** *The building was wrecked because it was unsafe.* —*n.* 1. anything that has been badly damaged, broken, or ruined. **Ex.** *The house was a wreck after the fire.* 2. the act of badly damaging, breaking, or ruining. **Ex.** *The wreck of the ship was reported yesterday.* —**wreck'age,** *n.* 1. act of wrecking. 2. pieces of a wreck. **Ex.** *There was much wreckage on the ground.* —**wreck'er,** *n.* 1. that which or the one who wrecks. 2. a truck which carries away wrecks. **Ex.** *The wrecker towed the car to a garage.*

wrench (4) [renč'], *n.* 1. a sudden pulling and twisting. 2. an injury by twisting or pulling. **Ex.** *He has a wrench in his shoulder.* 3. a sudden grief or emotional pain. **Ex.** *It was a wrench to leave her family.* 4. a tool for twisting nuts onto bolts, turning pipes, etc. —*v.* 1. twist and pull violently. **Ex.** *He wrenched the telephone from the wall.* 2. injure by twisting. **Ex.** *He wrenched his back trying to lift the heavy box.*

WRENCH 4

wrestle (4) [res'əl], *v.* 1. struggle to overcome another and force him to the ground. **Ex.** *The two boys wrestled for several minutes.* 2. try earnestly to overcome or solve a difficulty by thought. **Ex.** *He wrestled with the problem.* —**wres'tler,** *n.* one who wrestles. —**wres'tling,** *n.* a sport or contest in which people wrestle.

wretch (4) [reč'], *n.* 1. a person in great pain or in a very unhappy condition. **Ex.** *The poor wretch asked for food and a place to sleep.* 2. a person despised for his bad character. **Ex.** *She would not speak to the wretch.* —**wretch'ed,** *adj.*

wring (3) [riŋ'], *v.* 1. twist and press with force, as to remove water from wet cloth. **Ex.** *Wring the clothes until they are dry.* 2. obtain by force and threats of force. **Ex.** *He tried to wring a confession from the prisoner.* —**wring'er,** *n.* a mechanical device used for forcing water out of clothes when washing them.

wrinkle (4) [riŋ'kəl], *n.* a small fold or ridge on a smooth surface. **Ex.** *There were wrinkles in her face from age.*

—*v.* form wrinkles; become wrinkled. **Ex.** *This material wrinkles easily.*

wrist (4) [rist'], *n.* the joint where the hand and the arm meet. **Ex.** *He wore a watch on his wrist.*

write (1) [rayt'], *v.* 1. form letters and words on something with a pencil, pen, etc. **Ex.** *The child is learning to write.* 2. communicate with or send a message to in writing. **Ex.** *He writes me a letter every week.* 3. be the author of a book, poem, etc.; be the composer of a musical work. **Ex.** *He is writing a short story.* —**writ'er**, *n.* one who writes words, letters, books, etc. —**writ'ing**, *n.* the act of one who writes; something written. **Ex.** *I have read all of his writings.* —**write down**, write on paper. **Ex.** *Write down what he says.* —**write up**, write a report of. **Ex.** *Write that news up for tomorrow's paper.*

writhe (5) [rayð'], *v.* make twisting, bending movements, as in pain. **Ex.** *The wounded man writhed in agony.*

written (1) [rit'ən], *v.* past participle of *write.* **Ex.** *Has he written to you?* —*adj.* in writing. **Ex.** *They have a written agreement.*

wrong (1) [rɔ:ŋ'], *adj.* 1. not correct; mistaken. **Ex.** *His answers were wrong.* 2. bad; not lawful; not morally right. **Ex.** *It was wrong of her to take his book.* 3. not right for the purpose. **Ex.** *She wore the wrong dress to the party.* 4. not right in operation or condition. **Ex.** *There is something wrong with the car.* —*adv.* 1. not according to morals. **Ex.** *She did wrong in taking the money.* 2. not correctly. **Ex.** *She did the work wrong.* —*n.* 1. a morally bad thing. **Ex.** *They are teaching their children to know right from wrong.* 2. an injury or injustice. **Ex.** *She did him a great wrong.* —*v.* do an injustice or injury to. **Ex.** *She wronged him by making a false accusation.*

wrongdoer [rɔŋ'duw˺ər], *n.* one who does wrong. **Ex.** *They will punish wrongdoers.* —**wrong'do·ing**, *n.* a wrongful act.

wrote (1) [rowt'], *v.* past tense of *write.* **Ex.** *She wrote to him every day.*

wrung (3) [rəŋ'], *v.* past tense and participle of *wring.* **Ex.** *The machine wrung the clothes almost dry.*

---

a, far; æ, am; e, get; ey, late; i, in; iy, see; ɔ, all; ow, go; u, put; uw, too; ə, but, ago; ər, fur; aw, out; ay, life; oy, boy; ŋ, ring; θ, think; ð, that; ž, measure; š, ship; ǰ, edge; č, child.

X

X, x [eks'], *n.* the twenty-fourth letter of the English alphabet.

x-ray (3) [eks'rey'], *n.* 1. a ray similar to light which can pass through solid substances, like the human body, and affect film in the same way as light. **Ex.** *X-rays are used to study the body structures and in the treatment of some diseases.* 2. a photograph made with such rays. **Ex.** *The doctor studied the x-ray of the broken leg.* —*v.* examine or photograph with such rays. **Ex.** *His teeth were x-rayed.* —*adj.* referring to such rays. **Ex.** *The doctor bought a new x-ray machine.*

Y

Y, y [way'], *n.* the twenty-fifth letter of the English alphabet.

-y (1) [iy], *suffix.* 1. the act or action of. **Exs.** *Recover, recovery; deliver, delivery; discover, discovery.* 2. full of; characterized by. **Exs.** *Dirt, dirty; rain, rainy; salt, salty.* 3. the state or quality of being. **Exs.** *Difficult, difficulty; honest, honesty; jealous, jealousy.* 4. having the characteristics of; like. **Exs.** *Bush, bushy; silk, silky; wave, wavy.*

Yankee (4) [yæŋ'kiy], *n.* a familiar name given to English colonists before and during the American Revolution, Northerners during the Civil War in the United States, American soldiers in both World Wars, and citizens of the United States by people of other countries. **Ex.** *He was surprised to hear himself called a Yankee.*

yard (1) [yard'], *n.* a measure of length; 3 feet; 36 inches. **Ex.** *She bought two yards of material.* See **Weights and Measures.**

yard (1) [yard'], *n.* 1. the ground around a house or building. **Ex.** *They have many flowers in their back yard.* 2. an enclosed space that is used for a special purpose. **Ex.** *We bought some boards from the lumberyard.*

yardstick [yard'stik'], *n.* a stick 36 inches in length, used for measuring.

yarn (4) [yarn'], *n.* a special thread made from cotton, wool, etc., and used in making knitted and other kinds of material. Ex. *She bought some yarn for a sweater.*

yawn (4) [yɔ:n'], *v.* open the mouth wide without wanting to, as when bored or tired. Ex. *He yawned several times during the lecture.* —*n.* the act of opening the mouth in this way. Ex. *His suggestion was received with a yawn.*

year (1) [yi:r'], *n.* 1. a time period of twelve months or 365 days beginning on January 1 and ending on December 31; a time period as long as a year beginning at any mentioned time. Ex. *We are leaving next month and will be gone a year.* 2. a period within a year having its limits set according to some yearly activity. Ex. *The school year begins in September and ends the following June.* 3. an indefinite time or period. Ex. *They met years later.* —**year'ly,** *adj.* done, made, or occurring once in each year or every year. Ex. *The group had a yearly dance.* —*adv.* once in each year. Ex. *We see them yearly.*

yearn (4) [yərn'], *v.* want very much; desire. Ex. *He yearns to go home.*

yeast (5) [yiyst'], *n.* a yellowish substance in powder or cake form containing agents which cause chemical change. Ex. *She added yeast to the bread mixture to make it rise.*

yell (3) [yel'], *v.* scream loudly. Ex. *The boy yelled with pain.* —*n.* 1. such a cry. Ex. *The child's yell of anger could be heard in the next house.* 2. a shout of encouragement. Ex. *During the game the students often shouted the school yell.*

yellow (1) [yel'ow], *adj.* of the color of gold, of a ripe lemon, of a banana, or of butter. Ex. *She is wearing a yellow dress.* —*n.* a color like that of gold, of a lemon, etc. Ex. *They like yellow.*

yes (1) [yes'], *adv.* used to express: 1. agreement. Ex. *Yes, I like this book.* 2. consent. Ex. *Yes, I will come here tomorrow.* —*n.* the act of agreeing or consenting. Ex. *They replied with a "yes."*

yesterday (1) [yes'tərdiy, yes'tərdey'], *n.* the day before this present day. Ex. *Yesterday was the first day of the month; today is the second.* —*adv.* on the day before this present day. Ex. *It happened yesterday.*

yet (1) [yet'], *adv.* 1. at some time before now. Ex. *Has he* *come yet?* 2. now; at this time. **Ex.** *I cannot tell you just yet.* 3. at some future time. **Ex.** *I will learn this yet.* —*conj.* however; nevertheless. **Ex.** *She tries hard, yet she does not understand.*

yield (2) [yiyld¹], *v.* 1. produce; bear. **Ex.** *That field yielded a good crop.* 2. surrender; quit; give possession of something to another because of pressure or demand. **Ex.** *The troops yielded to the enemy.* 3. move back or away because of pressure or demand. **Ex.** *The door would not yield when we pushed it.* —*n.* that which is yielded; the amount produced. **Ex.** *The yield of milk from that cow was heavy.*

yoke (4) [yowk¹], *n.* 1. a device in the form of a frame of wood, placed on the necks of a pair of animals so that they can pull a plow or a load. **Ex.** *He put the yoke on the oxen.* 2. condition of slavery or of YOKE 1 submission to the control of another. **Ex.** *They were under the yoke of a foreign power.* —*v.* join by means of a yoke. **Ex.** *He yoked the oxen together and tied them to the plow.*

yonder (5) [yan¹dər], *adv.* at or in the place indicated or pointed to; over there. **Ex.** *Go yonder, where the two roads cross.* —*adj.* in the place indicated or pointed to; over there. **Ex.** *Yonder fields belong to this farm.*

you (1) [yuw¹], *pron.* 1. the person or persons to whom one's words are directed. **Exs.** *You should go now. I saw you yesterday. Did he give all of it to you?* 2. one; any person. **Ex.** *You never know what may happen.*

young (1) [yəŋ¹], *adj.* 1. not old; in the first years of life. **Ex.** *Our children are young.* 2. fresh and active. **Ex.** *He looks young for his age.* —*n.* 1. young people as a group. **Ex.** *The young often have little time for the old.* 2. young animals. **Ex.** *The birds fed their young.*

your (1) [yu:r¹], *adj.* of or belonging to you. **Ex.** *Is she your sister?*

yours (2) [yurz¹], *pron.* that which belongs to you. **Ex.** *Is this book yours?*

yourself [yərself¹], *pron.* 1. your own self. **Ex.** *Do it yourself.* 2. your usual self. **Ex.** *You are not acting like yourself today.*

youth (2) [youθ¹], *n.* 1. the period of life when one is young; the period of life between childhood and adulthood. **Ex.**

She played the piano in her youth. 2. a young man. **Ex.** *He was a youth of eighteen.* 3. young people, as a group. **Ex.** *The youth of the community are interested in politics.* 4. the quality or condition of being young, active, etc. **Ex.** *He had the youth and strength of a much younger man.*

Z

Z, z (1) [ziy¹], *n.* the twenty-sixth letter of the English alphabet.

zeal (4) [ziyl¹], *n.* strong, active interest; enthusiasm. **Ex.** *He worked for the cause with great zeal.* —**zeal¹ous,** *adj.* —**zeal¹ous·ly,** *adv.*

zero (4) [zi:r¹ow], *n.* 1. the figure "0" which symbolizes an absence of quantity; nothing. **Ex.** *Six taken from six equals zero.* 2. a line or point, as on a thermometer, on which a scale measured in degrees is based. **Ex.** *The temperature is going below zero tonight.*

zinc (5) [ziŋk¹], *n.* a bluish-white metal used as a protective coat for certain other metals and in mixtures with other metals, etc. **Ex.** *Zinc is combined with copper to make brass.*

zone (3) [zown¹], *n.* 1. an area which can be distinguished from the areas around it by some distinctive feature. **Ex.** *Cars must move slowly in a school zone.* 2. any one of the five areas into which imaginary lines running east and west divide the earth's surface by climate and location. —*v.* divide into zones.

ZONE 2

Ex. *This section of the city is zoned for business.*

zoo (5) [zuw¹], *n.* an enclosed area, usually in a park, where animals are kept for exhibition to the public. **Ex.** *The children saw the lions at the zoo.*

---

a, far; æ, am; e, get; ey, late; i, in; iy, see; ɔ, all; ow, go; u, put; uw, too; ə, but, ago; ər, fur; aw, out; ay, life; oy, boy; ŋ, ring; θ, think; ð, that; ž, measure; š, ship; j, edge; č, child.

Appendix I

Marks, Signs, and Symbols

I. In Writing

' **apostrophe** [əpas'trəfiy], 1. used at the end of nouns to show ownership or possession by that noun of something mentioned later in the sentence. (The apostrophe is usually but not always followed by an "s" in such nouns.) Exs. *John's book; the boy's dog (one boy); the boys' house (several boys)*. 2. used to show that a word has been shortened by omitting a letter or letters. Most common forms are: *-'m = am (I'm); -'re = are (you're); -'s = is (he's)* or *has (he's); -'ve = have (we've); -n't = not (isn't); -'ll = will (they'll); -'d = would (I'd)*. 3. used to show the plural of letters, signs, and figures. Ex. *Look in the A's and B's of this book.*

* **asterisk** [æs'tərisk`], used to show that the word in front of the asterisk is explained elsewhere where there is another asterisk, usually in a footnote at the bottom of the page.

: **colon** [kow'lən], 1. used in a sentence before a series of things, a long quotation, examples, etc. Ex. *I have the following: one hammer, two saws, and many nails.* 2. used at the end of the opening greeting in a business letter. Ex. *Dear Sir:*

, **comma** [kam'ə], 1. used to show a pause within a sentence shorter than the pause for a semicolon. Exs. *She laughed, and he cried. When he called, I was eating dinner. Ethel, my friend, is a teacher.* 2. used between words or numbers in a series including the last two which are separated by *"and."* Ex. *He bought meat, milk, bread, and fruit.*

— **dash** [dæš'], used to show a break in thought. Ex. *If we buy it now—and I would like to buy it—we will pay too much.* See **hyphen** below.

! **exclamation point** [eks`kləmey'šən poynt'], used after a word or at the end of a sentence to show surprise or other strong feeling. Exs. *You went there alone! Quiet!*

- **hyphen** [hay'fən], 1. used in a word to show that it is formed from two or more other words or from a prefix and another word. Exs. *Self-control; ex-smoker.* 2. used to show the syllables of a word, especially when part of

655

a word appears at the end of one line and the rest of the word appears on the next line. Ex. *Hy-phen.*

( )   **parentheses** [pəren'θəsiyz'], used around a word or words, figures, etc. which explain or make clearer in some way the other words or the sentence to which the words in parentheses are added. Ex. *The guest speaker (I knew him as a boy) is staying at my house.*

(or)   **parenthesis** [pəren'θəsis], one of a pair of parentheses.

.   **period** [pi:r'iyəd], 1. used to show a complete stop at the end of a sentence. Ex. *He went home.* 2. used to show that a word is an abbreviated form. Exs. *Doctor, Dr.; Senior, Sr.* 3. used to show that words are omitted. Ex. *About the book, the magazine said, ". . . one of the best."*

?   **question mark** [kwes'čən mark'], used after a word or at the end of a sentence to show a question has been asked. Exs. *Where did you go? Why?*

" "   **quotation marks** [kwowtey'šən marks'], 1. used before and after the words of the person speaking. Ex. *"When will I see you again?" he asked.* 2. used before and after words which are an exact repetition of something previously written or said. Ex. *The song begins with the words, "Tell me, pretty maiden."* 3. used before and after the name of a book, story, movie, etc. Ex. *When did you first see "Gone with the Wind"?*

' '   **quotation marks, single** [kwowtey'šən marks'], used before and after a quotation which is inside of another quotation. Ex. *"That man is the one who called 'Fire!' the policeman told me."*

;   **semicolon** [sem'iykow'lən], used to show a pause within a sentence 1. between clauses not joined by *"and," "but," "for," "nor," "or,"* or *"yet."* 2. between such clauses when one or more of the clauses contain commas. Ex. *It rained on the way to school; and our hats, coats, and shoes were soaked.* 3. between groups of words containing commas. Ex. *Three boxes were lost: one containing books, magazines, and papers; one containing paintings; and one containing silverware.*

II. In Arithmetic, Measures, and Weights

@   **at** [æt'], in the amount or rate of for each. Ex. *Six books @ $.05 cost $.30.*

¢   **cent(s)** [sent(s)¹], unit of money written after the number; one cent equals .01 of a dollar. **Ex.** *The books are priced at 5¢ each.*

°   **degree** [dəgriy¹], 1. a measure of temperature. **Ex.** *It is only 10° above zero today.* 2. a measure of angle. **Ex.** *A 90°-angle is a right angle. 90°.*

÷   **divided by** [dəvay¹did bay`]. **Ex.** *4 ÷ 2 = 2.*

$ **dollar(s)** [dal¹ər(z)], unit of money written before the number; one dollar equals one hundred cents. **Ex.** *The price of the book is $5.*

=   **equals** [iy¹kwəlz]. **Ex.** *2 + 2 = 4.*

′   **foot, feet** [fut¹, fiyt¹], a measure of length equal to 12 inches or ⅓ of a yard. **Ex.** *This window is 3′ wide and 6′ high.*

″   **inch(es)** [inč¹(əz)], a measure of length equal to ¹⁄₁₂ of a foot. **Ex.** *This material is 54″ wide.*

—   **minus** [may¹nəs], **Ex.** *3 − 2 = 1.*

%   **percent** [pərsent¹], out, in, or part of 100. **Ex.** *6% of 100 is 6.*

+   **plus** [pləs¹], and; added to. **Ex.** *2 + 2 = 4.*

×   **times** [taymz¹], multiplied by. **Ex.** *3 × 2 = 6.*

0   **zero** [zi:r¹ow], 1. nothing. **Ex.** *1 − 1 = 0.* 2. a point on the thermometer from which other degrees of temperature are measured. **Ex.** *It was 20° below 0 last night.*

&   **and** [ænd¹], with. **Ex.** *Jones & Sons is a company owned by Jones and his sons.*

%   **in care of** [in ke:r¹ əv], used in addresses to show that a person is located at the address of another or can be reached through that person. **Ex.** *His address is:*

                     John Jones
                     % Henry Smith
                     711 Box Street

Appendix II

Abbreviations

The following is a partial list of the most frequently used shortened forms in written American English. In many instances, an abbreviation may be written with periods or without them and have the same meaning. (Ex. *N.W. and NW*). Also, many abbreviations may be written in capital letters or in small letters and have the same meaning. (Ex. *P.M. and p.m.*). Only when the differing forms have differing meanings are they listed separately. (Ex. *mo., monthly and Mo., Missouri*).

A

A.B.	Bachelor of Arts. See **B.A.**
A.C.	alternating current, one of two common forms of electrical current. Electrical devices marked A.C. or D.C. can use only the current indicated.
A.D.	in the year of our Lord; the stated number of years since the birth of Christ.
adj.	adjective.
adv.	adverb.
Ala.	Alabama, a U.S. state.
Alas.	Alaska, a U.S. state.
A.M., a.m.	any hour between midnight and noon.
ans.	answer.
Apr.	April, the fourth month.
Ariz.	Arizona, a U.S. state.
Ark.	Arkansas, a U.S. state.
arr.	arrive.
Aug.	August, the eighth month.
Ave.	Avenue.

B

B.A.	Bachelor of Arts, first university degree, usually received after four years of study.
B.C.	before Christ; the stated number of years before the birth of Christ.

B.S.	Bachelor of Science, degree in science equivalent to B.A.
bu.	bushel(s), a measure.

C

Calif.	California, a U.S. state.
C.O.D., c.o.d.	Collect On Delivery. Payment to be collected when goods are delivered.
conj.	conjunction.
Conn.	Connecticut, a U.S. state.
C.S.T.	Central Standard Time, official time in the Central U.S.

D

D.C.	direct current. See **A.C.**
D.C.	District of Columbia, site of U.S. capital.
Dec.	December, the twelfth month.
Del.	Delaware, a U.S. state.
dept.	department.
D.S.T.	Daylight Saving Time, time during the period from the end of April to the end of October when clocks are turned ahead one hour to have more daylight at the end of the day. Ex. *4:30 E.S.T. = 5:30 D.S.T.*

E

E	East, a direction. Eastern.
e.g.	for example; as one example.
esp.	especially.
E.S.T.	Eastern Standard Time, official time in the Eastern U.S.
est.	1. established. 2. estimated.
etc.	et cetera.
ex.	example.

F

Feb.	February, the second month.
Fla.	Florida, a U.S. state.
ft.	foot or feet, a measure of length.

G

Ga.	Georgia, a U.S. state.
gal(s).	gallon(s), a liquid measure.
Govt., govt.	government.

H

hp, h.p.	horsepower, a measure of energy.
hr(s).	hour(s), a measure of time.

I

Ia.	Iowa, a U.S. state.
Id., Ida.	Idaho, a U.S. state.
i.e.	that is.
Ill.	Illinois, a U.S. state.
in(s).	inch(es), a measure of length.
Inc., inc.	Incorporated. Formed into a corporation.
Ind.	Indiana, a U.S. state.
interj.	interjection.
IOU, I.O.U.	I owe you, a signed paper promising to pay a debt.
I.Q.	intelligence quotient, a measure of a person's mental development.

J

Jan.	January, the first month.
Jr., jr.	junior.
Jul.	July, the seventh month.
Jun.	June, the sixth month.

K

Kan., Kans.	Kansas, a U.S. state.
Ky.	Kentucky, a U.S. state.

L

La.	Louisiana, a U.S. state.
lat.	latitude.
lb(s).	pound(s), a measure of weight.
L.L.B.	first degree in study of law.
long.	longitude.
lv.	leave.

M

M.A.	Master of Arts, next higher degree after a B.A.
Mar.	March, the third month.
Mass.	Massachusetts, a U.S. state.
math	mathematics.
M.D.	Doctor of Medicine.
Md.	Maryland, a U.S. state.
Me.	Maine, a U.S. state.
mi(s).	mile(s), a measure of length.
Mich.	Michigan, a U.S. state.
min(s).	minute(s), a measure of time.
Minn.	Minnesota, a U.S. state.
Miss.	Mississippi, a U.S. state.
mo(s).	month(s).
Mo.	Missouri, a U.S. state.
Mont.	Montana, a U.S. state.
mph, m.p.h.	miles per hour, a measure of speed.
Mr.	Mister, a title used before a man's name.
Mrs.	a title used before a married woman's last or full name.
Mt(s)., mt(s).	mountain(s).

N

N	North, a direction. Northern.
n.	noun.
N.C., N. Car.	North Carolina, a U.S. state.
N.D., N. Dak.	North Dakota, a U.S. state.
NE, N.E.	Northeast, a direction.
Neb.	Nebraska, a U.S. state.
Nev.	Nevada, a U.S. state.
N.H.	New Hampshire, a U.S. state.
N.J.	New Jersey, a U.S. state.
N.M., N. Mex.	New Mexico, a U.S. state.
Nov.	November, the eleventh month.
NW, N.W.	Northwest, a direction.
N.Y.	New York, a U.S. state.
N.Y.C.	New York City, a U.S. city.

O

O.	Ohio, a U.S. state.
Oct.	October, the tenth month.
Okla.	Oklahoma, a U.S. state.
Ore.	Oregon, a U.S. state.
oz(s).	ounce(s), a measure of weight and of liquids.

P

p.	page.
Pa.	Pennsylvania, a U.S. state.
pd.	paid.
Ph.D.	Doctor of Philosophy, the highest university degree; next highest degree after an M.A.
pk(s).	peck(s), a dry measure.
P.M., p.m.	any hour between noon and midnight.
P.O.	Post Office.
pp.	pages.
pr.	pair.
prep.	preposition.
pron.	pronoun.
P.S.	postscript, words added to a letter below the signature.
pt(s).	pint(s), a measure of volume.

Q

qt(s).	quarts(s), a measure of volume.

R

rd.	1. road. 2. rod, a measure of length.
Rep.	Representative.
Rev.	Reverend, a title before the name of a man of religion.
R.I.	Rhode Island, a U.S. state.
rpm, r.p.m.	revolutions per minute, a measure of speed.
R.R.	railroad.
Ry.	railway.

S

S	South, a direction. Southern.
S.C., S. Car.	South Carolina, a U.S. state.
S.D., S. Dak.	South Dakota, a U.S. state.
SE, S.E.	Southeast, a direction.
sec(s).	second(s), a measure of time.
Sen.	Senator.
Sept.	September, the ninth month.
Sr., sr.	Senior.
SS, S.S.	steamship.
St.	1. saint when used before a name. **Ex.** *St. John.* 2. street when used after a name. **Ex.** *Main St.*
SW, S.W.	Southwest, a direction.

T

Tenn.	Tennessee, a U.S. state.
Tex.	Texas, a U.S. state.
TV	television.

U

U.	University.
UN, U.N.	United Nations.
US, U.S.	United States.
USA, U.S.A.	1. United States of America. 2. United States Army.
USAF, U.S.A.F.	United States Air Force.
USCG, U.S.C.G.	United States Coast Guard.
USMC, U.S.M.C.	United States Marine Corps.
USN, U.S.N.	United States Navy.
USS, U.S.S.	United States Ship.
Ut.	Utah, a U.S. state.

V

v.	verb.
Va.	Virginia, a U.S. state.
vol(s).	volume(s).
Vt.	Vermont, a U.S. state.

W

W	West, a direction. Western.
w.	width.
Wash.	Washington, a U.S. state.
Wash., D.C.	Washington, D.C., capital city of the U.S.
Wis., Wisc.	Wisconsin, a U.S. state.
wk.	week.
wt.	weight.
W. Va.	West Virginia, a U.S. state.
Wyo.	Wyoming, a U.S. state.

XYZ

yd(s).	yard(s), a measure of length.
yr(s).	year(s).

Appendix III

Weights and Measures

Unit	Abbreviation	Value in Other U.S. Units	Metric Value[1]
Weight			
ounce	oz.	$\frac{1}{16}$th of one pound	28.349 grams
pound	lb.	16 ounces	0.453 kilogram
ton	—	2,000 pounds	0.907 metric ton
Dry Measure			
pint	pt.	$\frac{1}{2}$ of 1 quart	0.550 liter
quart	qt.	2 pints	1.101 liters
peck	pk.	8 quarts	8.809 liters
bushel	bu.	4 pecks or 32 quarts	35.238 liters
Liquid Measure			
pint	pt.	$\frac{1}{2}$ of 1 quart	0.473 liter
quart	qt.	2 pints	0.946 liter
gallon	gal.	4 quarts	3.785 liters
Length			
inch	in.	$\frac{1}{12}$th of 1 foot	2.540 centimeters
foot	ft.	12 inches or $\frac{1}{3}$ of 1 yard	30.480 centimeters
yard	yd.	3 feet or 36 inches	0.914 meter
rod	rd.	16½ feet	5.029 meters
mile	mi.	5,280 feet	1.609 kilometers

United States Money

Unit	Value		Symbol	Compared[2]
1 penny	1	cent	1¢	$1 = 7.600 rupees (India)
1 nickel	5	cents	5¢	360.0 yen (Japan)
1 dime	10	cents	10¢	5.03 shillings (England)
1 quarter	25	cents	25¢	4.955 francs (France)
1 half dollar	50	cents	50¢	6.110 dollars (Hong Kong)
1 dollar	100	cents	$1.00 or $1	12.49 pesos (Mexico)
				350.00 pesos (Argentina)

Heat

Degrees Centigrade	Degrees Fahrenheit	Condition
0°	32°	Freezing point
100°	212°	Boiling point

[1] System used in most parts of the world.
[2] As of February, 1969

Appendix IV

Place Names

This section provides the American spelling and pronunciation together with the identification of the continents, major geographic features and countries of the world, their capitals, and large cities of those countries in which English is an important language. All the states of the United States are listed as well as at least one major city from each state, major United States mountain systems, and major bodies of water. The letters N, S, E, and W refer to directions (North, South, East, and West) and are intended to make map location easier.

Names of natives of countries or areas are usually formed by adding the letter "n" to the names of the countries or areas ending in "a" (America; American), "an" to the names ending in "e," "i," "o," or "u" (Europe; European), and "ian" to names ending with other letters. Exceptions to this rule are shown in the list (Ex. *China; Chinese*). The same rule and exceptions apply in writing the adjective form. Ex. *A Mexican friend introduced me to Mexican food.*

A

Abidjan [æˈbiyĭan], capital of the Ivory Coast.

Accra [əkraˈ], capital of Ghana.

Addis Ababa [ædˈis aˈbəbə], capital of Ethiopia.

Afghanistan [æfgænˈəstænˈ], country in W central Asia. —**Afˈghan,** *n.* and *adj.*

Africa [æfˈrikə], second largest continent.

Alabama [ælˈəbæmˈə], SE U.S. state.

Alaska [əlæsˈkə], U.S. state NW of Canada.

Albania [ælbeyˈniyə], country in SE Europe.

Albany [ɔːlˈbəniy], capital of New York.

Albuquerque [ælˈbəkəːrˈkiy], capital of New Mexico.

Algeria [ælʤiːrˈiyə], country in NW Africa.

Algiers [ælʤiːrzˈ], capital of Algeria.

Amazon [æmˈəzanˈ], world's longest river, in **Brazil.**

America [əmeːrˈəkə], 1. the United States. 2. either North or South America.

Amman [aˈman, amanˈ], capital of Jordan.

Anchorage [æŋˈkərɪʤ], largest city in Alaska.

Andes [æn'diyz], large mountain system extending the length of W South America.

Angola [æŋgow'lə], Portuguese overseas territory in SW Africa.

Ankara [æŋ'kərə], capital of Turkey.

Annapolis [ənæp'ələs], capital of Maryland.

Antarctic [æntark'tik], area and ocean at the South Pole. —**Ant·arc'ti·ca**, land at the South Pole.

Appalachian Mountains [æp'əley'čən mawnt'ənz], longest mountain system of E U.S., extending from Canada to Alabama.

Arabia [ərey'biyə], peninsula of SW Asia. See **Saudi Arabia**. —**A·ra'bi·an Sea'**, sea between Arabia and Asia.

Arctic [ark'tik], area and ocean at the North Pole.

Argentina [a:r'jəntiy'nə], country in SE Latin America.

Arizona [e:r'əzow'nə], SW U.S. state.

Arkansas [ark'ənsɔ:'], 1. S central U.S. state. 2. river extending from Colorado to Arkansas, joining Mississippi.

Asia [ey'žə, ey'šə], largest continent.

Asuncion [asən'siyown'], capital of Paraguay.

Athens [æθ'ənz], capital city of Greece. —**A·the'ni·an,** *n.* and *adj.*

Atlanta [ætlæn'tə], capital of Georgia.

Atlantic [ætlæn'tik], ocean between the Americas and Africa and Europe.

Augusta [əgəs'tə], 1. capital of Maine. 2. city of Georgia.

Australia [ɔstreyl'yə], continent and country in the S Pacific.

Austria [ɔs'triyə], country in central Europe.

B

Baltic Sea [bɔl'tik siy'], sea in N Europe extending from Denmark to the USSR.

Baltimore [bɔl'təmɔr], seaport and largest city of Maryland.

Bamako [bæm'əkow], capital of Mali.

Bangkok [bæŋ'kak], capital of Thailand.

Bangui [bæn'giy], capital of Central African Republic.

Bathurst [bæθ'ərst], capital of Gambia.

Baton Rouge [bæt'ən ruwž'], capital of Louisiana.

Beirut [beyruwt', bey'ruwt], capital of Lebanon.

Belgium [bel'jəm], country in Europe, N of France. —**Bel'gian,** *n.* and *adj.*

Belgrade [bel'greyd, bel'græd], capital of Yugoslavia.

Bengal [ben'gɔl], bay of Indian Ocean.

Berlin [bərlin'], largest city of Germany.

Bern [bərn', bern'], capital of Switzerland.

Bhutan [buw'tan], country NE of India.

Birmingham [bər'miŋhæm], 1. largest city of Alabama. 2. city in W central England.

Bismarck [biz'mark], capital of North Dakota.

Black Sea [blæk' siy'], sea between Turkey and Russia.

Blantyre [blæn'tayr], capital of Malawi.

Bogota [bow'gəta], capital of Colombia.

Boise [boy'siy, boy'ziy], capital of Idaho.

Bolivia [bəliv'iyə], country in W central Latin America.

Bombay [bambey'], seaport in W India.

Bonn [ban'], capital of the Federal Republic of Germany (West Germany).

Boston [bɔs'tən, bas'tən], capital of Massachusetts.

Botswana [bats`wa'nə], country in S Africa.

Brazil [brəzil'], country in E South America.

Brazzaville [braz'əvil], capital of the Congo.

Britain [brit'ən], Great Britain. —**Brit'ish,** *adj.* —**the Brit'ish,** *n.*

British Commonwealth [brit'iš kam'ənwelθ`], association of Britain and independent countries formerly British colonies.

British Isles [brit'iš aylz'], islands of Great Britain and Ireland, NW Europe.

Brunei [bruwnay'], country of East Asia.

Brussels [brəs'əlz], capital of Belgium.

Buenos Aires [bwey'nəs ay'riyz, bow'nəs e:r'iyz], capital of Argentina.

Bujumbura [bəjəm`bər'ə], capital of Burundi.

Bulgaria [bəlge:r'iyə], country in SE Europe.

Burma [bər'mə], country in SE Asia. —**Bur`mese',** *n.* and *adj.*

Burundi [bəruwn'diy], country in central Africa.

C

Cairo [kay'row], capital of Egypt.

Calcutta [kælkət'ə], seaport in E India.

California [kæl`əfɔrn'yə], W U.S. state on the Pacific.

Cambodia [kæmbow'diyə], country in SE Asia.

Cameroon [kæm'əruwn'], country in W Africa.

Canada [kæn'ədə], country in North America. —**Ca·na'di·an,** *n.* and *adj.*

Canberra [kæn'bərə], capital of Australia.

Capetown [keyp'tawn`], seaport in S Africa.

Caracas [kəra'kəs], capital of Venezuela.

Caribbean Sea [kæ:r`əbiy'ən siy', kərib'iyən siy'], part of the Atlantic, SE of North America.

Caspian Sea [kæs'piyən siy'], sea between the USSR and Iran.

Central African Republic [sen'trəl æf'rikən ripəb'lik], country in N central Africa.

Central America [sen'trəl əme:r'əkə], countries and area between Mexico and South America.

Ceylon [silan'], country and island SE of India. —**Cey`lon·ese',** *n.* and *adj.*

Chad [čæd'], country in N central Africa.

Charleston [čarl'stən], 1. capital of West Virginia. 2. seaport of South Carolina.

Chesapeake Bay [čes'əpiyk` bey'], large Atlantic bay between Maryland and Virginia.

Chicago [šəka'gow, šəkɔ:'gow], largest city of Illinois, on Lake Michigan.

Chile [čil'iý], country in SW Latin America. —**Chil'e·an,** *n.* and *adj.*

China [čay'nə], largest country of Asia, divided into People's Republic of China and Republic of China (see **Taiwan**). —**Chi`nese',** *n.* and *adj.*

China Sea [čay'nə siy'], part of the W Pacific Ocean from Japan S to Singapore.

Cleveland [kliyv'lənd], largest city of Ohio, on Lake Erie.

Colombia [kələm'biyə], country in NW South America.

Colombo [kələm'bow], capital of Ceylon.

Colorado [kal`era'dow, kal`eræd'ow], W U.S. state.

Columbia [kələm'biyə], river flowing through Washington and Oregon to the Pacific.

Conakry [kan'əkriy], capital of Guinea.

Congo [kaŋ'gow], river in central Africa, boundary of the Congo.

Congo [kaŋ'gow], 1. Democratic Republic of the Congo, former Belgian Congo. 2. Congo, Brazzaville, former French Congo. —**Con'go·lese'**, *n*. and *adj*.

Connecticut [kənet'əkət], NE U.S. state on the Atlantic.

Copenhagen [kow'pənhey`gən, kow`pənhey'gən], capital of Denmark.

Costa Rica [kows'tə riy'kə], country in S Central America.

Cotonou [kow'tənuw], capital of Dahomey.

Cuba [kyuw'bə], country and largest island in the Caribbean.

Cyprus [say'prəs], country and island SW of Turkey. —**Cyp' ri·ot**, *n*. and *adj*.

Czechoslovakia [ček`əslowva'kiyə], country in central Europe.

D

Dacca [da'kə], city in E Pakistan.

Dahomey [da'howmey], country in W Africa.

Dakar [dəkar'], capital of Senegal.

Damascus [dəmæs'kəs], capital of Syria.

Danish [dey'niš], *n*. and *adj*. See **Denmark.**

Dar-es-Salaam [da:r' es səlam'], capital of Tanzania.

Delaware [del'əwer], E U.S. state on Atlantic.

Denmark [den'mark], country in NW Europe. —**Dane'**, *n*. citizen of Denmark. —**Dan'ish,** *n*. and *adj*.

Denver [den'vər], capital of Colorado.

Des Moines [də moyn'], capital of Iowa.

Detroit [ditroyt'], largest city of Michigan.

District of Columbia [dis'trikt əv kələm'biyə], site of Washington, U.S. capital, between Maryland and Virginia.

Djakarta [jəkar'tə], capital of Indonesia.

Dominican Republic [dəmin'ikən ripəb'lik], country on a Caribbean island with Haiti. —**Do·min'i·can,** *n*. and *adj*.

Dover [dow'vər], capital of Delaware.

Dublin [dəb'lən], capital of Ireland.

Dutch [dəč], *n*. and *adj*. See **Netherlands.**

E

East Indies [iyst' in'diyz], SE Asia.

Ecuador [ek'wədɔr], country in NW South America.

Egypt [iy'ǰipt], United Arab Republic.

El Salvador [el sæl'vədɔr], country in S Central America.

England [iŋ'glənd], S Britain except Wales. —**Eng'lish**, *n.* and *adj.*

English Channel [iŋ'gliš čæn'əl], body of water between England and France.

Equatorial Guinea [ek'wətɔr'iyəl gin'iy], country of W Africa.

Erie [i:r'iy], one of the five Great Lakes, central North America.

Ethiopia [iy'θiyow'piyə], country in NE Africa.

Europe [yu:r'əp], a continent.

F

Far East [fa:r' iyst'], E Asia.

Far West [fa:r' west'], western U.S.

Filipino [fil'əpiy'now], *n.* see **Philippines.**

Finland [fin'lənd], country in NE Europe. —**Finn'**, *n.* —**Finn'ish**, *n.* and *adj.*

Florida [flɔ:r'ədə], SE U.S. state on the Atlantic.

Formosa [fɔrmow'sə], Taiwan.

Fort Lamy [fɔrt' la'miy], capital of Chad.

France [fræns'], country in W central Europe. —**French'**, *n.* and *adj.*

Freetown [friy'tawn'], capital of Sierra Leone.

French [frenč'], *n.* and *adj.* See **France.**

French Guiana [frenč' giyæn'ə], French overseas department in NE South America.

G

Gabon [gæbɔ:n'], country in W central Africa.

Gambia [gæm'biyə], country in NW Africa.

Ganges [gæn'ǰiyz], river in NW India, flowing S to E India.

Georgetown [ǰɔrǰ'tawn'], capital of Guyana.

Georgia [ǰɔr'ǰə], SE U.S. state on the Atlantic.

Germany [ǰər'məniy], country, now divided, in central Europe. Federal Republic capital at Bonn. —**Ger'man**, *n.* and *adj.*

Ghana [ga'nə], country in W Africa.

Gibraltar [jibrɔl'tər], Strait of, body of water joining the Atlantic and the Mediterranean, SW Europe.

Great Britain [greyt' brit'ən], kingdom and island, NW Europe.

Great Lakes [greyt' leyks'], group of five large lakes, in central North America.

Greece [griys'], country in SE Europe. —**Greek'**, *n.* and *adj.* —**Gre'cian,** *adj.*

Greenland [griyn'lənd], an island in the N Atlantic.

Guatemala [gwa'təma'lə], country in Central America. —**Gua`te·ma'la Ci'ty,** capital of Guatemala.

Guinea [gín'iy], country in W Africa on the Atlantic.

Guyana [giyæn'ə, giya'nə], country in NE South America.

H

Hague, The [heyg'], capital of the Netherlands.

Haiti [hey'tiy], country on a Caribbean island with the Dominican Republic. —**Hai'tian,** *n.* and *adj.*

Hanoi [ha'noy'], capital of North Vietnam.

Hartford [hart'fərd], capital of Connecticut.

Havana [həvæn'ə], capital of Cuba.

Hawaii [həway'iy], U.S. state in the N central Pacific. —**Ha·wai'ian Is'lands,** island group forming the state.

Helena [hel'ənə], capital of Montana.

Helsinki [hel'siŋkiy], capital of Finland.

Holland [hal'ənd], the Netherlands.

Honduras [handu:r'əs, handyu:r'əs], country in Central America. —**Hon·du'ran,** *n.* and *adj.*

Hong Kong [hɔ:ŋ' kɔ:ŋ'], British colony on the coast of SE China.

Honolulu [han'əluw'luw], capital of Hawaii.

Houston [hyuws'tən], largest city of Texas.

Hudson [həd'sən], 1. river in New York State. 2. bay in NE Canada.

Hungary [həŋ'gəriy], country in E central Europe. —**Hun·gar'i·an,** *n.* and *adj.*

Huron [hyu:r'an, hyu:r'ən], one of the five Great Lakes, central North America.

I

Iceland [ays'lənd], country and island in the N Atlantic. —Ice'land'er, n. —Ice·lan'dic, adj.

Idaho [ay'dəhow`], NW U.S. state.

Illinois [il`ənoy', il`ənoyz'], N central U.S. state.

India [in'diyə], country in S Asia. —In'di·an, n. and adj. 1. of or concerning India. 2. of or concerning natives settled in America before Europeans.

Indiana [in`diyæn'ə], N central U.S. state.

Indianapolis [in`diyənæp'əlis], capital of Indiana.

Indian Ocean [in'diyən ow'šən], ocean S of Asia, E of Africa.

Indochina [in'dowčay'nə], part of a peninsula of SE Asia (Vietnam, Cambodia, Laos).

Indonesia [in`dəniy'žə], country of islands in SE Asia.

Indus [in'dəs], river, flowing NE to SW, from Tibet to the Arabian Sea (Pakistan).

Iowa [ay'əwə, ay'əwey`], N central U.S. state.

Iran [iran', iræn'], country in SW Asia.

Iraq [iræk', irak'], country in Near East. —I·raq'i, n. and adj.

Ireland [ayr'lənd], country in W British Isles, NW Europe. —I'rish, n. and adj.

Islamabad [izlam'əbæd], capital of Pakistan.

Israel [iz'riyəl], country in Near East. —Is`rael'i, n. and adj.

Italy [it'əliy], country in S central Europe. —I·tal'i·an, n. and adj..

Ivory Coast [ay'vəriy kowst'], country in W Africa.

J

Jackson [jæk'sən], capital of Mississippi.

Jamaica [jəmey'kə], country and island in the W Atlantic, SE of U.S.

Japan [jəpæn'], country and islands in E Asia, NW Pacific. —Jap`a·nese', n. and adj.

Jerusalem [jəruw'sələm], holy ancient city of the Near East.

Jidda [jid'ə], capital of Saudi Arabia.

Jordan [jɔr'dən], 1. country in the Near East. 2. river in the Near East.

K

Kabul [kabuwl'], capital of Afghanistan.

Kampala [kampa'lə], capital of Uganda.

Kansas [kæn'zəs], N central U.S. state. —**Kan'sas Ci'ty,** city in Missouri and Kansas.

Karachi [kəra'čiy], city in W Pakistan.

Kathmandu [kat'mənduw], capital of Nepal.

Kentucky [kəntək'iy], N central U.S. state.

Kenya [kiyn'yə, ken'yə], country in E Africa.

Khartoum [kartuwm'], capital of Sudan.

Kigali [kiygal'iy], capital of Rwanda.

Kingston [kiŋz'tən], capital of Jamaica.

Kinshasa [kinšha'sə], capital of the Republic of the Congo.

Korea [kɔriy'ə], country in NE Asia, divided into Democratic People's Republic of Korea (North Korea) and Republic of Korea (South Korea).

Kuala Lumpur [kwa'lə lumpu:r', kwa'lə lum'pur], capital of Malaysia.

Kuwait [kuwayt'], country and its capital city, NE of Saudi Arabia.

L

Lagos [ley'gɔs, la'gows], capital of Nigeria.

Lahore [ləhɔ:r'], city in W Pakistan.

Laos [la'ows, ley'ɔs], country in SE Asia. —**La·o'tian,** *n.* and *adj.*

La Paz [la paz'], capital of Bolivia.

Las Vegas [las vey'gəs], large city of Nevada.

Latin America [læt'ən əme:r'əkə], South and Central America and Mexico.

Lebanon [leb'ənən], country in the Near East. —**Leb`a·nese',** *n.* and *adj.*

Lesotho [ləsow'tow], country in S Africa.

Liberia [laybi:r'iyə], country in W Africa.

Libreville [liy'brəvil], capital of Gabon.

Libya [lib'iyə], country in N Africa.

Lima [liy'mə], 1. capital of Peru. 2. city in Ohio.

Lincoln [liŋ'kən], capital of Nebraska.

Lisbon [liz'bən], capital of Portugal.

Little Rock [lit'əl rak'], capital of Arkansas.

Lome [low'miy], capital of Togo.

London [lən'dən], capital of the United Kingdom and the British Commonwealth.

Long Island [lɔ:ŋ' ay'lənd], Atlantic island near U.S. coast and part of New York State.

Los Angeles [lɔs æn'jələs, lɔs æŋ'gələs], largest city in California.

Louisiana [luwiy`ziyæn'ə], S central U.S. state on the Gulf of Mexico.

Lusaka [luwsa'kə], capital of Zambia.

Luxembourg [lək'səmbərg`], country NE of France.

M

Madras [mədræs', mədras'], city in S India.

Madrid [mədrid'], capital of Spain.

Maine [meyn], NE U.S. state on the Atlantic.

Malagasy [mal`əga'siy], country and island SE of Africa.

Malawi [məla'wiy], country in SE Africa.

Malaya [məley'ə], peninsula in SE Asia.

Malaysia [məley'šə], country in SE Asia.

Mali [ma'liy], country in NW Africa.

Managua [mana'gwə], capital of Nicaragua.

Manchester [mæn'čes`tər], city in NW England.

Manhattan [mænhæt'ən], island and part of New York City.

Manila [mənil'ə], capital of the Philippines.

Maryland [me:r'ələnd], E U.S. state on the Atlantic.

Maseru [mas'əruw], capital of Lesotho.

Massachusetts [mæs`əčuw'sits], NE U.S. state on the Atlantic.

Mauritania [mɔ:r`ətey'niyə], country in NW Africa.

Mauritius [mɔriš'əs], island country E of Malagasy.

Mecca [mek'ə], holy city in Saudi Arabia.

Mediterranean Sea [med`ətərey'niyən siy'], sea between Africa and Europe.

Melbourne [mel'bərn], city in SE Australia.

Mexico [mek'sikow], country in S North America. —**Mex'i·co Ci'ty,** capital of Mexico. —**Mex'i·can,** *n.* and *adj.*

Mexico, Gulf of [mek'sikow`, gəlf' əv], body of water E of Mexico, S of U.S.

Miami [mayæm'iy], largest city in Florida.

Michigan [miš'əgən], 1. N central U.S. state. 2. one of the five Great Lakes, central North America.

Middle East [mid'əl iyst'], Near East and SW Asia.

Middle West [mid'əl west'], N central U.S. states.

Milwaukee [milwɔ:'kiy], large city in Wisconsin.

Minneapolis [min`iyæp'ələs], large city in Minnesota.

Minnesota [min`əsow'tə], N central U.S. state.

Mississippi [mis`əsip'iy], 1. SE U.S. state on the Gulf of Mexico. 2. river flowing S in central U.S. from Minnesota to the Gulf of Mexico.

Missouri [mizu:r'iy, mizu:r'ə], 1. N central U.S. state. 2. river flowing SE from Montana and joining the Mississippi River in Missouri.

Mogadiscio [mow'gədiy'šow], capital of Somalia.

Mongolia [maŋgow'liyə], country of NE central Asia. —**Mon'gol**, n. —**Mon·go'li·an**, n. and adj.

Monrovia [manrow'viyə], capital of Liberia.

Montana [mantæn'ə], NW U.S. state.

Montevideo [mantəvədey'o], capital of Uruguay.

Montreal [man'triyɔ:l'], city of E Canada.

Morocco [mərak'ow], country in NW Africa. —**Mo·rocc'an**, n. and adj.

Moscow [mas'kaw], capital of the USSR. —**Mus'co·vite**, n. and adj.

Mozambique [mow`zæmbiyk'], Portuguese overseas territory in SE Africa.

N

Nairobi [nayrow'biy], capital of Kenya.

Near East [ni:r' iyst'], countries of Asia nearest to Mediterranean.

Nebraska [nəbræs'kə], N central U.S. state.

Nepal [nəpɔ:l'], country NE of India. —**Nep`a·lese'**, n. and adj.

Netherlands [neð'ərləndz], country in NW Europe. —**Dutch**, n. and adj.

Nevada [nəvæd'ə, nəva'də], SW U.S. state.

Newark [nuw'ərk, nyuw'ərk], large city of New Jersey.

New Delhi [nuw' del'iy], capital of India.

New England [nuw' iŋ'glənd], NE U.S. states.

New Hampshire [nuw' hæmp'šər], NE U.S. state.

New Jersey [nuw' jər'ziy], E U.S. state on the Atlantic.

New Mexico [nuw' mek'sikow`], SW U.S. state.

New Orleans [nuw' ɔrliynz', nuw' ɔr'lənz], Louisiana seaport on the Gulf of Mexico.

New York [nuw' yɔrk'], 1. NE U.S. state on the Atlantic. 2. seaport and largest city of New York State.

New Zealand [nuw' ziy'lənd], country in the S Pacific.

Niamey [niy'amey], capital of Niger.

Nicaragua [nik`ərá'gwə], country in Central America.

Nicosia [nik`əsiy'ə], capital of Cyprus.

Niger [nay'jər, nay'gər], country in W Africa.

Nigeria [nayji:r'iyə], country in W Africa.

Nile [nayl'], African river flowing S to N into the Mediterranean. The White Nile and the Blue Nile join to form the Nile at Khartoum.

Norfolk [nɔr'fək], seaport in SE Virginia.

North America [nɔrθ' əme:r'əkə], a continent.

North Carolina [nɔrθ' ke:r`əlay'nə], SE U.S. state on the Atlantic.

North Dakota [nɔrθ' dəkow'tə], N central U.S. state.

North Pole [nɔrθ' powl'], farthest N point of the earth.

North Sea [nɔrθ' siy'], part of the Atlantic Ocean, between Britain and Denmark.

Norway [nɔr'wey], country in N Europe. —**Nor·we'gian,** *n.* and *adj.*

O

Ohio [owhay'ow], 1. N central U.S. state. 2. river flowing from Pennsylvania through Ohio joining the Mississippi River in Illinois.

Oklahoma [ow`klǝhow'mə], S central U.S. state. —**O`kla·ho'ma Ci'ty,** capital of Oklahoma.

Omaha [ow'məha`, ow'məhɔ:`], large city of Nebraska.

Ontario [antə:r'iyow], one of the five Great Lakes, central N America.

Oregon [ɔ:r'əgan`, ɔ:r'əgən], NW U.S. state on Pacific.

Orient [ɔ:r'iyənt], E Asia.

Oslo [as'low, az'low], capital of Norway.

Ottawa [at'əwə, at'əwaˋ], capital of Canada.

Ouagadougou [wa'gəduwˋguw], capital of Upper Volta.

P

Pacific [pəsif'ik], ocean between Asia and Australia and the Americas.

Pakistan [pæk'istænˋ, pak'istan'], country in S Asia in two parts NW and NE of India. —**Pak**ˋ**i·stan**'**i**, *n.* and *adj.*

Palestine [pæl'əstaynˋ], area and ancient holy country in the Near East, at E end of the Mediterranean Sea. —**Pal**ˋ**es·tin**' **i·an**, *n.* and *adj.*

Panama [pæn'əmaˋ], 1. country and its capital city in Central America. 2. canal between Atlantic and Pacific in Panama. —**Pan**ˋ**a·ma**'**ni·an**, *n.* and *adj.*

Paraguay [pæ:r'əgweyˋ, pæ:r'əgwayˋ], country in S central South America.

Paris [pæ:r'is], capital of France.

Peking [piy'kiŋ'], capital of People's Republic of China, located in E central China.

Pennsylvania [penˋsəlveyn'yə], E central U.S. state.

Persia [pər'žə], Iran.

Persian Gulf [pər'žən gəlf'], body of water in SW Asia between Arabia and Iran.

Peru [pəruw'], country in W South America. —**Pe·ru**'**vi·an**, *n.* and *adj.*

Philadelphia [filˋədel'fiyə], largest city in Pennsylvania.

Philippines [fil'əpiynzˋ], country and islands in the W Pacific. —**Fil**ˋ**i·pi**'**no**, *n.* and *adj.*

Phoenix [fiy'niks], capital of Arizona.

Pittsburgh [pits'bərg], large city in W Pennsylvania.

Poland [pow'lənd], country in E Europe. —**Pole**', *n.* —**Pol**'**ish**, *n.* and *adj.*

Polynesia [palˋəniy'žə], islands of S central Pacific.

Port-au-Prince [portˋowprins'], capital of Haiti.

Portland [port'lənd], 1. seaport in Oregon. 2. seaport in Maine.

Port-of-Spain [port' əv speyn'], capital of Trinidad.

Portugal [por'čəgəl], country in SW Europe. —**Por**'**tu·guese**, *n.* and *adj.*

Potomac [pətow'mək], river in Virginia and Maryland.

Prague [prag'], capital of Czechoslovakia.

Pretoria [pritɔ:r'iyə], capital of the Union of South Africa.

Providence [pra'vədəns], capital of Rhode Island.

Puerto Rico [pwer'tə riy'kow, pɔr'tə riy'kow], commonwealth and island in the W Atlantic, associated with U.S. —**Puer'to Ri'can,** *n.* and *adj.*

Pyongyang [pyɔ:ŋya:ŋ], capital of Democratic People's Republic of Korea (North Korea).

Q

Quito [kiy'tow], capital of Ecuador.

R

Rabat [rəbat'], capital of Morocco.

Rangoon [ræŋguwn'], capital of Burma.

Rawalpindi [ra'wəlpin'diy], capital of Pakistan.

Red Sea [red' siy'], sea between Africa and Arabia.

Reykjavik [rayk'yəvik], capital of Iceland.

Rhine [rayn'], river in Europe flowing from Switzerland N to North Sea.

Rhode Island [rowd' ay'lənd], NE U.S. state on the Atlantic.

Richmond [rič'mənd], capital of Virginia.

Rio de Janeiro [riy'ow dey žəne:r'ow], seaport of Brazil.

Rio Grande [riy'ow grænd'], border river between U.S. and Mexico.

Rocky Mountains [rak'iy mawnt'ənz], longest mountain system in W North America, extending from Alaska to Mexico.

Romania [ruwmey'niyə], country in E Europe.

Rome [rowm'], capital of Italy. —**Ro'man,** *n.* and *adj.*

Russia [rəš'ə], USSR.

Rwanda [ruwan'də], country in central Africa.

S

Sahara [səhæ:r'ə, səha'rə], desert in N Africa.

St. Lawrence [seynt' lɔ:r'əns], border river in E North America between the U.S. and Canada.

St. Louis [seynt' luw'is], largest city of Missouri.

St. Paul [seynt' pɔ:l'], capital of Minnesota.

Saigon [saygan', say'gan], capital of South Vietnam.

Salisbury [sɔlz'bəriy], capital of Southern Rhodesia.

Salt Lake City [sɔlt' leyk' sit'iy], capital of Utah.

San Francisco [sæn' frənsis'kow], seaport in N California.

San Jose [sæn' howzey'], capital of Costa Rica.

San Juan [sæn' hwan'], capital of Puerto Rico.

San Salvador [sæn' sæl'vədɔr], capital of El Salvador.

Sante Fe [sæn'tə fey'], capital of New Mexico.

Santiago [sæntiya'gow], capital of Chile.

Santo Domingo [sæn'tow domiŋ'ow], capital of Dominican Republic.

Saudi Arabia [sɔ:'diy əre'biyə, saw'diy ərey'biyə], country in the Near East, Arabia.

Scandinavia [skæn'dəney'viyə], N Europe (Denmark, Finland, Norway, and Sweden).

Scotland [skat'lənd], N Britain. —**Scot'**, *n.* —**Scotch'**, *n.* and *adj.* —**Scot'tish,** *adj.*

Seattle [siyæt'əl], seaport of Washington.

Senegal [sen'əgɔl, sen'əgæl], country in NW Africa. —**Sen'e·gal·ese,** *n.* and *adj.*

Seoul [sowl'], capital of South Korea.

Siam [sayæm'], Thailand. —**Si'a·mese',** *n.* and *adj.*

Sierra Leone [siye:r'ə liyown', siye:r'e liyown'iy], country in W Africa.

Sikkim [siyk'kim], country NE of India.

Singapore [siŋ'əpɔ:r`], country and city in SE Asia.

Somalia [səma'liyə], country in NE Africa.

South Africa [sawθ' æf'rikə], Union of South Africa.

South America [sawθ' əme:r'əkə], a continent.

South Carolina [sawθ' kæ:r`əlay'nə], SE U.S. state on the Atlantic.

South Dakota [sawθ' dəkow'tə], N central U.S. state.

Southern Rhodesia [səð'ərn rowdiy'žə], country in S central Africa.

South Pole [sawθ' powl'], farthest S point of the earth.

South Yemen [sawθ' yem'ən], country in S Arabia.

Soviet [sow'viyət], *n.* and *adj.* See **USSR.**

Soviet Russia [sow'viyət rəš'ə], USSR.

Soviet Union [sow'viyət yuwn'yən], USSR.

Spain [speyn'], country in SW Europe. —**Span'ish,** *n.* and *adj.*

683

Spanish Sahara [spæn'iš səhæ:r'ə], Spanish overseas territory in NW Africa.

Stockholm [stak'howm], capital of Sweden.

Sudan [suwdæn'], country in NE Africa. —**Su`da·nese'**, *n.* and *adj.*

Suez [suw'ez, suwez'], canal in Egypt between the Mediterranean and Red Seas.

Superior [səpi:r'yər], one of the five Great Lakes, central North America.

Surinam [sər'ənam], part of Netherlands in NE South America.

Swaziland [swa'ziylænd], country in S Africa.

Sweden [swiyd'ən], country in N Europe. —**Swede'**, *n.* —**Swed'ish**, *n.* and *adj.*

Switzerland [swit'sərlənd], country in central Europe. —**Swiss'**, *n.* and *adj.*

Sydney [sid'niy], city in E Australia.

Syria [si:r'iyə], country in the Near East.

T

Taipei [tay'pey'], capital of the Republic of China, Taiwan.

Taiwan [tay'wan'], island in the W Pacific, Republic of China. —**Tai`wa·nese'**, *n.* and *adj.*

Tananarive [tænæn'əriyv], capital of Malagasy.

Tanzania [tæn`zəniy'ə], country in E Africa.

Tegucigalpa [təguw`siygəl'pa], capital of Honduras.

Tehran, Teheran [te`əran'], capital of Iran.

Tel Aviv [tel' əviyv'], capital of Israel.

Tennessee [ten`əsiy'], SE U.S. state.

Texas [tek'səs], S central U.S. state on the Gulf of Mexico.

Thailand [tay'lænd], country in SE Asia. —**Thai'**, *n.* and *adj.*

Thames [temz'], river in S England, flowing from N to SE.

Tibet [tibet'], country in central Asia. —**Ti·bet'an**, *n.* and *adj.*

Togo [tow'gow], country in W Africa. —**To`go·lese'**, *n.* and *adj.*

Tokyo [tow'kiyow`], capital of Japan.

Topeka [təpiy'kə], capital of Kansas.

Toronto [təran'tow], city in E central Canada.

Transjordan [trænsjɔr'dən], Jordan.

Trinidad [trin'ədæd], island country NE of South America.

684

Tripoli [trip'əliy], capital of Libya.

Tulsa [təl'sə], city of Oklahoma.

Tunis [tuw'nis, tyuw'nis], capital of Tunisia.

Tunisia [tuwniy'žə, tuwniš'ə], country in N Africa.

Turkey [tər'kiy], country in the Near East on the Mediterranean. —**Turk'**, *n.* —**Turk'ish**, *adj.*

U

Uganda [yuwgæn'də], country in E central Africa.

Union of South Africa [yuwn'yən əv sawθ' æf'rikə], country in S Africa.

Union of Soviet Socialist Republics [yuwn'yən əv sow'viyət sow'šəlist ripəb'liks], country in E Europe and N Asia. —**So' viet**, *n.* and *adj.*

United Arab Republic [yuwnay'tid ær'əb ripəb'lik], Egypt; country in NE Africa, considered part of Near East.

United Kingdom [yuwnay'tid kiŋ'dəm], country including Britain and Northern Ireland, NW Europe.

United States of America [yuwnay'tid steyts' əv əme:r'əkə], country in North America.

Upper Volta [əp'ər vowl'tə], country in W Africa.

Uruguay [yu:r'əgwey`, yu:r'əgway`], country in SE central South America.

USSR [yuw' es' es' a:r'], Union of Soviet Socialist Republics.

Utah [yuw'tɔ, yuw'ta], NW U.S. state.

V

Venezuela [ven`əzwey'lə], country in N South America.

Vermont [vərmant'], NE U.S. state.

Vienna [viyen'ə], capital of Austria.

Vientiane [viyen'tiyan], capital of Laos.

Vietnam, Viet Nam [viyet'nam'], country in SE Asia, divided into Republic of South Vietnam and North Vietnam. —**Viet' nam·ese`**, *n.* and *adj.*

Virginia [vərjin'yə], E U.S. state on the Atlantic.

W

Wales [weylz'], W Britain. —**Welsh'**, *n.* and *adj.*

Warsaw [wɔr'sɔ], capital of Poland.

Washington [waš'iŋtən], NW U.S. state.

Washington, D.C. [waš'iŋtən diy' siy'], U.S. capital on the Potomac.

Wellington [wel'iŋtən], capital of New Zealand.

West Indies [west' in'diyz], islands in the Caribbean.

West Virginia [west' vər∫in'yə], E U.S. state.

Wisconsin [wiskan'sən], N central U.S. state.

Wyoming [wayow'miŋ], NW U.S. state.

XYZ

Yaoundé [yauwn'dey], capital of Cameroon.

Yemen [yem'ən, yey'mən], country in SW Arabia. —**Yem'en·ite,** *n.* and *adj.*

Yugoslavia [yuw`gowsla'viyə], country in SE Europe. —**Yu'go·slav,** *n.* and *adj.*

Yukon [yuw'kan], river in Alaska flowing into the Pacific.

Zambia [zæm'biyə], country in S central Africa.